SECOND EDITION

CHILTON'S EASY CAR CARE

Editorial Staff
Executive Editor, KERRY A. FREEMAN, S.A.E.
Manager, Editing and Design, DEAN F. MORGANTINI
Senior Editor, RICHARD J. RIVELE
Technical Editors   JOHN M. BAXTER
                    MARTIN J. GUNTHER
                    TONY MOLLA, S.A.E.
                    W. CALVIN SETTLE, JR.
                    RICHARD T. SMITH
                    RON WEBB

Officers
President, LAWRENCE A. FORNASIERI
Vice President & General Manager, JOHN P. KUSHNERICK

CHILTON BOOK COMPANY · RADNOR, PENNSYLVANIA

Part Numbers

Part numbers listed in this reference are not recommendations by Chilton for any product by brand name. They are references that can be used with interchange manuals and aftermarket supplier catalogs to locate each brand supplier's discrete part number.

Safety Notice

Proper service and repair procedures are vital to the safe, reliable operation of all motor vehicles, as well as the personal safety of those performing repairs. This book outlines procedures for servicing and repairing vehicles using safe, effective methods. The procedures contain many **NOTES, CAUTIONS** and **WARNINGS** which should be followed along with standard safety procedures to eliminate the possibility of personal injury or improper service which could damage the vehicle or compromise its safety.

It is important to note that repair procedures and techniques, tools, and parts for servicing motor vehicles, as well as the skill and experience of the individual performing the work vary widely. It is not possible to anticipate all of the conceivable ways or conditions under which vehicles may be serviced, or to provide cautions as to all of the possible hazards that may result. Standard and accepted safety precautions and equipment should be used when handling toxic and flammable fluids, and safety goggles or other protection should be used during cutting, grinding, chiseling, prying, or any other processes that can cause material removal or projectiles.

Some procedures require the use of tools specially designed for a specific purpose. Before substituting another tool or procedure, you must be completely satisfied that neither your personal safety, nor the performance of the vehicle will be endangered.

Although information in this guide is based on industry sources and is as complete as possible at the time of publication, the possibility exists that manufacturers made later changes which could not be included here. While striving for total accuracy, Chilton Book Company can not assume responsibility for any errors, changes, or omissions that may occur in the compilation of this data.

Contents

1. Tools and Supplies   1
Analyze Your Needs, 1
Basic Tools, 1
Specialty Tools, 9
General Maintenance Tools, 9
Tune-Up Tools, 10
Jacks and Jackstands, 16
Shop Supplies, 17
Types of Sealants, 18
Servicing Your Vehicle Safely, 20

2. Buyer's Guide to   23
Parts and Supplies
Sources for Parts, 24
Kinds of Parts, 27
Using Automotive Catalogs, 29

3. Fasteners   33
Screws, 33
SAE Bolts, 33
Metric Bolts and Nuts, 35
Whitworth Bolts, 36
Nuts, 36
Lockwashers, 36
Cotter Pins, 36
Loosening Seized Nuts and Bolts, 36
Repairing Damaged Threads, 37

4. Safety Systems and   39
Safety Check
Automotive Safety, 39
On-Board Warning Systems, 39
Seatbelts and Interlocks, 41
Troubleshooting the Interlock System, 42
Energy-Absorbing Bumpers, 44
Air Bags, 44
Deterrents for Drug- and Alcohol-Impaired Driving, 46
Walk-Around Safety Check, 47
Vibration Diagnosis, 48
Noises, 50
Safety on the Road, 51

5. Fuels, Lubricants   53
Gasoline, 53
Diesel Fuel, 56
Oils and Additives, 56
Motor Oil Guide, 58
Gluids and Greases, 60

6. Body and   62
Chassis Maintenance
Proper Maintenance Pays, 62
Underhood Maintenance Intervals, 63
Maintenance Intervals, 65
Recommended Lubricants, 67

7. Tune-Up   68
Necessary Tools, 68
Compression, 69
Checking Engine Vacuum, 69
Spark Plugs, 69
Distributor Service, 70
Electronic Ignition, 72
Ignition Timing, 72
Carburetor Adjustments, 72
Valve Adjustment, 73
Tune-Up Check List, 73

8. The Engine   74
How It Works, 74
Turbocharging, 77
The Diesel Engine, 78
The Wankel Engine, 78
Two Stroke Engines, 81
Troubleshooting Basic Performance, 82
Periodic Maintenance, 83
Compression, 83
Changing Your Oil, 86
Valve Adjustment, 87
Engine Identification, 85
Using a Vacuum Gauge, 88

9. The Cooling System   90
How the Cooling System Works, 90
What to Do When the Engine Overheats, 91
How to Spot Worn V-Belts, 92
How to Spot Bad Hoses, 93
Periodic Maintenance, 94
Checking and Replacing Thermostat, 96
Replacing Fan Belt, 97
Installling a Coolant Flush Kit, 101
Replacing Radiator Hoses, 102
Troubleshooting Basic Problems, 103
Air-Cooling Systems, 103
Installing a Transmission Oil Cooler, 104

10. Air-Conditioning   106
Theory of Air Conditioning, 106
How the Air Conditioner Works, 107
Safety Precautions, 108
Periodic Maintenance, 109
Troubleshooting Basic Problems, 111

11. Electrical System   113
Battery and Cables
Parts of the Battery, 113
How the Battery Works, 115
Battery Rating System, 116
Periodic Maintenance, 117
Troubleshooting Basic Problems, 117
Specific Gravity and Charge, 119
Replacing Battery Cables, 121
Jump Starting, 121
Keeping Battery Terminals Clean, 121
Jump Starting a Dead Battery, 122
Battery Chargers, 123
Replacing a Battery, 124

12. Electrical System   126
Starting and Charging
The Starting System, 126
Troubleshooting Basic Starting System Problems, 128
The Charging System, 128
Troubleshooting Basic Charging System Problems, 131
Periodic Maintenance, 132
Replacing the Alternator Belt, 133
How to Spot Worn V-Belts, 134

13. Electrical System   135
Ignition
How the Ignition System Works, 135
Periodic Maintenance, 140
Troubleshooting Basic Point-Type Ignition System Problems, 143
Checking the Distributor Cap, Points and Rotor, 146
Replacing Spark Plugs, 147
Reading Spark Plugs, 148
Breaker Point/Condenser/Rotor Replacement, 151
Setting the Dwell, 153
Timing the Ignition, 154

14. Electrical System Lights, Fuses, Flashers 156

Light Bulbs, 156
Headlights, 157
Fuses, Fusible Links and Circuit Breakers, 158
Flashers, 160
Troubleshooting Basic Lighting Problems, 161
Troubleshooting Basic Turn Signal and Flasher Problems, 162
Replacing Headlights, 163
Rewiring, 166

15. Fuel System and Emission Controls 167

The Fuel System, 167
How Carburetors Work, 169
Emission Control Systems, 169
Troubleshooting Basic Fuel System Problems, 173
Symptoms of Faulty Emissions Systems, 173
Periodic Maintenance, 174
Fuel Filter Replacement, 175
Air Filter Replacement, 176
Pump Your Own Gas, 179
Carbon Canister Filter Replacement, 180
Servicing the Fuel System, 180
Idle Speed Adjustment, 181

16. Windshield Wipers, Washers 184

Windshield Wipers, 184
Windshield Washers, 186
Periodic Maintenance, 186
Troubleshooting Basic Windshield Wiper Problems, 187
Troubleshooting Basic Windshield Washer Problems, 188
Servicing the Wipers, 189
Replacing Wiper Refills, 190
Replacing Windshield Wiper Blades, 192

17. Interior Care 194

Cleaning Fabric and Vinyl, 194
Repairing Seats and Dash, 194
How to Remove Stains from Fabric, 195
Vinyl Repair, 196
Door Panels, 197
Rug Care, 197
Rug Repair, 197
Glass and Plastic, 198
Keeping the Interior Clean, 198
Replacing Inside Rear-View Mirror, 199

18. Dash Gauges 20

Types of Gauges, 202
How to Read Gauges, 203
Troubleshooting Basic Problems, 205
Installing Dash Gauges, 206

19. Radios, Stereos, Tape Players 207

Tape Decks, 207
Radios, 207
Speakers, 208
Antennas, 209
Installing Stereo, 210
Troubleshooting Basic Radio Problems, 212

20. CB Radio, Radar Detectors 214

Why CB Radio?, 214
CBs and the FCC, 214

Choosing a CB Set, 215
Installing Mobile CBs and Antennas, 215
Noise Suppression for CB Radios, 217
Radar Detectors, 218
Troubleshooting CB Antenna Problems, 219
Installing CB and Antenna, 220
How Radar and Detectors Work, 221
Hooking Up the Detector, 224

21. Clutch and Manual Transmission 225

How the Clutch Works, 225
Troubleshooting Basic Problems, 227
How the Transmission Works, 228
Clutch Maintenance, 231
Transmission Maintenance, 232

22. Automatic Transmission 234

How the Automatic Transmission Works, 234
Towing Automatic Transmission Cars, 238
Replacing Fluid and Filter, 240
Periodic Maintenance, 241
Transmission Identification, 242
Transmission Fluid Indications, 243
Troubleshooting Basic Problems, 244

23. Driveshafts, Drive Axles 246

Driveshafts, 246
Universal Joints, 247
Front-Wheel Drive, 248
Rear (Drive) Axle and Differential, 249
Four-Wheel Drive, 251
Periodic Maintenance, 253
Basic Drive Axle Problems, 254
Checking Lubricant Level, 255
Troubleshooting Basic Driveshaft Problems, 256

24. Suspension and Steering 257

Types of Front Suspensions, 257
Manual Steering, 258
Power Steering, 261
Steering Geometry, 262
Rear Suspensions, 265
Periodic Maintenance, 265
Troubleshooting Basic Problems, 268
Servicing the Steering System, 269

25. Wheels 272

Wheel Construction, 272
Wheel Capacity, 273
Wheel Dimensions, 273
Caring for Wheels, 274
Troubleshooting Basic Problems, 275
Wheel Lug Torque Specifications, 276

26. Tires 277

Types of Tires, 277
New Tire Technology, 278
Tire Selection, 280
Tire Grading, 282
Reading the Tire Sidewall, 283
Tire Care, 286
Tire Size Comparison Charts, 288
Inflation Pressure Conversion Chart, 290
How to Read Tire Wear, 292
When You Have a Flat Tire, 293
Troubleshooting Basic Tire and Wheel Problems, 294

27. Brakes 295

Hydraulic System, 295
Drum Brakes, 296

Disc Brakes, 297
Power Brake Boosters, 298
Emergency Brake, 298
Periodic Maintenance, 298
Troubleshooting Basic Problems, 299
Brake System Tuneup Procedure, 303
Wheel Bearing Adjustment, 305

28. Trailer Towing 306

Trailer Weight, 306
Hitch Weight, 306
Wiring the Vehicle, 307
Recommended Equipment Checklist, 308
Cooling, 309
Handling a Trailer, 310
Hooking Up the Trailer, 312

29. Body Care and Repair 314

Washing, 314
Cleaners, Waxes and Polishes, 315
Special Surfaces, 317
Rust, Undercoating and Rustproofing, 317
Repairing Minor Body Damage, 318
Rustproofing Your Car, 319
Repairing Minor Surface Rust or Scratches, 320
Repairing Minor Dents and Deep Scratches, 322
Repairing Rust Holes with Fiberglass, 324

30. Anti-Theft Systems 327

Simple Steps You Can Take to Protect Your Car, 327
Insurance, 330
How Anti-Theft Systems Work, 330
CB Radios, Stereos and Accessories, 333

31. Buying and Owning a Car 336

Buying a New Car, 336
Buying Used Cars, 340
Warranties, 342
Emission Control Systems Warranty, 342
Costs of Owning a Car, 343
Insurance, 345

32. How to Deal with Vehicle Emergencies 348

Stopping on the Highway, 348
Throttle Sticking, 348
Brake Failure, 349
Loss of Steering, 349
Fires, 349
Loss of Oil Pressure, 350
Windshield Wiper Failure, 350
Hood Popup, 350
Submersion in Water, 351
Loss of Lug Nuts on the Wheels, 351
Exhaust System Failures, 351
Flat Tires and Blowouts, 351
Driving on Flooded Roads or in Heavy Rain, 352
Driving on Snow and Ice, 352
First Aid Supplies for Your Car, 353

33. 55 Ways to Save Fuel 355

Fuel Economy, 355
Care and Maintenance, 357
Driving Habits, 358
Buying a Car, 359

34. Chilton Tips 360
35. Glossary 368
Tune-up Specifications 378
Index 565

1
Tools and Supplies

Analyze Your Needs

Nearly everybody needs some tools, whether they're just for fixing the kitchen sink, or overhauling the engine in the family car. As far as car repairs go, pliers and a can of oil aren't going to get you very far down the path of do-it-yourself service. But, you don't have to equip your garage like the local service station either. Somewhere between these two extremes, there's a level that suits the average do-it-yourselfer. Just where that point is depends on your needs, your ability and your interest. The trick is to match your tools and equipment to the jobs you're willing and able to tackle.

Choose Your Own Level

To sort things out in an orderly manner, think about your repair work in three levels: basic, average and advanced. Before you purchase any tools, sit down and determine your present level of mechanical expertise. After you have determined that (be honest), determine just how far you intend to progress as an amateur mechanic. Knowing what you can and/or will do in the way of automotive repairs is the most important step you can take. Obviously, if all you ever intend to do is to change the oil and the plugs now and then, you won't need very many tools. If, however, you plan some fairly extensive repair work, you're going to end up with a pretty complete collection of tools.

Once you have determined your level of mechanical involvement, evaluate your tool purchases on a "must have" and a "nice-to-have" basis.

Basic Level

At a basic level of involvement, you'll probably do such things as check the coolant, oil, battery and other fluid levels, and change the oil and filter. You also might perform basic maintenance, keep an eye on the tire pressures, keep the car waxed and polished, and perhaps perform some minor body touch-up.

Average Level

The average level involvement will probably include replacing belts and hoses, replacing shocks, and engine tune-up.

Advanced Level

At the advanced level, you might dig deeply enough to re-line the brakes, check compression, perform major engine tuning, install a trailer hitch, replace a bad muffler, or repair body damage.

Basic Tools

After you've determined your level of mechanical expertise and

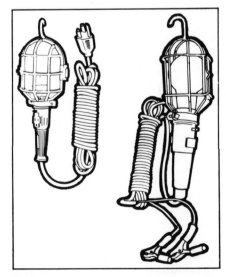

Trouble lights can be AC powered (left) or battery powered (right).

1

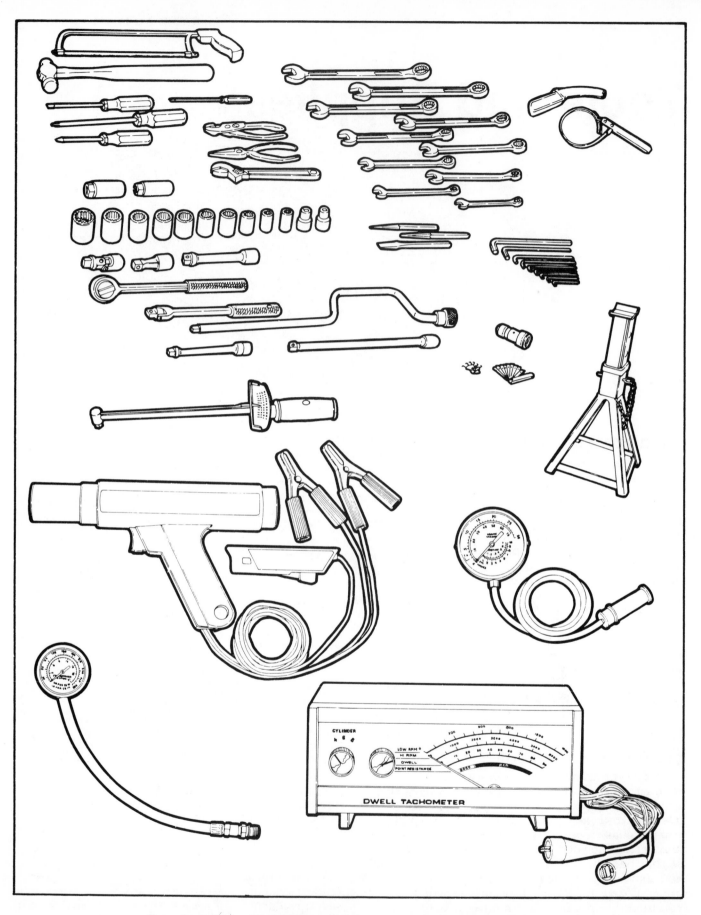

These basic tools will handle the majority of your automotive service needs.

2

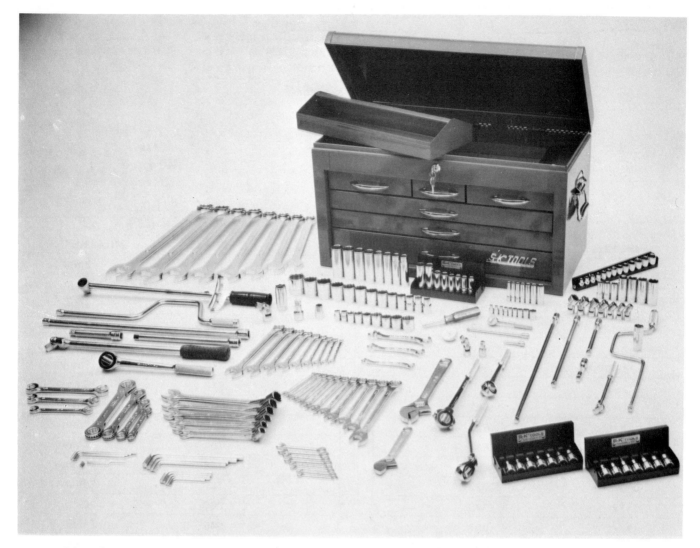

Depending on your level of involvement, you may need considerably more than a basic assortment of hand tools.

TOOLS AND EQUIPMENT PLANNER

Basic level	Average level		Advanced level
pliers	jacks	fender covers	battery charger
screwdrivers	drive-on ramps	fire extinguisher	volt/amp/ohmmeter
hammers	safety stands	first aid kit	tubing tools
wrenches	bench vise	grease gun	screw extractors
hacksaw	inspection mirror	funnels	taps, dies, thread file
files	wire wheels	magnet	pullers
cable/terminal cleaners	socket set	ruler	power tools
spark plug gage	thickness gages	putty knife/scraper	compression tester
tire pressure gage	brake adjusting tool		bench grinder
battery hydrometer	hex-key wrenches		continuity tester
antifreeze hydrometer	terminal crimper/stripper		torque wrench
trouble light	soldering gun		
oil can	tach/dwell meter		
workbench	timing light		
jumper cables	oil drain pan		
lug wrench	tread depth gage		

SAE/METRIC WRENCH SIZES

Many import cars and a few American cars use metric wrench sizes. In a few cases, an SAE wrench or socket may appear to fit a metric bolt, but a chewed up bolt and skinned knuckles will be the only result. It's always best to use the right size wrench. The following chart compares common SAE and metric wrench sizes.

SAE Wrench Sizes			*Metric Wrench Sizes*	
INCHES	**DECIMAL**		**DECIMAL**	**MILLIMETERS**
1/8"	.125		.118	3mm
3/16"	.187		.157	4mm
1/4"	.250		.236	6mm
5/16"	.312		.354	9mm
3/8"	.375		.394	10mm
7/16"	.437		.472	12mm
1/2"	.500		.512	13mm
9/16"	.562		.590	15mm
5/8"	.625		.630	16mm
11/16"	.687		.709	18mm
3/4"	.750		.748	19mm
13/16"	.812		.787	20mm
7/8"	.875		.866	22mm
15/16"	.937		.945	24mm
1"	1.00		.984	25mm

how far you want to progress as an amateur mechanic, you have to buy some tools. No matter what level you have decided on, there are some tools you cannot do without. These include pliers, open and box end wrenches, a ratchet and sockets, various types of screwdrivers, some punches and chisels, a hammer and hacksaw.

It will be worth your while to buy *quality* hand tools. You can buy tools in supermarkets but they'll probably only cause you

grief. Stick to the name-brand tools and you won't go wrong. Manufacturers like Craftsman, Mac, Snap-On, Proto, etc. make top-quality tools that will last a lifetime. Many brand-name tools are also sold with a "no questions" guarantee. If you break it, just take it back and it will be replaced, no questions asked. So buy your tools from a reputable tool manufacturer. You'll pay a little more, but it's worth it to avoid skinned knuckles and rounded-off bolts.

Metric or SAE?

Deciding whether you needed metric or SAE tools wasn't a problem until recently. All American cars used SAE fasteners, and foreign cars weren't all that popular. Now the picture has changed. Not only do foreign cars represent a sizable portion of the market, but a number of American auto makers are using metric sizes. The Chevette, for instance, uses more metric fasteners than SAE fasteners. So, if you own a foreign car, more than likely you'll need metric tools. Likewise, if you have a late-model American car, you might need some metric tools.

Common metric fasteners and the wrench size required are listed in the following chart.

Before you buy any tools, check with your dealer to determine just what kind of fasteners your car is put together with. Some American cars (such as the Vega) are entirely metric, while

Fastener Size (Millimeters)	Required Wrench
4 × .7	7 mm
5 × .8	8 mm
6.3 × 1	10 mm
8 × 1.25	13 mm
10 × 1.5	15 mm
12 × 1.75	18 mm
14 × 2	21 mm
16 × 2	24 mm

some are part metric and part SAE. Most American cars are still entirely SAE, however. Also keep in mind that some foreign cars (such as Volvo) utilize some SAE fasteners.

While there are some points of interchange between the metric and inch sizes, it's not a good idea to use metric wrenches on SAE fasteners and vice versa. In an emergency, you can use anything that will fit, but prolonged use will only ruin the fastener.

Pliers

Pliers come in a variety of shapes and sizes and you'll probably need at least three different kinds for a beginning tool kit. The regular slipjoint kind that everyone is familiar with is an absolute necessity. Long-nosed or needle-nosed pliers should be in everyone's tool kit also. The number of jobs these two tools are good for is endless. Locking pliers (commonly called vise grips) are so useful, you'll won-

der how you ever got along without them. A good pair of cutting pliers are a must for any kind of wiring job.

Eventually, you may want to add specialized pliers. There are pointed-tip pliers for spreading circlips and hooked pliers for removing brake springs. Some pliers have a groove in the end to compress the wire hose clamps used on many radiator hoses, although these can be made from a pair of old pliers by filing a groove in the end.

Wire strippers are also handy for electrical work. Most have special grooves for stripping various gauges of wire without cutting the wire inside.

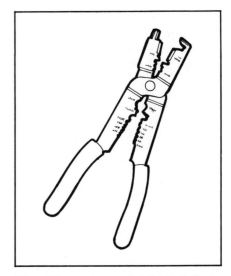

Wire strippers are a handy tool if you are doing much electrical work.

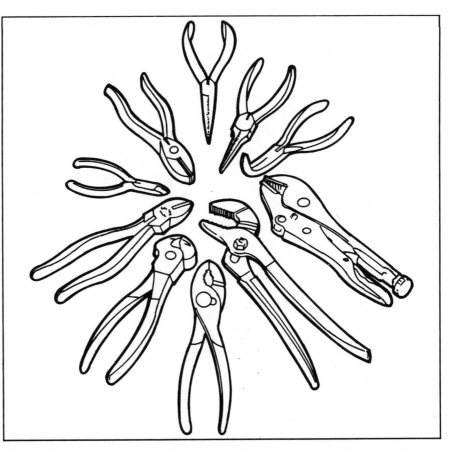

Pliers come in all shapes and sizes. The locking pliers (3 o'clock), channel locks or common slip joint pliers (6 o'clock) and combination wire cutters (10 o'clock) are the most useful.

Hammers

Hammers come in four basic types—machinist's (ball peen), claw, plastic (soft faced) and rubber. The basic hammer for a mechanic is the ball peen, but you needn't spend the six to twelve dollars for a quality ball peen hammer if you already have a good claw hammer available.

If you are going to buy a hammer, get one with an 8- or 12-ounce head that is drop forged and heat treated. The handle of a quality hammer will be hickory, ash or fiberglass.

A plastic mallet is useful in situations where less force is required and rubber mallets are good for installing snap-on hubcaps and other jobs where you don't want to mar the surface. This is the one case where an inexpensive tool works almost as well as an expensive one.

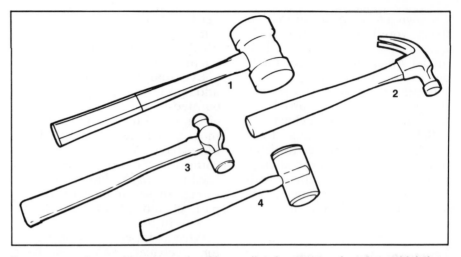

Four common types of hammers: 1. rubber mallet, 2. common claw, 3. machinist's or ball peen and 4. plastic or soft-faced.

Screwdrivers

Screwdrivers are another must for anyone planning to do any sort of automobile repair work. There are two general types of screwdrivers—phillips head screwdrivers and slot head screwdrivers. Keep in mind that these types of screwdrivers come in various sizes, so just because you have a slotted head screwdriver, and a phillips head doesn't mean you're going to be able to fit every screw you come across. Screwdrivers are often sold in sets containing all the common types.

Other specialized screwdrivers (Reed and Prince tips, clutch head, butterfly) are only useful if your vehicle uses screws that they will fit. The best practice is to acquire them as necessary. If you plan on changing your points and condenser, a magnetic screwdriver is indispensable to handle tiny screws in awkward locations. There are also locking screwdrivers known as screw starters that are handy for this operation. Many of the magnetic

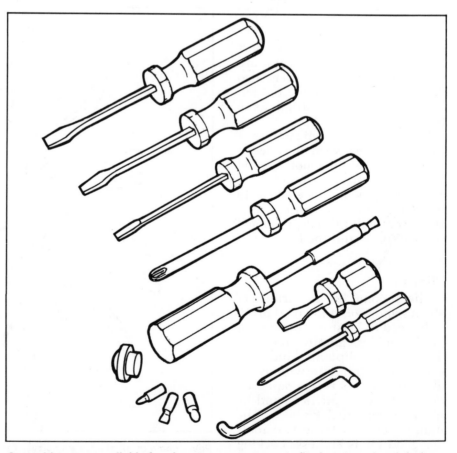

Screwdrivers are available for almost any purpose or to fit almost any head design.

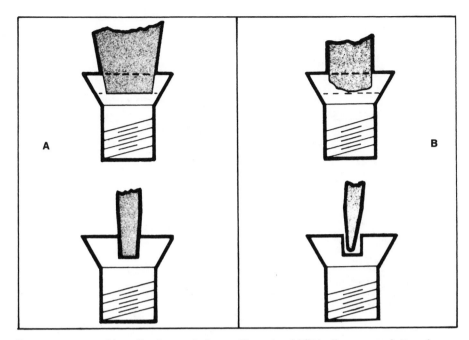

Keep your screwdriver tips in good shape. They should fit in the screw slot as shown in "A." If they look like the ones shown in "B," they need grinding or replacing.

Adjustable open wrenches are also very handy, but the cheap kind are no good at all, since they won't hold their setting. Good quality adjustables are available in various lengths, and you should have at least one.

Allen Wrenches and Star Wrenches

Allen and star (Torx®) wrenches are required more and more to work on cars. Allen wrenches are hexagonal and Torx® bits are multi-serrated inserts that fit inside a bolt or screw head rather than fitting around the outside of

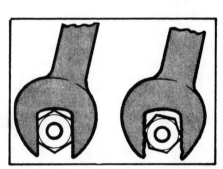

When you're using an open end wrench, use the correct size and position it properly on the flats of the nut or bolt.

screwdrivers have interchangeable bits for various types of screw heads.

Wrenches

Wrenches come in two kinds—open end and box end. Both kinds are necessary for any sort of tool kit. The box end wrenches are ordinarily of the twelve point type, and offer a better grip than the open end type, although obviously they cannot be used for some jobs.

Wrench offset is a consideration when buying wrenches. The head may be angled to make access to some bolts or nuts easier. Standard offset is 15° to 30°, but most wrenches are available from straight (0°) to right angle (90°) offsets. Many tool manufacturers offer combination wrenches which are an open end wrench on one end and a box end on the other. Box end wrenches are also available in ratcheting models, although their usefulness is limited for the amateur mechanic.

For fuel and brake line work, a special type of wrench known as a line wrench is available. It is nothing more than a box end wrench with one of the flats cut out so that it can be slipped over the line.

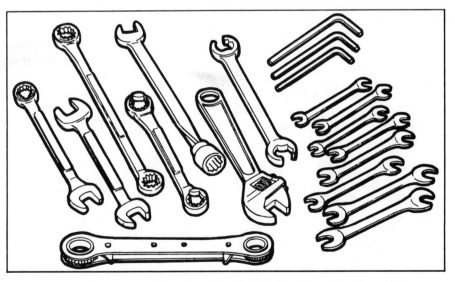

A sampling of the variety of wrench styles. The ratchet (bottom), adjustable (center) and combination open/box end (left) are the most useful.

the head. They can be L-shaped tools with their own handles or are available to fit a ratchet handle.

Ratchet and Sockets

A ratchet and socket set will probably be one of the most expensive purchases you make in assembling a basic tool kit. Ratchet drives come in three sizes, ½", ⅜" and ¼" drive. (There is also a ¾" drive ratchet, but it is of little use, unless you own a very large truck.) When buying a ratchet, pick the size you think you'll use the most. The ¼" size is only useful for smaller jobs, and the ⅜" size is the most popular and useful. Sockets come in six- and twelve-point faces, and in standard and deep lengths.

There are plenty of specialty tools for socket sets. Universal joints allow you to get into tight places, but are frequently hard to maneuver. Adaptors let you use different size drive sockets on other ratchet handles. Crowfoot wrenches are simply open-end wrench heads that fit a ratchet drive. Speeder handles, super-deep sockets, magnetic inserts, and screwdriver bits are all nice to have, if you have a use for them. If not, don't bother cluttering up your toolbox. Spark plugs require a deep socket, while the standard length is suitable for most of the other jobs you will encounter. The six-point sockets are heavier, but the twelve-point sockets give a better grip on the bolt and more turning positions for working in tight places.

You can also do yourself a big favor and choose a flexible head ratchet over a regular ratchet. A flex head ⅜" drive ratchet with a 6" extension will enable you to do most any job you want to do.

The ratchet handle comes in various lengths with a varying number of teeth on the ratchet. If you have a choice, pick the shorter ratchet handle and the one with the most teeth on the ratchet mechanism (most clicks

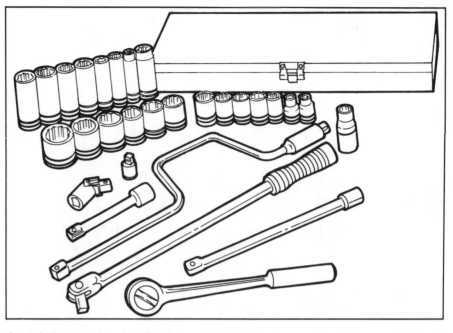

A ratchet, extension, breaker bar and selection of normal and deep sockets will handle most jobs.

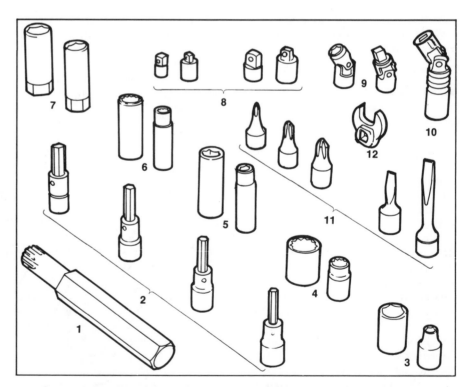

Some of the socket bits available for ratchet sets.

1. Star, serrated or Torx bit
2. Allen wrenches
3. ¼" drive 6-point sockets
4. ¼" drive 12-point sockets
5. ½" or ⅜" drive 6-point sockets
6. ½" or ⅜" drive 12-point sockets
7. ⅝" (right) and ¹³/₁₆" (left) spark plug sockets
8. Ratchet drive adaptors
9. Universal joints
10. Universal joint with socket wrench
11. Screwdriver socket bits

GUIDE TO TOOLS FOR DO-IT-YOURSELF REPAIRS

Type of repair (columns):

- Engine tuning
- Filter, oil changing & lube
- Cooling system
- Tire & wheels
- Body care
- Body repair
- Brakes
- Battery
- Starting/charging
- Stereo & radio
- Washers & wipers
- Air conditioning
- Towing & R/V
- Lighting
- Shock absorbers & suspension
- Safety services
- Exhaust systems
- Maintenance

Tools needed

Basic level
- pliers
- screwdrivers
- hammers
- wrenches
- hacksaw
- cable/terminal cleaners
- spark plug gage
- tire pressure gage
- battery hydrometer
- antifreeze hydrometer
- trouble light
- oil can
- workbench
- jacks
- drive-on ramps
- safety stands
- bench vise
- socket set
- oil drain pan
- tread depth gage
- lug wrench
- fender covers
- fire extinguisher
- first aid kit
- grease gun
- funnels

Average level
- bench grinder
- soldering gun
- tach/dwell meter
- timing light
- punches and chisels
- files
- inspection mirror
- electric drill
- wire wheels
- thickness gages
- compression tester
- continuity tester
- brake adjusting tool
- torque wrench
- hex-key wrenches
- terminal crimper/stripper
- magnet
- ruler
- putty knife/scraper

Advanced level
- micrometers
- battery charger
- volt/amp/ohmmeter
- tubing tools
- screw extractors
- taps, dies, thread file
- pullers
- power tools
- stud puller
- belt tension gage

Need to have ▮ Nice to have ▯

per turn of the handle). This will give you the greatest flexibility to reach tight places and the fewest bruised knuckles.

Torque Wrench

If you plan on doing anything more involved than changing the oil, you'll need a torque wrench. The beam-type models are perfectly adequate, although the click-type models are much more precise. Keep in mind that if you're tightening a part that has a torque value given, it's there for a reason. So use the torque wrench.

Click-type (or breakaway) torque wrenches can be set to any desired setting and will automatically release once the setting is reached. These are used mostly by professionals, and are not really necessary for the backyard mechanic. The beam-type torque wrench, while not quite as accurate or as fast to use as the click-type, is perfectly adequate for everyday use, and quite inexpensive. When using a torque wrench on any fasteners, keep the socket as straight as possible on the fastener. Trying to torque something on an angle just won't work.

Specialty Tools

In addition to basic tools, you'll find a number of small specialty tools that will make your life as a do-it-yourselfer much easier. A battery terminal puller costs only a dollar or so, and will save you a lot of trouble when you remove your battery cables. A combination cable and terminal cleaner is also handy. A tire pressure gauge is an absolute must if you plan on getting the most wear out of your tires. Buy a good one, since tire pressure is critical to tire life. A battery hydrometer and an antifreeze hydrometer are necessary to keep an eye on the state of your coolant and your battery.

General Maintenance Tools

The list of general maintenance tools is practically endless, depending on the degree of your involvement. However, a basic list for the average do-it-yourself mechanic would include:

· An oil filter wrench,
· An oil filler spout,
· A grease gun,
· A container for draining oil,
· A suction gun,

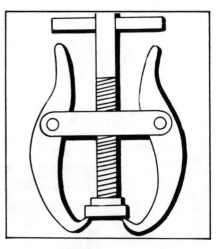

Battery terminal puller.

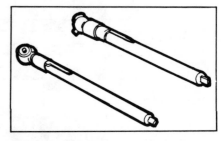

Tire pressure gauges should be included in every glove compartment.

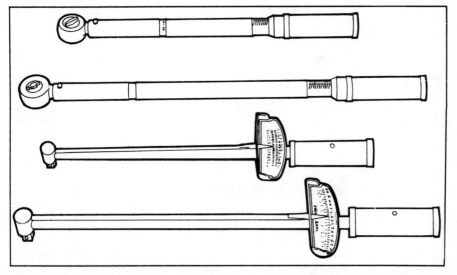

Torque wrenches (top to bottom): Click type (in./lb.); Click type (ft./lb.); Beam type (in./lb.); Beam type (ft./lb.).

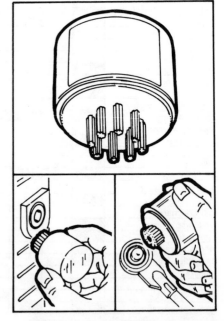

Side terminal battery cleaning tool.

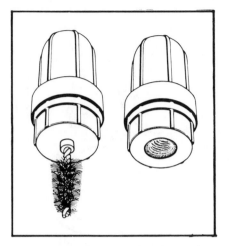

Top terminal battery cleaning tool.

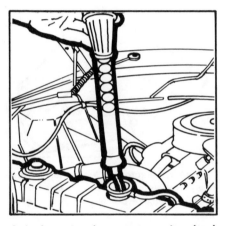

A hydrometer is necessary to check anti-freeze protection.

· Battery terminal cleaners, and

· Many rags for cleaning up the inevitable mess.

Oil filter wrenches come in four basic types. The strap wrench is the most common and will handle most filters. A more sophisticated filter wrench combines a strap or band wrench with a ratchet drive. This type is useful when the filter is located in an out-of-the-way place. The filter on the Dodge Omni and Plymouth Horizon, for instance, can only be removed with this type of wrench.

The other two types of filter wrenches are applied to the end of the oil filter, and both are designed for use with a ratchet drive. An oil filler spout is the only way to get oil from the can into the engine with a minimum

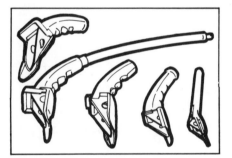

Oil can spouts.

of mess. Any other way will surely result in oil spilled on the engine, which will turn to smoke when the engine gets hot. Other types of fillers have flexible spouts for filling automatic transmissions and other hard-to-reach filler tubes.

A grease gun is also the only way to lubricate the car's chassis. The grease gun comes in various sizes that accept cartridges of different kinds of grease and a wide variety of flexible and odd-shaped fittings to reach hard-to-get-at grease nipples.

A fluid suction gun is almost a necessity to add (or remove) oil from a differential. The filler plugs on differentials and manual transmissions are frequently in a spot that you cannot fill directly from the container. You will probably have to transfer the fluid from the container into a suction gun first. The fluid is also frequently a heavy oil which does not flow easily, which further complicates the problem. To remove fluid from a unit without a drain plug, a suction gun is invaluable.

Battery cleaning tools are inexpensive and make battery terminal cleaning easier and quicker. They generally come in two styles, one for top terminals and one for side terminals. The one for side terminals is nothing more than a miniature wire brush, which you can easily substitute.

Tune-Up Tools

NOTE: *The word "tune-up" actually applies only to older cars, on which you can perform the traditional work associated with "tune-up"—spark plug replacement, ignition contact point replacement, dwell adjustment, ignition timing adjustment and carburetor idle and mixture adjustment.*

Engine performance maintenance is a more accurate term. Most modern cars and light

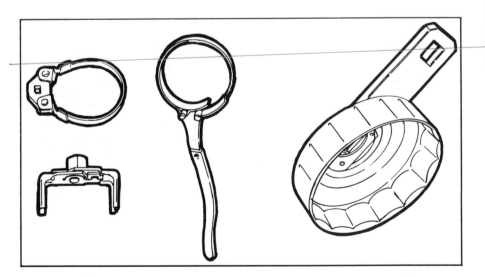

Various oil filter wrench styles. All but the one on the bottom are for use with ratchet drive.

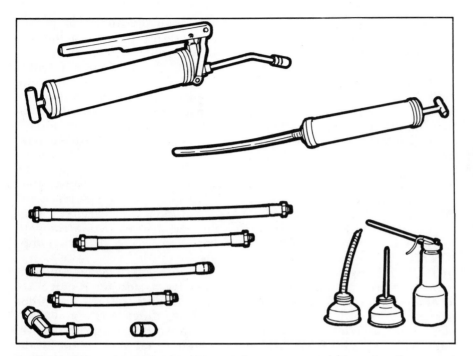

Lubrication tools—clockwise from upper left: grease gun, suction gun, oil cans and hose adaptors for grease gun.

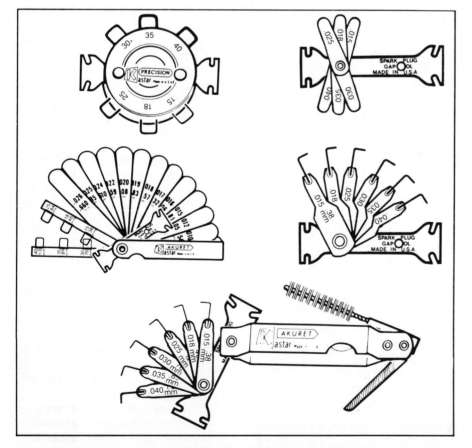

Feeler gauges are available in either leaf, wire or combination styles.

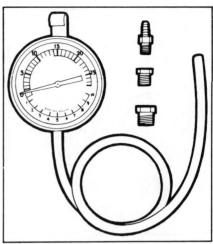

Vacuum gauge/fuel pump tester.

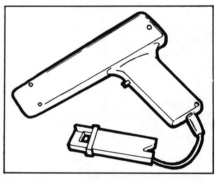

A modern electronic timing light. Note the inductive pick-up clamp. This type is more expensive but is of a better quality.

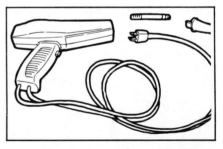

AC powered timing lights are powered by house current. They are generally the least expensive and produce the weakest light.

trucks are equipped with electronic ignition (no points) and an on-board computer that automatically adjusts the ignition timing, fuel mixture and idle speed. In fact, on modern computer-controlled vehicles, it's impossible to adjust these yourself.

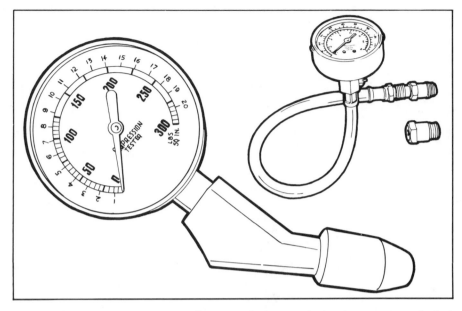

Two styles of compression gauges. The screw-in type on the top is more accurate, but more expensive. The push-in type (bottom) is more popular with do-it-yourself mechanics.

Sunlight will overpower the timing light flashes, so try and stay out of it.

flat feeler gauges to check point gap (if you have conventional ignition) and you'll need the round wire gauge to check and set the plug gap.

Professional mechanics never perform a tune-up on a car until they take a compression reading, and it's probably a habit you should get into yourself, particularly if you own an older car with a lot of miles on it. Compression gauges are available as screw-in types and hold-in types. The screw-in type is slower to use, but eliminates the possibility of a faulty reading due to escaping pressure. A compression reading will uncover many problems that can cause rough running. Normally, these are not the sort of problems that can be cured by a tune-up. Vacuum gauges are also handy for discovering air leaks, late ignition or valve timing, and a number of other problems.

Timing Lights

There are two basic kinds of timing lights—DC powered timing lights, which operate from your car's battery, and AC powered timing lights, which operate on 110 volt house current. Of the two, the DC light is preferable because it produces more light to see the timing marks in bright daylight.

Regardless of what kind is used, the light normally connects in series with the No. 1 spark plug using an adaptor. More expensive models sometimes use an inductive pickup which simply clamps around the plug wire and senses firing impulses. Inexpensive models use alligator clips; one clamps onto the connection between the plug and the plug wire, and the others clamp onto the car battery terminals.

■

Chilton Tip

Some timing lights will not work on electronic ignition systems, so if your car is equipped with electronic ignition, check to

If you have the need for, and plan on doing, your own tune-ups, there are some specialized tools you are going to need. You'll need both round wire and flat feeler gauges, a timing light, and a dwell-tach. A compression gauge and a manifold vacuum gauge are also handy, though not absolutely necessary. You'll need the

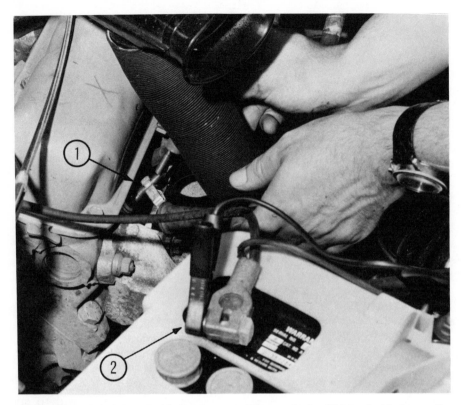

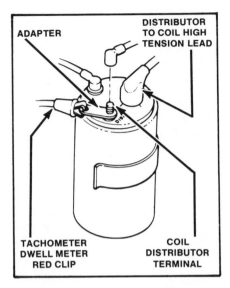

Typical dwell-tach connections.

Most DC powered timing lights are connected to an adaptor (1) inserted between No. 1 spark plug and the cable and to the (+) and (−) battery terminals (2).

make sure the timing light you buy will work. ■

The biggest problem you will probably have when using a timing light is trying to see the timing marks on the crankshaft pulley. Before you time the engine, mark the appropriate timing mark with fluorescent paint or chalk. Stay out of direct sunlight when you time the engine and buy a timing light with a xenon light, not a neon light. Timing lights which use a xenon tube provide a much brighter flash than those which use a neon tube.

Dwell-Tachometer

It's a fact of life that you can't do a good tune-up without a dwell-tach. You don't need one of those gigantic analyzers to set the dwell and rpm on your car,

but you just can't get along without a dwell-tach to measure the point dwell and the engine rpm. Prices range from less than $10 to $50 and more. All have a switch to go from the dwell scale to the rpm scale. Make sure you get a dwell-tach that is compatible with your car's ignition system.

Dwell-tachs are simple to hook up. Some dwell-tachs are powered by the circuit being tested, some operate off the car battery, and some have their own power source. On conventional ignition systems, one lead from the dwell-tach connects to the distributor primary terminal on top of the coil. Electronic ignition systems have specific connection procedures and you'll have to check with your dealer to determine the tach hook-up. Naturally, dwell readings cannot be obtained on electronic ignition systems, since dwell is electronically controlled and cannot

be altered. Rpm readings are still valid, of course.

Test Lights

A test light is nothing more than a light bulb connected to a lead and a probe or two leads. Test lights are normally used to determine whether or not a particular wire, circuit or component is "hot," that is, whether or not current is flowing through it.

To use a test light to check for the presence of current, simply attach the ground wire on the light to a good metal ground. Then touch the probe end of the test light to the end of the power supply wire that has been disconnected from the component using the power (light bulb, horn, gauge, etc.). If the component has been receiving current, the test light will go on. If the test light does not go on, then the problem is farther back in the circuit.

Volt/Ohmmeters

A voltmeter is used to measure the difference in electrical "pressure" between two points in a circuit. Just as water pressure is measured in pounds per square

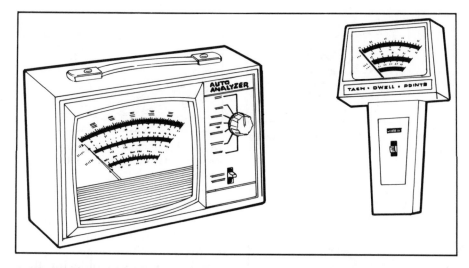

A hand-held dwell-tach tester (right) will do the job for the occasional mechanic. Those who are more serious will appreciate the multiple testing functions of the analyzer (left).

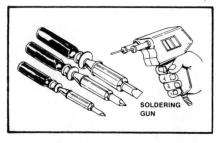

There are several types of soldering irons and guns.

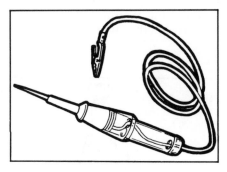

A simple test light.

inch, electrical pressure is measured in volts. When a voltmeter's two probes are placed on two "live" portions of an electrical circuit with different electrical pressures, current will flow through the voltmeter and produce a reading which indicates the difference in electrical pressure between the two parts of the circuit.

An ohmmeter differs from a voltmeter in that it incorporates its own source of power so that a standard voltage is always present. An ohmmeter is connected in the same way as a voltmeter, but since it is self-powered, all the power in the circuit to be measured should be off.

Remember that a voltmeter is measuring volts or electrical pressure, while an ohmmeter is measuring ohms, or circuit resistance. Volt/ohmmeters are only useful if you have some knowledge of electricity and of course have the factory specifications for whatever you are testing. It does you no good to know that a certain circuit has twelve volts unless you know what the factory specification for that circuit is. They are not used very often but are handy in certain situations.

Soldering Gun

Soldering is a quick, efficient method of joining metals permanently. Everyone who has the occasion to make electrical repairs should know how to solder. Electrical connections that are soldered are far less likely to come apart and will conduct electricity far better than connections that are only "pig-tailed" together.

The most popular (and preferred) method of soldering is with an electric soldering gun. Soldering irons are available in many sizes and wattage ratings. Irons with high wattage ratings deliver higher temperatures and recover lost heat faster. A small soldering iron rated for no more than 50 watts is recommended for home use, especially on electrical projects where excess heat can damage the components being soldered.

There are three ingredients necessary for successful soldering—proper flux, good solder and sufficient heat.

Flux

A soldering flux is necessary to clean the metal of tarnish, prepare it for soldering and to enable the solder to spread into tiny crevices. When soldering electrical work, always use a resin flux or resin core solder, which is non-corrosive and will not attract moisture once the job is finished. Other types of flux (acid-core) will leave a residue that will attract moisture, causing the wires to corrode.

Good Solder

Tin is a unique metal with a low melting point. In a molten state, it dissolves and alloys easily with many metals. Solder is made by mixing tin (which is very expensive) with lead (which is very inexpensive). The most common proportions are 40/60, 50/50 and 60/40, the percentage of tin always being listed first.

Low-priced solders often contain less tin, making them very difficult for a beginner to use because more heat is required to melt the solder. A common solder is 40/60 which is well suited for all-around general use, but 60/40 melts easier, has more tin for a better joint and is preferred for electrical work.

Sufficient Heat

Successful soldering requires that the metals to be joined be heated to a temperature that will melt the solder, usually somewhere around 360–460°F., depending on the tin content of the solder. Contrary to popular belief, the purpose of the soldering iron is not to melt the solder itself, but to heat the parts being soldered to a temperature high enough to melt solder when it is touched to the work. Melting flux-cored solder on the soldering iron will usually destroy the effectiveness of the flux.

How to Solder

1. Soldering tips are made of copper for good heat conductance, but must be "tinned" regularly for quick transference of heat to the project and to prevent the solder from sticking to the iron. To "tin" the iron, simply heat it and touch flux-cored solder to the tip; the solder will flow over the tip. Wipe the excess off with a rag.

2. After some use, the tip may become pitted. If so, simply dress the tip smooth with a smooth file and "tin" the tip again.

3. An old saying holds that "metals well-cleaned are half soldered." Flux-cored solder will remove oxides, but rust, bits of insulation and oil or grease must be removed with a wire brush or emery cloth.

4. For maximum strength in soldered parts, the joint must

Wipe the excess tin from the iron while hot.

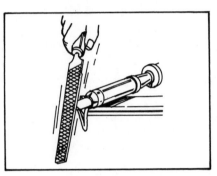

Dress the tip with a smooth file.

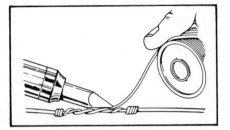

The correct method of soldering. Let the heat transferred to the work melt the solder.

start off clean and tight. Weak joints will result in gaps too wide for the solder to bridge.

5. If a separate soldering flux is used, it should be brushed or swabbed on only those areas that are to be soldered. Most solders contain a core of flux and separate fluxing is unnecessary.

6. Hold the work to be sol-

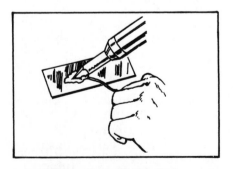

Tinning the soldering iron.

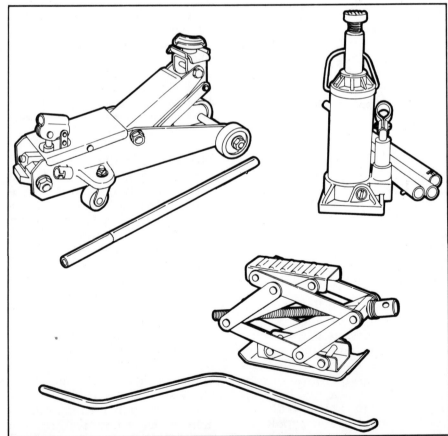

Three types of jacks. Clockwise from bottom, the scissors jack, hydraulic "trolley" jack and stationary hydraulic jack.

dered firmly. It is best to solder on a wooden board, because a metal vise will only rob the piece to be soldered of heat and make it difficult to melt solder. Hold the soldering tip with the broadest face against the work to ·be soldered. Apply solder under the tip close to the work as shown. Apply enough solder to give a heavy film between the iron and piece being soldered, moving slowly and making sure the solder melts properly. Keep the work level or the solder will run to the lowest part, and favor the thicker parts, because these require more heat to melt the sol-

der. If the soldering tip overheats (the solder coating on the face of the tip burns up), it should be re-tinned.

7. Once the soldering is completed, let the soldered joint stand until cool.

Jacks and Jackstands

A car must be raised in order to lubricate the chassis, change the oil and gain access to various parts under the car. Above all, a car must be raised and supported safely. Never attempt to work under a vehicle supported only by a jack.

The *bumper jack* that comes with the car is suitable for raising the car, but is not suitable for supporting the car while you work under it. Once the car is raised, place safety stands under it before attempting any work.

Scissors jacks are the least expensive type of jacks. These are mechanically operated by a threaded rod that is turned inside a diamond-shaped frame. Cranking the screw causes the diamond-shaped frame to expand or contract, raising or lowering the car. These are more reliable than bumper jacks, but are still no substitute for jackstands.

Hydraulic jacks are the best and quickest means of lifting a car off the ground. Hydraulic jacks run anywhere from $8-200, depending on the size and quality of the jack. They are available as small units which can be picked up easily in one hand and placed where needed, or as large, heavy units equipped with wheels to move them about. The smaller models work slowly and tip over easier.

Hydraulic jacks use a pump to push hydraulic fluid against a ram which operates the lifting pad. They have seals that are prone to leak. This is one good reason why you shouldn't work under a vehicle supported by a hydraulic jack. If the seals leak, the jack will lose pressure and the car will slowly (or quickly) fall to the ground.

Jackstands are the safest way to support a car. They consist of stands made of heavy metal, and are adjustable for different working levels. Once you have raised the car or truck to a convenient height, the jackstands are adjusted underneath it and the vehicle is lowered onto the stands.

Professional jackstands are the easiest to use, but cost the most. Occasionally, if you're very fortunate, they can be picked up used from a service station that is going out of business.

Drive-on ramps are the alternative to jacking and supporting

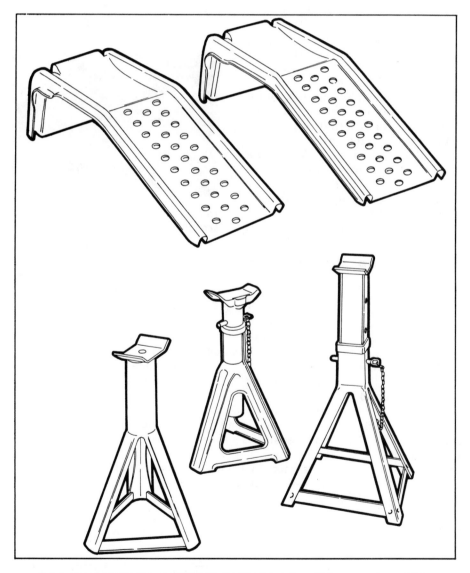

Drive-on ramps (top) or jackstands (bottom) are a must to support a vehicle.

the vehicle. A good set of pressed steel ramps can cost as much as $40–50, but they are often worth the expense.

Shop Supplies

When you plan your shop supplies, you should follow the same format as you used for your tools—if you intend to perform only basic level work, you need only acquire a minimum number of supplies, and so forth.

At the basic level, you're going to need mostly replacement fluids. Things such as motor oil, antifreeze, automatic transmission fluid and brake fluid should be kept on hand. You'll also need some clean rags or wiping towels and some hand cleaner.

At the average level, things get a little more complex. You'll probably need chassis and wheel bearing grease, spare hoses and belts, plugs, points, penetrating oil, parts cleaner and a variety of other supplies.

The list of supplies needed for the advanced level could be endless, but if you're operating at the advanced level, you probably already have most supplies. Take a look at the list prepared here, keeping in mind that it's only a partial list, and these are all just suggestions. Remember the advanced level includes all the other levels as well.

Sealants

If you're not already familiar with the terms "aerobic," "anaerobic" and "RTV", you probably should be. These are kinds of sealants that are gradually replacing cork and rubber gaskets on car assemblies.

The terms refer to the curing properties of the sealants. Aerobic means that the sealant cures in the presence of air and can be used on flexible flanges and between machined parts. But it should not be used where it might squeeze out and plug small passages. Parts must be assembled immediately or the sealant will harden.

RTV sealant is another name for a type of aerobic sealant, standing for Room Temperature Vulcanizing. Aerobic sealants are often identified as RTV silicone rubber compounds, under names such as GM, GE, Permatex, Devcon, Dow Corning, MOPAR, Fel-Pro or Loctite.

Anaerobic sealants are those that cure in the absence of air. In other words, the sealant will not cure (harden) until the parts are assembled and the air is denied. Anaerobic sealants are for use between smooth, machined surfaces, but should not be used between flexible mounting flanges. They should also be applied sparingly in a continuous bead to a clean surface.

Uncured aerobic or RTV sealants can be wiped off with a rag. Cured sealants can be removed with a scraper, wire brush or common shop solvents.

Universal Thread Sealant

There are more thread sealants than can be counted. Add to these the several tapes now on

Thread locking compounds are used to keep nuts and bolts from vibrating loose.

SHOP SUPPLIES PLANNER

Basic Level	Average level		Advanced level
motor oil	chassis grease	assorted electrical connectors	vacuum hose
antifreeze/coolant	wheel bearing grease	assorted fuses	oil seals for wheel bearings
fuel line antifreeze	penetrating oil	spare battery terminals	gear oil
automatic transmission fluid	parts cleaning solvent	sandpaper	fuel line
power steering fluid	carburetor cleaner	assorted bulbs	thermostat
hand cleaner	oil absorbent compound	solder	assorted gaskets
car wash chemicals	cotter pins	spray paint	muffler clamps and brackets
windshield washer solvent	nut and bolt assortment	spray undercoating	thread repair kit
windshield wiper blades	flat and lock washer assortment	body repair kits	brake system parts
brake fluid	spare belts	battery terminal spray	thermostat
wiping towels (cloth/paper)	spare hoses	gasket/sealer	
electrical tape	hose clamps	fuel filter	
masking tape	radiator cap		
air filter	spare wire		
oil filter	tune-up parts		
	spark plugs		

The Average level is in addition to Basic level; Advanced includes Basic and Average.

TYPES OF SEALANTS

Type Product	Description	Characteristics
Lubricants	High temperature anti-seize lubricant	High temp anti-seize lube that does not harden with heat. Prevents corrosion. Good to temperatures of 1800°F.
	Dry spray lubricant with Teflon	Dry spray contains Teflon. Prevents sticking and squeaking on most moving parts, even non-metallic ones. Better than oil, silicone or graphite.
	Multi-purpose penetrating lubricant	Fast-acting penetrating oil. Also displaces moisture and prevents corrosion when applied prior to assembly.
	Degreasing agent	Cuts grease and washes it away . . . leaves no film or residue. Good on glass, metal or rubber. Excellent on brake assemblies.
Sealers	Thread sealing tape made of Teflon	A tape thread sealant and lubricant made of Teflon in a handy roll. Replaces pipe dopes and hardening sealants.
	High performance thread sealant	Lubricates threads, then seals by hardening without shrinkage or cracking. Vibration resistant.
	Fast, hard-setting gasket sealer	Fast-setting gasket supplement in paste form. Dries to a hard film. Fills voids.
	Pliable, non-hardening gasket sealer	Dries to a pliable seal. Fills voids, protects threaded parts, too.
	Liquid gasket sealer	Brush-on type for non-rubber gaskets before assembly to ease reassembly and insure a leak-resistant seal.
	Spray adhesive sealant	A fast-drying adhesive sealant in an aerosol can.
	Form-in-place gasket compound	Self-forming gasket compound to fill gaps up to .030″ and up to 350°F applications. Can be used as a substitute for a gasket in an emergency when pre-cut soft gaskets are not available.
	Black silicone rubber adhesive and sealant	Room temperature vulcanizing silicone especially useful in sealing joints and threads, or use in attaching weather stripping. Good low temperature flexibility.
Bonders	Clear silicone rubber adhesive and sealant	Room Temperature Vulcanizing silicone dries to a transparent film to function where appearance is vital.
	Instant adhesive	Instant adhesive for high strength bonding of rubber, metal, hard woods and plastic.
	Quick-drying contact adhesive	Quick-drying contact adhesive for bonding all types of gaskets, including rubber, to parts before assembly. Resists impact, water proofs, mends and reinforces.
	General purpose epoxy adhesive	A multi-purpose epoxy that forms a tough bond in minutes.
Lockers	Self-curing locking compound	Self-curing compound replaces lock washers in nut and bolt applications.
	High strength locking compound	High strength version of above, used on sleeves, studs, and other parts that don't need frequent disassembly.
Patchers	Steel reinforced patching compound	Steel reinforced epoxy compound for repair of engine blocks, axle housings, pump castings, body work, etc.
	Aluminum reinforced patching compound	Aluminum reinforced epoxy for use in repairing aluminum castings, aluminum heads or blocks, transmission cases, etc.

the market and the confusion can be great. Mechanics should be aware of a new anaerobic sealant with a Teflon filler which can be used on all joints. (GM Truck has adopted it as universal sealant.) "Pipe Sealant with Teflon" is applied to threads. It creates an instant seal, but does not cure for 24 hours. This permits making changes if needed. Once hardened it prevents vibration-induced loosening.

How to Use Sealants

Anaerobics: clean surfaces with solvent and apply bead to one surface. Material will not begin to cure until parts are assembled. Sealing is effective in half an hour. Full cure is complete in 2½ to 10 hours depending upon temperature. Cold slows cure.

Silicone sealant: clean and dry surfaces. Apply bead and let cure for two hours. To make a gasket that will cling to only one surface, apply bead to one surface and allow it to cure. Then apply grease to other surface, and assemble. Or, to make a gasket that will bond to both surfaces, apply and assemble. This will provide maximum blowout resistance. Material will cure to depth of ¼" in 24 hours.

When to Use Sealants

The basic guide in choosing a sealant is the size of the gap. Anaerobic materials are used only on smooth, rigid, machined-surfaced flanges which have a total gap less than .030 inch. Silicones are used in parts that may flex (such as metal-stamping covers) and which have gaps that are more than .030 inch but not more than .25 inch.

Both materials are impervious to the normal automotive fluids such as gas, oil, coolants and hydraulics. Anaerobics have a temperature range of −60°F to 300°F, and silicones will handle −100°F to 450°F.

Anaerobics: Common applications for the anaerobic materials include fuel pumps, timing covers, oil pumps, water pumps, thermostat housings, oil filter adapters, manual transmission housings, differential covers and other rigid parts. Bear in mind that anaerobic materials add rigidity to the assembly because they help lock the surfaces.

Silicone sealant: Many silicone applications involve stamped metal housings such as oil pans, valve covers, and other parts such as intake manifolds, transmission covers, axle covers and rear main bearing seals.

Solvent release: Non-hardening sealants are used to repair cut gaskets on both rigid and flexible assemblies that operate at high temperatures up to 600°F. On semipermanent assemblies the materials set quickly to bolster the conventional gasket. By remaining pliable, they permit easy removal at a later date.

Hardening sealants dry fast and hard and are used on permanent assemblies to aid the conventional gasket, particularly when the flanges are damaged.

Most sealants also aid in assembly by holding the gasket in place during assembly. When such positioning problems are extremely difficult, a gasket adhesive can be used to hold the gasket in perfect alignment during assembly.

Arranging Your Shop

Obviously, the arrangement of your shop depends a great deal on just what kind of shop you have in the first place. If you have very limited floor space, careful use of wall space will be the key to allowing yourself working room. If you're like most of us, you probably have a million things in the garage already, which isn't going to help matters. Put up some shelves or get some pegboard to hang tools on. Make sure you have plenty of lighting in the garage. If you don't have enough lights, install some more. There's nothing worse than trying to work by the light of a flashlight or a troublelight. Keep the floor clean and make sure you have adequate ventilation. Keep flammable liquids outside, and anchor all the benches and any heavy equipment you may have.

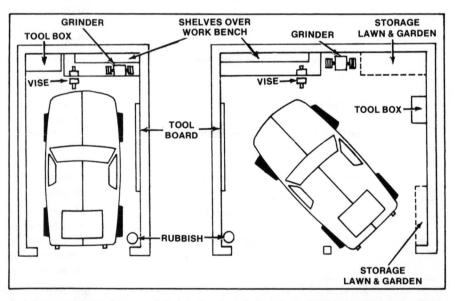

A one-car garage takes careful planning in order to make the best use of its available space. Careful use of wall space is the key, since floor space is so limited. With a two-car garage you can make increased use of peripheral floor space. Some points to remember:
(1) *Make sure that you have good lighting.*   (4) *Have good ventilation.*
(2) *Make sure the electrical supply is adequate.*   (5) *Keep flammable liquids outside.*
(3) *Keep the floor clean.*   (6) *Anchor benches and equipment.*

Servicing Your Vehicle Safely

It is virtually impossible to anticipate all of the hazards involved with automotive maintenance and service, but care and common sense will prevent most accidents.

The rules of safety for mechanics range from "don't smoke around gasoline," to "use the proper tool for the job." The trick to avoiding injuries is to develop safe work habits and take every possible precaution.

Dos

· Do keep a fire extinguisher and first aid kit within easy reach.

· Do wear safety glasses or goggles when cutting, drilling, grinding or prying, even if you have 20–20 vision. If you wear glasses for the sake of vision, then they should be made of hardened glass that can serve also as safety glasses, or wear safety goggles over your regular glasses.

Whenever you are working under the car, it should be supported on jack-stands.

· Do shield your eyes whenever you work around the battery. Batteries contain sulphuric acid; in case of contact with the eyes or skin, flush the area with water or a mixture of water and baking soda and get medical attention immediately.

· Do use safety stands for any under-car service. Jacks are for raising vehicles; safety stands are for making sure the vehicle stays raised until you want it to come down. Whenever the vehicle is raised, block the wheels remaining on the ground and set the parking brake.

· Do use adequate ventilation when working with any chemicals. Like carbon monoxide, the asbestos dust resulting from brake lining wear can be poisonous in sufficient quantities.

· Do disconnect the negative battery cable when working on the electrical system. The primary ignition system can contain up to 40,000 volts.

· Do follow manufacturer's directions whenever working with potentially hazardous materials. Both brake fluid and antifreeze are poisonous if taken internally.

· Do properly maintain your tools. Loose hammerheads, mushroomed punches and chisels, frayed or poorly grounded electrical cords, excessively worn screwdrivers, spread wrenches (open end), cracked sockets, slipping ratchets or faulty droplight sockets can cause accidents.

· Do use the proper size and type of tool for the job being done.

· Do, when possible, pull on a wrench handle rather than push on it, and adjust your stance to prevent a fall.

· Do be sure that adjustable wrenches are tightly adjusted on the nut or bolt and pulled so that the face is on the side of the fixed jaw.

· Do select a wrench or socket that fits the nut or bolt. The wrench or socket should sit straight, not cocked.

· Do strike squarely with a hammer—avoid glancing blows.

· Do set the parking brake and block the drive wheels if the work requires that the engine be running.

Don'ts

· Don't run an engine in a garage or anywhere else without proper ventilation—EVER! Carbon monoxide is poisonous; it takes a long time to leave the human body and you can build up a deadly supply of it in your system by simply breathing in a little every day. You may not realize you are slowly poisoning yourself. Always use power vents, windows, fans or open the garage doors.

· Don't work around moving parts while wearing a necktie or other loose clothing. Short sleeves are much safer than long, loose sleeves and hard-toed shoes with neoprene soles protect your toes and give a better grip on

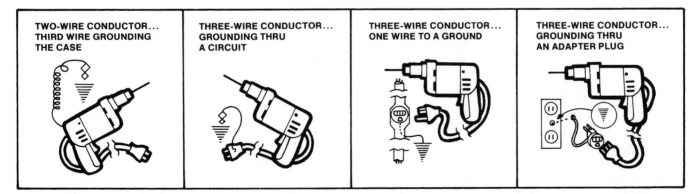

TWO-WIRE CONDUCTOR... THIRD WIRE GROUNDING THE CASE

THREE-WIRE CONDUCTOR... GROUNDING THRU A CIRCUIT

THREE-WIRE CONDUCTOR... ONE WIRE TO A GROUND

THREE-WIRE CONDUCTOR... GROUNDING THRU AN ADAPTER PLUG

If you're using portable electric tools, make sure they're grounded, preferably at the plug by a three-wire connector.

Don't wear a necktie or loose clothing while working near a running engine.

Cleaning parts in gasoline is not a good idea.

· Don't use pockets for toolboxes. A fall or bump can drive a screwdriver deep into your body. Even a wiping cloth hanging from the back pocket can wrap around a spinning shaft or fan.

· Don't smoke when working around gasoline, cleaning solvents or other flammable material.

· Don't smoke when working around the battery. When the battery is being charged, it gives off explosive hydrogen gas.

· Don't use gasoline to wash your hands; there are excellent soaps available. Gasoline may contain lead, and lead can enter the body through a cut, accumulating in the body until you are very ill. Gasoline also removes all the natural oils from the skin so that bone-dry hands will suck up oil and grease.

· Don't service the air conditioning system unless you are equipped with the necessary tools and training. The refrigerant, R-12, is extremely cold and when exposed to the air, will instantly freeze any surface it comes in contact with, including your eyes. Although the refrigerant is normally non-toxic, R-12 becomes a deadly poisonous gas in the presence of an open flame. One good whiff of the vapors from burning refrigerant can be fatal.

slippery surfaces. Jewelry such as watches, fancy belt buckles, beads or body adornment of any kind are not safe when working around a car. Long hair should be hidden under a hat or cap.

2
Buyer's Guide to Parts and Supplies

Do-it-yourself has become an economic necessity for many of us today. It's an opportunity to save some money and have some measure of fun working on the old buggy at the same time.

You'll find, if you haven't already, that it's easy to change the oil and filters and handle minor repairs, but you have to be sure you're getting the correct parts, at the best price.

Today, manufacturers and retailers know you're interested in do-it-yourself repairs to save money. That's why you'll find parts packaged or displayed with application charts to help you select the right parts for your vehicle.

Auto supply stores, discount and department stores, automotive jobbers, and other sources sell complete lines of quality parts for auto repair enthusiasts like yourself. You may want to comparison shop these outlets to see where you can get the most for your money. It's wise to compare price tags and quality all year, instead of expecting to find bargains on infrequent shopping tours. Sales on replacement

parts are common. Weekly specials, holiday, and seasonal promotions all offer a chance to save on your automotive needs.

It doesn't really matter whether you buy name-brand or store-brand tune-up parts. You can save a little money on the store-brand items as opposed to OEM (Original Equipment Manufactured) parts, but you may end up replacing them a little sooner if you buy too far down on the price scale.

The main thing is to be sure to get the correct part for your car. An incorrect tune-up part can adversely affect the engine performance, fuel economy, and emissions, and will cost you more money and aggravation in the end. To avoid buying the parts piecemeal, many manufacturers have taken to offering do-it-yourself tune-up packages, containing points, condenser, plugs, rotor, and sometimes distributor cap. Spark plug wires can be purchased already cut to length and ready to install, or as a kit, in which case you cut the necessary lengths yourself.

To get the proper parts for

your car, you will probably need to know some or all of the following information:

Make: Chevrolet, Datsun, etc.
Model: Impala, 710 Station wagon, etc.
Year: 1976 (example)
Engine size: The engine size is usually designated in cubic inches (350, 260, etc.) or in cubic centimeters (cc) on imports (1600, 2000, etc.). Occasionally, it will be given in liters (1.6, 2.0, etc.). If you are not sure, there is usually a sticker on the air cleaner or under the hood that tells you the engine size. There may be a letter with the number which you should copy down, too.
Number of cylinders: 4, 5, 6, 8, etc., for example
Carburetor (or fuel injection): If the engine is carbureted, you'll need to know if the carburetor is a 1, 2, 3, or 4 barrel (abbreviated bbl) model. You may also find the word venturi (abbreviated V) used interchangeably with the word barrel when describing carburetors.
Air conditioner: Yes or No

QUICK REFERENCE SPECIFICATIONS

For quick and easy reference, you can use this form to jot down frequently used information concerning parts available for your vehicle.

Tune-Up Data

Firing Order _____

Spark Plugs:
  Type (Manufacturer/No.) _____
  Gap (in.) _____

Points (if equipped):
  Part Number _____
  Gap (in.) _____

Dwell Angle (°) _____

Ignition Timing (°) _____
  Vacuum (Connected/Disconnected) _____

Valve Clearance (in.)
  Intake _____ **Exhaust** _____

Capacities

Engine Oil (qts)
  With Filter Change _____
  Without Filter Change _____
  Type of Lubricant _____

Cooling System (qts) _____

Manual Transmission (pts) _____
  Type of Lubricant _____

Transfer Case (pts.) _____
  Type of Lubricant _____

Automatic Transmission (pts) _____
  Type of Lubricant _____

Differential (pts) _____
  Type of Lubricant _____

Commonly Forgotten Part Numbers

Use these spaces to record the part numbers of frequently replaced parts.

PCV VALVE
Manufacturer _____
Part No. _____

OIL FILTER
Manufacturer _____
Part No. _____

AIR FILTER
Manufacturer _____
Part No. _____

FUEL FILTER
Manufacturer _____
Part No. _____

Quantity of oil: How many quarts
Engine code: Since 1976, this code has been important to domestic cars. The engine code is part of the VIN (Vehicle Identification Number), which is visible through the front windshield on the driver's side. On AMC cars, the engine code is the 7th digit of the VIN; on GM, Ford and Chrysler cars, the engine code is the 5th digit.
Electronic ignition: Yes or No

On imports, in addition to the above, you may need to know the distributor number (located on a metal tag on the distributor), the chassis serial number (located on a plate on the body), and the engine serial number (located on a pad on the engine).

Sources for Parts

There are many sources for the parts you will need. Where you shop for parts will be determined by what kind of parts you need, how much you want to pay for the parts, and the types of stores in your neighborhood.

New Car Dealers

New car dealers almost always have parts for your car, but the prices are almost always higher than other sources. The dealer carries what are known in the auto trade as OEM (Original

Equipment Manufactured) parts. OEM parts are those supplied by the car manufacturer and are the same parts installed on the car when it was built. Because of the higher overhead expenses, these parts are generally a little more expensive than the same item available through other outlets.

The higher cost of OEM parts does not necessarily indicate a better value, or higher quality. Automotive jobbers and auto discount stores regularly stock high-quality replacement parts in addition to OEM parts. Even though the car manufacturer will recommend that you use OEM parts for replacement or service work, he will also specify that you can use an equivalent replacement part. Many replacement parts are made by or sold by reputable companies and are built to the same specifications as OEM parts. In many cases, replacement parts may even be identical to OEM parts, since many parts manufacturers sell parts to car makers as OEM parts and also sell the same part to other companies, who market the part under a different brand name. The parts you have to be careful of are "gypsy" parts, which are discussed later in this section. Fortunately there are very few of them.

There are some parts for your vehicle—cylinder heads, crankshafts, body parts, and other slow movers—that you will be unlikely to obtain anywhere but at your dealer. These parts are not sold in sufficient quantities to make it attractive for any other outlet to stock them.

Service Stations

Your local service station can supply you with many of the common parts you require, though they stock these parts mainly for their own use in the repair end of the business. The problem, from the consumer's standpoint, is the cost—it will be high. The reason is that the service station operator buys the

The automotive jobber carries a full line of parts and supplies, and many jobbers do a sizeable do-it-yourself business. Most jobbers carry parts behind the counter, in contrast to the auto discount stores.

same part from a jobber that you can buy over the counter. Although he buys at a discount, he must make a profit on the resale of the item, whether through direct sale of the item or as part of repair charges. Really, when your service station sells parts to you over the counter, they are competing with the local parts stores and discount merchandisers, and most service stations do not buy or sell parts in sufficient volume to offer a competitive price. They are in business to sell "service," not to sell parts.

Parts Jobber

The local parts jobber, who is usually listed in the yellow pages or whose name can be obtained from the local gas station, supplies most of the parts that are purchased by service stations and repair shops. He also does a sizeable business in over-the-counter parts sales for the do-it-yourselfer, and this may constitute as much as 30% to 50% of his

business. Lately, jobbers have been offering more do-it-yourself items as the number of backyard mechanics increases.

The jobber usually has at least two prices—one for the local mechanic or service station and an over-the-counter retail price. The reason for this is that local mechanic, like the service station, does not pay the retail price for a given part. They pay less than retail (a mechanic's discount may range from 15–40% depending on the item) and mark up the price of the part to their customer, making a profit on the resale. Many jobbers will offer you a 10% to 15% discount off the retail prices on over-the-counter sales, and most jobbers run periodic sales on both private brand and brand name do-it-yourself items.

The prices charged by jobbers are usually lower than the new car dealers and service stations but slightly higher than discount or mass merchandisers. The reason is that the jobber is used to dealing with professional mechanics and usually sells name-brand or OEM parts. His volume is such that he sells more than a service station, but less than a discount merchandiser, and thus his prices fall somewhere between the two.

The people who work the counters in the jobber stores know a great deal about cars—far more than the clerk in a discount store or the salesperson in the auto section of a department store. Unless they are extremely busy or very rushed, they can usually offer valuable advice on quality parts or tools needed to do the job right.

Automotive Chain Stores

Almost every community has one or more convenient automotive chain stores, the equivalent of a Pep-Boys or Penn-Jersey. These stores often offer the best retail prices and the convenience of one-stop shopping for all your automotive needs. Since they cater to the automotive do-it-

yourselfer, these stores are almost always open weekday nights, Saturdays, and Sundays, when the automotive jobbers are usually closed.

Chain stores are the automotive "supermarkets." Hardly a week goes by that they are not running advertised specials or a seasonal promotion of some type. The ads normally appear in the local newspapers and offer substantial savings on both name- and store-brand items. In contrast to the traditional jobber stores, where most merchandise is located behind the counter, you can walk through the auto chain stores and browse among most products, picking and choosing from a large stock of brand names.

Prices in the auto chain stores will normally be competitive with the discount stores and mass merchandisers, and they will usually be slightly lower than the jobber. Counter personnel working in the chain stores are slightly less experienced than those working for the jobber, but

they are usually familiar with their products and common automotive problems and can offer good advice.

Discount Stores

The lowest prices for parts are most often found in discount stores or the auto department of mass merchandisers, such as K-Mart, Sears, and Woolco. Parts sold here are name- and private-brand parts bought in huge quantities, so they can offer a competitive price. Private-brand parts are made by major manufacturers and sold to large chains under a store label.

You have to have a good idea of what you're looking for when you buy from these outlets. Many are self-serve, in direct contrast to the older, traditional jobbers where they still look up the part number and get the part for you.

Auto Junkyard

Wrecking yards, junkyards, salvage yards, previously owned parts yards—call them what you will—are good sources of parts, particularly for older cars or limited budgets, although most parts available from salvage yards are beyond the scope of this book. Auto wrecking yards range from the incredibly sophisticated computer-run inventories to stumblebum one-man operations where nobody knows exactly what they have except the inevitable snarling dog.

In most cases, don't expect the wrecking yards to supply the smaller parts. They prefer to deal in complete assemblies. Among the better deals in wrecking yards are engines, transmissions, rear axles, body parts, and wheels. The cost of these parts from a yard is generally about one-half the cost of new parts. Most junkyards are not interested in selling carburetors, voltage regulators, and other small parts, but if they do, their cost will be negligibly less than the cost of rebuilt parts, and rebuilt parts are a far better deal.

The auto chain stores carry name brand as well as store brand replacement parts. Most parts are on display in the aisles, allowing inspection.

The automotive sections of discount stores take a "supermarket" approach to replacement parts.

Some wrecking yards may have two prices—one if they remove the parts and one if you do it. Most yards will prefer to remove parts themselves, but be careful. Time is money when removing parts, so a lot of yards, particularly the less organized, will remove an engine or rear axle with a cutting torch instead of unbolting it. This makes it necessary for you to buy small parts, such as motor mounts, brake lines, spring hangers, and other hardware, that were destroyed by the cutting torch.

Kinds of Parts

New or Rebuilt Parts

Many times you will be required to return your old starter, alternator, fuel pump, or carburetor when you buy a new one. These old parts are returned to a professional parts rebuilding service and are reconditioned to be sold over the counter as remanufactured or rebuilt parts.

Most parts stores will carry both new and rebuilt parts. There is nothing wrong with buying remanufactured parts. Many are just as good as the new ones but can be bought at a considerable savings. Compare the price and warranty on a remanufactured part with that of a new part. In general, the higher the quality of a remanufactured part, the closer the price will be to a new part and the better the warranty.

Inordinately low prices for remanufactured parts usually mean shorter parts life and earlier failures. In this case, it will be worthwhile to spend a little extra money for higher quality.

Counterfeit Parts

Caveat Emptor—let the buyer beware—was a reasonable attitude when the buyer could easily judge the quality of the merchandise he was buying.

But, as automobiles have become increasingly sophisticated, with electronic engine control systems and other hi-tech hardware, there are fewer manifestly clear ways by which to judge the quality of replacement parts.

Reputable manufacturers of replacement parts have built their reputations of repeat business. Their products meet or exceed the OE (Original Equipment) specifications. If they don't perform, you're not going to come back and buy many more of the same.

Counterfeiting, as applied to auto parts, is a broad term that covers any form of deception designed to trick the buyer into believing that he or she is purchasing a part produced by the original equipment manufacturer or a reputable aftermarket manufacturer.

Counterfeit products should not be confused with "generic" or "no-brand" products such as those found in the food industry. It's fully understood that these types of products are not branded products. The key to counterfeit parts lies in the fact that no attempt is made to identify the source of manufacture and that the counterfeit part and packaging closely resembles the real thing.

Packaging of reputable parts manufacturers is often unique and highly recognizable, but those who buy replacement parts by appearance or packaging alone should beware. Counterfeit parts are made to look like the real thing both in packaging and appearance.

Counterfeit packaging usually involves the unauthorized use of a registered trademark on the packaging or the simulation of a part using original equipment characteristics and is designed to

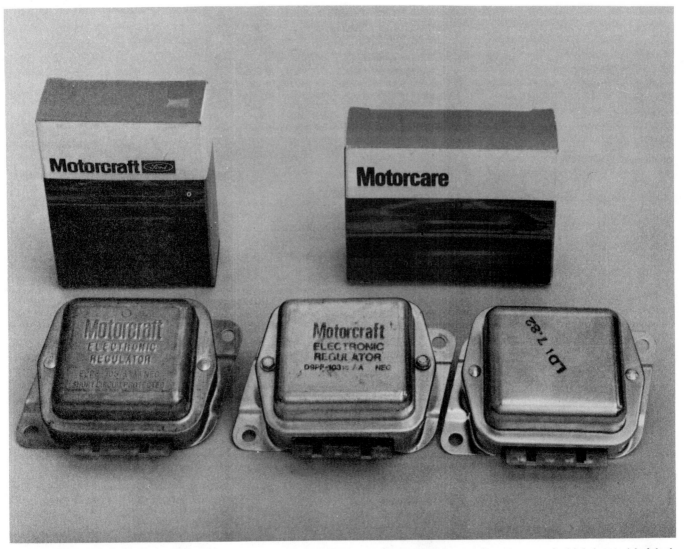

A genuine electronic voltage regulator and its box are shown on the left beside two counterfeit parts, one of which (center) is falsely labeled and another of which (right) came in a simulated package. The counterfeit parts can be spotted because one lacks the brand name identification, and the other uses hex-head screws instead of rivets to fasten the cover.

pass off generally sub-standard parts as the genuine article. Counterfeit parts have the right number of wires and connectors. They look official, durable and reliable.

But looks are deceiving. Not only can counterfeit parts cost you money in the long run due to premature failure or an unknown manufacturer who will not guarantee the part's performance, the shortcuts often taken in the manufacture of counterfeit parts could jeopardize your safety or the vehicle's performance. Some coun-

terfeit brake shoes have been found to be deficient in braking power. Some counterfeit gas tank caps have no safety valves, designed to prevent spillage and fire in the event of an accident.

How can you recognize counterfeit parts? Often, it's extremely difficult.

· Buy brand-name products. A name brand manufacturer's reputation for quality can only have been earned by selling quality merchandise.

· Be suspicious of packaging that very closely, but not exactly,

replicates the packaging of a known, name brand manufacturer.

· Recognize that in a competitive marketplace, there will be variations in price among reputable manufacturers. But, be suspicious of extremely low prices.

· If someone other than yourself is installing the part, ask to see the package in which it came. Even mechanics are not immune to assuming, mistakenly, that they are buying name brand replacement parts.

· If possible, compare the orig-

ORIGINAL
FORD BRAND

SOLD BY FORD AND LINCOLN-MERCURY DEALERS

COUNTERFEIT
FORD
BRAND

UNIVERSAL JOINT KIT

ORIGINAL
MOTORCRAFT
BRAND

SOLD BY FORD AND LINCOLN-MERCURY DEALERS
AND INDEPENDENT DISTRIBUTORS, WHOLESALERS,
REPAIR SHOPS AND RETAIL STORES

Motorcraft

COUNTERFEIT
MOTORCRAFT
BRAND

Motorcraft

The authentic parts packages are shown on the left; the counterfeit parts packages are shown on the right. The colors are the same and both feature the manufacturer's ghosted car symbol.

inal equipment part with the replacement part before purchasing the replacement part. There are often subtle differences between counterfeit and original equipment or reputable replacement parts.

Using Automotive Catalogs

For the person looking for a part for his or her car, the catalog is the most important tool to know how to use. Automotive parts catalogs are what you

make them—a confusing foreign language or an easy-to-understand reference to get the correct part number, and price the first time.

Almost all manufacturers of hard parts make a catalog listing the part number, application, and sometimes the price of the item. The catalog may take the form of a large book with thousands of entries if the manufacturer makes many parts for a lot of applications, or it may be as simple as a single card if the manufacturer has relatively few variations. If you are purchasing

oil filters, air filters, PCV valves, belts, hoses, and similar common parts, you will usually find the catalog near the merchandise in the parts store, though from time to time they will disappear. Wherever they are located and whatever form they take, learning to use them will assure that you get the correct part the first time, saving a lot of time and energy to return parts that don't fit.

General Layout

Catalogs normally contain a descriptive and dated (sometimes coded) cover, a table of

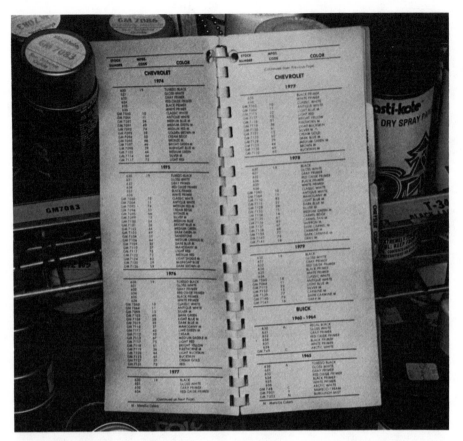

Many catalogs and application charts are found on the store's parts shelves along with the merchandise. This one is the application chart for automotive parts.

Parts catalogs, giving part number and application, are provided by manufacturers for most replacement parts.

contents, index, illustrations, and then the meat of the catalog, the applications. The applications are normally arranged two ways—(1) alphabetically by car name, and (2) numerically by part number. Jobbers may store their catalogs using the Weatherly filing system, a three-digit number on the front of the catalog, but this is of little interest to the do-it-yourselfer. What does interest you is the alphabetical listing of vehicles by make and model.

Many manufacturers print their parts catalogs every year, but some only print every two years and supply a supplement during the off year. It is essential to check the date of the catalog to be sure it has the latest information. Working with an outdated catalog is sometimes worse than working with no catalog at all.

Locating Applications

Let's say you want to look up the spark plug for your 1973 Oldsmobile 350 V8 engine. The first thing you do is find a spark plug catalog and check the date to make sure it is current. Then you look in the index for "Oldsmobile." In this particular catalog there is no listing by make and model in the index. The spark plug applications are broken down by American Passenger Cars, Import Passenger Cars, and several other listings. Turn to the page starting American Passenger Cars.

Under American Passenger Cars, you'll find they are broken down into individual makes starting with American Motors and working back to Willys. Scan the pages until you find the heading Oldsmobile. Under Oldsmobile you'll find the applications are further broken by 6-cylinder and V8 engines. Your Oldsmobile has a V8, so look under the appropriate heading. V8 engines are, then, further categorized by year, beginning with the most recent, and by engine size (260, 305, 350, 455, etc). Running down the entries under V8 engines show three possible listings:

1973–74 350 cu. in. 4-bbl. A/T
1971–74 350 cu. in. 2- and 4-bbl. M/T
1971–74 350 cu. in. 2-bbl. A/T

There are a number of variables that could affect the part number, such as whether the engine has high-energy (electronic) ignition or whether it is a California or Federal car, but since your engine is a 350-cubic-inch V8 with a 4-barrel carburetor (you can find out by consulting the tune-up decal under the hood) and automatic transmission, read across the column from the first entry and find the number of the spark plug.

Abbreviations and Footnotes

If you have trouble deciphering the abbreviations used in the parts catalog, they are usually identified in the front of the catalog.

The biggest distraction in all automotive catalogs are the footnotes. Asterisks, daggers, numerals, and letters that appear after a part number or listing indicate that you are up against a footnote. If such a notation is present, you must look further for more information. Most likely you will go to the bottom of the page for an explanation of why the notation was used. And the explanation could be almost anything. Special kits, superceded parts, special applications, and a myriad of other pieces of information all are deserving of footnotes. To get the right part for your car you cannot afford to skip over the footnotes.

Cross-Reference

Many catalogs include a cross-reference so you can double check information. A cross-reference could be original equipment to independent supplier part numbers, or applica-

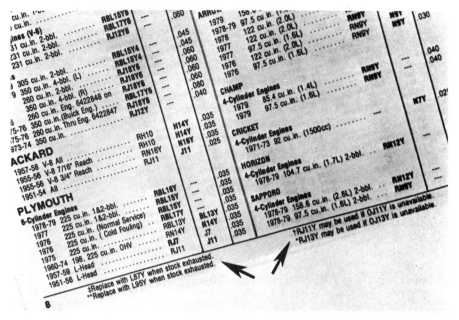

Catalog footnotes are important for getting the proper application. They frequently contain replacement part numbers or other pertinent information.

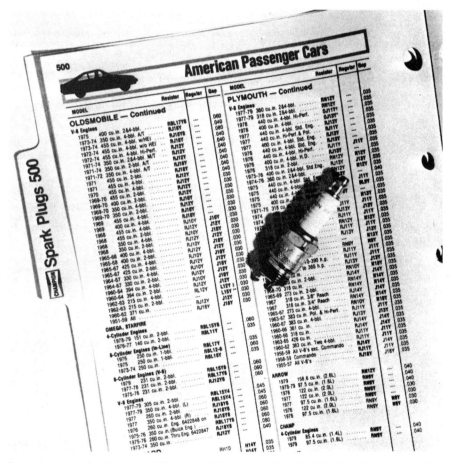

A good way to check your ability to read the catalog is to first look up the part number and then check the actual number on the part.

tion by part number. Let's assume we are looking for a standard equipment alternator belt for a 1972 Ford F100 truck with a 351V8 engine. We get the belt catalog and turn to the table of contents. Belts are listed by part number under vehicle and application. Since we don't know the part number, we turn to Application by Vehicle. The top listing is American Motors, so you know you are working with an alphabetical listing, but you have to be careful because sometimes American Motors vehicles are listed under "Rambler."

Scanning from American Motors through Willys (Kaiser-Jeep) does not locate the vehicle you have, so turn the page. Imported cars are next, listed alphabetically from Alpha-Romeo to Volvo. The next page is headlined Trucks, so you have the right spot. The first listing on this page is probably Chevrolet and the last is Studebaker.

It is an alphabetical listing by make and model, so go down the line to Ford. This listing starts with 1959–69 model, so proceed until you come to 1972. A 1972 listing of the F100 shows "351V8 except air conditioning." Continuing down the column you come across "F100, 351V8 with air conditioning." Read across the page and you will find the replacement belt number.

Common Catalog Mistakes

Catalogs are designed for using, not confusing, but it is not unusual for catalog users to make mistakes in tracking down part numbers. Simple goofs are the most common and costly. For instance, often the user will find the correct listing, but then he or she reads across the wrong line. Or everything is done correctly, but a mistake is made in copying or trying to remember the part number. Or you can get mixed up in using a cross-reference, or working with an outdated catalog, or overlooking a footnote. Such mistakes happen every day to even the most experienced. All you can do is try your best to avoid them.

3
Fasteners

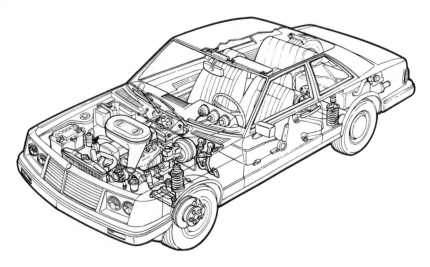

Threaded fasteners are the basic couplers holding your vehicle together. There are many different kinds, but they all fall into three basic types:

Bolts—Bolts go through holes in parts that are attached together and require a nut that is turned onto the other end. A lockwasher of some sort is usually used under the nut.

Studs—Studs are similar to bolts, except that they are threaded at both ends (they have no heads). One end is screwed into a threaded hole and a nut is turned onto the other end. Lockwashers are usually used under the nuts.

Screws—Screws are turned into drilled or threaded holes in metal or other materials

There are a great variety of screws and bolts, but most are hex headed or slot headed for tightening. Because the fastener is the weakest link in an assembly, it is useful to know the relative strength of the fastener, determined by the size and type of material. It is also important to understand the sizes of bolts, to avoid the expense and work of rethreading stripped holes.

Screws

Screws are supplied with slotted or Phillips heads for screwdrivers or with hex heads for wrenches. Most of the screws used on cars and trucks are sheet metal, hexagon or pan type. Occasionally, you'll find a self-tapping sheet metal screw, with slots in the end to form a cutting edge. These types cut their own threads when turned into a hole.

The size of a screw is designated as 8-32, 10-32 or ¼-32. The first number indicates the size of the thread at the root or minor diameter, and the second number indicates the number of threads per inch.

SAE Bolts

Most bolts used on US produced cars and trucks are measured in inches, and standards for these bolts are established by the Society of Automotive Engineers (SAE). Special markings on the head of the bolt indicate its tensile strength (resistance to breaking). The SAE grade num-

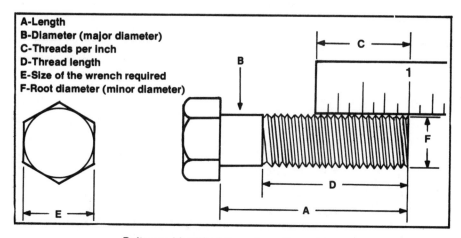

A-Length
B-Diameter (major diameter)
C-Threads per inch
D-Thread length
E-Size of the wrench required
F-Root diameter (minor diameter)

Bolts are identified by various dimensions.

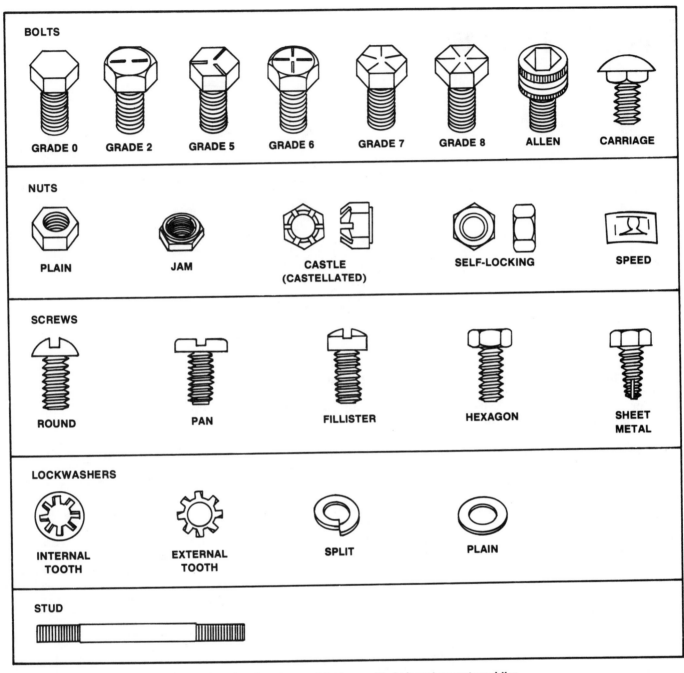

Examples of various types of fasteners likely found on automobiles.

ber, corresponding to the special markings, is an indication of the relative strength of the bolt. Grade 0 bolts (no markings) are usually made of a mild steel and are much weaker than a grade 8, usually made from a mild carbon steel alloy, though a grade 0 or 2 bolt is sufficient for most fasteners.

SAE fasteners are also iden-

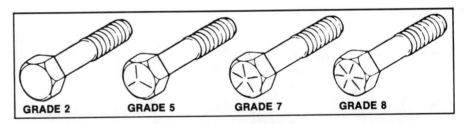

The markings on SAE bolts indicate the relative strength of the bolt.

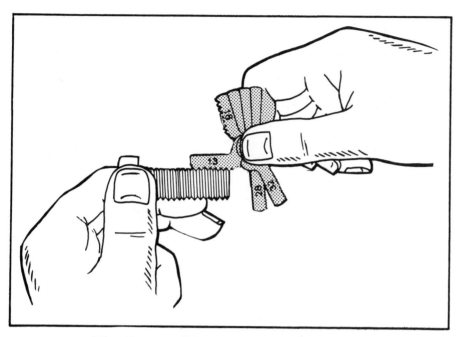

A thread gauge will instantly identify the thread size.

tified by size. As an example, a ⅜-24 bolt means that the major (greatest) thread diameter is ⅜" and that there are 24 threads per inch. The head diameter is always ³/₁₆" larger than the bolt diameter. A ½-16 bolt would be ½" in diameter and have 16 threads per inch. More threads per inch are called "fine" threads and less threads per inch are "coarse" threads. Generally, the larger the bolt diameter, the coarser the threads. There are actually six different classes of threads, but most bolts are UNC (Unified National Coarse) or UNF (Unified National Fine). The term "Unified" refers to a thread pattern to which US, British and Canadian machine screw threads conform.

Metric Bolts and Nuts

The International Standards Organization (ISO) has designated the metric system as the world standard of measurement.

Ever since Ford introduced the 2300 cc, 4-cylinder engine in the Pinto, Bobcat, Mustang II and Capri II, the use of metric fasteners has become more preva-

lent in the US. Chevettes, for instance, have more metric fasteners than the inch-size (SAE) type.

The mixture of metric and SAE fasteners on the same car means that you have to be very careful when removing bolts to note their locations and to keep metric nuts and bolts together. At first glance, metric fasteners may appear to be the same size as their SAE counterparts, but they're not. While the size may be very close, the pitch of the threads (distance between threads) is different. It is possible to start a metric bolt into a hole with SAE threads and run it down several turns before it binds. Any further tightening will strip the threads. The opposite could occur also; a nut could be run all the way down

and be too loose to provide sufficient strength.

Fortunately, metric bolts are marked differently than SAE bolts. An ISO metric bolt larger than 6 mm in diameter has either "ISO M" or "M" embossed on top of the head. In addition, most metric bolts are identified by a number stamped on the bolt head, such as 4.6, 5.8 or 10.9. The number has nothing to do with the size, but does indicate the relative strength of the bolt. The higher the number, the stronger the bolt. Some metric nuts are also marked with a single-digit number to indicate the strength, and some may have the M and strength grade embossed on the flats of the hex.

Metric nuts with an ISO thread are marked on one face of the hex flats with the strength grade (4, 5, 6, 8, 12, 14). Some nuts with a 4, 5 or 6 strength grade may or may not be marked.

A clock face system is used as an alternate means of strength grade designation. The external chamfers or face of the nut are marked with a dash at the appropriate hour mark corresponding to the relative strength grade. One dot indicates the 12 o'clock position and, if the grade is above 12, 2 dots identify 12 o'clock.

Metric Grade	Nominal Diameter (mm)	Corresponds to SAE Grade
4.6	M5 thru M36	1
4.8	M1.6 thru M16	—
5.8	M5 thru M24	2
8.8	M16 thru M36	5
9.8	M1.6 thru M16	—
10.9	M5 thru M36	8
12.9	M1.6 thru M36	—

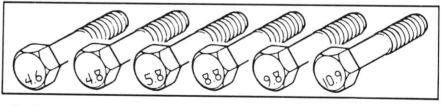

Metric bolts are marked with numbers that indicate the relative strength of the bolt. These numbers have nothing to do with the size of the bolt.

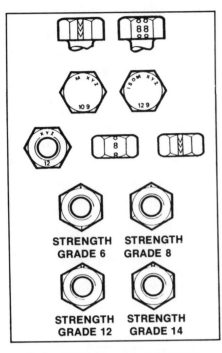

Typical ISO bolt and nut markings.

The size of a metric fastener is also identified differently than an SAE fastener. A metric fastener could be designated M12 x 2, for example. This means that the major diameter of the threads is 12 mm and that the thread pitch is 2 mm (there are 2 mm between threads). Most importantly, metric threads are not classed by number of threads per inch, but by the distance between the threads, and the distance between threads does not exactly correspond to number of threads per inch (2 mm between threads is about 12.7 threads per inch).

The 25 standard metric diameter and pitch combinations are

M1.6 × 0.35	M20 × 2.5
M2 × 0.4	M24 × 3
M2.5 × 0.45	M30 × 3.5
M3 × 0.5	M36 × 4
M3.5 × 0.6	M42 × 4.5
M4 × 0.7	M48 × 5
M5 × 0.8	M56 × 5.5
M6.3 × 1.0	M64 × 6
M8 × 1.25	M72 × 6
M10 × 1.5	M80 × 6
M12 × 1.75	M90 × 6
M14 × 2	M100 × 6
M16 × 2	

shown here. The first number in each size is the nominal diameter (mm) and the second number is the thread pitch (mm).

Whitworth Bolts

Unless you own a British automobile, you probably won't ever run across a Whitworth thread. The British have been using the Whitworth thread on screws, bolts and nuts for years. The screw thread form is the basis of the British Standard Whitworth (BSW) and British Standard Fine (BSF) system, both of which were replaced by metric bolts around the mid-1960's.

You may occasionally run across a few replacement parts still manufactured with Whitworth threads, but these will be rare.

THREAD FORMS REPLACED BY ISO METRIC

BSW	BSF	UNC	UNF	ISO Metric Size
		10	10	M5
3/16	3/16			
		12	12	M6
1/4	1/4	1/4	1/4	M6
5/16	5/16	5/16	5/16	M8
3/8	3/8	3/8	3/8	M10
7/16	7/16	7/16	7/16	
1/2	1/2	1/2	1/2	M12

Nuts

There are a variety of nuts used on cars. Slotted and castle (castellated) nuts are designed for use with a cotter pin. These are mainly used for front-end and wheel-bearing fasteners, where it is extremely important that the nuts do not work loose.

Other nuts have a self-locking feature. A soft metal or plastic collar inside the nut is slightly smaller than the bolt threads. When the nut is turned down, the bolt cuts a thread in the collar and the collar material jams in

the bolt threads to keep the nut from loosening.

Other nuts include jam nuts and speed nuts. A jam nut is merely a second nut to hold the first nut in place and is widely used where an adjustment is involved. A speed nut is a rectangular piece of sheet metal that is pushed down over a screw or stud.

Lockwashers

A lockwasher is a split or toothed washer installed between a nut or screwhead and a flat washer or the actual part. The split washer is crushed flat and locks the nut in place by spring tension, while the toothed lockwasher, usually used for smaller bolts, provides many edges to improve the locking effect.

Cotter Pins

Cotter pins are used with slotted or castle nuts. The bolt has a hole in it and when the nut is tightened, the slots are aligned with the bolt hole. The cotter pin is inserted through the nut and bolt and the legs of the cotter pin bent over.

Loosening Seized Nuts and Bolts

Occasionally, nuts and bolts that are rusted resist the ministrations of mere mortals and refuse to budge. Most of the time, penetrating oil or a sharp rap with a hammer will loosen stubborn nuts.

Another method, used in extreme cases, is to saw away two sides of the nut with a hacksaw. The idea is to weaken the nut as much as possible by sawing away two sides as close to the bolt as possible without actually damaging the bolt threads. A wrench will usually remove the remaining portion of the nut.

STANDARD TORQUE SPECIFICATIONS

The Newton-metre has been designated the world standard for measuring torque and will gradually replace the foot-pound and kilogram-meter. In the absence of specific torques, the following chart can be used as a guide to the maximum safe torque of a particular size/grade of fastener.

There is no torque difference for fine or coarse threads.

Torque values are based on clean, dry threads. Reduce the value by 10% if threads are oiled prior to assembly.

The torque required for aluminum components or fasteners is considerably less.

SAE Bolts

SAE Grade Number	1 or 2			5			6 or 7		
Bolt Markings Manufacturers' marks may vary—number of lines always two less than the grade number.									
Usage	Frequent			Frequent			Infrequent		
Bolt Size (inches)—(Thread)	Maximum Torque			Maximum Torque			Maximum Torque		
	Ft-Lb	kgm	Nm	Ft-Lb	kgm	Nm	Ft-Lb	kgm	Nm
¼—20	5	0.7	6.8	8	1.1	10.8	10	1.4	13.5
—28	6	0.8	8.1	10	1.4	13.6			
5/16—18	11	1.5	14.9	17	2.3	23.0	19	2.6	25.8
—24	13	1.8	17.6	19	2.6	25.7			
3/8—16	18	2.5	24.4	31	4.3	42.0	34	4.7	46.0
—24	20	2.75	27.1	35	4.8	47.5			
7/16—14	28	3.8	37.0	49	6.8	66.4	55	7.6	74.5
—20	30	4.2	40.7	55	7.6	74.5			
½—13	39	5.4	52.8	75	10.4	101.7	85	11.75	115.2
—20	41	5.7	55.6	85	11.7	115.2			
9/16—12	51	7.0	69.2	110	15.2	149.1	120	16.6	162.7
—18	55	7.6	74.5	120	16.6	162.7			
5/8—11	83	11.5	112.5	150	20.7	203.3	167	23.0	226.5
—18	95	13.1	128.8	170	23.5	230.5			
¾—10	105	14.5	142.3	270	37.3	366.0	280	38.7	379.6
—16	115	15.9	155.9	295	40.8	400.0			
7/8—9	160	22.1	216.9	395	54.6	535.5	440	60.9	596.5
—14	175	24.2	237.2	435	60.1	589.7			
1—8	236	32.5	318.6	590	81.6	799.9	660	91.3	894.8
—14	250	34.6	338.9	660	91.3	849.8			

Repairing Damaged Threads

Several methods of repairing damaged threads are available. Heli-Coil® (shown here), Keenserts® and Microdot® are among the most widely used. All involve basically the same principle—drilling out stripped threads, tapping the hole and installing a prewound insert—making welding, plugging and oversize fasteners unnecessary.

Two types of thread repair inserts are usually supplied—a standard type for most inch-coarse, inch-fine, metric-coarse and metric-fine thread sizes and a spark plug type to fit most spark plug port sizes. Consult the individual manufacturer's catalog to determine exact applica-tions. Typical thread repair kits will contain a selection of pre-wound threaded inserts, a tap (corresponding to the outside diameter threads of the insert) and an installation tool. Spark plug inserts usually differ because they require a tap equipped with pilot threads and a combined reamer/tap section. Most manu-facturers also supply blister-packed thread repair inserts sep-

STANDARD TORQUE SPECIFICATIONS, continued
Metric Bolts

Relative Strength Marking	4.6, 4.8			8.8		
Bolt Markings						
Usage	Frequent			Infrequent		
Bolt Size	Maximum Torque			Maximum Torque		
Thread Size x Pitch (mm)	Ft-Lb	Kgm	Nm	Ft-Lb	Kgm	Nm
6 x 1.0	2–3	.2–.4	3–4	3–6	.4–.8	5–8
8 x 1.25	6–8	.8–1	8–12	9–14	1.2–1.9	13–19
10 x 1.25	12–17	1.5–2.3	16–23	20–29	2.7–4.0	27–39
12 x 1.25	21–32	2.9–4.4	29–43	35–53	4.8–7.3	47–72
14 x 1.5	35–52	4.8–7.1	48–70	57–85	7.8–11.7	77–110
16 x 1.5	51–77	7.0–10.6	67–100	90–120	12.4–16.5	130–160
18 x 1.5	74–110	10.2–15.1	100–150	130–170	17.9–23.4	180–230
20 x 1.5	110–140	15.1–19.3	150–190	190–240	26.2–46.9	160–320
22 x 1.5	150–190	22.0–26.2	200–260	250–320	34.5–44.1	340–430
24 x 1.5	190–240	26.2–46.9	260–320	310–410	42.7–56.5	420–550

arately plus a master kit containing a variety of taps and inserts plus installation tools.

Before effecting a repair to a threaded hole, remove any snapped, broken or damaged bolts or studs. Penetrating oil can be used to free frozen threads; the offending item can be removed with locking pliers or with a screw or stud extractor. After the hole is clear, the thread can be repaired.

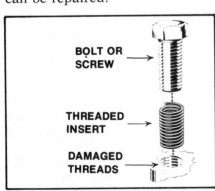

Damaged bolt holes can be repaired with thread repair inserts

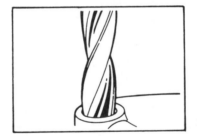

1. Drill out the damaged threads with the specified drill. Drill completely through the hole or to the bottom of a blind hole.

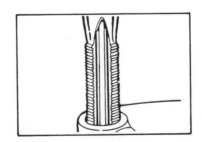

2. With the tap supplied, tap the hole to receive the threaded insert. Keep the tap well oiled and back the tap out frequently to avoid clogging the threads.

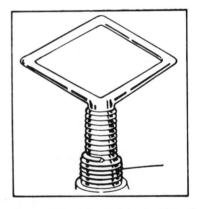

3. Screw the thread insert onto the thread installation tool until the tang engages the slot. Screw the insert into the tapped hole until it is ¼–½ turn below the top surface. After installation break the tang off with a hammer and punch.

Safety Systems and Safety Check

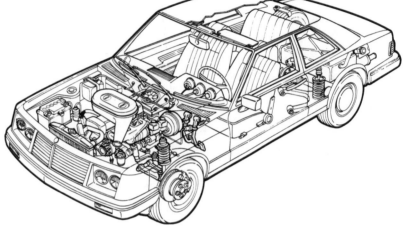

TOOLS AND SUPPLIES

Tools
  Screwdrivers
  Wrenches
  Pliers
  Jumper wire
  Wire cutters
Supplies
  Wire
  Electrical tape
  Duct tape

Automotive Safety

Believe it or not, automotive safety is not a recent invention of Washington legislators. Safety has always been a concern of automakers, even before Federal standards were initiated.

As far back as 1900, when cars were still "horseless carriages," the steering wheel replaced the rudder-like steering stick, adding safety as well as convenience to the vehicle.

In the next decade, the industry introduced the all-steel body, rearview mirror, shock absorbers and the electric horn.

Automobiles of the 1920s were revolutionized by steel wheels, twin-beam headlights, laminated windshield glass, hydraulic brakes on all four wheels, balloon tires and windshield wipers.

The 1930s brought improved steering gears, power brakes, defrosters and sealed-beam headlights.

In the 1940s double hood latches, padded instrument panels, and self-adjusting brakes were first used, in addition to one of the most important safety innovations—the turn signal.

In the post-war 1950s, the population of automobiles increased dramatically and safety became even more important. Seat belts, head restraints, energy-absorbing steering wheels and impact-resistant door latches were added to most new cars.

The '60s and '70s saw the advent of dual braking systems, collapsible steering columns, wear indicators for various parts of the vehicle, side impact door beams, warning lights and buzzers, seatbelt interlock systems and energy-absorbing bumper systems.

There are currently over 50 National Highway Traffic and Safety Administration (NHSTA) standards that directly affect vehicle safety, with more (including air bags, drunk-driver interlocks and 50 mile-per-hour crash protection) sure to make it onto the books during the 1980s.

Most of the cost of regulatory compliance has been passed on to the consumer in the form of retail price increases. The accompanying chart shows how much car prices have risen—above normal price increases—between 1968 and 1978 due to compliance with Federally mandated safety and air quality regulations. The chart also estimates that the consumer will be footing the bill for an extra $1,000—above normal price increases—between 1979 and 1984 for cars to comply with Federal safety standards.

On-Board Warning Systems

Turn on the ignition switch in almost any new or late-model car and watch the instrument panel. The modern automobile has an abundance of warning lights that provide valuable information. In addition to the familiar oil, temperature and ammeter lights, the list could also include:

· Brake system warning
· Windshield washer fluid level

- Coolant level
- Brake fluid level
- Door ajar
- Headlamp door position
- EGR or emission check
- High beam indicator
- Seatbelt light
- Cold engine warning
- Turn signals

A few cars with air bags also have a function indicator, and some import cars have a brake lining wear indicator light. The high price of fuel is creating a demand for yet another light—the fuel economy warning system. When the light comes on, it tells the driver he or she is pushing too hard on the gas pedal. High manifold vacuum equals good gas mileage and vice versa. The system simply reads manifold vacuum from a sensor, and when it drops to a predetermined level, a circuit is completed and the light is lit.

If a warning light comes on, you must find out why. There's either a problem in the system being monitored or in the warning lamp circuit. Finding the actual fault is important and not very difficult. But a wiring diagram is the basic tool needed to prevent confusion.

Looking at the typical warning light circuit, you'll see that the bulb is most often supplied with current through the ignition switch. Further examination reveals the most common way of completing the circuit and getting the bulb to light is by means of a sensor which completes the ground connection. In this case, sensor is a fancy word for a switch that turns on or off according to specific conditions.

Consider the oil pressure warning light system. Current from the ignition switch flows through the warning lamp and from there to ground through the oil pressure switch. This particular switch is normally closed and the circuit is complete until the switch opens in response to oil pressure in the engine.

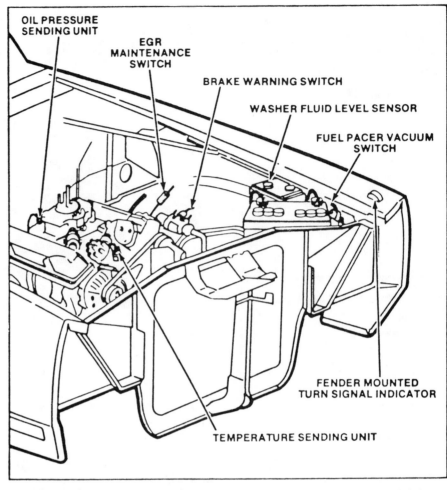

Warning light related parts can be found almost anywhere under the hood. It is important that any check of the system include the wiring, which exists in a hostile environment.

Just the opposite is true with the water temperature sensor. It is normally open and only completes the circuit when an internal element expands (in response to heat) to close the contacts. If the car has a cold engine warning lamp, the sensor includes two sets of contacts. One set is normally closed and opens as the internal element expands. This action breaks the ground circuit to the warning lamp. The other set of contacts functions if the temperature rises far enough to close them, turning on the high temperature warning.

If either of the temperature lights is lit while the engine seems normal, just unplugging the wires from the sensor will provide valuable diagnostic information. If the lights remain lit, there's a short to ground in the wiring from the lamp to the sensor. The service needed isn't to the cooling system, but the warning system.

If the lights go out with the wires unplugged and the engine seems normal, it's entirely possible that the sensor has failed and needs to be replaced. But don't just unplug the wires and forget about them. This could be disastrous for the car owner should a cooling problem develop without warning.

Seatbelts and Interlocks

Seatbelts have been used on cars for years, but 1974 and 1975 cars also have a seatbelt interlock system which, depending on your viewpoint, was either a godsend or simply another example of government interference with your private life.

The seatbelt interlock uses the same warning buzzer as earlier cars, but in addition, requires that you buckle your seatbelt before the car can be started. Switches imbedded in the seats sense the presence of a predetermined amount of weight and prevent the car from starting unless the belt is buckled. A small logic module (actually a mini-computer) is programmed to accept only one sequence of events to start the car. If you sit down, buckle up and turn the key, in exactly that sequence, the module will allow the car to start. If you do it any other way the module is programmed to refuse to allow the car to start. Leaving the seatbelts buckled is not the solution either. The belt must be retracted when you remove weight from the seat or the module is programmed to reject these conditions.

The problem is, what do you do when the car won't start even with the belts buckled in the proper sequence?

The seatbelt system doesn't fail often, but when it does, the fault usually lies in the electronic control module, a small gadget either under the seat or behind the instrument panel. The module cannot think, but it is programmed to determine the sequence of events in starting the car.

The first thing to do if your car won't start is to make sure there is nothing on the front seat that might depress the sensor switches. Also make sure all the front seat belts are unbuckled. If the seat and belts are okay, turn

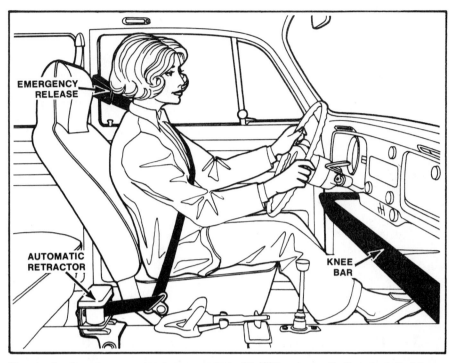

No warning buzzers or sensors are needed with VW's new seatbelt system that is undergoing "real world" testing in the U.S. The upper end of the shoulder belt is anchored to the door and the other end to an inertia reel retractor. When the door is closed, the belt automatically adjusts to the wearer.

the switch off, unbuckle, and get out of the car. Wait three minutes for the module to realize that you are actually out. Make sure the parking brake is on and the transmission is in Neutral or Park. Then, reach in through the window and start the car. This is called the "mechanic's start" and is a feature of all the interlock systems. Parking attendants make use of the mechanic's start by putting pressure with their back against the seat and raising off the cushion so the seat switch is not depressed. This works, but may eventually break the seat.

If your car will start by using the mechanic's start, you can continue to use it indefinitely. But it is inconvenient, and difficult to use when the engine is cold, because you have to reach in and pump the throttle once to set the choke, without sitting on the seat.

If the mechanic's start won't do the job, the next easiest ma-

neuver is to turn on the ignition switch, open the hood, push the override button, and try again to start the car. This button allows you one start, bypassing the interlock system completely. Do not attempt to tape or wire the button down permanently. The override switch is designed to allow you one start only.

If pushing the override button doesn't let you start the car, turn on the headlights. Are they bright, with full brilliance? If they are completely dead, or only a dim glow, you have a dead battery, and there is probably nothing wrong with the interlock.

A quick way to eliminate the interlock is to unplug the override relay and use a jumper wire across two of the wires in the plug, as follows:

American Motors: Connect the green (with tracer) and green wires together.

Chrysler Corp.: Connect the two yellow wires together.

Ford Motor Co.: Connect the

No. 32 red/blue stripe wire to the No. 33 white/pink dot wire. If the No. 32 and No. 33 terminals have more than one wire, connect all the wires from No. 32 to No. 33.

General Motors: Connect the green or green/black wire (purple/white on Cadillac) to the purple wire.

After making the connection, leave the override relay unplugged. The car should start normally, using the key. If it doesn't, the trouble is not in the interlock, but in the starting system. If the car does start, it may be driven indefinitely with the above connections, and the interlock will not be heard from again.

Disconnecting the Interlock System

As of October 29, 1974, a special Act of Congress made it legal to disconnect the seatbelt interlock and buzzer, although the warning light portion of the system must remain functional.

AMC

The logic module is located under the center of the instrument panel. The starter relay/by-pass switch is mounted under the hood, next to the starter solenoid on the right-hand inner fender panel.

The interlock may be disabled by unplugging the override relay

and connecting the green (with tracer) wire, and the green wire together.

Chrysler Corporation

The underhood bypass switch is located near the electronic control unit on the firewall on all intermediate models, and near the right-hand hood hinge plate on all full-size models.

The remaining components are found in the following locations: Buzzer—at the right side of the instrument panel above the parking brake on intermediates, and at the left side of the brake support bracket on full-size models; Interlock Unit—on the instrument panel to the left of the glovebox on intermediates, and above the buzzer on full-size models.

To disconnect the continuous seat-belt warning buzzer:

1. Remove the nine-cavity connector from the control unit.

2. Momentarily ground the wire in cavity No. 6 to see if the buzzer operates. This is done to positively identify the buzzer wire.

3. Cut off the wire at cavity No. 6 and tape it back into the wiring harness.

Disconnecting the interlock feature itself is not for the amateur mechanic. All dealers have received a service bulletin on how to modify the electronic control unit for customers requesting it. It involves disconnecting the buzzer wire (you could easily do this yourself) and making some internal wiring changes to the printed circuit board in the interlock module (the bulletin recommends that this be done by a radio repair shop).

Chilton Tip

Although the interlock can be disabled by disconnecting the seat sensor wires at the connectors under the seat, this is not the proper method, since it also disables the seatbelt warn-

TROUBLESHOOTING THE INTERLOCK SYSTEM

ENGINE WILL NOT START

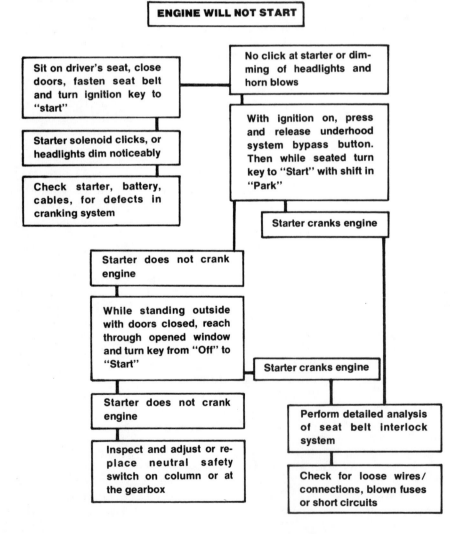

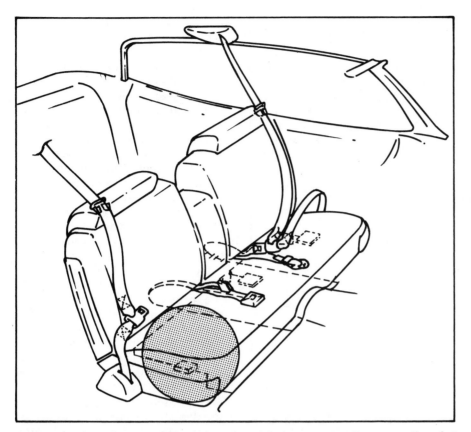

Simply disconnecting the interlock control module lets you start the car anytime, but the warning light is required by law.

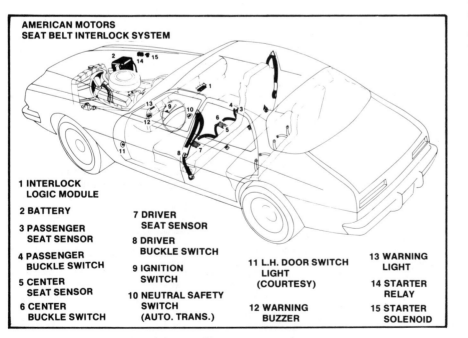

**AMERICAN MOTORS
SEAT BELT INTERLOCK SYSTEM**

1 INTERLOCK
LOGIC MODULE

2 BATTERY

3 PASSENGER
SEAT SENSOR

4 PASSENGER
BUCKLE SWITCH

5 CENTER
SEAT SENSOR

6 CENTER
BUCKLE SWITCH

7 DRIVER
SEAT SENSOR

8 DRIVER
BUCKLE SWITCH

9 IGNITION
SWITCH

10 NEUTRAL SAFETY
SWITCH
(AUTO. TRANS.)

11 L.H. DOOR SWITCH
LIGHT
(COURTESY)

12 WARNING
BUZZER

13 WARNING
LIGHT

14 STARTER
RELAY

15 STARTER
SOLENOID

AMC seatbelt interlock parts locator.

ing light. The seatbelt warning light is still required. ∎

Ford Motor Co.

To disable the interlock on Ford Motor Co. cars:

1. Apply the parking brake and remove the ignition key.

2. Locate the system emergency override switch and connector under the hood. Remove the connector.

3. Cut the white wire(s) with the pink dots (#33 circuit) and the red wire(s) with the light blue stripe (#32 circuit).

4. Splice the two (four) wires together and tape the splice. Use a "butt" connector if available.

∎

Chilton Tip

Do not cut and splice the other connector wires. If the red/yellow hash wire is spliced to any of the other wires the car will start in gear.

∎

5. Install the connector back on the override switch. Close the hood.

6. Apply the parking brakes, buckle the seat belt, and turn the key to the "ON" position. If the starter cranks in "ON" or any gear selected, the wrong wires have been cut and spliced. Repeat steps 3–6.

7. Unbuckle the belt and try to start the car. If the car doesn't start, repeat steps 3–6. If the car starts, everything is OK.

8. To stop the warning buzzer from operating, remove it from its connector and throw it away. Tape the connector to the wiring harness so that it can't rattle.

General Motors

To disconnect the seatbelt interlock system on GM cars:

1. Disconnect the negative battery cable.

2. Locate the interlock harness connector under the left side of the instrument panel on or near the fuse block.

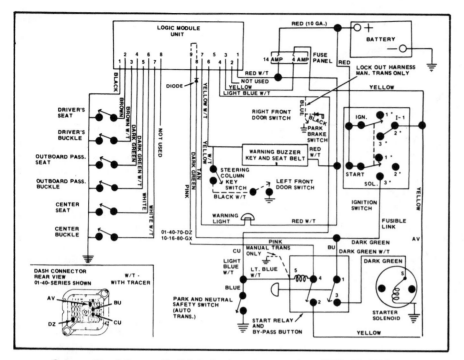

Schematic of the seatbelt interlock system used on 1974–75 AMC cars.

3. Cut and tape the ends of the green wire on the body side of the connector.

4. To disconnect the buzzer remove it from the fuse block or connector.

Energy-Absorbing Bumpers

Energy-absorbing bumpers in some form, capable of absorbing impact up to 5 mph, have been required by law on passenger cars since 1973. Basically, a piston is charged with an inert gas and a cylinder is filled with hydraulic fluid. The cylinder tube is crimped around the piston tube. The crimping is backed by a grease ring to prevent the entrance of moisture and/or dirt. The piston tube is attached to the bumper and the cylinder tube is attached to the frame. Extension is limited by a stop ring.

Some oil wetting is normal due to seepage of the grease ring behind the crimp. Hydraulic fluid leakage in the form of noticeable dripping indicates a failed unit.

Some scuffing of the piston is normal in average use. Obvious damage to the unit, such as dents or torn mounts, indicates a failed unit. Repair is not possible. Defective units must be replaced.

Air Bags

The Federal government has mandated the use of air bags ac-cording to the following timetable:

  1982—all full-size cars
  1983—all intermediate and compact cars
  1984—all passenger cars

The air bag, or air cushion restraint system (A.C.R.S.) as it is technically known, is one of the more controversial automotive safety devices, and is intended to replace the familiar (and inexpensive) seatbelt.

Although different manufacturers' systems vary slightly, the air bag system is composed of a few basic parts. A sensor in the area of the front bumper, and, in some cases, a second sensor in the firewall area, sense the impact. The sensors activate inflator(s) that inflate a passenger air bag in the right-hand side of the dashboard, a driver air bag located in the steering wheel hub and a knee restraint for driver and passenger located beneath the dash to prevent submarining.

The system has an indicator lamp activated by the ignition key to let you know the system is working. If the car is involved in a frontal crash equivalent to running into a stationary barrier at at least 10–12 mph, the sudden deceleration (impact) causes the sensor to activate a nitrogen gas inflator which instantly inflates the air bag preventing the oc-

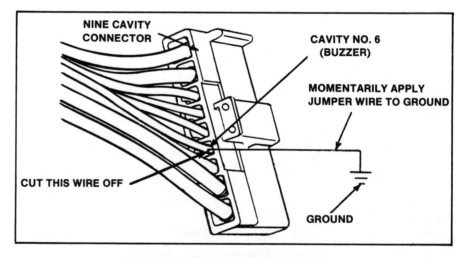

The Chrysler Corp. nine-cavity connector.

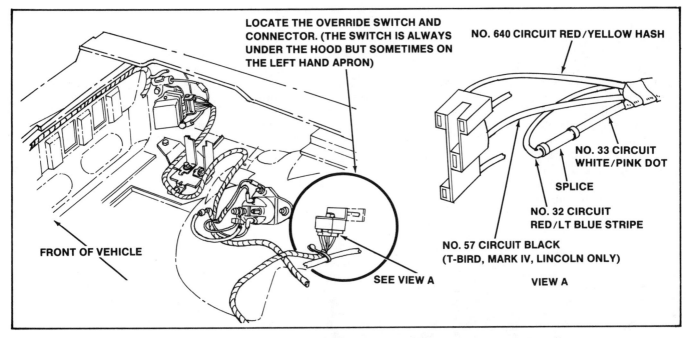

Disconnecting the Ford Motor Co. seatbelt interlock.

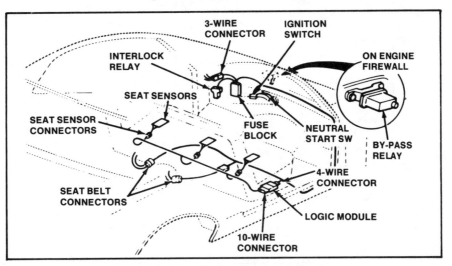

GM seatbelt interlock system parts locator.

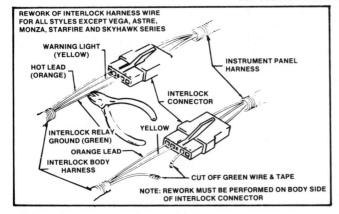

Disconnecting the GM starter interlock on all models except Vega, Monza, Astre, Starfire and Skyhawk.

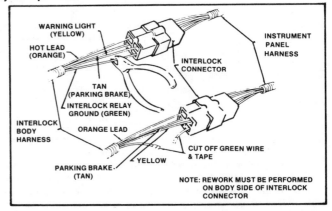

Disconnecting the Vega, Monza, Astre, Starfire and Skyhawk interlock.

cupants from contacting the inside of the vehicle. The air cushions absorb the impact.

The air bags themselves are porous and the air is actually beginning to escape as they are being inflated. The entire process (sensing, inflation and partial deflation) is completed in about 1/25th of a second, or about the time it takes to blink your eye.

Although the system has been proven effective in frontal impact crashes (but not as effective as seatbelts), it has several drawbacks:

· The system is expensive. Private business and the government differ on the cost, but it is staggering. Manufacturers of components and the car companies agree that the installed price per car will be about $325, and the replacement cost in the event of accidental deployment or an accident will run two and a half to three times the cost of the original system.

· In all, the air bags will cost about $25 billion over the next 20 years, or more than the total of all other safety features mandated since 1966.

· The air bags are only supposed to inflate in *frontal* accidents. Air bags are not intended to offer protection from side or rear impacts, or from rollovers.

· The propellent used to inflate the air bags is sodium azide, a Class B poison and hazardous material used in the production of smokeless gunpowder. In its pure form, it is relatively stable, but converts to nitrogen gas when triggered by a spark. Aside from this, it has been identified as a potent mutagen and potential carcinogen.

Deterrents for Drug- and Alcohol- Impaired Driving

Determining when driving skills have been impaired by drugs or alcohol is often a matter of opinion, which may vary widely from state to state. Alcohol, for instance, is absorbed directly into the bloodstream very rapidly and is eliminated slowly. It takes the body about one hour to dispose of an ounce of whiskey. If alcohol is consumed faster than it's eliminated, the alcohol will build up in measurable amounts which will affect an individuals' judgment, perception, coordination and reflexes. If alcohol constitutes as little as 0.1% of the volume of blood (five ounces of 86-proof alcohol in one hour), the chances of being involved in an accident are six to seven times greater than if the person consumed no alcohol. If the alcohol concentration reaches 0.15%, the chances of being involved in an accident are 25 times greater than the person with no alcohol.

Auto manufacturers have come up with many deterrents to alcohol- or drug-impaired drivers.

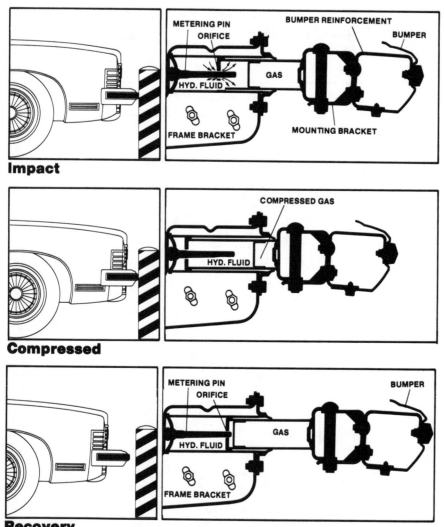

Impact

Compressed

Recovery

On impact, the bumper makes contact with the barrier. As the bumper is pushed back, hydraulic fluid is pushed past the tapered metering pin, absorbing the impact. As the bumper is stopped, hydraulic fluid in the front chamber has forced the floating piston forward, compressing the gas to return the bumper. On recovery, compressed gas forces the fluid to return to its original chamber and the bumper is returned to its original position.

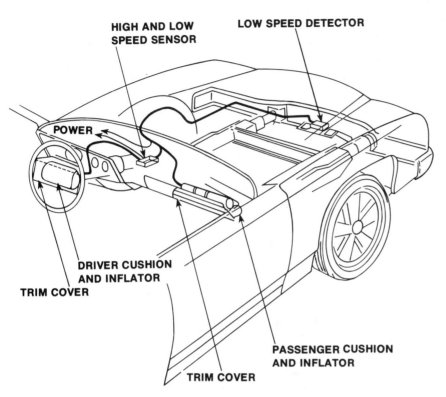

HIGH AND LOW SPEED SENSOR

LOW SPEED DETECTOR

POWER

DRIVER CUSHION AND INFLATOR

TRIM COVER

PASSENGER CUSHION AND INFLATOR

TRIM COVER

Typical installation of a gas-powered air bag restraint system.

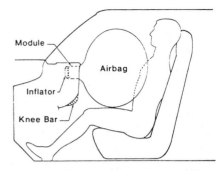

Module

Airbag

Inflator

Knee Bar

High mounted passenger air bags are designed to provide head and upper torso restraint in frontal impacts.

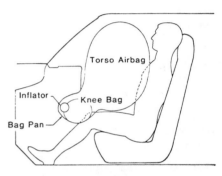

Torso Airbag

Inflator

Knee Bag

Bag Pan

Low mounted passenger air bags are designed to give lower torso protection in frontal impact situations.

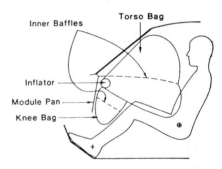

Inner Baffles

Torso Bag

Inflator

Module Pan

Knee Bag

Driver air bag uses a steering wheel mounted air bag for protection in frontal impacts.

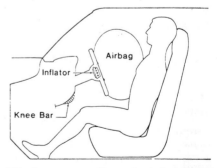

Inflator

Airbag

Knee Bar

This is a composite system developed for small cars such as Omni and Chevette.

One of the latest, but typical of the systems being tested, is this unit being evaluated by General Motors. It is installed in the vehicle and operates whenever the ignition is turned on. When the ignition is turned on, a sensitive needle on the instrument panel begins to fluctuate, and its movements can be controlled by slight motions of the steering wheel. If the driver's actions are impaired, erratic motion of the steering wheel will cause the needle to swing uncontrolled back and forth outside the middle (shaded) area. A red reset button will light, indicating the starter is "locked out" and will not operate. The driver has two more chances to pass the test. Pushing the reset button reactivates the needle, and if the driver keeps the needle in the center area for a predetermined amount of time, a "pass" button will light and the car can be started.

Experiments indicate that half of all persons with a blood alcohol concentration of 0.1% will fail the test.

Walk-Around Safety Check

Take a few minutes to walk around your car or truck every now and then, especially during a long trip. Checking out all of the things that affect your driving safety won't take more than five minutes and could uncover a small problem before it gets dangerous or expensive.

Tires and Wheels

Check for uneven wear patterns, excessive wear, nails, cuts or other damage. Uneven wear may indicate alignment problems in the front end or uneven inflation pressure. Check the inflation pressure with a gauge.

MECHANICAL VIBRATION DIAGNOSIS

Vibration Category	Correction Codes For Vibrations Within Specific mph Ranges								
	10	20	30	40	50	60	70	80	90
Vehicle Speed Sensitive				UJ and TEB	WB	TRR	TB PSY	TLR	
Torque Sensitive		UJA		UJ and TEB				UJA	
Engine Speed Sensitive		EA DEM							

Diagnosis Chart Correction Codes

ADB—Accessory Drive Belts. Excessive wear or looseness may cause droning noise or flutter.

AN—Rear Axle Noise. May be caused by gears or bearings.

DEM—Damaged Engine Mounts. May allow engine or accessories to contact body.

EA—Engine Accessories. Loose or broken accessories: power steering pump, air conditioning compressor, alternator, water pump, etc.

PSY—Propeller Shaft and Yokes. Undercoating, runout, and balance not a cause for vibration below 45 mph. Possible cause of audible vibration only between 55 and 75 mph.

TB—Tire Balance. Not a cause of vibration below 30 mph. Dynamic unbalance not a cause below 40 mph. Check balance of wheels and tires.

TEB—Transmission Extension Housing Bushing. Looseness usually accompanied by oil seal leakage.

TLR—Tire and Wheel Lateral Runout. Not usually a cause of vibration below 60 mph.

TRR—Tire and Wheel Radial Runout. Not a cause of vibration below 20 mph. The speed required to cause vibration increases as runout decreases.

TW—Tire Wear. Uneven wear patterns (cupped) may generate a singing whine at higher speeds and degenerate to a growl at lower speeds and may be accompanied by vibration similar to that caused by wheel bearings.

UJ—Universal Joints. Universal joints can cause vibrations at any speed.

UJA—Universal Joint Angles. Incorrect angles may cause mechanical vibration below 15 mph and mechanical or audible vibration between 30 and 55 mph.

WB—Wheel Bearings. If rough or damaged, will cause a growling or grinding noise at low speeds, or a whining noise at high speeds. Loose wheel bearings can cause mechanical vibrations at 50 to 60 mph.

AUDIBLE VIBRATION DIAGNOSIS

Vibration Category	Correction Codes For Vibrations Within Specific mph Ranges								
	10	20	30	40	50	60	70	80	90
Vehicle Speed Sensitive				UJA UJ and TEB	WB	TW	PSY		
Torque Sensitive					AN UJ and TEB				
Engine Speed Sensitive			DEM	ADB	EA				

HIGHWAY EMERGENCY CHECKLIST

Item	Car	Glove Comp.	Trunk
Fire extinguisher	√		
This manual	√		
Coins for meters and phone		√	
Tire Gauge		√	
Flashlight		√	
First aid kit		√	
Road maps		√	
Spare fuses		√	
Flares			√
4-way lug wrench/jack			√
Jumper cables			√
Hand tools			√
Paper towels/rags			√
Work gloves			√
Hand cleaner			√
Fan belt			√
Plastic jug of water			√
Duct tape			√
Silicone spray lube			√

Prototype deterrent system for alcohol- or drug-impaired driver.

Lighting System

Check the headlights, turn signals and taillights for proper operation. Take a look at the operation of all exterior lights while someone else operates them.

Clean the headlights with a rag. You'll be amazed at the difference it makes at night.

Mirrors

Be sure that the mirrors are clean and adjusted properly for the best view of what's behind you.

Windshield and Wipers

Clean the windshield for maximum visibility. While you're about it, take a quick look at the wiper blades. They should be in good condition for when they're needed.

Tailpipe

Checking the color of the tailpipe is a good habit to get into. It can provide a quick check on how your engine is operating.

On a long trip, or when the car has been run at highway speeds for a while, the inside of the tailpipe should be a light gray or white. This indicates that the engine is running properly.

A blackish or sooty tailpipe indicates that the carburetor is set too rich and probably needs adjusting.

Fluid Leaks

Look for fuel, oil, or water leaks. The location of the spots under the car can give a clue to the source of the leak, just as the color of the spots gives valuable clues.

Red is probably automatic transmission fluid.

Black or brown is most likely engine oil or rear axle lube.

Clear water will usually come

NOISES

Noises are the most common indicator of something gone wrong in your car, and also the most difficult to interpret. Noises come in hundreds of variations (knocks, rattles, squeaks, grinds, etc.), each with its own particular sound and nearly impossible to describe accurately. The other problem is recognizing when the sound is perfectly normal and when it spells trouble.

Virtually any part can make almost any noise if the conditions are right. A stethoscope, piece of hose or a metal rod can be used carefully to pinpoint sounds coming from various parts.

Noise	Description	Could be Caused By
Buzz	A humming sound (bzzzz)	A buzz or whistle can be caused by a defective radiator cap. If loosening the cap stops the noise, replace the cap. Other causes include foreign debris on the radiator, loose radiator or fan, or a loose shroud.
Clang	Metallic ringing similar to the sound of a bell	This is normally due to a failing U-joint and you will hear it as you back off, or step on the gas. U-joints are serviced by replacement.
Click (tick)	A quick, sharp sound similar to a loud clock	A tick while starting is typical of older electrical fuel pumps and is not a malfunction. Other causes are stone in the tire tread (frequency varies with speed), damaged wheel bearing, shredded fan belt, windshield wiper motor/transmission, differential or transmission gears, heater motor, lack of radio suppression, or improperly adjusted valves.
Grinding Grating Growling	A harsh rubbing sound, like parts rubbing or scraping A deeper grinding sound	Check the fluid level in the power steering pump. U-joints will also occasionally make a grinding noise, as will a starter drive that is not engaging or disengaging completely. Other causes include a bad throwout bearing, dragging brakes, something non-metallic in contact with the brakes or brake drum, worn transmission gears, bad water pump or loose water pump pulley or fan belt contacting the shroud.
Hiss	A high pitched sound like steam escaping (sssssssss...)	The usual cause of this type of sound is steam escaping from the radiator or a broken hose, although it can be produced by a vacuum leak, a leaking tire, or a loose spark plug. All of these are fairly easy to cure. Other causes are wind leaks around the body or windows, or a plugged PCV valve. Watch the oil fill hole; if smoke is coming out accompanied by a hiss, chances are you have worn piston rings.
Howl	A prolonged wailing sound	A howling sound is usually from the transmission gears (check the fluid level before assuming the worst), but could also be due to wind leaks around the body or windows.
Hum	A low droning noise (hummmmmm...)	A hum from the rear probably indicates a defective rear axle, especially if it is louder coasting, but before having it torn down, check other causes. Snow tires produce a constant hum, as do certain road surfaces. Check the rear axle oil level, wheel bearings and U-joints.
Knock	A pounding or striking of metal parts	A constant knocking noise is usually due to worn crankshaft or connecting rod bearings. A knock under load can be caused by worn connecting rod bearings, fuel octane too low, or loose wrist pins in the piston. Remove a spark plug wire from each cylinder in turn. If the knock stops, you've located the cylinder.
Rattle	Rapid succession of sharp sounds	Rattles are normal to the aging process. If it doesn't seem to affect the handling or running of the car, don't worry.
Squeal	A prolonged, shrill squeaking	A squeal normally comes from an improperly tightened fan belt, but could be due to a bad water pump, brakes not fully releasing, improper toe-in, worn brake linings, low tires or worn alternator bearings.
Thud, Thump	A dull knocking sound	These sounds are caused by low, flat-spotted or out-of-round tires, worn U-joints (they give a slight thud as you let off the gas), loose battery or contents of the trunk, bad throwout bearing (check by applying and releasing the clutch), excessive play in the crankshaft or broken engine mounts.

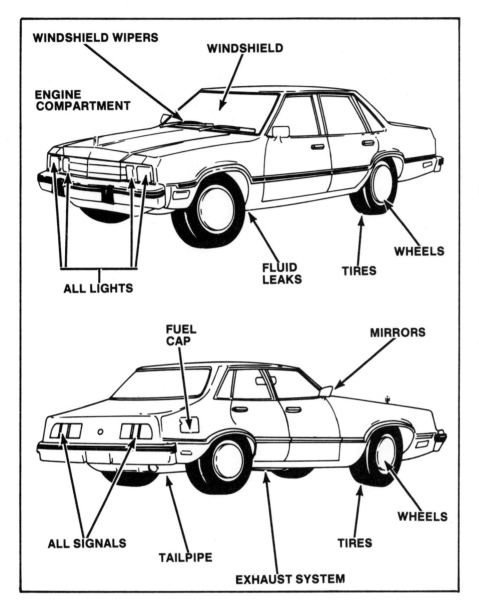

COMMON SENSE GUIDE TO SAFETY

Sight	Besides routine inspection, be alert to the very appearance. Look for sagging on either end or side, puddles underneath or anything that doesn't look right.
Sound	If you've got a strange noise, try to associate it with a particular function, such as braking or accelerating. Then you'll know where to look for it.
Smell	Smells are deceptive. Does it smell like burned rubber, oil, or insulation? Gas or exhaust fumes point out leaks in their systems.
Feel	If car handles strangely, is it a constant feel, or does it only pull while braking? Associate behavior of car with particular action.

from the air conditioning condenser on a hot day.

Greenish water is usually antifreeze.

It's normal for the air conditioner to drip a small amount of water under the front of the car when it's used on a hot day.

Fuel Cap

If you just stopped for fuel, be sure that the fuel cap was put back.

Underhood Check

Engine oil—Check the engine oil level.

Coolant—Check the radiator coolant level.

Battery—Check the electrolyte level.

Automatic transmission–Check the fluid level.

Master cylinder—Check the fluid level.

Windshield washer—Check the fluid level.

Belts & hoses—Visually check all belts and hoses for wear.

Safety on the Road

While you're on the road, pay attention to your car; it may be trying to tell you something. Look, listen, smell and feel for possible problems. Warning signals come in many forms—noises, different handling and vibrations.

Sights

Part of any walk-around inspection of your vehicle should include checking underneath for spots and drips. Get into the habit of doing this regularly, especially after the car has been driven for a while.

· Red spots under the transmission area indicate leaking transmission fluid. Try to find out where the leak is coming from. It could be the problem is as simple as an overfilled transmission. The fluid could be foaming out the dipstick tube and running down the case.

· Rust spots of water under the

front of the car may indicate a leaking radiator, leaking radiator hoses or simply overflow from the radiator or air conditioning condenser.

· Dark oil spots under the differential probably indicate that the differential rear cover bolts are loose and should be tightened. Oil spots under the engine can mean anything from leaking valve cover gaskets (the oil runs down the engine) to a host of more serious problems. Try to find the source of the leak and fix it.

Feel

All good drivers learn to recognize when the car is behaving differently than normal. Vibrations often preface a great many mechanical problems that can be located and corrected before they become serious. Be suspicious of any vibrations that are out-of-the-ordinary—be alert and train yourself to recognize the warning signs.

Smell

Strange odors are often a clue to something gone (or about to go) wrong.

· An overheated radiator gives off a steamy vapor and a mild odor something like burning paint. It should warn you to check the temperature gauge or to stop and check the coolant level.

· Overheated brake linings give off a strong definite odor of something burning. Usually overheated linings are accompanied by squeaking sounds from the wheels, indicating that the linings are glazed from heat. The best thing to do is stop and let the brakes cool for about half an hour, but have the brakes checked as soon as possible.

· Burning oil or grease is a strong, pungent odor, usually more noticeable when the car is not moving. Occasionally, there will be wisps of smoke coming from under the hood. The problem could be as simple as oil leaking from valve cover gaskets onto hot exhaust manifolds, or it could be just accumulated grease from a delayed engine cleaning.

· A frequent smell associated with newer cars equipped with catalytic converters is the rotten egg smell, which is unmistakable for anything else. One of the by-products of the reaction in the catalytic converter is sulphur dioxide (SO_2), which is responsible for the odor. It does not indicate a malfunction, but is extremely unpleasant.

5
Fuels and Lubricants

Gasoline

Gasoline is a hydrocarbon (composed of hydrogen and carbon), produced by refining crude oil or petroleum. When gasoline burns, these compounds separate into hydrogen and carbon atoms and unite with oxygen atoms. The results obtained from burning gasoline are dependent on its most important characteristics: octane rating, volatility, lead content, and density.

Octane Rating

Simply put, the octane rating of a gasoline is its ability to resist knock, a sharp metallic noise resulting from detonation or uncontrolled combustion in the cylinder. Knock can occur for a variety of reasons, one of which is the incorrect octane rating for the engine in your car. To understand why knock occurs, you must understand why knock doesn't occur. So let's take a look at the normal combustion process.

Under normal operating conditions, the firing of the spark plug initiates the burning of the fuel/air mixture in the combustion chamber. Once the plug fires, a wall of flame starts out-

ward from the plug in all directions at once. This flame front moves evenly and rapidly throughout the entire combustion chamber until the entire fuel/air mixture is burned. This even, rapid progress of the burning fuel/air mixture is highly dependent on the octane rating of the gasoline.

If the octane rating is too low, the last part of the compressed fuel/air mixture may ignite before the flame front reaches it, in effect creating two areas of combustion within the cylinder. However, while the original combustion is proceeding at a care-

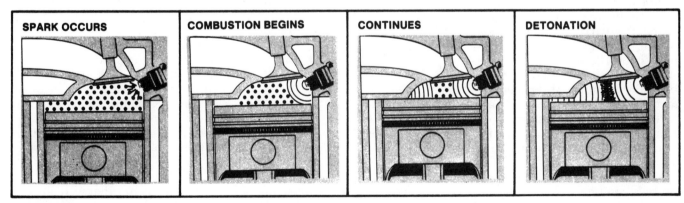

Detonation occurs when the anti-knock quality of the fuel used does not meet the engine's requirements. Note the two flame fronts. Detonation, like preignition can cause severe engine damage.

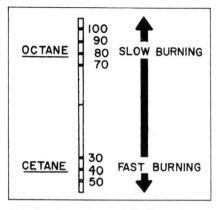

Cetane diesel fuel rating compared to octane gasoline fuel rating.

fully controlled rate, this new combustion is simply a sudden sharp explosion. This abrupt increase in pressure is what creates the knocking sound in the combustion chamber.

As far as the piston is concerned, the damage it inflicts is exactly like striking the piston top with a heavy hammer. Knock is very damaging to the engine, since it causes extraordinary wear to bearings, piston crowns, and other vital engine parts. Engines can actually be destroyed through excessive engine knock.

Engine knock can be controlled by using a gas with the proper octane rating. Octane measurements made under laboratory conditions have led to "Research" and "Motor" octane ratings. In general, the research octane number tends to be about 6 to 10 points higher than the motor octane rating (for what is essentially the same gasoline). Since the early seventies, most octane ratings on gas pumps have been the average of the research and motor octane numbers. For instance, if the gasoline formerly had a research octane rating of 100, and a motor octane rating of 90, the octane rating found on the pump now would be 95.

Your owner's manual will probably indicate the type of gasoline and octane recommended for use in your car. Since the 1971 model year, most cars have been designed to operate satisfactorily on 91 Research octane gasoline. However, octane requirements can vary according to the vehicle and the conditions under which it is operating. If you encounter sustained engine knock, wait until your tank is nearly empty, then try a gasoline with a higher octane rating. Don't overbuy—it's a waste of money to buy gasoline of a higher octane than your engine requires in order to satisfy its anti-knock need.

As a new car is driven, combustion deposits build up and the octane requirement increases until an equilibrium level, normally between four and six octane numbers higher than the new-car requirement, is reached. Other factors which can increase the octane an engine requires are higher air or engine temperatures, lower altitudes, lower humidity, a more advanced ignition spark timing, a leaner carburetor setting, sudden acceleration, and frequent stop-and-go driving which increases the build-up of combustion chamber deposits.

Catalytic Converters and Unleaded Fuel

Since 1975, most cars have been equipped with catalytic converters, making the use of unleaded fuel mandatory. If you own a car equipped with a catalytic converter, you're well aware of this fact. All cars equipped with catalytic converters have a restricted filler neck opening which will only permit the use of the smaller nozzle used on unleaded gas pumps. The use of leaded gas will not harm the engine, but will destroy the effectiveness of the converter and void your warranty.

Lead Content

Older, higher-compression engines usually require a gasoline with a higher octane rating. The most efficient way of increasing the octane rating of a gasoline is to add a compound called tetraethyl lead. Therefore, if your owner's manual specifies the use of "premium" gasoline, you may have to use leaded fuels in order to avoid having your engine knock. However, should circumstances force you to use a low-lead or no-lead gasoline with lower octane than the car manufacturer specifies, you should temporarily retard the ignition timing very slightly in order to lessen the possibility of knocking. Some cars, though designed to operate on leaded gasoline, may be able to use the new low-lead and no-lead fuels. Again, experimentation is helpful in determining the gasoline octane which your car and your driving require. Don't automatically rule out a low-lead gasoline.

Volatility

The volatility of any liquid is its ability to vaporize, and gasoline must vaporize in order to burn. A highly volatile gasoline will help a cold engine start easily and run smoothly while it is warming up. However, the use of a highly volatile gasoline in warm weather tends to cause vapor lock, a condition in which the gasoline actually vaporizes before it arrives at the carburetor jet where vaporization is supposed to take place. This premature vaporization may occur in the fuel line, fuel pump, or in a section of the carburetor. When use of highly volatile fuel leads to vapor lock, the engine becomes starved for fuel and will either lose power or stall. Although refiners vary the percentage of volatile fuel in their gasoline according to season and locality, vapor lock is more likely to occur in the early spring, when some stations may not have received supplies of less volatile gasoline.

Density

Density is another property of gasoline which can affect your fuel economy. It indicates how much chemical energy the gasoline contains. Density is generally measured in BTU's per gallon (the BTU, or British Thermal Unit, is a standard unit of energy), and usually varies less than 2% among most gasolines but can vary as much as 4–8%. This indicates that gas mileage could vary by as much as 4 to 8%, depending on the density of the gasoline you happen to choose.

Additives

Practically as important as octane rating and volatility are the additives that refiners put into their gasolines. Carburetor detergent additives help clean the tiny passages in the carburetor, ensuring consistent fuel/air mixtures necessary for smooth running and good gas mileage. Winter additives include fuel line de-icers to reduce carburetor icing at the throttle plate. Other additives are used to help control combustion chamber deposits, gum formation, rust, and wear. One additive you may have noticed in your late-model car is manganese. Since the advent of the catalytic converter and the resultant widespread use of unleaded gas, manganese has been used by an increasing number of refiners as an anti-knock additive in unleaded gasoline. Manganese works, but it leaves reddish deposits on spark plugs. So if you pull your spark plugs and notice that they are covered with what looks like rust, don't panic. It's only manganese and it's as harmless as the lead deposits it replaces.

Gasoline Blends

The disruption of oil supplies from the Middle East in 1973, and again in 1979, spurred an effort try and curb the U.S. dependence on foreign petroleum sources. Interest in alternative fuels was also created by the reduction or elimination of lead anti-knock additives in gasoline. The lead was removed because of its incompatibility with the catalytic converter, now standard on almost every car and light truck.

Vast deposits of shale rock and tar sands in North America contain huge reserves of rich, but expensive-to-recover, oil. A far less complicated and more economical method is to blend alcohol, in the form of ethanol or methanol, with gasoline. Interest in these blends, generally known as gasohol, had been slight, prior to 1973, because the fuel would have been more expensive than gasoline.

But, all that changed when gasoline soared past $1.00 per gallon.

Ethanol has attracted the most attention as a blend. It can be fermented from a variety of bases, including grain and sugar cane, much the same way wine is produced from grapes. The U.S. Environmental Protection Agency (EPA) allows a 10% ethanol mixture with gasoline and it is being sold as "super unleaded" or "premium unleaded" gasoline, gasohol, or with no specific identification.

Methanol comes from natural gas, but the technology is known to produce it from coal, wood and a variety of other materials. Like ethanol, methanol raises the octane of gasoline and reduces engine "knock" or "ping", without affecting the efficiency of the catalytic converter. A 5% blend of methanol may raise the octane rating at the pump by 1–1.5 numbers.

Methanol also reduces carbon monoxide exhaust emissions, but the trade-offs can be high.

Methanol has an adverse affect on fuel economy, especially in late model vehicles. A 5% blend of methanol with gasoline has an energy content 2.5% less than gasoline.

Evaporative emissions rise substantially when methanol is blended with gasoline. And, methanol may increase the oxides of nitrogen emissions and affect the capacity of the charcoal in the evaporative emissions canister.

Methanol causes both hot and cold weather driveability problems. Methanol can change the stoichiometric (chemically correct) air/fuel ratio in the fuel delivery system. The higher volatility of the fuel increases the chance of vapor lock and the increased heat of vaporization of methanol increases cold start and stalling problems in winter.

Methanol, when water is present even in trace (minute) amounts will separate gasoline into 2 layers—gasoline rich on top and alcohol and water on the bottom. The net effect is unsatisfactory vehicle operation. Since the engine draws fuel from the bottom of the tank, it will not run properly, even at idle. Some refiners add heavier alcohols, known as "cosolvents", to counter the separation, but they are not 100% effective.

Methanol has an effect on the parts of the fuel system and is measured more in time than in mileage. Rubber, plastic and metal fuel system components in most motor vehicles were designed for use with gasoline and are subject to attack by methanol blended fuels. Water tends to cling to methanol, and any water in the fuel tank will be carried through the entire fuel system. Metal components (excluding brass) are subject to water corrosion. Plastic and rubber compounds, tend to swell, lose strength and stretch when subjected to high concentrations of methanol.

Several fuel suppliers are successfully marketing blends of methanol and cosolvents with gasoline, but the long-term effects on engines and fuel systems are not known and vehicle manufacturers will not give unqualified sanction to the use of methanol blended fuels. Most vehicle manufacturers specifically warn that gasoline blended with methanol can adversely affect your vehicle and some indicate that the use of methanol could void the manufacturer's warranty.

Check your owner's manual to be sure.

Diesel Fuel

Because of their unique compression-ignition principle, diesel engines run on fuel oil instead of gasoline. The fuel is injected into the cylinder at the end of the compression stroke and the heat of compression ignites the mixture. Diesel fuel used in automotive applications comes in two grades, No. 1 diesel fuel and No. 2 diesel fuel. No. 1 diesel is the more volatile of the two and is designed for engines which will operate under varying load and speed conditions. No. 2 diesel is designed for a relatively uniform speed and high loads. The two grades of fuel will mix and burn with no ill effects, although the engine manufacturer will undoubtedly recommend one or the other. Some of the important characteristics of diesel fuel are its cetane number and its viscosity.

Cetane Number

The cetane number of a diesel fuel refers to the ease with which a diesel fuel ignites. Don't confuse cetane ratings with octane ratings. Octane ratings refer to the slowing or controlling of the burning of gasoline. Cetane ratings refer only to the ease or speed of the ignition of diesel fuel. High cetane numbers mean that the fuel will ignite with relative ease or that it ignites well at low temperatures. Naturally, the lower the cetane number, the higher the temperature must be to ignite the fuel. Most commercial fuels have cetane numbers that range from 35 to 65. No. 1 diesel fuel is generally about 50 cetane, and is usually suitable for automotive applications. Most diesel manufacturers recommend fuel with a minimum cetane rating of about 45.

Viscosity

Viscosity is the ability of a liquid to flow. Water, for instance, has a low viscosity since it flows so easily. The viscosity of diesel fuel is important since it must be low enough that it flows easily through the injection system, while at the same time being high enough to lubricate the moving parts in the injection system. Number 2 diesel fuel has a higher viscosity than No. 1, which means it lubricates better, but does not flow as well. Because of this and its lower cetane rating, No. 2 diesel is not as satisfactory as No. 1 in extremely cold weather.

Where to Get Diesel Fuel

It wasn't too long ago that the only place you could get diesel fuel was at a truck stop. You can still get it there, and many other places as well. Estimates place the number of diesel stations in the U.S. as high as 12,000. While it's true that quite a few of these are tiny, out-of-the-way gas stations that sell diesel fuel to farmers, that still leaves a lot of major stations which are quite easily found. Most diesel car manufacturers (Mercedes-Benz, Oldsmobile, Peugeot, Volkswagen) publish diesel fuel directories which are quite complete. Check with your dealer to obtain one.

One more word on diesel fuels. No matter what you've heard elsewhere, *don't* thin diesel fuel with gasoline in cold weather. The lighter gasoline, which is more explosive, will cause rough running at the very least, and may cause extensive engine damage if enough is used.

Oils and Additives

Three ways you can improve your car's mileage and insure that it delivers good economy for a longer time are: 1) understand the functions of oil in your engine, 2) choose the proper oil for various operating conditions, and 3) have the oil and filter changed at the recommended intervals.

The Functions of Engine Oil

What does oil do in your car's engine? If you answered "lubricate," you're only partially right. While oil is primarily a lubricant, it also performs a number of other functions which are vital to the life and performance of your engine.

In addition to being a lubricant, oil also dissipates heat and makes parts run cooler; it helps reduce engine noise; it combats rust and corrosion of metal surfaces; it acts as a seal for pistons, rings, and cylinder walls; it combines with the oil filter to remove foreign substances from the engine.

When combustion occurs, temperatures can reach 2000–3000° F., while pistons can easily reach a temperature of 1000° F. The high heat load travels down the connecting rods to the bearings. Both tin and lead are commonly used in bearings and become very soft around 350° F.

Oil in the crankcase can reach 250° F. after warm-up and is supplied to the bearings at these temperatures.

As the oil circulates, it picks up heat, and may be 50° F. hotter than the crankcase oil. Flow and recirculation of the oil keeps the bearings at a safe heat level and is essential to limiting bearing temperatures. A continuous circulation of large quantities of oil is essential to long engine life.

Types of Engine Oil

Engine oil service classifications have been provided by the American Petroleum Institute and include "S" (normal gasoline engine use) and "C" (commercial and fleet) applications. The following chart compares the latest API oil classifications with those previously used.

Oil Viscosity

In addition to meeting the SE classification of the American Petroleum Institute, your oil should be of a viscosity suitable for the outside temperature in which you'll be driving.

Oil must be thin enough to get between the close-tolerance moving parts it must lubricate. Once there, it must be thick enough to separate them with a slippery oil film. If the oil is too thin, it won't separate the parts; if it's too thick, it can't squeeze between them in the first place—either way, excess friction and wear takes place. To complicate matters, cold-morning starts require a thin oil to reduce engine resistance, while high-speed driving requires a thick oil which can lubricate vital engine parts at temperatures up to 250° F.

According to the Society of Automotive Engineers' viscosity classification system, an oil with a high viscosity number (e.g., 40) will be thicker than one with a lower number (e.g., 10W). The "W" in 10W indicates that the oil is desirable for use in winter driving. Through the use of special additives, multiple-viscosity oils are available to combine easy starting at cold temperatures with engine protection at turnpike speeds. For example, a 10W-40 oil will have the viscosity of a 10W oil when the engine is cold and that of a 40 oil when the engine is warm. The use of such an oil will decrease engine resistance and improve your gas mileage during short trips in which the oil doesn't have a chance to warm up.

Some of the more popular multiple-viscosity oils are 5W-20, 5W-30, 10W-30, 10W-40, 20W-40, 20W-50, and 10W-50. Some manufacturers feel that fuel economy is about 1% greater with 10W-30 as opposed to 10W-40, and that 10W-30 oils produce less piston and ring deposits, decreasing oil consumption and decreasing the chance of stuck rings.

Consult the chart in this section, your owner's manual or a reputable oil dealer for the recommended viscosity range for your car and the outside temperature in which it operates.

Additives

A high-quality engine oil will include a number of chemical compounds known as additives. These are blended in at the refinery and fall into the following categories.

Pour point depressants help cold starting by making the oil flow more easily at low temperatures. Otherwise, the oil would tend to be a waxy substance just when you need it the most.

Oxidation and bearing corrosion inhibitors help to prevent the formation of gummy deposits which can take place when engine oil oxidizes under high temperatures. In addition, these inhibitors place a protective coating on sensitive bearing metals, which would otherwise be attacked by the chemicals formed by oil oxidation.

Rust and corrosion inhibitors protect against water and acids formed by the combustion process. Water is physically separated from the metal parts vulnerable to rust, and corrosive acids are neutralized by alkaline chemicals. The neutralization of combustion acids is an important key to long engine life.

Detergents and dispersants use teamwork. Detergents clean up the products of normal combustion and oxidation while dispersants keep them suspended until they can be removed by means of the filter or an oil change.

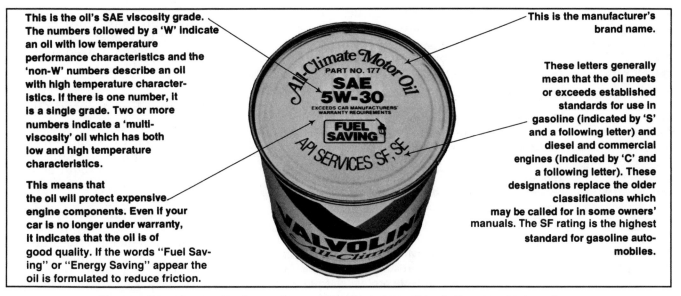

This is the oil's SAE viscosity grade. The numbers followed by a 'W' indicate an oil with low temperature performance characteristics and the 'non-W' numbers describe an oil with high temperature characteristics. If there is one number, it is a single grade. Two or more numbers indicate a 'multi-viscosity' oil which has both low and high temperature characteristics.

This means that the oil will protect expensive engine components. Even if your car is no longer under warranty, it indicates that the oil is of good quality. If the words "Fuel Saving" or "Energy Saving" appear the oil is formulated to reduce friction.

This is the manufacturer's brand name.

These letters generally mean that the oil meets or exceeds established standards for use in gasoline (indicated by 'S' and a following letter) and diesel and commercial engines (indicated by 'C' and a following letter). These designations replace the older classifications which may be called for in some owners' manuals. The SF rating is the highest standard for gasoline automobiles.

The top of the oil can will tell you all you need to know about the oil. Note that this is an SF oil.

MOTOR OIL GUIDE

The American Petroleum Institute (API) has classified and identified oil according to its use. The API service recommendations are listed on the top of the oil can and all car manufacturers use API letters to indicate recommended oils.

Almost all oils meet or exceed the highest service rating (SE), but viscosity should be selected to match the highest anticipated temperature before the next oil change.   S=Gasoline   C=Diesel

API Symbol	Use & Definition
SF	SF is the most severe service. It is an improved version of SE quality oil with improved oxidation stability and anti-wear quality. It replaces SE oil for all model years.
SE	SE is recommended for use in all 4-cycle gasoline engines, and cars used for stop and start or high speed, long distance driving. It has increased detergency and can withstand higher temperatures, while providing maximum protection against corrosion, rust and oxidation. Meets all service requirements for classifications SD, SC, SB and SA.
SD (formerly MS 1968)	These oils provide more protection against rust, corrosion and oxidation than oils classified SC. Meets minimum gasoline engine warranties in effect from 1968-70.
SC (formerly MS 1964)	These oils control rust and corrosion and retard the formation of high and low temperature deposits and meets minimum warranty requirements in effect for 1964-67 gasoline engines.
SB (formerly MM)	These oils have anti-scuff properties and will slow down oxidation and corrosion. Oils designed for this service afford minimum protection under moderate operating conditions.
SA (formerly ML)	These oils have no protective properties and have no performance requirements.
CD (formerly DS)	These oils provide protection from high temperature deposits and bearing corrosion in diesel engines used in severe service.
CC (formerly DM)	These oils provide protection from rust, corrosion and high temperature deposits in diesel engines used in moderate to severe service.
CB (formerly DM)	These oils are designed to provide protection from bearing corrosion and deposits from diesel engines using high sulphur fuel. Service is meant for engines used in mild to moderate service with lower quality fuels.
CA (formerly DG)	This is a general diesel service classification. These oils should not be used when sulphur content of fuel exceeds 0.4%. Oils will provide protection from bearing corrosion when high quality fuels are used.

Foam inhibitors prevent the tiny air bubbles which can be caused by fast-moving engine parts whipping air into the oil. Foam can also occur when the oil level falls too low and the oil pump begins sucking up air instead of oil (like when the kids finish a milkshake). Without foam inhibitors, these tiny air bubbles would cause hydraulic valve lifters to collapse and reduce engine performance and economy significantly.

Viscosity index improvers reduce the rate at which an oil thins out when the temperature climbs. These additives are what makes multiple-viscosity oils possible. Without them, a single-weight oil which permitted easy starting on a cold morning might thin out and cause you to lose your engine on a hot afternoon. If you use a multiple-viscosity oil, it's this additive that helps your gas mileage during those short trips in cold weather.

Friction modifiers and extreme pressure additives are valuable in so-called boundary lubrication, where there is metal-to-metal contact due to the absence or breaking down of the oil film between moving parts. Friction modifiers, or anti-wear agents, deposit protective surface films which reduce the friction and heat of metal-to-metal contact. Extreme pressure additives work by reacting chemically with metal surfaces involved in high-pressure contact.

Specially Formulated Oils

The use of a turbocharger on an engine requires a specially-formulated motor oil to satisfy the unique lubrication requirements of turbocharging.

At highway speeds, a turbocharger spins extremely fast, often in excess of 100,000 rpm. To put that speed in perspective, the engine may only be turning at 2000–4000 rpm. As a result, the turbocharging process builds up tremendous heat. Motor oil is used, not only to lubricate the turbocharger bearings, but also to dissipate a great deal of the heat. And, because the engine shares its oil supply with the turbocharger, a lot of the contaminants and filth in the engine find their way into the precisely machined turbocharger bearing housing.

As soon as the ignition is shut off, oil stops flowing to the turbocharger bearings and other vital components. Since the motor oil no longer carries away heat, temperatures around the turbo-charger bearings can build up to 600 F. in a few minutes. At those temperatures, ordinary motor oils, literally "cook" and leave behind harmful carbon deposits (coke) that will eventually plug the lubricating passages to the bearings and cause complete turbo failure. Dislodged coke deposits will abrade and corrode the turbocharger bearings, leading to premature failure.

New motor oils are available in a wide range of SAE grades, from 10W-30 to 20W-50, and are specially formulated to withstand the 600 F. oil "soak-down" temperatures that occur following ignition shut-off. These oils contain additional antioxidants and detergents to combat corrosion and heat build-up.

Synthetic Oils

Recently, a number of major oil companies have introduced synthetic oils, which are composed of manmade hydrocarbons instead of petroleum-based hydrocarbons. There are quite a few claims being made for synthetic oils, including increased gas mileage, extended oil drain intervals, improved hot and cold weather engine performance, and less wear and tear on engines. Whether or not these claims are true has yet to be decided. One thing is certain, however. Synthetic oil is expensive. At prices that range up to three dollars a quart, synthetic oils will have to live up to every one of their claims to be cost-effective, but as long as it has an SF rating, synthetic oil certainly will not harm your car.

Handling Used Motor Oil

The EPA has distributed the following warning intended for those who handle used motor oil on a REGULAR basis.

In a laboratory study, mice developed skin cancer after their skin was exposed to used motor oil twice a week, without being washed off, for most of their life span. While this one study is not conclusive, substances found to cause cancer in laboratory animals may also cause cancer in humans.

Those who handle used motor oil are advised to minimize skin contact with used motor oil, to promptly remove any used oil from their skin and to follow these safety precautions:

DO follow work practices that minimize the amount of skin exposed and the length of time used oil stays on the skin.

DO thoroughly wash off used oil

OIL RECOMMENDATIONS CHART
(SEE NOTE)

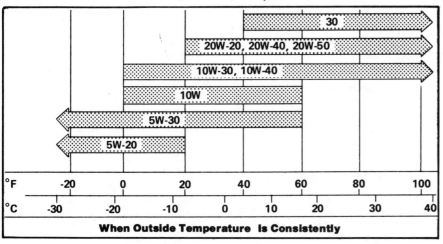

NOTE: Since 1980, the preferred viscosities of motor oil used in engines in GM (Buick, Cadillac, Chevrolet, Oldsmobile, Pontiac and GM Canadian) vehicles are:

Gasoline Engines
SAE 5W-30 (preferred for engines of 2.8 liters or less)
SAE 10W-30 (preferred for all other engines)
SAE 15W-40, 20W-20, 30 (acceptable for all engines)

Diesel Engines
SAE 30 (preferred above freezing*)
SAE 10W-30, 15W-40 (acceptable for all engines; use only for cold weather operation; helps starting)

*Except for 1.8 and 2.2 liter diesels, where SAE 10W-30 is preferred at all temperatures. Do not use SAE 10W-40 or, any other grade not specifically recommended.

GM does not recommend the use of 10W-40 engine oils in 1984 or later GM gasoline engines. The use of 10W-40 oil will not automatically void the GM new car warranty, but if the use of such oil is determined to have caused engine damage, the cost of repair will not be covered by the warranty, as GM does not cover any damage caused by the use of nonrecommended oils, or oils that do not meet API quality or viscosity grades.

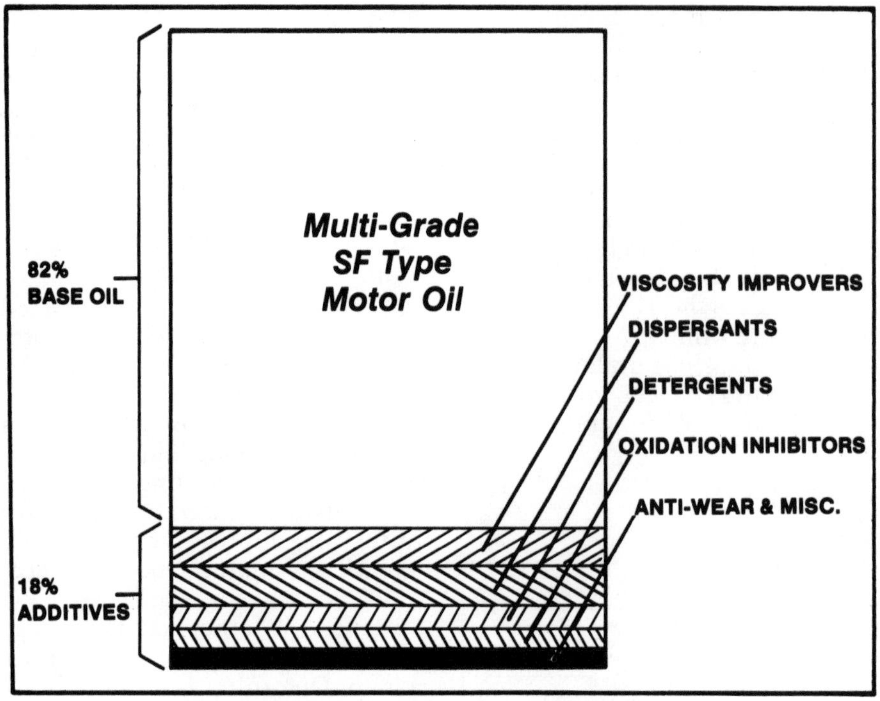
Multi-Grade
SF Type
Motor Oil
82%
BASE OIL
18%
ADDITIVES
VISCOSITY IMPROVERS
DISPERSANTS
DETERGENTS
OXIDATION INHIBITORS
ANTI-WEAR & MISC.

Breakdown of the additives in a can of motor oil.

as soon as possible with soap and water.

DO wash oil soaked clothing before wearing it again. Discard oil soaked shoes.

DO use gloves made of material that oil cannot penetrate if that is practical for your work.

DON'T use kerosine, gasoline or other thinners to wash oil off the skin. They remove the skin's natural oils and can cause dryness or have serious toxic effects.

DON'T over-use waterless hand cleaners. They also remove the skin's protective barriers.

DON'T put oil rags in your pockets. This can cause prolonged skin contact.

Fluids and Greases

Chassis Greases

Quite a few late-model cars, especially American ones, no longer require chassis lubrication, but for those that do, the correct grease is generally an EP (extreme pressure) chassis lube. There's not really much problem, since it's about the only thing you can get that will fit in your hand-operated grease gun, if you lube your own car.

Wheel Bearing Lubricant

There are two types of wheel bearing lubricant; low temperature (short fiber grease) and high temperature (long fiber grease). The high temperature wheel bearing lubricant is the only one suitable for modern cars.

Master Cylinder Fluid

Brake fluid is used for both the brake master cylinder and the clutch master cylinder (if your car is equipped with a hydraulic clutch). Use only brake fluid rated DOT 3 or 4 or conforming to SAE Standard J1709. The rating can be found on the can.

Automatic Transmission Fluid

Automatic transmission fluids are specific to the car using them. For instance, all late-model General Motors cars use Dexron® or Dexron II® ATF. Ford Motor Company uses a type of ATF known as Type F. See the section on Automatic Transmissions.

There are basically three types of fluids.

Type A, Suffix A, was recommended by GM, Chrysler and AMC between 1956 and 1967. Type A was superceded by Dexron®.

Dexron® was recommended by GM, Chrysler and AMC from 1967–75, and in any transmission that had previously specified Type A. Dexron II® superceded Dexron® as the recommendation for 1975 and later cars using this fluid.

Type F fluid is recommended by Ford Motor Co. and a few imported manufacturers, and contains certain frictional compounds required for proper operation in these transmissions. Containers marked with a qualification number 1P-XXXXXX are suitable for Ford transmissions prior to 1967, while a qualification number of 2P-XXXXXX is suitable in all Ford transmissions.

1977 and later Ford cars with a C6 automatic transmission use a new Type F fluid known as a CJ fluid. The dipstick of these transmissions is marked "Use ESP-M2C138-CJ Fluid Only".

Once again, there is really not much of a problem here, since the tops of all cans are clearly marked to indicate the type of fluid. If you are in doubt, check your owner's manual.

Manual Transmission Lubricant

Generally speaking, manual transmissions use a gear oil of about SAE 80 or 90 viscosity. This is a gear oil viscosity and has nothing to do with motor oil viscosity. For instance, an SAE 80W gear oil can have the same viscosity characteristics as an SAE 40 or 50 motor oil.

Not all manual transmissions use gear oil. For years, Chrysler Corporation specified the use of

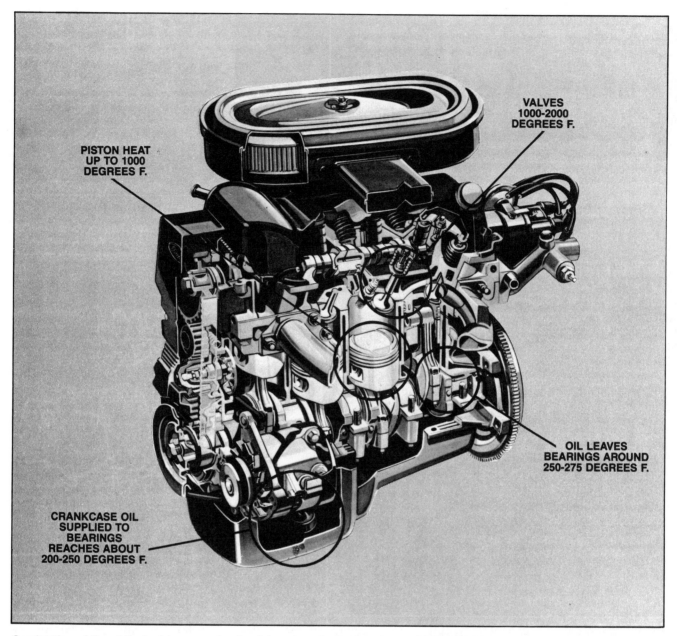

PISTON HEAT
UP TO 1000
DEGREES F.

VALVES
1000-2000
DEGREES F.

OIL LEAVES
BEARINGS AROUND
250-275 DEGREES F.

CRANKCASE OIL
SUPPLIED TO
BEARINGS
REACHES ABOUT
200-250 DEGREES F.

Combustion of the air/fuel mixture can develop internal engine temperatures of 2000–3000°F., The high heat load reaches many of the engine's operating parts. Oil flow is needed to help reduce operating temperatures.

automatic transmission fluid in their manual transmission cars. Some transaxles, both foreign and domestic use either ATF or engine oil to lubricate the transmission. For this reason, it is always best to consult your owner's manual or your dealer if you are unsure about what sort of lubricant to use in your manual transmission.

Rear Axle Lubricants

Conventional rear axles use gear oil of about 80 or 90 grade. Consult your owner's manual for more detail. Limited-slip or Positraction® rear axles require a special lubricant which is available from the dealer. If you do have a limited-slip differential, **make sure** you use only the correct lubricant, as the use of the incorrect lubricant can destroy the differential.

Power Steering Fluid

Power steering pumps are ordinarily lubricated with power steering fluid. Use the correct type for the car. Check the owner's manual if you are unsure.

Body and Chassis Maintenance

Proper Maintenance Pays

The automobile is a truly amazing machine. It is expected to function under a wide range of weather conditions and other adverse conditions, yet it is subjected to careless and hard driving and indifferent maintenance. Recommended service intervals are often ignored by the same car owners that wouldn't let a week go by without vacuuming all the rugs in the house.

Today the automobile is an integral part of our life. We have come to rely on the proper functioning of the family car and seldom if ever make a time allowance in case the car should fail to start. We expect it to start and move out every time, and fortunately, most of the time it does. But the rare instance that it doesn't, causes the owner to forget the thousands of times it started without a problem. The irony is, that chances are, it failed to start because of neglect.

A periodic maintenance program such as the one in this book can keep the car owner more aware of the condition of his or her car and will save money in three important areas—fuel economy, emissions and performance.

Champion Spark Plug Co. tested engine conditions and consumer maintenance habits over a two-year period. The tests covered 5,666 cars in 27 cities throughout the United States and Canada. Here are some of the results:

· Cars judged to be in need of tune-ups recorded an 11.36% improvement in fuel economy when tuned to manufacturer's specifications.
· New plugs alone accounted for an average 3.44% improvement in fuel economy.
· A complete tune-up lowered emissions of CO (carbon monoxide) at idle by an average 45.37%.
· Engine neglect affects not only safety, but starting dependability and general operation as well.
· More than 27% of all cars tested were more than a quart low on oil.
· Nearly 15% of all cars tested had dirty air filters.
· 79% (almost 8 cars out of 10) had maintenance deficiencies that adversely affected fuel economy, emissions or performance.

UNDERHOOD MAINTENANCE INTERVALS

This chart gives minimum maintenance intervals by miles or time, whichever comes first, based on average of 12,000 miles per year. Obviously, the type of driving you do will also affect your maintenance program. There are details on how to perform your own maintenance in each section.

Diagram Number	Item	Check Every	Refer to Section for more information
	Engine ▲		
1	Check oil, add if necessary	Fuel Stop	8
2	Drain oil	6000 miles/6 months	8
3	Replace oil filter	6000 miles/6 months	8
4	Check valve clearance, adjust if necessary	12,000 miles/12 months	8
	Ignition System ▲		
5	Replace points and condenser	12,000 miles/12 months	13
6	Replace spark plugs		
	Point-type ignition	12,000 miles/12 months	13
	Electronic ignition	18-24,000 miles/18-24 months	13
6	Check spark plug wires	12,000 miles/12 months	13
6	Replace spark plug wires	At least every 36,000 miles/3 years	13
5	Replace distributor cap/rotor	12,000 miles/12 months	13
7	Check/adjust ignition timing		
	Point-type ignition	12,000 miles/12 months	13
	Electronic ignition	12,000 miles/12 months (when plugs are replaced)	13
	Battery		
8	Check electrolyte level/charge	1000 miles/1 month	11
9	Check/clean terminals and cables	3000 miles/3 months	11
	Starter and Alternator ▲		
9	Check electrical connections	3000 miles/3 months	12
10	Check/adjust drive belt	3000 miles/3 months	12
10	Replace drive belt*	At least every 24,000 miles/2 years	12
	Cooling System ▲		
11	Check coolant level	1000 miles/1 month	9
12	Check condition of radiator hoses	1000 miles/1 month	9
11	Check condition of radiator cap	1000 miles/1 month	9
10	Check/adjust drive belt	3000 miles/3 months	9
10	Replace drive belt*	At least every 24,000 miles/2 years	9
12	Clean radiator of debris	3000 miles/3 months	9
12	Drain/replace coolant	12,000 miles/12 months (Each Fall)	9
	Fuel & Emissions System ▲		
16	Clean crankcase breather	12,000 miles/12 months	15
13	Replace air filter	12,000 miles/12 months	15
14	Replace fuel filter	12,000 miles/12 months	15
15	Check PCV valve	12,000 miles/12 months	15
10	Check/adjust air pump belt tension	3,000 miles/3 months	15
10	Replace drive belt*	At least every 24,000 miles/2 years	15
	Air Conditioning		
12	Clean condenser grille	3000 miles/3 months	10
17	Check for leaks at connections	3000 miles/3 months	10
17	Check refrigerant level	3000 miles/3 months	10
10	Check/adjust compressor belt	1000 miles/1 month	10
10	Replace compressor drive belt*	At least every 24,000 miles/2 years	10
	Automatic transmission ▲		
18	Check fluid level/condition	6000 miles/6 months	22

UNDERHOOD MAINTENANCE INTERVALS, continued

Diagram Number	Item	Check Every	Refer to Section for more Information
19	**Brakes** Check master cylinder fluid level	1000 miles/1 month	27
20	**Power Steering** Check pump fluid level	3000 miles/3 months	24
10	Replace drive belt*	At least every 24,000 miles/2 years	24
10	Check drive belt tension	1000 miles/1 month	24

▲ If the vehicle is used for severe service (trailer pulling, continual stop/start driving, off-road operation), cut the maintenance interval in ½.

*New drive belts will stretch with use. Recheck the tension of a newly installed belt after 200 miles.

4 AND 6 CYLINDER INLINE ENGINES

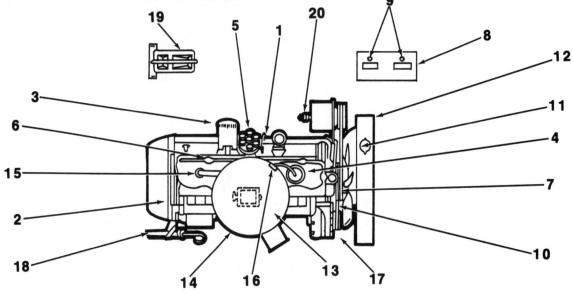

V6 AND V8 ENGINES

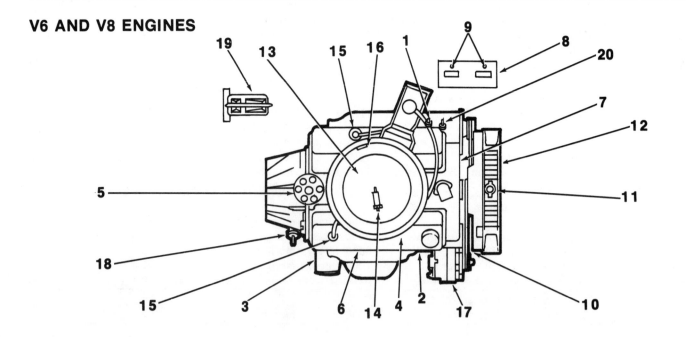

BODY AND CHASSIS MAINTENANCE INTERVALS

This chart gives minimum maintenance intervals in miles or time, whichever comes first, based on an average of 12,000 miles per year. Obviously, the type of driving will also affect your maintenance program. There are details on how to perform your own maintenance in each section.

Diagram Number	Item	Check Every	Refer to Section for more information
	Automatic Transmission ▲		
1	**Change fluid**	24,000 miles/2 years	22
1	**Replace filter or clean screen**	24,000 miles/2 years	22
	Clutch and Manual Transmission ▲		
2	**Check lubricant level**	3000 miles/3 months	21
2	**Change lubricant**	24,000 miles/2 years	21
3	**Check clutch pedal free-play**	6000 miles/6 months	21
2	**Lubricate shift linkage**	6000 miles/6 months	21
	Brakes ▲		
4	**Check condition of brake pads or brake shoes**	6000 miles/6 months	27
4	**Check wheel cylinders, return springs, calipers, hoses, drums and/or rotors**	6000 miles/6 months	27
5	**Adjust parking brake**	As necessary	27
	Suspension ▲		
6	**Check shock absorbers**	12,000 miles/12 months	24
7	**Check tires for abnormal wear**	1000 miles/1 month	24
8	**Lubricate front end**	3000 miles/3 months	24
	Driveshaft ▲		
9	**Lubricate U-joints**	6000 miles/6 months	23
	Rear Axle ▲		
10	**Check level of rear axle fluid**	6000 miles/6 months	23
10	**Replace rear axle fluid**	24,000 miles/2 years	23
	Tires ▲		
11	**Clean tread of debris**	As necessary	26
12	**Check tire pressure**	Each fuel stop/2 weeks	26
11	**Rotate tires**	6000 miles/6 months	26
11	**Check tread depth**	6000 miles/6 months	26
	Wheels		
12	**Clean wheels**	As necessary	25
12	**Check wheel weights**	Each fuel stop/2 weeks (when you check tire pressure)	25
11	**Rotate wheel/tire**	6000 miles/6 months	25
	Windshield wipers		
	Check wiper blades	3000 miles/3 months	16
	Replace wiper blades	12,000 miles/12 months	16
	Lubricate linkage and pivots	6000 miles/6 months	16
	Check hoses and clean nozzles	3000 miles/3 months	16
	Windshield		
	Clean glass	Each fuel stop	16
	Air Conditioner		
13	**Operate air conditioner for a few minutes**	Once a week	10

*New drive belts will stretch with use. Recheck the tension of a newly installed belt after 200 miles.
▲ If the vehicle is used for severe service (trailer pulling, continual stop/start driving, off-road operation) cut the maintenance interval in ½.

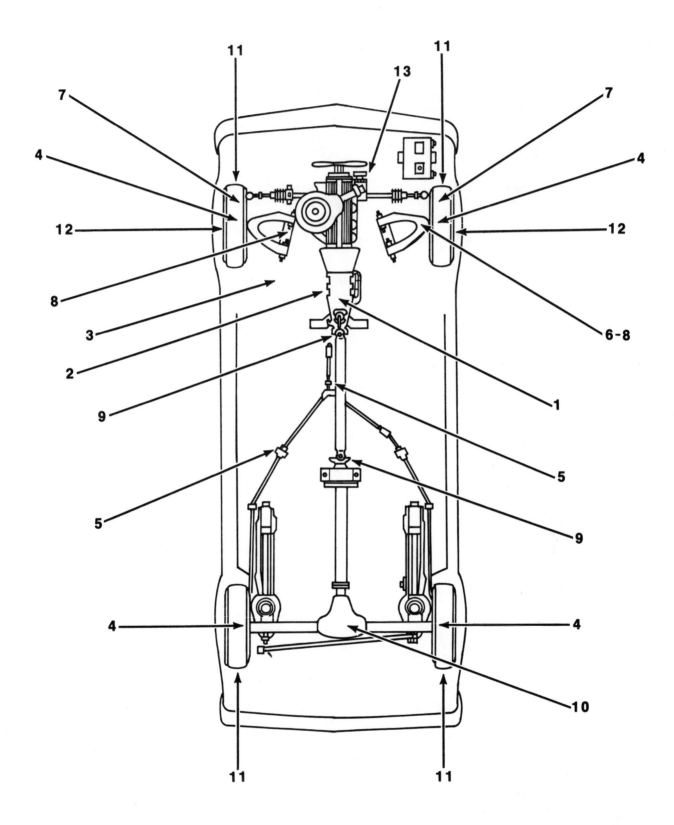

RECOMMENDED LUBRICANTS

Every manufacturer has specific recommendations for fluids and lubricants used in their vehicles. These are generally listed in the owners manual. In the absence of specific recommendations, use the following as a general guide.

Part	Symbol	Lubricant
Engine	A	Engine oil SE viscosity determined by anticipated temperatures before next oil change
Manual transmission	B	SAE 80W-90 gear lubricant (API-GL4)
Manual transmission (with overdrive)	B	SAE 80W-140 gear lubricant (API-GL4)
Automatic transmission	C	Automatic transmission fluid Dexron® Dexron II® Type F
Power steering pump		Power steering fluid
Conventional rear axle	B	SAE 80W-90 gear lubricant (API-GL5)
Limited slip rear axle	B	SAE 80W-90 limited slip gear lubricant (API-GL5). NOTE: Special limited slip additive may be required
Front wheel bearings	D	High melting point, long fiber wheel bearing grease
Brake master cylinder (drum or disc brakes)	E	Heavy duty brake fluid meeting DOT-3 minimum
Clutch master cylinder	E	Heavy duty brake fluid meeting DOT-3 minimum
Manual steering gear, suspension, ball joints, U-joints, clutch and gear shift linkage, steering linkage and other chassis lubrication points	F	Lithium base, multi-purpose chassis lubricant
Doors, hood, trunk and tailgate locks, seat tracks, parking brake	G	White grease
Accelerator linkage, door hinges, trunk and hood hinges	A	SAE 30 motor oil
Lock cylinders	H	Silicone spray lubricant or thin oil applied to key and inserted in lock
Weather stripping	H	Silicone spray lubricant

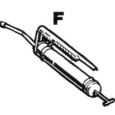

7
Tune-Up

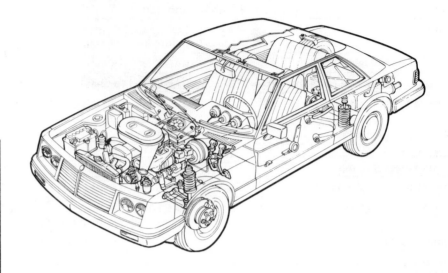

```
┌─────────────────────────────────┐
│       TOOLS AND SUPPLIES        │
│ Tools                           │
│   Spark plug socket (either     │
│     13/16" or 5/8" depending on │
│     model)                      │
│   Screwdriver                   │
│   Wrenches                      │
│   Feeler gauges (flat and wire  │
│     type)                       │
│   Dwell/tachometer              │
│   Timing light                  │
│   Compression tester            │
│   Voltmeter/ohmmeter    (op-    │
│     tional)                     │
│   Vacuum gauge (optional)       │
│   Golf tee                      │
│ Supplies                        │
│   Replacement parts (plugs,     │
│     points, condenser, rotor,   │
│     cap, wires, etc.)           │
│   Penetrating oil               │
│   Tape                          │
└─────────────────────────────────┘
```

NOTE: *The word "tune-up" actually applies only to older cars, on which you can perform the traditional work associated with "tune-up"—spark plug replacement, ignition contact point replacement, dwell adjustment, ignition timing adjustment and carburetor idle and mixture adjustment.*

Engine performance maintenance is a more accurate term. Most modern cars and light trucks are equipped with electronic ignition (no points) and an on-board computer that automatically adjusts the ignition timing, fuel mixture and idle speed. In fact, on modern computer-controlled vehicles, it's impossible to adjust these yourself.

An automotive tune-up is an orderly process of inspection, diagnosis, testing, and adjustment that is periodically necessary to maintain peak engine performance or restore the engine to original operating efficiency.

Tests by the Champion Spark Plug Company show that an average 11.36% improvement in gas economy could be expected after a tune-up. A change to new spark plugs alone provided a 3.44% decrease in fuel use. As for emissions, significantly lower emissions were recorded at idle after a complete tune-up on a car needing service. An average 45.37% reduction of CO (carbon monoxide) emissions was recorded at idle after a complete tune-up. HC (hydrocarbon) emissions were cut 55.5%.

The tune-up is also a good opportunity to perform a general preventive maintenance check on everything in the engine compartment. Look for failed or about to fail components such as loose or damaged wiring, leaking fuel lines, cracked coolant hoses, and frayed fan belts.

This section will lead you through the various elements of a tune-up in their proper order. Later sections, as mentioned below, give specific details on how to perform the various procedures. Operations should be performed in the order listed.

Necessary Tools

In order to perform a proper tune-up, several specific tools are needed; a dwell-tach, a timing light, a spark plug socket, feeler gauges (both the flat type and the round wire type for gapping plugs), and a compression tester. If you have a late-model car with electronic ignition, you won't need a dwell-meter since dwell is nonadjustable on these cars. Also keep in mind that some tachometers will not operate on cars equipped with electronic ignition, and neither will some timing lights. So before you buy anything, check to make sure it will work on your particular car.

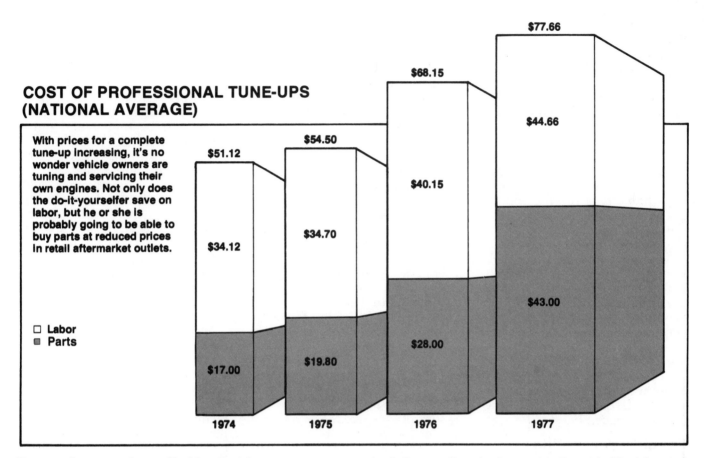

COST OF PROFESSIONAL TUNE-UPS (NATIONAL AVERAGE)

With prices for a complete tune-up increasing, it's no wonder vehicle owners are tuning and servicing their own engines. Not only does the do-it-yourselfer save on labor, but he or she is probably going to be able to buy parts at reduced prices in retail aftermarket outlets.

□ Labor
■ Parts

	1974	1975	1976	1977
Total	$51.12	$54.50	$68.15	$77.66
Labor	$34.12	$34.70	$40.15	$44.66
Parts	$17.00	$19.80	$28.00	$43.00

The cost of a tune-up is steadily rising. By doing your own tune-ups, the do-it-yourself mechanic can save the cost of the labor and can even buy parts at discount prices.

Compression

NOTE: *See also Section 8.*

Along with vacuum gauge readings and spark plug condition, cylinder compression test results are extremely valuable indicators of internal engine condition. Most professional mechanics automatically check an engine's compression as the first step in a comprehensive tune-up. Obviously, it is useless to try and tune an engine with extremely low or erratic compression readings, since a simple tune-up will not cure the problem. However, before we go any further, it might be wise to review just exactly what compression is.

In the description of engine operation in Section 8, it is mentioned that, after the intake valve closes, the air/fuel mixture is trapped in the cylinder as the piston rises. The volume of the combustion chamber after the piston reaches TDC (top dead center) is about ⅛ to 1/11 of the volume of the whole cylinder. Compressing the mixture in this manner raises the pressure and temperature in the combustion chambers during the power stroke, thus improving combustion and increasing the amount of power delivered to the piston on the downstroke. Any leakage in the combustion chamber will reduce the pressure created during the compression stroke.

The pressure created in the combustion chamber may be measured with a gauge that remains at the highest reading it measures during the action of a one-way valve. This gauge is inserted into the spark plug hole. A compression test will uncover many mechanical problems that can cause rough running or poor performance.

Checking Engine Vacuum

Strictly speaking, vacuum gauge readings are not a necessary part of the everyday tune-up, which is why a vacuum gauge is considered optional equipment. Properly used, however, a vacuum gauge is an extremely useful diagnostic tool. Gauge readings and their meanings are given in Section 8.

Spark Plugs

Spark plug life and efficiency depend upon the condition of the engine and the combustion chamber temperatures to which the plug is exposed. These temperatures are affected by many factors, such as compression ratio of the engine, air/fluel mixtures, exhaust emission equipment, and the type of driving you do.

Factory-installed plugs are, in a way, compromise plugs, since the factory has no way of knowing what sort of driving you do, but most people never have reason to change their plugs from the factory-recommended heat range. Nevertheless, when picking a spark plug, follow this general rule of thumb for choosing the heat range: If most of your driving is long distance, high speed travel, use a colder plug; if most of your driving is stop and go, use a hotter plug.

See Section 13, "Electrical System Ignition," for more detailed information on the procedures described below.

Reading Spark Plugs

Your spark plugs are the single most valuable indicator of your engine's internal condition. Study your spark plugs carefully every time you remove them. Compare them to the chart in Section 13 to identify the most common plug conditions.

Replacing Spark Plugs

A set of spark plugs usually requires replacement after 10,000 to 12,000 miles on cars with conventional ignition systems and after about 15,000 to 30,000 miles on cars with electronic ignition. These figures are dependent on your particular style of driving, however. The electrode on a new spark plug has a sharp edge, but with use, this edge becomes rounded by erosion, causing the plug gap to increase. In normal operation, plug gap increases about 0.001 inch for every 1,000 to 2,500 miles. As the gap increases, the plug's voltage requirement also increases. It requires a greater

voltage to jump the wider gap and about two to three times as much voltage to fire a plug at high speeds than at idle.

Tools needed for spark plug replacement include a ratchet handle, short extension, spark plug socket (there are two types; either $^{13}/_{16}$ inch or $^{5}/_{8}$ inch, depending upon the type of plug), a combination spark plug gauge and gapping tool, and a can of penetrating oil.

When removing spark plugs, work on one at a time. Don't start by removing the plug wires all at once, because unless you number them, they may become mixed up. Take a minute before you begin and number the wires with tape. The best location for numbering is near where the wires come out of the cap.

Checking and Replacing Spark Plug Wires

Visually inspect the spark plug cables for burns, cuts, or breaks in the insulation. Check the spark plug boots and the nipples on the distributor cap and coil. Replace any damaged wiring. If no physical damage is obvious, the wires can be checked with an ohmmeter for excessive resistance. To do this, remove the distributor cap and leave the wires connected to the cap. Connect one lead of the ohmmeter to the corresponding electrode inside the cap and the other lead to the spark plug terminal (remove it from the spark plug for the test). Replace any wire which shows over 50,000 ohms. (Generally speaking, resistance should not run over 35,000 ohms and 50,000 ohms should be considered the outer limit of acceptability.)

Test the coil wire by connecting the ohmmeter between the center contact in the cap and either of the primary terminals at the coil. If the total resistance of the coil and wire is more than 25,000 ohms, remove the wire from the coil and check the resistance of the wire alone. If the re-

sistance is higher than 15,000 ohms, replace the wire. Wire resistance is a function of length, and the longer the wire, the greater the resistance. Thus, if the wires on your car are longer than the factory originals, resistance will be higher and quite possibly outside of these limits.

When installing a new set of spark plug wires, replace the wires one at a time so there will be no mixup. Start by replacing the longest wire first. Install the boot firmly over the spark plug. Route the wire exactly the same as the original. Insert the nipple firmly into the tower on the distributor cap. Repeat the process for each wire.

Distributor Service

(*Note:* More detailed information on the procedures described below is given in Section 13.)

Essentially, a distributor performs two functions: It switches primary current on and off at the coil, and it distributes secondary current to the spark plugs through the distributor cap. To do this in a conventional ignition system, it relies on breaker points and a condenser.

If you have ever wondered why it is necessary to tune your engine occasionally, consider the fact that the distributor system must complete the above cycle each time a spark plug fires. On a six-cylinder, four-cycle engine, three of the six plugs must fire once for every engine revolution. If the idle speed of your engine is 800 revolutions per minute (800 rpm), the breaker points open and close two times for each revolution. For every minute your engine idles, your points open and close 1,600 times ($2 \times 800 = 1600$). And that is just at idle. What about at 65 mph?

Proper gap between the breaker points is essential to efficient operation of your engine. Breaker point gap can be checked and set with a feeler gauge or with a dwell meter.

When you set the points, you are really adjusting the amount of time (in degrees of distributor rotation) that the points will remain open. If you adjust the points with a feeler gauge, you are setting the maximum amount the points will open when the rubbing block on the points is on a high point of the distributor cam.

When you adjust the points with a dwell meter, you are measuring the number of degrees of distributor cam rotation during which the points will remain closed before they start to open as a high point of the distributor cam approaches the rubbing block of the points.

There are two rules that should always be followed when adjusting or replacing points. First, the points and condenser are a matched set, and you must never replace one without replacing the other. Second, if you change the point gap or dwell of the engine, you also change the ignition timing. Therefore, if you adjust the points, you must also adjust the timing.

Points Inspection and Replacement

Remove the distributor cap and the rotor. Insert a screwdriver between the stationary and breaker arms of the points and examine the condition of the contacts. Replace the points if the contacts are blackened, pitted, or if the metal deposits have disrupted the specified point gap. Also replace the points if the breaker arm has lost its tension or if the rubbing block is excessively worn.

Contact points that have become slightly burned (light gray) may be cleaned with a point file. In order for the points to function properly, the contact faces must be aligned. The alignment must be checked with the points closed. If the contact faces are not centered, bend the stationary arm to suit. Never bend the breaker arm. Discard the points if they cannot be centered correctly.

Inspect the Distributor Components

Inspect the inside surface of the distributor cap for cracks, carbon tracks, or badly burned contacts. To remove carbon tracks, wash the cap in soap and water and dry thoroughly. Replace the cap if it is cracked or if the contacts are badly eroded.

Inspect the rotor for cracks, excessive burning of the contacts, and mechanical damage, and replace as necessary. Slightly burned contacts should be sanded smooth.

While primary wiring is less perishable than the secondary circuit, it should be checked for cracked insulation or loose connections. Tighten connections or replace wires as necessary.

Adjusting Point Gap

A dwell meter is the most reliable method of setting the points and should always be used to make a final point gap adjustment. But a preliminary setting of the dwell angle can be made manually using a feeler gauge. This is a good method of making an initial setting even if a dwell meter is available. Install the points and condenser, making sure all connections are pushed on or screwed together securely. If the mounting screw on the ignition points assembly is also used to make the gap adjustment, tighten it just enough to hold the contacts apart. Rotate the engine until the tip of one of the distributor cams sits squarely under the cam follower on the movable contact arm.

Now, using a leaf type feeler gauge (gap the points as specified in the manual), move the base plate of the point assembly back and forth until the gauge just slips between the two contacts when it is forced straight through. If the mounting screw

serves as the adjusting lock, the contact assembly can usually be moved by wedging a screwdriver between a slot in the contact base plate and a protrusion on the surface of the distributor plate. In assemblies with an adjusting screw which is accessible from outside the distributor, an allen wrench is inserted into the head of the adjusting screw and rotated to make the adjustment.

When the points are pitted, make sure the gauge does not come in contact with the built-up portion on one of the contact surfaces. A wire feeler gauge may help to make a more accurate preliminary adjustment when the points are pitted.

NOTE: *Make sure all gauges are clean in gapping the points. An oily gauge will cause rapid point burning.*

Setting Dwell Angle

The dwell angle is the number of degrees of distributor cam rotation through which the breaker points remain fully closed (conducting electricity). Increasing the point gap decreases dwell, while decreasing the point gap increases dwell.

Using a dwell meter of known accuracy, connect the red lead (positive) wire of the meter to the distributor primary wire connection on the positive (+) side of the coil, and the black ground (negative) wire of the meter to a good ground on the engine (e.g. thermostat housing nut).

The dwell angle may be checked either with the distributor cap and rotor installed and the engine running, or with the cap and rotor removed and the engine cranking at starter speed. The meter gives a constant reading with the engine running. With the engine cranking, the reading will fluctuate between zero degrees dwell and the maximum figure for that angle. While cranking, the maximum figure is the dwell angle at that breaker point setting. Never attempt to change dwell angle while the ignition is on. Touching the point contacts or primary wire connection with a metal screwdriver can result in a 12 volt shock.

To change the dwell angle, loosen the point retaining screw slightly and make the approximate correction. Tighten the retaining screw and test the dwell with the engine cranking. On General Motors V8 engines, dwell angle is set with an allen wrench through the window in the distributor.

If the dwell appears to be correct, install the breaker point protective cover, if so equipped, the rotor and distributor cap, and test the dwell with the engine running. Take the engine through its entire rpm range and observe the dwell meter. The dwell should remain within specifications at all times. Great fluctuation of dwell at different engine speeds indicates worn distributor parts.

After adjusting the dwell angle, the ignition timing must be checked.

Electronic Ignition

Most domestic cars and light trucks since 1975 and most late model import cars have an electronic ignition system. This means that the distributor has no breaker points or condenser to be replaced periodically. The function of the breaker points and condenser is replaced by solid state circuitry.

About the only thing you can do to "tune-up" these units is periodically inspect the distributor cap much as you would a conventional distributor cap. The dwell on electronic ignition systems is electronically controlled and generally not adjustable. You may get a reading on a dwell/tachometer, but the dwell cannot be adjusted.

Ignition Timing

Ignition timing is the measurement in degrees of crankshaft ro-

tation of the point at which the spark plugs fire in relation to the point at which the piston reaches top dead center (TDC) in the cylinder. The plugs may fire either before or after TDC.

Ignition timing is adjusted by loosening the distributor locking device and turning the distributor in the engine. The paragraphs below outline the steps in checking and adjusting the ignition timing. See also Section 13.

1. If the timing light operates from the battery, connect the red lead to the battery positive terminal, and the black lead to a ground. With all lights, connect the trigger lead in series with no. 1 spark plug wire.

2. Disconnect and plug the required vacuum hoses, as in the manufacturer's specifications. Connect the red lead of a tachometer to the distributor side of the coil and the black lead to ground. Start the engine, put the (automatic) transmission in gear (if required), and read the tachometer. Adjust the carburetor idle screw to the proper speed for setting the timing. Aim the timing light at the crankshaft pulley to determine where the timing point is. If the point is hard to see, it may help to stop the engine and mark it with chalk.

3. Loosen the distributor holding clamp and rotate the distributor slowly in either direction until the timing is correct. Tighten the clamp and observe the timing mark again to determine that the timing is still correct. Readjust the position of the distributor, if necessary.

4. Accelerate the engine in neutral, while watching the timing point. If the distributor advance mechanisms are working, the timing point should advance as the engine is accelerated. If the engine's vacuum advance is engaged with the transmission in neutral, check the vacuum advance operation by running the engine at about 1,500 rpm and connecting and disconnecting the vacuum advance hose.

Carburetor Adjustments

Carburetors are fairly complex instruments, but since they have relatively few moving parts, they are not normally as vulnerable to wear and tear as are distributor components. It is safe to say that modern carburetors are quite reliable and a correctly set-up carburetor is probably good for 50,000 maintenance-free miles. Any recurring carburetor problems indicate incorrect set-up or faulty repair work, since carburetor wear is very gradual.

Essentially, there are only two carburetor adjustments which may be necessary during the course of a normal tune-up. It is entirely possible that no adjustments will be necessary at all. Nonetheless, it is always a good idea to check.

(For more information on the procedures outlined below, see Section 15, "Fuel System.")

Idle Speed Adjustment

Generally, the idle speed is adjusted before the idle mixture is adjusted. You will need a tachometer to adjust the carburetor to the specified rpm. On a conventional ignition system, connect the tachometer red lead to the negative terminal of the coil and connect the black lead to ground. Electronic ignition systems generally have specific tach hook-up procedures and may not work with all tachometers. (See Section 13 or manufacturer's instructions.)

Locate the idle speed screw (See Section 15) or the idle solenoid. With the engine at operating temperature, adjust the screw or the solenoid until the correct idle speed is reached. On cars equipped with idle solenoids, there are usually two idle speeds listed. The higher of the two speeds is with the solenoid connected, the lower is with the solenoid disconnected. Set both speeds and then go on to the mixture adjustment.

Idle Mixture Adjustment

Locate the idle mixture screw or screws. Idle mixture screws on all vehicles manufactured after 1972 are capped in accordance with federal emission control regulations, so there is only a limited range of adjustment possible. To comply with emission regulations, the caps should not be removed or the mixture adjusted without them. After you have found the mixture screws, adjust them according to the manufacturer's instructions. These instructions vary, but in general, the procedure is this:

1. On early vehicles without capped mixture screws, adjust the mixture screw(s) for the highest idle speed you can obtain on the tachometer. Or use a vacuum gauge and adjust the screws until the highest possible vacuum reading is obtained.

2. On vehicles with capped screws, adjust the mixture screws within the limits imposed by the caps until the highest possible idle is obtained. Then adjust the screws inward from highest idle until the specified rpm drop is obtained.

After the mixture has been adjusted, it is often necessary to reset the idle speed with the idle speed screw or solenoid. As a general rule, idle mixture adjustments will raise the idle speed above that which is called for.

Valve Adjustment

Periodic valve adjustments are not required on most modern engines with hydraulic valve lifters. In fact, many engines no longer have any provision for valve adjustment, hydraulic valve lifter technology being what it is. Most import car engines, however, have adjustable valves, since a tightly controlled valve lash is the key to wringing horsepower out of these smaller motors. See Section 8 for procedures.

Tune-Up Check List
Point-Type Ignition

On a conventional ignition system, the basic tune-up procedures are as follows:

· Check decal under the hood for manufacturers' specifications.

· Remove spark plugs one at a time.

· Test compression in each cylinder.

· Clean and/or replace spark plugs and gap plugs to manufacturer's specifications and install in engine.

· Check distributor cap and rotor for cracks and wear. Replace if necessary.

· Check points for wear and excessive resistance. Repair and replace.

· Use dwell/tachometer to set points to specifications.

· Use dwell/tachometer to set rpm to specifications.

· Use timing light to set correct timing.

· Adjust the valves if necessary.

Electronic Ignition

On an electronic ignition system, the basic tune-up procedures are as follows.

· Remove spark plugs.

· Test compression in each cylinder.

· Clean and/or replace spark plugs and gap spark plugs to manufacturer's specifications and install in engine.

· Check distributor cap and rotor for cracks and wear. Replace if necessary.

· Use tachometer to set idle speed to specifications.

· Use timing light to set initial timing. (Most electronic ignition systems do not require adjustments.)

Both of the lists given above represent only the "bare bones" facts about tune-ups. Other functions that could be performed are using an emissions analyzer to check for compliance with emissions standards and for fuel economy, and measuring vacuum and checking for leaks with a vacuum gauge.

8
The Engine

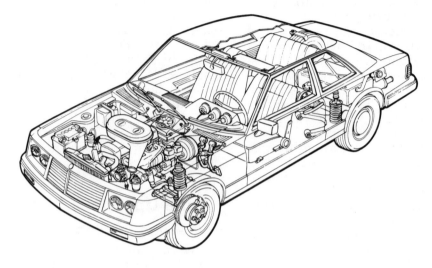

How it Works

The basic piston engine is a metal block containing a series of chambers. The upper engine block is usually an iron or aluminum alloy casting, consisting of outer walls that form hollow jackets around the cylinder walls. The lower block, which provides a number of rigid mounting points for the bearings that hold the crankshaft in place, is known as the crankcase. The hollow jackets of the upper block add rigidity to the engine and contain the liquid coolant which carries heat away from the cylinders and other engine parts.

An air cooled engine block consists of a crankcase which provides a rigid mounting for the

Cutaway view of an overhead camshaft four-cylinder engine.

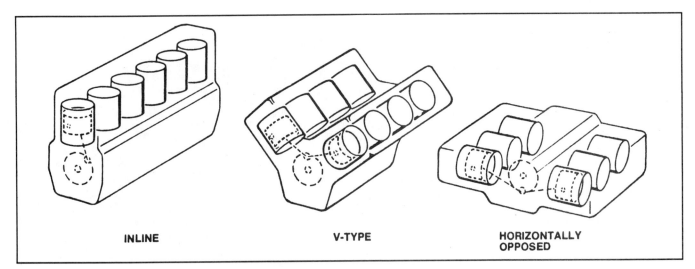

INLINE V-TYPE HORIZONTALLY OPPOSED

Common automotive engine cylinder arrangements

THE FOUR STROKE CYCLE

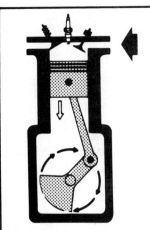

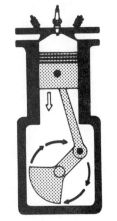

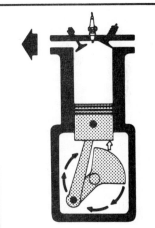

1. Intake

The intake stroke begins with the piston near the top of its travel. As the piston begins its descent, the exhaust valve closes fully, the intake valve opens and the volume of the combustion chamber begins to increase, creating a vacuum. As the piston descends, an air/fuel mixture is drawn from the carburetor into the cylinder through the intake manifold. The intake stroke ends with the intake valve closed just after the piston has begun its upstroke.

2. Compression

As the piston ascends, the fuel/air mixture is forced into the small chamber machined into the cylinder head. This compresses the mixture until it occupies ⅛th to 1/11th of the volume that it did at the time the piston began its ascent. This compression raises the temperature of the mixture and increases its pressure, increasing the force generated by the expansion of gases during the power stroke.

3. Ignition

The fuel/air mixture is ignited by the spark plug just before the piston reaches the top if its stroke so that a very large portion of the fuel will have burned by the time the piston begins descending again. The heat produced by combustion increases the pressure in the cylinder, forcing the piston down with great force.

4. Exhaust

As the piston approaches the bottom of its stroke, the exhaust valve begins opening and the pressure in the cylinder begins to force the gases out around the valve. The ascent of the piston then forces nearly all the rest of the unburned gases from the cylinder. The cycle begins again as the exhaust valve closes, the intake valve opens and the piston begins descending and bringing a fresh charge of fuel and air into the combustion chamber.

The four-stroke cycle of a gasoline-powered, spark ignition engine.

crankshaft and has studs to hold the cylinders in place. The cylinders are individual, single-wall castings, finned for cooling, and they are usually bolted to the crankcase, rather than cast integrally with the block.

In a water-cooled engine, only the cylinder head is bolted to the top of the block. The water pump is mounted directly to the block.

The crankshaft is a long iron or steel shaft mounted rigidly at a number of points in the bottom of the crankcase. The crankshaft is free to turn and contains several counterweighted crankpins (one centered under each cylinder) that are offset several inches from the center of the crankshaft and turn in a circle as the crankshaft turns. Pistons are connected to the crankpins by steel connecting rods. The rods connect the pistons at their upper ends with the crankpins at their lower ends. Circular rings seal the small space between the pistons and wall of the cylinders.

When the crankshaft spins, the pistons move up and down in the cylinders, varying the volume of each cylinder, depending on the position of the piston. Two openings in each cylinder head (above the cylinders) allow the intake of the air/fuel mixture and the exhaust of burned gasses. After intake, the pistons compress the fuel mixture at the top of the cylinder, the fuel is ignited, and, as the pistons are forced downward by the expansion of burning fuel, the connecting rods convert the up and down motion of the pistons into rotary (turning) motion of the crankshaft. A round flywheel at the rear of the crankshaft provides a large, stable mass to smooth out the rotation.

The cylinder heads form tight covers for the tops of the cylinders and contain chambers into which the fuel mixture is forced as it is compressed by the pistons reaching the upper limit of their travel. Each combustion chamber contains one intake valve, one exhaust valve, and one

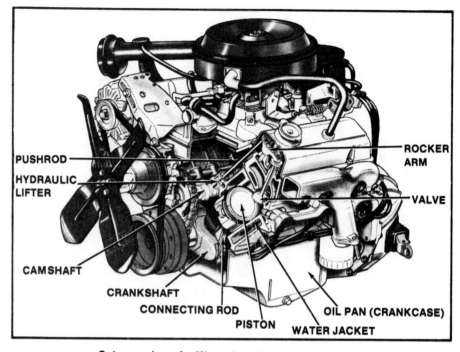

Cutaway view of a V6 engine with overhead valves.

spark plug per cylinder. The tips of the spark plugs protrude into the combustion chambers.

The valve in each opening in the cylinder head is opened and closed by the action of the camshaft. The camshaft is driven by the crankshaft through a chain or belt at ½ crankshaft speed (the camshaft gear is twice the size of the crankshaft gear). The valves are operated either through

rocker arms and pushrods (overhead valve engine) or directly by the camshaft (overhead cam engine).

Lubricating oil is stored in a pan at the bottom of the engine and is force fed to all parts of the engine by a gear-type pump, driven from the crankshaft. The oil lubricates the entire engine and also seals the piston rings, giving good compression.

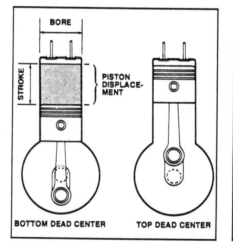

Basic engine cylinder dimensions

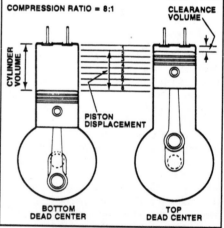

The ratio between the total cylinder volume and clearance volume is the compression ratio

Turbocharging

Turbocharging, sometimes called supercharging, has been under investigation practically since the invention of the automobile. Gottlieb Daimler, generally credited with development of the first auto, sought to boost the volumetric efficiency of his first vertical gasoline engine in 1885, but was unable to make it work. It wasn't until 1921 that Mercedes-Benz introduced the first production supercharged cars.

Between 1921 and the end of World War II, various companies exploited the use of superchargers and turbochargers for racing, marine, and large truck engines. In 1962, General Motors introduced the Oldsmobile F-85 Jetfire, powered by a turbocharged V8 engine and quickly followed that with a turbocharged version of the Chevrolet Corvair. With gasoline prices going rapidly out of sight, the number of manufacturers offering turbocharging has rapidly increased as manufacturers try to maintain performance, reduce engine size and emissions, and increase fuel economy, all at the same time. Models available now run the gamut from the Porsche 930 Turbo and the Mercedes-Benz 300SD Turbodiesel to the four-cylinder Ford Mustang.

The word turbocharger is an abbreviation of the word turbo-supercharging. Although there is a difference between turbocharging and supercharging, the principle is the same—to drive a small compressor which will increase the quantity of fuel/air mixture going into the combustion chamber as it is needed, increasing the volumetric efficiency of the engine and increasing the power output.

Supercharging accomplishes this by operating the compressor mechanically, through a gear-driven shaft. The supercharger is normally activated on demand, when the accelerator pedal is pushed to the floor. A turbocharger is actually a small turbine, which uses exhaust gasses to spin a turbine wheel mounted on a common shaft with a compressor. As the turbine turns at high speed, it causes the compressor to pack a greater charge of air into the engine's cylinders.

In both systems, air enters through an air intake, passes through an air cleaner, and travels through a duct (usually funnel shaped) to the compressor inlet portion of the turbocharger. From there air is forced through a diffuser into the intake manifold, to the individual cylinders.

The turbocharger itself and the principle are extremely simple, but sophisticated engineering problems are created by its application. The most critical problem is controlling the manifold or boost pressure. This is the amount of additional boost or pressure created by the turbocharger. The boost must be controlled or the engine will begin to detonate and eventually burn holes in the pistons and self destruct.

The solution lies in the wastegate or safety valve, which is keyed to intake manifold pressure, exhaust pressure, or a combination of both. At a predetermined pressure, the wastegate valve will open, allowing some of the exhaust gas to pass directly into the exhaust system bypassing the turbocharger. This keeps the intake manifold pressure at a preset maximum.

The second problem with turbocharging is the generally inconsistent quality of gasoline available. If the octane of the fuel is unpredictable, then so is the point at which the engine begins to detonate, making it difficult to set the maximum manifold pressure. The answer to this problem is a *knock sensor*, a device that detects the harmful pressure waves of detonation in the cylinders and instantly retards the ignition timing to prevent detonation.

The turbocharger itself spins at a maximum speed of about 110,000 rpm at highway speeds and is capable of supplying boost pressure of up to 60 to 70 psi on

The GM turbocharged V6 engine. The turbocharger is mounted on the right rear of the engine (arrow).

Some of the different components needed to turbocharge an engine. Clockwise from left: exhaust manifold, additional piping, turbocharger/wastegate assembly, carburetor adaptor, and intake manifold.

sion ratios used in automotive diesels run anywhere from 16:1 to 23:1. A typical spark-ignition engine has a ratio of about 8:1. This is why a spark-ignition engine which continues to run after you have shut off the engine is said to be "dieseling." It is running on combustion chamber heat alone.

Designing an engine to ignite on its own combustion chamber heat poses certain problems. For instance, although a diesel engine has no need for a coil, spark plugs, or a distributor, it does need what are known as "glow plugs." These look like spark plugs, but are only used to warm the combustion chambers when the engine is cold. Without these plugs, cold starting would be impossible. Also, since fuel timing (rather than spark timing) is critical to a diesel's operation, all diesel engines are fuel-injected rather than carbureted, since the precise fuel metering necessary is not possible with a carburetor.

professional racing engines. But for the average auto or light truck, 3 to 9 psi is about the maximum boost pressure expected.

The Diesel Engine

Diesel engines, like gasoline-powered engines, have a crankshaft, pistons, camshaft, etc. Also, four-stroke diesels require four piston strokes for the complete combustion cycle, exactly like a gasoline engine. The difference lies in how the fuel mixture is ignited. A diesel engine does not rely on a conventional spark ignition to ignite the fuel mixture. Instead, heat produced by compressed air in the combustion chamber ignites the fuel and produces a power stroke. This is known as a compression-ignition engine.

No fuel enters the cylinder on the intake stroke, only air. Since only air is present on the intake stroke, only air is compressed on the compression stroke. At the

end of the compression stroke, fuel is sprayed into the combustion chamber and the mixture ignites.

The fuel/air mixture ignites because of the very high temperatures generated by the high compression ratios used in diesel engines. Typically, the compres-

The Wankel Engine

Like a conventional piston engine, the Wankel engine is an internal combustion engine and operates on a four-stroke cycle. Also, it runs on gasoline and the

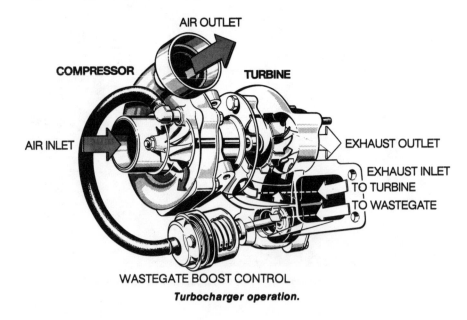

Turbocharger operation.

AIR OUTLET

COMPRESSOR

TURBINE

AIR INLET

EXHAUST OUTLET

EXHAUST INLET
TO TURBINE
TO WASTEGATE

WASTEGATE BOOST CONTROL

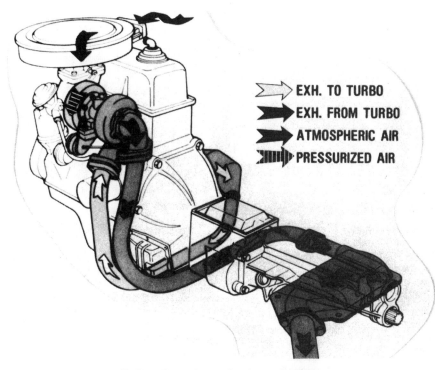

EXH. TO TURBO
EXH. FROM TURBO
ATMOSPHERIC AIR
PRESSURIZED AIR

Air flow through a turbocharged engine.

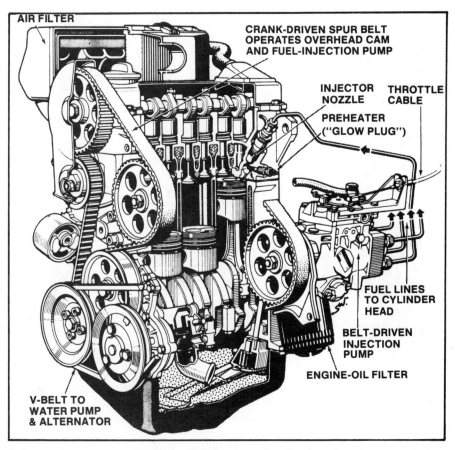

AIR FILTER

CRANK-DRIVEN SPUR BELT
OPERATES OVERHEAD CAM
AND FUEL-INJECTION PUMP

INJECTOR
NOZZLE

THROTTLE
CABLE

PREHEATER
("GLOW PLUG")

FUEL LINES
TO CYLINDER
HEAD

BELT-DRIVEN
INJECTION
PUMP

ENGINE-OIL FILTER

V-BELT TO
WATER PUMP
& ALTERNATOR

Cutaway view of an overhead camshaft four-cylinder diesel engine. Notice its similarity to the gasoline four-cylinder pictured earlier.

THE DIESEL FOUR STROKE CYCLE

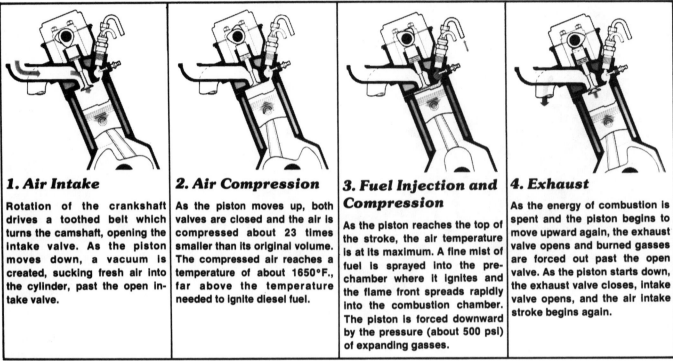

1. Air Intake

Rotation of the crankshaft drives a toothed belt which turns the camshaft, opening the intake valve. As the piston moves down, a vacuum is created, sucking fresh air into the cylinder, past the open intake valve.

2. Air Compression

As the piston moves up, both valves are closed and the air is compressed about 23 times smaller than its original volume. The compressed air reaches a temperature of about 1650°F., far above the temperature needed to ignite diesel fuel.

3. Fuel Injection and Compression

As the piston reaches the top of the stroke, the air temperature is at its maximum. A fine mist of fuel is sprayed into the pre-chamber where it ignites and the flame front spreads rapidly into the combustion chamber. The piston is forced downward by the pressure (about 500 psi) of expanding gasses.

4. Exhaust

As the energy of combustion is spent and the piston begins to move upward again, the exhaust valve opens and burned gasses are forced out past the open valve. As the piston starts down, the exhaust valve closes, intake valve opens, and the air intake stroke begins again.

The four-stroke principle applied to a diesel engine.

spark is generated by a conventional distributor-coil ignition system. However, the similarities end there.

In a Wankel engine, the cylinders are replaced by chambers, and the pistons are replaced by rotors. The chambers are not circular, but have a curved circumference that is identified as an epitrochoid. An epitrochoid is the curve described by a given point on a circle as the circle rolls around the periphery of another circle of twice the radius of the generating circle.

The rotor is three-cornered, with curved sides. All three corners are in permanent contact with the epitrochoidal surface as the rotor moves around the chamber. This motion is both orbital and rotational, as the rotor is mounted off center. The crankshaft of a piston engine is replaced by a rotor shaft, and crank throws are replaced by ec-

THE ROTARY ENGINE POWER CYCLE

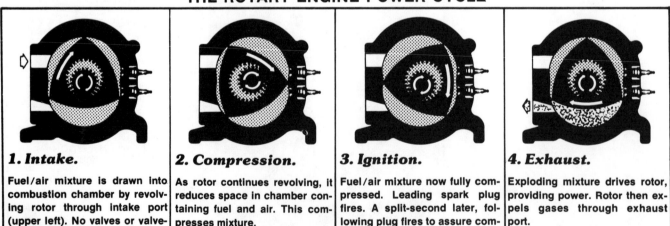

1. Intake.

Fuel/air mixture is drawn into combustion chamber by revolving rotor through intake port (upper left). No valves or valve-operating mechanism needed.

2. Compression.

As rotor continues revolving, it reduces space in chamber containing fuel and air. This compresses mixture.

3. Ignition.

Fuel/air mixture now fully compressed. Leading spark plug fires. A split-second later, following plug fires to assure complete combustion.

4. Exhaust.

Exploding mixture drives rotor, providing power. Rotor then expels gases through exhaust port.

The path of the rotor in a Wankel engine. Note the constantly varying shape of the combustion chamber and the two spark plugs per cylinder.

Cutaway view of Mazda's rotary engine. Note that this is a two rotor engine.

opposite the ports, and the exhaust phase takes place in the area preceding the exhaust port, overlapping with the latter part of the expansion phase. All three rotor faces are engaged in one of the four phases at all times.

Two Stroke Engines

Several cars imported into the United States use two-stroke engines. These operate with only a compression stroke and a power stroke. Intake of fuel and air mixture and expulsion of exhaust gases takes place between the power and compression strokes while the piston is near the bottom of its travel. Ports in the cylinder walls replace the cylinder heads valves of the four-stroke engine. The crankcase is kept dry of oil, and the entire engine is lubricated by mixing the oil with the fuel so that a fine mist of oil covers all moving parts.

The ports are designed so the fuel and air are trapped in the engine's crankcase during most of the downstroke of the piston. This makes the crankcase into a

centrics. Each rotor is carried on an eccentric. Any number of rotors is possible, but most engines have one or two rotors. The valves of the piston engine are replaced by ports in the Wankel engine housing. They are covered and uncovered by the path of the rotor.

One of the key differences between the Wankel rotary engine and the piston engine is in the operational cycle. In the piston engine, all the events take place at the top end of the cylinder (intake, compression, expansion, and exhaust). The events are spaced out in time only. The Wankel engine is the opposite. The events occur at the same time but at different places around the rotor housing surface.

The intake phase takes place next to the intake port and overlaps with the area used for compression. Expansion takes place

THE TWO STROKE CYCLE

1. Compression
The compression stroke of a two-stroke engine; the intake port is open and the air/fuel mixture is entering the crankcase.

2. Power
The power stroke of a two-stroke engine; the intake port is closed, and the piston is being forced down by the expanding gases. The air/fuel mixture is being compressed in the crankcase.

3. Exhaust
The exhaust stroke of a two-stroke engine; the piston travels past the exhaust port, thus opening it, then past the intake port, opening that. As the exhaust gases flow out, the air/fuel mixture flows in due to being under pressure in the crankcase. The next stroke of the piston is the compression stroke and the series of events starts over again.

TROUBLESHOOTING BASIC ENGINE PERFORMANCE

Most basic engine problems are caused by neglect or lack of maintenance. This chart will help locate the basic problems you can easily handle yourself. Obviously there are other, more serious causes (broken or worn parts) that will require the services of a professional mechanic.

Some ignition components can only be checked with special equipment. One way to eliminate these as a cause of a problem is by substituting a component known to be good. Further information on a possible cause can be found in the section listed after each cause.

Symptom(s)	Possible Cause(s)
ENGINE RUNS WELL, BUT IS HARD TO START WHEN COLD	• Wrong oil viscosity for prevailing temperature (see recommended viscosity chart in section 8) • Stuck or improperly adjusted choke (Section 15) • Inadequate fuel pump volume, clogged fuel filter (Section 15) • Cracked distributor cap (Section 13) • Improper ignition timing/dwell angle (Section 13)
ENGINE IDLES POORLY OR STALLS The engine runs rough; in extreme cases the whole car will shake. The engine may quit running while idling or driving.	• Idle speed/mixture improperly adjusted (Section 15) • Air leak at carburetor base, intake manifold or vacuum hoses (Section 15) • Clogged PCV valve/hose (Section 15) • Stuck or improperly adjusted choke (Section 15) • Incorrect timing/dwell; fouled spark plugs (Section 13) • Worn valves (Section 13)
ENGINE MISFIRES AT HIGH SPEEDS ONLY	• Spark plug gaps too wide (Section 13) • Weak coil or spark plug wires; improper dwell angle (Section 13) • Inadequate fuel pump volume, clogged fuel filter (Section 15)
ENGINE MISSES AT VARIOUS SPEEDS Steady jerking usually more pronounced as engine load increases. Exhaust has steady spitting sound at idle.	• Water/foreign matter in fuel • Insufficient dwell angle (Section 13) • Late ignition timing (Section 13) • Weak coil or condenser (Section 13)
ENGINE LACKS POWER Engine delivers limited power under load or at high speed. Won't accelerate normally, loses power going up hills.	• Wrong ignition timing (Section 13) • Fouled or improperly gapped spark plugs (Section 13) • Incorrect dwell angle, weak coil or condenser (Section 13) • Weak coil or condenser (Section 13) • Improper adjusted valves (Section 8) • Worn piston rings, rings, valves (Section 8) • Inadequate fuel pump volume (Section 15)
ENGINE HESITATES ON ACCELERATION Momentary lack of response as accelerator is depressed, most pronounced when pulling away from stop.	• Incorrect ignition timing (Section 13) • Inadequate fuel pump volume (Section 15)
ENGINE DETONATES (PINGS) Detonation is a mild to severe ping, usually worse under acceleration. Engine makes a sharp metallic knock that sounds like a bolt rattling	• Ignition timing over-advanced (Section 13) • Spark plug heat range too high (Section 13) • Stuck heat riser (Section 13) • Excessive carbon deposits in combustion chamber • Too low octane fuel (Section 5)
HIGH OIL CONSUMPTION More than 1 quart every 500 miles	• Oil level too high (Section 8) • Oil of too light viscosity (Section 8) • External oil leaks (Section 4) • Worn cylinders or rings (Section 8)
NOISY VALVES	• Improperly adjusted valves (Section 8) • Incorrect engine oil level (Section 8) • Piece of carbon stuck underneath valve

compression chamber that force-feeds the combustion chambers after the ports are uncovered. The pistons serve as the valves, covering the ports whenever they should be closed.

Periodic Maintenance

Keeping Your Engine Clean

There are a variety of cleaners and degreasers available to help you keep your engine and engine compartment clean. No one wants to work on an engine that is nearly invisible underneath the grease. The most effective way to clean an engine is to steam clean it. However, this takes equipment which the average backyard mechanic does not ordinarily have, though steam cleaning is available at some car washes. It is possible, of course, to have your engine professionally steam cleaned, although this is generally not necessary unless the engine is extraordinarily dirty. Ordinary commercial degreasers, available at auto parts stores, will generally do the job.

Checking Oil

Maintaining the correct oil level in your car is probably the most important single item of periodic engine maintenance you

ENGINE MAINTENANCE INTERVALS

To keep your engine operating efficiently, maintain it at the following intervals.

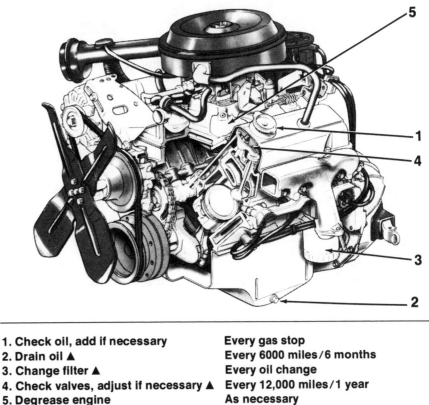

1. **Check oil, add if necessary**	**Every gas stop**
2. **Drain oil ▲**	**Every 6000 miles/6 months**
3. **Change filter ▲**	**Every oil change**
4. **Check valves, adjust if necessary ▲**	**Every 12,000 miles/1 year**
5. **Degrease engine**	**As necessary**

▲If the vehicle is used for severe service, (trailer pulling, constant stop/start driving, off-road operation), cut the maintenance interval in half.

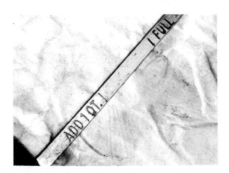

The oil marks on most dipsticks are self-explanatory. The distance between the marks on the dipstick usually corresponds to one quart of oil. Maintain the oil level between the two marks. Keep in mind that too much oil is almost as bad as too little oil.

can perform. There are many reason's an engine uses up oil, but keep in mind that it is not unusual for even a showroom-fresh car to use oil at the rate of about 1000 miles to the quart. Therefore, it can be assumed that almost every engine will use a certain amount of oil.

Frequent oil checks are a necessity. Make it a habit to check the oil at least once a week or at every gas stop. whichever occurs more frequently. When checking the oil, the engine should be warm, but not running, and the car should be parked on a level surface. Be sure to give the oil a few minutes to drain back into the pan from the upper regions of the engine. Otherwise you will get a false reading.

Compression

A check of cylinder compression is the first step in any comprehensive tune-up. It is useless to try to tune an engine with insufficient compression because other tune-up procedures will not cure the problem.

Any leak in the combustion chamber will reduce the pressure created during the compression stroke. The pressure created in the combustion chamber can be measured with a gauge that remains at the highest reading it measures, through the action of a one-way valve. There are two types of compression gauge—the hand-held type and the screw-in type. The hand-held type is less expensive, but more difficult to

OIL RECOMMENDATIONS CHART—GASOLINE ENGINE
(SEE NOTE)

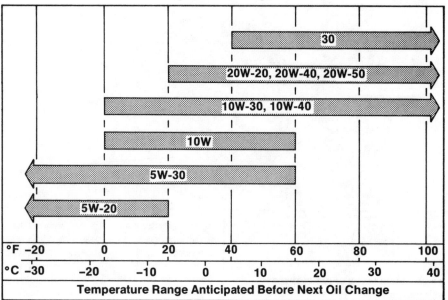

				30				
		20W-20, 20W-40, 20W-50					
	10W-30, 10W-40						
	10W						
5W-30							
5W-20							

°F	−20	0	20	40	60	80	100
°C	−30	−20	−10	0	10	20	30	40

Temperature Range Anticipated Before Next Oil Change

NOTE: Since 1980, the preferred viscosities of motor oil used in engines in GM (Buick, Cadillac, Chevrolet, Oldsmobile, Pontiac and GM Canadian) vehicles are:

Gasoline Engines
SAE 5W-30 (preferred for engines of 2.8 liters or less)
SAE 10W-30 (preferred for all other engines)
SAE 15W-40, 20W-20, 30 (acceptable for all engines)

Diesel Engines
SAE 30 (preferred above freezing*)
SAE 10W-30, 15W-40 (acceptable for all engines; use only for cold weather operation; helps starting)

* Except for 1.8 and 2.2 liter diesels, where SAE 10W-30 is preferred at all temperatures. Do not use SAE 10W-40 or, any other grade not specifically recommended.

GM does not recommend the use of 10W-40 engine oils in 1984 or later GM gasoline engines. The use of 10W-40 oil will not automatically void the GM new car warranty, but if the use of such oil is determined to have caused engine damage, the cost of repair will not be covered by the warranty, as GM does not cover any damage caused by the use of nonrecommended oils, or oils that do not meet API quality or viscosity grades.

get a good reading with, since it all depends on how tightly you hold the gauge in the spark plug hole. If you have the screw-in type, you don't have this problem, although on some engines it's difficult to thread the gauge into the spark plug hole.

A compression test will uncover many mechanical problems that can cause rough running or poor performance. Also,

while you have the spark plug removed, it would be an excellent idea to check spark plug condition. Refer to Section 13 "Electrical System/Ignition" for information on reading spark plugs.

Caution

Do not try to check compression on diesel or rotary engines. A normal compression gauge

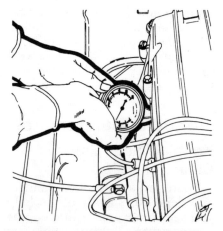

Hand-held compression gauges such as the type shown are the most common, although screw-in types are also available and more accurate. When checking compression, remove all the spark plugs before taking any readings. Also be sure the engine completes at least one full revolution (intake, compression, power and exhaust) to ensure an accurate reading.

cannot handle the extreme pressure of a diesel engine, and special equipment is necessary to check compression on a rotary engine.

Checking Compression

Prepare the engine for a compression test as follows:

1. Run the engine until it reaches operating temperature. The engine is at operating temperature a few minutes after the upper radiator hose gets hot. If the test is performed on a cold engine, the readings will be considerably lower than normal, even if the engine is in perfect mechanical condition.

2. Note the position of the spark plug wires and remove the plug wires from the plugs.

3. Clean all dirt and foreign material from around the spark plugs, and then remove all the plugs. Block the throttle plates wide open.

4. Have an assistant crank the engine over while you hold the gauge in the spark plug hole. The engine should be cranked over for at least one full revolution.

OIL RECOMMENDATIONS CHART—DIESEL ENGINES
(SEE NOTE)

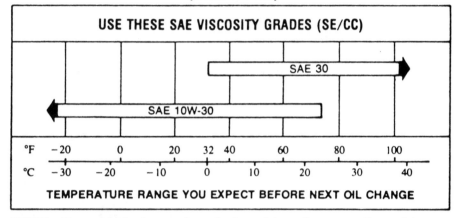

NOTE: Since 1980, the preferred viscosities of motor oil used in engines in GM (Buick, Cadillac, Chevrolet, Oldsmobile, Pontiac and GM Canadian) vehicles are:

Gasoline Engines
SAE 5W-30 (preferred for engines of 2.8 liters or less)
SAE 10W-30 (preferred for all other engines)
SAE 15W-40, 20W-20, 30 (acceptable for all engines)

Diesel Engines
SAE 30 (preferred above freezing*)
SAE 10W-30, 15W-40 (acceptable for all engines; use only for cold weather operation; helps starting)

* Except for 1.8 and 2.2 liter diesels, where SAE 10W-30 is preferred at all temperatures. Do not use SAE 10W-40 or, any other grade not specifically recommended.

GM does not recommend the use of 10W-40 engine oils in 1984 or later GM gasoline engines. The use of 10W-40 oil will not automatically void the GM new car warranty, but if the use of such oil is determined to have caused engine damage, the cost of repair will not be covered by the warranty, as GM does not cover any damage caused by the use of nonrecommended oils, or oils that do not meet API quality or viscosity grades.

Probably the best idea is to crank the engine until you record the highest reading.
5. Record the compression reading from that cylinder (noting which cylinder it was), and repeat the test for all the other cylinders.

All engines will not exhibit the same compression readings. In fact two identical engines may not have the same compression. Generally, the rule of thumb is that the lowest cylinder should be within 25% of the highest. The lower limit of normal compres-sion on a V8 engine with normal wear is 100 psi; on a 4- or 6-cylinder engine, it is 90 psi.

Low Compression

Compression readings that are generally low indicate worn rings, valves, or pistons, and generally indicate a high-mileage engine. If all cylinders read low, squirt a tablespoon of oil into the cylinder, crank the engine a few times, and recheck compression. If the readings come up to normal, the problem is worn rings, pistons, or cylinders. If compres-sion does not increase, the problem is in the valves.

Low compression in two adjacent cylinders (with normal compression in the other cylinders) indicates a blown head gasket between the low-reading cylinders. Other problems are possible (broken ring, hole burned in a piston), but a blown head gasket is most likely.

Engine Identification

Since 1976, on engines used in domestically produced cars, it is important for servicing and ordering parts, to know which engine you have. The place to start identifying an engine is with the VIN (Vehicle Identification Number) of the car. The VIN is visible through the windshield on the driver's side of the dash and contains a lot of data encoded into a lengthy combination of letters and numbers. A specific letter or number is used to designate the installed engine and engines are identified in the specifications charts by the engine code letter.

Up to and including 1980, the engine number appears in the VIN as follows:

American Motors Corp. (AMC)—the seventh figure in the VIN indicates the installed engine
Chrysler Corporation—the fifth figure in the VIN indicates the installed engine
Ford Motor Company—the fifth figure in the VIN indicates the installed engine
General Motors Corp.—the fifth figure in the VIN indicates the installed engine. However, GM occasionally used the same letter or number to identify different engines (as long as they were made by different divisions). For instance, the letter S was used in 1976 to identify the 454 CID V8 used in Chevrolets. It was also used to identify the 455 CID V8 used in Pontiacs. Because of this, it is
(Text continues on page 91.)

CHANGING YOUR OIL

Oil changes are not difficult. As a matter of fact, it's one of the simplest (and most valuable) operations you can perform on your car. Although it may seem somewhat complicated at first glance, if you follow these simple instructions, you'll discover that it's one of the easiest ways to save money you'll ever find. All you'll need is the oil, an oil filter, a drain pan of some type, an oil spout, an adjustable wrench, and an oil filter wrench.

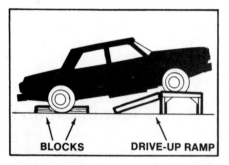

1. Warm the car up before changing your oil. Raise the front end of the car and support it on drive-on ramps or jackstands.

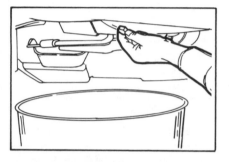

2. Locate the drain plug on the bottom of the oil pan and slide a low flat pan of sufficient capacity under the engine to catch the oil. Loosen the plug with a wrench and turn it out the last few turns by hand. Keep a steady inward pressure on the plug to avoid hot oil from running down your arm.

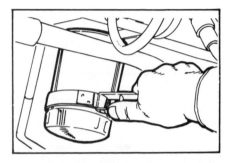

3. Remove the oil filter with a filter wrench. The filter can hold more than a quart of oil, which will be hot. Be sure the gasket comes off with the filter and clean the mounting base on the engine.

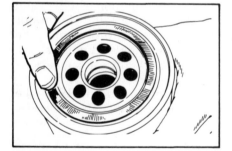

4. Lubricate the gasket on the new filter with clean engine oil. A dry gasket may not make a good seal and will allow the filter to leak.

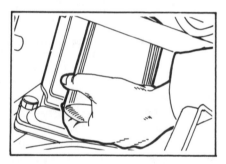

5. Position a new filter on the mounting base and spin it on by hand. Do not use a wrench. When the gasket contacts the engine, tighten it another ½–1 turn by hand.

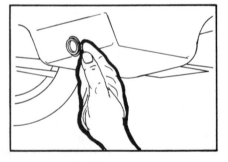

6. Using a rag, clean the drain plug and the area around the drain hole in the oil pan.

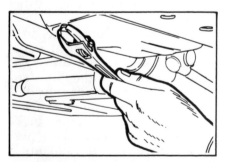

7. Install the drain plug and tighten it finger-tight. If you feel resistance, stop and be sure you are not cross-threading the plug. Finally, tighten the plug with a wrench.

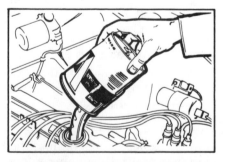

8. Locate the oil cap on the valve cover. An oil spout is the easiest way to add oil, but a funnel will do just as well.

9. Start the engine and check for leaks. The oil pressure warning light will remain on for a few seconds; when it goes out, stop the engine and check the level on the dipstick.

VALVE ADJUSTMENT

Periodic valve adjustments are not required on most modern engines with hydraulic valve lifters. In fact, some engines no longer have any provision for valve adjustment, given today's hydraulic valve lifter technology. However, the relatively recent proliferation of small, economy cars has brought about a resurgence in the popularity of adjustable valves and solid lifters, which are more common to smaller engines.

Exact valve adjustment procedures for all cars is impossible to detail here, but the following illustrations are typical of almost all types of valve adjustment, and should serve as a general guide. Consult the Tune-Up Specifications section for valve clearances on those engines requiring periodic adjustment.

Following are some tips that can make valve adjustment a little easier and more accurate:
• Before removing a valve cover, be sure to have a valve cover gasket on hand.
• Check the specifications to be sure if the valves are adjusted with the engine "hot" or "cold."
• If you set the valves with the engine running, run the engine as slow as possible.
• The gauge should pass through with a slow steady drag. With the engine running, if you force the gauge or the engine misses when the gauge is inserted, the clearance is too tight.
• It's better to have the clearance a little loose than a little tight. Valves adjusted too tight will cause valve burning.

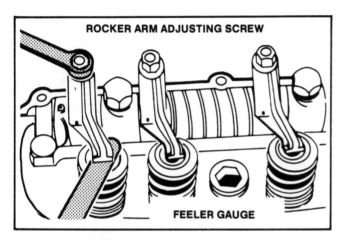

This is an example of one of the most common types of valve adjustment procedure. The rocker on this overhead valve engine arm is equipped with an adjusting nut, and valve clearance is checked by inserting a feeler gauge between the rocker arm and the tip of the valve stem. If the clearance is correct, the correct size feeler gauge should just fit with a slight drag. Adjustments are made simply by turning the adjusting nut. Some adjusters are slotted so that a flat-bladed screwdriver may be used for adjustment.

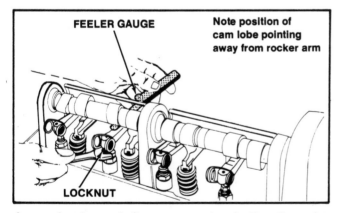

An overhead camshaft arrangement actuating the valves through rocker arms. Clearance is checked when the camshaft lobe is pointing away from the contact point on the rocker arm. Adjustment is made by loosening the locknut and turning the adjusting nut.

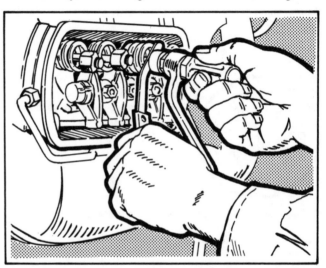

Volkswagen beetle motors utilize a simple overhead valve arrangement, although the horizontal arrangement of the engine makes adjusting the valves somewhat awkward.

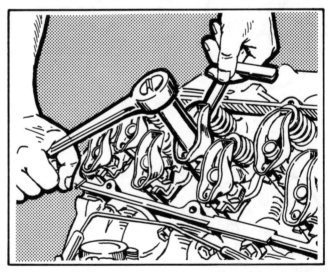

Adjusting the valves on a General Motors solid lifter V8. Clearance is checked between the rocker arm and the valve stem. Adjustment is made simply by turning the nut in the top of the rocker arm.

USING A VACUUM GAUGE

White needle = steady needle   Dark needle = drifting needle

The vacuum gauge is one of the most useful and easy-to-use diagnostic tools. It is inexpensive, easy to hook up, and provides valuable information about the condition of your engine.

Indication: Normal engine in good condition

Gauge reading: Steady, from 17–22 in./Hg.

Indication: Sticking valve or ignition miss

Gauge reading: Needle fluctuates from 15–20 in./Hg. at idle

Indication: Late ignition or valve timing, low compression, stuck throttle valve, leaking carburetor or manifold gasket.

Gauge reading: Low (15–20 in./Hg.) but steady

Indication: Improper carburetor adjustment, or minor intake leak at carburetor or manifold

Gauge reading: Drifting needle

Indication: Weak valve springs, worn valve stem guides, or leaky cylinder head gasket (vibrating excessively at all speeds).

Gauge reading: Needle fluctuates as engine speed increases

Indication: Burnt valve or improper valve clearance. The needle will drop when the defective valve operates.

Gauge reading: Steady needle, but drops regularly

Indication: Choked muffler or obstruction in system. Speed up the engine. Choked muffler will exhibit a slow drop of vacuum to zero.

Gauge reading: Gradual drop in reading at idle

Indication: Worn valve guides

Gauge reading: Needle vibrates excessively at idle, but steadies as engine speed increases

necessary to be sure of the make and model year of the car before a positive identification of the engine can be made according to the fifth figure letter code.

Beginning in 1981, all manufacturersd adopted a uniform, 17-digit VIN. The tenth digit of the VIN indicates the model year and the eighth digit indicates the engine code.

The VIN is visible through the driver's side windshield.

9

The Cooling System

Your engine needs a cooling system to protect it from self-destruction. Burning gases inside the cylinders can reach a temperature of 4500° F and produce enough heat to melt a 200 lb engine block.

About one-third of the heat produced in the engine must be carried away by the cooling system. Some is utilized for heating the passenger compartment. And, strange as it seems, your car's air conditioner produces heat in the process of cooling and dehumidifying the air. This heat must also be dispersed by the cooling system.

How the Cooling System Works

The main parts of the engine cooling system are the radiator, radiator pressure cap, hoses, thermostat, water pump, fan, and fan belt. The system is filled with coolant, which should be a 50-50 mixture of antifreeze and water. No matter where you live or how hot or cold the weather becomes, the mixture should be maintained the year around.

The water pump and engine cooling fan are mounted on the same shaft and driven by a belt connected to the engine. The pump draws coolant from the bottom of the radiator and forces it through passages surrounding the hot area—the cylinders, combustion chambers, valves and spark plugs. From there the coolant flows through a hose into the top of the radiator, then downward through tubes attached to cooling fins and surrounded by air passages. Heat is transferred from the coolant to air forced through the radiator passages by the fan and the forward motion of the car.

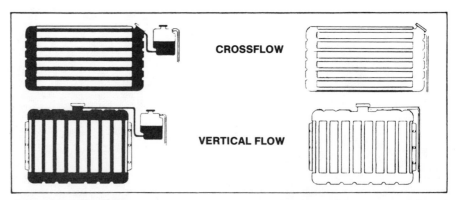

Conventional automotive radiators with coolant recovery systems (left) and without coolant recovery system (right).

CROSSFLOW

VERTICAL FLOW

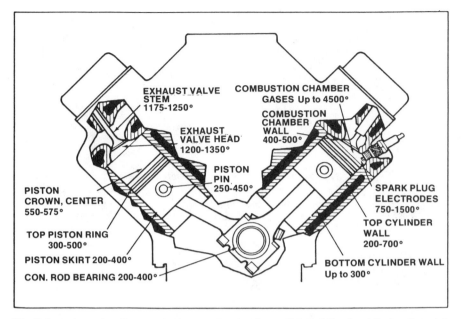

EXHAUST VALVE STEM 1175-1250°

COMBUSTION CHAMBER GASES Up to 4500°

EXHAUST VALVE HEAD 1200-1350°

COMBUSTION CHAMBER WALL 400-500°

PISTON PIN 250-450°

PISTON CROWN, CENTER 550-575°

SPARK PLUG ELECTRODES 750-1500°

TOP CYLINDER WALL 200-700°

TOP PISTON RING 300-500°

PISTON SKIRT 200-400°

CON. ROD BEARING 200-400°

BOTTOM CYLINDER WALL Up to 300°

The internal combustion engine converts about one-third of the heat it develops into power. Another third is lost in the exhaust system and the remaining third must be carried away by the cooling system. The operating temperatures are typical of a modern engine.

What is Coolant

Coolant in late model cars is a 50-50 mixture of ethylene glycol and water. This mixture in older cars was required only in the winter to prevent freezing, but modern cars with air-conditioning must also use it in the summer as well.

Late-model car manufacturers also require their engines to run at a higher temperature because it results in better engine efficiency and improves the effectiveness of emission control devices. This temperature is controlled by the thermostat, most of which are in the 192° F or 195° F range.

Good quality antifreezes also contain water pump lubricants, rust inhibitors, and other corrosion inhibitors along with acid neutralizers. Antifreeze mixtures should not remain in the cooling system beyond one year.

Controlling the Temperature

It's important to get the coolant up to normal operating temperature as quickly as possible to ensure smooth engine operation, free flow of oil, and ample heat for the occupants. When the engine is cold, the thermostat blocks the passage from the cylinder head to the radiator and sends coolant on a shortcut to the water pump. The cooling fluid is not exposed to the blast of air from the radiator, so it warms up rapidly. As temperature increases, the thermostat gradually opens and allows coolant to flow through the radiator.

Cooling systems on older cars were limited to a maximum temperature of 212° F—the boiling point of water. To get rid of the extra heat generated by more powerful engines, automatic transmissions, and air conditioning, modern cars have pressurized systems using a 50-50 mixture of antifreeze and water which enables them to operate at temperatures up to 263° F without boiling. At this temperature, plain water alone would boil away.

Transmission Oil Cooler

Automatic transmission oil is cooled by a small, separate radiator, usually located in the lower tank or alongside the main radiator. It serves the same purpose for the transmission as the main radiator does for the engine.

Most cars can benefit from the installation of a transmission oil cooler, especially if the car is used to pull a trailer or for some other kind of heavy service. See the installation procedures later in this chapter.

What to Do When the Engine Overheats

Air conditioning, automatic transmission, and power-operated accessories put an extra burden on the engine cooling system. The hot light is designed to come on as the engine begins to overheat. This gives the driver a chance to correct the cause of overheating with minimum delay. If you are stuck in heavy traffic and the temperature gauge shows the engine is overheated or the hot light comes on, shut off the air conditioner. Whenever you come to a stop, shift into neutral and speed up the engine a little to increase circulation of the coolant and air flow from the fan.

If the hot light turns on or the temperature gauge indicates overheating when the air conditioner is running, follow these steps:

1. Turn off the air conditioning. If the light doesn't go out in about a minute, pull over in a safe place and set the parking brake. Then place the transmission selector lever in park.

2. Don't turn off the engine, instead, speed up the engine so it sounds as if it's idling twice as fast as normal. Lift the engine hood and check for fluid leaks at the radiator hoses, radiator, or radiator overflow outlet. Check to see that drive belts are intact, fan is turning, and radiator cap is sealed. The overheating should subside.

HOW TO SPOT WORN V-BELTS

V-Belts are vital to the efficient cooling system operation—they drive the fan and water pump. They require little maintenance (occasional tightening) but they will not last forever. Slipping or failure of the V-belt will lead to overheating. If your V-belt looks like any of these, it should be replaced.

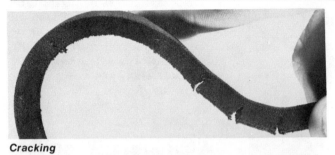

Cracking

This belt has deep cracks, which cause it to flex. Too much flexing leads to heat build-up and premature failure. These cracks can be caused by using the belt on a pulley that is too small. Notched belts are available for small diameter pulleys.

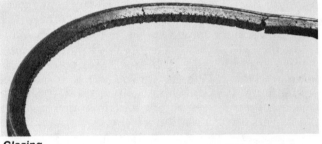

Softening (grease and oil)

Oil and grease on a belt can cause the belt's rubber compounds to soften and separate from the reinforcing cords that hold the belt together. The belt will first slip, then finally fail altogether.

Glazing

Glazing is caused by a belt that is slipping. The more the belt slips, the more glazing will be built up on the surface of the belt. The more the belt is glazed, the more it will slip. If the glazing is light, tighten the belt.

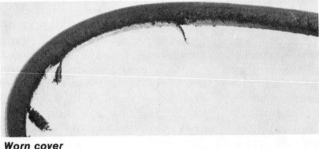

Worn cover

The cover of this belt is worn off and is peeling away. The reinforcing cords will begin to wear and the belt will soon break.

Separation

This belt is on the verge of breaking and leaving you stranded. The layers of the belt are separating and the reinforcing cords are exposed. It's just a matter of time before it breaks completely.

HOW TO SPOT BAD HOSES

Both the upper and lower radiator hoses are called upon to perform difficult jobs in an inhospitable environment. They are subject to nearly 18 psi at under hood temperatures often over 280°F., and must circulate nearly 7500 gallons of coolant an hour—3 good reasons to have good hoses.

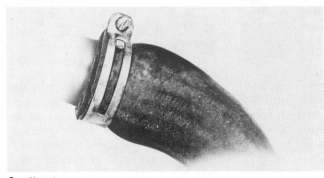

Swollen hose

A good test for any hose is to feel it for soft or spongy spots. Frequently these will appear as swollen areas of the hose. The most likely cause is oil soaking. This hose could burst at any time, when hot or under pressure.

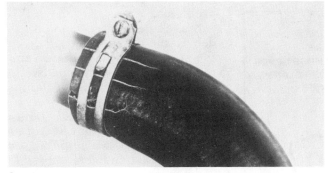

Cracked hose

Cracked hoses can usually be seen, but feel the hoses to be sure they have not hardened; a prime cause of cracking. This hose has cracked down to the reinforcing cords and could split at any of the cracks.

Frayed hose end (due to weak clamp)

Weakened clamps frequently are the cause of hose and cooling system failure. The connection between the pipe and hose has deteriorated enough to allow coolant to escape when the engine is hot.

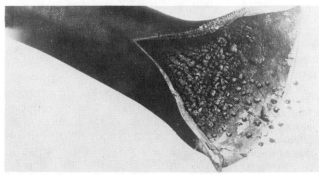

Debris in the cooling system

Debris, rust and scale in the cooling system can cause the inside of a hose to weaken. This can usually be felt on the outside of the hose as soft or thinner areas.

3. When the overheating has passed, proceed on the road a little slower, and don't resume normal driving for 10 minutes.

4. If the radiator starts boiling over, pull off the road as soon as possible. Shut off the engine. When the boiling stops, raise the hood, but don't touch the radiator cap. Allow the system to cool. Then place a cloth over the cap and slowly turn it to the first notch to relieve the pressure. Remove the cap, start the engine, and slowly add water. Replace the cap.

5. Never open the radiator cap when the engine is hot; the release of pressure will precipitate boiling and further overheating—and may scald anyone nearby in the process. If the engine is losing coolant, or a fan belt is broken or loose, or if the overheating persists, stop the engine until the cause of the overheating is corrected.

6. At the first opportunity, check the system to find out why it overheated. Refill with the correct mix of the antifreeze and water.

Periodic Maintenance

At least once a year, the engine cooling system should be inspected, flushed, and refilled with fresh coolant. If the coolant is left in the system too long, it loses its ability to prevent rust and corrosion. If the coolant has too much water, it won't protect against freezing.

The pressure cap should be checked for signs of age or deterioration. Fan belt and other drive belts should be inspected and adjusted to the proper tension. If a belt is cracked, frayed along the edges, or shows signs of peeling, it should be replaced before it fails and causes more serious problems.

Leaves, dead insects, and other debris should be removed from the surfaces of the radiator and the air conditioning condenser so air can get through. Hose clamps should be tightened, and soft or cracked hoses replaced. Damp spots or accumulations of rust or dye near hoses, water pump, or other areas indicate possible leakage, which must be corrected before filling the system with fresh coolant.

Check Coolant Level

Once a month or every 1000 miles, whichever comes first, check the level of the coolant in the radiator. If you do a lot of hard driving or trailer pulling, check more often.

Coolant level should be checked on a cold engine. If there is a chance the engine is hot, cover the radiator cap with a heavy cloth. Turn the radiator cap to the first stop and let the pressure release. The pressure is gone when the hissing stops. Push down on the cap and turn it all the way around to remove it.

Many late-model cars come equipped with a coolant recovery system. They allow coolant that would normally overflow to be caught in an expansion tank; it will automatically be drawn back into the radiator when the

COOLING SYSTEM LEAKS

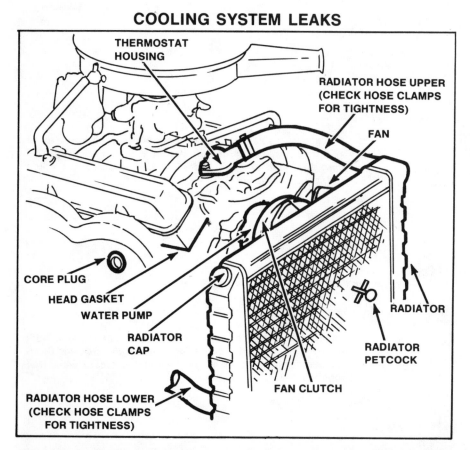

THERMOSTAT HOUSING

RADIATOR HOSE UPPER (CHECK HOSE CLAMPS FOR TIGHTNESS)

FAN

CORE PLUG

HEAD GASKET

WATER PUMP

RADIATOR CAP

RADIATOR

RADIATOR PETCOCK

FAN CLUTCH

RADIATOR HOSE LOWER (CHECK HOSE CLAMPS FOR TIGHTNESS)

Loss of engine coolant is usually not mysterious if you know what to look for. Most car manufacturers purposely keep the coolant level an inch or so below the filler neck to allow for expansion when the engine is hot. If the system is filled to the filler neck, coolant will be forced out the overflow tube as it expands. Then, when you check the level after the engine has cooled, it appears as though you are losing coolant. Coolant system leaks usually show up as a puddle of coolant on the garage floor or driveway. External coolant leaks are likely to occur at: loose hose clamps, leaking hoses, leaking radiator, leak at thermostat housing, leak at radiator petcock, loose water pump housing bolts, faulty radiator cap, loose freeze plugs (located at side of block), leaking heater core (this will sometimes leak coolant inside the passenger compartment).

COOLING SYSTEM MAINTENANCE INTERVALS

Your car's cooling system will work efficiently if it is maintained at these intervals.

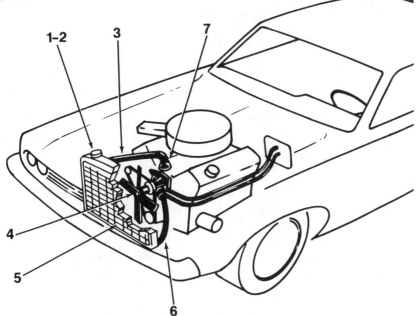

1. Check coolant level ▲	Every month/1000 miles
2. Check condition of radiator cap	Every month/1000 miles
3. Check condition of radiator hoses ▲	Every month/1000 miles
4. Check condition/adjust drive belt ▲	Every 3 months/3000 miles*
5. Clean radiator of debris	Every 3 months/3000 miles
6. Change coolant	Every year/12,000 miles (Preferably each Fall)
7. Check thermostat	Every 2 years/24,000 miles

*New drive belts will stretch and should be checked and adjusted after the first 200 miles.

▲ If the vehicle is used for severe service (trailer pulling, continuous stop/start driving, off-road operation), cut the maintenance interval in half.

Cover the radiator cap with a thick rag before removing it.

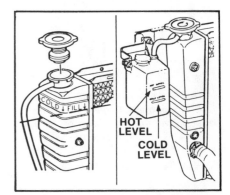

Coolant level should be 1" to 2" below the filler neck on systems without coolant recovery (left). This will allow for coolant expansion when the engine gets hot. On coolant recovery systems (right) maintain the level at the mark (arrow) on the plastic tank.

Cars with coolant overflow systems use a plastic bottle to catch coolant overflow. On these systems, do not open the radiator cap. Check the level and add coolant at the plastic bottle.

Lever-type radiator caps make releasing the pressure easier and safer. When the system is hot, lifting the lever will release the pressure and the cap can be removed.

CHECKING AND REPLACING THERMOSTAT

The thermostat can be checked for leakage (especially if you have a problem of insufficient heat) by holding it up to a light at room temperature. A slight leakage of light at one or 2 places is normal; if you can see light all around the center in a ring, replace the thermostat.

Most thermostats are designed to begin opening at the rated temperature (stamped on the thermostat), and be fully open at approximately 212°F., the boiling point of water. Immerse the thermostat in boiling water. If it does not open about ¼" or more, it should be replaced.

1. Drain enough coolant to bring the level down below the level of the upper hose. The coolant can be saved and reused if it's not old.

2. Remove the thermostat housing bolts. The hose is removed for clarity, but it's easier to leave it attached. Tap the housing lightly to break the gasket seal and lift the housing off. Note the position of the thermostat.

3. Remove the thermostat and stuff a clean rag in the opening. Scrape the old gasket off the engine and thermostat housing.

4. Thermostats sometimes stick closed when they're new. "Exercising" the new thermostat will help prevent this.

5. Insert the new thermostat with the spring end pointing down. Use a new gasket or one of the types of RTV silicone gasket sealers.

6. Replace the thermostat housing and tighten the bolts evenly (the radiator hose is removed for clarity). Refill the system with coolant, bring the engine to operating temperature and check for leaks.

coolant cools down. Radiator caps for these systems are not interchangeable. Replace only with the proper cap for the system.

Keep the coolant level 1" to 2" below the filler neck on a cold engine. On cars equipped with a coolant recovery system, simply check the level in the plastic tank, located near the radiator. On these types, add coolant to the plastic tank, not the radiator.

If the coolant level is constantly low, check for leaks.

Check the Radiator Cap

While you are checking the coolant level, check the radiator cap for a worn or cracked gasket. If the cap doesn't seal properly, fluid will be lost and the engine will overheat.

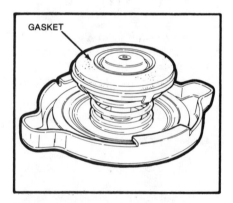

Check radiator cap occasionally for worn or cracked gasket. If cap doesn't seal properly, fluid will be lost and engine will overheat.

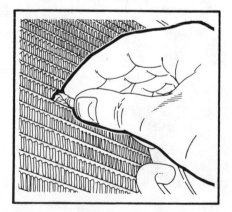

Keep the radiator grille clear of debris, bugs and leaves.

REPLACING FAN BELT

The fan belt runs the water pump and the alternator on most cars. Depending on the number of other accessories, it may be necessary to disengage other drive belts, in order to remove the fan belt.

Adjust the drive belt to proper tension (about ½" deflection under light thumb pressure).

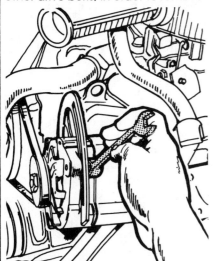

1. Loosen the alternator adjusting bolt. If necessary loosen the bolt that the alternator pivots on. This will give you enough freedom to move the alternator.

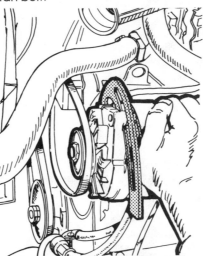

2. Push the alternator in until there is enough slack in the belt to remove it. Remove the alternator belt from the alternator pulley and crankshaft pulley. If fan belt is behind another belt, the interfering belt will also have to be removed.

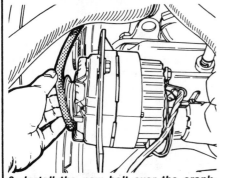

3. Install the new belt over the crankshaft, water pump and alternator pulleys. Be sure you have the right belt. It should fit even with the top of the pulley groove and should not require too much movement of the alternator to properly tension it.

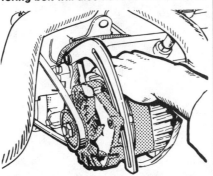

4. Pull the alternator outward to tighten the belt. Do not pry on the alternator. Tighten the alternator adjusting bolt and pivot bolt (if loosened). Check the belt tension, and recheck it in about 200 miles; new belts will stretch with use.

A worn cap should be replaced with a new one.

Clean Radiator of Debris

Periodically clean any debris—leaves, paper, insects, etc.—from the radiator fins. Pick the large pieces off by hand. The smaller pieces can be washed away with water pressure from a hose.

Carefully straighten any bent radiator fins with a pair of needle nose pliers. Be careful—the fins are very soft.

Drive Belts

Modern V-Belts Don't Show Their Age

On today's cars it's very difficult to tell the difference between an automotive V-belt with 50,000 miles of wear, and another belt with 10,000 miles of wear. A ba-sic change in engine belt construction—one that produces a longer-lasting belt—also makes it difficult to spot indications of belt wear.

Until recently, standard automotive V-belts were produced with a rubberized fabric cover. As these "banded" belts were used, the cover would gradually wear through on the sides, due to abra-

Check the degree of protection afforded by the coolant. A small, inexpensive (less than $1.00) tester like the one shown will do fine. Squeeze the bulb and suck some coolant into the glass tube. A scale on the side of the glass tube will convert the number of balls that are floating into coolant protection (°F).

Because modern bandless belts no longer show signs of potential failure, it's difficult to tell which belt has been in service for 45,000 miles (outside) or for 2400 miles (inside).

Because this type of failure takes place inside the belt, there is no easy way to determine when the belt is about to break. Statistics show the chance of V-belt failure on an average car goes up sharply after four years.

For this reason many V-belt manufacturers recommend that all engine V-belts be replaced on a four-year basis.

In this way, the replacement can be done at the car owner's convenience, rather than on an emergency basis.

The other major cause of V-belt failure is improper tension. This causes the belt to slip as it travels around the pulleys, generating heat build-up. Excessive heat eventually causes the rubber compounds in the belt to break down, and crack, leading to belt failure.

Indicators of belt tension problems include:

· Belt squeal, especially on the fan or power steering drives.

· Battery discharge, sometimes caused by a slipping alternator belt.

· Excessive sidewall wear that allows the belt to ride lower than normal in the pulley grooves.

· Absence of overcord (the belt's top protective covering).

· Cracking of the bottom and sides of the belt.

Also, small engine compartments on today's cars make belts more susceptible to heat and contamination from petroleum products. High temperatures can cause belts to dry, harden and crack. If a belt becomes oil soaked, it cannot grip the pulley. Petroleum products also break down the rubber compounds in the belt.

The best way to check belt tension is with a tension gauge. Because of smaller engine compartments and shorter belt spans between pulleys, the old finger deflection method of checking tension is not as accurate.

Adjustment

The most crucial procedure in belt installation is proper ten-

sion from the accessory drive pulleys. When the belt cover became frayed or worn, the car owner or auto mechanic had an easy-to-spot, built-in wear indicator (see "How To Spot Worn V-Belts").

Now, virtually all automotive V-belts produced in the U.S. and Europe are made without a cover. These "bandless" belts don't show wear like their predecessors. Although bandless belts are designed to outlast banded belts on similar drives, they provide no early warning of failure.

There are two main causes of V-belt failure. The most common is fatigue of the load-bearing, tensile cords leading to belt failure from the inside out. Tensile cord failure is due to a gradual weakening of the tensile cords that results from a combination of side stress, bending stress, and centrifugal force imposed on the belt as it travels around the pulleys.

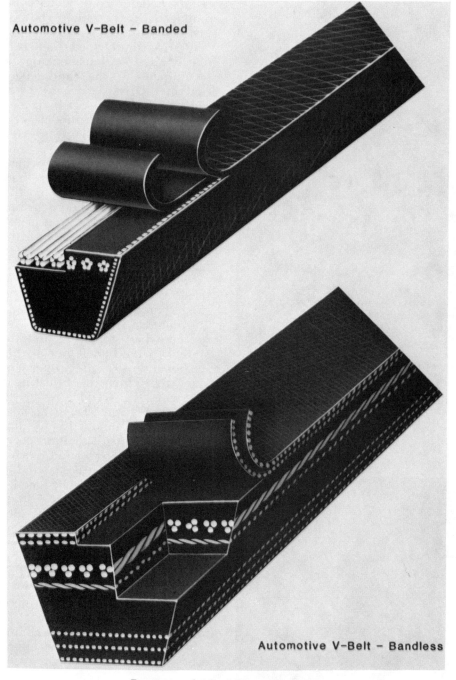

Automotive V–Belt – Banded

Automotive V–Belt – Bandless

Two types of drive belt construction.

crack and break prematurely. Also, heat may be transferred from the pulley to the accessory drive shaft, and burn up the bearing lubricants.

Belt slip also can lead to failure of the accessory system. For example, a slipping alternator belt probably will not charge the battery properly, and could lead to alternator damage due to heat. Or, the power steering will become inoperative if the belt fails.

Low belt tension or tension loss may have been caused by improper maintenance, improper installation or lack of a run-in, loose or bent adjustment brackets, pulley groove wear, or belt sidewall wear.

When replacing a V-belt, follow these steps:

1. To determine proper tension for belts, check the recommended tension ranges in the belt manufacturer's catalog. Also, tension ranges usually are available in service guides and shop manuals.

2. You also will need the proper tools: box-end wrenches or sockets with ratchets, a pry bar, such as a wooden hammer handle or piece of pipe, and a tension gauge.

3. It also is very important to be sure the car won't start accidentally or the electric fan won't engage. For safety, disconnect the ground cable (negative post) from the battery terminal.

4. Loosen the pivot and adjustment bolts, move the accessory or take-up idler to the minimum position, and remove the old belt.

5. Loop the new belt over the pulleys. Never pry a belt onto a pulley with a screwdriver or bar. This usually damages the belt's tensile member and causes the belt to fail prematurely.

6. Once the belt is installed and seated into the pulley grooves, pull back the accessory or take-up idler by hand until the belt is snug. Then with the pry bar, apply force on the accessory until the belt is tight. But, be careful to pry on the engine and accessory at

sioning. Improper tension can damage the belt, and in time, lead to failure of the accessory system the belt drives. It's important to follow correct tensioning procedures when replacing belts.

Improperly tensioned belts are either too tight or too loose. Tensioning below the recommended range is the most common cause of belt failure.

Belt tension determines how much horsepower, or torque, a belt can transmit without slipping. A belt that lacks proper tension will slip, generating excessive heat. Heat hardens the materials in a belt, causing it to

Use of a belt tension gauge is recommended to assumre accurate belt tension.

Simple, inexpensive belt tension gauges are available for use in place of more expensive models.

points where neither will be damaged. Next, tighten the adjustment bolt.

7. To accurately determine belt tension, use of a tension gauge is recommended. The hand-deflection method is as accurate because of the relatively high tension ranges on late-model cars, higher accessory loads, shorter spans between pulleys, and smaller belt cross sections, which make belts appear tighter than they really are. In addition, the hand-deflection method is a subjective measurement, and is dependent on the strength of the individual who is checking for tension.

With a tension gauge, check the tension. The higher figure of the range listed in the catalog, plus 15 pounds, is the tension required when a belt is first installed. If the belt is not at this tension, adjust to the proper tension and tighten the adjustment bolt using the wrench.

8. Next, give the belt a short run-in period (about 15–20 minutes). This seats the belt properly in the pulley groove, and relaxes the tension. Once it is seated, the new belt should be retensioned.

9. If a belt loses its tension, or slips, tighten it. Properly tensioned belts should hold the correct tension within the recommended range for several months. Belt tension, however, should be rechecked periodically.

The condition and adjustment of the drive belt are vital to proper cooling. Check the condition of the drive belts about every three months.

Drain and Refill Cooling System

Completely draining and refilling the cooling system at least every two years will remove accumulated rust, scale and other deposits. This will increase the ability of the coolant to cool the engine.

1. Drain the existing antifreeze and coolant. Open the ra-

INSTALLING A COOLANT FLUSH KIT

Rust, scale and dirty coolant are frequently responsible for overheating and engine damage. A coolant flushing kit will give you a reverse flush to loosen accumulated rust and scale.

Drain some coolant out of the radiator to bring the level down below the thermostat. Some cars have no petcock; loosen the lower radiator hose to drain.

There are 2 heater hoses. One runs from the water pump to the firewall; the other from top of the engine to the firewall. Cut into the hose running from the top of the engine to firewall.

Slide hose clamps over the ends of the heater hose and insert the flushing tee into each end of the hose. Tighten the hose clamps.

Remove the radiator cap and insert the splash tube in its place. Set the heater controls on "high." Turn the water on (low pressure) and flush until the water runs clear from the splash tube.

Connect a garden hose to the coupler and screw the coupler onto the flushing tee.

Remove the splash tube. Remove the garden hose and coupler from the flushing tee. Install the cap on the flushing tee.

■

Chilton Tip

If your car has air conditioning, start the engine and let it run during the entire flush. Shut the engine off before turning off the water.

If your car has a cross-flow radiator (radiator cap on the sidetank), open the radiator drain as well as using the splash tube.

■

diator and engine drain petcocks, or, if necessary, disconnect the bottom radiator hose, at the radiator outlet.

2. Close the petcock or re-connect the lower hose and fill the system with water.

3. Add a can of quality radiator flush.

4. Idle the engine until the upper radiator hose gets hot.

5. Drain the system again.

6. Repeat this process until the drained water is clear and free of scale.

7. Close all petcocks and connect all the hoses.

8. If equipped with a coolant recovery system, flush the reservoir with water and leave empty.

9. Determine the capacity of your cooling system. The capacity will probably be listed in the specifications section of this book. Add a 50/50 mix of quality antifreeze (ethylene glycol) and water to provide the desired protection.

10. Run the engine for 15 minutes with the radiator cap removed.

11. Stop the engine and check the coolant level. It should be 1"–2" below the filler neck. With a coolant recovery system, the level should be at the overflow tube level in the radiator and at the "FULL" mark on the coolant reservoir.

12. Check the level of protection with a hydrometer, replace the cap and check for leaks.

REPLACING RADIATOR HOSES

Coolant drain and refill can be done easily. When changing hoses, coolant must be drained. If coolant is less than a year old, it can be re-used. Replace coolant over 1 year old. Check hose clamps for tightness and replace all cracked or soft hoses.

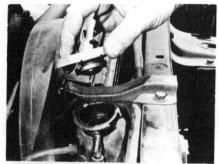

1. Remove the radiator cap.

2. Open the radiator petcock to drain coolant. Squirt some penetrating oil on the petcock to loosen it first. If there is no petcock, disconnect lower radiator hose. If the coolant is over a year old, discard it.

3. Remove the hose clamps and the hoses. Be careful. The radiator necks are made of soft metal. Wipe the hose connections and remove residue with emery cloth.

4. Replace all hose clamps badly rusted or damaged.

5. Slide new hose clamps over each hose end. Slide the hoses over the hose connections.

6. Position each hose clamp about ¼' from the end of the hose and tighten. Close petcock and refill with 50/50 antifreeze/water mix.

7. Start the engine and idle it for 15 minutes with the radiator cap off. Check for leaks. Check the coolant level and add coolant if necessary. Install the radiator cap.

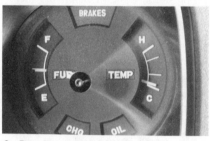

8. Road test the car. Watch temperature gauge to avoid overheating.

COOLING SYSTEM CAPACITY CHART

Cooling System Capacity (QTS.)	QUARTS OF ANTIFREEZE REQUIRED								
	3	4	5	6	7	8	9	10	11
6	−34°								
7	− 17								
8	−7	−34°							
9	0	−21							
10	4	−12	−34°						
11	8	−6	−23						
12	10	0	−15	−34°					
13		3	−9	−25					
14		6	−5	−17	−34°				
15		8	0	−12	−26				
16		10	2	−7	−19	−34°			
17			5	−4	−14	−27			
18			7	0	−10	−21	−34°		
19			9	2	−7	−16	−28		
20			10	4	−3	−12	−22	−34°	

For Best Year Round Operation under all driving conditions, install a 50/50 mix of ANTIFREEZE and water. Protects against freeze-ups down to −34°F. Protects against boilover up to 266°F.*

*Using a 15-lb. pressure cap in good condition

TROUBLESHOOTING BASIC COOLING SYSTEM PROBLEMS

The most common troubles you'll have with your car's cooling system will show up as overheating. It will first show up when the high temperature warning light (on the dash) comes on or when the temperature gauge shows abnormally high operating temperatures (above 230°F.). Occasionally, a weakened hose will rupture and cause immediate overheating.

YOUR CAR'S ENGINE OVERHEATS BECAUSE...
COOLANT LEVEL IS LOW—Check and correct level
LOOSE OR BROKEN FAN BELT—Tighten or replace fan belt
FAULTY RADIATOR CAP—Replace cap
INACCURATE GAUGE OR WARNING LIGHT—Have gauge and sending unit checked
CLOGGED COOLING SYSTEM—Drain coolant and flush system
DEBRIS ON RADIATOR—Clean the radiator
THERMOSTAT STUCK CLOSED—Replace thermostat
WATER PUMP IS FAULTY—Have water pump checked and/or replaced
ANTIFREEZE HAS BEEN USED TOO LONG—Drain coolant and fill with fresh mix.
WATER HAS HIGH MINERAL CONTENT—
Radiator HOSE HAS WEAKENED AND COLLAPSED—Replace hose
IGNITION TIMING IS RETARDED—Check and set ignition timing
ENGINE OIL LEVEL IS LOW—Check and refill engine oil
CYLINDER HEAD GASKET LEAKS—This is usually accompanied by bubbles in the radiator (engine running) and poor compression in the cylinders adjacent to the leak.

YOUR CAR'S HEATER DOES NOT PRODUCE HEAT BECAUSE...
THE THERMOSTAT IS STUCK—Replace the thermostat
THE HEATER CORE IS CLOGGED—Have the heater core checked
HEATER CONTROL IS FAULTY—Check the control mechanism

YOUR CAR'S ENGINE WARMS UP SLOWLY BECAUSE...
THE THERMOSTAT IS STUCK OPEN—Replace the thermostat

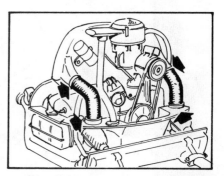
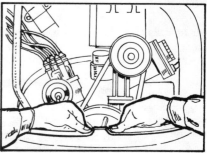
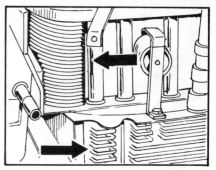

Air-Cooling Systems

Air-cooling systems are generally trouble-free and require less maintenance than a water-cooling system. A few problems can occur, however. They usually show up as an engine that operates sluggishly after a short period of driving.

· Check the drive belt for glazing or cracks. If necessary, replace the belt. While the belt is off, check the fan to be sure it rotates freely.

· Check all ducting for loose or missing screws, bent or missing parts, cracks or leaks.

· Check the ignition timing and valve adjustment. Poor tuning can cause high operating temperatures.

· Be sure you are using engine oil of the proper viscosity for the outside temperatures.

· If the problem persists, it may be necessary to remove the ducting and clean the engine of accumulated dirt, especially around the cylinder cooling fins. A clogged oil cooler can also cause overheating, since this is the only method of cooling the engine oil. If there is any evidence of sludge in the engine or oil, the oil should be drained and replaced. It is extremely important that the oil be kept clean.

INSTALLING A TRANSMISSION OIL COOLER

The recommended method of installation is "in-series," using the existing cooling system. The "replacement" method should only be used if the existing cooler is damaged. The replacement method may void a new car warranty and will provide less total cooling.

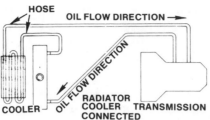

"In-series" installation is recommended. (Photo courtesy Hayden, Inc.)

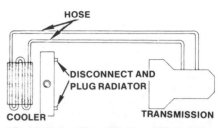

"Replacement" installation. (Photo courtesy Hayden, Inc.)

1. Identify the oil return line. It is usually located toward the rear of the transmission. It is also the cooler of the two lines after the engine has run a few minutes.

4. Hold the cooler in place and insert the plastic mounting rods through from the front.

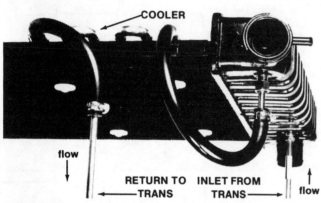

2. A few hand-tools are all that's needed to install a cooler.

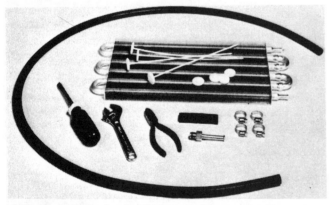

5. Place the rods to hold the cooler in a stable position.

3. Install the rubber mounting pads on the cooler.

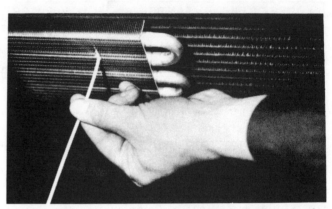

6. Lock the cooler in place with the special locking nut. Don't pull it so tight that the plastic rods are cut by the radiator fins.

7. *Slip a hose clamp over each end of the hose.*

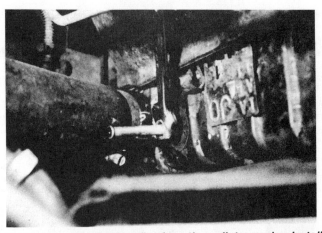

10. **Remove the oil return line from the radiator cooler. Install the special adaptor in its place. If the adaptor cannot be used, you will have to cut the oil return line (at least 4" from the radiator). Remove the burrs and slightly flare the line.**

8. **Without cutting the hose, slide each end onto one of the cooler fittings.**

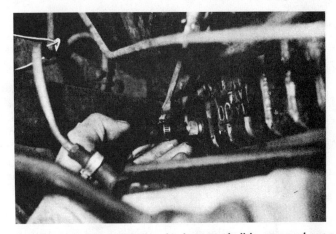

11. **Measure and cut the cooler hose and slide one end over the adaptor or oil return line (at least 1"). Tighten the clamp until the rubber shows through the clamp slots. Bends in the hose should have a radius of 2" or more. Position them where they won't chafe.**

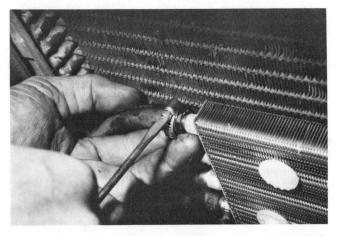

9. *Tighten the hose clamps until rubber appears through the slots and is flush with the metal clamp.*

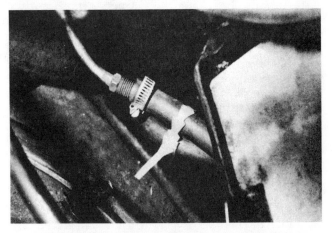

12. **Connect the other cooler hose to the oil return line. If you used the adaptor, you'll have to slide the fitting back. Tighten the clamp. Check the fluid level. Run the engine and check for leaks.**

10
Air-Conditioning Systems

Theory of Air Conditioning

In order to understand how air conditioning works, it is necessary to understand several basic laws about the flow of heat. While it may seem puzzling to talk about heat in the same breath as air conditioning, heat is all you are really concerned with. An air conditioner does not cool the air, but rather, removes the heat from a confined space.

The law of entropy states that all things must eventually come to the same temperature; there will always be a flow of heat between adjacent objects which are at different temperatures. When two objects at different temperatures are placed next to each other, heat will flow from the warmer of the two objects to the cooler one. The rate at which heat is transferred depends on how large the difference is be-

tween their temperatures. If the temperature difference is great, the transfer of heat will be great, and if the temperature difference lessens, the transfer of heat will be reduced until both objects reach the same temperature. At that point, heat transfer stops.

Because of entropy, the interior of an automobile tends to remain at approximately the same temperature as the outside air. To cool an automobile interior, you have to reverse the natural flow of heat, no matter how thoroughly insulated the compartment might be. The heat which the body metal and glass absorb from the outside must constantly be removed.

The refrigeration cycle of the air-conditioning system removes the heat from a car's interior by making use of another law of heat flow, the theory of latent heat. This theory says that during a change of state, a material can absorb or reject heat without changing its temperature. A material is changing its state when it is freezing, thawing, boiling or condensing. Changes of state differ from ordinary heating and cooling in that they occur with-

out the **temperature** of the substance changing, although they cause a visible change in the **form** of the substance. While many materials can exist in solid, liquid, or gaseous form, the best example is plain water.

Water is a common material that can exist in all three states. Below 32° F., it exists as ice. Above 212° F., at sea level air pressure, it exists as steam, which is a gas. Between these two temperatures, it exists in its liquid form.

Since a change in state occurs at a constant temperature, it follows that a material can exist as both a liquid and a gas at the same temperature without any exchange of heat between the two states. As an example, when water boils, it absorbs heat without changing the temperature of the resulting gas (steam).

The change from a solid to a liquid and vice versa is always practically the same for a given substance (32° F. for water), but the temperature at which a liquid will boil or condense depends upon the pressure. For example, water will boil at 212° F., but only at sea level. The boiling

106

The same substance can exist in three states, depending on the temperature.

point drops slightly at higher altitudes, where the atmospheric pressure is lower. We also know that raising the pressure 15 lb above normal air pressure in an automobile cooling system will keep the water from boiling until the temperature reaches about 260° F.

One additional aspect of the behavior of a liquid at its boiling point must be clarified to understand how a refrigeration cycle works. Since liquid and gas can exist at the same temperature, either the evaporation of liquid or the condensation of gas can occur at the same temperature and pressure conditions. It's just a matter of whether the material is being heated or cooled.

As an example, when a pan of water is placed on a hot stove, the heat travels from the hot burner to the relatively cool pan and water. When the water reaches its boiling point, its temperature will stop rising, and all the additional heat forced into it by the hot burner will be used to turn the liquid material into a gas (steam). The gas thus contains slightly more heat than the liquid material.

If the top of the pan were now to be held a couple of inches above the boiling water, two things would happen. First, droplets of liquid would form on the lower surface of the lid. Second, the top would get hot very quickly. The top becomes hot because the heat originally used to turn the water into steam is being recovered. As the vapor comes in contact with the cooler surface of the metal, heat is removed from it and transferred to the metal. This heat is the same heat that was originally required to change the water into a vapor, and so it again becomes a liquid.

Since water will boil only at 212° F. and above, it follows that the steam must have been 212° F. when it reached the top and must have remained that hot until it became a liquid. The cooling effect of the top (which started out at room temperature) caused the steam to condense, but both the boiling and the condensation took place at the same temperature.

To sum up, refrigeration is the removal of heat from a confined space and is based on three assumptions:

1. Heat will only flow from a warm substance to a colder substance.

2. A refrigerant can exist as both a liquid and a gas at the same temperature if it is at its "boiling point." A refrigerant at its boiling point will boil and absorb heat from its surroundings if the surroundings are warmer than the refrigerant. A refrigerant at its boiling point will condense and become liquid, losing heat to its surroundings, if they are cooler than the refrigerant.

3. The boiling point of the refrigerant depends upon the pressure of the refrigerant, rising as the pressure rises and falling as the pressure falls.

The operation of the refrigeration cycle illustrates how these three laws are put to use.

How the Air Conditioner Works

Refrigeration Cycle

Any automotive air-conditioning system employs four basic parts—a mechanical compressor, driven by the car's engine; an expansion valve, which is a restriction the compressor pumps against; and two heat exchangers, the evaporator and the condenser. In addition, there is the

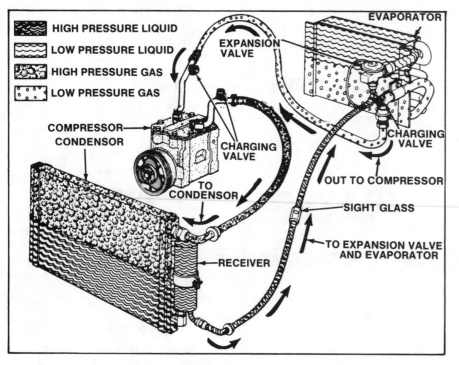

HIGH PRESSURE LIQUID
LOW PRESSURE LIQUID
HIGH PRESSURE GAS
LOW PRESSURE GAS

EVAPORATOR

EXPANSION VALVE

COMPRESSOR
CONDENSOR

CHARGING VALVE

CHARGING VALVE

TO CONDENSOR

OUT TO COMPRESSOR

SIGHT GLASS

TO EXPANSION VALVE AND EVAPORATOR

RECEIVER

Basic components of an air conditioning system and the flow of refrigerant.

refrigerant which flows through this system.

The belt-driven compressor uses engine power to compress and circulate the refrigerant gas throughout the system. The refrigerant passes through the condenser on its way from the compressor outlet to the expansion valve. The condenser is located **outside** the passenger compartment, usually in front of the car's radiator. The refrigerant passes from the expansion valve to the evaporator, and after passing through the evaporator tubing, it is returned to the compressor through its inlet. The evaporator is located **inside** the car's passenger compartment.

When the compressor starts running, it pulls refrigerant from the evaporator coil and forces it into the condenser coil, thus lowering the evaporator pressure and increasing the condenser pressure. When proper operating pressures have been established, the expansion valve will open and allow refrigerant to return to the evaporator as fast as the com-

pressor is removing it. Under these conditions, the pressure at each point in the system will reach a constant level, but the condenser pressure will be much higher than the evaporator pressure.

The pressure in the evaporator is low enough for the boiling point of the refrigerant to be well below the temperature of the vehicle's interior. Therefore, the liquid will boil, remove heat from the interior, and pass from the evaporator as a gas. The heating effect produced as the refrigerant passes through the compressor keeps the gas from liquifying and causes it to be discharged from the compressor at very high temperatures. This hot gas passes into the condenser. The pressure on this side of the system is high enough so that the boiling point of the refrigerant is well beyond the outside temperature. The gas will cool until it reaches its boiling point, and then condense to a liquid as heat is absorbed by the outside air. The liquid refrigerant is then

forced back through the expansion valve by the condenser pressure.

Refrigerant

A liquid with a low boiling point must be used to make practical use of the heat transfer which occurs when a liquid boils. Refrigerant-12 (R-12) is the refrigerant which is universally used in automotive air-conditioning systems. At normal temperatures, it is a colorless, odorless gas which is slightly heavier than air. Its boiling point at atmospheric pressure is −21.7° F. Whenever liquid R-12 is spilled into the open air, it can be seen for a brief period as a rapidly boiling, clear liquid.

R-12 is **nearly** an ideal refrigerant. It operates at low pressure and condenses easily at the temperature ranges found in automotive air-conditioning systems. It is also non-corrosive, non-toxic (except when exposed to an open flame), and non-flammable. However, due to its low boiling point and the fact that it is stored under pressure, certain safety measures must be observed when working around the air-conditioning system.

Air Conditioning Safety Precautions

There are two particular hazards associated with air-conditioning systems and they both relate to the refrigerant gas.

First, R-12 is an extremely cold substance. When exposed to air, it will instantly freeze any surface it comes in contact with, including your eyes. The other hazard relates to fire. Although normally non-toxic, refrigerant gas becomes highly poisonous in the presence of an open flame. In fact, one good whiff of the vapors formed by burning refrigerant can be fatal. So keep all forms of fire (including cigarettes) well clear of the air-conditioning system.

Any repair work to an air-conditioning system should be left to a professional. Do not, under any circumstances, attempt to loosen or tighten any fittings or perform any work other than that outlined here.

Periodic Maintenance

Any in-depth troubleshooting of air-conditioning systems requires expensive equipment and, more importantly, specialized training. However, there are some general checks you can make periodically to ensure that your air conditioner is working efficiently. Remember, refrigerant gas is extremely harmful. DO NOT attempt to work on any air-conditioning system without specialized tools and training.

Checking for Oil Leaks

Refrigerant leaks show up as oily areas on the various components because the compressor oil is transported around the entire system along with the refrigerant. Look for oily spots on all the hoses and lines, and especially on the hose and tubing connections. If there are oily deposits, the system may have a leak, and you should have it checked by a qualified repairman.

■

Chilton Tip

A small area of oil on the front of the compressor is normal and no cause for alarm.

■

Keeping the Condenser Clear

Periodically inspect the front of the condenser for bent fins or foreign material (dirt, bugs, leaves, etc.). If any cooling fins are bent, straighten them carefully with needle-nosed pliers. You can remove any debris with a stiff bristle brush.

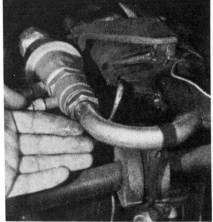

Run your hand along the underside of all hose connections and check for leaks. If you find a leak, have it fixed by an air-conditioning specialist. Do not attempt repairs yourself.

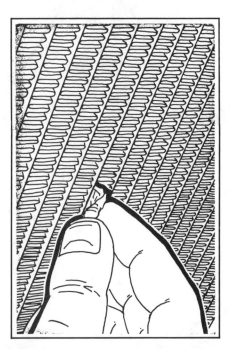

The position of the condenser in front of the radiator makes it particularly susceptible to collecting debris. Periodically, remove the accumulated bugs, leaves and other trash from the condenser.

Check the Compressor Belt

Periodically check the condition and tension of the compressor belt. Cracks that will affect operation of the belt will appear as a separation of a large portion

of the belt. Glazing is the result of slippage and is indicated by an extremely smooth appearance on the side of the belt that bears against the pulley grooves. See Section 9. Cooling System for more information on "How to Spot Bad V-Belts." Check the belt for the correct tension by applying thumb tension to the belt midway between the two pulleys. A correctly tensioned belt should have about ½"–¾" of deflection. New belts should be slightly tighter to allow for tension loss during break-in. If the belt needs to be tightened, use the following procedure.

1. Loosen the mounting bolt(s) on the compressor.

2. Position a pry bar where you can get some leverage and pry the compressor outward until the belt is correctly tensioned.

3. Tighten the bolts while holding the compressor in the correct position. This often requires a third hand. When tightened, belts should have a springy feel to them and there should be no slack in them.

Checking the Refrigerant Level

There are two ways to check refrigerant level. On cars equipped with sight glasses, checking the refrigerant level is a simple matter. Many late model cars, however, do not have a sight glass, and you have to check the temperature of the lines to determine the refrigerant level.

With Sight Glass

The sight glass is normally located in the head of the receiver/drier. The receiver/drier is not hard to locate. It's a large metal cylinder that looks something like a fire extinguisher. Sometimes the sight glass is located in one of the metal lines leading from the top of the re-

AIR-CONDITIONING SYSTEM MAINTENANCE INTERVALS

Your car's air conditioning system will work efficiently if it is maintained at these intervals

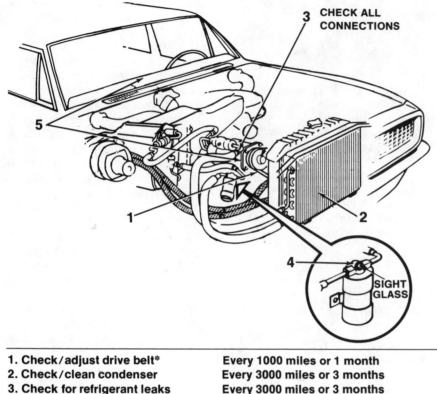

3 CHECK ALL CONNECTIONS

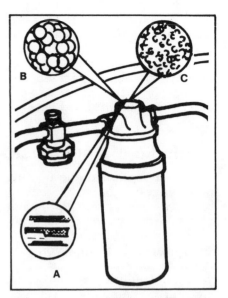

Oil streaks (A), constant bubbles (B) or foam (C) indicate there is not enough refrigerant in the system. Occasional bubbles during initial operation is normal. A clear sight glass indicates a proper charge of refrigerant or no refrigerant at all, which can be determined by the presence of cold air at the outlets in the car. If the glass is clouded with a milky white substance, have the receiver/drier checked professionally.

1. Check/adjust drive belt*	Every 1000 miles or 1 month
2. Check/clean condenser	Every 3000 miles or 3 months
3. Check for refrigerant leaks	Every 3000 miles or 3 months
4. Check refrigerant level	Every 3000 miles or 3 months
5. Operate compressor	Once a week for a few minutes (regardless of season)

*New belts will stretch with use. Recheck the tension after 200 miles of operation.

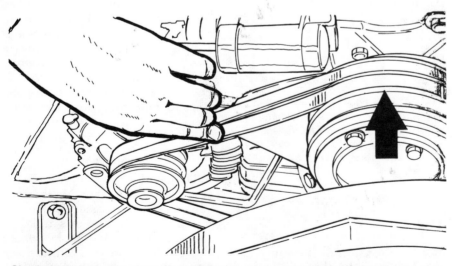

Check the belt tension of the air-conditioning compressor (arrow) using a belt tension gauge. This compressor uses two belts and the belts also drive the alternator. If one belt is replaced, both should be replaced.

ceiver/drier. Once you've found it, wipe it clean and proceed as follows:

1. With the engine and the air-conditioning system running, look for the flow of refrigerant through the sight glass. If the air conditioner is working properly, you'll be able to see a continuous flow of clear refrigerant through the sight glass, with perhaps an occasional bubble at very high temperatures.

2. Cycle the air conditioner on and off to make sure what you are seeing is clear refrigerant. Since the refrigerant is clear, it is possible to mistake a completely discharged system for one that is fully charged. Turn the system off and watch the sight glass. If there is refrigerant in the system, you'll see bubbles during the off cycle. If you observe no bubbles when the system is running, and the air flow from the unit in the car is delivering cold air, everything is OK.

TROUBLESHOOTING BASIC AIR CONDITIONING PROBLEMS

Most problems with the air conditioning system are best left to experts with the knowledge and proper equipment. There are, however, a number of problems that you can check out yourself.

Problem	Is Caused By	What to Do
There's little or no air coming from the vents (and you're sure it's on)	• The A/C fuse is blown • Broken or loose wires or connections • The on/off switch is defective	• Check and/or replace fuse • Check and/or repair connections • Have switches checked and/or replaced
The air coming from the vents is not cool enough	• Windows and air vent wings open • The compressor belt is slipping • Heater is on • Condenser is clogged with debris • Refrigerant has escaped through a leak in the system • Receiver/drier is plugged	• Close windows and vent wings • Tighten or replace compressor belt • Shut heater off • Clean the condenser • Have system checked • Have system serviced
The air has an odor	• Vacuum system is disrupted • Odor producing substances on the evaporator case • Condensation has collected in the bottom of the evaporator housing	• Have the system checked/repaired • Clean the evaporator case • Clean the evaporator housing drains
System is noisy or vibrating	• Compressor belt or mountings loose • Air in the system	• Tighten or replace belt; tighten mounting bolts • Have the system serviced

Sight glass condition
    Constant bubbles, foam or oil streaks
    Clear sight glass, but no cold air
    Clear sight glass, but air is cold
    Clouded with milky fluid
	• Undercharged system (see text)
	
	• No refrigerant at all
	• System is OK
	• Receiver/drier is leaking desiccant
		• Have system charged/checked
		
		• Have system charged/checked
		
		• Have system checked

Large difference in temperature of lines	• System undercharged	• Have system charged/checked

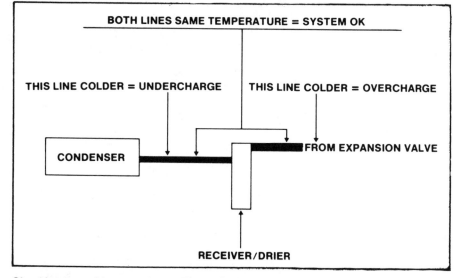

Checking the refrigerant charge if the system has no sight glass. See text for explanation.

3. If you observe bubbles in the sight glass while the system is operating, the system is low on refrigerant. Have it checked by a professional.

4. Oil streaks in the sight glass are an indication of trouble. Most of the time, if you see oil in the sight glass, it will appear as a series of streaks, although occasionally it may be a solid stream of oil. In either case, it means that part of the charge has been lost.

Without Sight Glass

On vehicles that are not equipped with sight glasses, it is necessary to feel the temperature difference in the inlet and outlet lines at the receiver/drier to gauge the refrigerant level. Use the following procedure:

1. Locate the receiver/drier. It will generally be up front near the condenser. It is shaped like a small fire extinguisher and will always have two lines connected to it. One line goes to the expansion valve and the other goes to the condenser.

2. With the engine and the air conditioner running, hold a line in each hand and gauge their relative temperatures. If they are both the same approximate temperature, the system is correctly charged.

3. If the line from the expansion valve to the receiver/drier is a lot colder than the line from the receiver/drier to the condenser, then the system is overcharged. It should be noted that this is an extremely rare condition.

4. If the line that leads from the receiver/drier to the condenser is a lot colder than the other line, the system is undercharged.

5. If the system is undercharged or overcharged, have it checked by a professional air-conditioning mechanic.

Operate the Air Conditioner Periodically

A lot of problems can be avoided by simply running the air conditioner at least once a week, regardless of the season. Simply let the system run for at least five minutes a week (even in the winter), and you'll keep the internal parts lubricated as well as preventing the hoses from hardening.

11
Electrical System/Battery and Cables

All batteries used in modern automotive applications are of the lead-acid storage type. Essentially, a lead-acid storage battery is an electro-chemical device for storing energy in chemical form so that this energy can be released as electricity when connected to an outside circuit. A battery can perform this operation repeatedly.

Parts of the Battery

Plate Grids

The plate grids are the vital elements of the battery, for they support the active material, and although they are not an active part in the production of electricity they must be a good conduc-

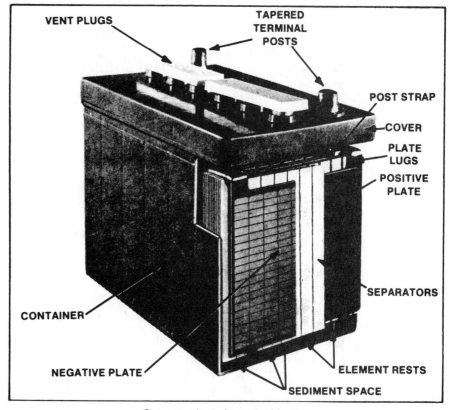

Cutaway view of a typical battery.

tor to support the flow of electricity. There are two types of plates—positive plates and negative plates. The positive plates con-

sist of a grid over which active lead peroxide is placed. This is a dark brown crystalline material which has a high degree of poros-

113

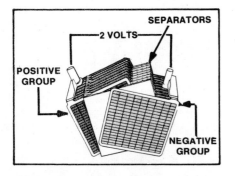

Compound battery element or cell showing positive plates, negative plates, and separators.

ity in order to allow the electrolyte to penetrate the plate freely. Negative plates are grids pasted with a type of lead referred to as sponge lead, which is simply finely ground lead. Grinding the lead allows the electrolyte to penetrate the grid.

There may be any number of plates used in a battery; it all depends on how much energy you want to store. The more plates (or the larger the plates), the more energy the battery can store and release. The negative plates will always outnumber the positive plates by one for reasons of improved performance.

Separators

No positive plate may touch a negative plate, or all the plates in the cell will lose their stored energy. This is called a short. To prevent the plates from touching, thin sheets of non-conductive porous material called separators are used. These are placed between every positive and negative plate.

Battery Elements

An element is the desired number of positive and negative plates placed together with a separator between each plate. The simplest unit you could construct would be a single positive plate and a single negative plate, kept apart by a porous separator. This would be a single element. If this element is put in a solution of sulfuric acid and water (elec-

trolyte), a simple two-volt cell is formed. Electricity will flow if these plates are connected to an electrical load. When six of these cells are connected in series, a group or battery of cells is formed. This battery of cells will produce six times as much electrical pressure as a simple two-volt cell, or 12 volts.

Electrolyte

Electrolyte is a mixture of sulfuric acid and water. Ordinarily, the electrolyte used in a fully charged battery contains about 25% sulfuric acid and 75% water. The strength or percentage of the sulfuric acid in the solution is measured by its specific gravity, that is, the density of the electrolyte versus the density of pure water. The specific gravity or electrolyte strength of a fully charged battery is in the range of 1.260 to 1.275. This means that its electrolyte is at least 1.260 times heavier than pure water. This is only true at 80° F. however. Above or below that temperature, the reading must be corrected to allow for the tem-

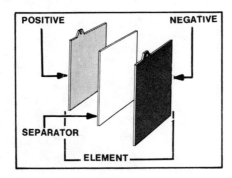

A simple battery element.

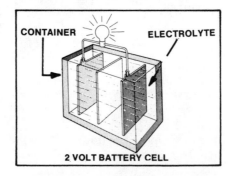

A two volt cell connected to a load.

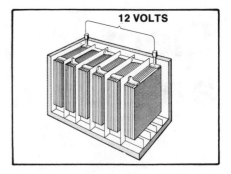

Typical 12 volt battery cell arrangement.

perature. See the section on checking electrolyte level.

Containers and Terminals

Battery containers are simply tanks which hold all the various elements; plates, separators and electrolyte. Usually, the case is constructed of molded hard rubber or polypropylene (plastic). The containers are designed to withstand extremes of heat and cold, as well as shock. In addition, all containers have a series of four bridges on the bottom. The elements rest on these bridges, allowing a space for the active material to settle during the life of the battery.

The battery terminals are the external electrical connections. They are connected inside the battery to the positive plates (+ terminal) and the negative plates (− terminal). For years, the terminals were located on the top of the battery, and in many cases, still are. Recently, however, side terminal batteries have been developed to minimize or eliminate the problem of dirt, acid spray, or moisture corroding the terminals or cables.

Covers and Vent Caps

Vent plugs or covers are there for a number of reasons. In addition to keeping impurities out of the battery, the vent plugs provide a convenient way to check and/or add electrolyte. With the new "maintenance-free" or "lifetime" batteries, there is no way (or necessity) to add electrolyte since the battery top is sealed.

How the Battery Works

Every storage battery used in an automobile has three key functions:

· To provide current for the starter and ignition system when cranking.

· To provide current (in addition to alternator current) to operate the radio, lights, etc.

ACCESSORY CURRENT DRAW (AMPS)

Lights

Headlights (high beam)	18
Headlights (low beam)	14
Taillights	8
Total	**40**

Safety

Emergency brake light	4
Emergency flasher	20
Turn signals	20
Windshield wipers	6
Horn	20
Brake lights	20
Running lights	8
Total	**98**

Ignition

Winter starting	225–500
Summer starting	100–400
Approx. Avg.	**300**

Courtesy

Cigarette lighter	25
Interior lights	25
Trunk light	25
Instrument panel lights	4
Total	**79**

Entertainment

Radio	10
Stereo Tape	10
Electric antenna	20
Total	**40**

Comfort

Air conditioner	15
Heater	7
Defroster	25
Electric seat	20
Electric windows	20
Total	**87**

· To act as a voltage stabilizer or reservoir in the electrical system.

While the first two functions are obvious, the third may require some explanation. To understand it, first consider the battery and alternator (or generator) as opposing forces. Current will flow from the greater force to the lesser force. For example, after running the starter motor, the battery will be discharged since some of the acid has been absorbed into the plates. If the car is driven immediately, (which is usually the case) current will flow back into the battery from

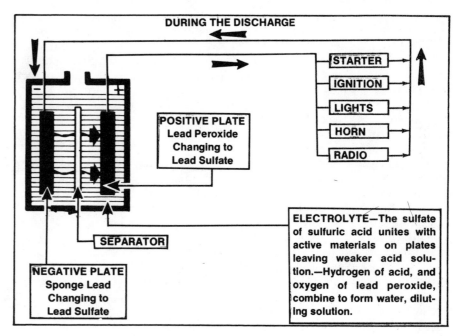

The discharge process.

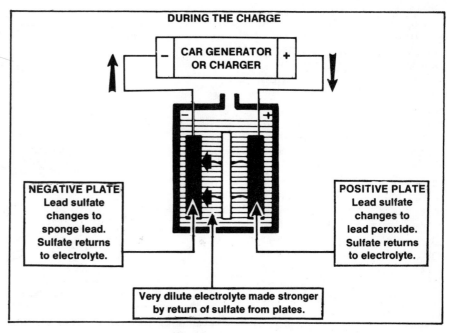

The charging process.

the alternator. The voltage regulator will cut off the current when the battery is recharged.

The most important attribute of a lead-acid storage battery is its chemical reversability. This means that unlike a dry cell battery, a storage battery is capable of being recharged by passing an electric current through it in the opposite direction of discharge. Through a chemical reaction, the battery's active chemicals will be restored to a state of charge.

To understand the charging process, you first have to understand how a battery is discharged.

The discharge process in a battery is begun as soon as an electrical circuit is completed, such as turning on the car lights. Current flows from the battery through the positive terminal. During the time that there is a drain on the battery (it is discharging), sulfuric acid in the battery works on both the positive and negative plates' active material, lead peroxide and sponge lead respectively. Hydrogen in the sulfuric acid combines with oxygen available at the positive plate to form water, which reduces the concentration of acid in the electrolyte. This is why the state of charge can be determined by measuring the strength (specific gravity) of the electrolyte.

The amount of acid consumed by the plates is in direct proportion to the amount of energy removed from the cell. When the acid is used up to the point where it can no longer deliver electricity at a useful voltage, the battery is effectively discharged.

To recharge the battery, it is only necessary to reverse the flow of current provided by the alternator through the positive terminal and out the negative battery terminal. The sulphate that formed on the plates during discharge is changed back to sponge lead and the sulphur returns to the electrolyte forming sulfuric acid again. At the posi-

tive plate, the lead sulfate changes to lead peroxide and returns even more sulfuric acid to the electrolyte.

Battery Rating System

Under the new battery rating system, there are two standards used to determine battery power.

The *cold power rating* is used for measuring battery starting performance and provides an approximate relationship between battery size and engine size. To pick a battery with the correct cold power rating for your car, simply match the cold power rating to the engine size in cubic inches. For instance, if your car has a 350-cubic-inch engine, select a battery with a cold power rating of 350 or greater.

The *reserve capacity rating* is used for measuring electrical capacity. It shows how long (in minutes) the battery will operate the car's electrical system in the event of a charging system failure. For example, if your battery has a reserve capacity rating of 135, this means you have approximately 2 hours and 15 minutes before the battery goes completely dead and to get to a service station.

BATTERY MAINTENANCE INTERVALS
Your car's battery will perform efficiently if it is maintained at these intervals.

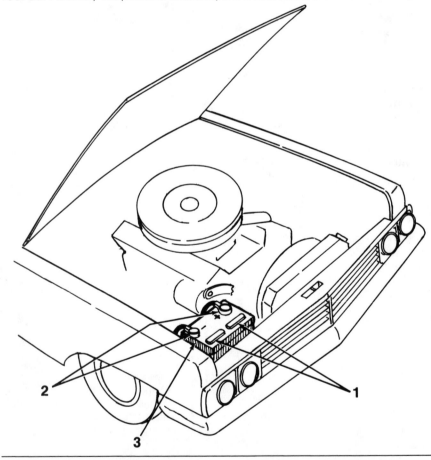

1. Check electrolyte level/add water Check State of Charge	**Every month or 1000 miles**
2. Check/clean terminals and cables	**Every 3 months or 3000 miles**
3. Tighten battery hold-downs	**As needed**

Periodic Maintenance

Difficulty in starting cars accounts for almost half of the service calls that the American Automobile Association makes each year.

A survey by Champion Spark Plug Company recently indicated that roughly one third of all cars experienced one "can't start" condition in a given year.

When a car won't start, most people blame the battery, when in fact, it may be that the battery has run down in a futile attempt to start a car with other problems.

Battery output is affected by ambient temperatures; the battery becomes less efficient at low temperatures, while the power required to start the engine becomes greater. All this means

TROUBLESHOOTING BASIC BATTERY PROBLEMS

Battery problems can be linked to any number of causes; old age, cold weather, starting and charging system problems, an out-of-tune car, etc. Fortunately, troubleshooting battery problems is fairly simple.

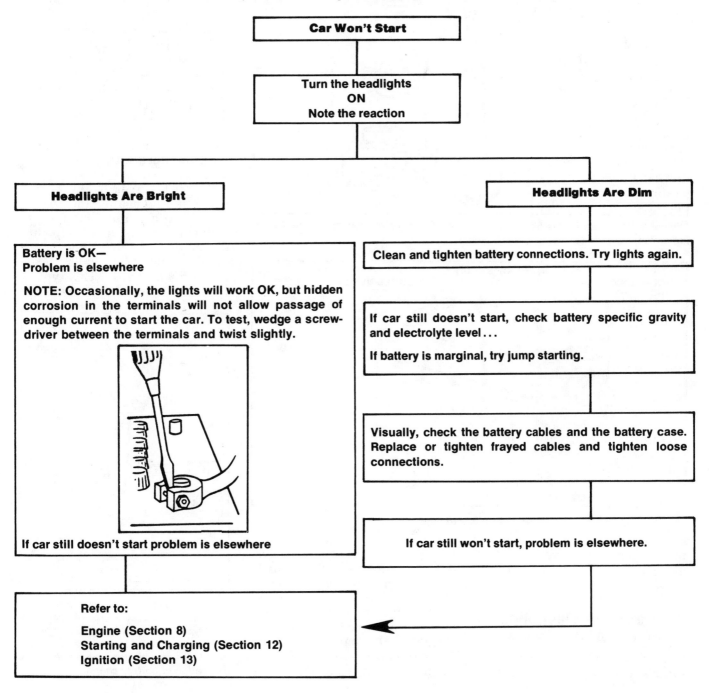

Car Won't Start

Turn the headlights ON Note the reaction

Headlights Are Bright

Headlights Are Dim

Battery is OK—
Problem is elsewhere

NOTE: Occasionally, the lights will work OK, but hidden corrosion in the terminals will not allow passage of enough current to start the car. To test, wedge a screwdriver between the terminals and twist slightly.

If car still doesn't start problem is elsewhere

Clean and tighten battery connections. Try lights again.

If car still doesn't start, check battery specific gravity and electrolyte level . . .

If battery is marginal, try jump starting.

Visually, check the battery cables and the battery case. Replace or tighten frayed cables and tighten loose connections.

If car still won't start, problem is elsewhere.

Refer to:

Engine (Section 8)
Starting and Charging (Section 12)
Ignition (Section 13)

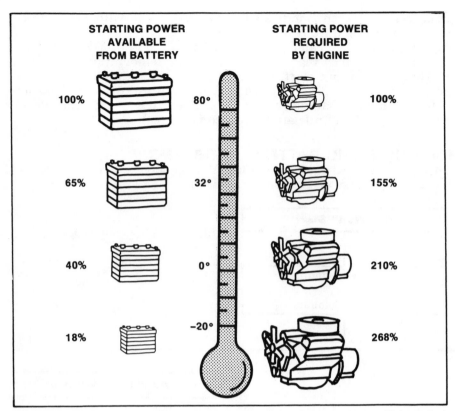

STARTING POWER AVAILABLE FROM BATTERY		STARTING POWER REQUIRED BY ENGINE	
100%	80°		100%
65%	32°		155%
40%	0°		210%
18%	−20°		268%

The colder the weather, the healthier the battery has to be to provide sufficient starting power.

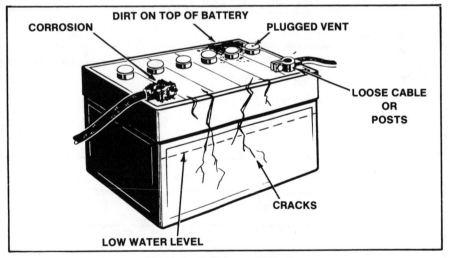

Check the battery periodically.

CORROSION

DIRT ON TOP OF BATTERY

PLUGGED VENT

LOOSE CABLE OR POSTS

CRACKS

LOW WATER LEVEL

that it pays to keep your battery in good shape, so that power is there when it's needed.

Checking the Electrolyte Level and Adding Water

A hydrometer is used to check the electrolyte specific gravity.

The specific gravity is determined by the amount of sulfuric acid remaining in the electrolyte. The amount of sulfuric acid remaining in the electrolyte is directly proportional to the state of charge of the battery, because the acid is absorbed by the plates during discharge, leaving only

water behind. To test the battery specific gravity:

1. Remove the filler or vent caps from the battery top.

2. Check the level of the electrolyte. It should be approximately ¼ in. above the level of the plates. If it isn't, add water.

3. Insert the hydrometer into the battery cell and draw enough electrolyte into the tube to float the balls or the float. The ball-type hydrometers are probably easier to obtain than the float-type, but either one will work.

4. Remove the hydrometer from the battery cell and hold it up to eye level in a vertical position. If you are using a ball-type hydrometer, check the number of floating balls against the chart on the hydrometer. If you are using a float-type hydrometer, read the float scale at the point where the surface of the liquid meets it. Disregard any curvature of liquid against the float.

5. Read and interpret the hydrometer results. A ball-type hydrometer will simply give you a reading like "3 balls floating—75% charged." This type of hydrometer is easier to read, but

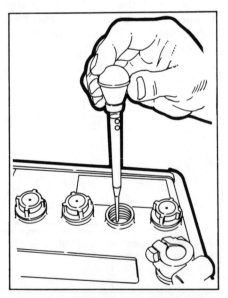

Float-type hydrometers work best, since they can be corrected for temperature. Ball-type hydrometers are inexpensive and can be stored in the glove compartment. These will also give an accurate indication of battery charge.

SPECIFIC GRAVITY (@ 80° F.) AND CHARGE

Specific Gravity Reading (use the minimum figure for testing)

Minimum	Battery Charge
1.260	100% Charged
1.230	75% Charged
1.200	50% Charged
1.170	25% Charged
1.140	Very Little Power Left
1.110	Completely Discharged

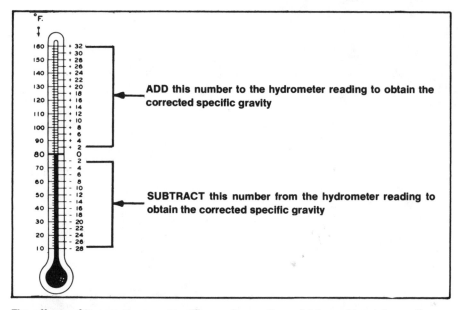

The effects of temperature on specific gravity readings. Add or subtract depending on temperature.

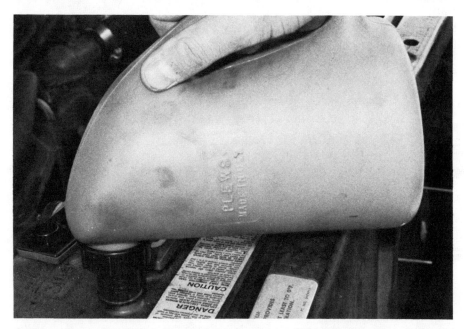

Adding water to the battery. The best way is to use a filling can like the one used in service stations. It automatically shuts off water flow at the proper level. However, any type of bulb syringe or measuring cup can be used to add water.

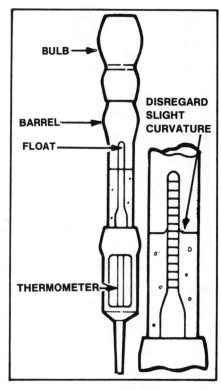

Float-type hydrometer.

not as accurate as a float-type hydrometer. With a float-type hydrometer, a reading of 1.260 indicates a fully charged battery (reading corrected for temperature). Any reading below 1.220 is indicative of a poor charge condition. A reading of 1.150 or below indicates that the cell is dead. If any one cell is lower than the others by 0.50 or more, that cell is shorted and the battery must be replaced.

Chilton Tip

If water is added to the battery during freezing weather, be sure the car is driven a few miles to mix the water with electrolyte. If not, water will lay on top of the electrolyte and could freeze.

Checking the Charge on Delco-Remy Batteries

For years Delco batteries have been equipped with an electrolyte level indicator in the cap of

Some Delco batteries have a unique electrolyte level indicator in the cap of one of the cells (shown removed here).

is OK. The dark condition with a green dot means the battery is functioning properly. The completely dark condition means that the battery might need a charge if you have been experiencing cranking problems. The light condition means that the battery needs to be replaced.

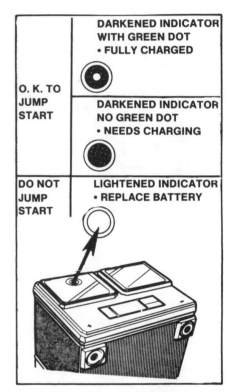

Charge indicator on a sealed battery.

one of the cells. This is a transparent rod which extends through the center of the cap. When the electrolyte is at the correct level, the end of the rod is immersed and the top will be very dark. When the level is low, the rod will seem to glow.

Checking the Charge on Maintenance-Free Batteries

While some maintenance-free batteries, such as the Delco "Freedom" battery, have a charge indicator in the top of the battery, others have no indicator at all and cannot be checked in any way. When checking the state of charge on a maintenance-free battery, keep in mind that there are three ways the charge indicator can look—it can be completely dark, it can be dark with a green dot in the middle, or it can be completely light. The only one you really have to worry about is the completely light condition. The other two conditions mean the battery

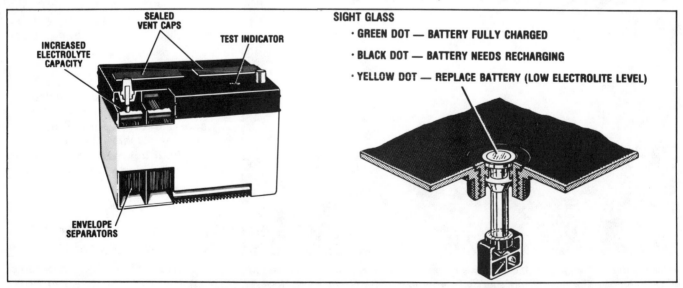

Most maintenance-free batteries have a charge indicator to check the state of charge.

Replacing Battery Cables

Battery cables don't go bad very often, but like anything else, they can wear out. If the cables on your car are cracked, frayed or broken, they should be replaced. When replacing the cables, unhook the negative cable from the battery first so you don't get any sparks. A terminal puller is handy for this operation although not strictly necessary. Replace the cables with one of the same length, or you will increase resistance and possibly cause hard starting. Smear the battery posts with a light film of petroleum jelly once you've installed the new cables. If you replace the cables one at a time, you won't mix them up.

Jump Starting

If you should ever find it necessary to have to jump start your car (and you probably will), there are certain precautions to follow to avoid injury to yourself or damage to either car.

Precautions

1. Batteries of the two vehicles must be of the same voltage. Never try to start a 12-volt battery from a 6-volt battery or vice versa.
2. Batteries must be of the same polarity—that is, the same terminal must be grounded on each battery. On almost every modern car, the grounded side is the negative (−) side. In this case, the positive (+) cable will run to the starter or starter relay. In most cases, the terminals will be marked −, N, Neg or +, P or Pos.
3. Batteries contain sulfuric acid; shield your eyes whenever you work near the battery. In case of acid contact with the eyes or skin, flush the area with water or a mixture of water and baking soda and get medical attention immediately.
4. Be sure the vent cap holes are not obstructed by grease or

KEEPING BATTERY TERMINALS CLEAN/REPLACING BATTERY CABLES

Loose, dirty, or corroded battery terminals are a major cause of so-called battery failure. It's a good idea every three months or so to remove and clean the battery terminals and give them a light coating of grease. While you're at it, check the cables for signs of wear or chafing. Replace any cable or terminal that looks marginal. While battery terminals can be cleaned without them, terminal cleaning tools are an excellent investment and will pay for themselves many times over. They can be purchased at any auto parts store. Side-terminal batteries require a special tool which is available for cleaning the threads in the battery case. See Tools and Supplies, Section 1.

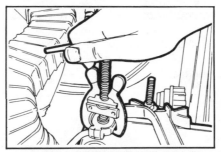

1. Clean the top of the battery with a solution of baking soda and water.

2. Loosen the terminal nuts.

3. A battery terminal puller works best to remove the terminal from the post. You can pry the terminal off, but you'll probably weaken the post.

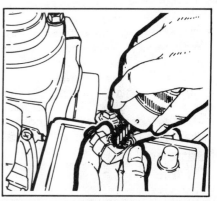

4. Clean the battery terminal with a battery terminal cleaning tool. Use the pointed end of the brush to clean the inside of the clamp until it shines.

5. Use the other end of the cleaner and clean the post until it shines. Use a rotating motion.

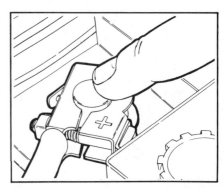

6. Reinstall the cables and apply a liberal amount of petroleum jelly to the terminals.

JUMP STARTING A DEAD BATTERY

Many motorists have probably left their headlights on in a parking lot or put off buying a new battery just long enough to find themselves in need of an emergency start. A jump start permits a dead or weakened battery to borrow power from a fully charged battery through booster cables. A pair of jumper cables kept in the trunk and the knowledge of how to use them correctly will sometimes prove invaluable.

JUMP STARTING PRECAUTIONS (see text)

1. Be sure both batteries are of the same voltage.
2. Be sure both batteries are of the same polarity (have the same grounded terminal).
3. Be sure the vehicles are not touching.
4. Be sure the vent cap holes are not obstructed.
5. Do not smoke or allow sparks around the battery.
6. In cold weather, check for frozen electrolyte in the battery.
7. Do not allow electrolyte on your skin or clothing.
8. If using jumper cables to start diesel-engined vehicles, the external power source must not exceed vehicle system voltage (13.5) volts.

JUMP STARTING PROCEDURE

1. Determine voltages of the two batteries; they must be the same.
2. Bring the starting vehicle close (they must not touch) so that the batteries can be reached easily.
3. Turn off all accessories and both engines. Put both cars in Neutral or Park and set the handbrake.
4. Cover the cell caps with a rag—do not cover terminals.
5. If the terminals on the run-down battery are heavily corroded, clean them.
6. Identify the positive and negative posts on both batteries and connect the cables in the order shown.
7. Start the engine of the starting vehicle and run it at fast idle. Try to start the car with the dead battery. Crank it for no more than 10 seconds at a time and let it cool off for 20 seconds in between tries.
8. If it doesn't start in 3 tries, there is something else wrong.
9. Disconnect the cables in the reverse order.
10. Replace the cell covers and dispose of the rags.

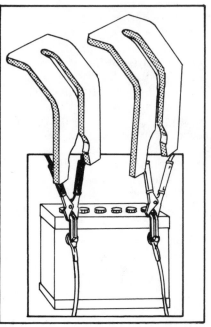

Late-model side terminal batteries can pose a problem when connecting jumper cables. Often there isn't enough room between the battery and the fender to connect the cables without touching the sheet metal. Side terminal adaptors are available to alleviate this problem and should be removed after use.

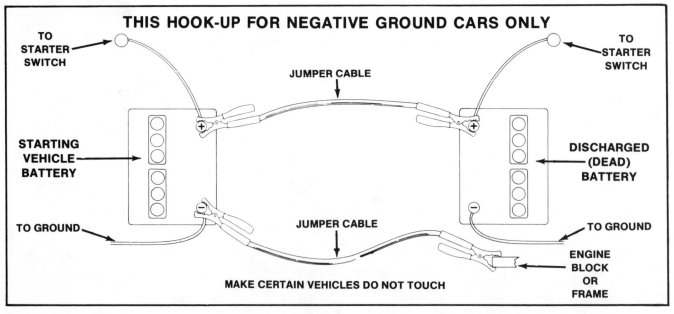

THIS HOOK-UP FOR NEGATIVE GROUND CARS ONLY

TO STARTER SWITCH

JUMPER CABLE

TO STARTER SWITCH

STARTING VEHICLE BATTERY

DISCHARGED (DEAD) BATTERY

TO GROUND

JUMPER CABLE

TO GROUND

ENGINE BLOCK OR FRAME

MAKE CERTAIN VEHICLES DO NOT TOUCH

dirt. The vent holes allow hydrogen gas (which is formed by chemical reaction in the battery) to escape safely.

5. Do not smoke or allow sparks around the battery. The chemical reaction in the battery (see above) gives off hydrogen gas, which when combined with oxygen, is potentially explosive.

6. In extremely cold weather, remove the cell caps and check for frozen electrolyte. Never attempt to jump start or boost a frozen battery.

7. Once you have all the cables hooked up, start the engine of the booster vehicle, and let it run at high idle. Now attempt to start the engine of the disabled vehicle. Once the vehicle starts, remove the jumper cables immediately to avoid damage to either car's electrical system. Do not touch the cables terminals together until they're completely unhooked, or you're going to see a lot of sparks.

Jumper Cables

There are four things to consider when buying jumper cables.

Conductor (Cable)

Cables are usually made from copper, which minimizes power loss due to heating of the conductor, since copper has less resistance to electrical current (more resistance produces more heat). Aluminum is sometimes used, but the gauge size should be at least two numbers smaller to deliver the same power. The package should say "all copper conductor"; if not, push the insulation back to be sure it is copper.

The gauge (size) of the conductor is also important. The smaller the gauge number, the larger the wire. A larger conductor will carry more current longer, without overheating.

Clamps

Check the feel of the clamps. They should resist twisting from side to side, have a strong spring and good gripping power. A higher amperage rating means the clamps will withstand more current.

Insulation

The conductor is insulated with vinyl or rubber to protect the user. Quality cables will retain their flexibility in sub-zero temperatures without cracking or breaking.

Length

Buy the shortest cables possible to safely do the job. Longer cables mean increased resistance and power loss, but they should be at least 8–10 feet to reach between two cars.

Battery Chargers

Before using any battery charger, consult the manufacturer's instructions for its use.

Battery chargers are electrical devices that change house current (AC) to a lower voltage of direct current (DC) that can be used to charge an auto battery. There are two types of battery chargers—manual and automatic.

NOTE: *On diesel-engined vehicles, do not operate the glow plug system while using an external battery charger to charge the battery.*

A manual battery charger must be physically disconnected

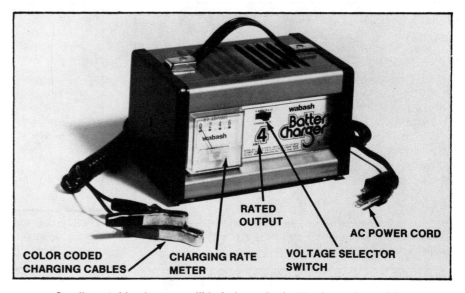

RATED OUTPUT

AC POWER CORD

COLOR CODED CHARGING CABLES

CHARGING RATE METER

VOLTAGE SELECTOR SWITCH

Small, portable chargers will help keep the battery in peak condition.

APPROXIMATE CHARGING TIME

Specific Gravity	Charger Rated Output		
Before Charging*	4 amps	6 amps	10 amps
1.250	————Charge at 2 amps or less————		
1.225	2-4 hrs	2-3 hrs	½-1 hr
1.200	5-7 hrs	3-5 hrs	1-2 hrs
1.175	8-10 hrs	5-7 hrs	2-4 hrs
1.150	10-14 hrs	6-8 hrs	3-5 hrs

*Temperature corrected—check with hydrometer

NOTE: Due to condition temperature, etc. a given battery may require more or less time. This chart is only a guide. Check the state of charge periodically with a hydrometer.

REPLACING A BATTERY

When a battery finally goes dead, it is often very difficult to get the car and battery to a shop to have a new battery installed. Usually you wind up taking the old battery out of the vehicle and exchanging it for a new battery. Most stores will give a credit of several dollars for the old battery.

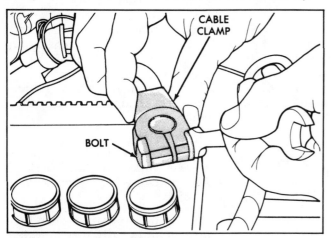

1. Loosen the battery cable clamps. Note which is the positive and which is the negative cable.

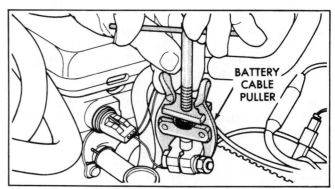

2. Remove the battery cable clamps from the posts.

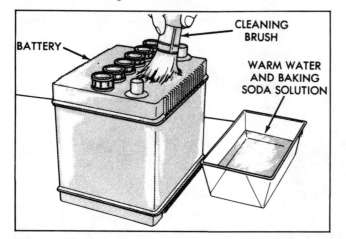

3. Remove the battery and clean the top with a solution of baking soda and water.

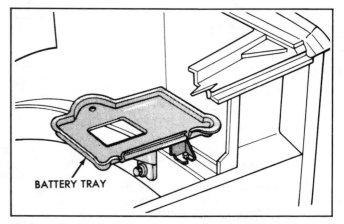

4. Clean the battery tray or compartment with a solution of baking soda and water. Install the battery and hold-down clamp. Be sure it is securely positioned.

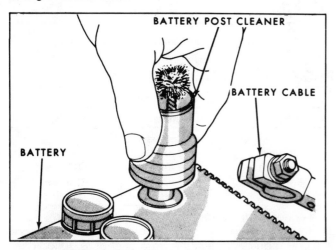

5. Clean the battery posts with a cleansing tool or wire brush.

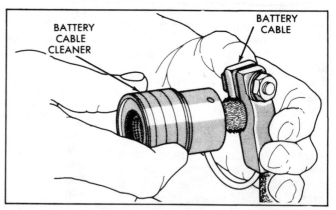

6. Clean and install the battery clamps. The positive cable (the one that runs to the starter) should be connected first. Coat each terminal and clamp with a light coat of petroleum jelly to retard corrosion.

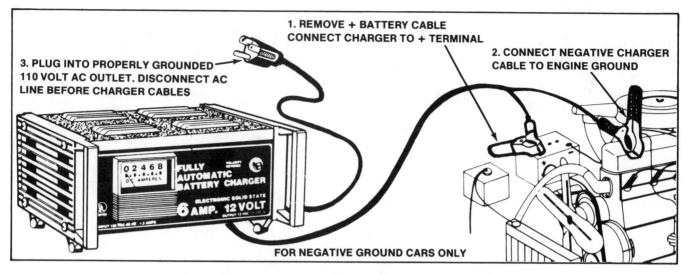

3. PLUG INTO PROPERLY GROUNDED 110 VOLT AC OUTLET. DISCONNECT AC LINE BEFORE CHARGER CABLES

1. REMOVE + BATTERY CABLE CONNECT CHARGER TO + TERMINAL

2. CONNECT NEGATIVE CHARGER CABLE TO ENGINE GROUND

FOR NEGATIVE GROUND CARS ONLY

Typical battery charger hook-up with the battery in the vehicle.

when the battery has become fully charged. If not, the battery can be overcharged, and possibly fail. Excess charging current at the end of the charging cycle will heat the electrolyte, resulting in loss of water and active material, substantially reducing battery life. As a general rule, on manual chargers, when the ammeter on the charger registers half the rated amperage of the charger, the battery is fully charged. This can vary, and it is recommended to use a hydrometer to accurately measure state of charge.

Automatic battery chargers have an important advantage—they can be left connected (for instance, overnight) without the possibility of overcharging the battery. Automatic chargers are equipped with a sensing device to allow the battery charge to taper off to near zero as the battery becomes fully charged. When charging a low or completely discharged battery, the meter will read close to full rated output. If only partially discharged, the initial reading may be less than full rated output, as the charger responds to the condition of the battery. As the battery continues to charge, the

sensing device monitors the state of charge and reduces the charging rate. As the rate of charge tapers to 0 amps, the charger will continue to supply a few milliamps of current—just enough to maintain a charged condition.

Battery and Charging Safety Precautions

Always follow these safety precautions when charging or handling a battery.

1. Wear eye protection when working around batteries. Batteries contain corrosive acid and produce explosive gas a byproduct of their operation. Acid on the skin should be neutralized with a solution of baking soda and water made into a paste. In case acid contacts the eyes, flush with clear water and seek medical attention immediately.

2. Avoid flame or sparks that could ignite the hydrogen gas produced by the battery and cause an explosion. Connection and disconnection of cables to battery terminals is one of the most common causes of sparks.

3. Always turn a battery

charger off, before connecting or disconnecting the leads disconnecting the leads. When connecting the leads, connect the positive lead first, then the negative lead, to avoid sparks.

4. When lifting a battery, use a battery carrier or lift at opposite corners of the base.

5. Be sure there is good ventilation in a room where the battery is being charged.

6. Do not attempt to charge or load-test a maintenance-free battery when the charge indicator dot is yellow or clear.

7. Disconnect the negative battery cable if the battery is to remain in the vehicle during the charging process.

8. Be sure the ignition switch is OFF before connecting or turning the charger ON. Sudden power surges can destroy electronic components.

9. Use proper adaptors to connect charger leads to side terminal batteries.

10. When turning the charger ON, slowly increase the charge rate. If gassing or spewing occurs turn the charger OFF. If smoke or dense vapor comes out of the battery during the charging process, turn the charger OFF.

12

Electrical System/Starting and Charging

TOOLS AND SUPPLIES

Tools
   Wrenches
   Pry bar or long screwdriver
Supplies
   Belt
   Belt dressing

The Starting System

The storage battery (see Section 11—Battery and Cables) is the source of electrical power, providing the current to fulfill the many electrical demands of the modern car. The battery, however, is limited in its electrical capacity, and a means must be supplied to assist the battery.

How the Starting System Works

A generator or alternator is used to provide the added current necessary to maintain a specific voltage level to operate the electrical system, and to recharge the battery while the engine is running. When the key is turned, a small amount of current is sent to the starter solenoid, where it flows through a coil of wire wrapped around a metal core, encasing a metal plunger. As the current flows through the coil, a magnetic field

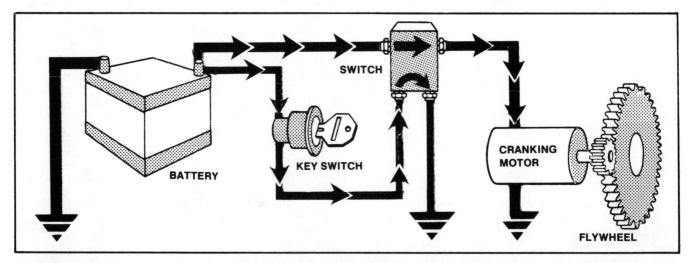

A typical starting system converts electrical energy into mechanical energy to turn the engine. The components are: Battery—to provide electricity to operate the starter; Ignition switch—to control the energizing of the starter relay or solenoid; Starter relay or solenoid—to make and break the circuit between the battery and starter; Starter—to convert electrical energy into mechanical energy to turn the engine; Starter drive gear—to transmit starter rotation to the engine flywheel.

126

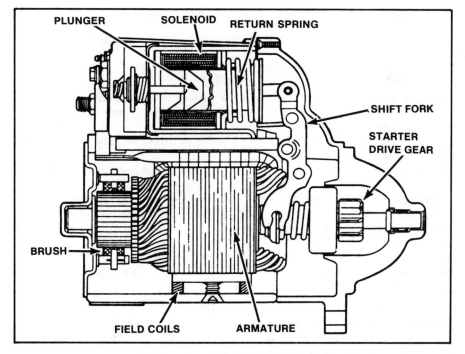

Cutaway view of typical starter motor.

is produced and the plunger is pulled into contact with the heavy wires of the battery-to-starter circuit. As contact is made, the current flows from the battery to the starter. The use of a starter switch or a relay controls the closing of the circuit between the battery and the starter only, and the drive gear is pushed into mesh with the flywheel by centrifugal force as the starter begins to rotate.

The solenoid is mounted on the starter and also used as an interrupter switch. Two functions must be performed; first, the closing of the circuit between the battery and the starter, and second, the starter drive gear moved to mesh with the engine flywheel gear teeth. The plunger is connected to the starter drive gear through mechanical linkage, and both the closing of the electrical circuit and the engagement of the starter drive gear occur at the same time.

Current to the starter is directed to the stationary coils around pole pieces or field coils, and causes an increase in the magnetic field between them. A movable armature, made by looping heavy wire around a shaft, is placed between the opposite field pieces. Part of the applied current is directed through brushes to a commutator, to which the ends of the wire loops on the armature are attached. The result is to produce a variable magnetic field in both the armature and the field coils, which causes a repelling or kicking action between the two magnetic fields. The armature is the only part of the starter that is able to rotate and the mechanical force developed is transmitted to the engine by the starter drive unit.

The starting of the engine signals the driver to release the ignition key from the start position, stopping the flow of current to the solenoid or relay. The plunger is pulled out of contact with the battery-to-starter cables by a coil spring, and the flow of electricity is interrupted to the starter. This weakens the magnetic fields and the starter ceases its rotation.

As the solenoid plunger is released, its movement also pulls the starter drive gear from its engagement with the engine flywheel.

There is one other component; on cars with automatic transmissions a neutral safety switch on the side of the transmission is wired to the relay or solenoid. Some manual transmission cars have a clutch switch to prevent starting the car unless the clutch

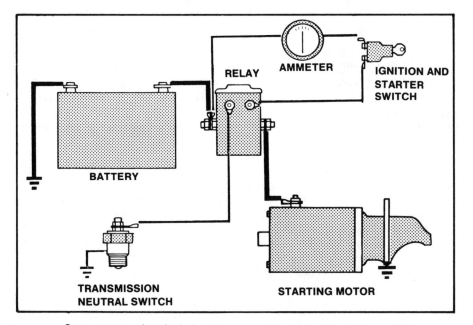

Some starter electrical circuits use a relay as an interrupter switch.

TROUBLESHOOTING BASIC STARTING SYSTEM PROBLEMS

Many starting system problems are the result of neglect. This chart will show you which problems you can fix yourself and which require professional service.

Problem	Is Caused by	What to do
Engine does not crank (Solenoid or relay does not click)	• "Dead" battery • Loose, corroded or broken connections • Corroded battery terminals (lights will usually light) • Faulty ignition switch • Faulty neutral safety switch or clutch switch (To test: push on brake pedal, hold key in start position and move shift lever or clutch pedal) • Defective starter switch, relay or solenoid.	• Charge or replace battery • Clean or repair connections • Clean terminals (see Section 11) • Have ignition switch checked/replaced • Have neutral safety switch or clutch switch checked or replaced • Have defective component replaced
Engine will not crank (Solenoid or relay clicks)	• Low or "dead" battery • Corroded battery terminals or cables • Defective starter solenoid or relay (test by bridging contacts with a screwdriver or remote starter switch) • Defective starter motor (if current is passed through relay or solenoid)	• Charge or replace battery • Clean or replace terminals or cables • Have defective component replaced • Have starter replaced or overhauled
Starter motor cranks slowly	• Low battery • Loose, corroded or broken connections • Cable size too small • Internal starter motor problems • Engine oil too heavy • Ignition timing too far advanced	• Charge or replace battery • Clean, repair or replace connections • Replace with proper size cable (see Section 14) • Have starter replaced or overhauled • Use proper oil viscosity for temperature (see Section 8) • Set timing to specifications
Starter spins, but will not crank engine	• Broken starter drive gear • Broken flywheel teeth	• Have drive gear replaced • Have flywheel checked
Noisy starter motor	• Starter mounting loose • Worn starter drive gear or flywheel teeth • Worn starter bushings	• Tighten mounting bolts • Have starter or flywheel checked • Have starter replaced or overhauled

is depressed. Its function is to prevent activation of the starter (by creating a open circuit) when the transmission is in any gear other than Park or Neutral. The car can only be started in Park or Neutral.

The Charging System

When the engine is not running, the source of electricity to operate the starter and other components is the battery. If the battery continued providing electricity after the engine started, it would quickly exhaust its supply of energy. To provide electrical power when the engine is running and to recharge the battery, generators and alternators are used. Neither can produce electricity, however, unless the engine is running.

For many years, the generator was used exclusively to provide electrical power, but the growing popularity of power-consuming electrical accessories found the generator incapable of producing the required power at low engine speeds.

Since the alternator (really an AC generator) has the ability to produce high electrical output at relatively low engine speeds, it

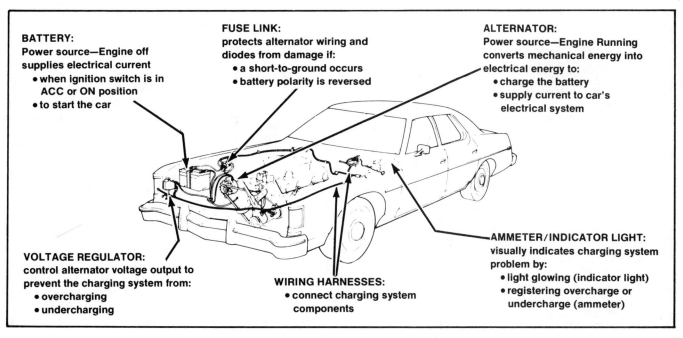

BATTERY:
Power source—Engine off supplies electrical current
- when ignition switch is in ACC or ON position
- to start the car

FUSE LINK:
protects alternator wiring and diodes from damage if:
- a short-to-ground occurs
- battery polarity is reversed

ALTERNATOR:
Power source—Engine Running converts mechanical energy into electrical energy to:
- charge the battery
- supply current to car's electrical system

VOLTAGE REGULATOR:
control alternator voltage output to prevent the charging system from:
- overcharging
- undercharging

WIRING HARNESSES:
- connect charging system components

AMMETER/INDICATOR LIGHT:
visually indicates charging system problem by:
- light glowing (indicator light)
- registering overcharge or undercharge (ammeter)

The components of a typical automotive charging system.

neatly solved the problem. Due to the need for large, externally mounted rectifiers, however, alternators were first used on cars and trucks with special electrical load requirements.

The dawn of the space age in the early 1960's saw the development of inexpensive diodes. Rectifiers could now be mounted on the interior of the alternator housing, allowing the construction of a light and compact unit, which today is used as standard equipment on all cars and trucks.

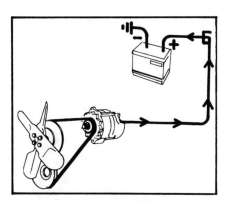

The alternator converts mechanical energy into electrical energy to charge the battery, using the engine as a source of turning power.

How the Charging System Works

When the ignition key is turned on, current movement is indicated by the glowing of the

red charging indicator light or by the movement of the needle to the discharge side of the ammeter gauge.

Current passes through the ignition switch to the voltage regu-

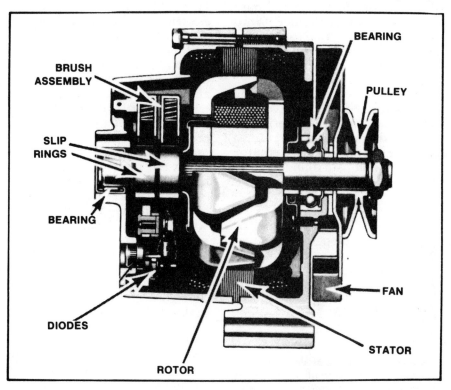

BRUSH ASSEMBLY

BEARING

PULLEY

SLIP RINGS

BEARING

DIODES

ROTOR

STATOR

FAN

Cutaway view of a typical automotive alternator.

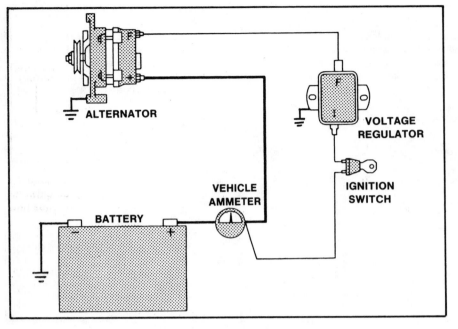

A typical automotive charging system.

complete the circuit for another phase winding.

The direct current, flowing from the alternator output terminal to the battery, is used to provide the current to operate the electrical system and to recharge the battery. As electrical demand increases, the voltage regulator senses the low voltage condition and directs more current to pass through the rotor, which increases the magnetic field. This causes greater induction voltage to be produced, which increases the output of the alternator. As the voltage increases and the requirements of the electrical system decrease, the voltage regulator reduces the current flowing through the rotor, thereby lowering the magnetic field and decreasing the output of the alternator.

lator. The voltage regulator, through a series of resistors and transistors, sends a small amount of current to the alternator post which is connected to the brushes. The brushes contact slip-rings on the rotor, and pass the small amount of current into the windings of the rotor. This current passing through the rotor coils creates a magnetic field within the alternator.

As the engine is started and the rotor is rotated by the drive belt, the rotor induces a magnetic current in the stationary windings or stator located in the alternator housing and surrounding the rotor.

This induced current is alternating current (AC) and must be changed to direct current (DC); diodes are used for this purpose. The technical explanation of how a diode works is not important. Think of the diode as a form of an electrical check valve, allowing current to flow in one direction and blocking the current flow in the opposite direction. A negative diode will pass current traveling in a negative direction, while the positive diode will pass current traveling in a positive direction. The positive diodes make up the positive rectifier, while the negative diodes make up the negative rectifier.

The stationary windings or stator are wound into three sets of windings or phrases. Each phase winding is connected to a positive and a negative diode. When the phase winding is passing positive current, the current will flow through the positive diode and to the output terminal of the alternator.

When the phase winding is passing negative current, the negative diode allows the returning current from the ground circuit to pass into the windings to

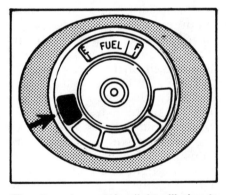

The alternator warning light will glow to indicate a problem in the charging system.

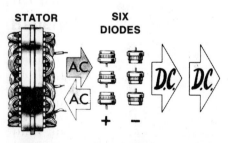

Negative and positive diodes convert AC current into DC current. Note the AC current reversing direction while the DC current flows in only one direction.

Ammeter gauges are sometimes used as indicators of charging system condition.

STARTING AND CHARGING SYSTEM MAINTENANCE INTERVALS

To keep the starting and charging system operating efficiently, it should be maintained at the following intervals.

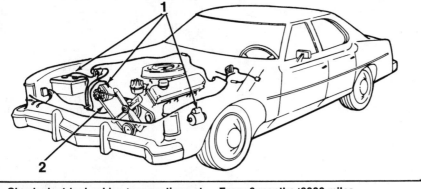

1. Check electrical cables/connections at:
   Battery
   Relay or solenoid
   Starter
   Alternator
	Every 3 months/3000 miles

2. Check condition/adjust drive belt Replace drive belt	Every 3 months/3000 miles* As necessary*

*New drive belts will stretch with use. Recheck the tension of new belts after 200 miles of use.

The Warning Indicator Light or Ammeter

Most modern cars have an indicator light located on the dash to alert the driver of a malfunction in the charging system. It is also used to pass a small amount of battery current to the alternator rotor to excite and produce the magnetic field until the alternator begins to charge and can assume this function itself.

Because the bulb circuit is connected to both the battery and alternator sides, any movement of current between the two units will cause the bulb to light. As the alternator begins to charge and the produced voltage reaches the battery voltage, the current between the two units ceases to move and the bulb will go out. If either the battery or the alternator should fail as the car is being driven, the difference of

TROUBLESHOOTING BASIC CHARGING SYSTEM PROBLEMS

There are many charging system problems you can fix yourself. This chart will show you which ones you can fix and which ones require professional service.

Problem	Is Caused by	What to Do
Noisy Alternator	• Loose mountings • Loose drive pulley • Worn bearings • Brush noise • Internal circuits shorted (High pitched whine)	• Tighten mounting bolts • Tighten pulley • Have bearings replaced • Have brushes cleaned/replaced • Have alternator replaced or overhauled
Squeal when starting engine or accelerating	• Glazed or loose belt	• Replace or adjust belt
Indicator light remains on or ammeter indicates discharge (engine running)	• Broken fan belt • Broken or disconnected wires • Internal alternator problems • Defective voltage regulator	• Install belt • Repair or connect wiring • Have alternator overhauled/replaced • Have voltage regulator replaced
Car light bulbs continually burn out—battery needs water continually	• Alternator/regulator overcharging	• Have voltage regulator/alternator overhauled or replaced
Car lights flare on acceleration	• Battery low • Internal alternator/regulator problems	• Charge or replace battery • Have alternator/regulator overhauled or replaced
Low voltage output (alternator light flickers continually or ammeter needle wanders)	• Loose or worn belt • Dirty or corroded connections • Internal alternator/regulator problems	• Replace or adjust belt • Clean or replace connections • Have alternator or regulator overhauled or replaced

voltage between the two units will allow current to flow and the bulb to light, warning the driver of a malfunction.

Chilton Tip

Frequently a loose or slipping belt is the cause of a glowing or flickering alternator warning light.

An ammeter also indicates the condition of the charging system. A low battery will be indicated by a high charging current to-

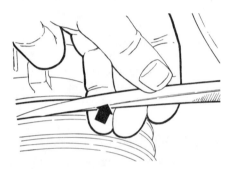

Check the condition of the alternator belt. See "How to Spot Worn V-Belts."

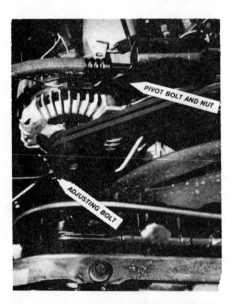

To adjust the belt, loosen the adjusting bolt and, if necessary, the pivot bolt.

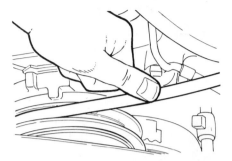

Check the belt tension by applying light thumb pressure to the belt at the midpoint of its longest span.

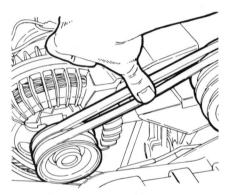

Replace dual belts in sets to maintain proper tension on the pulleys.

ward (+) side of the gauge. A wiring short or faulty accessory will show as a high rate of discharge toward (−) side of the gauge. It's normal for the gauge to move a slight amount in either direction.

Periodic Maintenance

The only periodic maintenance that can be performed on the starting and charging systems is to inspect the electrical cables and wires for fraying and breakage (refer to Section 11—Battery

and Cables), and to inspect the alternator drive belt for proper tension, wear or damage and replace or adjust the belt as necessary. Follow the maintenance intervals in this section, but make a general visual check each time the hood is opened.

Adjusting the Belt

The alternator belt should be inspected for the proper tension by checking the deflection of the belt at the middle of its longest span, under light thumb pressure. If the deflection is over ½", the belt should be adjusted. If it cannot be adjusted, it should be replaced.

To adjust the belt, loosen the adjusting bracket bolt and/or the alternator pivot bolt and nut. Force the alternator outward toward the fender and tightly against the belt; do not pry on the alternator housing. Tighten the adjusting pivot and bolts and check the deflection. Do not over tighten the belt, as damage may result to the alternator bearings. A belt which is too loose will not drive the alternator and provide enough electricity.

Chilton Tip

If two belts are used to drive the alternator and a difference is noted in the deflection of the two belts or that one belt needs to be replaced while the other is good, replace both belts to maintain the proper tension pressure on the pulleys.

REPLACING THE ALTERNATOR BELT

The fan belt runs the water pump and alternator on most cars and trucks. Depending on the number and type of other accessories, it may be necessary to disengage other drive belts in order to gain access to the alternator (fan) belt.

1. Loosen the alternator adjusting bolt. If necessary loosen the bolt that the alternator pivots on. This will give enough freedom to move the alternator.

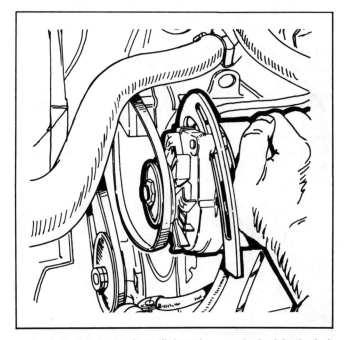

2. Push the alternator in until there is enough slack in the belt to remove it. Remove the alternator belt from the alternator pulley and crankshaft pulley. If fan belt is behind another belt, the interfering belt will also have to be removed.

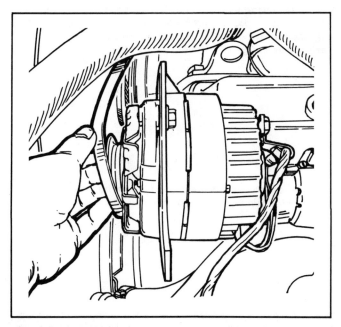

3. Install the new belt over the crankshaft, water pump and alternator pulleys. Be sure you have the right belt. It should fit even with the top of the pulley groove and should not require too much movement of the alternator to properly tension it.

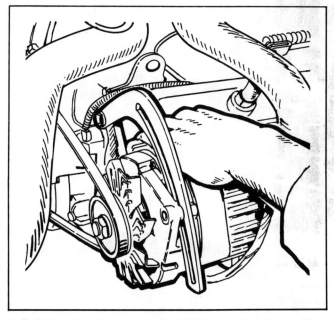

4. Pull the alternator outward to tighten the belt. Do not pry on the alternator. Tighten the alternator adjusting bolt and pivot bolt (if loosened). Check the belt tension, and recheck it in about 200 miles; new belts will stretch with use.

HOW TO SPOT WORN V-BELTS
(See "Drive Belts" in Section 9.)

V-belts are vital to efficient charging system operation—they drive the alternator or generator. They require little maintenance (occasional tightening) but they will not last forever. Slipping or failure of the V-belt will lead to undercharging. If your V-belt looks like any of these, it should be replaced.

Cracking

This belt has deep cracks, which cause it to flex. Too much flexing leads to heat build-up and premature failure. These cracks can be caused by using the belt on a pulley that is too small. Notched belts are available for small diameter pulleys.

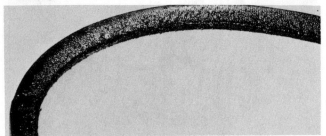

Softening (grease and oil)

Oil and grease on a belt can cause the belt's rubber compounds to soften and separate from the reinforcing cords that hold the belt together. The belt will first slip, then finally fail altogether.

Glazing

Glazing is caused by a belt that is slipping. The more the belt slips, the more glazing will be built up on the surface of the belt. The more the belt is glazed, the more it will slip. If the glazing is light, tighten the belt.

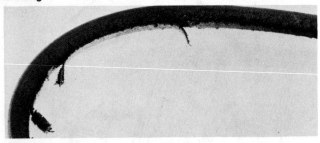

Worn cover

The cover of this belt is worn off and is peeling away. The reinforcing cords will begin to wear and the belt will soon break.

Separation

This belt is on the verge of breaking and leaving you stranded. The layers of the belt are separating and the reinforcing cords are exposed. It's just a matter of time before it breaks completely.

13
Electrical System/Ignition

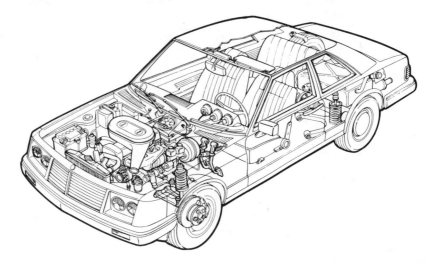

TOOLS AND SUPPLIES

Tools
  Assorted wrenches
  Spark plug socket, either 13/16 or 5/8, depending on the size of your plug
  Ratchet and extension
  Feeler gauges, both flat and wire type
  Assorted screwdrivers
  Dwell-tachometer
  Timing light
  Volt/ohmmeter
Supplies
  Spark plugs
  Points, condenser, and rotor
  Cap, wires, etc. (if necessary)
  Can of penetrating oil

How the Ignition System Works

Conventional (Point-Type) Ignition Systems

The automotive ignition system has two basic functions: it must control the spark and timing of the spark plug firing to match varying engine requirements, and it must increase battery voltage to a point where it will overcome the resistance offered by the spark plug gap and fire the plug.

To accomplish this, an automotive ignition system is divided into two electrical circuits. The primary circuit carries low voltage. This circuit operates

Close-up of the distributor components you will be concerned with. Note that the points are open and the rotor has been removed for clarity.

135

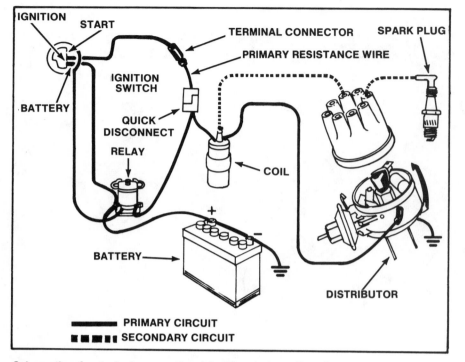

Schematic of a typical conventional ignition system. Not all systems use a starter relay, although in all other respects, they are the same.

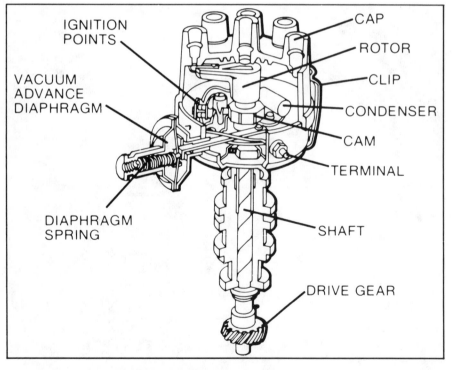

A conventional distributor with all the parts in place.

distributor cap and rotor, the spark plug leads, and the spark plugs.

The distributor is the controlling element of the system. It switches the primary current on and off and distributes the current to the proper spark plug each time a spark is needed. The distributor is basically a stationary housing surrounding a rotating shaft. The shaft is driven at one-half engine speed by the engine's camshaft through the distributor drive gears. A cam near the top of the distributor shaft has one lobe for each cylinder of the engine. The cam operates the contact points, which are mounted on a plate within the distributor housing.

A rotor is attached to the top of the distributor shaft. When the distributor cap is in place, a spring-loaded piece of metal in the center of the cap makes contact with a metal strip on top of the rotor. The outer end of the rotor passes very close to the contacts connected to the four, six, or eight spark plug leads around the outside of the distributor cap.

The coil is the heart of the ignition system. Essentially, it is nothing more than a transformer which takes the relatively low voltage (12 volts) available from the battery and increases it to a point where it will fire the spark plug as much as 40,000 volts. The term "coil" is perhaps a misnomer since there are actually *two* coils of wire wound about an iron core. These coils are insulated from each other and the whole assembly is enclosed in an oil-filled case. The primary coil, which consists of relatively few turns of heavy wire, is connected to the two primary terminals located on top of the coil. The secondary coil consists of many turns of fine wire. It is connected to the high tension connection on top of the coil (the tower into which the coil wire from the distributor is plugged).

Under normal operating conditions, power from the battery is

only on battery current and is controlled by the breaker points and the ignition switch. The secondary circuit consists of the sec-

ondary windings in the coil, the high tension lead between the distributor and the coil (commonly called the coil wire), the

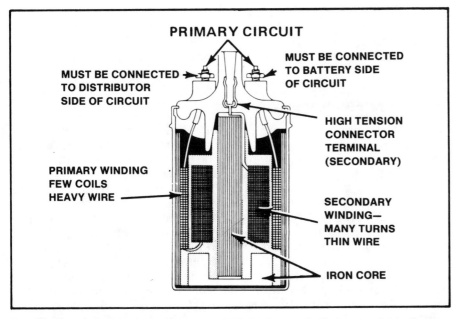

PRIMARY CIRCUIT

MUST BE CONNECTED TO BATTERY SIDE OF CIRCUIT

MUST BE CONNECTED TO DISTRIBUTOR SIDE OF CIRCUIT

HIGH TENSION CONNECTOR TERMINAL (SECONDARY)

PRIMARY WINDING FEW COILS HEAVY WIRE

SECONDARY WINDING— MANY TURNS THIN WIRE

IRON CORE

Simplified cutaway of a conventional coil. The primary windings connect to the two small terminals on the top of the coil, while the secondary winding connects to the central tower.

fed through a resistor or resistance wire to the primary circuit of the coil and is then grounded through the ignition points in the distributor (the points are closed). Energizing the coil primary circuit with battery voltage produces current flow through the primary windings, which induces a very large, intense magnetic field. This magnetic field remains as long as current flows and the points remain closed.

As the distributor cam rotates, the points are pushed apart, breaking the primary circuit and stopping the flow of current. Interrupting the flow of primary current causes the magnetic field to collapse. Just as current flowing through a wire produces a magnetic field, moving a magnetic field across a wire will produce a current. As the magnetic field collapses, its lines of force cross the secondary windings, inducing a current in them. Since there are many more turns of wire in the secondary windings, the voltage from the primary windings is magnified considerably—up to 40,000 volts.

The voltage from the coil secondary windings flows through the coil high-tension lead to the center of the distributor cap, where it is distributed by the rotor to one of the outer terminals in the distributor cap. From there, it flows through the spark plug lead to the spark plug. This process occurs in a split second and is repeated every time the points open and close, which is up to 1500 times a minute in a 4-cylinder engine at idle.

To prevent the high voltage from burning the points, a condenser is installed in the circuit. It absorbs some of the force of the surge of electrical current that occurs during the collapse of the magnetic field. The condenser consists of several layers of aluminum foil separated by insulation. These layers of foil are capable of storing electricity, making the condenser a sort of electrical surge tank.

Voltages just after the points open may reach 250 volts because of the amount of energy stored in the primary windings and the subsequent magnetic field. A condenser which is defective or improperly grounded will not absorb the shock from the fast-moving stream of electricity when the points open and the current can force its way across the point gap, causing pitting and burning.

Electronic Ignition Systems

Electronic Ignition systems are not as complicated as they may first appear. In fact, they differ

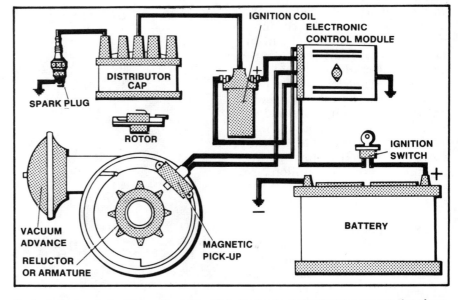

IGNITION COIL

ELECTRONIC CONTROL MODULE

DISTRIBUTOR CAP

SPARK PLUG

ROTOR

IGNITION SWITCH

VACUUM ADVANCE

RELUCTOR OR ARMATURE

MAGNETIC PICK-UP

BATTERY

Typical electronic ignition schematic. Note its basic similarity to a conventional system.

only slightly from conventional ignition systems. Like conventional ignition systems, electronic systems have two circuits: a primary circuit and a secondary circuit. The entire secondary circuit is exactly the same as in a conventional ignition system. Also, the section of the primary circuit from the battery to the battery terminal at the coil is exactly the same as in a conventional ignition system.

Electronic ignition systems differ from conventional ignition systems in the distributor component area. Instead of a distributor cam, breaker plate, points, and condenser, an electronic ignition system has an armature (called variously a trigger wheel, reluctor, etc.), a pickup coil (stator, sensor, etc.), and an electronic control module.

Essentially, all electronic ignition systems operate in the following manner: With the ignition switch turned on, primary (battery) current flows from the battery through the ignition switch to the coil primary windings. Primary current is turned on and off by the action of the armature as it revolves past the pickup coil or sensor. As each tooth of the armature nears the pickup coil, it creates a voltage which signals the electronic module to turn off the coil primary current. A timing circuit in the module will turn the current on again after the coil field has collapsed. When the current is off, however, the magnetic field built up in the coil is allowed to collapse, which causes a high voltage in the secondary windings of the coil. It is now operating on the secondary ignition circuit, which is exactly the same as in a conventional ignition system.

Troubleshooting electronic ignition systems ordinarily requires the use of a voltmeter and/or an ohmmeter. Sometimes the use of an ammeter is also required. Because of differences in design and construction, trou-

bleshooting is specific to each system. If you suspect trouble in your electronic ignition system, have it looked at by a professional mechanic.

Hall Effect Electronic Ignition

The Omni/Horizon uses a Hall Effect electronic ignition in conjunction with the Chrysler Lean Burn System. It consists of a sealed Spark Control Computer, Hall Effect pickup assembly, coil, spark plugs, ballast resistor, and the various wires needed to connect the components.

The distributor contains the Hall Effect pickup assembly, which replaces the breaker points assembly in conventional systems. The pickup assembly supplies the computer with information on engine speed and crankshaft position, and it is one of five signals which the computer uses to determine ignition timing. The Hall Effect is a shift in magnetic field, caused, in this installation, when one of the rotor blades passes between the two arms of the sensor.

There are essentially two modes of operation connecting the Hall Effect distributor with the Spark Control computer: the start mode and the run mode. The start mode is used only during engine cranking. During cranking, only the Hall Effect pickup signals enter the computer. These signals are interpreted to provide a fixed number of degrees of spark advance. The computer shuts off coil primary current in accordance with the pickup signals. As in conventional ignition systems, primary current shutdown causes secondary field collapse, and the high voltage is sent from the coil to the distributor, which then sends it to the spark plug.

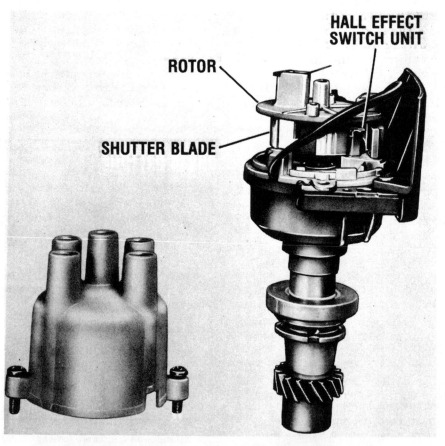

ROTOR

SHUTTER BLADE

HALL EFFECT SWITCH UNIT

Hall Effect distributor used on Omni, Reliant and Aries models.

After the engine starts, and during normal engine operation, the computer functions in the run mode. In this mode, the Hall Effect pickup serves as only one of the five signals to the computer. It is a reference signal of maximum possible spark advance. The computer then determines, from information provided by the other sensors, how much of this advance is necessary, and shuts down the primary current accordingly to fire the spark plug at the exact moment when this advance (crankshaft position) is reached.

There is a third mode of operation which becomes functional only when the computer fails. This is the limp-in mode. This mode functions on signals from the pickup only, and results in very poor engine performance. However, it does allow the car to be driven to a repair shop. If a failure occurs in the pickup assembly or the start mode of the computer, the engine will neither start nor run.

Ignition Timing

Ignition timing is a measurement, in degrees of crankshaft rotation, of the point at which the spark plug fires in relation to when the piston reaches top dead center (TDC) on its compression stroke.

Ignition timing is adjusted by loosening the distributor locknut and turning the distributor in the engine.

Ideally, the air/fuel mixture in the cylinder will be ignited (by the spark plug) and just beginning its rapid expansion as the piston passes top dead center (TDC) of the compression stroke. If this happens, the piston will be beginning the power stroke just as the compressed and ignited air/fuel mixture starts to expand. The expansion of the air/fuel mixture will then force the piston down on the power stroke and turn the crankshaft.

It takes a fraction of a second for the spark from the plug to

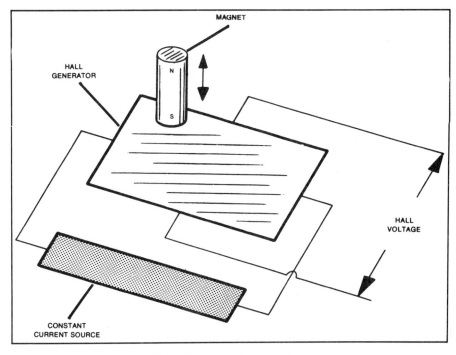

Hall Effect operating principle.

completely ignite the mixture in the cylinder. Because of this, the spark plug must fire before the piston reaches TDC if the mixture is to be completely ignited as the piston passes TDC. This measurement is given in degrees of crankshaft rotation *before* (the piston reaches) *top dead center* (BTDC).

If the ignition timing setting is six degrees (6°) BTDC, this means that the spark plug must fire at a time when the piston for that cylinder is 6° before top dead center of its compression stroke. However, this only holds true while the engine is at idle speed. As the engine accelerates from idle, the speed of the engine (rpm) increases, meaning that the pistons are now traveling up and down much faster. Because of this, the spark plugs will have to fire even sooner if the mixture is to be completely ignited as the piston passes TDC. To accomplish this, the distributor advances the timing of the spark as engine speed increases.

The distributor has two ways of advancing the ignition timing. In one, centrifugal advance

weights are thrown out by centrifugal force as engine speed increases, causing the points to open sooner. Springs pull the weights back as speed decreases. The other is called vacuum advance and is controlled by the large circular housing on the side of the distributor. Diaphragm springs are compressed at low engine speed (when vacuum is high), causing a diaphragm link to be pulled, which moves the breaker plate to advance spark timing.

In addition, some distributors have a vacuum-retard mechanism which is contained in the same housing as the vacuum advance. Its function is to retard the timing of the ignition spark under certain engine conditions. This causes more complete burning of the air/fuel mixture in the cylinder and consequently lowers exhaust emissions.

Because these mechanisms change ignition timing, it is necessary to disconnect and plug the one or two vacuum lines from the distributor when setting the basic ignition timing.

If ignition timing is too ad-

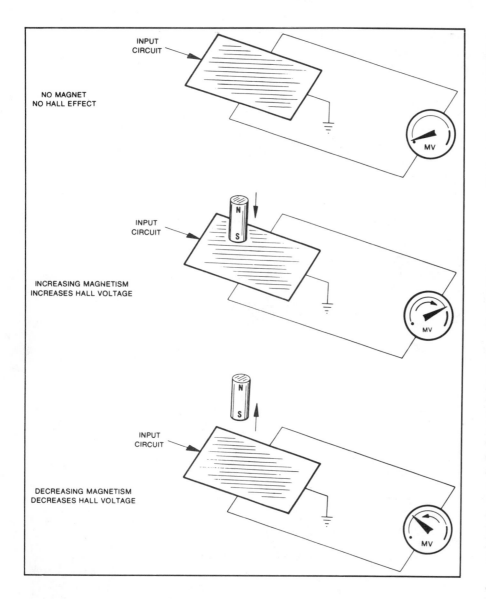

INPUT CIRCUIT

NO MAGNET
NO HALL EFFECT

INPUT CIRCUIT

INCREASING MAGNETISM
INCREASES HALL VOLTAGE

INPUT CIRCUIT

DECREASING MAGNETISM
DECREASES HALL VOLTAGE

or a rattle in the engine. If the ignition timing is too retarded (after, or ATDC), the piston will have already started down on the power stroke when the air/fuel mixture ignites and expands. This will cause the piston to be forced down only a portion of its travel. This will result in poor engine performance and lack of power.

Periodic Maintenance

Periodic maintenance of the ignition system will keep your engine running smoothly, maintain good fuel economy, and prevent expensive repairs and troublesome breakdowns.

Tests by the Champion Spark Plug Company showed that an average 11.36% improvement in gas economy could be expected after a tune-up. A change to new spark plugs alone provided a 3.44% decrease in fuel use. As for emissions, significantly lower emissions were recorded at idle after a complete tune-up on a car needing service. An average 45.37% reduction of carbon monoxide emissions was recorded at idle after a complete tune-up. Hydrocarbon emissions were cut 55.5%.

Normally, the breaker points, condenser, and spark plugs need replacement after 10–12,000 miles (1 year) on cars equipped with conventional Point-type ignition. Electronic ignitions, of course, do not need regular distributor maintenance, since there is nothing to wear out. Also, because of the higher voltages delivered, spark plugs should last anywhere from 18,000–24,000 miles.

When performing a tune-up, do not neglect the other components of the ignition system, such as the plug wires and distributor cap. These components fail from simple fatigue just like the points and plugs. The only difference is it takes them a little longer. So keep an eye on them.

vanced (BTDC), the ignition and expansion of the air/fuel mixture in the cylinder will try to force the piston down the cylinder

while it is still traveling upward. This causes engine "ping," a sound which resembles marbles being dropped into an empty can

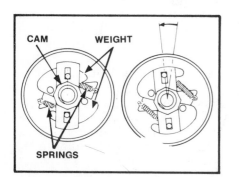

Centrifugal advance is controlled by engine speed.

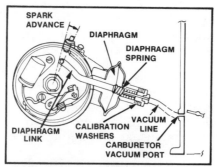

Vacuum advance is controlled by throttle position and engine load.

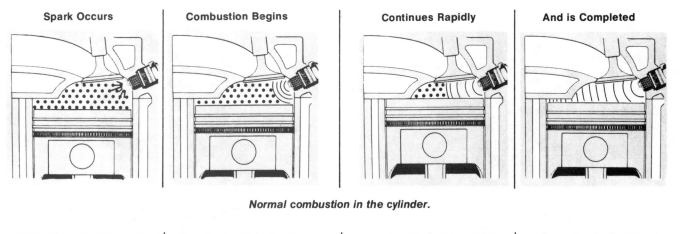

| Spark Occurs | Combustion Begins | Continues Rapidly | And is Completed |

Normal combustion in the cylinder.

| Ignited by a Hot Deposit | Regular Ignition Spark | Ignites Remaining Fuel | Flame Fronts Collide |

Detonation. This occurs when the anti-knock quality of the fuel used does not meet the engine requirements. Note the two flame fronts. Detonation, like pre-ignition, can cause severe engine damage.

| Ignited by a Hot Deposit | Regular Ignition Spark | Ignites Remaining Fuel | Flame Fronts Collide |

Preignition. This is just what the term implies—ignition of the fuel charge prior to the time of the spark. Any hot spot within the combustion chamber such as glowing carbon deposits, rough metallic edges, or overheated spark plugs can cause preignition.

Silicone Lubricants

Modern electronic ignition systems generate extremely high voltages and high heats. The spark plug boots can soften and actually fuse to the ceramic insulator of the spark plugs after long exposures to high temperature and voltage. If this happens, the boot (and possibly the wire) must be replaced, adding to the cost and complexity of a tune-up.

To help alleviate this condition, many manufacturers are using new silicone compounds (called greases in the trade, although they're not really greases) to slow the deterioration caused by heat and high voltage. The compounds are generally nonconductive, protective lubricants that will not dry out, harden, or melt away. They form a weathertight seal between rubber or plastic and metal and are found in several typical locations:

· Inside the insulating boots of spark plug wires to improve insulation, prevent aging, and ease removal and installation from the spark plug.

· Inside primary ignition cir-

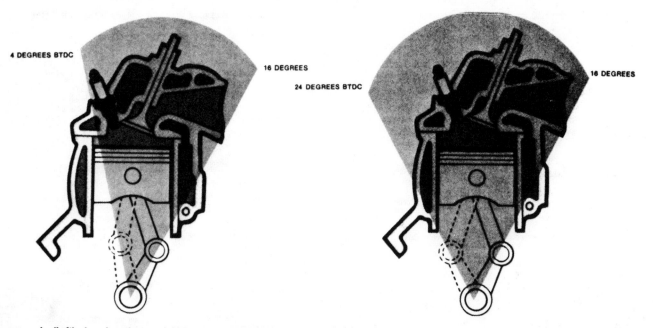

An example (left) showing that at 1,000 rpm a spark occurring at 4° BTDC will cause combustion to exert maximum pressure on the piston at 16° ATDC. At 2,000 rpm (right) a spark occurring at 24° BTDC will still cause combustion to exert maximum force on the piston at 16° ATDC.

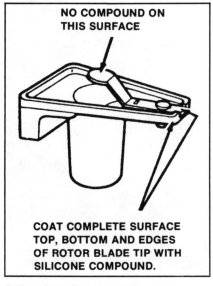

NO COMPOUND ON THIS SURFACE

COAT COMPLETE SURFACE TOP, BOTTOM AND EDGES OF ROTOR BLADE TIP WITH SILICONE COMPOUND.

Before installing a new Ford rotor, coat the surfaces with a silicone compound.

Anytime a spark plug boot is removed, it is wise (and often necessary) to apply a small amount of silicone boot release or similar material to the inside of the boot. This also applies to the distributor end of the spark plug wire.

cuit cable connectors to improve insulation.

· On distributor and rotor cap electrodes to improve RFI (Radio Frequency Interference) suppression.

· Under the GM Hall Effect ignition (HEI) control module to improve heat transfer.

Most domestic manufacturers supply the silicone compounds through their own parts depart-

Application Point	Silicone Compound
General Motors: under HEI module	**Supplied with new module, or use GE-642 or DC-340**
Ford Motor Company: inside spark plug boots, on end of cable when installing new boot, and on rotor and cap electrodes	**Ford part number D7AZ-19A331-A or use GE-627 or DC-111**
Chrysler Corporation: ¼" deep within spark control computer connector cavity coating rotor electrode	**Use Mopar part number 2932524 or NLGI Grade 2 EP (not a silicone) Supplied with new rotor, or use GE-628 or DC-111**
American Motors (Prestolite system): distributor primary connector—coat male terminal, fill female ¼ full	**AMC part number 8127445 or GE-623**
International Harvester (Prestolite system): coat all secondary terminals, including spark plug boots	**IHC part number 472141-C1 only**

TROUBLESHOOTING BASIC POINT-TYPE IGNITION SYSTEM PROBLEMS

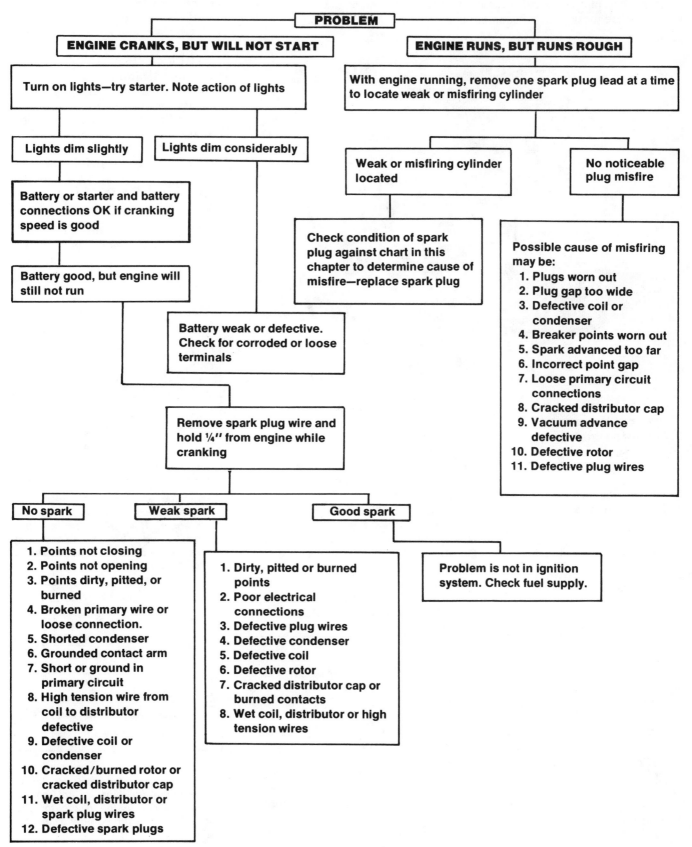

IGNITION SYSTEM MAINTENANCE INTERVALS

In order to maintain peak efficiency in your car's ignition system, periodic maintenance should be performed at the following intervals:

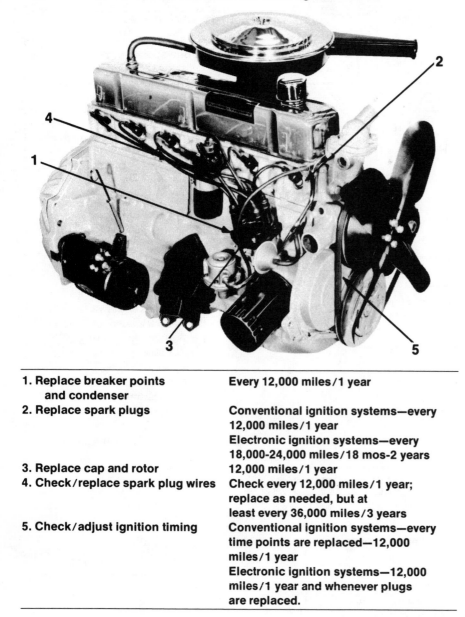

1. Replace breaker points and condenser	Every 12,000 miles/1 year
2. Replace spark plugs	Conventional ignition systems—every 12,000 miles/1 year Electronic ignition systems—every 18,000-24,000 miles/18 mos-2 years
3. Replace cap and rotor	12,000 miles/1 year
4. Check/replace spark plug wires	Check every 12,000 miles/1 year; replace as needed, but at least every 36,000 miles/3 years
5. Check/adjust ignition timing	Conventional ignition systems—every time points are replaced—12,000 miles/1 year Electronic ignition systems—12,000 miles/1 year and whenever plugs are replaced.

ments in one-application packages or supply a small quantity of the compounds with the new rotor, cap, or module. Equivalent compounds are also available from jobbers and retailers under General Electric (GE) or Dow Corning (DC) brand names. The most common are the following:

· GE-623, 627, and 628 are interchangeable in automotive applications. They insulate, form a watertight seal, prevent heat aging, and provide RFI suppression when applied to the rotor electrode.

· GE Silicone Spark Plug Boot Release is specially formulated to resist high temperature and ease spark plug boot removal. It must be applied each time the boot is removed or the seal is broken.

· DC-111 is thermally stable and provides a good seal between rubber or plastic and metal. It is similar to GE-623, 627, and 628.

· GE-642 is a heat-transfer compound.

· DC-340 is a heat-transfer compound, similar to GE-642.

The chart on page 133 lists specific manufacturers' application points and recommended greases. One nonsilicone application, for the Chrysler spark control computer, is included.

Checking Spark Plug Wires

Plug wires are one of the most overlooked components of the ignition system, which is understandable since they seldom show any visible signs of deterio-

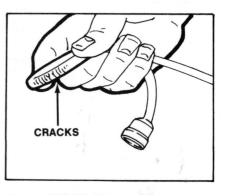

Spark plug wires can be checked visually by bending them in a loop over your finger. This will reveal any bad cracks, burned or broken insulation. Any wire showing cracked insulation should be replaced.

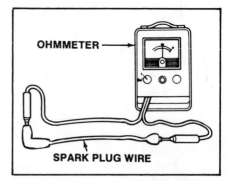

On cars with point-type ignition systems, check the spark plug wires as shown. On electronic ignitions, do not remove the wire. Remove the distributor cap and test the wire through the distributor cap terminal.

Check both ends of the spark plug wires for corrosion or cracking. The end of this cable is badly corroded and should be replaced.

Test the plug wires inside the cap at the terminals. Test the coil wire at the center terminal.

ration or failure. It is a good idea to visually inspect the plug wires at every tune-up. Bending the wires in a tight loop will show signs of brittleness, cracking, or burn marks, but the only reliable way to check plug wires is with an ohmmeter.

For cars equipped with conventional ignition, the best way to check the wires is to remove the plug wire from the plug *and* the distributor cap and test the wire alone. Simply insert the ends of the ohmmeter in the terminals of the spark plug wire. As a general rule, resistance should not exceed 3,000 to 7,000 ohms per foot. Replace any wire which

shows readings well outside these limits.

The procedure for checking plug wires on cars equipped with electronic ignition is slightly different. For one thing *do not,* under any circumstances, pierce the plug wires. Test the wires at their terminals only. When checking the wire, do not remove it from the distributor cap. Test the wire through the distributor cap. If resistance is marginal, remove the wire from the cap carefully and retest it. If resistance is outside the values given, replace the wire.

Resistance values for electonic

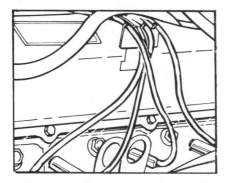

Misfiring can be the result of spark plug leads to adjacent, consecutively firing cylinders running parallel and too close together.

ignition plug wires vary from manufacturer to manufacturer. However, as a general rule, you should replace any wire which shows a resistance of over 50,000 ohms total. If you don't have an ohmmeter, count on replacing your plug wires approximately every 36,000 miles.

When replacing wires on cars with electronic ignition, use plug wires rated for use with electronic ignition *only.* Ordinary plug wires will quickly fail due to the high heat conditions.

■

Chilton Tip

Engine misfire is sometimes the result of spark plug wires grouped together and running parallel for a long distance. The high voltage tends to jump from wire to wire, and will most likely occur in consecutive firing cylinders that are located close together.

Make sure that adjacent cables of consecutively firing cylinders are far apart or crossed at right angles.

■

Replacing Spark Plug Wires

Replace one spark plug wire at a time. This will keep you out of trouble with crossed wires. When removing the wires, twist back and forth as you pull up. This will help free up stuck wires. Pull only on the spark plug boot, never on the wire itself.

Take the old wire and match it with a new one for length. If you are cutting your own, make sure there is good contact between the end of the wire and the pinch-on connector.

Make sure each wire seats all the way down in the distributor cap. First push the wire down, then the boot. The wire should click into place.

After you are done, make sure all wires are clear of the choke, throttle linkage, or hot exhaust manifolds.

CHECKING THE DISTRIBUTOR CAP, POINTS AND ROTOR

Under normal operating conditions, the breaker points, and condenser should last a minimum of 12,000 miles/1 year. The rotor and distributor cap should last a good deal longer. However, it is a good idea to check the condition of the distributor components every 6,000 miles (6 mos) or so, especially if the car is subjected to severe usage or adverse weather conditions.

Remove the distributor cap and check the inside of it carefully for any signs of pitting or burning on the terminals. Also, wipe it out carefully and check for cracks in the bakelite surface itself. Check it in a good strong light, since quite often cracks are very difficult to see.

After you've checked the cap, pull the rotor off and check it for pitting, burning, or cracks. Rotors don't wear out nearly as fast as breaker points or the condenser, but they do wear out. If you didn't replace the rotor at every tune-up, make sure you replace it at least once a year.

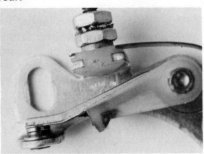

Check the points very carefully. They'll probably be your main source of trouble. If the points are in correct alignment, they should be flat against each other, as shown.

Incorrectly aligned points. This condition is correctable when the points are new, but at this point, it makes more sense to simply replace them.

These points are worn out. Note the deeply pitted areas, cracked contact face, and the fact that the pitted area is off-center indicating probable misalignment when they were installed.

These points show only slight graying of the contact surfaces, which indicates normal wear. They may be filed slightly before being returned to use, but it is not necessary. If you do file them, be sure you reset the point gap.

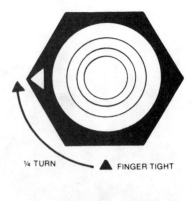

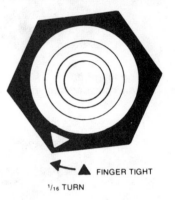

In the absence of specified torque, tighten plugs as shown.

Replacing Spark Plugs

Tools you will need for spark plug replacement include at least a ratchet handle, extension, spark plug socket ($^{13}/_{16}$" for some cars, $^{5}/_{8}$" for others), combination spark plug gapping gauge and bending tool, and a can of penetrating oil. A torque wrench makes for more accurate plug tightening, but it is not generally used. Only doing the job will tell you exactly what tools and acrobatics you'll need for the really hard-to-reach plugs on some cars.

When removing spark plugs, work on one at a time. Don't start by removing all the plug wires at once, because you'll probably get them mixed up. Take a minute before you begin and number the wires with tape. The best location for numbering is near where the wires come out of the distributor cap.

REPLACING SPARK PLUGS

Regular spark plug replacement is one of the surest ways to achieve optimum performance and fuel economy, regardless of what you drive. Follow these simple steps to replace each spark plug in your cars' engine. Also see the text under "Spark Plug Replacement"

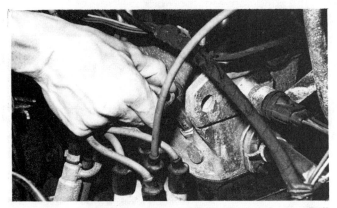

1. To remove the boot, twist it gently on the spark plug. Pull the boot off the plug, but don't tug on the wire.

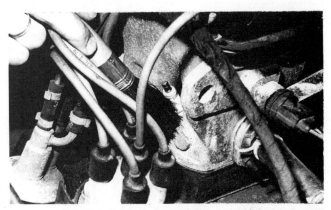

2. Brush away any dirt from around the plug, so that none will fall into the hole after the plug is removed.

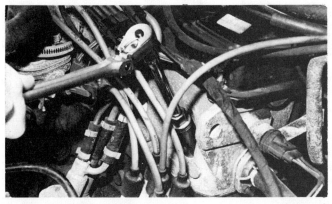

3. Remove the spark plug using the proper size socket and the necessary extensions. Be sure the socket is seated straight on the plug and turn it counterclockwise to remove it.

4. Once the plug is removed, compare it with the plugs pictured in this section to determine engine condition. Check the spark plug gap and adjust it if you plan to re-use the plugs.

5. There is only one correct way to adjust the spark plug gap. Use a tool such as the one illustrated. Use of other tools or methods will risk breaking the electrode.

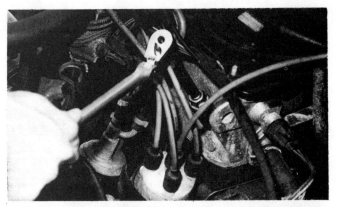

6. Squirt a drop of penetrating oil on the spark plug threads and start the plug in by hand to avoid cross-threading. Tighten it snugly with a spark plug socket.

Chilton Tip

It will ease spark plug removal if the engine is at operating temperature.

Use a wire gauge to check the spark plug gap. Flat gauges are not accurate when used on spark plugs. The correct size feeler gauge should pass through the gap with a slight drag.

If the gap is incorrect, bend the side electrode to adjust the gap. Never bend or try to adjust the center electrode.

Chilton Tip

When installing plugs that are hard to reach, slip a piece of vacuum hose over the plug and start it by turning the hose.

Replacing Points, Condenser, and Rotor

Like a lot of other jobs, this is one that looks hard until you actually do it. You'll need a couple (*Text continues on page 144.*)

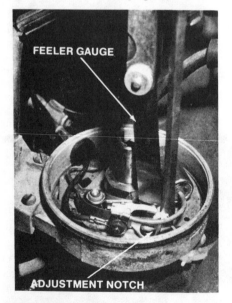

When you're gapping the points, make sure you don't have the feeler gauge on an angle. It takes a little bit of practice to wield the screwdriver and the feeler gauge at the same time.

READING SPARK PLUGS

A close examination of spark plugs will provide many clues to the condition of an engine. Keeping the plugs in order according to cylinder location will make the diagnosis even more effective and accurate. The following diagrams illustrate some of the conditions that spark plugs will reveal.

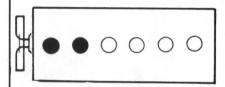

Two adjacent plugs are fouled in a 6-cylinder engine, 4-cylinder engine or either bank of a V8. This is probably due to a blown head gasket between the two cylinders.

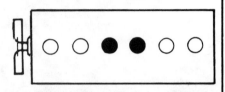

The two center plugs in a 6-cylinder engine are fouled. Raw fuel may be "boiled" out of the carburetor into the intake manifold after the engine is shut-off. Stop-start driving can also foul the center plugs, due to overly rich mixture. Proper float level, a good needle and seat or use of an insulating spacer may help this problem.

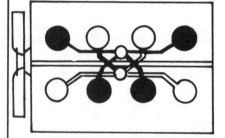

An unbalanced carburetor is indicated. Following the fuel flow on this particular design shows that the cylinders fed by the right-hand barrel are fouled from overly rich mixture, while the cylinders fed by the left-hand barrel are normal.

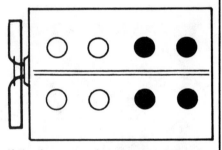

If the four rear plugs are overheated, a cooling system problem is suggested. A thorough cleaning of the cooling system may restore coolant circulation and cure the problem.

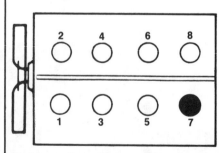

Finding one plug overheated may indicate an intake manifold leak near the affected cylinder. If the overheated plug is the second of two adjacent, consecutively firing plugs, it could be the result of ignition cross-firing. Separating the leads to these two plugs will eliminate cross-fire.

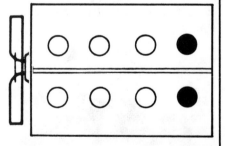

Occasionally, the two rear plugs in large, lightly used V8's will become oil fouled. High oil consumption and smoky exhaust may also be noticed. It is probably due to plugged oil drain holes in the rear of the cylinder head, causing oil to be sucked in around the valve stems. This usually occurs in the rear cylinders first, because the engine slants that way.

Normal

APPEARANCE: *This plug is typical of one operating normally. The insulator nose varies from a light tan to grayish color with slight electrode wear. The presence of slight deposits is normal on used plugs and will have no adverse effect on engine performance. The spark plug heat range is correct for the engine and the engine is running normally.*
CAUSE: *Properly running engine*
RECOMMENDATION: *Before reinstalling this plug, the electrodes should be cleaned and filed square. Set the gap to specifications. If the plug has been in service for more than 10–12,000 miles, the entire set should probably be replaced with a fresh set of the same heat range.*

Incorrect Heat Range

APPEARANCE: *The effects of high temperature on a spark plug are indicated by clean white, often blistered insulator. This can also be accompanied by excessive wear of the electrode, and the absence of deposits.*
CAUSE: *Check for the correct spark plug heat range. A plug which is too hot for the engine can result in overheating. A car operated mostly at high speeds can require a colder plug. Also check ignition timing, cooling system level, fuel mixture and leaking intake manifold.*
RECOMMENDATION: *If all ignition and engine adjustments are known to be correct, and no other malfunction exists, install spark plugs one heat range colder.*

Oil Deposits

APPEARANCE: *The firing end of the plug is coverered with a wet, oily coating.*
CAUSE: *The problem is poor oil control. On high mileage engines, oil is leaking past the rings or valve guides into the combustion chamber. A common cause is also a plugged PCV valve, and a ruptured fuel pump diaphragm can also cause this condition. Oil fouled plugs such as these are often found in new or recently overhauled engines, before normal oil control is achieved, and can be cleaned and reinstalled.*
RECOMMENDATION: *A hotter spark plug may temporarily relieve the problem, but the engine is probably in need of engine work.*

Carbon Deposits

APPEARANCE: *Carbon fouling is easily identified by the presence of dry, soft, black, sooty deposits.*
CAUSE: *Changing the heat range can often lead to carbon fouling, as can prolonged slow, stop-and-start driving. If the heat range is correct, carbon fouling can be attributed to a rich fuel mixture, sticking choke, clogged air cleaner, worn breaker points, retarded timing or low compression. If only one or two plugs are carbon fouled, check for corroded or cracked wires on the affected plugs. Also look for cracks in the distributor cap between the towers of affected cylinders.*
RECOMMENDATION: *After the problem is corrected, these plugs can be cleaned and reinstalled if not worn severely.*

Ash Deposits

APPEARANCE: *Ash deposits are characterized by light brown or white colored deposits crusted on the side or center electrodes. In some cases it may give the plug a rusty appearance.*

CAUSE: *Ash deposits are normally derived from oil or fuel additives burned during normal combustion. Normally they are harmless, though excessive amounts can cause misfiring. If deposits are excessive in short mileage, the valve guides may be worn. Reddish or rusty deposits are caused by manganese, an anti-knock compound replacing lead in unleaded gas. No engine malfunction is indicated.*

RECOMMENDATION: *Ash-fouled plugs can be cleaned, gapped and reinstalled.*

Splash Deposits

APPEARANCE: *Splash deposits occur in varying degrees as spotty deposits on the insulator.*

CAUSE: *These usually occur after a long delayed tune-up. By-products of combustion have accumulated on pistons and valves because of a delayed tune-up. Following tune-up or during hard acceleration, the deposits loosen and are thrown against the hot surface of the plug. If the deposits accumulate sufficiently, misfiring can occur.*

RECOMMENDATION: *These plugs can be cleaned, gapped and reinstalled.*

High Speed Glazing

APPEARANCE: *Glazing appears as shiny coating on the plug, either yellow or tan in color.*

CAUSE: *During hard, fast acceleration, plug temperatures rise suddenly. Deposits from normal combustion have no chance to fluff-off; instead, they melt on the insulator forming an electrically conductive coating which causes misfiring.*

RECOMMENDATION: *Glazed plugs are not easily cleaned. They should be replaced with a fresh set of plugs of the correct heat range. If the condition recurs, using plugs with a heat range one step colder may cure the problem.*

Detonation

APPEARANCE: *Detonation is usually characterized by a broken plug insulator.*

CAUSE: *A portion of the fuel charge will begin to burn spontaneously, from the increased heat following ignition. The explosion that results applies extreme pressure to engine components, frequently damaging spark plugs and pistons.*

Detonation can result by over-advanced ignition timing, inferior gasoline (low octane) lean air/fuel mixture, poor carburetion, engine lugging or an increase in compression ratio due to combustion chamber deposits or engine modification.

RECOMMENDATION: *Replace the plugs after correcting the problem.*

BREAKER POINT/CONDENSER/ROTOR REPLACEMENT (EXCEPT GM V8)

The following procedures are typical of just about every distributor made, except for the General Motors V8's, which are covered next.

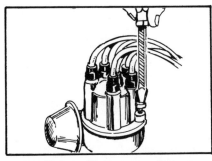

1. *The first step is to remove the screws which hold the distributor cap down. Some distributors have wire clips instead of screws. You can set the cap off to one side without removing any wires. If you haven't checked the inside of the cap lately, now is a good time.*

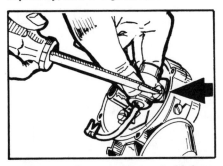

4. *Remove the condenser hold-down screw and remove the condenser. Be sure to use a magnetic screwdriver for this job. The condenser on many cars, especially imported ones, is located on the outside of the distributor. Sometimes these are quite difficult to reach and require a very small screwdriver or a small ignition wrench to remove them.*

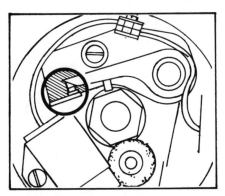

7. *After the points are installed, check to make sure the contact faces are aligned. Although it doesn't show it is best to have the points on one of the high sides of the cam lobes to do this. If you have to adjust the alignment, move the stationary arm carefully with a pair of needle nosed pliers.*

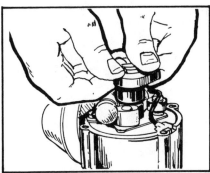

2. *Remove the rotor by pulling straight up. Check it for cracks, burning, or pitting.*

5. *Remove the screw which holds the points and remove the points. Use the magnetic screwdriver or you'll lose the screw.*

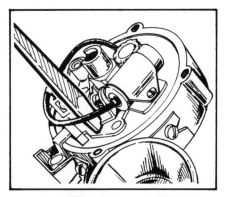

8. *You'll probably need an assistant to help you for this part. Bump the engine over gently until the rubbing block on the points set is on one of the high spots of the distributor cam. Take a look at the picture in the beginning of this section to see just how the points should look. After you have the points correctly positioned, adjust the point gap by inserting a screwdriver in the adjusting slot and twisting.*

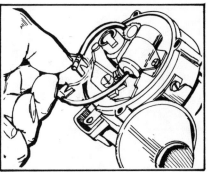

3. *Remove the wires from the points. Some simply slip in and out, while others are held in place by a small screw or nut.*

6. *Install the new set of points after wiping off the cam lobes to remove any grease. Put a small amount of new grease on the rubbing block. It is generally supplied with the new points. On almost all points sets, there is a locating pin that must go in a hole to keep the points stationary. Install the hold-down screw using the magnetic screwdriver or a screw starter. Install the condenser in the same manner. Hook up the wires to the points.*

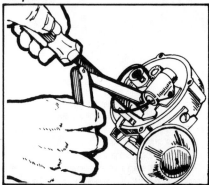

9. *Insert the correct size feeler gauge to check the gap. The gauge should pass through the contact faces with just a slight drag if the gap is correct. It takes a little practice to get this just right. Once you have the gap correct, replace the rotor and cap.*

BREAKER POINT/CONDENSER/ROTOR REPLACEMENT—GM V8

Installing points and condenser in a General Motors V8 engine is slightly different from the majority of other cars. There's nothing difficult about it and in some ways it's easier.

1. *Remove the distributor cap by depressing the screw in the cap and rotating the latch off the distributor. There are two latches. Lift the cap off and set it to one side.*

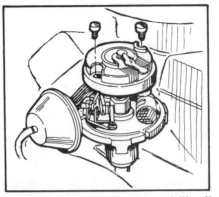

2. *Remove the two screws and lift off the rotor. If it's cracked, or the metallic tip is badly burned, replace it.*

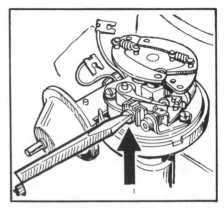

3. *Disconnect the two wire terminals connected to the points set. Note that the condenser connector is on the outside.*

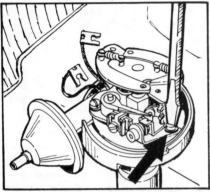

4. *Loosen, but do not remove the two points attaching screws. Slide the points off the screws.*

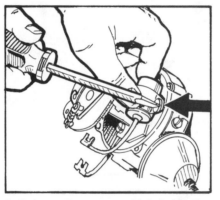

5. *Remove the screw which holds the condenser. Use a magnetic screwdriver or you'll probably drop the screw.*

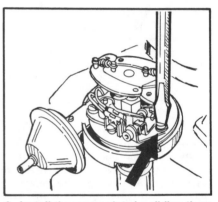

6. *Install the new points by sliding them onto the breaker plate under the screws. Tighten the screws down. Install the condenser and hook up the wires. Some manufacturers now supply a point and condenser set as one piece, simplifying installation.*

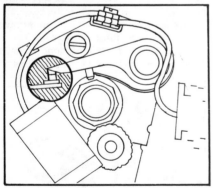

7. *Once you have the new points installed, check to make sure the point contact surfaces are correctly aligned. If they aren't, straighten them out by gently bending the stationary arm with a pair of needle nosed pliers. Turn the engine over until the rubbing block on the points set is resting on one of the high spots of the distributor cam. The easiest way to do this is to have someone gently bump the ignition key until you have the points in the correct position.*

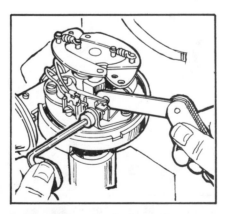

8. *Insert the correct size feeler gauge into the point gap. Point gap is adjusted with a ⅛ in. allen wrench or special tools available for this. Adjust the gap with the allen wrench until the feeler gauge can be moved in and out between the contacts with only a slight drag. Make sure you keep the gauge straight. The points can also be set with the engine running using a dwell meter.*

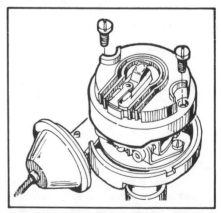

9. *Install the rotor on the advance weight assembly. Make sure you have the round peg in the round hole and the square peg in the square hole. Install the cap.*

of screwdrivers, a small ignition wrench, a set of flat feeler gauges, and a magnetic or screwholding screwdriver. The screws that hold the point and condenser are very small and they have a nasty habit of disappearing down inside the distributor. When that happens, you have to remove the distributor to retrieve them. This is not a job done for amusement.

Remove the distributor cap and rotor and take a close look at everything in the distributor so you'll know where everything goes before you start taking things out.

Checking Spark Plugs

The single most accurate indicator of the engine's condition is the firing end of the spark plugs. Although the spark plug has no moving parts, it is exposed to more stress than any other engine part.

The plug must deliver a high voltage spark thousands of times a minute, at precisely timed intervals, under widely varying conditions. Because it is inside the combustion chamber, it is exposed to the corrosive effects of chemical additives in fuel and oil, and to extremes of temperature and pressure. The terminal end may be as cold as ice, but the firing tip will be exposed to flame temperatures in excess of 3000° F.

It's easy to see that the efficiency of an engine is dependent on the ability of the spark plug to function properly. If the efficiency of the engine is impaired, the first place it will show up is in the condition of the spark plugs.

It is a good idea to remove a couple of spark plugs every 5,000 to 6,000 miles (twice a year), just to check on the condition of the engine. Compare the appearance of the firing end of the plug with those illustrated here, which represent eight of the most common conditions found in cars today.

Learning to read the plugs can provide valuable information about the performance of your engine and help keep little problems from becoming big ones.

Setting the Dwell

Conventional Ignition Systems

A good dwell-tachometer is an invaluable tool for the do-it-yourselfer and need not cost a lot. You can purchase a reliable hand-held dwell-tach for less than $10. Simply setting the point gap is adequate, of course, but in order to obtain the highest efficiency from your engine, you should use a dwell meter.

Dwell (or cam angle) is the amount of time the breaker points remain closed and is measured in degrees of distributor rotation. Dwell will vary according to the point gap. If the points are set too wide, they open gradually and dwell angle (the time they remain closed) is small. This wide gap causes excessive arcing at the points, leading to point burning. The insufficient dwell doesn't give the coil sufficient time to build up maximum energy, so coil output decreases. If the point gap is too narrow, dwell is increased, and the idle becomes rough and starting is difficult.

The wider the point opening, the smaller the dwell, and the smaller the point opening, the larger the dwell. A point gap of .019" on a V8 engine might produce a dwell of 28°, while a gap of .016" might produce a dwell of 34°.

To hook up the dwell-tach, connect one lead of the dwell meter (usually the black one) to a good ground on the engine, and the other lead (the positive or red lead) to the negative side of the coil. The terminal is easy to find: look for the terminal which has the small wire that leads to the distributor. Also, there will always be a small minus sign next to the terminal, though it frequently is covered with grease.

Once the dwell meter is connected, the dwell can be checked

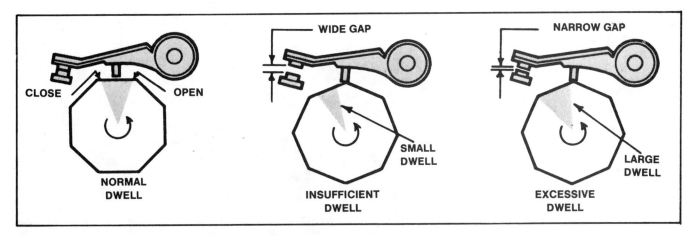

Dwell angle is a function of point gap.

Distributor terminal on the coil (arrow). It is identified by the wire leading to the distributor.

Setting the dwell on a General Motors V8.

with the engine either idling or cranking. The easiest way, of course, is to have the engine running. (If you came anywhere close when you gapped the points, the engine will run.) Compare the dwell to the point dwell in the tune-up specifications in the back of this book. If the dwell needs adjusting, shut the engine off, and adjust the point gaps (see Breaker Point/Condenser/Rotor Replacement in this section). If the dwell is too low, the point gap is too wide. If the dwell is too high, the point gap is too narrow.

On General Motors V8's, you can set the dwell while the engine is running, which simplifies the procedure considerably. Simply shut the engine off, insert the dwell adjusting tool (⅛" allen wrench will do) through the "window" in the distributor, turn the engine on, and adjust the dwell by gradually turning the tool.

Electronic Ignition Systems

Dwell is controlled electronically on solid-state ignition systems and, as a result, is non-adjustable.

Timing the Ignition

Ignition timing should be checked and adjusted every time the point dwell is altered. The reason for this is that changing the point dwell changes ignition timing (although changing the timing does not affect dwell). To visualize the relationship between dwell and ignition timing, remember that increasing the dwell retards the timing and decreasing the dwell advances the timing. For example, a 1° increase in dwell results in the ignition timing being retarded 2°. (Distributor degrees are always ½ of crankshaft degrees.)

Ignition timing is checked with a timing light. Use the following procedure:

1. If the timing light operates from the battery, connect the red lead to the battery positive terminal and connect the black lead to a ground. With all lights, connect the trigger lead to No. 1 spark plug wire. (See Section for hookups of timing lights.)

2. Disconnect and plug the vacuum hose to the distributor (if required).

3. Check the timing at idle. (See the tune-up specifications in the back of this book.) Aim the timing light at the crankshaft pulley or timing marks. The light will flash and momentarily "freeze" the timing marks and pointer. If the point is hard to see, it may help to stop the engine and mark the timing scale with chalk.

4. Loosen the distributor lock

Stay out of direct sunlight when you're timing the engine since the sunlight will overpower the timing light flashes. Keep your hands and the timing light clear of the fan blades. Always shut off the engine to make distributor adjustments.

Timing marks are generally quite difficult to see. This particular timing scale has the degrees clearly marked on it. Many timing scales do not. Notice that the mark on the pulley is also visible. It is always a good idea to mark the appropriate point on the scale with paint or chalk. Mark the point on the pulley while you're at it.

nut and rotate the distributor slowly in either direction until the timing is correct. Tighten the clamp and observe the timing mark again to make sure that the timing is still correct. Readjust the position of the distributor, if necessary.

5. Accelerate the engine in Neutral, while watching the timing point. If the distributor advance mechanisms are working, the timing point should advance as the engine is accelerated. If the engine's vacuum advance is engaged with the transmission in Neutral, check the vacuum advance operation by running the engine at about 1,500 rpm and connecting and disconnecting the vacuum advance hose.

14
Electrical System/Lights, Fuses & Flashers

```
TOOLS AND SUPPLIES
Tools
    Soldering gun
    Wire strippers/cutters
    Screwdrivers
    Fuse removal tool
    Pliers
Supplies
    Electrical tape
    Terminal hardware
    Rosin core solder
    Flux
    Fuses (assorted)
    Flasher
    Light bulbs (assorted)
```

Modern cars use dozens of bulbs to light everything from the road to the ash tray. Servicing the system is easy; over half of all lighting problems are caused by burned out bulbs, corroded sockets or burned out fuses.

Light Bulbs

Small bulbs, used for most automotive applications, come in four basic types—single contact bayonet base, double contact bayonet base with opposed or staggered indexing lugs, cartridge types for a small, flat installation, and wedge-base light bulbs.

Small bulbs show a broken filament when burned-out and are easily replaced. Turn them about ¼ turn and pull them from the socket. The single contact bayonet base is usually used for instrument panel lights in a small snap-in socket. The major difficulty in replacing these is finding them.

The double contact bayonet base is commonly used for turn signals, parking and taillights. The staggered indexing lugs allow one-way installation so the filament connection is correct. These bulbs are reached by removing the lens or light assembly; inside the trunk is also a common place to hide the light housings.

Don't forget to install the gasket under the lens or housing, if one is used. The gasket seals out moisture, a major cause of bulb troubles. While the bulb is out of the socket, check the socket for corrosion and if necessary, clean it.

Poor grounding is a major cause of non-functioning bulbs, especially when the bulb fila-

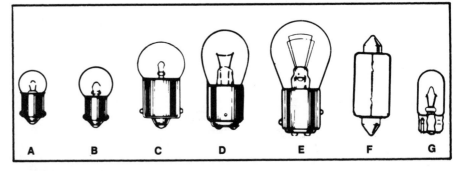

Common automotive bulbs:
A,B—Miniature bayonet for indicator and instrument lights
C—Single contact bayonet for license and courtesy lights
D—Double contact bayonet for trunk and underhood lights
E—Double contact bayonet with staggered indexing lugs for stop, turn signals and
    brake lights
F—Cartridge type for dome lights
G—Wedge base for instrument lights

Burned bulbs show a broken filament (arrows).

ments are OK. Scraping the terminal sockets and polishing the bulb contacts is frequently all that's required. Also check the ground between the bulb housing and the fender, and between the fender and the body. The electricity has to get back to the ground (negative) side of the battery. If it can't because of poor grounding, the bulb won't work. Many times, running a ground wire from the bulb housing directly to the frame of the car is easier than trying to make a ground through rusted sheet metal.

Headlights

There are five different types of sealed beam headlights. The code is molded into the lens.

1—Type 1 lamps are for four-lamp systems that have a single high-beam filament in a circular 5-¾-inch diameter housing.

1A—Type 1A lamps are for four-lamp systems that have a single high-beam filament in a rectangular 4 x 6½-inch housing.

2—Type 2 lamps have both a high-beam and a low-beam filament in a circular housing. Type 2 lamps for four-lamp systems

To replace a license plate light, remove the lens from the bumper and push the bulb in, turning it counterclockwise.

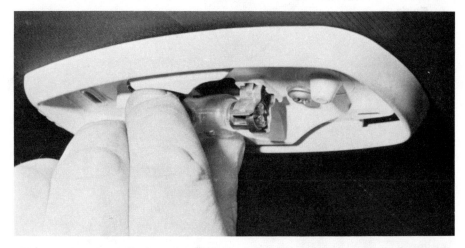

This is a cartridge bulb; be sure to get the correct replacement. Pry the dome lens from the housing. Make sure the dome light switch is off and the doors are closed to avoid blowing a fuse. Lever the bulb straight out of the housing and install a new bulb.

To replace a turn signal, stop light or back-up light bulb, push down on the bulb while turning it counterclockwise. When installing the new bulb be sure the indexing lugs match the socket; the bulb will only fit one way.

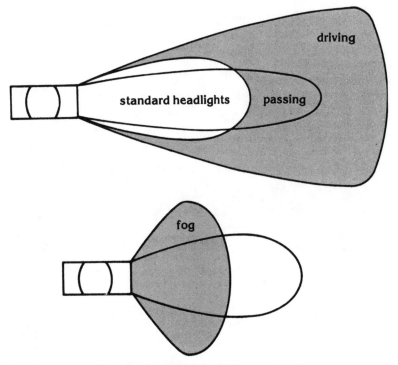

Beam patterns of different types of lights

Remove the screws holding the lens or lens retainer.

Remove the lens and/or the retaining ring.

Remove the bulb from the socket by pushing in and turning ¼ turn counterclockwise. On some cars, the light housing must be removed from the fender for access to the snap-in light socket at the rear of the housing.

All headlights have three aiming pads, which are small glass bumps molded into the lens at specific points. These are used when the headlamps are being aimed with a mechanical aimer. So that mechanical aimers can be used on all headlamp installations, fixed transparent lamp covers have been prohibited on all new cars sold in the U.S. since 1967.

Headlamps are installed in a circuit with multiple-plug connectors. Type 1 and 1A lamps are installed in the inner or lower positions in four-lamp systems. They have two connecting prongs. Type 2, 2A, and 2B lamps have three connecting prongs. In four-lamp systems, Type 2 and 2A lamps are installed in the outer or upper positions.

A new type of sealed beam headlight is the halogen light, which has been standard equipment on European cars for years, but not approved for use in the United States until 1979. The halogen lights increase the candlepower of the headlight from 75,000 to almost 150,000, and boost the distance a driver can see at night by almost 20% over the present tungsten lights. Auto makers have started installing them on top-of-the-line models in 1980 and their use will spread on 1981 models.

Like today's lights, the new lights use a tungsten filament, but it is contained in a halogen gas environment, which allows the filament to be heated to a much higher temperature to produce a much brighter and whiter light. They also require less power, so that a smaller and lighter alternator can be used.

are 5-¾ inches in diameter. Type 2 lamps for 2-lamp systems are 7 inches in diameter.

2A—Type 2A lamps are for four-lamp systems that have the same filaments as a Type 2 lamp in a 4 x 6½-inch rectangular housing.

2B—Type 2B lamps are for two-lamp systems which have the same filaments as a Type 2 lamp in a rectangular housing made to metric dimensions of 142 x 200 mm (5.6 x 7.9 inches). Tentative approval has been given by NHTSA to a smaller, rectangular, 4-lamp system known as Type F.

Fuses, Fusible Links and Circuit Breakers

All wires must be insulated and protected from overload. If the insulation breaks (creating a path for electricity that was not intended) or if the circuit is over-

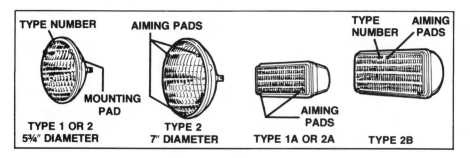

Basic types of headlights.

loaded, the fuse, circuit breaker or fusible link that protects the circuit will "blow."

Fuses

Fuses never blow because of high voltage. High amperage in the circuit, greater than the capacity of the fuse, causes the metal strip to heat up, melt and open the circuit, preventing the flow of electricity. A fuse could carry 200 volts as well as 2 volts, but will only tolerate its rated amperage plus about 10% to han-

dle minor current surges before it blows.

Auto fuses come in several designs, but consist basically of a zinc strip or a piece of wire. Heavier load fuses have a notch in the middle of the zinc strip. The wider section at each end is

to give better temperature-carrying capability. The heat from a temporary overload is transferred to the wider metal and slows down fuse burn-out. In the event of a heavy overload, the metal strip will melt in a fraction of a second and protect the circuit.

On 1977 and later GM cars, you'll likely find a fuse that is different from all others. It's a miniaturized, blade-type design that GM calls "Auto-fuse." The new Autofuse was developed in conjunction with the new, smaller fuse block. Fuses of different ratings are interchangeable but amperage ratings are molded in color-coded numbers that match

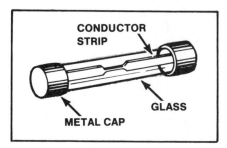

Typical automotive fuse.

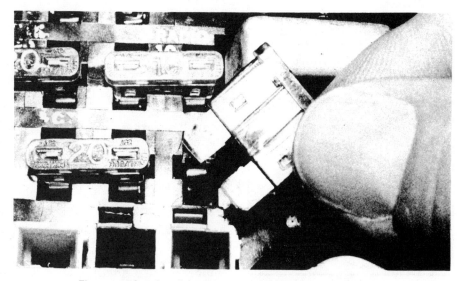

The new "Autofuse" found on some 1977 and later GM cars.

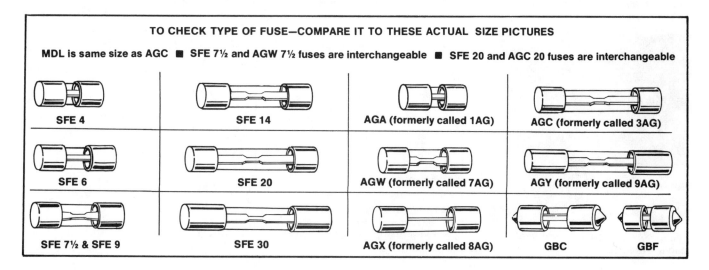

the fuse ratings on the fuse block.

The following chart identifies the amperage and color code.

Amps	Color
3	violet
5	tan
7½	brown
10	red
20	yellow
25	white

■ Chilton Tip

Even if you have the new GM "minifuse," don't throw away the old glass fuses. Adaptors are available to use the older fuses in the new GM fuse block.

■

Normally the fuse box is somewhere under the dash or in the engine compartment. Burned out fuses are readily identified by the burned zinc element in the mid-

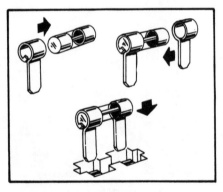

Adaptors are available to use older fuses in the new GM fuse block.

Small, plastic fuse removal tools are readily available.

dle of the glass or ceramic insulator. Small, inexpensive plastic tools are available to easily replace a burned fuse. Never replace a fuse with one of a higher load capacity (the amperage is usually stated on the fuse), and if a fuse continues to "blow," have the circuit checked, since it is probable there is a defective component, somewhere.

Circuit Breakers

Circuit breakers are sealed assemblies that perform the same job as the fuse, but in the event of an overload, will cut current for an instant. Unlike a fuse, things will return to normal. They rarely go bad but must be replaced with an identical unit should one blow. As with fuses, if a circuit breaker continues to fail, the source of the trouble should be found and corrected.

You never know exactly where to look for a circuit breaker, but many times they are located near the fuse box or near the component they protect. On some cars the circuit breaker that protects the headlights is an integral part of the headlight switch, which must be replaced in its entirety.

Fusible Links

Fusible links are a piece of wire about 6" long which is spliced into another wire, usually a gauge or two smaller than the wire it protects. Fusible links can be found almost anywhere. Many times they are identified by a col-

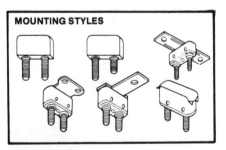

Circuit breakers come in a variety of styles and sizes, and can be mounted almost anywhere. They may be mounted in the line they protect, or plugged into the circuit at the fuse box.

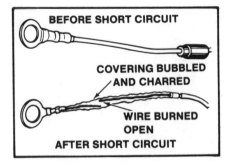

Most fusible links show a melted, charred insulation when they burn out.

ored flag on the link, or by a loop to make it stand out from other wires, and are almost always the same color as the protected circuit. Some fusible links may burn in half with no change in appearance, but most are covered with a special insulation that will bubble and char when the fusible link burns.

Fusible links should always be replaced with an original-equipment type; never use a standard piece of wire.

1. Disconnect the negative battery cable.

2. Disconnect the eyelet of the fuse link from the component.

3. Cut the other end of the fuse link from the wiring harness at the splice.

4. Connect the eyelet end of a new fuse link to the component.

5. Splice the open end of the new fuse link into the wiring harness.

6. Solder the splice with rosin-core solder and wrap the splice with electrical tape. This splice must be soldered. See Section 1 "Tools and Supplies" for tips on soldering.

7. Connect the negative battery cable.

8. Start the engine to check that the new connections complete the circuit.

Flashers

Flashers are found in all sorts of out-of-the-way places. They are usually small metal (round or square) units that plug into the (*Text continues on page 171.*)

TROUBLESHOOTING BASIC LIGHTING PROBLEMS

The ability to see and be seen is vital to safety. Fortunately, most lighting problems are relatively uncomplicated and easily corrected.

The Problem	Is Caused By	What to Do
Lights		
One or more lights don't work, but others do	• Defective bulb(s) • Blown fuse(s) • Dirty fuse clips or light sockets • Poor ground circuit	• Replace bulb(s) • Replace fuse(s) • Clean connections • Run ground wire from light socket housing to car frame
Lights burn out quickly	• Incorrect voltage regulator setting or defective regulator • Poor battery/alternator connections	• Have voltage regulator checked/replaced • Check battery/alternator connections
Lights go dim	• Low/discharged battery • Alternator not charging • Corroded sockets or connections • Low voltage output	• Check battery • Check drive belt tension; repair or replace alternator • Clean bulb and socket contacts and connections • Have voltage regulator checked/replaced
Lights flicker	• Loose connection • Poor ground • Circuit breaker operating (short circuit)	• Tighten all connections • Run ground wire from light housing to car frame • Check connections and look for bare wires
Lights "flare"—Some flare is normal on acceleration—if excessive, see "Lights Burn Out Quickly"	• High voltage setting	• Have voltage regulator checked/adjusted
Lights glare—approaching drivers are blinded	• Lights adjusted too high • Rear springs or shocks sagging • Rear tires soft	• Have headlights aimed • Check rear springs/shocks • Check/correct rear tire pressure
Turn Signals		
Turn signals don't work in either direction	• Blown fuse • Defective flasher • Loose connection	• Replace fuse • Replace flasher • Check/tighten all connections
Right (or left) turn signal only won't work	• Bulb burned out • Right (or left) indicator bulb burned out • Short circuit	• Replace bulb • Check/replace indicator bulb • Check/repair wiring
Flasher rate too slow or too fast	• Incorrect wattage bulb • Incorrect flasher	• Replace bulb • Replace flasher (use a variable load flasher if you pull a trailer)
Indicator lights do not flash (burn steadily)	• Burned out bulb • Defective flasher	• Replace bulb • Replace flasher
Indicator lights do not light at all	• Burned out indicator bulb • Defective flasher	• Replace indicator bulb • Replace flasher

TROUBLESHOOTING BASIC TURN SIGNAL AND FLASHER PROBLEMS

Most problems in the turn signals or flasher system, can be reduced to defective flashers or bulbs, which are easily replaced. Occasionally, problems in the turn signals are traced to the switch in the steering column, which will require professional service.

F=Front   R=Rear   ✳=Lights off   O=Lights on

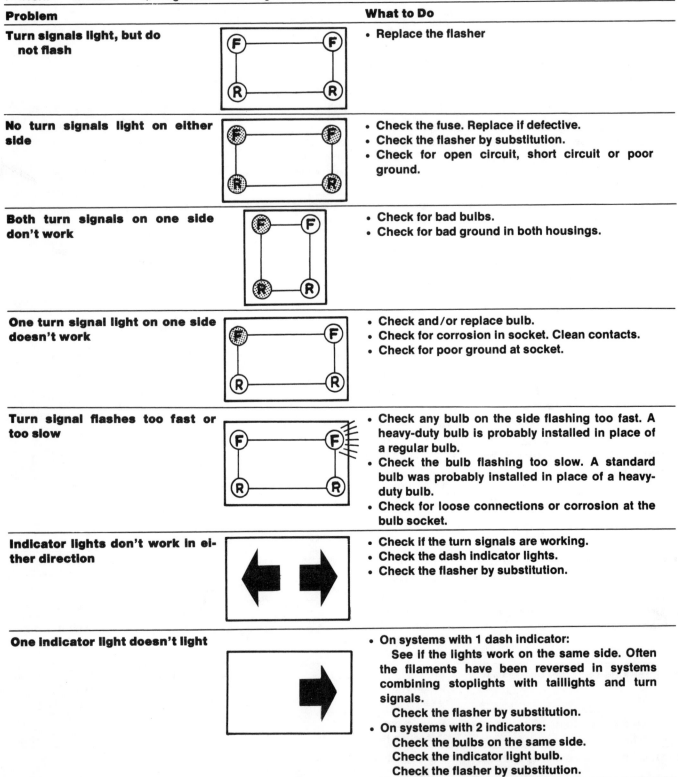

Problem		What to Do
Turn signals light, but do not flash		• Replace the flasher
No turn signals light on either side		• Check the fuse. Replace if defective. • Check the flasher by substitution. • Check for open circuit, short circuit or poor ground.
Both turn signals on one side don't work		• Check for bad bulbs. • Check for bad ground in both housings.
One turn signal light on one side doesn't work		• Check and/or replace bulb. • Check for corrosion in socket. Clean contacts. • Check for poor ground at socket.
Turn signal flashes too fast or too slow		• Check any bulb on the side flashing too fast. A heavy-duty bulb is probably installed in place of a regular bulb. • Check the bulb flashing too slow. A standard bulb was probably installed in place of a heavy-duty bulb. • Check for loose connections or corrosion at the bulb socket.
Indicator lights don't work in either direction		• Check if the turn signals are working. • Check the dash indicator lights. • Check the flasher by substitution.

One indicator light doesn't light		• On systems with 1 dash indicator:
		  See if the lights work on the same side. Often the filaments have been reversed in systems combining stoplights with taillights and turn signals.
		  Check the flasher by substitution.
		• On systems with 2 indicators:
		  Check the bulbs on the same side.
		  Check the indicator light bulb.
		  Check the flasher by substitution.

REPLACING HEADLIGHTS

Headlights are easily replaced. There are basically 2 kinds (round and rectangular) even though they are found in any number of configurations. The lights illustrated are typical of either kind. Be sure that the headlight adjusting screws are not disturbed when removing the headlight bezel or retaining ring. They are easily recognized by the thick plastic head (usually Phillips) as opposed to the sheet metal screws usually holding the retaining rings in place.

Rectangular Headlights

1. Remove the headlight bezel retaining screws. Don't disturb the headlight adjusting screws (arrows).

2. Remove the headlight bezel.

3. Remove the headlight retaining ring screws. Don't disturb the headlight adjusting screws (arrows).

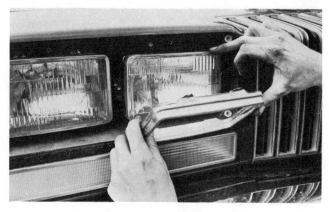

4. Remove the headlight retaining ring.

5. Remove the sealed beam and unplug the wiring harness from the rear of the lamp.

6. Connect the plug to a new sealed beam. Install the lamp, retaining ring and headlight bezel.

Round Headlights

1. Remove the headlight bezel retaining screws and the headlight bezel.

2. Sometimes the light retaining ring is held to the headlight bucket by a spring in addition to screws.

3. Remove the screws holding the headlight retaining ring.

4. Remove the headlight retaining ring.

5. Remove and unplug the headlight.

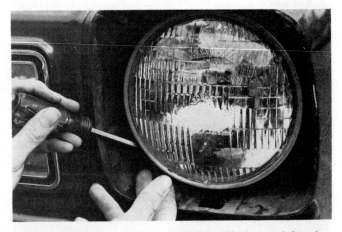

6. Connect the new lamp and install it with the retaining ring. Install the retaining ring screws and/or spring and install the headlight bezel.

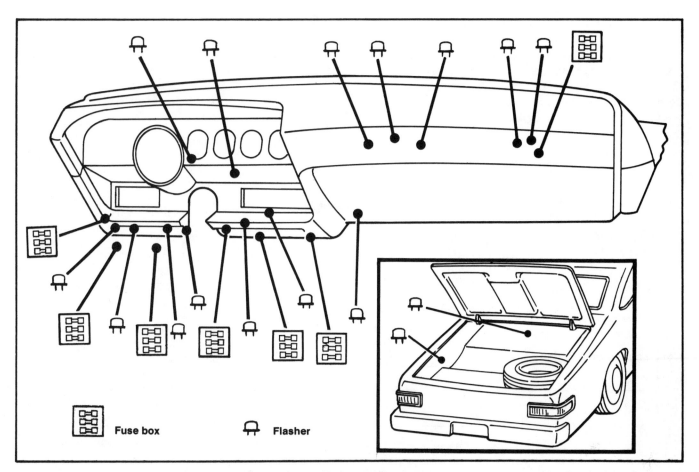

The flasher or fuse block can be found almost anywhere depending on the year and car model.

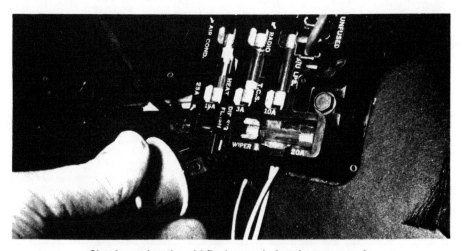

Simply unplug the old flasher and plug the new one in.

fuse box, and they operate the turn signal indicators and the hazard warning system. These don't go bad very often, but suspect the flasher if all the bulbs are in good condition. Con-versely, check the bulbs first, be-cause the flashers are designed to stop working when a bulb burns out alerting the driver to a prob-lem.

If you can't find the flasher right away, turn on the ignition and the turn signals and start hunting for the noise. When you find it, you'll be able to feel the vibration in the relay. Most flashers plug in and can usually be replaced by feel, even if you can't see them. Older cars use a three-pronged flasher, while newer ones use a two-pronged unit.

The flasher consists of a blade and resistance ribbon, which holds the blade in a bent posi-tion, until the flashered-circuit is activated. Current flows through the ribbon, heating it so that it elongates and relaxes its tension on the blade. The blade snaps away from the ribbon, breaking the circuit. In the absence of cur-rent, the ribbon cools rapidly and shrinks in length until the blade is pulled back into contact with the ribbon. This heating

PERIODIC MAINTENANCE FOR LIGHTS, FUSES AND FLASHERS

Lights, fuses and flashers give little warning before they go bad. About the only thing you can do is to periodically check the bulbs to be sure they are working. Fuses and flashers will give immediate evidence that they have ceased functioning.

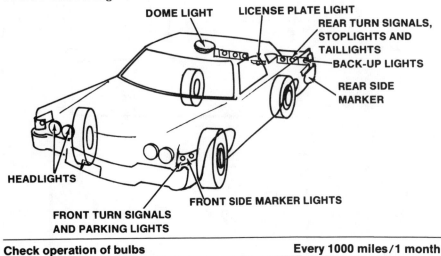

DOME LIGHT
LICENSE PLATE LIGHT
REAR TURN SIGNALS, STOPLIGHTS AND TAILLIGHTS
BACK-UP LIGHTS
REAR SIDE MARKER
HEADLIGHTS
FRONT SIDE MARKER LIGHTS
FRONT TURN SIGNALS AND PARKING LIGHTS

Check operation of bulbs	Every 1000 miles/1 month

and cooling cycle causes the flashing action in the circuit.

Rewiring

Almost anyone can replace frayed or otherwise damaged wires, as long as the proper tools and parts are available. Automotive wire terminals and connectors are available to fit almost any need. Be sure the ends of all wires are fitted with the proper terminal hardware and connectors. Wrapping a wire around a stud is never a permanent solution and will only cause trouble later.

Be sure that wires are replaced one at a time to avoid confusion, and route them neatly and out-of-the-way.

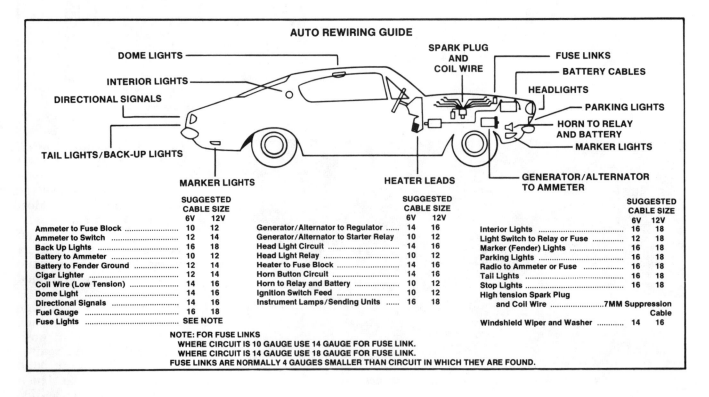

AUTO REWIRING GUIDE

DOME LIGHTS
INTERIOR LIGHTS
DIRECTIONAL SIGNALS
TAIL LIGHTS/BACK-UP LIGHTS
MARKER LIGHTS
HEATER LEADS
SPARK PLUG AND COIL WIRE
FUSE LINKS
BATTERY CABLES
HEADLIGHTS
PARKING LIGHTS
HORN TO RELAY AND BATTERY
MARKER LIGHTS
GENERATOR/ALTERNATOR TO AMMETER

	SUGGESTED CABLE SIZE			SUGGESTED CABLE SIZE			SUGGESTED CABLE SIZE	
	6V	12V		6V	12V		6V	12V
Ammeter to Fuse Block	10	12	Generator/Alternator to Regulator	14	16	Interior Lights	16	18
Ammeter to Switch	12	14	Generator/Alternator to Starter Relay	10	12	Light Switch to Relay or Fuse	12	18
Back Up Lights	16	18	Head Light Circuit	14	16	Marker (Fender) Lights	16	18
Battery to Ammeter	10	12	Head Light Relay	10	12	Parking Lights	16	18
Battery to Fender Ground	12	14	Heater to Fuse Block	14	16	Radio to Ammeter or Fuse	16	18
Cigar Lighter	12	14	Horn Button Circuit	14	16	Tail Lights	16	18
Coil Wire (Low Tension)	14	16	Horn to Relay and Battery	10	12	Stop Lights	16	18
Dome Light	14	16	Ignition Switch Feed	10	12	High tension Spark Plug		
Directional Signals	14	16	Instrument Lamps/Sending Units	16	18	and Coil Wire	7MM Suppression	Cable
Fuel Gauge	16	18				Windshield Wiper and Washer	14	16
Fuse Lights	SEE NOTE							

NOTE: FOR FUSE LINKS
WHERE CIRCUIT IS 10 GAUGE USE 14 GAUGE FOR FUSE LINK.
WHERE CIRCUIT IS 14 GAUGE USE 18 GAUGE FOR FUSE LINK.
FUSE LINKS ARE NORMALLY 4 GAUGES SMALLER THAN CIRCUIT IN WHICH THEY ARE FOUND.

15
Fuel System and Emission Controls

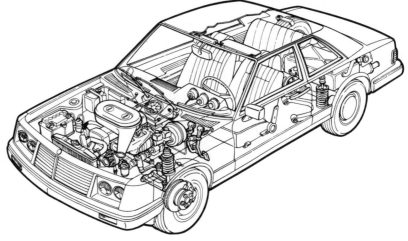

The Fuel System

An automotive fuel system consists of everything between the fuel tank and the carburetor or fuel injection unit. This includes the tank itself, all the lines, one or more fuel filters, a fuel pump (mechanical or electric), and the carburetor or fuel injection unit.

With the exception of the carburetor or fuel injection unit, the operation of the fuel system is quite simple. Fuel is drawn from the tank through the fuel line by the fuel pump, which forces it to the fuel filter and on to the carburetor where it is distributed to the cylinders.

Fuel Tank

Fuel tanks are normally located at the rear of the vehicle, although on rear-engined cars they are located at the front. The tank contains a fuel gauge sending unit and a filler tube. In most tanks, there is also a screen of some sort in the bottom of the tank near the pickup to filter out impurities.

Since the advent of emission controls, tanks are equipped with a control system to prevent fuel vapor from being discharged into the atmosphere. A vent line in the tank is connected to a filter in the engine compartment. Vapors from the tank are trapped in the filter canister, where they are routed back to the fuel tank, making the system a closed loop. All the fumes are prevented from escaping to the atmosphere. These systems also require the use of a special gas cap with an airtight seal.

Fuel Pump

There are two types of fuel pumps in general use: the mechanical pump and the electric pump. Mechanical pumps are the more common of the two and are used on nearly all American cars. Electric pumps are used on all fuel-injected cars (and some carburetor-equipped cars, such as the Vega) as well as a number of imported cars.

Mechanical fuel pumps are usually mounted on the side of the block and operated by an eccentric on the engine's camshaft. A pump rocker arm rests against the camshaft eccentric, and as the camshaft rotates, it causes

Typical mechanical fuel pump. Not all fuel pumps are this accessible, but they can all be found by following the fuel line backwards from the carburetor.

167

the rocker arm to rock back and forth. Inside the fuel pump, the rocker arm is connected to a flexible diaphragm. A spring, mounted underneath, maintains pressure on the diaphragm. As the rocker arm rocks, it pulls the diaphragm down and then releases it. Once the diaphragm is released, the spring pushes it back up. This continual diaphragm motion causes a partial vacuum and pressure in the space above the diaphragm. The vacuum sucks the fuel from the tank and the pressure pushes it toward the carburetor.

As a general rule, mechanical fuel pumps are quite dependable. When trouble does occur, it is usually caused by a cracked or broken diaphragm that does not draw sufficient fuel. Occasionally, the pump arm or spring will become so worn that the fuel pump can no longer produce an adequate supply of fuel, but this condition can be easily checked. Older fuel pumps can be rebuilt, but late-model pumps have a crimped edge and must be replaced if defective.

There are two general types of electric fuel pumps in use today. The impeller-type pump uses a vane or impeller which is driven by an electric motor. These pumps are often mounted in the fuel tank, though they are sometimes found below or beside the tank.

The bellows-type pump is becoming rare. The bellows pump ordinarily is mounted in the engine compartment and contains a flexible metal bellows operated by an electromagnet.

Most electric fuel pumps cannot be rebuilt and must be replaced if defective. Minor service is usually confined to checking electrical connections and checking for a blown fuse.

Fuel Filters

In addition to the screen located in the bottom of the fuel tank, all fuel systems have at least one other filter located

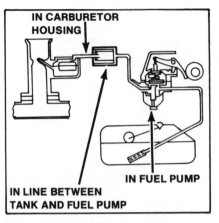

Likely fuel filter locations.

somewhere between the fuel tank and the carburetor. On some models, the filter is part of the fuel pump itself, on others it is located in the fuel line, and still others locate the filter in the carburetor inlet or the carburetor body itself. If you replace the fuel filter, you'll be amazed at the bits of sediment and dirt trapped by the filter.

In-line Filters

In-line filters are located between the fuel pump and the carburetor. They are connected to the metal fuel line by rubber hoses and clamps. Most are "throw-away" units with a paper element encased in a see-through plastic housing that allows you to view the amount of dirt trapped in the filter.

Some in-line filters consist of a replaceable pleated paper cartridge installed in a permanent filter housing. Their use is limited mostly to gasoline engine trucks. Most cars use the throw-away type.

In-the-Carburetor Filters

Fuel filters located in the carburetor are found mostly on GM cars and trucks. They consist of a small paper or bronze filter that is installed in the carburetor housing. They are extremely simple in design and are about as efficient as an in-line type.

The bronze filter is the least common and must be installed

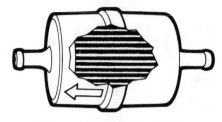

A disposable, throw-away filter.

A replaceable cartridge filter.

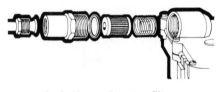

An in-the-carburetor filter.

A sintered bronze in-the-carburetor fuel filter.

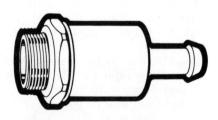

A screw-in, throw-away filter.

with the small cone section facing out. Both types are held in place by a threaded metal cap that attaches to the fuel line and screws into the carburetor fuel inlet.

Screw-In Filters

Screw in filters are very common on Ford vehicles. A screw in filter is threaded into the carburetor housing. The other end connects directly to the fuel line. Inside the filter housing is either a fine paper mesh or nylon element that filters out impurities. Like other in-line types, these are designed as throw-aways.

Fuel Filter/Water Separator

This type of filter is usually found on diesel cars and trucks and is being offered as an option on gasoline engine vehicles in areas where water in the fuel is a serious problem. It is designed for in-line installation and consists of a replaceable cartridge inside a corrosion-resistant housing.

Most operate as a two-stage filter. The lower stage removes dirt particles down to 1 micron in size and allows the water to form large droplets. In the second stage, fuel freely passes through the filter, but water will not. Water collects in the bottom of the filter housing, and a drain plug on the bottom of the housing is usually provided.

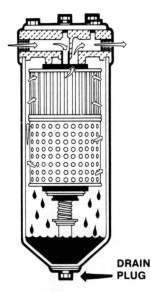

A fuel filter/water separator.

DRAIN PLUG

How Carburetors Work

The carburetor is the most complex part of the entire fuel system. Carburetors vary greatly in construction, but they all operate basically the same way. Their job is to supply the correct mixture of fuel and air to the engine in response to varying conditions.

Despite their complexity, carburetors function because of a simple physical principle, known as the venturi principle. Air is drawn into the engine by the pumping action of the pistons. As the air enters the top of the carburetor, it passes through a venturi, which is nothing more than a restriction in the throttle bore. The air speeds up as it passes through the venturi, causing a slight drop in pressure. This pressure drop pulls fuel from the float bowl through a nozzle into the throttle bore, where it mixes with the air and forms a fine mist, which is distributed to the cylinders through the intake manifold.

There are six different systems (fuel/air circuits) in a carburetor that make it work: the float system, main metering system, idle and low-speed system, accelerator pump system, power system, and the choke system. The way these systems are arranged in the carburetor determines the carburetor's size and shape.

It is hard to believe that the little single-barrel carburetor used on 4- or 6-cylinder engines have the same basic systems as the enormous 4-barrel carburetors used on V8 engines. Of course, the 4-barrels have more throttle bores ("barrels") and a lot of other hardware you won't find on the single-barrels. But, basically, all carburetors are similar, and if you understand a simple single-barrel, you can use that knowledge to understand a 4-barrel. If you'll study the explanations of the various systems, you'll discover that carburetors aren't as tricky as you thought they were. In fact, they're fairly simple, considering the job they have to do.

It's important to remember that carburetors seldom give trouble during normal operation. Other than changing the fuel and air filters and making sure the idle speed and mixture are ok at every tune-up, there's not much maintenance you can perform on the average carburetor.

Since they have so few moving parts, there isn't a lot in a carburetor to wear out. The only parts you might occasionally have trouble with are the throttle shaft, accelerator pump, and maybe the power valve. Ordinarily, carburetor problems are caused by dirt or gummy fuel deposits. Most other so-called carburetor problems are caused by other sources such as faulty breaker points, ignition timing, spark plugs, or even a clogged air filter. So if you suspect a problem in your carburetor, be sure you check everything else first.

Emission Control Systems

When viewed as a whole, emission control systems can be extremely confusing. But it is possible to ease some of the confusion by dividing the overall emissions system into several easily understood smaller systems.

There are four main systems in use on almost all cars today: the catalytic converter system, the positive crankcase ventilation (PCV) system, the air injection reactor (AIR) system, and the exhaust gas recirculation (EGR) system.

CARBURETOR OPERATING PRINCIPLES

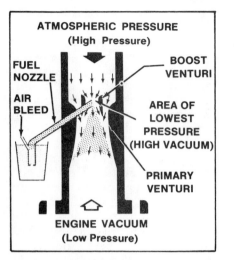

The venturi principle in operation. The pumping action of the pistons creates a vacuum which is amplified by the venturi in the carburetor. This pressure drop will pull fuel from the float bowl through the fuel nozzle. Unfortunately, there is not enough suction present at idle or low speed to make this system work, which is why the carburetor is equipped with an idle and low speed circuit.

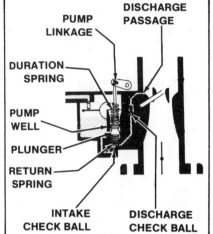

Accelerator pump system. When the throttle is opened, the air flowing through the venturi starts flowing faster almost immediately, but there is a lag in the flow of fuel out of the main nozzle. The result is that the engine runs lean and stumbles. It needs an extra shot of fuel just when the throttle is opened. This shot is provided by the accelerator pump, which is nothing more than a little pump operated by the throttle linkage that shoots a squirt of fuel through a separate nozzle into the throat of the carburetor.

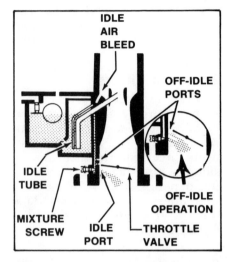

Idle and low-speed system. The vacuum in the intake manifold at idle is high because the throttle is almost completely closed. This vacuum is used to draw fuel into the engine through the idle system and keep it running. Vacuum acts on the idle jet (usually a calibrated tube that sticks down into the main well, below the fuel level) and sucks the fuel into the engine. The idle mixture screw is there to limit the amount of fuel that can go into the engine.

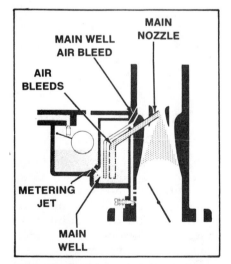

The main metering system may be the simplest system of all, since it is simply the venturi principle in operation. At cruising speeds, the engine sucks enough air to constantly draw fuel through the main fuel nozzle. The main fuel nozzle or jet is calibrated to provide a metering system. The metering system is necessary to prevent an excess amount of fuel flowing into the intake manifold, creating an overly rich mixture.

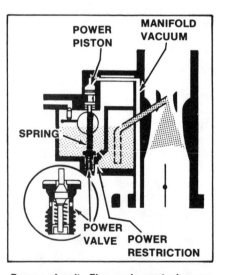

Power circuit. The main metering system works very well at normal engine loads, but when the throttle is in the wide-open position, the engine needs more fuel to prevent detonation and give it full power. The power system provides additional fuel by opening up another passage that leads to the main nozzle. This passageway is controlled by a power valve.

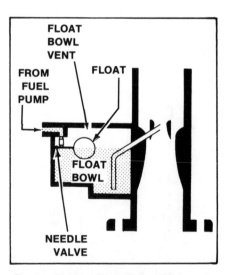

Float circuit. When the fuel pump pushes fuel into the carburetor, it flows through a seat and past a needle which is a kind of shutoff valve. The fuel flows into the float bowl and raises a hinged float so that the float arm pushes the needle into the seat and shuts off the fuel. When the fuel level drops, the float drops and more fuel enters the bowl. In this way, a constant fuel supply is maintained.

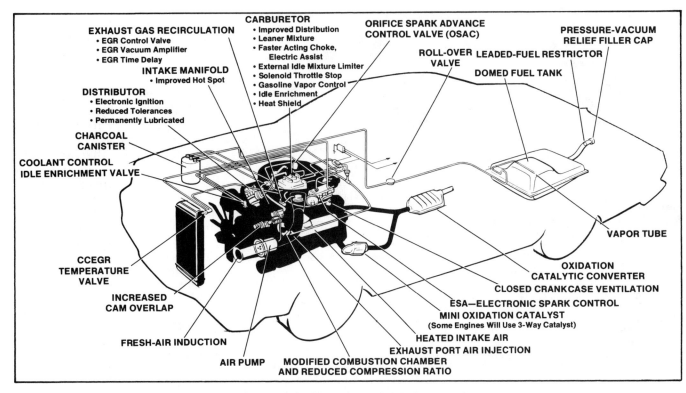

Most of the emission control systems in use today.

Catalytic Converter

The catalytic converter is a device inserted in the exhaust system that treats the exhaust gases so that harmful carbon monoxide (CO) and hydrocarbons (HC) are converted to harmless carbon dioxide and water vapor.

The converter is installed in the exhaust system as close to the engine as possible, usually under the front seat or slightly forward of the seat. It looks a little like a muffler, but does not function as a muffler in any way. Instead it functions as a catalyst, encouraging a reaction between two or more substances without being involved in the end product. The catalyst used in converters is platinum, which is efficient and long-lived, but expensive.

While catalytic converters are built in a wide variety of shapes and sizes, they all fall into two general types, the pellet, or bead type and the monolithic type. Construction may differ slightly, but the object is the same—to present the largest possible surface area to passing exhaust gases.

There are some problems associated with catalytic converter usage that most of us are aware of. One is that the converters tend to run extremely hot and require shielding. Another problem is that converter-equipped cars require unleaded gasoline. The use of a leaded gasoline will poison the catalyst and render the converter useless.

Catalytic Converter Precautions

The catalytic converter operates at extreme temperatures, well over 1000° F, so many converter problems can be traced to overheating. To prevent catalytic converter overheating, avoid the following:

1. Use of fuel system additives or cleaning agents.

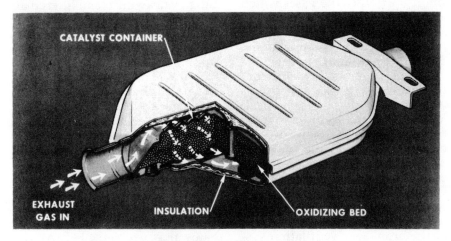

Cutaway of a catalytic converter.

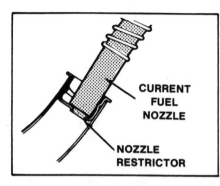

Cars with catalytic converters have a restrictor in the filler neck to prevent filling from leaded gas pumps which have a larger pump nozzle.

2. Operating the car with an inoperative choke.
3. Extended periods of dieseling (run-on).
4. Shutting off the ignition with the car in motion.
5. Ignition or charging system failure.
6. Misfiring of one or more plugs.
7. Disconnecting a plug wire with the engine running.
8. Push or tow starting the car when the engine is hot.
9. Pumping the gas pedal to start a hot engine.

Positive Crankcase Ventilation Systems

Since the early sixties, all cars have been equipped with crankcase ventilation systems.

When the engine is running, a small portion of the gases which are formed in the combustion chamber leak past the piston rings and enter the crankcase. Since these gases are under pressure, they tend to escape from the crankcase and enter the atmosphere. If these gases are allowed to remain in the crankcase for any length of time, they contaminate the engine oil and cause sludge to build up in the crankcase. If the gases are allowed to escape to the atmosphere, they pollute the air with unburned hydrocarbons. The job of the crankcase ventilation system is to recycle these gases back

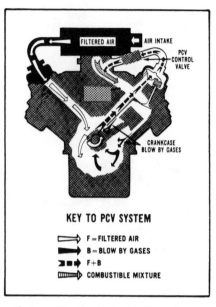

KEY TO PCV SYSTEM

F = FILTERED AIR
B = BLOW BY GASES
F + B
COMBUSTIBLE MIXTURE

Schematic of a typical PCV system.

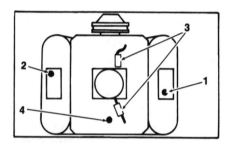

Likely PCV valve locations—(1-2) in either valve cover, (3) at the carburetor or (4) in the intake manifold.

into the engine combustion chamber where they are reburned.

The crankcase (blow-by) gases are recycled as the engine is running by drawing clean filtered air through the air filter and into the crankcase. As the air passes through the crankcase, it picks up the combustion gases and carries them out of the crankcase, through the oil separator, through the PCV valve, and into the induction system. As they enter the intake manifold, they are drawn into the combustion chamber where they are reburned.

The most critical component in the system is the PCV valve which controls the amount of gases that are recycled. At low engine speeds, the valve is par-

tially closed, limiting the flow of gases. As engine speed increases, the valve opens to admit greater quantities of air to the intake manifold.

If the PCV valve becomes blocked or plugged, the gases will be prevented from escaping from the crankcase by the normal route. Since they are under pressure, they will find their own way out of the crankcase. This alternate route is usually a weak oil seal or gasket in the engine. As the gas escapes by the gasket, it usually creates an oil leak. Besides causing oil leaks, a clogged PCV valve also allows these gases to remain in the crankcase for an extended period of time, promoting the formation of sludge in the engine.

Air Injection Systems

Sometimes called air pump systems, these systems have been around since the middle sixties. Air pump or air injection systems have a lot of hardware, with hoses and lines running all over the place, which makes them look very complicated. But in actuality air injection systems are one of the simplest emission control systems.

The air pump is driven by a belt at the front of the engine, and it pumps air under a pressure of only a few pounds into each exhaust port. The hydrocarbons and carbon monoxide that come out of the port are very hot, and mixing in extra air causes them to burn in the exhaust manifold. The carbon monoxide and hydrocarbons are converted to carbon dioxide and water, the harmless by-products of combustion. Stainless steel nozzles are used to direct air into the port as close to the exhaust valve as possible (stainless steel is used so that the nozzle will not burn up).

Between the nozzles and the pump is a check valve to keep the hot exhaust gases from flowing back into the pump and hoses and destroying them. Pumps also utilize a gulp valve or a diverter

TROUBLESHOOTING BASIC FUEL SYSTEM PROBLEMS

Many problems in the fuel system can be traced to dirt or moisture in the system, or to clogged fuel or air filters. Changing filters at regular intervals will eliminate most problems.

The Problem	Is Caused By	What to Do
Engine cranks, but won't start (or is hard to start) when cold	• Empty fuel tank • Incorrect starting procedure • Defective fuel pump • No fuel in carburetor • Clogged fuel filter • Engine flooded • Defective choke • Water in fuel has frozen	• Check for fuel in tank • Follow correct procedure • Check pump output—See "Servicing the Fuel System" • Check for fuel in the carburetor —See "Servicing the Fuel System" • Replace fuel filter • Wait 15 minutes; try again—See "Servicing the Fuel System" • Check choke plate—See "Servicing the Fuel System" • See "Servicing the Fuel System"
Engine cranks, but is hard to start (or does not start) when hot —(presence of fuel is assumed)	• Defective choke • Vapor lock	• Check choke plate—See "Servicing the Fuel System" • See "Servicing the Fuel System"
Rough idle or engine runs rough	• Dirt or moisture in fuel • Clogged air filter • Faulty fuel pump	• Replace fuel filter • Replace air filter • Check fuel pump output—See "Servicing the Fuel System"
Engine stalls or hesitates on acceleration	• Dirt or moisture in the fuel • Dirty carburetor • Defective fuel pump • Incorrect float level, defective accelerator pump	• Replace fuel filter • Clean the carburetor—See "Servicing the Fuel System" • Check fuel pump output—See "Servicing the Fuel System" • Have carburetor checked
Poor gas mileage	• Clogged air filter • Dirty carburetor • Defective choke, faulty carburetor adjustment	• Replace air filter • Clean carburetor—See "Servicing the Fuel System" • Have carburetor checked
Engine is flooded (won't start accompanied by smell of raw fuel)	• Improperly adjusted choke or carburetor	• Wait 15 minutes and try again, without pumping gas pedal. See "Servicing the Carburetor" • If it won't start, have carburetor checked

SYMPTOMS OF FAULTY EMISSIONS SYSTEMS

Symptom	Possible Cause
Rough Idle	Faulty PCV valve or clogged lines Faulty EGR valve
Hesitation on acceleration	Faulty PCV valve
Backfiring	Faulty air pump check valve
Overheating	Heater air cleaner defective

valve. Early systems used a gulp valve, while later systems use diverter valves. They both operate on the same principle.

During deceleration, when the throttle is closed, the high vacuum in the intake manifold pulls a lot of fuel into the engine and out the exhaust system. If the pump continued pumping during deceleration, you could cause an explosion in the exhaust system that could blow the muffler apart. To prevent this, a valve is connected between the pump and the intake manifold. A small sensing line leads from the valve diaphragm to the intake manifold. During deceleration, the vacuum through the sensing line acts on the diaphragm, which

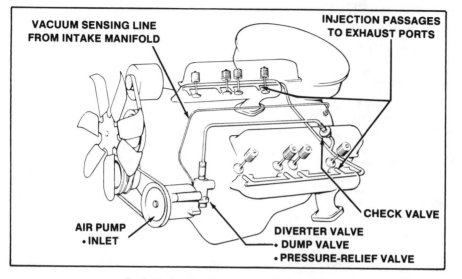

Typical air injection reactor(AIR) system.

pulls the valve open, allowing all of the air from the pump to flow directly into the intake manifold.

There were several problems associated with the gulp valve (most noticeably a tendency for the engine to continue running during deceleration), so it was replaced by the diverter valve, which is simply a more sophisticated version of the gulp valve.

EGR Systems

Exhaust gas recirculation (EGR) systems have been in use since 1973. They are used primarily to lower peak combustion chamber temperatures and control the formation of nitrous oxide (NOx). NOx emissions at low combustion temperatures are not severe, but when the combustion temperature goes over 2500° F, the production of NOx in the combustion chambers shoots way up.

You can lower the peak combustion temperatures by retarding the spark or by introducing an inert gas to dilute the fuel/air mixture. Introducing exhaust gases into the combustion chamber is a little like throwing water-soaked wood on a blazing fire. The water-soaked wood won't burn, so the fire cools down and doesn't roar as much. Put a little exhaust gas in the

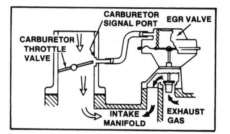

EGR system operation.

combustion chamber and it takes the place of a certain amount of the air/fuel mixture. When the spark ignites the mixture, there isn't as much to burn, so the fire is not as hot. Also, the engine doesn't put out as much power.

The amount of exhaust gas recirculated is kept to a minimum. It's surprising how little exhaust gas it takes to cool down the peak combustion temperatures.

The controlling element in the EGR system is the EGR valve. The EGR valve is mounted on the intake manifold so that when the valve opens, exhaust gases are allowed to pass from the crossover passage into the throat under the carburetor.

The EGR valve is vacuum operated, sometimes by intake manifold vacuum, and sometimes by ported (carburetor) vacuum. The ported vacuum systems are the simplest. At idle, the

port is above the throttle blade, so that the EGR valve stays closed. When the throttle is opened, vacuum acts on the port and the EGR valve opens. At wide-open throttle, there is no intake manifold vacuum, so the EGR valve closes to give the engine maximum power.

Most EGR systems also use a temperature control of some kind. The control can be electric or mechanical. When the engine coolant temperature is below a specified level, the EGR system is locked out.

Periodic Maintenance

The major components of the fuel system—the carburetor and the fuel pump—are quite reliable in themselves. Fuel system maintenance consists mostly of keeping them clean and changing them at regular intervals. Dirt and foreign matter of any sort are the major enemies of the fuel system.

About the only component of the emission control system that requires regular replacement is the PCV valve. If you do a lot of high-speed driving, it's a good idea to check the PCV valve more frequently than the recommended intervals, especially if the car is older.

Checking/Replacing the PCV Valve

PCV valves are generally, though not always, located in the valve cover. If you are unsure of the location of the valve, check the owners manual.

A general test is to remove the PCV valve from the valve cover and shake it. If a rattle is heard, the valve is usually OK.

A more accurate test is:
1. Connect a tachometer to the engine.
2. With the engine idling, remove the PCV valve from its mount.
3. Check the tachometer reading. Place a finger over the valve

FUEL FILTER REPLACEMENT

Replace the fuel filter every 12,000 miles or 12 months, whichever comes first. There are basically only 3 types of fuel filters. The one on your car or truck will be similar to one of these.

General Motors (filter located in carburetor housing)

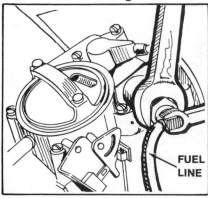

The fuel filter is located behind the large fuel line inlet nut on the carburetor.

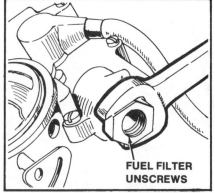

Remove the larger filter retaining nut from the carburetor. The spring behind the filter will push the filter out.

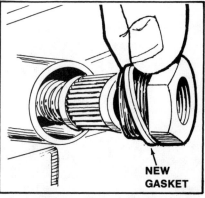

Install the new filter and the spring. Some carburetors have a paper element; others have a bronze element.

Ford Motor Company (filter located externally on carburetor housing)

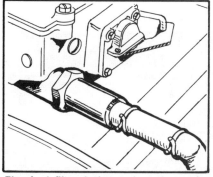

The fuel filter is located at the carburetor inlet.

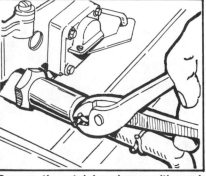

Remove the retaining clamps with a pair of pliers.

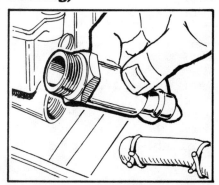

Unscrew the old filter and remove it from the carburetor. Install the new filter.

Inline Filters (AMC, Chrysler and most imports, etc.)

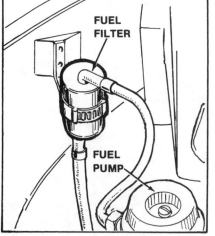

Inline fuel filters are very common and easily replaced. Locate the filter and remove the hose clamps from the hoses.

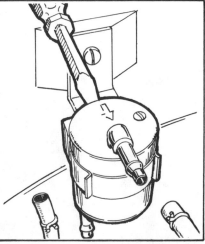

If the filter is held by a retaining clip, remove it from the clip and disconnect the hoses.

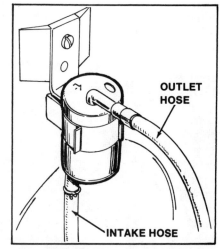

Install the fuel filter, making sure you connect the inlet and outlet hoses correctly. Fuel flow is usually marked on the filter.

AIR FILTER REPLACEMENT

The air filter is never very difficult to find. It is almost always inside a large can-type housing on top of the carburetor or fuel injection air intake. It will only take a few minutes to replace the air filter and it will go a long way toward allowing your engine to operate at maximum efficiency. Tests have shown that a completely clogged air cleaner can reduce gas mileage as much as 1-3 miles per gallon.

1. *Unscrew the wingnut and put it aside. Sometimes there are several clips that have to be released before the cover can be removed.*

2. *Remove the old air filter. If only slightly dirty, it can be gently tapped on a hard surface to dislodge dirt. If it is extremely dirty, discard it.*

3. *Check the small crankcase breather filter. If it's dirty, remove and discard it also.*

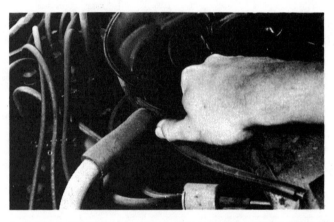

4. *Remove the clip, crankcase filter elbow, and the filter (if equipped).*

5. *Install a new crankcase filter. Put the elbow back on the filter neck.*

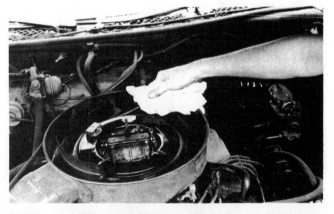

6. *Wipe the inside of the filter housing clean and install a new filter. Reinstall the air cleaner cover.*

A magnified view of a section of a typical air filter. The air filter stops dirt and dust from getting into the engine.

FUEL AND EMISSIONS SYSTEM MAINTENANCE INTERVALS

Your car's fuel and emissions systems will work efficiently if it is maintained at these intervals.

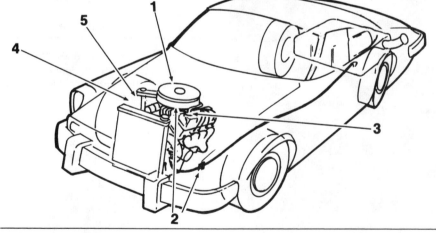

1. **Replace air filter and crankcase breather filter** — Every 12,000 miles/12 months
2. **Replace fuel filter** — Every 12,000 miles/12 months
3. **Check/replace PCV valve** — Check every 12,000 miles/12 months Replace every 24,000 miles/2 years
4. **Replace carbon canister filter element** — Every 15,000 miles
5. **Check/adjust air pump belt tension** — Every 3000 miles/3 months*

*New belts will stretch. Check tension after new belt is installed after 200 miles.

or hose opening. A suction should be felt.

4. Check the tachometer again. The engine speed should have dropped at least 50 rpm. It should return to normal when you remove your finger from the opening.

5. If the engine does not change speed or if the change is less than 50 rpm, the hose is clogged or the valve is defective. Check the hose first. If the hose is not clogged, replace the PCV valve.

6. Test the new valve to make sure that it is operating properly.

Check Air Pump Belt Tension

The condition and proper tensioning of the drive belt are vital to the proper operation of the air pump. A belt which is too loose will not drive the air pump fast enough, and a belt that is too tight will damage the bearings. The belt should produce about

The air pump drive belt should have about ½" play at the middle of its longest span under thumb pressure.

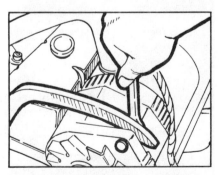

Loosen the adjusting bolt to adjust the air pump belt tension.

Pull the PCV valve from its grommet on the valve cover to test or replace it.

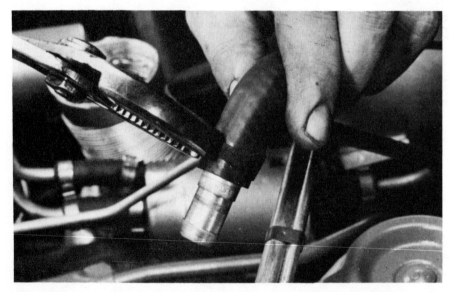

Squeeze the clamp with pliers and slide the clamp up the hose. Pull the PCV valve out of the hose.

the tachometer red (+) lead to the distributor side of the coil (the side that connects to the small wire leading from the distributor). Connect the black lead to ground. Electronic ignitions have specific tachometer hookup procedures and not all tachometers will work on an electronic ignition. Check with the tachometer manufacturer to determine if your tach will work on electronic ignition.

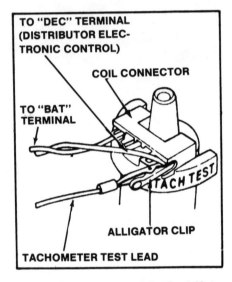

This is the tach hook-up for Ford Motor vehicles with electronic ignition. The tachometer connects to the terminal marked "tach-test."

The tach terminal on GM electronic ignitions distributors is shown by arrow.

½" deflection in the middle of its longest span under thumb pressure. If the tension is not correct, loosen the adjusting and/or pivot bolts and tighten the belt. Do not pry on the air pump housing.

Replacing the belt is very similar to replacing the alternator or fan belt. See Section 12 "Starting and Charging System" or Section 9 "Cooling System" for belt replacement and information on how to spot bad drive belts.

Idle Speed Adjustment

You will need a tachometer to adjust the idle speed. On conventional ignition systems, connect

PUMP YOUR OWN GAS

By some estimates, ⅓ of all the gasoline pumped in the U.S. is at self-service pumps. More and more drivers are trading the privilege of being waited on for the 2¢-5¢ per gallon saving, which can add up to as much as $1.00 on every fill-up. Self-service gasoline is now legal in all 50 states and is increasing in popularity. It doesn't take much more effort to pump your own gas and pocket the savings.

1. Pull the car into a lane so that the filler cap is on the same side as the pump. If you have a center filler cap, don't go too far past the pump. At some stations you'll have to pay first, but it's easier to overpay and get a refund than to underpay.

3. Remove the filler cap and put it where you'll remember it. Insert the pump nozzle about half-way into the filler pipe and squeeze the trigger. If the flow stops immediately, you're pumping too fast or the nozzle is inserted too far. Release the trigger and squeeze it gently.

2. Gasoline pumps will only function when the numbers are at zero. Most self-service pumps have directions. Remove the nozzle from its holder and turn the lever ¼ turn (depending on the pump). This will return all numbers to zero and start the pump.

4. When the tank is full, the flow will stop automatically. Don't try to squeeze in too much gas; it will only overflow onto the fender or you. Return the operating lever and nozzle to their original positions and replace the gas cap.

CARBON CANISTER FILTER REPLACEMENT

To prevent fuel vapors from escaping into the atmosphere, a carbon canister is used to trap fumes. Keep the canister operating efficiently by changing the filter every 12,000 miles or 12 months, whichever comes first.

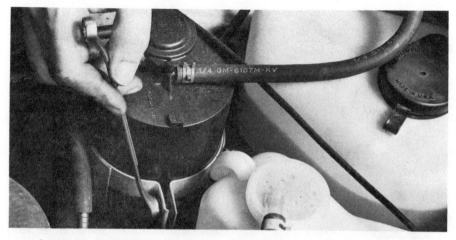

Locate the carbon canister and loosen the clamp to remove the canister.

The filter is located in the bottom of the canister. Remove and discard the old filter. Install the new filter.

Reinstall the canister in the clamp and check to be sure the hoses are tight.

Servicing the Fuel System

To help locate the source of a suspected problem in the fuel system, check the following points, in conjunction with the troubleshooting chart.

Fuel in the Tank

Make sure there is fuel in the tank. Normally, the easiest way to do this is to trust the fuel gauge. Gauges do not normally go bad, though they have been known to read erratically.

Fuel at the Carburetor

To check if fuel is getting to the carburetor, remove the air cleaner and open the choke butterfly flap, which is located at the top of the carburetor. If the engine is warm, the flap should already be open. Look down into the carburetor as someone operates the gas pedal several times or as you move the throttle linkage yourself.

Each time the throttle is moved, a small stream of gas should squirt into the carburetor. If not, the fuel filter could be clogged or the fuel pump could be at fault.

Fuel Pump Output

If there is no fuel at the carburetor and the fuel filter is not clogged, the problem is most likely the fuel pump. Before testing the pump, tighten the pump diaphragm screws around the

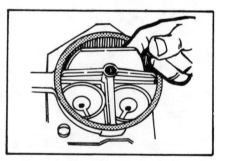

Check for gas at the carburetor by looking down the carburetor throat while someone moves the accelerator. Do not attempt to start the engine while looking into the carburetor.

IDLE SPEED ADJUSTMENT

The most important external carburetor adjustment, and the one most often necessary, is the idle speed adjustment.

Idle speed adjustment is made on a warm engine and the transmission in Drive (automatic) or neutral (manual). When setting the idle in gear, be sure to block the wheels and set the parking brake. You'll need a tachometer to tell the idle speed and the specification can be found in the back of this book or on the tune-up decal under the hood. If there is no decal, the car should creep slightly in Drive, with your foot off the brake.

Idle Speed Screws

The idle speed screw is usually located down low on the carburetor next to the throttle lever. Don't mistake the idle speed screw for the fast idle screw. The fast idle screw provides a faster idle speed while the engine is warming up and operates against a stepped cam. The difference will be obvious on a warm engine; the fast idle screw won't touch anything and turning it will have no effect on idle speed.

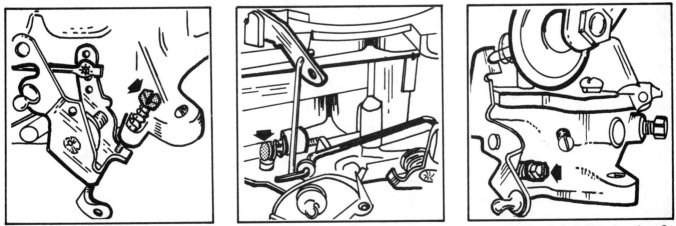

On most carburetors (1, 2, 3) the throttle screws are in plain view and easily accessible after removing the air filter housing. On cars without solenoids, the throttle screw is the only curb idle adjustment.

Throttle Solenoids

Since the early 1970's, most manufacturers have used a throttle solenoid to prevent "run-on" or dieseling.

Solenoids usually have 2 settings—the "curb idle" and the "low or off-idle" speed. Curb idle is the normal idle speed on a warm engine. Low or off-idle is set with a throttle screw after electrically disconnecting the solenoid and is always lower than the curb idle speed.

Some cars (principally early 70's GM) have a CEC (Combination Emission Control) valve, which resembles a solenoid but is not to be used to adjust idle speed. CEC valves (regardless of manufacture) are usually labeled.

A positive test for a solenoid is to shut off the A/C, open the throttle by hand, and have someone turn the ignition key to ON (don't start the engine). If the solenoid stem extends, you have an idle solenoid and curb idle is set with the solenoid.

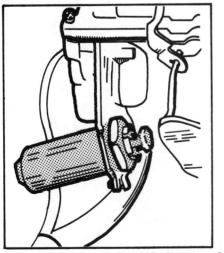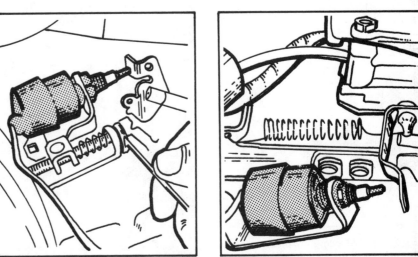

The most common solenoid is found on GM vehicles (1). Idle speed is adjusted by turning the hex-headed end of the shaft. Other cars (2) have a rack that moves the whole solenoid bracket or a threaded body and locknut (3) to rotate the entire solenoid.

flange and be sure the fuel lines are tight.

There are two ways to check the fuel pump output. Ordinarily, vacuum gauges double as fuel pump testers, so you get two tools for the price of one. A simple volume test can be performed by unhooking the fuel line from the carburetor and holding it over a can or jar. Have someone crank the engine for a couple of seconds. Be sure to direct the gas line away from hot manifolds and other components. If the fuel pump is operating properly, it should pump fuel out in steady, regular spurts. Intermittent spurts or very little fuel probably indicate a problem in the pump.

Dirt or Water in the Fuel

Occasionally, you can get a tankful of "bad" gas, contaminated with dirt or water, which will cause the engine to hesitate or run rough. Dirt can get lodged around the small jets and orifices in the carburetor, and in cold weather, water can freeze around the pick-up screen or filter. Fuel additives are available to dissolve the ice in the line.

Small specks of dirt in the carburetor can be dislodged by removing the air cleaner and covering the top of the carburetor with the palm of your hand while someone operates the starter briefly. This draws heavily on fuel in the float bowl and tends to wash away small particles of dirt.

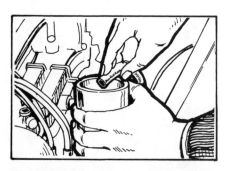

Check the fuel pump by disconnecting the output line (fuel pump to carburetor) at the carburetor and operating the starter briefly.

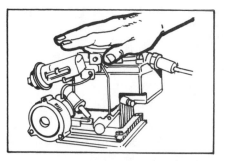

Specks of dirt can be dislodged from the carburetor by holding the palm of your hand over the carburetor and operating the starter.

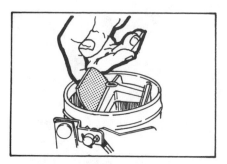

If the engine floods repeatedly, check the choke butterfly flap.

Dirty Carburetor

There are many commercial carburetor cleaners for the inside and outside of the carburetor. Gum, varnish, and carbon tend to build up on the inside of the carburetor and clog the small

jets and holes. Regular applications of carburetor cleaner can prevent this build-up. Follow the manufacturers directions on the can.

Oil and grease also build up on the outside of the carburetor and can cause the throttle and choke shafts to bind. Spray a carburetor linkage lubricant on the linkage and the choke and throttle shafts where they enter the carburetor housing.

Flooded Engine

A flooded engine is the result of too much gas entering the cylinders, either due to a sticking choke or the inability of the plugs to fire. It is usually accompanied by the smell of raw gas.

If the engine floods repeatedly, check that the choke butterfly flap is not stuck. Remove the air cleaner and move the butterfly flap with your finger. It should open freely (all the way) if the engine is hot and return to almost completely closed if the engine is cold.

The best cure for a flooded engine is to open the hood and let it stand for 15 to 20 minutes to let the accumulated raw fuel evaporate. Try not to pump the gas when restarting the car.

Choke cap showing the index marks and notches (arrow).

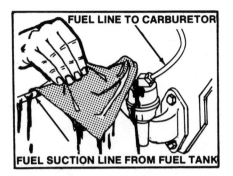

Vapor lock can be cured faster by draping a wet cloth over the fuel pump.

Vapor Lock

Vapor lock occurs on hot days, usually because fuel lines are routed too close to a hot exhaust manifold or other heated part.

Fuel begins to boil in the lines and the resulting bubbles block the flow of fuel. Vapor lock is recognizable when the car stops running for no apparent reason and, after standing for a time, starts again.

The cure for vapor lock is to raise the hood and let the engine cool until the bubbles blocking the flow of fuel condense. You can hasten the cooling process by draping a wet rag over the fuel pump or fuel line (suction line) running between the tank and fuel pump.

Another temporary cure on the road is to wrap the fuel line in tin foil anywhere it passes very close to a hot engine component. The tin foil will tend to reflect the heat from the engine.

Choke Adjustment

A properly adjusted choke should seldom require attention. However, there are occasions when it is necessary to either enrich or lean out the mixture to ease starting. Loosen the screws holding the choke cap in place and rotate the cap.

■

Chilton Tip

Mark the original setting of the choke cap with a screwdriver or white paint. Most caps are marked to indicate which direction is lean and rich. Normally, you will want to enrich the mixture about 2 notches in the winter and lean it out about 2 notches in summer.

■

16
Windshield Wipers and Washers

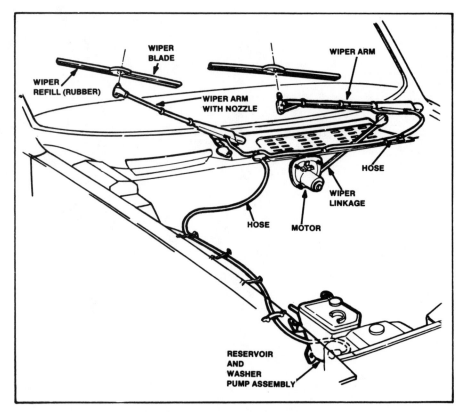

Windshield Wipers

The first windshield wipers were an inside, hand-operated crank connected to an outside arm holding a rubber wiper blade, and operated back and forth by the driver. Later, for the convenience of the passenger, a blade and arm was installed on the passenger's side of the windshield and connected to the arm on the driver's side by linkage and operated in tandem with the driver's wiper.

This was unsatisfactory and was replaced by the vacuum wiper motor which operated the wiper arms using the vacuum from the car engine. This type of motor was used as late as the early '20's, mounted along the

Typical windshield wiper system.

roof line and later moved to the cowl panel, directly below the windshield.

The major difficulty plaguing

the vacuum motor was its inability to maintain a constant wiper blade speed. As the engine vacuum was lowered (when the car

184

went uphill for instance), the wipers would stop and cause visibility problems.

Vacuum holding tanks with one-way check valves and mechanical vacuum pumps were used to maintain a constant vacuum supply, but as the car designs changed, the windshield became larger and the wiper motor's work load increased. The added work load could not be handled by vacuum wipers.

Vacuum wipers gave way to electric wiper motors, first installed on cars as an option as early as 1940. The electric motor was dependable and could operate the wipers independent of the fluctuation in engine vacuum, and by 1972, all original equipment vacuum wiper motor installations had ceased.

Electric wiper motors are generally one or two speed units, with three speed units used as options. A delayed or intermittent wiper control is also available to use in a mist or light drizzle when the wipers are not continually needed. An adjustable time interval of three to twenty seconds is usually provided for the delayed wiper operation.

How Vacuum Wipers Work

Although the vacuum wiper motors have been discontinued as standard equipment on the new cars, many older cars are still equipped with them, continually harassing unfortunate drivers.

The vacuum wiper motor is a semi-circular, enclosed chamber housing a neoprene coated paddle to which the wiper linkage drive arm is attached.

An air intake tube or opening, a vacuum tube, a movable valve mechanism, and a slide control unit are mounted on or near the top of the wiper motor to operate and control the linkage.

Theoretically, vacuum (low pressure) and atmospheric pres-

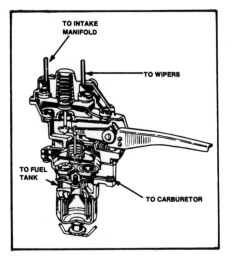

Vacuum pump and fuel pump combined in one unit supplies vacuum to operate vacuum windshield wipers.

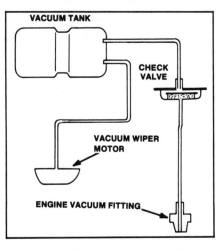

Vacuum holding tank and check valve are needed for vacuum wiper systems.

sure (high pressure) are regulated in the motor chamber and act upon the opposite sides of the paddle, forcing it to move from the high pressure side to the low pressure side. As the paddle moves to its limit within the chamber, a valve mechanism is tripped by a cam on the paddle, which causes the vacuum and atmospheric pressure to change sides within the chamber, reversing the reaction on the paddle, pushing it back to the other side where the valve mechanism is again tripped, and the sequence is reversed.

All this assumes that a high vacuum is available from the

engine. Unfortunately, whenever the throttle is opened (to go up a hill) engine vacuum falls off, and the pressure on the vacuum side of the paddle nearly equals the atmospheric pressure on the other side. The net result is that the paddle does not move and neither do the wipers, until you take your foot off the gas, creating more engine vacuum.

When the wiper motor is turned off, the paddle is held in the park position by the valve mechanism (which is prevented from tripping) and a vacuum reaction on the paddle.

If the wiper motor becomes defective, the entire motor must be replaced.

How the Electric Wiper Motor Works

The electric wiper motor is a permanent magnet, rotary electric motor. A worm gear machined on the armature shaft drives the output shaft and gear through an idler gear and shaft. The output shaft operates the output arm, which is connected to the wiper linkage. As the electric motor revolves the output arm, the linkage is forced to move in a back and forth motion.

The speed of the electric motor is controlled by resistors, located on or in the control switch, and connected to the wiper motor electrical windings. The control switch directs the current through certain circuits of the wiper motor, as the driver desires.

Wiper Linkage

Regardless of the type of drive motor used, the wiper linkage remains basically the same.

As the drive output arm is revolved or moved back and forth by the operation of the wiper motor, the force of this movement is transmitted by the linkage, to the linkage pivots, to which the wiper arms and blades are attached. As the linkage pivots are forced to rotate, the arms and blades move on the windshield in a predetermined arc.

Two types of linkages are used—depressed and non-depressed. The depressed types are hidden below the hood line when in the park position, while the non-depressed types are visible above the hood line when in their park position.

Windshield Washers

Windshield washers are installed in different cars in different ways.

A few cars have the washers operated by foot pressure, while others have the washers operated by electric motors, mounted separately or mounted in combination with the wiper motor. All types are controlled by the driver.

The nozzle arrangements are different in the respect that the locations can range from a single base with adjustable offset nozzles, to a single nozzle for the right and left sides, mounted on the cowl panel and individually aimed at the windshield.

Another location of the washer nozzles are on the wiper arms, distributing the fluid spray over the windshield as the arms go through their cleaning arcs.

On certain car models, the washer pump can be activated and the wipers will automatically start and stop after a predetermined time, while on others the wipers must be stopped manually.

Plastic or rubber tubing is used to route the washer fluid from the reservoir, through the pump and check-valves, and to the washer nozzles.

Periodic Maintenance

Changing Wiper Blades

First, don't forget that many vehicles have rear wipers as well as front wipers.

Normally, the wiper blade rubber refills should be changed at least once a year (see "Servicing the Wipers"), depending upon

the type of weather and the amount of use. If the wipers receive greater than average use or if the car is left outdoors much of the time, both the blades and the refills should be replaced more often.

The blade base should be inspected for kinks along the frame, bent or broken lever or yoke jaws and broken or rusted blade saddles at each refill replacement.

Always replace refills or blades in pairs. If one side has worn out, the other side is likely to follow suit in the near future.

Chattering is the noise and the jerking motion resulting from the wiper blade rubber getting hard and not gliding smoothly over the windshield.

Make sure the wiper blade and rubber is properly installed and in good condition. If the rubber is soft and pliable, chattering should not occur.

Worn linkage and connections can also cause chattering of the wiper blades, but replacement of the linkage parts is beyond the scope of the casual do-it-yourselfer.

Wiper Motor and Linkage Lubrication

The wiper motor, regardless of the type used, does not require regular maintenance. It is sometimes located in an unaccessible position and can only be exposed by removal of cover panels or other parts when replacement is necessary. If the linkage pivot arms or pivot shafts are exposed, apply a silicone spray lubricant to them at least twice a year.

Cleaning the Windshield

The windshield should be kept clean to avoid grinding the dirt into the wiper blades and scratching the glass.

Keep waxes and solvents from the windshield. Waxes leave an invisible film that can create a serious hazard when rain or road grime becomes mixed in the wax coating. The wiper blades cannot cut through this coating during their cleaning action. Clean the waxes from the windshield surface as soon as possible, using commercial cleaners designed for this purpose.

WINDSHIELD WIPER AND WASHER MAINTENANCE INTERVALS

Windshield wiper problems can be kept to a minimum and you'll be able to see a lot better by keeping the system in good shape.

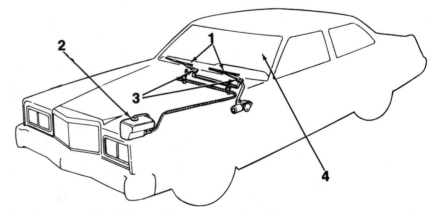

1. Check wiper blades	Every 3 months/3000 miles
2. Check windshield washer fluid level	Every 3 months/3000 miles
Check hoses and clean nozzles	Every 3 months/3000 miles
3. Lubricate linkage and pivots	Every 6 months/6000 miles
4. Clean windshield	Each gas stop

TROUBLESHOOTING BASIC WINDSHIELD WIPER PROBLEMS

Most windshield wiper problems are traced to the motor, but there are a few areas to eliminate before assuming the motor is bad.

TROUBLESHOOTING ELECTRIC WIPERS

The Problem	Is Caused By	What to Do
Wipers do not operate— Wiper motor heats up or hums	• Internal motor defect • Bent or damaged linkage • Arms improperly installed on linkage pivots	• Have motor serviced • Repair or replace linkage • Position linkage in park and reinstall wiper arms
Wipers do not operate— No current to motor	• Fuse or circuit breaker blown • Loose, open or broken wiring • Defective switch • Defective or corroded terminals • No ground circuit for motor or switch	• Replace fuse or circuit breaker • Repair wiring and connections • Replace switch • Repair or clean terminals • Repair ground circuits
Wipers do not operate— Motor runs	• Linkage disconnected or broken	• Connect wiper linkage or replace broken linkage

TROUBLESHOOTING VACUUM WIPERS

The Problem	Is Caused By	What to Do
Wipers do not operate	• Control switch or cable inoperative • Loss of engine vacuum to wiper motor (broken hoses, low engine vacuum, defective vacuum/ fuel pump) • Linkage broken or disconnected • Defective wiper motor	• Repair or replace switch or cable • Check vacuum lines, engine vacuum and fuel pump • Have linkage repaired • Have wiper motor replaced
Wipers stop on engine acceleration	• Leaking vacuum hoses • Dry windshield • Oversize wiper blades • Defective vacuum/fuel pump	• Repair or replace hoses • Wet windshield with washers • Replace with proper size wiper blades • Replace pump

COMMON PROBLEMS WITH WIPER REFILLS

The part of the wiper requiring the most attention is the wiper refill, or rubber strip that actually wipes the windshield. Car washes, constant back-and-forth motion, windshield solvents, cold weather and the drying effects of the sun all take their toll on wiper elements. Any of the following conditions will result in poor wiper performance and are cause to replace the element.

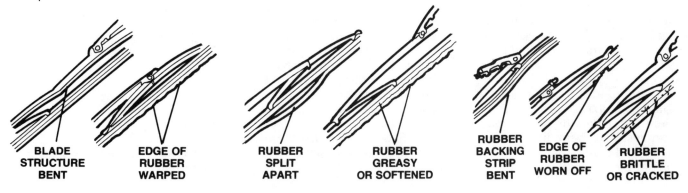

BLADE STRUCTURE BENT   EDGE OF RUBBER WARPED   RUBBER SPLIT APART   RUBBER GREASY OR SOFTENED   RUBBER BACKING STRIP BENT   EDGE OF RUBBER WORN OFF   RUBBER BRITTLE OR CRACKED

TROUBLESHOOTING BASIC WINDSHIELD WASHER PROBLEMS

Windshield washer problems can usually be traced to minor details such as clogged hoses or jets. Check the little things before assuming the worst.

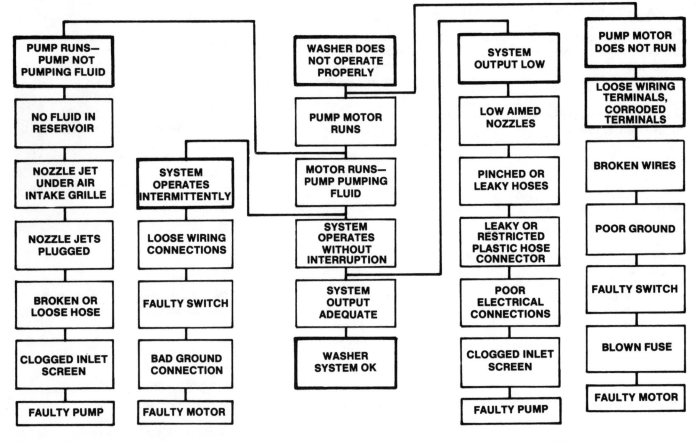

PUMP RUNS— PUMP NOT PUMPING FLUID		WASHER DOES NOT OPERATE PROPERLY	SYSTEM OUTPUT LOW	PUMP MOTOR DOES NOT RUN
NO FLUID IN RESERVOIR		PUMP MOTOR RUNS	LOW AIMED NOZZLES	LOOSE WIRING TERMINALS, CORRODED TERMINALS
NOZZLE JET UNDER AIR INTAKE GRILLE	SYSTEM OPERATES INTERMITTENTLY	MOTOR RUNS— PUMP PUMPING FLUID	PINCHED OR LEAKY HOSES	BROKEN WIRES
NOZZLE JETS PLUGGED	LOOSE WIRING CONNECTIONS	SYSTEM OPERATES WITHOUT INTERRUPTION	LEAKY OR RESTRICTED PLASTIC HOSE CONNECTOR	POOR GROUND
BROKEN OR LOOSE HOSE	FAULTY SWITCH	SYSTEM OUTPUT ADEQUATE	POOR ELECTRICAL CONNECTIONS	FAULTY SWITCH
CLOGGED INLET SCREEN	BAD GROUND CONNECTION	WASHER SYSTEM OK	CLOGGED INLET SCREEN	BLOWN FUSE
FAULTY PUMP	FAULTY MOTOR		FAULTY PUMP	FAULTY MOTOR

Keep solvents from the windshield to avoid damage to the wiper blade rubber and to the sealing rubber of the windshield. Certain solvents can destroy the rubber by swelling or disintegration. Use only solutions that have been designed for use on the windshield surface.

Winter Wiper Maintenance

If you live in the snow belt or your area is subjected to freezing rains, remove any packed snow or ice from the windshield before starting and stopping the wiper motor.

If the blades are frozen to the glass or snow is packed over them, starting the wiper motor can result in bent linkage, bent arms and blades, and possible internal motor damage.

Clean the park position area of packed snow and ice, remembering that the arms and blades will stop at a lower position than the lowest point of the normal wiper blade sweep. This can cause the wiper motor to continue to run which can result in blown fuses or circuit breakers, or internal damage to the wiper motor.

As the wiper blades free themselves from the glass, lift them carefully to prevent the rubber from cracking or tearing. Clean the snow and ice from the rubber before using them.

Similarly, with the washer system, make sure the nozzles are always free of snow and ice. Be sure a non-freezing solution (available as pre-mix or concentrate) is added to the washer fluid. Follow the instructions on the solution container when mixing.

Nozzle Adjustment

Centered Single Post— Non-Adjustable Nozzles

This type is usually located on the rear center of the hood panel, directly in front of the windshield. By loosening the body retaining nut from under the hood,

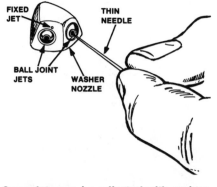

Some jets can be adjusted with a piece of fine wire.

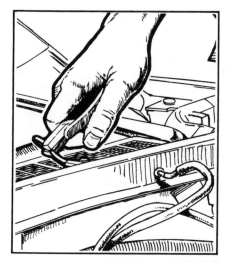

This type of jet is adjusted with pliers or by hand.

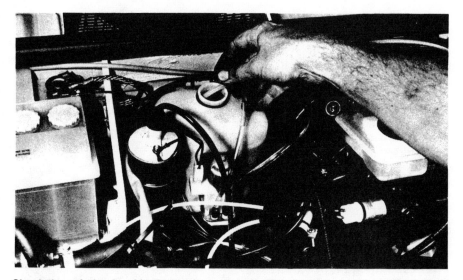

Check the solution level in the washer reservoir. Also check the screen in the bottom of the pick-up tube for clogging. Note the washer pump on the side of the bottle. Some pumps are mounted in a remote location.

the nozzle body can be turned to provide the best spray discharge to cover the majority of the windshield area. Tighten the retaining nut while holding the nozzle body in position.

Centered Single Post—Adjustable Nozzles

The nozzle is adjusted with a wrench, screwdriver or pliers. If the nozzle has no gripping area, the adjustment is done by inserting a stiff wire into the nozzle aperture and moving the nozzle in the direction desired. When using the wire as an adjuster tool, do not force the nozzles; the wire could be broken within the nozzle aperture.

Individual Nozzles

A tab is normally fastened to the nozzle stem to assist in the aiming of the nozzle. If a tab is not present, use a pair of pliers and **gently** move the nozzle in the proper direction.

Wiper Arm Nozzles

No adjustment is necessary on this type nozzle, as the aperture is centered on the wiper arm and moves with the arm action.

Windshield Washers

If the bottom of the washer fluid reservoir has accumula-

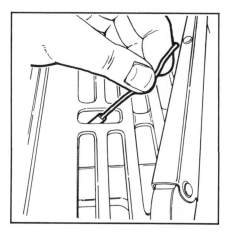

Clean the nozzles with a piece of fine wire.

tions of dirt, remove it from the car and clean the inside thoroughly and reinstall, connecting all hoses and wires.

Examine the plastic or rubber hoses for cracks or breaks, and replace them as needed.

By following the mixing instructions on the solution container, fill the reservoir to the specified height with the proper mixture.

Using a long pin or a piece of fine wire, loosen any dirt deposited in the nozzles, hoses or screens. Rinse the exposed areas with clear water.

Operate the pump or motor

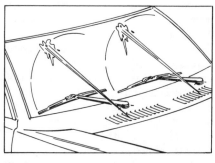

Washer nozzles should be adjusted to hit the windshield above center.

and flush the washer system out with the new solution until all traces of deposits are gone.

Observe the washer nozzle aim and if necessary, correct it, remembering that the washer nozzles are provided in different forms and have different methods of adjustment.

■

Chilton Tip

Don't confuse the windshield washer bottle with the plastic coolant overflow tank.

■

Servicing the Wipers

It may be necessary to move the wiper arms and blades higher on the windshield before attempting to replace the arms, blades or refills.

In the case of the vacuum wiper, operate the engine and pull the vacuum line from the wiper motor to stop the arms in a workable position. Reinstall the arms in the same position as they were removed.

If the car is equipped with an electric wiper, turn the ignition switch on first, and then turn the wiper switch on. When the wipers are in their farthest point of their arc, turn the ignition switch off. Mark the position of the arms so that the replacement will be installed in the same location as the original.

Wiper Refill Replacement

There are several different types of refills, differing in their method of replacement. One type (known as Anco) has two release buttons, approximately one-third of the way up from the ends of the blade frame. Pushing the buttons down releases a lock and allows the rubber filler to be removed from the wiper blade frame. The new rubber refills slide back into the frame and lock in place.

Another type (known as Trico) of refill has two metal tabs that unlock at one end of the wiper frame, by squeezing the tabs together. The rubber filler can then be withdrawn from the wiper frame jaws. A new refill is installed by inserting the refill into the front frame jaws and sliding it rearward to engage the remaining frame jaws. At the end of its travel, the tabs will lock into place on the front jaws of the wiper blade frame.

A third type is the refill made from polycarbonate. This refill has a simple locking device at one end which flexes downward out of the groove into which the jaws of the holder fit, allowing easy release. By sliding the new refill through all the jaws and pushing through the slight resistance when it reaches the end of

REPLACING WIPER REFILLS (ELEMENTS)

There are several different kinds of standard equipment and aftermarket wiper refills. Depending on who services the car or where you purchase parts, you may have almost any type. Each is removed and installed in its own unique way.

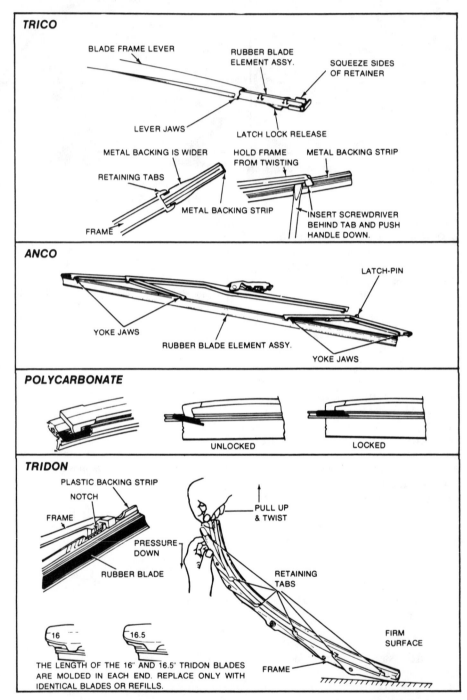

its travel, the refill will lock into position.

A fourth type (known as Tridon) uses a rubber element mounted on a plastic backing strip. A notch in the backing strip engages the blade frame.

The length of the Tridon blade

(16″ or 16½″) is molded into the end of the refill. These should be replaced only with identical refills.

Regardless of the type of refill used, make sure that all the frame jaws are engaged as the refill is pushed into place and locked.

The metal blade holder and frame can easily scratch the glass surface, if allowed to touch it.

The non-metallic polycarbonate type refills are universal, fitting nearly all makes of wiper frames, and you may be able to save some inconvenience by using this type of refill.

Wiper Blade Replacement

Trico Bayonet Blade

Press down on the arm to unlatch the top stud. Depress the tab on the saddle and pull the blade from the arm. When installing the blade, the locking studs should snap into place.

Anco Bayonet Blade

Press inward on the tab and pull the blade from the arm. To install, slide the blade into the arm so that the locking studs snap into place.

Trico or Anco Pin Type

Insert a screwdriver into the spring release opening of the blade saddle and depress the spring clip. Pull the blade from the arm. To install, push the blade saddle onto the mounting pin so that the spring clip engages the pin. Be sure that the blade is securely attached to the arm.

Universal Types

Numerous universal blades and adapters have been provided to install other than the original equipment wiper blades.

To install the universal type, push the blade adapter onto the arm until the lugs click into place. Push the blade onto the adapter until the locking lugs

click closed. To remove the adapter from the blade, a tab is provided as in the Anco bayonet type and by pressing on the tab, the adapter can be pulled from the arm.

Replacing the Wiper Arm

The wiper arm attachment to the pivot shaft varies from car to car, and should be known before any attempt is made to remove the arm from the pivot.

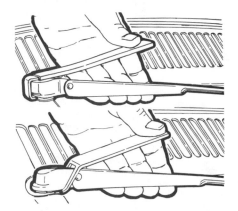

These two styles of wiper arm removal tools are inexpensive and will remove the arm from the drive shaft without damaging shaft or arm.

Pin and Hole Type

This type of arm has a pin hole near the arm's pivot pin. To remove the arm, raise the blade end off the glass and insert a $^3/_{32}$ inch pin or pop rivet into the hole. This locks the arm in the released position, allowing the arm to be lifted off the pivot shaft without the aid of tools.

To install this type of arm, the pin must be left in place. (New service replacement arms have the pins already installed to hold them in the released position). Position the wiper motor in the park position and install the wiper arm over the pivot shaft, in its proper arm-to-glass position. Push the arm downward over the pivot shaft so that the retaining clip will engage the drive head of the pivot shaft. Remove the pin from the wiper arm.

Slide Latch Type

This wiper arm has a slide latch that locks under the drive head of the pivot shaft. To remove this type, raise the blade end from the glass and at the same time, move the slide latch

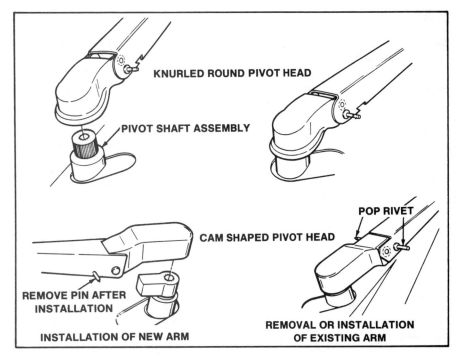

Pin and hole type arm replacement.

REPLACING WINDSHIELD WIPER BLADES

Just as there are several different kinds of refills, there are several different designs to attach the wiper blade to the arm. Each is removed in its own way, which is not always obvious. These are the most popular types in use today.

Side Pin Type

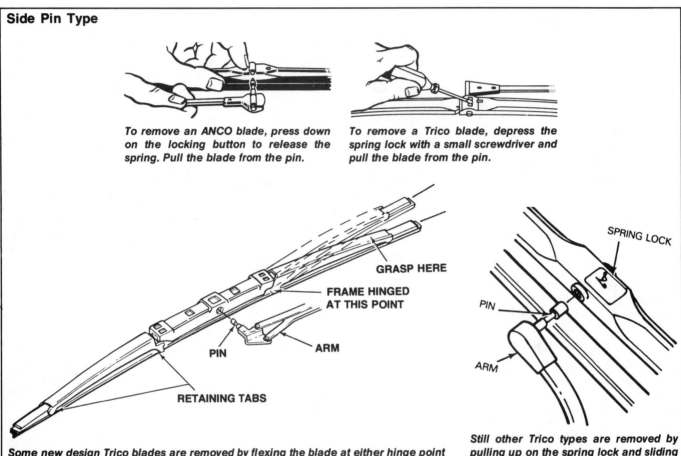

To remove an ANCO blade, press down on the locking button to release the spring. Pull the blade from the pin.

To remove a Trico blade, depress the spring lock with a small screwdriver and pull the blade from the pin.

Some new design Trico blades are removed by flexing the blade at either hinge point to release the lock. Pull the blade from the pin.

Still other Trico types are removed by pulling up on the spring lock and sliding the blade off the pin.

Bayonet Type

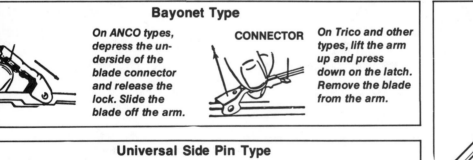

On ANCO types, depress the underside of the blade connector and release the lock. Slide the blade off the arm.

On Trico and other types, lift the arm up and press down on the latch. Remove the blade from the arm.

Universal Side Pin Type

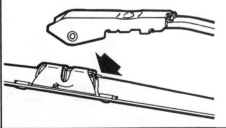

Most deadlock types are released by depressing the small arm beneath the wiper arm. This releases the lock. The blade can be removed from the pin in the adaptor. If necessary, the adaptor can be removed from the arm.

Dead Lock Type

Universal blades replace the standard blade on a side pin type arm. The universal blade simply snaps onto the pin and will rotate freely when properly installed. It is removed by pulling it off the pin.

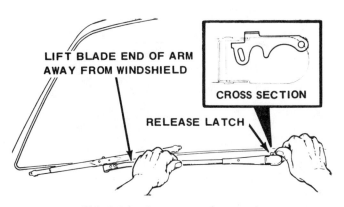

Side latch wiper arm replacement.

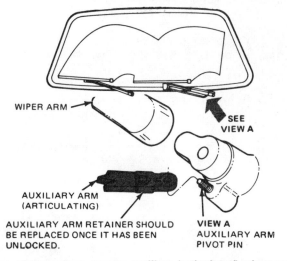

Some wiper systems use an auxiliary (articulated) wiper arm. It is secured to an auxiliary pivot by a sliding lock.

outward, away from the pivot shaft. This holds the arm in the off-glass position and permits it to be removed from the pivot head without the aid of tools.

To install this type arm, push the wiper arm onto the pivot head while holding the arm in the off-glass position. Push the slide latch into the lock under the pivot shaft. Lower the blade to the windshield. If the blade does not touch the glass, the slide latch is not completely locked.

Conventional Arm

This type of arm has no pins or latches to work with. To remove the arm, lift the blade end from the glass and with the aid of a special tool, pull the assembly from the pivot shaft.

To install the arm, hold the blade and arm in the swing out position and push the arm onto the serrated drive end of the pivot shaft. The special tool may be needed to assist in the installation.

Bolt or Nut Retainer Type

A bolt or nut is used to retain the wiper arm to the drive end of the pivot shaft.

To remove this arm, the bolt or nut must be removed from the pivot shaft. The arm can then be lifted from the pivot shaft.

To install the arm, position it over the pivot shaft and engage the serrations of the wiper arm and the pivot shaft drive end. Install the bolt or nut and tighten securely.

Auxiliary Arm

Some cars are equipped with a small auxiliary arm in addition to the main arm, mounted on the driver's side. This arm assembly is sometimes called an articulating arm, meaning to be connected by joints, and the main purpose is to change the angle of the blade as it travels through its arc, to clear more of the windshield glass area in front of the driver.

To remove this arm, first re-

move the main arm from the pivot shaft. Unlock the auxiliary arm from the lug on the pivot shaft, by sliding the retaining clip back onto the auxiliary arm.

To install the auxiliary arm, position the arm on the lug of the pivot shaft and engage the retaining clip. Install the main arm as previously outlined.

Universal Arms and Blades

Universal arms and blades are sold by aftermarket outlets to take the place of original equipment. One such item is an adjustable arm, having an angling swivel for the blade, and a tension controller screw.

Certain universal wiper blades have adapters to fit existing wiper arms, so that the entire arm and blade assembly need not be replaced.

Other blades incorporate a wind deflector to help keep the blades flat on the windshield when the car is traveling at high speeds. These are called anti-lift wiper blades.

17
Interior Care

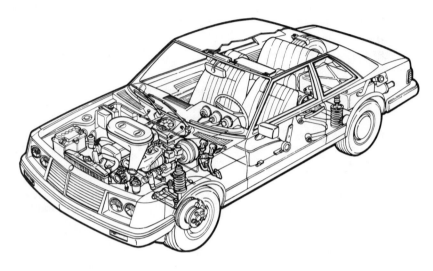

One way to preserve a "new-car" feeling is to keep the interior clean and protected. You have to use some common sense and not let the dirt accumulate. The more dirt that gets ground into carpeting and seats, the faster they will wear out. Keep the seats clean and the rugs vacuumed.

Cleaning Fabric and Vinyl

There are a number of products on the market that will clean vinyl or fabric interiors, but mild soap and water is still one of the best (and cheapest) cleaners and should be used at least three or four times a year. Household cleaners like 409, Fantastik and multi-purpose cleaners such as Armor All® will also clean vinyl well. As with any cleaner, test it in an out-of-the-way place before using it.

A whisk broom or vacuum cleaner will keep the rugs clean and free of loose dirt build-up. To clean the carpet, rug shampoo can be used as well as the foamy types in aerosol cans, but the foam types are more of a spot cleaner than an overall cleaner. When working with chemicals and spot removers, be sure that you follow directions on the product and work in a well ventilated area.

Repairing Seats and Dash

Vinyl seats and dashboards are subject to cracking and tearing with hard use. Wear and tear in these areas is very noticeable, but not too difficult to repair. Cloth-covered seats are harder to repair, unless you're handy with a tailor's needle and thread. If you're not and the seams are coming apart, invest in a set of seat covers in lieu of a trip to the upholstery shop.

Any retail auto store sells pre-fitted seat covers at a fraction of the cost of new upholstery. Seat covers are sold as "fits-all" (universal application), or more expensively by make and model of car. Be sure to check if the covers fit bench, bucket or split-back seats. The covers are tied or wired under the seats.

Burn marks in vinyl seats, arm-rests and dashboards can be repaired with the help of a good vinyl repair kit. Rips in the vinyl and seams that have come apart are slightly more difficult but are well worth the time and effort in the end.

About the best way to repair a rip is to heat both sides of the tear with a hair drier. Lift up the material and place a 2″ wide strip of fabric tape under one side of the vinyl. Stretch the other side over the tape and line it up carefully. When you have it lined up, press down. Hold it in place while someone applies vinyl repair liquid over the area to be re-

HOW TO REMOVE STAINS FROM FABRIC INTERIOR

For best results, spots and stains should be removed as soon as possible. Never use gasoline, lacquer thinner, acetone, nail polish remover or bleach. Use a 3″ x 3″ piece of cheesecloth. Squeeze most of the liquid from the fabric and wipe the stained fabric from the outside of the stain toward the center with a lifting motion. Turn the cheesecloth as soon as one side becomes soiled. When using water to remove a stain, be sure to wash the entire section after the spot has been removed to avoid water stains. Encrusted spots can be broken up with a dull knife and vacuumed before removing the stain.

Type of Stain	How to Remove It
Surface spots	Brush the spots out with a small hand brush or use a commercial preparation such as K2R to lift the stain.
Mildew	Clean around the mildew with warm suds. Rinse in cold water and soak the mildew area in a solution of 1 part table salt and 2 parts water. Wash with upholstery cleaner.
Water stains	Water stains in fabric materials can be removed with a solution made from 1 cup of table salt dissolved in 1 quart of water. Vigorously scrub the solution into the stain and rinse with clear water. Water stains in nylon or other synthetic fabrics should be removed with a commercial spot remover.
Chewing gum, tar, crayons, shoe polish (greasy stains)	Do not use a cleaner that will soften gum or tar. Harden the deposit with an ice cube and scrape away as much as possible with a dull knife. Moisten the remainder with cleaning fluid and scrub clean. Stains other than chewing gum or tar should be sponged thoroughly with cool water. If stain remains, soak it for several hours and sponge it with a detergent solution. Rinse again. If the stain still remains, sponge with dry-cleaning fluid.
Ice cream, candy	Most candy has a sugar base and can be removed with a cloth wrung out in warm water. Oily candy, after cleaning with warm water, should be cleaned with upholstery cleaner. Rinse with warm water and clean the remainder with cleaning fluid.
Wine, alcohol, egg, milk, soft drink (non-greasy stains)	Do not use soap. Scrub the stain with a cloth wrung out in warm water. Remove the remainder with cleaning fluid.
Grease, oil, lipstick, butter and related stains	Use a spot remover to avoid leaving a ring. Work from the outside of the stain to the center and dry with a clean cloth when the spot is gone.
Coffee, tea, soft drinks, beer, grass, foliage	Sponge with cool water immediately. Rub in mild liquid detergent and soak for 30 minutes. Rinse with cold water. If fabric permits, pour boiling water through from a distance of 2–3 feet. On non-washable articles, stain can sometimes be removed by sponging with rubbing alcohol.
Headliners (cloth)	Mix a solution of warm water and foam upholstery cleaner to give thick suds. Use only foam—liquid may streak or spot. Clean the entire headliner in one operation using a circular motion with a natural sponge.
Headliner (vinyl)	Use a vinyl cleaner with a sponge and wipe clean with a dry cloth.
Seats and Door panels	Mix 1 pint upholstery cleaner in 1 gallon of water. Do not soak the fabric around the buttons.
Leather or vinyl fabric	Use a multi-purpose cleaner full strength and a stiff brush. Let stand 2 minutes and scrub thoroughly. Wipe with a clean, soft rag.
Nylon or synthetic fabrics	For normal stains, use the same procedures you would for washing cloth upholstery. If the fabric is extremely dirty, use a multi-purpose cleaner full strength with a stiff scrub brush. Scrub thoroughly in all directions and wipe with a cotton towel or soft rag.

paired. Let it dry completely before using it. The repair should look like new and last quite a while.

Other methods of repairing vinyl involve vinyl repair compounds that require heat. The kits contain a repair compound, applicator and several different graining papers. If the hole is deep, it will have to be filled with foam or anything to provide a

VINYL REPAIR

Small tears and rips in vinyl can be repaired using a number of vinyl repair kits. The one shown here works well on flat areas and must be cured by heat from an iron (the cotton setting works well).

1. Vinyl repair kits requiring heat work best on tears in flat areas.

2. If the hole is deep, stuff some foam rubber into the hole to fill it.

3. Apply some vinyl patch compound to the tear and smooth it out. Don't put too much on the surrounding area.

4. Select a graining paper that closely matches the grain in your vinyl.

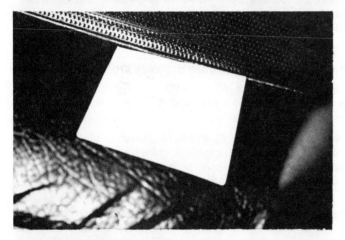

5. Place the graining paper over the tear with the grain in the paper facing down.

6. Use a hot iron (set at Cotton) and heat the patch for 60 seconds. Do not let the iron directly contact the vinyl.

backing. Spread the vinyl patch compound over the blemish. Select a graining paper to closely match the grain of your material and place it over the patch, grain side down. Heat it with an iron set at COTTON for about 60 seconds. DO NOT LET THE IRON CONTACT THE VINYL. The result should be a longlasting and nearly invisible repair.

Repairing Door Panels

It's easy to fix door panels. Treat them the same way you would a vinyl seat. The panels are usually fastened to the door with clips behind the panel. If

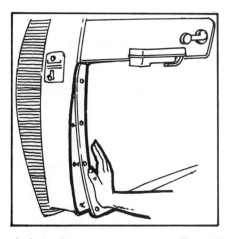

A few sharp raps with your fist will usually snap a door panel back into place.

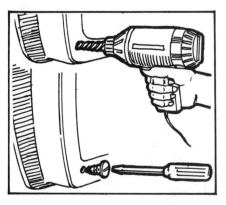

If the clips are sprung, drill some small holes where the panel is pulled away and install some screws with countersunk washers.

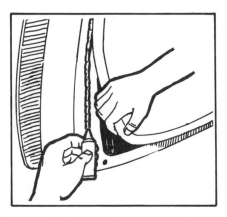

If drilling holes and screws is not practical, use one of the superstrength glues available.

these won't hold any more, screw or glue the panel in place.

Door Panels

Vinyl door panels can be cleaned with a solution of 1 pint of upholstery cleaner mixed in 1 gallon of water. If the panels are extremely dirty, use more cleaner in the solution.

Scrub the panel thoroughly, doing one section at a time. Clean between all seams, in cracks and underneath the beading.

Wipe off the dirt and excess cleaner with a soft rag or clean cotton towel.

If the door panels have pulled away from the door, they can be easily put back in place. The panels are usually fastened to the door with clips at the back and a groove at the bottom.

A few raps with your fist will normally put them back in place. If not, drill a couple of small holes through the panel and door and screw the panels in place with screws and countersunk

Use screws and countersunk washers to attach door panels.

washers. Be careful not to drill through any window mechanisms or hit the door glass. If drilling isn't practical, use one of the superstrength glues available.

Rug Care

Before doing anything about cleaning carpets, thoroughly vacuum everything to remove all loose dirt. The foaming rug shampoos (aerosol cans) are good for spot cleaning.

Overall cleaning can be done with 1 pint of upholstery cleaner in 1 gallon of water. If the carpet is faded, spotted, or discolored, add an upholstery tint to the solution. To get the right color shade add tint in small quantities and test the solution by dipping a white cloth in and wringing it out. The color will usually dry a shade or two darker.

Apply the solution with a stiff brush and scrub the carpet vigorously in one direction. When it dries, fluff the carpet with a dry brush.

Salt stains (from winter weather) can be removed by soaking the stained area in a heavy solution of table salt and water. Use a stiff brush, if necessary, and wash the entire carpet. You may have to repeat this several times.

Rug Repair

Repairing burns, rips, tears, or worn spots in rugs can be done simply and quickly. The only things you'll need are a razor

Use a razor blade to trim away the frayed or burned ends of the hole.

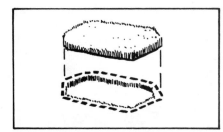

Cut a piece of carpet from under the seat or some other inconspicuous location to match the size of the hole to be repaired. The patch should be about ⅛" larger than the hole.

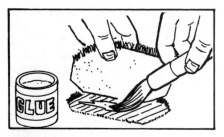

Glue the patch in place and let it dry completely.

Rake the nap of the rug with a dull nail to hide the seams in the carpet where it was repaired.

blade, glue, carpet cut from under a seat and a nail.

Glass and Plastic

Interior glass should be cleaned at least once a week to remove deposits of smoke and other films.

Water alone will seldom cut through the haze from cigarette smoke and usually only succeeds in rearranging the film.

Household, blue-liquid cleaners for glass work best. In the absence of these, or for stubborn dirt, use about 4 table-spoons of ammonia in 1 quart of water.

Clean the excess dirt and grime with a paper towel. Apply the cleaner, use a paper towel to clean the dust and dirt from the glass and another to polish the glass.

Chilton Tip

Be careful you do not break the grid on rear window defoggers when cleaning the rear window. Do not use abrasive cleaners.

To remove paint overspray and masking tape residue from glass, use a strong professional glass cleaner.

Exterior glass surfaces are best cleaned with commercial window cleaning solutions. Smears, bugs and road tar can be removed with a rubber or plastic scraper and window cleaner. Don't use razor blades (except as below), putty knives or steel wool.

To remove stubborn stickers, scotch tape or masking tape, wet a paper towel or cloth with cigarette lighter fluid and moisten the residue. Let it soak in and very carefully scrape it away with a single-edge razor blade.

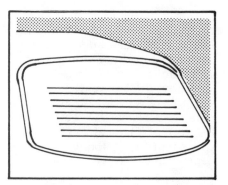

Do not clean the inside of the rear window with abrasive cleaners. This could destroy the defroster grid.

If you have any clear plastic, use a plastic cleaner that has no harsh abrasives. Inexpensive plastic polishes are available that will remove minor scratches and restore the finish.

Keeping the Interior Clean

Once you've gone to the trouble of cleaning the interior, it'll be worth your while to keep it clean. It makes it much easier to clean up the next time around.

Common sense plus these tips will help keep the interior clean.

Vacuum the carpets regularly. The hardest thing to get out of carpets is ground-in dirt.

If careless cleaning has damaged the defroster grid, use a repair kit to paint a new conductive bridge across the gap.

REPLACING THE INSIDE REAR-VIEW MIRROR

Occasionally, after many adjustments the inside rear-view mirror may fall off the windshield. To replace it, use only adhesives specially formulated to bond close-mated, smooth-surfaced materials. The adhesive should also attain at least half its strength in a few minutes.

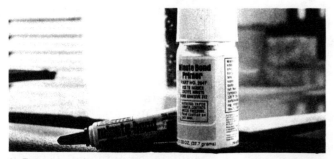

1. To cement the rear-view mirror mount to glass, use only adhesives specially formulated to bond smooth surfaces.

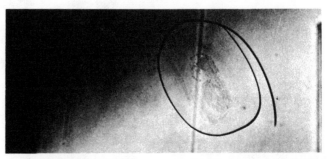

2. Circle the area with grease pencil where the mirror mount was originally located.

3. Loosen the allen screw which holds the rear view mirror to the mount.

4. Scrape the old adhesive off the mount. It must be clean. Apply a thin coat of glue (1 drop per square inch) to the mount.

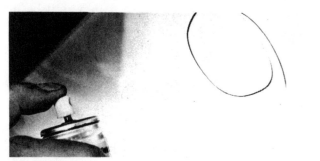

5. Clean the windshield where the mirror is to be mounted and spray a light film of catalyst on the windshield.

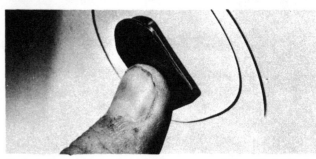

6. Locate the mirror mount where you want it and hold in place for 1 minute. The adhesive attains 50% strength in 1 minute, so be sure you have it where you want it. Be sure the proper end is up.

7. Slip the mirror on the mount.

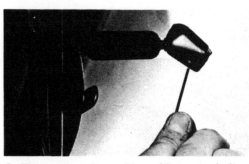

8. Tighten the mirror with an Allen wrench. It only needs to be snugged up.

Use electrical tape or plastic bundling straps to keep wires secured underneath the dash.

Floor mats are a good investment. They take a lot of wear that carpets would normally get.

· If you don't have floor mats, invest in a set. They are much cheaper to replace than carpets and take a lot of the wear carpets would normally get.

· Don't be too heavy handed with waxes, polishes and dressings. Too much build-up of wax and polish only traps more dirt.

· Don't use dressings or wax on dirty vinyl. Spend a little time to clean it properly before applying a vinyl dressing.

· A combination cleaner/protectant or saddle soap used on vinyl will keep it soft and pliable but will also make the seats slippery. A good buffing with a soft cloth will reduce the slippery feeling.

· If your fabric upholstery is fairly new and absolutely clean, Scotch-garding® will keep stains from setting in the fabric and make them easier to clean. But, if the fabric is already dirty or old, you're only wasting your time.

· If possible, park your car in the shade. If you can't park in the shade, at least cover the seat back and dash if they will be in the sun's rays.

· Clean spots and stains as quickly as possible before they have a chance to set in the material. You stand a better chance of completely removing the stain if you remove it while it's wet.

18
Dash Gauges

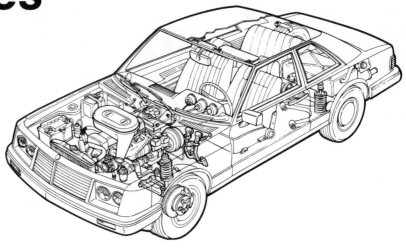

TOOLS AND SUPPLIES

Tools
  Electric drill
  Hole saw
  Screwdrivers
  Pliers
  Wrenches
  Drill
  Wire strippers
Supplies
  Wire terminals
  Wire
  Electrical tape
  Tap connectors

Most engine problems develop slowly and telegraph their warning signs clearly. If you are equipped to read them. About 15 years ago, the auto industry began a trend to eliminate dash gauges. The oil pressure, ammeter and coolant temperature gauges were replaced with small warning lights—quickly and aptly named "idiot" lights. The difference is that the idiot light tells you when something has already happened; the gauge will tell you when it's starting to happen, and will indicate a trend.

Fortunately, auto makers are beginning to offer gauges again—as optional equipment, sometimes in addition to the standard warning lights. Equipping your car or truck with gauges in addition to the warning lights can in-

dicate a pattern that will point out irregularities in plenty of time to correct them and save the expense of more serious problems.

As an example, watching the coolant temperature gauge climb slightly above normal over a period of time can indicate slipping belts, low coolant level, worn hoses or incorrect ignition timing. Any of these problems

are easily corrected before they cause the warning light to come on, when the engine has already overheated.

As the age of electronics increases the sophistication of the automobile, more and more use is being made of the electronic module. These modules are virtually a small on-board computer that monitors hundreds of inputs from various sensors on

Several years ago, the auto makers replaced the oil pressure, ammeter and coolant temperature gauges with "idiot" lights (arrows).

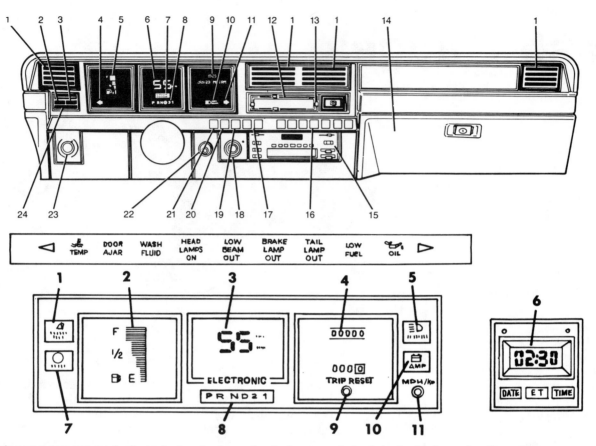

Electronic computers are gradually replacing simple mechanical gauges. A single logic chip in conjunction with sensors can easily monitor every system of the car, providing warning lights and instant read out of information from tire pressure to fuel economy to elapsed time to your destination.

the car. Based on the information it receives, the module makes decisions to alter ignition timing or alter the fuel metering system.

Manufacturers have also found that the module is capable of handling more functions than there is a practical use for. As a result, more equipment is being offered to feed the driver a constant stream of information—everything from tire pressure to fuel economy to elapsed time or mileage.

Types of Gauges

There are basically, two types of gauges—mechanical and electrical.

Mechanical Gauges

Mechanical gauges measure speed or pressure at the source and send the information to the gauge mechanically. The speedometer and Bourdon tube oil pressure gauges are examples of this type.

Bourdon tube oil pressure gauges are connected directly to a small tube in the main engine oil passage, by a plastic or copper line. The gauge consists of a flattened tube bent in the form of a curve that tends to straighten under engine oil pressure. The curved tube is linked to a needle that registers on a calibrated scale. They are easily distinguished by the copper or nylon line running from the engine to the gauge.

Electrical Gauges

Electrical gauges monitor functions at the source and send the information to the gauge electrically.

Thermal (bi-metallic) electric gauges are activated by the difference in the expansion rate of a bi-metal bar. A sending unit controls the flow of current to a heating element coiled around a bi-metal bar in the gauge. These gauges can be recognized by a pointer that moves slowly to its position when the ignition is turned ON.

Magnetic electric gauges move the indicator needle by changing the balance between the magnetic pull of two coils built into the gauge. When the ignition is OFF, the needle may rest anywhere. Balance is controlled by the action of a sending unit which will vary current flow, depending on temperature, pressure or movement of a float arm. A magnetic gauge can be recognized by a needle that jumps to its position when the ignition is turned ON. A 90° scale is also the maximum that can be used, since the needle must swing between the poles of a magnet.

Many electric gauges use an instrument voltage regulator to control the supply of voltage to the gauge. This prevents fluctuations in the gauge due to varying voltage.

How to Read Gauges

The problem with gauges is in knowing how to read them, it doesn't do much good to have gauges, if you can't interpret the reading.

Most gauges are marked with green (OK) or red (danger) areas or with calibrated faces. No gauge should be considered totally accurate; an indication of change is far more important than a totally accurate reading.

You should be able to quickly familiarize yourself with the normal readings on the gauges, and to easily spot a sudden or developing change in the readings.

Coolant Temperature

These gauges monitor the temperature of the engine coolant. As the engine warms up, the temperature will probably rise to somewhere around the 180°–200° F range. If you're stuck in traffic, the temperature will rise slightly. It will also rise slightly immediately after shutting the engine off, because the coolant is not being cooled, but will return

to normal when the engine is started.

Variations in temperature as shown on the gauge are not normal, unless you happen to suddenly get caught in heavy traffic or some other conditions cause the temperature to change. Too cool temperatures indicate a faulty thermostat. Too hot readings indicate low coolant level, worn hoses, defective radiator cap, incorrect ignition timing or slipping belts. If the normal operating temperature rises over the course of time, and the above factors are OK, suspect a worn water pump or a clogged system.

Oil Pressure

The oil pressure gauge will tell you if your engine is getting proper lubrication. At fast idle when the engine (and oil) are cold, the pressure will probably be at maximum on the gauge, around 60 psi. Depending on the car, rpm and condition of the engine, oil pressure should be constant, somewhere around 30–40 psi at cruising speed, and less at idle. Under load you can expect the oil pressure to rise slightly and to fall off with deceleration.

Low oil pressure can warn of low oil level, wrong viscosity oil, overheating, clogged oil filter or worn engine (lots of miles).

Ammeter

The ammeter will indicate the condition of the charging system.

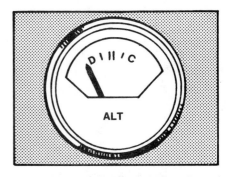
The ammeter monitors the rate of charge or discharge of the battery.

It will show charge (+) when the battery is being charged and discharge (−) when the battery is being used. Just after cranking the engine, the ammeter will show a charging condition if lights and accessories are off. As the energy spent in cranking is restored to the battery, the pointer will gradually move back toward the center, but should stay slightly on the charge (+) side. If the battery is low, it will show a charge condition for an indeterminate period.

At speeds above 30 mph, with lights and accessories on, the ammeter should read on the charge side, depending on the condition of the battery. At road speeds, the ammeter should never show discharge. If it does, check the belts or charging system.

A battery that appears to charge rapidly, then discharge rapidly, is failing and replacement time is near. Slower than normal charging rates indicate a slipping belt or a problem in the alternator.

Voltmeter

Voltmeters are used on some cars in place of an ammeter because they give a more complete indication of battery condition. Even though the car uses a 12-volt system, the system operates at slightly over 13 volts. If the voltmeter reads under approximately 13 volts after the engine has been running a while, look for slipping belts or too low a voltage regulator setting on cars

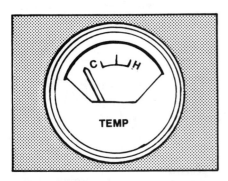
The coolant temperature gauge reads coolant temperature in degrees Fahrenheit, or is merely marked "Cold" and "Hot."

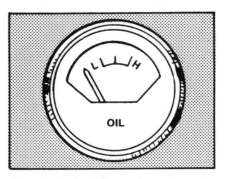
Oil pressure is monitored in psi (pounds per square inch), or marked "Low" and "High."

The voltmeter shows the battery condition at any given moment, more accurately than an ammeter.

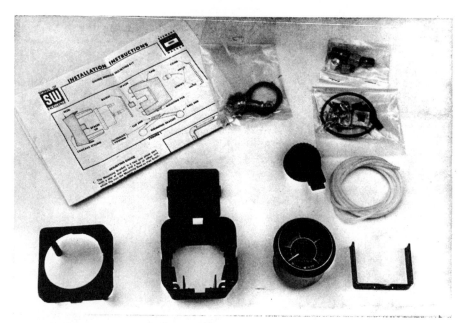

Variations of the vacuum gauge use colors and words to replace the readings in in./ Hg normally associated with a vacuum gauge.

with adjustable regulators. Continuously high (above approximately 15 volts) or low (below 13 volts) voltage may also indicate a defective alternator or defective battery.

Vacuum Gauge

Vacuum gauges are always mechanical types which measure manifold pressure (engine vacuum), which relates directly to fuel consumption. Engine vacuum varies inversely with engine speed, so you should also drive at the highest indicated vacuum. Try to maintain the highest vacuum under all conditions.

The vacuum gauge readings are also a good indication of the condition of your engine. Actually, the readings are not as important as a steady needle. At idle, the vacuum gauge should show a steady reading of anywhere from 8–16 in./Hg on an engine in good tune and operating condition. A needle that twitches at idle indicates fouled plugs, stuck or worn valves. A

low reading at idle that stays low usually means a leaking vacuum hose, incorrect ignition timing or worn valves or valve guides.

As engine speed increases, erratic readings may mean a blown head gasket or worn valves.

Recently, public interest in fuel economy has given birth to a variation of the vacuum gauge, called a "motor minder." This gauge is basically a vacuum gauge with words ("Poor," "Fair," "Good" and "Excellent") and color bands (red/yel-

low/green) replacing the numbers on the face of the vacuum gauge. Since there is a direct correlation between in./Hg (vacuum) and fuel economy, gauge manufacturers have already interpreted the numbers for the driver.

Tachometer

Tachometers are among the most popular of gauges, possibly because of their identification with racing.

While they are not completely

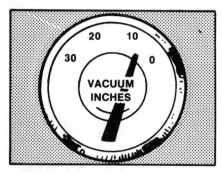

Vacuum gauges monitor engine vacuum in in./Hg (inches/mercury).

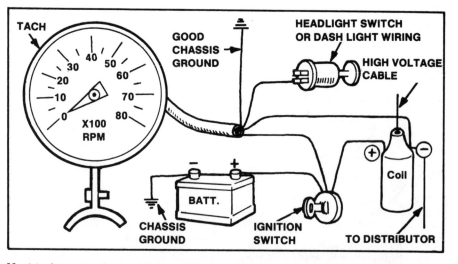

Most tachometers have only four connections to make. One goes to ground, one to power (ignition switch), one for lights and one to the distributor side of the coil.

TROUBLESHOOTING BASIC DASH GAUGE PROBLEMS

Most problems with dash gauges can be traced to faulty wiring or a defective sending unit. Occasionally, the gauge itself will be at fault.

The Problem	Is Caused By	What to Do
Coolant Temperature Gauge		
Gauge reads erratically or not at all	• Loose or dirty connections • Defective sending unit • Defective gauge	• Clean/tighten connections • Bi-metal gauge: remove the wire from the sending unit. Ground the wire for an instant. If the gauge registers, replace the sending unit. • Magnetic gauge: Disconnect the wire at the sending unit. With ignition ON gauge should register COLD. Ground the wire; gauge should register HOT.
Ammeter Gauge—Turn Headlights ON (do not start engine). Note reaction		
Ammeter shows charge Ammeter shows discharge Ammeter does not move	• Connections reversed on gauge • Ammeter is OK • Loose connections or faulty wiring • Defective gauge	• Reinstall connections • Nothing • Check/correct wiring • Replace gauge
Oil Pressure Gauge		
Gauge does not register or is inaccurate	• On mechanical gauge, Bourdon tube may be bent or kinked. • Low oil pressure • Defective gauge • Defective wiring • Defective sending unit	• Check tube for kinks or bends preventing oil from reaching the gauge. • Remove sending unit. Idle the engine briefly. If no oil flows from sending unit hole, problem is in engine. • Remove the wire from the sending unit and ground it for an instant with the ignition ON. A good gauge will go to the top of the scale. • Check the wiring to the gauge. If it's OK and the gauge doesn't register when grounded, replace the gauge. • If the wiring is OK and the gauge functions when grounded, replace the sending unit.
All Gauges		
All gauges do not operate All gauges read low or erratically All gauges pegged	• Blown fuse • Defective instrument regulator • Defective or dirty instrument voltage regulator • Loss of ground between instrument voltage regulator and car. • Defective instrument regulator	• Replace fuse • Replace instrument voltage regulator • Clean contacts or replace • Check ground • Replace regulator
Warning Lights		
Light(s) do not come on when ignition is ON, but engine is not started	• Defective bulb • Defective wire • Defective sending unit	• Replace bulb • Check wire from light to sending unit • Disconnect the wire from the sending unit and ground it. Replace the sending unit if the light comes on with the ignition ON.
Light comes on with engine running	• Problem in individual system Defective sending unit	• Check system • Check sending unit (see above)

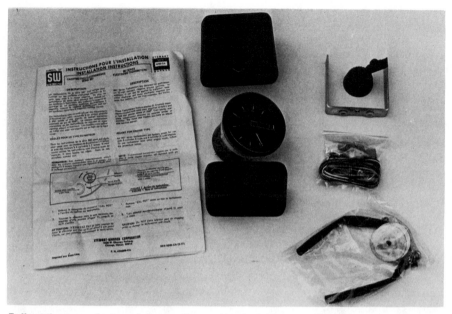

Follow the manufacturer's instructions when installing gauges. Many gauges can either be installed in the dash or can be installed in a custom housing available from the manufacturer.

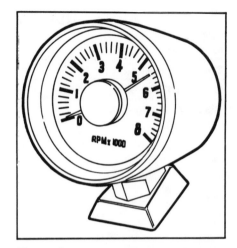

The tachometer measures engine rpm (1000's of engine revolutions per minute).

A normal vacuum gauge can be used to determine the most fuel efficient driving conditions.

accurate, they are useful during tune-ups for setting idle speed, and while driving, to keep the engine at its most efficient rpm.

Installing Dash Gauges

Before buying gauges, make a survey of likely mounting spots. Gauges should be placed within easy viewing and should not interfere with driving. Give some thought to the location based on priority. The ones you're going to watch the most should be most convenient.

Be sure the gauge faces are clear and readable. They should leave no doubt as to the readings. An accessory mounting bracket is the easiest way to mount gauges, but they can be installed on the dashboard if you want to cut holes in the dash.

Installation is usually a matter of following the manufacturer's instructions for hook-up. Mechanical gauges should be placed where the plumbing for the gauge provides a minimum of routing problems. Be sure all wires are well secured, protected against chafing and have enough slack to absorb engine vibrations. Plastic tap connectors are useful for splicing into wires. These eliminate the need for cutting and taping wires and give a clean, quick connection.

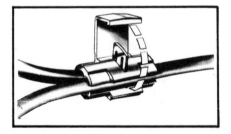

Tap connectors making splicing into wires easy.

19
Radios, Stereos and Tape Players

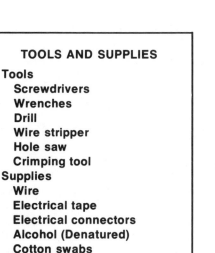

As with all equipment, you should learn as much as possible about the various components before purchasing anything.

Tape Decks

There are basically two types of automotive tape players: 8-tracks and cassettes. Your choice is a matter of personal preference. If you already have one type in a home player, you'll likely choose the same type for your car. Tape player prices can range from $20 to several hundred dollars, with the more expensive units generally offering better tone response, less distortion and greater power output.

The 8-track system allows you to hear exactly what you want to hear in stereo. 8-track systems are highly dependable, offer excellent sound reproduction and a wide range of programming.

The cassette system is newer and offers several advantages over 8-track. The tape used is half the width of 8-track tape and moves at half the speed. Because of this, it can store the same recording in a case about a quarter of the size of an 8-track. If you have limited installation space and want a radio/tape combination, this is the way to go.

Caring for Tape Cartridge

Whether you prefer 8-track cartridges or cassettes, they will give better sound reproduction and last longer if you take care of them.

· Do not expose the tape cartridge to direct sunlight or extremes of temperature.

· If the cartridge is accidentally exposed to high temperatures, allow the tape to run for several minutes at low volume before playing it normally.

· Remove the cartridge from the tape player when not in use.

· Protect the open end of the cartridge from dust and dirt.

Store tapes with the open end down.

· Never try to pry the cartridge open or pull the tape out.

Cleaning Tape Players

The playback head and capstan accumulate a coating of oxide from the tape. This accumulation can be removed with a cotton swab moistened in denatured alcohol. Do not use carbon tetrachloride. Hold the cartridge door open and swab the surfaces of the playback head and capstan; dry the parts with a clean cotton swab.

Radios

In radios, you have a choice of three types: AM, AM-FM, and AM-FM stereo. If all you ever listen to is AM, just get an AM unit and save your money. But if you demand a variety of programming plus quality sound reproduction, AM-FM stereo is the way to go.

AM Radio

In general, AM (amplitude modulation) has a greater range than FM (frequency modulation).

207

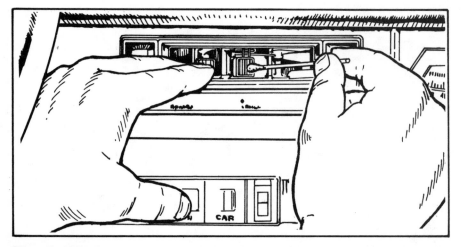

Clean the tape head and capstan every few hours of operation with a cotton swab and denatured alcohol.

AM can be heard as far away as 200–300 miles from a strong station at night, but suffers from several disadvantages.

First, even though AM stations can be heard at great distances, as the station gets weaker, the volume falls off. Second, AM stations are more susceptible to static from power lines and other man-made sources, especially when only distant stations are receivable. Traffic lights, electric signs and thunderstorms can make AM unlistenable. Third, AM stations fade under overpasses and in downtown areas.

FM Radio

FM radio is often called "line of sight," because the high frequencies will not bounce off the atmosphere like AM radio. Consequently, the range of FM is only 35–50 miles depending on terrain. A mountain can easily blank out an FM radio wave, but in downtown urban areas, the signal will bounce off buildings making FM reception possible when AM is not (for instance, in tunnels).

Though it is not static-free, FM is less susceptible to static. Like AM, it will pick up static from electrical disturbances, especially when operating in the fringe area of an FM station. But unlike AM, as the station gets weaker, the volume will stay the same, although background noise will increase.

Speakers

Speakers are one of the most neglected components of a car stereo system. You can have the best radio or tape player made, but without good speakers, it won't make a bit of difference, because poor-quality speakers create their own distortion and static.

Car speakers come in two basic types—flush mount or surface mount. Flush mount (also known as recessed) work best installed in doors, kick panels or rear decks, where they produce best sound and are out of the way. The large, open areas in doors and under the rear deck (behind the speakers) serve as acoustic enclosures, reinforcing the bass tones. Flush-mount speakers are usually 5″ round or 6″ x 9″ oval speakers.

Surface-mount (wedge or hang-on) speakers come with their own enclosures made of high-strength ABS plastic. They feature quick and easy installation on almost any flat surface, and can even be installed beneath the dash if they are attached to a flat board. However, the bass tones are not as good because of the reduced baffle space behind the speaker.

Whichever type you choose, a good rule of thumb is, "the heavier the magnet, the better the speaker." A good speaker will have a magnet weighing at least 3 to 5 ounces, often as much as 20 ounces. Also, larger speakers (diameter) are more effective, especially for low (bass) tones.

Stereo radios and tape players require the use of at least two

PARALLEL HOOK-UP 8 OHM UNIT 8 OHM SPEAKERS

4 OHM 4 OHM 8 OHM 8 OHM

8 OHM 8 OHM 4 OHM 4 OHM 8 OHM 8 OHM

SERIES PARALLEL 8 OHM UNIT 4 OHM SPEAKERS

PARALLEL HOOK-UP 4 OHM UNIT 8 OHM SPEAKERS

STEREO 8 OHM   STEREO 8 OHM   STEREO 4 OHM

Learn the impedance of your stereo or tape player before deciding on speakers. The impedance (ohms) for each speaker should be the same to avoid poor sound or blown speakers. The hook-ups shown here will accommodate multi-speaker installations.

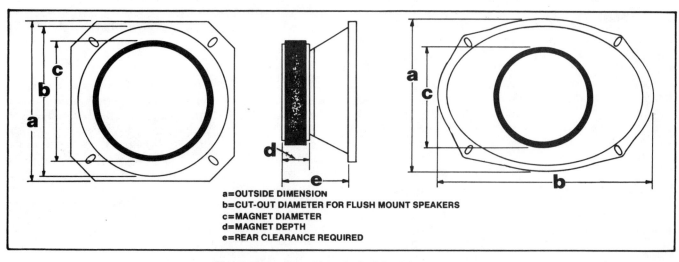

a=OUTSIDE DIMENSION
b=CUT-OUT DIAMETER FOR FLUSH MOUNT SPEAKERS
c=MAGNET DIAMETER
d=MAGNET DEPTH
e=REAR CLEARANCE REQUIRED

Check these dimensions before buying speakers.

speakers to achieve the proper stereo effect, though you can use four or even six. No matter how many speakers you use, remember stereo separation must be side-to-side.

The mounting location you pick will usually determine whether flush- or surface-mount speakers are used. Surface-mounted speakers are the easiest to install because they simply bolt in place. Flush-mount speakers produce a better bass response because they use the larger area behind them as a baffle. However, flush mounts are more complex to install.

Before you start cutting holes for them, its smart to make a couple of checks. Will the speaker's location affect the operation of the window crank, convertible top mechanism or removal of the spare tire? If yes, find another location. Also, be sure there's enough room to fit the speaker where you want it. Use a template to help you position the speakers exactly where you want them, and use a hole saw to cut the hole.

Antennas

Like the speakers, the antenna deserves some consideration if optimum performance is expected.

For best reception on AM, the antenna should be extended as high as possible. On FM, the optimum antenna height is approximately 31"; it also happens to work well on AM.

There are several types of antennas. The traditional extendable antenna is seldom seen anymore, giving way to the one-piece stainless steel antenna. These are probably the best compromise, because they are tuned for FM reception and offer the most resistance to casual vandals, who like to break the antennas off parked cars.

The windshield antenna supplied with many new cars works fine on AM, but leaves something to be desired on FM.

For those to whom price is not important, or who desire the latest in technology, electronic antennas are the thing. These incorporate an amplifier in the base of the antenna to boost the radio signal. Some of the signal in any antenna is lost through the cable before it reaches the receiver. If the signal can be amplified before it enters the cable, a stronger signal will eventually reach the receiver, allowing reception of stations that would normally go unheard.

Remove the cap nut holding the antenna mast.

The stainless steel antenna mast can usually be replaced without disturbing the mount.

Installing Stereo

In-dash installation is the most attractive and theft-resistant, but it's also the more difficult to perform. Under-dash mounting is far easier and sometimes your only choice. Whatever spot you decide on, be sure to mount the unit out of the way of passengers and vehicle controls.

When drilling mounting holes, a piece of masking tape makes it easier to mark hole locations and will prevent a slipping drill from scratching the paint. Be VERY careful that you don't drill into wires or other concealed components.

Wiring is easy. Most music machines have a fused power lead, a ground wire and two wires for each speaker. Simply follow the manufacturer's wiring diagram for proper hook-up. Use crimp-on terminals or soldered connections—they're much more reliable than just twisting wires together and taping them.

Installing the Speakers

The most important decision when installing stereo is the placement of the speakers. Acoustically, the best place for speakers is level with the listeners' ears, and where the baffle (space behind the speakers) is large enough for good bass tones. Unfortunately, most cars don't have a space that meets these conditions so you'll have to examine your car carefully. Consider these places as mounting locations for speakers:

Rear deck—There's plenty of room to act as a baffle, but the speakers are essentially mounted in the trunk, and while the rear deck is at ear level, the speakers face up.

Under the dash—The space under the dash of most cars will barely accommodate the radio, let alone a pair of stereo speakers.

Top of the dash—This is a favorite for factory-installed speakers, which can often (though not easily) be replaced if desired.

Kick panels—Kick panels sometimes cover cavities that make good baffles, but frequently only cover the inner fender wall.

In the door—This location is probably the best compromise for a good baffle, good listening position and ease of installation.

Rear Seat panels—This may be the only place in small cars.

Hopefully, you've decided on a location before buying speakers, so you know whether they'll fit with no interference. The next step is to wire the receiver to the speakers.

It's probably easiest to leave installation of the radio itself until last. The speaker wires are usually coded. Keep the wires with the color stripes or ridge going to the same terminal of each speaker. Use a flat, push-on spade connector or solder the connection. Keep the wires where they will be out of the way and won't be rubbed or chafed. Popular places to run wires are under the carpets or door sill plates. Where the wires run through a hole, protect them with a rubber grommet.

Be sure to leave enough slack in the wires to open doors, allow for vibration and to connect the wires to the radio.

Installing the Radio

Radio installations are either in-dash or under-dash. The in-dash route is neater and less tempting to thieves but generally harder than under-dash.

Look under the dash. Most cars have a clearing in the maze of hoses and wires for a factory-installed radio to fit. After-market

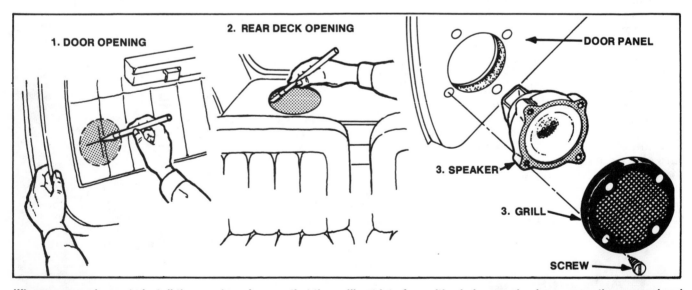

Wherever you choose to install the speakers, be sure that they will not interfere with window mechanisms, spare tire removal and the like. Also be sure the speaker dimensions will fit in the space available. Mark the hole pattern with a template (1). Cut the fabric with a knife (2) and finish the hole with a saw. Install the speaker and grille (3).

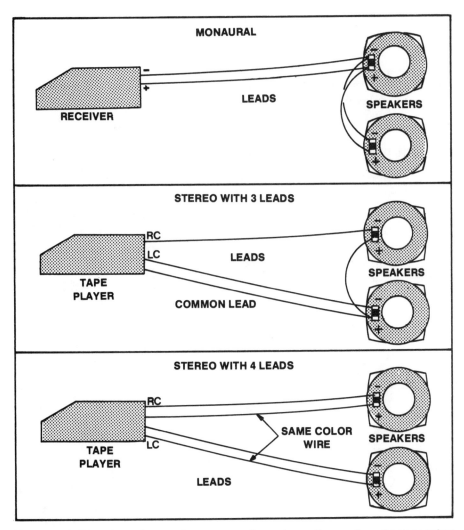

Use one of these examples to wire your speakers, depending on how many speaker leads come out of your radio or tape deck.

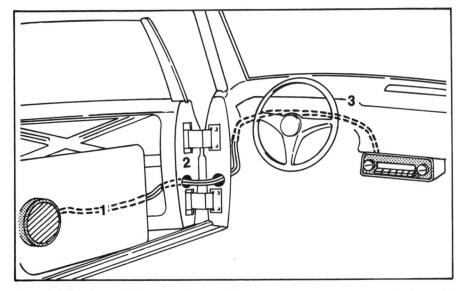

If your speakers are in the doors, the wires (1) can run through holes in the doors (2) and up under the dash (3).

radios generally resemble the factory item in size and shape and many are fitted with adjustable control shafts to fit different cars. Check before you buy the radio to be sure it will fit your particular installation.

Once you've chosen a location, check the following:

· Make sure the set doesn't block the flow of air or interfere with heater controls.

· Make sure you have a solid anchor point.

· Make sure the controls are within easy reach.

· Make sure a power source and chassis ground are convenient.

· Make sure there's nothing behind the anchor spot that could be damaged during installation.

Chilton Tip

A tape player should never be installed more than 30° from the horizontal unless specifically designed for vertical or off-horizontal operation.

Before actually installing the set, check for a source of power. Radios are most often connected to a source that is "hot" only when the ignition switch is ON. This way the radio will go off when the ignition is turned OFF. Tape players, however, should be connected to a power source that is always "hot." This prevents shutting off the power while the player is playing, avoiding flat spots on the roller. You can usually find either type of power source at the fuse block, which can be tapped with a push-on spade connector. For safety, insert a 1.5 amp fuse in the power line.

Before turning on the system, recheck all wiring. Pay special attention to grounding and speaker wiring.

TROUBLESHOOTING BASIC RADIO PROBLEMS

Radio problems are not normally caused by a defective radio. More often the cause is due to some less obvious fault. Follow the procedures in order before assuming the radio is defective.

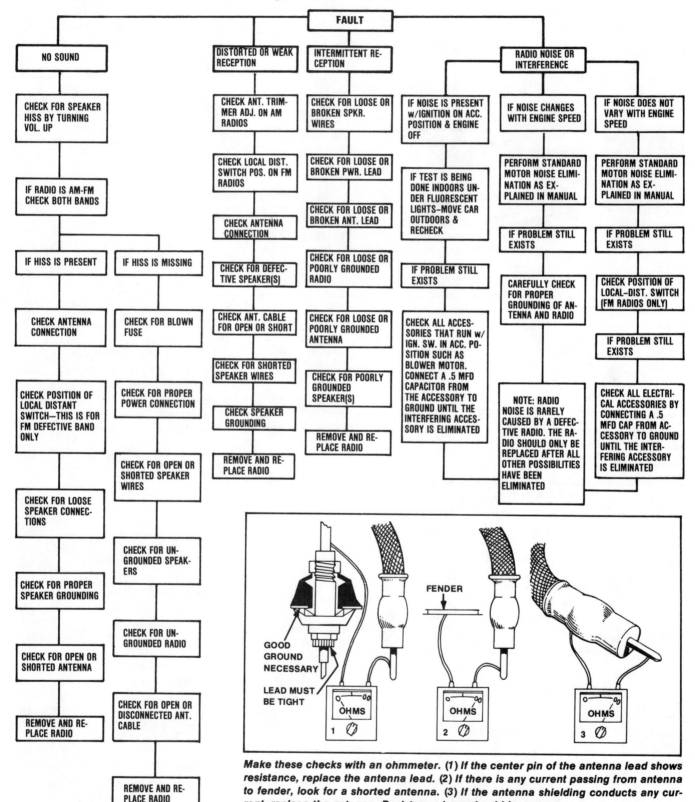

FAULT

NO SOUND

CHECK FOR SPEAKER HISS BY TURNING VOL. UP

IF RADIO IS AM-FM CHECK BOTH BANDS

IF HISS IS PRESENT   IF HISS IS MISSING

CHECK ANTENNA CONNECTION

CHECK POSITION OF LOCAL DISTANT SWITCH—THIS IS FOR FM DEFECTIVE BAND ONLY

CHECK FOR LOOSE SPEAKER CONNECTIONS

CHECK FOR PROPER SPEAKER GROUNDING

CHECK FOR OPEN OR SHORTED ANTENNA

REMOVE AND REPLACE RADIO

CHECK FOR BLOWN FUSE

CHECK FOR PROPER POWER CONNECTION

CHECK FOR OPEN OR SHORTED SPEAKER WIRES

CHECK FOR UNGROUNDED SPEAKERS

CHECK FOR UNGROUNDED RADIO

CHECK FOR OPEN OR DISCONNECTED ANT. CABLE

REMOVE AND REPLACE RADIO

DISTORTED OR WEAK RECEPTION

CHECK ANT. TRIMMER ADJ. ON AM RADIOS

CHECK LOCAL DIST. SWITCH POS. ON FM RADIOS

CHECK ANTENNA CONNECTION

CHECK FOR DEFECTIVE SPEAKER(S)

CHECK ANT. CABLE FOR OPEN OR SHORT

CHECK FOR SHORTED SPEAKER WIRES

CHECK SPEAKER GROUNDING

REMOVE AND REPLACE RADIO

INTERMITTENT RECEPTION

CHECK FOR LOOSE OR BROKEN SPKR. WIRES

CHECK FOR LOOSE OR BROKEN PWR. LEAD

CHECK FOR LOOSE OR BROKEN ANT. LEAD

CHECK FOR LOOSE OR POORLY GROUNDED RADIO

CHECK FOR LOOSE OR POORLY GROUNDED ANTENNA

CHECK FOR POORLY GROUNDED SPEAKER(S)

REMOVE AND REPLACE RADIO

IF NOISE IS PRESENT w/IGNITION ON ACC. POSITION & ENGINE OFF

IF TEST IS BEING DONE INDOORS UNDER FLUORESCENT LIGHTS—MOVE CAR OUTDOORS & RECHECK

IF PROBLEM STILL EXISTS

CHECK ALL ACCESSORIES THAT RUN w/ IGN. SW. IN ACC. POSITION SUCH AS BLOWER MOTOR. CONNECT A .5 MFD CAPACITOR FROM THE ACCESSORY TO GROUND UNTIL THE INTERFERING ACCESSORY IS ELIMINATED

RADIO NOISE OR INTERFERENCE

IF NOISE CHANGES WITH ENGINE SPEED

PERFORM STANDARD MOTOR NOISE ELIMINATION AS EXPLAINED IN MANUAL

IF PROBLEM STILL EXISTS

CAREFULLY CHECK FOR PROPER GROUNDING OF ANTENNA AND RADIO

NOTE: RADIO NOISE IS RARELY CAUSED BY A DEFECTIVE RADIO. THE RADIO SHOULD ONLY BE REPLACED AFTER ALL OTHER POSSIBILITIES HAVE BEEN ELIMINATED

IF NOISE DOES NOT VARY WITH ENGINE SPEED

PERFORM STANDARD MOTOR NOISE ELIMINATION AS EXPLAINED IN MANUAL

IF PROBLEM STILL EXISTS

CHECK POSITION OF LOCAL-DIST. SWITCH (FM RADIOS ONLY)

IF PROBLEM STILL EXISTS

CHECK ALL ELECTRICAL ACCESSORIES BY CONNECTING A .5 MFD CAP FROM ACCESSORY TO GROUND UNTIL THE INTERFERING ACCESSORY IS ELIMINATED

GOOD GROUND NECESSARY

LEAD MUST BE TIGHT

FENDER

OHMS   OHMS   OHMS

1   2   3

Make these checks with an ohmmeter. (1) If the center pin of the antenna lead shows resistance, replace the antenna lead. (2) If there is any current passing from antenna to fender, look for a shorted antenna. (3) If the antenna shielding conducts any current, replace the antenna. Resistance here should be zero.

Installing the Antenna

Antenna installation is usually fairly easy. The biggest problem is fishing the cable through the fender or firewall to connect it with the radio.

A single-piece antenna is already matched to the FM receiver, but you'll need to adjust the AM portion of the receiver.

Tune the radio to a weak station around 1400 on the AM dial and turn the trimmer adjustment until the station is strongest. The trimmer screw is either on the back or side of the set near the antenna jack, or on the front behind the tuning knob. Wherever it is hidden, it is usually labeled "ANT."

Noise Suppression

Static, hash and interference in the sound system is usually due to loose connections. Go over all wiring connections before assuming the set is defective. Be especially careful when checking the antenna and its lead-in. Looseness, rust, or failure to clean away the paint under ground connections destroys fidelity.

Make a preliminary check with all accessories turned off. Turn accessories on one at a time and listen for increased static. If a particular type of interference cannot be readily identified, a test capacitor can be easily constructed as shown. A grounded

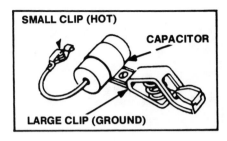

A home-made test capacitor can be constructed to locate static by the process of elimination.

capacitor touched to all "hot" electrical connections will identify the offending item if the static disappears.

20
CB Radio and Radar Detectors

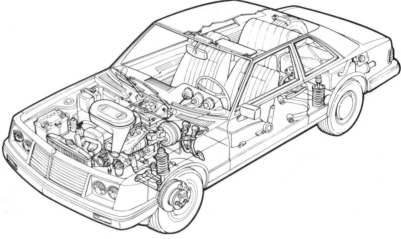

```
TOOLS AND SUPPLIES
Tools
  Screwdrivers
  Electric drill
  Wire stripper
  Single-edge razor blade
  Wrenches
  Pliers
  Soldering gun
Supplies
  Wire
  Electrical tape
  Solder and flux
  Electrical connectors
```

Why CB Radio?

Few events have affected the life of the average motorist more than the fuel shortage of 1973–74 and the subsequent lowering of the national speed limit to 55 mph. During the truckers' strike of 1974, a direct result of the fuel embargo, the motoring public became aware of the network of Citizens Band (CB) radios tracking the movements of "Smokey Bear." Millions of motorists rushed out and bought CBs to monitor truckers' conversations, receiving up-to-the-minute reports on traffic, weather conditions and speed traps. Since then, CBs have become so popular, that they rank second only to the telephone as the largest form of two-way communication.

Most CB owners wouldn't go far without their "rig," claiming it keeps them more alert, helps pass the time and provides the location of every speed trap for miles, in addition to other uses:

· Campground operators frequently monitor Channel 11, anticipating campers searching for accommodations in the peak seasons.

· Garages, service stations and private citizens monitor Channel 9 to assist in emergency situations or to help stranded motorists. Channel 9 is the official nationwide channel for emergencies, including such information as where to find food and lodging. Organized groups such as REACT (Radio Emergency Associated Citizens Teams), the largest, handle millions of emergency calls annually and are equipped to provide you with information or route your call to the proper authority.

Increasingly, state police are beginning to use CB radios. Highway patrols in several states have installed CBs in their patrol cars, and some troopers buy their own sets. Police and CBers have been known to cooperate in apprehending drunk or hit-and-run drivers.

CBs and the FCC

No operator's license is required for CB. The Federal Communications Commission (FCC) used to require that you obtain a Radio Service Class D station permit before operating a CB. However, the permit requirement has been suspended.

You should however, pick up a copy of Part 95 of the FCC Rules and Regulations, which is the bible as far as CB is concerned. These rules can be obtained from the Government Printing Office ($1.50), or are usually reprinted in any complete book on CB's.

The FCC is empowered by Congress to establish and enforce the rules and regulations governing the use of CB radio. Much of the problem is that most people don't understand the 20-odd pages of legal jargon that make up Part 95. To simplify things, the FCC has made the following modifications, which are currently in effect:

· The "hobby" restriction is removed. Citations will no longer be given for idle "chit-chat" except in cases of profanity, playing music or selling merchandise on the air.

· The use of "handles" is now approved, provided the station call sign is also given.

· The fee is no longer being collected.

· Effective Jan. 1, 1977, the number of channels was increased from 23 to 40. At the same time, the FCC stated that the 40-channel expansion was an interim measure, and that studies are underway considering the 220 and 900 MHz band for CB.

· The permit requirement has been suspended.

The FCC is concerned mainly with obscenity on the air and use of the linear (RF) amplifier.

Obscenity on the air is, fortunately, fairly rare. The linear (RF) amplifier is another matter. It can boost the output of a CB from 4 watts to over 100 and blank out large geographic areas, making it impossible for others to transmit. The FCC is so concerned about these that selling or owning one (it doesn't have to be hooked up) is a Federal offense punishable by a fine of up to $10,000 and a year in jail.

Choosing a CB Set

There are hundreds of models to choose from, and features are numbered in the tens. Your choice will probably depend on how much you want to spend, but here's a checklist to help you through the CB jungle.

1. Look for an FCC "Type Accepted" set. It will be marked as such and means it meets or exceeds FCC standards.

2. Learn to interpret the specifications.

Output power in watts (W) is regulated by the FCC to no more than 4 watts. Most sets give 2½–4 watts; look for a set that gives the highest output in watts.

Modulation is limited to 100%; the closer to 100% the set is

rated, the better its talking power.

Sensitivity in microvolts (uV) is the ability of the receiver to pick up weak signals. The smaller the number, the better the set; look for something under .8 microvolts.

Selectivity (dB) is the receiver's ability to reject signals on adjacent channels. This is important since signals are separated by very small frequency differences. The greater the dB rating, the more selective the receiver.

Spurious rejection in dB is the ability of a set to keep transmissions on the channel selected. A 60 dB rating is minimum; the higher the number the better the set.

3. If possible, try the set before buying. Check the squelch. As the squelch is turned up, the audio should suddenly go off; as the squelch is turned back, the audio should suddenly come on. If the squelch acts like a volume control (sound fades gradually), look at another set.

4. Look for a set with automatic noise limiter (ANL) and

noise blanker (NB); noise from your own ignition can play havoc with the receiver.

5. Look for a detachable mike. This will make repair or replacement easier.

6. Look for easily operated controls. Switches should leave no doubt as to their position and meters should be easily read.

Installing Mobile CBs & Antennas

Almost all new equipment comes with some sort of owner's manual or installation procedures. Follow the manufacturer's recommendations and supplement them with some ideas here.

Connecting the Set

Mobile installations are easy. The problem is deciding where to put the set so that it will be unobtrusive, fit neatly and be in easy reach. Most sets could fit in the glove compartment except that they are hard to operate from there.

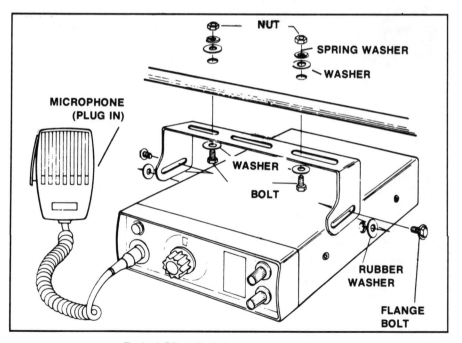

Typical CB radio below-dash installation.

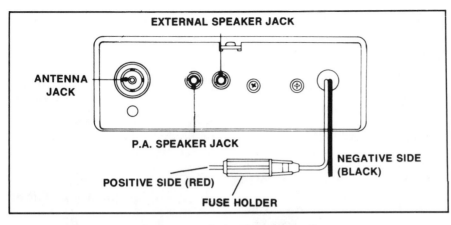

EXTERNAL SPEAKER JACK

ANTENNA JACK

P.A. SPEAKER JACK

POSITIVE SIDE (RED)

FUSE HOLDER

NEGATIVE SIDE (BLACK)

The rear panel of a typical CB radio.

CB's have become a popular item with thieves. Unless you plan to disconnect your set every time you leave the car, give some

Cigarette lighter adapters provide a convenient temporary 12-volt power source.

A CB slide mount on the console makes a neat installation.

thought to installing it where it will attract the least attention. A fairly good solution is to use the slide mounts popular with auto tape deck enthusiasts. You have only to disconnect the antenna and remove the set to stow it out of sight.

When installing your "rig";
· Observe battery polarity. Most sets are negative ground.
· Always connect a 1.5 amp fuse in the power line, using an automotive fuse holder.
· Be sure all connections are clean and tight. All connections should be soldered and taped.

Installing the Antenna

It is impossible to detail the installation of every antenna/mount combination—the possibilities are endless. They range from magnetic mounts to the popular trunk lid mount, which offers three advantages:
· an efficient antenna system (either base, top or center loaded);
· easily removable; and
· no holes need be drilled.

Tuning the Antenna

Most antennas are supplied ready to use and will give a satisfactory SWR (Standing Wave Ratio) reading. SWR is the amount of signal reflected back into the antenna from sheet metal body panels, nearby build-

Three types of antennas: top—magnetic roof-top mount; middle—cowl mount on fender; bottom—electric combination AM/FM/CB antenna.

NOISE SUPPRESSION FOR CB RADIOS

Radio interference (noise), falls into 2 classes—natural (lightning, atmospheric disturbances about which little can be done) or man-made (produced by the car's ignition and other machinery). Most CB's use noise limiters or blankers to filter out most of the man-made interference, but extreme cases will require additional noise suppression. Don't confuse background noise with interference; concern yourself with it only if it disrupts reception at normal volume.

Locating the Noise

Each type of interference you hear through the receiver has its own distinctive sound and characteristics, giving a clue to its source.

IGNITION: a popping sound, increasing with engine speed. It will disappear immediately when the ignition is turned off.

ALTERNATOR: a musical, high-pitched whine, increasing in frequency with engine speed. It will NOT shut off instantly when the key is turned off.

VOLTAGE REGULATOR: a ragged, rasping sound at an irregular rate that will not disappear immediately when the key is turned off.

INSTRUMENTS: hissing, crackling and clicking sounds at irregular intervals. They can be tested by disconnecting the gauges one at a time, or by jarring the dashboard.

WHEELS & TIRES: a popping or rushing sound on dry roads. Lightly apply the brakes; the noise should disappear.

ACCESSORIES: make a preliminary check with all accessories off. Turn them on one at a time and listen for increased noise.

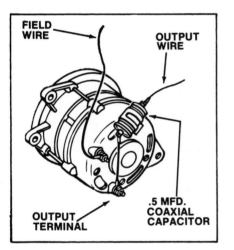

Voltage Regulator

Install a 0.5 mfd capacitor as close as possible to the **armature** and **battery** terminals. Do not connect a capacitor to the field terminal.

Instruments & Accessories

A 0.5 mfd capacitor installed at the gauge terminal or sending unit will reduce interference from these sources.

Electric windows, heater blowers, and the like can be quieted with a 0.25 mfd capacitor installed at the accessory terminal.

Wheels & Tires

Static collector rings, installed inside the front wheel caps, will prevent static from entering the radio.

Ignition Coil

Remove the ignition coil. Clean the paint from the back of the mounting bracket and reassemble it tightly.

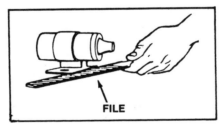

Bonding

Bonding straps are pieces of metal or copper braid which

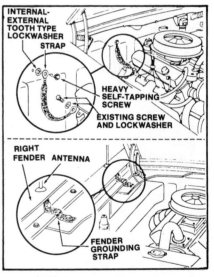

electrically connect components to ground.

Good places to use them are:
· Engine-to-frame
· Fenders-to-frame
· Trunk lid to fender and hood to firewall
· Exhaust pipe-to-frame

Use self-tapping screws, toothed lockwashers and heavy straps as short as possible.

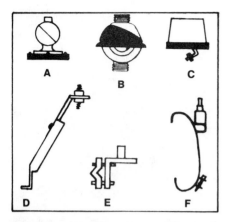

The most popular antenna mounts: A-Swivel ball; B-Cowl/fender mount; C-No hole trunk mount; D-Rain gutter mount; E-West coast mirror or roof rack mount; F-Bumper mount.

ings, etc. A 1.1:1 match is ideal, if seldom achieved. Anything below 1.5:1 is fine, and above 3:1 indicates danger.

Any CB specialist can check and/or tune your antenna. You can do it yourself, but an SWR meter will cost about $15 and you shouldn't be charged more than $5 for someone to do it. If you do it yourself, close all car doors and check the SWR in an open area. Trim the antenna in small (⅛") increments by trimming the bottom of the metal resonator rod (the top portion of the antenna).

An SWR meter is necessary to tune the antenna. Connect the antenna cable to the "antenna" end and connect the "transmitter" end to the set with a patch cord.

Caution

Before working on the car, disconnect the battery.

Preliminary Checks

1. Be sure all connections are clean and tight. All oil, paint and grease should be removed from areas where electrical contact is necessary.

2. Be sure the engine is tuned. More interference will be produced from worn plugs, points, cap and rotor.

3. Keep accessory leads away from the ignition system and other suspected noise producers.

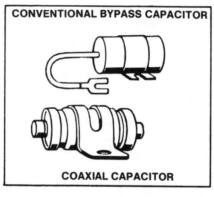

If absolutely necessary, accessory leads should cross ignition wires at right angles.

Capacitors

Man-made interference is almost always an alternating, impulse type. Capacitors are rated in microfarads (mfd) and pass this type of current to ground, without affecting the flow of direct current.

Caution

Never use capacitors on transistorized or electronic ignitions.

Alternator

To quiet the alternator, install a 0.5 mfd coaxial capacitor at the alternator output terminal. Be sure it is rated to handle the alternator output current.

Radar Detectors

Let's face it. The 55 mph speed limit is here to stay. Regardless of superior visibility, light traffic, or any other excuse you can offer "Smokey," the 55 mph speed limit has been mandated and states are required to enforce it. In fact, the Federal government has threatened to withhold Federal highway money from states with poor speed limit compliance records.

Radar is the states' prime weapon in enforcing the speed

The newest police radar units are hand-held, calculate speed in less than 1/100th second, and emit no radar beam until a trigger is released.

The traditional police radar. It is used as stationary radar or as a sophisticated and extremely accurate speedometer, when the radar and target are travelling in the same direction.

TROUBLESHOOTING CB ANTENNA PROBLEMS

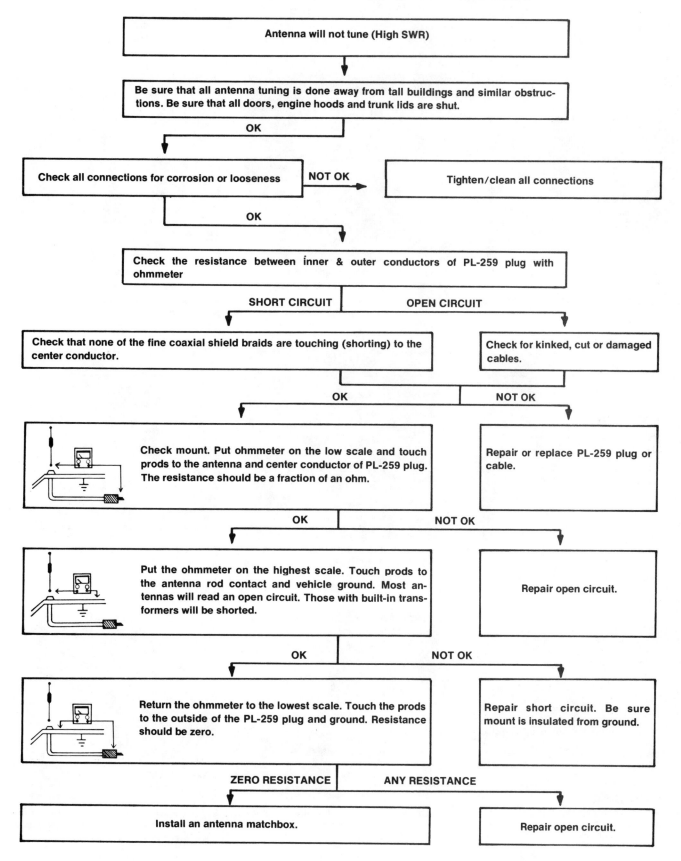

Antenna will not tune (High SWR)

↓

Be sure that all antenna tuning is done away from tall buildings and similar obstructions. Be sure that all doors, engine hoods and trunk lids are shut.

OK

Check all connections for corrosion or looseness — NOT OK → **Tighten/clean all connections**

OK

Check the resistance between inner & outer conductors of PL-259 plug with ohmmeter

SHORT CIRCUIT / OPEN CIRCUIT

Check that none of the fine coaxial shield braids are touching (shorting) to the center conductor.

Check for kinked, cut or damaged cables.

OK / NOT OK

Check mount. Put ohmmeter on the low scale and touch prods to the antenna and center conductor of PL-259 plug. The resistance should be a fraction of an ohm.

Repair or replace PL-259 plug or cable.

OK / NOT OK

Put the ohmmeter on the highest scale. Touch prods to the antenna rod contact and vehicle ground. Most antennas will read an open circuit. Those with built-in transformers will be shorted.

Repair open circuit.

OK / NOT OK

Return the ohmmeter to the lowest scale. Touch the prods to the outside of the PL-259 plug and ground. Resistance should be zero.

Repair short circuit. Be sure mount is insulated from ground.

ZERO RESISTANCE / ANY RESISTANCE

Install an antenna matchbox.

Repair open circuit.

INSTALLING CB & ANTENNA

There are many types of antennas and mounts available, and just as many places to put them. Probably the most common installation is the trunk mount, because it requires no holes in the vehicle body. This installation is typical of a trunk mount, but regardless of which mount and antenna combination you choose, the principles detailed here are the same.

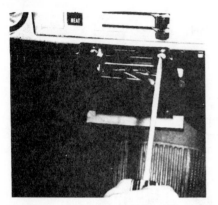

1. Install the male portion of the slide mount in the desired location. Mount the female portion of the slide mount on the radio. Be sure both parts are wired alike.

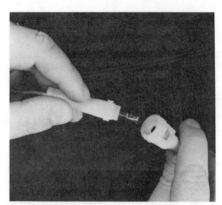

2. Splice a fuse holder and 1.5 amp fuse into the power line. Tape the connections securely.

3. Route the power line (with spade connector) to the fuse box and plug into an empty, fused terminal. Connect the ground wire to a screw using a toothed lockwasher.

4. Scrape away about ⅜" of foam from the center conductor. Attach terminal hardware to both leads, crimping it in place and soldering.

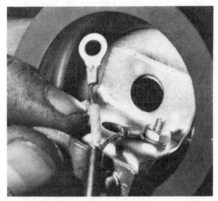

5. Assemble the trunk mount and attach the braided lead (ground side) to the screw provided.

6. Attach the copper wire (center conductor) to the antenna mount.

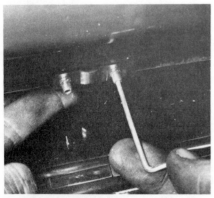

7. Slip the mount over the edge of the trunk lid and tighten the allen screws to hold it in place.

8. Lightly tighten the antenna into the mount.

9. Route the antenna cable through the trunk and under the door sill plates to keep it out of the way.

limit, and, as radar has become more sophisticated, so are the methods of avoiding it. The radar detector and the CB are the most effective countermeasures in the driver's arsenal.

CBers say the citizens band radio is still the best defense against speed traps. But, you could be rolling along, just as the radar trap is being set up, and be the first unlucky victim, which is where the radar detector can earn its keep.

Newer units may even replace CB as the motorist's early warning defense; manufacturers claim that detectors will soon be available which can pick up radar around curves and over hills.

Do You Need a Radar Detector?

Most of us, at one time or another, exceed the speed limit, either by design, casual indifference or righteous indignation. Forget the old wives' tales that covering your hubcaps with tin foil will jam police radar. If you regularly cruise the interstates and are inclined to exceed the speed limit, the savings from one ticket for more than 65 mph, coupled with the inevitable court costs, points on your license, inconvenience of a court appearance and resultant high insurance rates, will more than offset the cost of a decent radar detector.

It's estimated that between 70% and 85% of all interstate speeding arrests are made with radar. It's easy to operate, offers practically unbeatable evidence in court, and is versatile. Since inveterate and casual speeders alike are part of the game of psychological warfare, with your driver's license as the prize, you need as many odds a possible in your favor. The CB is still the favorite weapon, but while it provides an overkill of warning for stationary radar traps, it cannot provide much warning for the K-band portable units until an unwary offender is pulled over.

A radar detector offers several advantages:
· No complicated installation,
· No antenna,
· Not subject to weather conditions, interference or inane chatter,
· Works day or night (when a CB is less effective).

However, don't depend totally on the radar detector to protect your wallet. The newest police jewel is a hand-held, portable unit equipped with a hold-button to cut off the radar signal until the unit is activated. The trooper waits until he has reason to believe that a vehicle is speeding, aims the gun and releases the trigger. The speed is computed, and displayed in less than $1/100$th second. Only the CB will warn you of this fellow when he pulls someone over, unless your detector picks up the signal when the radar is "shot."

In 1979, a Florida judge ruled that radar clockings could not be used as evidence in some 80 cases pending under his jurisdiction. Even though other judges were not bound by his ruling, the judge questioned the reliability of the radar equipment.

Erroneous readings in the radar were apparently caused by interference from billboards, overpasses, car heaters near the radar unit, air conditioning fans in the vehicle, and CB and police radios.

Are Detectors Legal?

Radar detectors are legal in most states, or most states are indifferent to their use since more compliance with 55 mph is the net result. Only Virginia has an outright law prohibiting their use. Connecticut prohibits their use by order of the State Police, and New Jesey has an ordinance prohibiting windshield obstruction, a favorite mounting place for detectors. Possession of a detector in Denver or Washington, D.C. will likely get you a fine, and Virginia authorities may go as far as to confiscate a detector, whether it's in use or not.

Legal opinion holds that any or all prohibitions regarding radar detectors may be unconstitutional and that laws regulating their use are contrary to Federal Communications Commission regulations on the theory that a radar detector is merely a radio receiver. The Communications Act of 1934, As Amended, specifically gives the FCC—a Federal agency whose regulations supersede states' rights—the right to regulate interstate radio transmission and reception. The FCC gives the right to "receive telecommunications of any type on any frequency" to all the people of the United States. The only thing illegal is for you to divulge the information which you receive without the permission of the sender (i.e., get on your CB and say that your radar detector uncovered a radar trap at such-and-such a milepost).

The laws regulating use of radar detectors are currently being challenged in court. Electrolert, Inc., a detector manufacturer, will even offer legal decisions to those who feel that they were convicted of speeding through the indiscriminate use of radar. Until the question is decided, you're asking for trouble by advertising the detector's presence in hostile areas.

How Radar and Detectors Work

Radar, an acronym for Radio Detecting and Ranging, was first developed by the U.S. Navy during World War I to accurately determine the range for heavy artillery aboard ship.

Just as sound waves bounce around and produce an echo, ultrahigh frequency (uhf) radio waves can be sent out on a set frequency, reflected from an object and received again. The police radar is both a transmitter and receiver, sending and receiving signals in an almost continuous sequence. Most traffic radar works at an incredibly high frequency, allowing the continuous sequence of signals. More than 95% of all traffic radar works at 10.525 GHz (gigahertz), or over 10,000,000 cycles per second. These are known as the X-band. The remaining 5% (K-band) are the newest and operate at 24.150 GHz.

Stationary radar can track you coming or going. A special antenna is used to transmit the radio beam in a narrowly focused pattern, spreading out about 6 degrees. A moving object with a high metal content will cause the beam to be reflected (echoed) and received by the radar unit. Since the object is moving, the signal is echoed at a slightly different frequency than when it was transmitted. This frequency change is known as the Doppler effect. If the vehicle is coming toward the radar, the echoed frequency will be higher; if it's moving away, the echoed frequency will be lower. The radar measures the rate of frequency change (1 mph is equal to a frequency change of 31.4 cycles per second on the X-band) and computes the target's speed. A vehicle producing a frequency change of 2041 cycles per second will be "caught" at 65 mph, more than enough for a citation.

The computation is more complicated when the radar is in motion in a cruising patrol car. Actually two signals (a high Doppler and low Doppler) are sent from the same radio beam. The low Doppler is reflected from the road surface; to the radar, it is stationary and the road is moving towards it. The high Doppler portion of the beam is reflected from the moving vehicle. Through some complex circuitry, the radar computes the closing speed of the two vehicles, and subtracts the lower frequency speed of the road surface (which the radar believes is moving toward it, but at a slower rate) and arrives at the speed of the oncoming vehicle. Moving radar only works if the patrol car is coming at the target; it will not work once the target has passed in the opposite direction. If you are both heading in the same direction, "Smokey" must be behind you and going at the same speed. In this mode, the radar unit is an extremely accurate speedometer, recording the patrol car's own speed.

Range

Radar operates only on a line-of-sight basis; it can't see around corners or over hills. But, it can measure the speed of a vehicle practically anywhere it can get a clear line of sight at the target, for instance, just as the target crests a hill or rounds a curve.

It is generally agreed that X-band radar will give the trooper audio alert at about 1 mile, and speed readout at about ¾ mile on a clear, straight road. The newest, most sophisticated K-band units are capable of speed readout at up to a mile. Fortunately for the motorist, the practical range of traffic radar on a well-travelled interstate is about ¼ mile, and, most arrests are clocked within ⅛ mile.

Most radar in use today (ex-

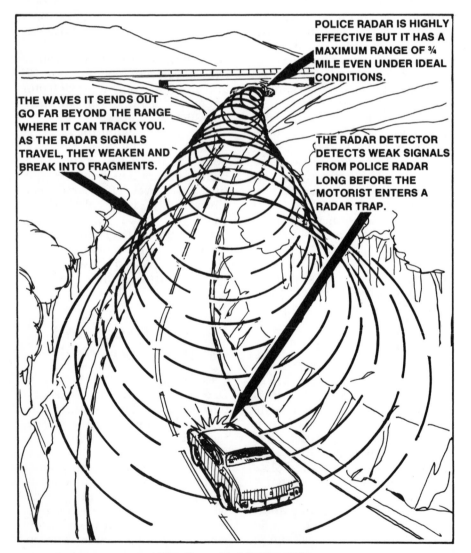

POLICE RADAR IS HIGHLY EFFECTIVE BUT IT HAS A MAXIMUM RANGE OF ¾ MILE EVEN UNDER IDEAL CONDITIONS.

THE WAVES IT SENDS OUT GO FAR BEYOND THE RANGE WHERE IT CAN TRACK YOU. AS THE RADAR SIGNALS TRAVEL, THEY WEAKEN AND BREAK INTO FRAGMENTS.

THE RADAR DETECTOR DETECTS WEAK SIGNALS FROM POLICE RADAR LONG BEFORE THE MOTORIST ENTERS A RADAR TRAP.

How the radar detector works.

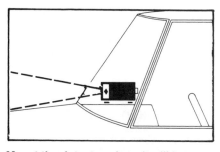

Mount the detector where it will have an unobstructed view of the road. Tilting it down a few degrees will sometimes increase the range.

Radar detectors are traditionally mounted on the dash.

cept for ultrasophisticated models that compute speed instantaneously) require a full second to lock in the target and register speed. But, once it locks onto a target, speed readout is instant. They also have a circuit that rejects inputs where deceleration of the target is more than about three miles per second. It's not hard to figure that if your radar detector goes off, and you can decelerate from 65 to 55 in slightly

over three seconds, the radar will reject your speed signal, giving you a chance to get down to the legal limit.

Size is another variable. The smaller the target, the closer it has to be to radar to get a reading. A speeding truck at ¼ mile may give a stronger signal than a closer, slower moving car. Since

radar will lock onto the strongest signal, the car could easily pay for the truck's sins. Typically, a large truck will reflect a stationary radar signal at 1200 yards, a full-size car at 800 yards and a small car at 400 yards.

How far away can a detector identify the presence of radar? Depending on conditions, as far as three miles away. Most traffic radar broadcasts its signal at about 1/10 watt; the average radar detector can identify a signal with a strength of 1/1,000,000 watt. Since it needs to see only the presence of a diffused beam, it will usually give advance warning. Its effectiveness however, is dependent on its sensitivity. Most detectors on an interstate will identify the presence of radar before the radar can get an accurate speed readout. Usually, 5–20 seconds of advance warning will be provided.

Radio waves are reflected from bridge abutments, lines of cars,

HOW FAST?

Many highways have a measured mile at intervals along the road. The purpose of these is to drive at a constant speed along the measured mile and convert the time it takes to cover the mile into speed as a check of your speedometer.

The accompanying chart can convert the time it takes to cover one (1) mile into an approximation of your miles per hour speed. To get an accurate speed it would be necessary to cover the entire mile at a constant speed however.

You can also figure your mph by using the relationship between speed (R), distance (D) and time (T), expressed by the formula:

$$R = \frac{D}{T}$$

Since 0.6818 mph = 1 ft/sec, the following calculation will give your speed.

$$R\,(\text{speed in mph}) = \frac{5280\,\text{feet}}{\text{time in seconds to cover 1 mile}} \times .6818$$

If it takes	To go	Your Speed to the nearest mph is
50 seconds	1 mile	72
51 seconds	1 mile	71
52 seconds	1 mile	70
53 seconds	1 mile	68
54 seconds	1 mile	67
55 seconds	1 mile	65
56 seconds	1 mile	64
57 seconds	1 mile	63
58 seconds	1 mile	62
59 seconds	1 mile	61
60 seconds	1 mile	60
61 seconds	1 mile	59
62 seconds	1 mile	58
63 seconds	1 mile	57
64 seconds	1 mile	56
65 seconds	1 mile	55
66 seconds	1 mile	54
67 seconds	1 mile	54
68 seconds	1 mile	52
69 seconds	1 mile	52
70 seconds	1 mile	51

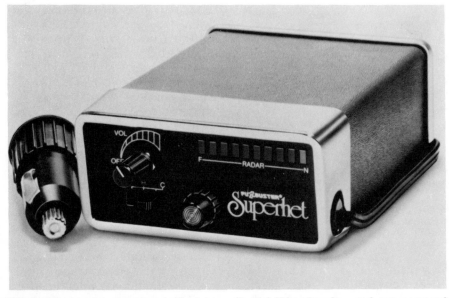

Most newer radar detectors will pick up K- and X-band radar, and are powered through the cigarette lighter socket.

tage. Since neither can see around corners, the radar can lock onto the car before the driver has a chance to react to the detector's warning.

Hooking Up the Detector

Any radar detector can be wired directly into the vehicle electrical system, though most detectors come with a power cord to plug into the cigarette lighter socket. The detector is mounted on the dash or clipped to the sunvisor; anywhere that it has an unobstructed view of the road. By aiming the detector down a few degrees, you can sometimes increase the range. The detector will read radar wave "bounce" off the road.

Truckers sometimes run another detector, facing back or aimed into a rear view mirror, along with the CB. You can't get much more protection from speed-traps—except to obey the speed limit.

chain link fences, guard rails, or even the roadway. This "bounce" will be picked up by the detector, and under most conditions, give ample warning. On hills, the situation is roughly the same. Radar waves will bounce off the road surface, enabling the detector to pick them up sooner. On open curves, however, with nothing around for the radar signal to bounce off, radar has the advan-

21
Clutch and Manual Transmission

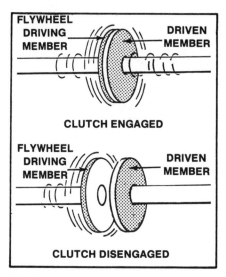

To overcome inertia and start the car moving, the automobile engine develops power which is transmitted as a twisting force (torque) from the engine crankshaft to the rear wheels. A smooth and gradual transfer of power and torque is accomplished through the use of a clutch friction unit to engage and disengage the power flow. A transmission is used to vary the gear ratio for the best speed and power, and to provide for car movement under the different conditions of starting, stopping, accelerating, maintaining speed and reversing. The various components necessary to deliver power to the rear wheels are the flywheel, pressure plate, clutch plate, release bearing, control linkages and the transmission.

How the Clutch Works

The clutch is a device to engage and disengage power from the engine, allowing the car to be stopped and started.

A pressure plate or "driving member" is bolted to the engine flywheel and a clutch plate or "driven member" is located between the flywheel and the pressure plate. The clutch plate is splined to the shaft extending from the transmission to the flywheel, commonly called a clutch shaft or input shaft.

When the clutch and pressure plates are locked together by friction, the clutch shaft rotates with the engine crankshaft. Power is transferred from the engine to the transmission, where it is routed through different gear ratios to obtain the best speed and power to start and keep the car moving.

The Flywheel

The flywheel is located at the rear of the engine and is bolted to the crankshaft. It helps absorb power impulses resulting in a smoothly idling engine and provides momentum to carry the

Clutch engagement and disengagement.

engine through its operating cycle. The rear surface of the flywheel is machined flat and the clutch components are attached to it.

The Pressure Plate

The driving member is commonly called the pressure plate. It is bolted to the engine flywheel and its main purpose is to exert pressure against the clutch plate, holding the plate tight against

225

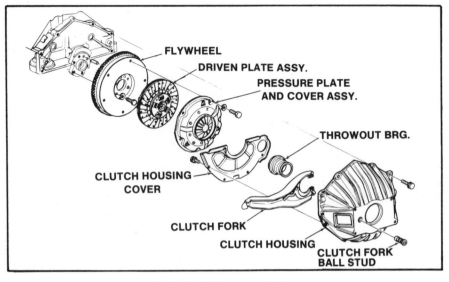

Typical clutch components.

the flywheel, and allowing the power to flow from the engine to the transmission. It must also be capable of interrupting the power flow by releasing the pressure on the clutch plate. This allows the clutch plate to stop rotating while the flywheel and pressure plate continue to rotate.

The pressure plate basically consists of a heavy metal plate, coil springs or a diaphragm spring, release levers (fingers), and a cover.

When coil springs are used, they are evenly spaced around the metal plate and located between the plate and the metal cover. This places an even pressure against the plate, which in turn presses the clutch plate tight against the flywheel. The cover is bolted tightly to the flywheel and the metal plate is movable, due to internal linkages. The coil springs are arranged to exert direct or indirect tension upon the metal plate, depending upon the manufacturers design. Three release levers (fingers) are used on most pressure plates, evenly spaced around the cover, to release the holding pressure of the springs on the clutch plate, allowing it to disengage the power flow.

When a diaphragm spring is used instead of coil springs, the internal linkage is necessarily different to provide an "over-center" action to release the clutch plate from the flywheel. Its operation can be compared to the operation of an oil can. When depressing the slightly curved metal on the bottom of the can, it would go over-center and give out a loud "clicking" noise; when released, the noise again would be heard and the metal would return to its original position. A click is not heard in the clutch operation, but the action of the diaphragm spring is the same as the oil can.

The Clutch Plate

The clutch plate or driven member, consists of a round metal plate attached to a splined hub. The outer portion of the round plate is covered with a friction material of molded or woven asbestos and is riveted or bonded to the plate. The thickness of the clutch plate and/or facings may be warped to give a softer clutch engagement. Coil springs are often installed in the hub to help provide a cushion against the twisting force of clutch engagement. The splined hub is mated to (and turns) a splined transmission shaft when the clutch is engaged.

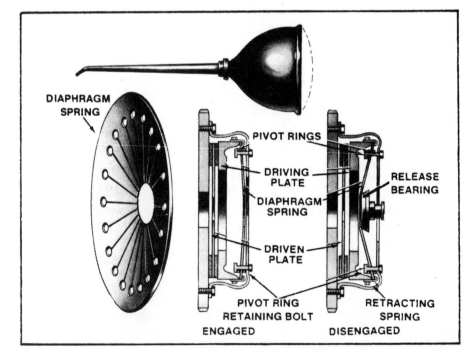

The operation of a diaphragm spring-type pressure plate can be compared to the effect of the bottom of an oil can.

TROUBLESHOOTING BASIC CLUTCH AND MANUAL TRANSMISSION PROBLEMS

As you drive your car, you become used to noises, vibrations and the feel of the car in different gears. Any changes in these sensations may indicate the beginning of a problem. It's important to note what gear you are in, at what speeds the problem occurs, noise level and whether it disappears from one gear to another.

Most problems in the clutch and transmission are a job for a mechanic, and usually require removal and service.

Problem	Cause(s)
Excessive clutch noise	**Throwout bearing noises** are more audible at the lower end of pedal travel. The usual causes are: • Riding the clutch • Too little pedal free-play • Lack of bearing lubrication **A bad clutch shaft pilot bearing** will make a high pitched squeal, when the clutch is disengaged and the transmission is in gear or within the first 2″ of pedal travel. The bearing must be replaced. **Noise from the clutch linkage** is a clicking or snapping that can be heard or felt as the pedal is moved completely up or down. This usually requires lubrication. **Transmitted engine noises** are amplified by the clutch housing and heard in the passenger compartment. They are usually the result of insufficient pedal free-play and can be changed by manipulating the clutch pedal.
Clutch slips (the car does not move as it should when the clutch is engaged)	This is usually most noticeable when pulling away from a standing start. A severe test is to start the engine, apply the brakes, shift into high gear and SLOWLY release the clutch pedal. A healthy clutch will stall the engine. If it slips it may be due to: • A worn pressure plate or clutch plate • Oil soaked clutch plate • Insufficient pedal free-play
Clutch drags or fails to release	The clutch disc and some transmission gears spin briefly after clutch disengagement. Under normal conditions in average temperatures, 3 seconds is maximum spin-time. Failure to release properly can be caused by: • Too light transmission lubricant or low lubricant level • Improperly adjusted clutch linkage
Low clutch life	Low clutch life is usually a result of poor driving habits or heavy duty use. Riding the clutch, pulling heavy loads, holding the car on a grade with the clutch instead of the brakes and rapid clutch engagement all contribute to low clutch life.
Transmission shifts hard	Common causes of hard shifting are: • Improper lubricant viscosity or lubricant level • Clutch linkage needs adjustment/lubrication
Transmission leaks lubricant	The general location of a leak can be found by putting a clean newspaper under the transmission overnight. • Lubricant level too high • Cracks in the transmission case • Loose or missing bolts • Drain or fill plug loose or missing • Vent hole plugged
Transmission is noisy in gear	Most problems such as this require the services of a mechanic. Causes include: • Insufficient lubricant • Worn gears (excessive end-play) • Worn bearings • Damaged synchronizers • Chipped gear teeth
Transmission is noisy in Neutral	Noises in Neutral are usually caused by: • Insufficient/incorrect lubricant • Worn reverse idler gear • Worn bearings or gear teeth

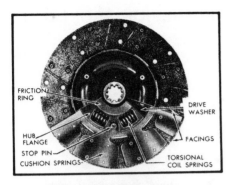

Typical clutch driven plate.

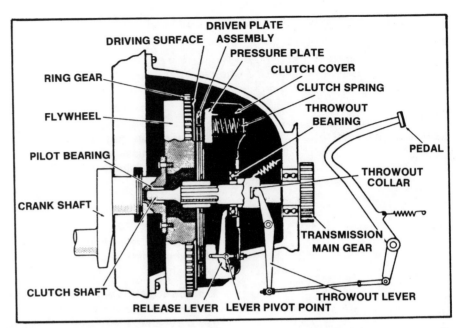

Cross-sectional view of typical clutch. Note the operation of the clutch pedal and linkage to engage and disengage the clutch.

The Release Bearing

The release (throwout) bearing is usually a ball bearing unit, mounted on a sleeve, and attached to the release or throwout lever. Its purpose is to apply pressure to the diaphragm spring or the release levers in the pressure plate. When the clutch pedal is depressed, the pressure of the release bearing or lever actuates the internal linkages of the pressure plate, releasing the clutch plate and interrupting the power flow. The release bearing is not in constant contact with the pressure plate. A linkage adjustment clearance should be maintained.

Power Flow Disengagement

The clutch pedal provides mechanical means for the driver to control the engagement and disengagement of the clutch. The pedal is connected to either a cable or rods, which are directly connected to the release bearing lever.

When the clutch pedal is depressed, the linkage moves the release bearing lever. The release lever is attached at the opposite end to a release bearing which straddles the transmission clutch shaft, and presses inward on the pressure plate fingers or the diaphragm spring. This inward pressure acts upon the fingers and internal linkage of the pressure plate and allows the clutch plate to move away from the fly-

wheel, interrupting the flow of power.

Power Flow Engagement

While the clutch pedal is depressed and the power flow interrupted, the transmission can be shifted into any gear. The clutch pedal is slowly released to gradually move the clutch plate toward the flywheel, under pressure of the pressure plate springs. The friction between the clutch plate and flywheel becomes greater as the pedal is released and the engine speed increased. Once the car is moving, the need for clutch slippage is lessened, and the clutch pedal can be fully released.

Coordination between the clutch pedal and accelerator is important to avoid engine stalling, shock to the driveline components, and excessive clutch slippage and overheating.

How the Transmission Works

The internal combustion engine creates a twisting motion or torque, which is transferred to

the rear wheels. But the engine cannot develop much torque at low speeds; it will only develop maximum torque at higher speeds. The transmission, with its varied gear ratios, provides a means of using this low torque to start the car.

The transmission gear ratios allow the engine to be operated most efficiently under a variety of driving and load conditions. Through the use of gear ratios, the need for extremely high engine rpm at high road speeds is avoided.

The modern transmission provides both speed and power through selected gear sizes that are engineered for the best all-around performance. A power (lower) gear ratio starts the car moving and speed gear ratios keep the car moving. By shifting to gears of different ratios, the driver can match engine speed to road conditions.

Gear Ratios

To obtain maximum performance and efficiency, gear ratios are engineered to each model of car, dependent upon such items as the size of the engine, the car

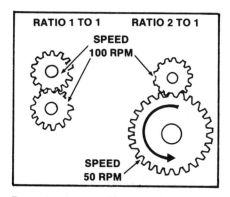

RATIO 1 TO 1   RATIO 2 TO 1

SPEED
100 RPM

SPEED
50 RPM

Example of determining gear ratio. Gear ratio can be found by dividing the number of teeth on the smaller gear into the number of teeth on the larger gear.

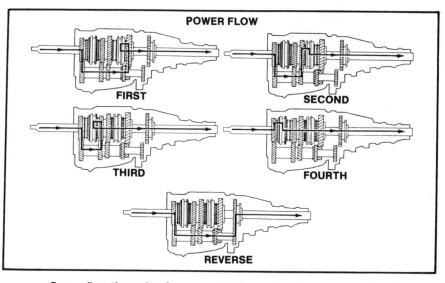

POWER FLOW

FIRST

SECOND

THIRD

FOURTH

REVERSE

Power flow through a four-speed, fully synchronized transmission.

weight and expected loaded weight, etc.

The gear ratio can be determined by counting the teeth on both gears. For example, if the driving gear has 20 teeth and the driven gear has 40 teeth, the gear ratio is 2 to 1. (The driven gear makes one revolution for every two revolutions of the drive gear.) If the driving gear has 40 teeth and the driven gear 20 teeth, the gear ratio is 1 to 2. (The driven gear revolves twice, while the drive gear revolves once.)

The transmissions used today may have three, four or five speeds forward, but all have one speed in reverse. The reverse gear is necessary because the engine rotates only in one direction and cannot be reversed. The reversing procedure must be accomplished inside the transmission.

By comparing gear ratios, you can see which transmission transmits more power to the rear wheels at the same engine rpm. The five-speed transmission's low or first gear with a ratio of 3.61 to 1 means that for 3.61 revolutions of the input or clutch shaft, (coupled to the engine by the clutch), the output shaft of the transmission will rotate once. This provides more power to the rear wheels, compared to the four-speed transmission's low gear of 2.33 to 1.

When the transmission is shifted into the high gear in the three- and four-speed transmission, and fourth gear in the five-speed transmission, the gear ratio is usually 1 to 1 (direct drive). For every rotation of the engine and input shaft, the output shaft is rotating one turn.

Fifth gear in a five-speed transmission is usually an overdrive. This gear is used for higher speed driving where very little load is placed on the engine. This gear ratio provides better economy by lowering the engine RPM to maintain a specific speed. The input shaft rotates only 0.87 of a turn, while the output shaft rotates one revolution, resulting in the output shaft rotating faster than the input shaft.

The overdrive is normally incorporated in the transmission

gearing of four- and five-speed transmissions, and is a separate unit attached to the rear of three-speed transmissions.

Synchromesh Transmissions

The power flow illustrated in a typical three-speed is a conventional, spur-geared transmission. To obtain a quiet operation and gear engagement, synchronizing clutches are added to the main-shaft gears. The addition of synchronizers allows the gears to be in constant mesh with the cluster gears (gears that provide a connection between input and output shafts), and the synchronizing clutch mechanism locks the gears together.

The main purpose of the synchronizer is to speed up or slow

TYPICAL TRANSMISSION GEAR RATIOS

	3-Speed	4-Speed	5-Speed
1st (Low)	2.7:1	2.23:1	3.61:1
2nd	1.6:1	1.77:1	2.05:1
3rd	1.0:1	1.35:1	1.36:1
4th	—	1.00:1	1.00:1
5th	—	—	0.87:1
Reverse	3.6:1	2.16:1	3.25:1

Note: The gear ratios are typical and do not represent any particular car.

CLUTCH AND TRANSMISSION MAINTENANCE INTERVALS

A little preventive maintenance in the clutch and transmission can prevent normal wear from causing more expensive problems.

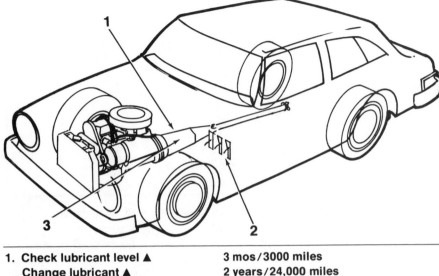

1. **Check lubricant level ▲**	**3 mos / 3000 miles**
Change lubricant ▲	**2 years / 24,000 miles**
2. **Check clutch pedal free-play ▲**	**6 mos / 6000 miles**
3. **Lubricate shift linkage**	**6 mos / 6000 miles**

▲If the vehicle is used for severe service (trailer pulling, constant stop/start driving, off-road operation), cut the maintenance interval in half.

down the rotation speeds of the shaft and gear, until both are rotating at the same speeds so that both can be locked together without a gear clash.

Since the car is normally standing still when shifted into reverse gear, a synchronizing clutch is ordinarily not used on reverse gear.

Four- and Five-Speed Transmissions

The power flow through the four- and five-speed transmissions can be charted in the same manner as the three-speed transmission.

As a rule, the power flow in high gear is usually straight through the transmission input shaft to the mainshaft, which would be locked together. When in the reduction gears, the power flow is through the input shaft, to the cluster gear unit, and

---

POWER FLOW THROUGH A THREE-SPEED MANUAL TRANSMISSION

Reverse Gear

A reverse idler gear is in constant mesh with a cluster gear, while the 1st gear (on the mainshaft) is moved rearward and engages the reverse idler gear. Since a third gear is added to the gear train, the result is a reversal of mainshaft (output) rotation causing the driveshaft and rear wheels to move in the opposite direction.

1st (Low) Gear

The 1st gear is splined to the mainshaft and is moved into mesh with the 1st gear machined on the cluster gear. The input gear on the mainshaft turns the cluster gear; since 1st gear is also splined to the mainshaft, the mainshaft will rotate.

2nd Gear

The 1st gear is moved to its neutral position while 2nd gear on the mainshaft is meshed with the 2nd gear on the cluster gear. The cluster gear is turned by the input shaft and this motion results in rotation of the mainshaft. Since the size of 2nd gear is smaller than 1st gear, the output shaft turns at a higher rate of speed than it would in 1st gear.

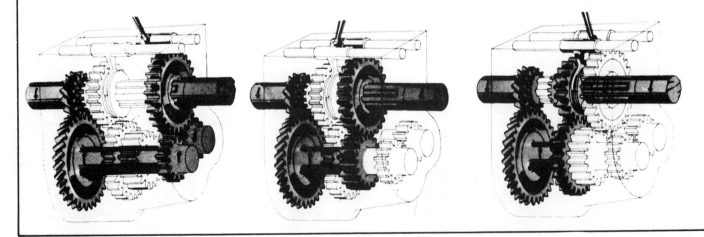

through the reduction gear to the mainshaft.

Transaxles

When the transmission and the drive axle are combined in one unit, it is called a "transaxle." The transaxle is bolted to the engine and has the advantage of being an extremely rigid unit of engine and driveline components. The complete engine-transaxle unit may be located at the front of the car (front-wheel drive) or at the rear of the car (rear-wheel drive).

The power flow through the transmission section of the transaxle is the same as through a conventional transmission.

Clutch Maintenance

The only maintenance associated with the clutch is to periodically check the distance be-

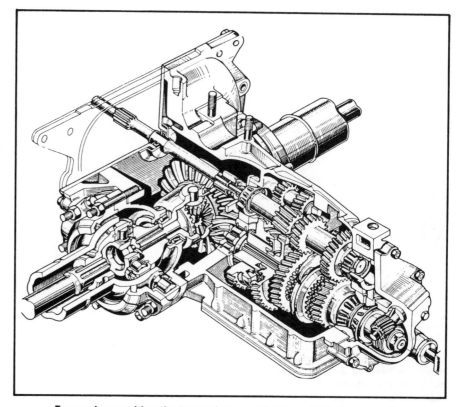

Transaxles combine the transmission and differential into one unit.

3rd (High) Gear

The power flow through 1st and 2nd gears enters the transmission through the input shaft and is transferred to the cluster gear in the lower part of the transmission case and back up to the mainshaft by meshing 1st and 2nd gears on the cluster with those on the mainshaft. The power route of 3rd gear is slightly different. The input shaft is locked to the mainshaft and allows the power to flow in a straight line through the transmission.

B Countershaft gear
C 2nd gear (cluster)
D 2nd gear (mainshaft)
E 1st gear (cluster)

F Low and reverse sliding gear (mainshaft)
G Reverse gear (cluster)
H Reverse idler gear

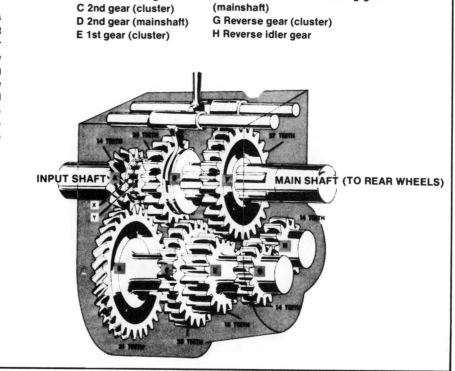

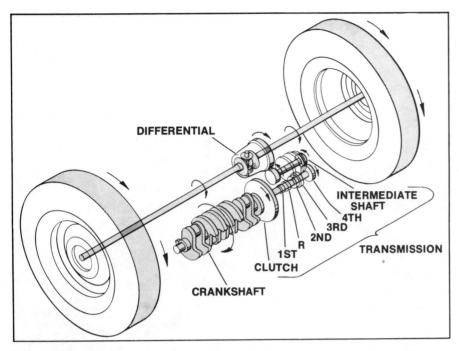

This simple model illustrates the power flow through a modern front-wheel drive system. Note how the direction of rotation of the engine crankshaft and axle shafts (attached to the wheels) are the same, made possible by the use of an intermediate shaft.

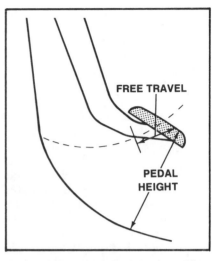

Check the clutch pedal free-play with an ordinary ruler.

tween the release bearing and the pressure plate. This clearance is commonly called "clutch pedal free-play" and is the distance the pedal moves before the slack is taken from the linkage and the release bearing begins to move the clutch away from the flywheel.

This distance can be measured by standing a 12-inch ruler on the floor board and measuring the height of the pedal in the released position. Take the slack from the clutch linkage (depress the pedal until resistance is felt) and remeasure. The difference between the two measurements is the amount of clutch linkage free-play (measured at the pedal). Generally, the clearance should be approximately ⅞" to 1". This clearance can be maintained by adjustment of the clutch linkage. If not, the clutch and pressure plate should be replaced as a set.

Transmission Maintenance

The transmission requires little maintenance, other than checking/changing the lubricant, and lubricating the shift linkage.

Internal problems usually require removal and overhaul of the transmission.

Lubricate the Shift Linkage

Periodically lubricate the trunnions, swivels, sliding surfaces and pivot points of the shift link-

This cutaway of the 1980 Citation (and other GM X-Body cars) shows the compactness of a transversely mounted V6 engine, automatic transmission and rack-and-pinion steering, for front-wheel drive applications.

The drain plug is always the lower of the two plugs. The fill plug is the upper plug and may or may not be on the same side of the transmission case.

age (if equipped with external shift linkage) with chassis grease. Make sure that the linkage is free and does not bind.

Checking the Lubricant Level

There are usually two plugs on the transmission. The lower plug is the drain plug and the upper plug the fill plug.

By removing the filler plug, the level of the lubricant can be checked. The lubricant should be level with or very close to the bottom of the filler hole. If no lubricant is visible, insert a finger or bent rod into the filler hole and try to touch the lubricant. Lubricant can be added as necessary. Since the gear oil is usually fairly thick, it is added with a suction gun or squeeze bulb of some type.

Changing Transmission Lubricant

The lubricant is usually changed every two years or 24,000 miles by removing the drain (lower) plug from the transmission case and draining the old lubricant into a catch

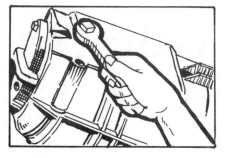

1. Remove road dirt from around the filler plug and remove the plug.

2. Check the fluid level with your finger or a bent rod. The level should be at, or just below the level of the hole.

3. If necessary, add fluid with a hand bulb syringe or a kitchen-type bulb for basting. It will help if the lubricant is warm when added.

pan. Be sure the fluid is at operating temperature.

The drain plug is sometimes magnetic to attract stray metal particles, keeping them out of the bearings and gear teeth. Be sure to clean the magnet of any metal particles before installing the drain plug.

A few transmissions have no

Some transmissions have no drain plug. In these cases, the lower bolt holding the extension housing to the transmission case is removed and serves as a drain plug.

drain plugs. In this case the lower rear extension housing bolt is removed to drain the transmission. Put a sealer on the bolt threads when replacing the bolt.

To fill the transmission, use a lubricant dispenser or hand bulb-type syringe through the fill hole, located on the side of the transmission case. Slightly over-fill and allow the lubricant to find its own level. Keep adding lubricant until the level is constant at the bottom of the filler hole. Install the fill plug and tighten securely. Clean any excess lubrication from the case surface to avoid road dirt build-up.

Lubricant Recommendation

The following lubricants are used in manual transmissions. Manufacturers differ in type and grade of lubricant usage; consult your owners manual for the proper lubricant to use in your transmission.

Engine oil—20, 30, 40, 20-40 weight
Automatic Transmission Fluid—Dexron®
80 or 90 weight gear oil:
    Above 32° F.—Use 90 weight
    Below 32° F.—Use 80 weight
Transaxles with common lubrication supply—80, 90 weight gear lubricant.

22
The Automatic Transmission

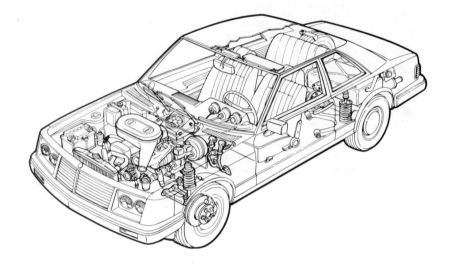

In recent years, the automobile has become so sophisticated and the automatic transmission so reliable, that automatic transmissions are the most popular option. Over 75% of all new cars are ordered with an automatic transmission. All the driver has to do is start the engine, select a gear and operate the accelerator and brakes. It may not be as much fun as shifting gears, but it is far more efficient if you haul heavy loads or pull a trailer.

The automatic transmission anticipates the engines needs and selects gears in response to various inputs (engine vacuum, road speed, throttle position, etc.) to maintain the best application of power. The operations usually performed by the clutch and manual transmission are accomplished automatically,

through the use of the fluid coupling, which allows a very slight, controlled slippage between the engine and transmission. Tiny hydraulic valves control the application of different gear ratios on demand by the driver (position of the accelerator pedal), or in a preset response to engine conditions and road speed.

How the Automatic Transmission Works

The automatic transmission allows engine torque and power to be transmitted to the rear wheels within a narrow range of engine operating speeds. The transmission will allow the en-

gine to turn fast enough to produce plenty of power and torque at very low speeds, while keeping it at a sensible rpm at high vehicle speeds.

The transmission uses a light fluid as the medium for the transmission of power. This fluid also operates the hydraulic control circuits and acts as a lubricant. Because the transmission fluid performs all of these three functions, trouble within the unit can easily travel from one part to another.

The automatic transmission operates on a principle that fluids cannot be compressed, and that when put into motion, will cause a similar reaction upon any resisting force. To under-

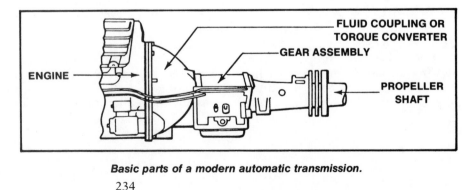

Basic parts of a modern automatic transmission.

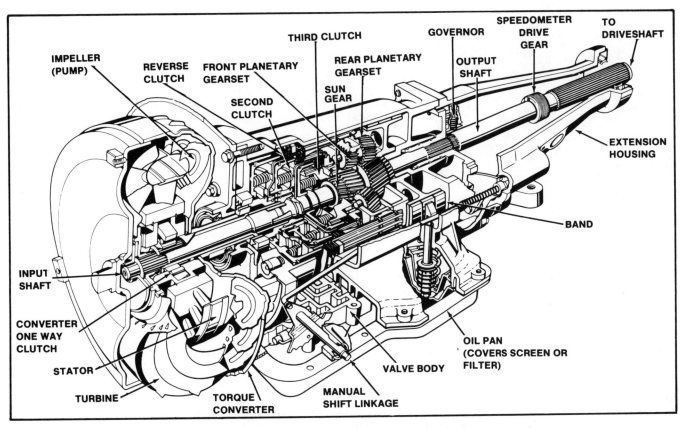

IMPELLER (PUMP) · REVERSE CLUTCH · FRONT PLANETARY GEARSET · SECOND CLUTCH · THIRD CLUTCH · REAR PLANETARY GEARSET · SUN GEAR · GOVERNOR · SPEEDOMETER DRIVE GEAR · OUTPUT SHAFT · TO DRIVESHAFT · EXTENSION HOUSING · BAND · INPUT SHAFT · CONVERTER ONE WAY CLUTCH · STATOR · TURBINE · TORQUE CONVERTER · MANUAL SHIFT LINKAGE · VALVE BODY · OIL PAN (COVERS SCREEN OR FILTER)

Cutaway view of typical automatic transmission showing basic components.

stand this law of fluids, think of two fans placed opposite each other. If one fan is turned on, it will begin to turn the opposite fan blades. This principle is applied to the operation of the fluid coupling and torque converter by using driving and driven members in place of fan blades.

Every type of automatic transmission has two sections. The front section contains the fluid coupling or torque converter and takes the place of the driver-operated clutch. The rear section contains the valve body assembly and the hydraulically controlled gear units, which take the place of the manually shifted standard transmission.

Torque Converter

The front section is called the torque converter. In replacing the traditional clutch, it performs three functions:

· It acts as a hydraulic clutch (fluid coupling), allowing the

engine to idle even with the transmission in gear.

· It allows the transmission to shift from gear to gear smoothly, without requiring that the driver close the throttle during the shift.

· It multiplies engine torque making the transmission more

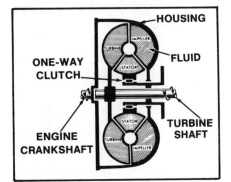

HOUSING · FLUID · ONE-WAY CLUTCH · ENGINE CRANKSHAFT · STATOR · TURBINE · TURBINE SHAFT

The torque converter housing is rotated by the engine crankshaft and turns the impeller. The impeller spins the turbine, which gives motion to the turbine (output) shaft to drive the gears.

responsive and reducing the amount of shifting required.

The torque converter is a metal case which is shaped like a sphere that has been flattened on opposite sides and is bolted to the rear of the engine's crankshaft. Generally, the entire metal case rotates at engine speed and serves as the engine's flywheel.

The case contains three sets of blades. One set is attached directly to the case forming the impeller or pump. Another set is directly connected to the output shaft, and forms the turbine. The third set (stator) is mounted on a hub which, in turn, is mounted on a stationary shaft through a one-way clutch. Rollers are wedged into slots, preventing backward rotation. When the rollers are not in the slots, the stator turns in the same direction as the impeller.

The pump, which is driven by the converter hub at engine speed, keeps the torque converter

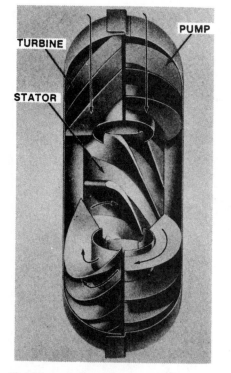

Fluid flows in two directions through the torque converter. It flows through the blades and it spins with the engine.

full of transmission fluid at all times. Fluid flows continuously through the unit to provide cooling.

A fluid coupling will only transmit the torque the engine develops; it cannot increase the torque. This is one job of the torque converter. The impeller drive member is driven at engine speed by the engine's crankshaft and pumps fluid, to its center, which is flung outward by centrifugal force as it turns. Since the outer edge of the converter spins faster than the center, the fluid gains speed. Fluid is directed toward the turbine driven member by curved impeller blades, causing the turbine to rotate in the same direction as the impeller. The turbine blades are curved in the opposite direction of the impeller blades.

In flowing through the pump and turbine the fluid flows in two separate directions. It flows through the turbine blades, and

it spins with the engine. The stator, whose blades are stationary when the vehicle is being accelerated at low speeds, converts one type of flow into another. Instead of allowing the fluid to flow straight back into the pump, the stator's curved blades turn the fluid almost 90° toward the direction of rotation of the engine. Thus the fluid does not flow as fast toward the pump, but is already spinning when the pump picks it up. This has the effect of allowing the pump to turn much faster than the turbine. This difference in speed may be compared to the difference in speed between the smaller and larger gears in any gear train. The result is that engine power output is higher, and engine torque is multiplied.

As the speed of the turbine increases, the fluid spins faster and faster in the direction of engine rotation. As a result, the ability of the stator to redirect the fluid flow is reduced. Under cruising conditions, the stator is eventually forced to rotate on its one-

way clutch and the torque converter begins to behave almost like a solid shaft, with the pump and turbine speeds being almost equal.

In 1978, Chrysler Corporation introduced a new automatic transmission, featuring what is called a "lock-up" clutch in the transmission's torque converter. The lock-up is a fully automatic clutch that engages only when the transmission shifts into 3rd gear or when needed based on a predetermined demand factor.

The lock-up clutch is activated by a piston. When engaged, the lock-up clutch gives the benefits of a manual transmission, eliminating torque converter slippage. In the engaged position, engine torque is delivered mechanically, rather than hydrodynamically (through fluid). This gives improved fuel economy and cooler transmission operating temperatures.

In 1980, Ford introduced what is known as the AOT (Automatic Overdrive Transmission). Essentially, this transmission uses a

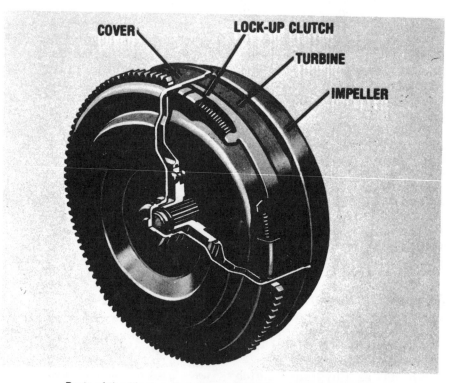

Parts of the "lock-up" clutch used by Chrysler Corporation.

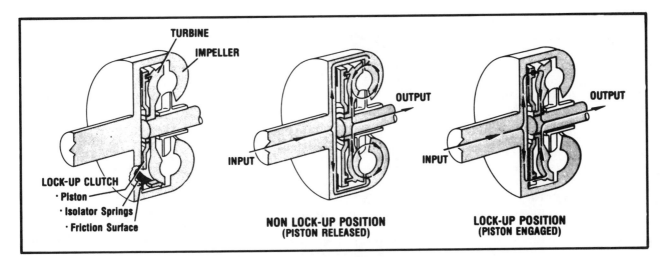

Operation of Chrysler's "lock-up" clutch and torque converter.

lock-up torque converter, by offering an additional refinement. The transmission is a four-speed unit, with fourth gear as an overdrive (0.67:1). Torque is transmitted via a full mechanical lock-up from the engine, completely bypassing the torque converter and eliminating hydraulic slippage.

In third gear (1:1 ratio), engine power follows a "split-torque" path, in which there is a 60% lock-up. Sixty percent of the power is transmitted through solid connections and 40% of the engine power is delivered through the torque converter.

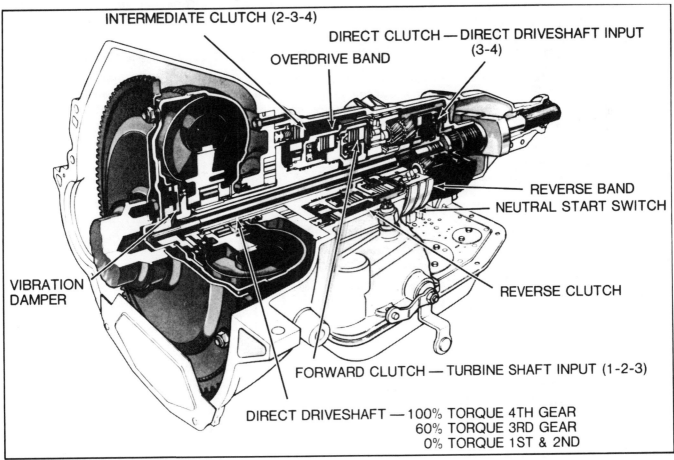

Cutaway of Ford's AOT four-speed automatic transmission. Most of the parts are similar to a conventional automatic transmission (shown earlier) except for the overdrive and lock-up parts.

The Planetary Gearbox

The rear section of the transmission is the gearbox, containing the gear train and valve body to shift the gears.

The ability of the torque converter to multiply engine torque is limited, so the unit tends to be more efficient when the turbine is rotating at relatively high speeds. A planetary gearbox is used to carry the power output from the turbine to the driveshaft to make the most efficient use of the converter.

Planetary gears function very similarly to conventional transmission gears. Their construction is different in that three ele-

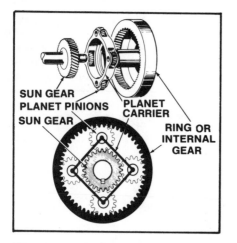

Planetary gears are similar to manual transmission gears, but are composed of three parts.

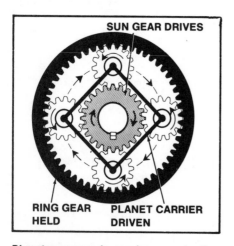

Planetary gears in maximum reduction (Low). The ring gear is held and a lower gear ratio is obtained.

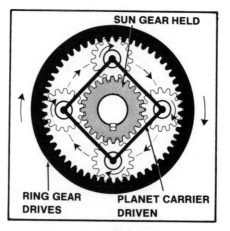

Planetary gears in minimum reduction (Drive). The ring gear is allowed to revolve, providing a higher gear ratio.

ments make up one gear system; an outer gear shaped like a hoop, with teeth cut into the inner surface; a sun gear, mounted on a shaft and located at the very center of the outer gear; and a set

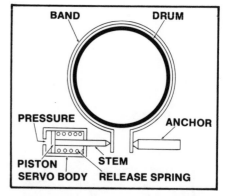

Servos, operated by pressure, are used to apply or release the bands to either hold the ring gear or allow it to rotate.

of three planet gears, held by pins in a ring-like planet carrier and meshing with both the sun gear and the outer gear. Either the outer gear or the sun gear may be held stationary, providing more than one possible torque multiplication factor for

TOWING AUTOMATIC TRANSMISSION CARS

When towing a disabled car, care must be used to avoid damage to the automatic transmission. The maximum distance and speed should be adhered to, or the transmission could be damaged. If extended distances or higher speeds are anticipated or if your car is not listed here, insist that the drive wheels be raised or the driveshaft disconnected.

Transmission	Towing Maximum Speed	Maximum Distance (miles)
AMC Shift Command	35	50
AMC Torque Command	30	50
Chrysler A-404 (Omni, Horizon)	25	15
Chrysler Torqueflite	30	*
Ford FMX, CW, C3, C4, C6, C6S thru '77	30	15
Ford FMX, CW, C3, C4, C6, C6S, AOT '78 and later	25	25
GM Powerglide	35	50
GM Type 200	35	50
GM Type 250, 350, 375B	35	50
GM Type 375, 400, 425	35	50

*—No mileage recommendation. Chrysler advises picking up the rear end or removing the driveshaft.

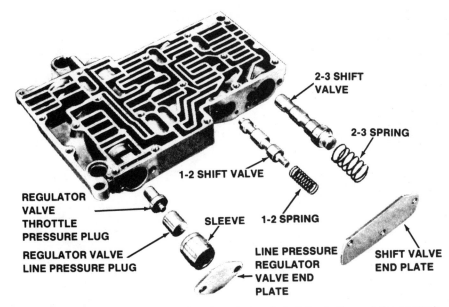

The valve body, containing the shift valves, is located at the bottom of the transmission. The shift valves (there are many more than shown) are operated by hydraulic pressure.

each set of gears. If all three gears are forced to rotate at the same speed, the gearset forms, in effect, a solid shaft.

Bands and clutches are used to hold various portions of the gearsets to the transmission case or to the shaft on which they are mounted.

Shifting Gears

Shifting is accomplished by changing the portion of each planetary gearset that is held to the transmission case or shaft.

A valve body contains small hydraulic pistons and cylinders. Fluid enters the cylinder under pressure and forces the pistons to move to engage the bands or clutches.

The hydraulic fluid used to operate the valve body comes from the main transmission oil pump. This fluid is channeled to the various pistons through the shift valves. There is generally a manual shift valve which is operated by the transmission selector lever and an automatic shift valve for each automatic upshift the transmission pro-

vides. Two-speed automatics have a low-high shift valve, while three-speeds will have a 1-2 shift valve, and a 2-3 shift valve.

There are two pressures which effect the operation of these valves. One (governor pressure) is determined by vehicle speed, while the other (modulator pressure) is determined by intake manifold vacuum or throttle position. Governor pressure rises with an increase in vehicle speed, and modulator pressure rises as the throttle is opened wider. By responding to these two pressures, the shift valves cause the upshift points to be delayed with increased throttle opening to make the best use of the engine's power output. If the accelerator is pushed further to the floor the upshift will be delayed longer (the car will stay in gear).

The transmission modulator also governs line pressure, used to actuate the servos. In this way, the clutches and bands will be actuated with a force matching the torque output of the engine.

Most transmissions also make use of an auxiliary circuit for down-shifting. This circuit may be actuated by the throttle link-

AUTOMATIC TRANSMISSION MAINTENANCE INTERVALS

To keep your automatic transmission as troublefree as possible, it should be maintained at the following intervals.

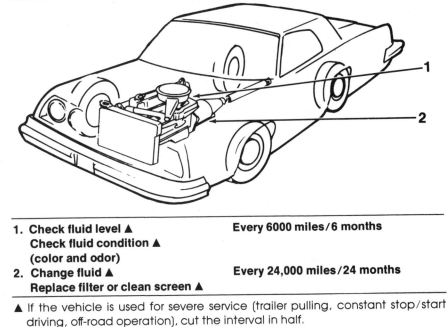

| 1. Check fluid level ▲ Check fluid condition ▲ (color and odor) | Every 6000 miles/6 months |
| 2. Change fluid ▲ Replace filter or clean screen ▲ | Every 24,000 miles/24 months |

▲ If the vehicle is used for severe service (trailer pulling, constant stop/start driving, off-road operation), cut the interval in half.

REPLACING AUTOMATIC TRANSMISSION FLUID AND FILTER

Replacing the automatic transmission fluid and filter is easy and the most valuable service you could do your transmission. Some transmissions have no filter, using a screen which can be cleaned and reinstalled. If your transmission has a filter, a new filter gasket and O-ring (for the intake pipe) usually come packed together. Always install a new gasket when the pan is removed.

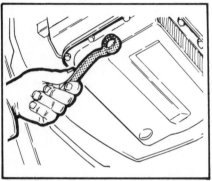

1. Position a catch pan under the transmission. If equipped, remove the drain plug. Be careful; the fluid may be hot.

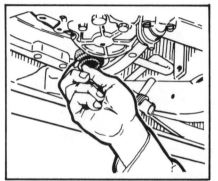

4. Remove the old O-ring from the filter neck and replace with new O-Ring supplied with filter kit.

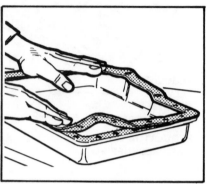

7. Install a new gasket on the pan.

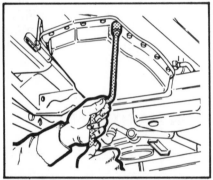

2. Many late-model vehicles have no drain plug. Loosen the pan bolts and allow one corner of the pan to tilt slightly to drain the fluid.

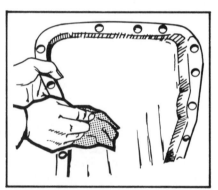

5. Clean the pan thoroughly with gasoline and allow to air dry completely.

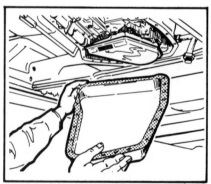

8. Install the new pan and gasket. Do not overtighten the screws.

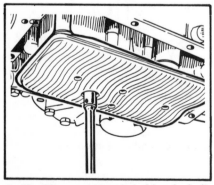

3. The filter or screen is held on by bolts or screws. Remove the filter or screen straight down.

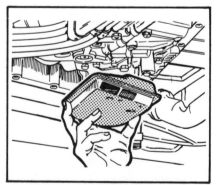

6. Install the new filter. Be sure the intake pipe is seated in the O-ring. Some transmissions use a screen which can be cleaned in gasoline and air dried.

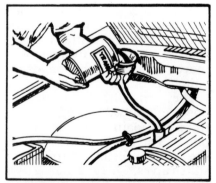

9. Fill the transmission with the required amount of fluid. Do not overfill. Start the engine and shift through all the gears. Check the fluid level and add fluid if necessary.

age or the vacuum line which actuates the modulator, or by a cable or solenoid. It applies pressure to a special downshift surface on the shift valve or valves, to shift back to low gear as vehicle speed decreases.

Periodic Maintenance

Types of Fluid

There are basically two classifications of automatic transmission fluids. The AF classification (Type A) is Dexron® or Dexron II®, approved for use in General Motors, Chrysler Corporation and American Motors automatic transmissions.

The FA classification (Type F) is for use in all Ford Motor Company automatics, except the 1977 and later C-6 model, which must use a special fluid conforming to Ford Motor Company Specification # ESP-M2C138-CJ.

The difference is that Dexron® and Dexron II® permit smoother clutch engagement. Type F uses an additive for quicker lock-up.

∎
Chilton Tip
The fluid type is marked on the dipstick of many cars; do not mix types of fluid.
∎

QUALIFICATION NUMBER

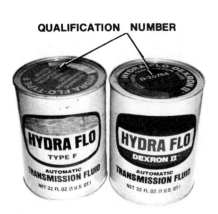

The type of fluid and the fluid qualification number are imprinted on the top of the can.

Import car owners should consult their owner's manual for the approved fluid to use.

Checking Fluid Level

Check the transmission fluid level every 6000 miles or 6 months, whichever comes first.

The vehicle should be on a level ·surface, transmission in Park, and the engine running. The fluid should be at normal operating temperature. If the vehicle has been used to haul a trailer or has been on an extended trip, wait half an hour before checking.

∎
Chilton Tip
On General Motor's dipsticks there are three fluid levels.

If the fluid feels cool (about room temperature), the fluid should be ⅛–⅜" below the ADD mark; two dimples mark this spot.

If the fluid feels warm, the level should be close to the ADD mark (slightly above or below).

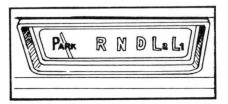

1. Check the automatic transmission fluid level in PARK, with the engine warm and running.

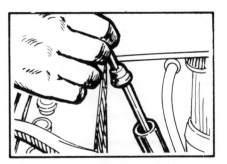

2. Remove the dipstick and wipe clean. Reinsert the dipstick all the way. Remove it again and check the fluid level.

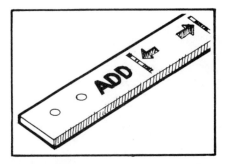

3. The fluid level should be between the ADD and FULL marks. Check the appearance of the fluid.

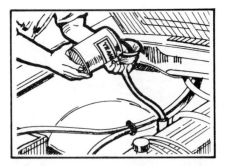

4. If the level is low, add fluid through the dipstick tube, using a long funnel. Do not mix fluid types and do not overfill. It takes only 1 pint to raise the level from ADD to FULL.

If the fluid is hot (cannot be held comfortably), the level should be between ADD and FULL.

∎

Fluid Temperature

Transmission fluid is designed to last many thousands of miles under normal conditions. But, one of the most important factors affecting the life of the fluid and the transmission is the temperature of the fluid. Overheated fluid forms sludge and particles of carbon that can block the minute passages and lines that circulate the fluid throughout the transmission. This causes the transmission to overheat even more and will lead to eventual failure of the transmission.

Anything that puts a load on the engine can cause the transmission to heat up and speed the

TRANSMISSION IDENTIFICATION

Pan gasket outlines are shown to aid in identifying the type of transmission used in domestic vehicles. It is useful to know the shape of the gasket when buying a replacement along with the refill capacity and fluid type; gasket and filters are normally ordered by transmission type.

Import car gasket outlines are not shown; in general, only one automatic transmission is used in any import car, and parts (gaskets, filters) are usually ordered by car name rather than transmission type.

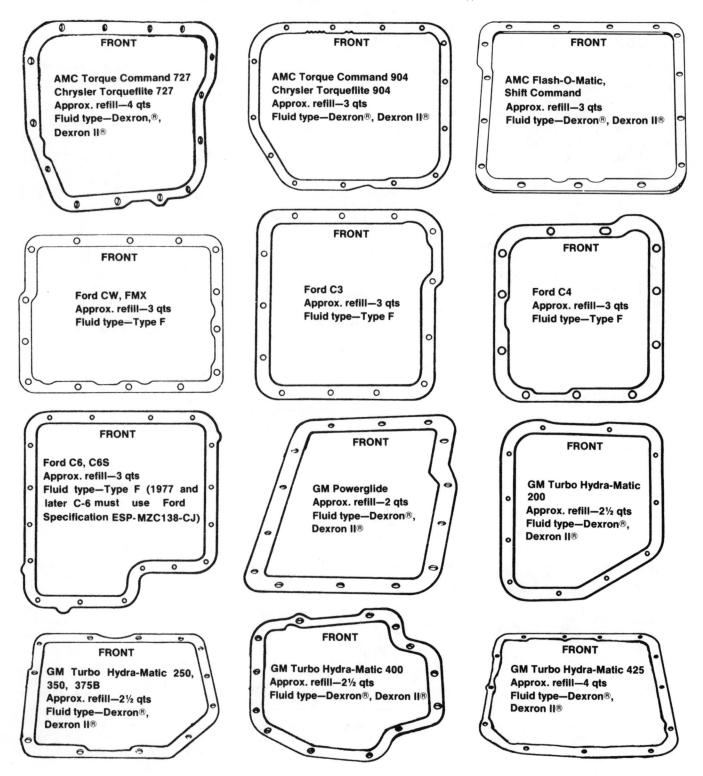

FRONT

AMC Torque Command 727
Chrysler Torqueflite 727
Approx. refill—4 qts
Fluid type—Dexron,®,
Dexron II®

FRONT

AMC Torque Command 904
Chrysler Torqueflite 904
Approx. refill—3 qts
Fluid type—Dexron®, Dexron II®

FRONT

AMC Flash-O-Matic,
Shift Command
Approx. refill—3 qts
Fluid type—Dexron®, Dexron II®

FRONT

Ford CW, FMX
Approx. refill—3 qts
Fluid type—Type F

FRONT

Ford C3
Approx. refill—3 qts
Fluid type—Type F

FRONT

Ford C4
Approx. refill—3 qts
Fluid type—Type F

FRONT

Ford C6, C6S
Approx. refill—3 qts
Fluid type—Type F (1977 and later C-6 must use Ford Specification ESP-MZC138-CJ)

FRONT

GM Powerglide
Approx. refill—2 qts
Fluid type—Dexron®, Dexron II®

FRONT

GM Turbo Hydra-Matic 200
Approx. refill—2½ qts
Fluid type—Dexron®, Dexron II®

FRONT

GM Turbo Hydra-Matic 250, 350, 375B
Approx. refill—2½ qts
Fluid type—Dexron®, Dexron II®

FRONT

GM Turbo Hydra-Matic 400
Approx. refill—2½ qts
Fluid type—Dexron®, Dexron II®

FRONT

GM Turbo Hydra-Matic 425
Approx. refill—4 qts
Fluid type—Dexron®, Dexron II®

TRANSMISSION FLUID INDICATIONS

The appearance and odor of the transmission fluid can give valuable clues to the overall condition of the transmission. Always note the appearance of the fluid when you check the fluid level or change the fluid. Rub a small amount of fluid between your fingers to feel for grit and smell the fluid on the dipstick.

If the fluid appears:	It indicates:
Clear and red colored	• Normal operation
Discolored (extremely dark red or brownish) or smells burned	• Band or clutch pack failure, usually caused by an overheated transmission. Hauling very heavy loads with insufficient power or failure to change the fluid, often result in overheating. Do not confuse this appearance with newer fluids that have a darker red color and a strong odor (though not a burned odor).
Foamy or aerated (light in color and full of bubbles)	• The level is too high (gear train is churning oil) • An internal air leak (air is mixing with the fluid). Have the transmission checked professionally.
Solid residue in the fluid	• Defective bands, clutch pack or bearings. Bits of band material or metal abrasives are clinging to the dipstick. Have the transmission checked professionally.
Varnish coating on the dipstick	• The transmission fluid is overheating

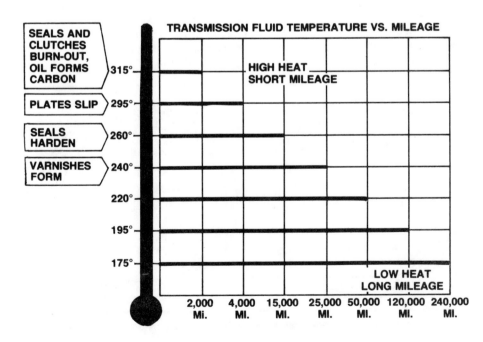

deterioration of the fluid. Towing a trailer, idling in traffic and climbing long hills are all hard on a transmission. The accompanying graph illustrates just how much transmission temperature affects the life of transmission components. Fluid that lasts 50,000 miles at a temperature of 220° F, will only last half that long if the temperature is consistently 20° F higher.

The secret to long transmission life is regular fluid changes and keeping an eye on the condition of the fluid—both temperature and color.

Checking for Leaks

If the fluid level is consistently low, suspect a leak. The easiest way is to slip a piece of clean newspaper under the car overnight, but this is not always an accurate indication, since some leaks will occur only when the transmission is operating.

Other leaks can be located by driving the car. Wipe the underside of the transmission clean and drive the car for several miles to bring the fluid temperature to normal. Stop the car, shut off the engine and look for leakage. Remember, however, that where the fluid is located may not be the source of the leak. Airflow around the transmission while the car is moving may carry the fluid to some other point.

Changing the Fluid and Filter

See "Changing Automatic Transmission Fluid and Filter." The fluid and filter should be changed about every 24,000 miles or 2 years, under normal usage. Some transmissions have a screen that only needs cleaning. If the vehicle is used in severe service (trailer pulling, extreme stop-and-start driving, etc.), cut the interval in half.

TROUBLESHOOTING BASIC AUTOMATIC TRANSMISSION PROBLEMS

Given proper maintenance and care, the automatic transmission will provide many miles of trouble-free operation. Most minor problems can be traced to fluid level; maintaining the proper fluid level will avoid these problems. Keeping alert to changes in the operation of the transmission (different shifting patterns, abnormal sounds, fluid leakage) can prevent small problems from becoming large ones. If the problem cannot be traced to loose bolts, fluid level, overheating or clogged filter seek professional service.

Problem	Is Caused By	What to Do
Fluid leakage	• Defective pan gasket • Loose filler tube • Loose extension housing to transmission case • Converter housing area leakage	• Replace gasket or tighten pan bolts • Tighten tube nut • Tighten bolts • Have transmission checked professionally
Fluid flows out the oil filler tube	• High fluid level • Breather vent clogged • Clogged oil filter or screen • Internal fluid leakage	• Check and correct fluid level • Open breather vent • Replace filter or clean screen (change fluid also) • Have transmission checked professionally
Transmission overheats (this is usually accompanied by a strong burned odor to the fluid)	• Low fluid level • Fluid cooler lines clogged • Heavy pulling or hauling with insufficient cooling • Faulty oil pump, internal slippage	• Check and correct fluid level • Drain and refill transmission. If this doesn't cure the problem, have cooler lines cleared or replaced. • Install a transmission oil cooler. See Section 9 • Have transmission checked professionally.
Buzzing or whining noise	• Low fluid level • Defective torque converter, scored gears	• Check and correct fluid level • Have transmission checked professionally
No forward or reverse gears or slippage in one or more gears	• Low fluid level • Defective vacuum or linkage controls, internal clutch or band failure	• Check and correct fluid level • Have unit checked professionally
Delayed or erratic shift	• Low fluid level • Broken vacuum lines • Internal malfunction	• Check and correct fluid level • Repair or replace lines • Have transmission checked professionally

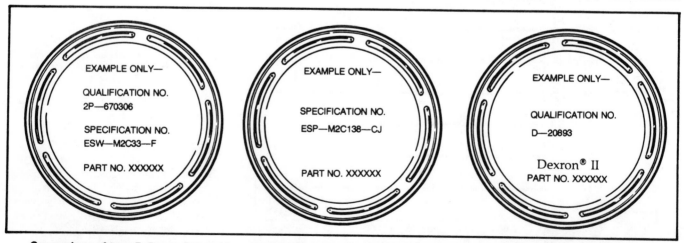

Comparison of type F, Dexron® II and type CJ fluid containers and their identifying code numbers (© Ford Motor Co.)

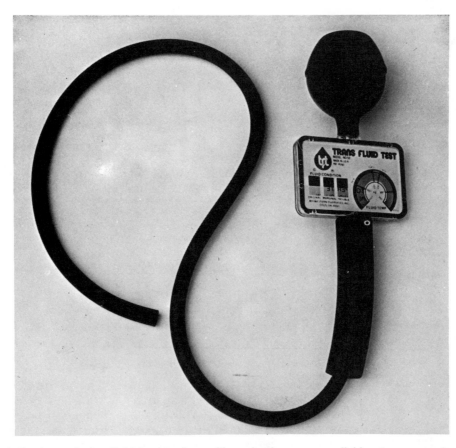

Check the transmission fluid temperature with a simple gauge available at many parts stores.

Chilton Tip

Some cars have no transmission drain plug. On these cars, the pan has to be removed to drain the fluid. Always replace the gasket if the pan is removed.

Servicing the Transmission

Aside from changing the fluid and filter and tightening nuts and bolts, servicing the automatic transmission should be left to professionals. Automatic transmissions are too complicated and too delicate for amateurs to service.

Chilton Tip

The fluid intended for many late-model automatic transmissions has a darker red color and stronger odor. Be suspicious only if the fluid has a distinct brownish color or definitely smells burned.

Driveshafts and Drive Axles

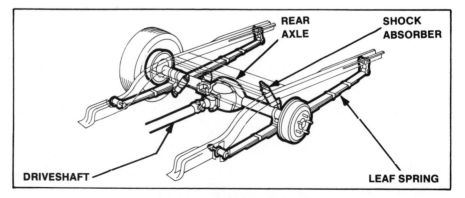

Driveshafts

In a conventional front-engine/rear-wheel-drive car, power is transmitted to the rear axle from the transmission through a tubular or solid shaft, called a driveshaft. Its only function is to connect the transmission and rear axle in the power flow.

As engine power is applied to the driveshaft (by the transmission) and it begins to rotate, the pinion drive gear in the rear axle, which is connected to the other end of the driveshaft, is forced to rotate. The pinion drive gear turns the ring gear which resists the effort because it is connected to the axle shafts and the rear wheels. As resistance is overcome and the wheels turn, the axle housing will tend to rotate in the opposite direction of wheel rotation.

To prevent excessive movement of the axle housing, and to attach the axle housing to the car body, several methods are used.

The *Hotchkiss drive* design transfers the thrust of the drive wheels from the axle housing to the car's frame through leaf springs or control arms if the rear suspension utilizes coil springs. The *torque tube drive* design transfers the thrust through the torque tube to the transmission, to the engine and to the frame through the crossmember and the engine mounts.

Hotchkiss Drive

An exposed tubular or hollow driveshaft is used with Hotchkiss-type rear axles. It is adaptable to longer lengths and can be used in two or more parts,

Solid driveshaft and components.

Hotchkiss drive with leaf springs.

246

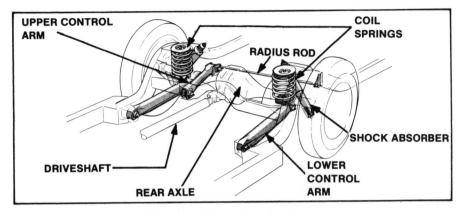

UPPER CONTROL ARM

COIL SPRINGS

RADIUS ROD

SHOCK ABSORBER

DRIVESHAFT

REAR AXLE

LOWER CONTROL ARM

Hotchkiss drive with coil springs.

with bearings to support the shaft and prevent whipping as the shaft rotates. Two or more universal joints are used for flexibility.

Hotchkiss-type rear axles use either coil or leaf springs to connect the drive axle housing to the car body. When leaf springs are used, the car is moved forward by thrust applied at the forward end of the springs, pushing against the frame. This thrust action results in flexing and distortion of the springs and allows the front of the axle housing to move upward to the limit of the springs.

When coil springs are used, the torque transfer is similar to leaf springs, but two control arms are used to connect the rear axle to the frame for transfer of driving force. The control arms stabilize the twisting action of the axle housing and assist in the transfer

of driving force to the car body. The control arms are attached to the frame and are allowed to pivot at the frame attaching point.

Torque Tube Drive

Torque tubes differ from the Hotchkiss design in that a solid drivesahft is encased in a hollow torque tube and rotates within a support bearing to prevent whipping. One universal joint is used at the front of the driveshaft, and the rear of the shaft is attached to the axle drive pinion through a flexible coupler.

The torque tube is connected to the rear of the transmission through a ball-type connection to permit flexibility as the car responds to road irregularities. Because the torque tube is fastened rigidly to the rear axle housing, the housing will not twist when engine power is applied.

Control arms (radius rods) extend from the outer ends of the axle housing to assist in controlling driving wheel thrust. The coil springs do not absorb or transmit any torque and are required for ride quality only.

The driving thrust is transmitted to the front of the torque tube, to the rear flange of the transmission housing and to the car crossmember and frame to push the car ahead.

Universal Joints

Because of changes in the angle between the driveshaft and axle housing, universal joints (U-joints) are used to provde flexibility. The engine is mounted rigidly to the car frame, while the driving wheels are free to move up and down in relation to the car frame. The angle between the driveshaft and rear axle changes constantly as the car responds to various road conditions.

To give flexibility and still transmit power as smoothly as possible, several types of universal joints are used.

The most common type of universal joint is the cross and yoke type. Yokes are used on the ends of the driveshaft with the yoke arms opposite each other. Another yoke is used opposite the

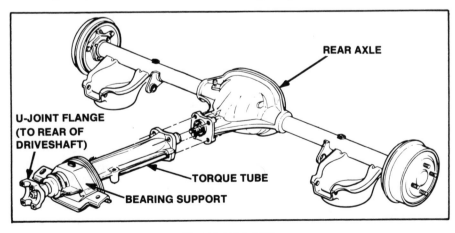

REAR AXLE

U-JOINT FLANGE (TO REAR OF DRIVESHAFT)

TORQUE TUBE

BEARING SUPPORT

Torque tube drive.

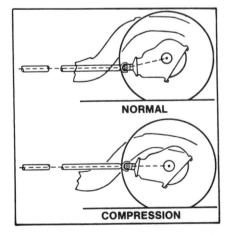

NORMAL

COMPRESSION

U-joints are necessary to compensate for changes in the angle between driveshaft and rear axle.

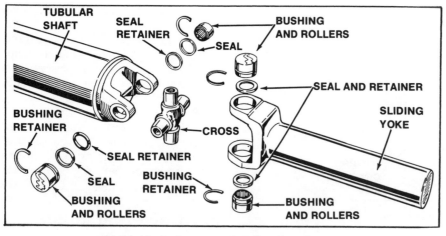

Parts of typical cross and yoke universal joint.

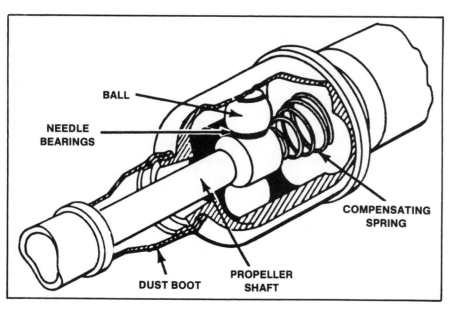

An enclosed ball and trunnion type U-joint.

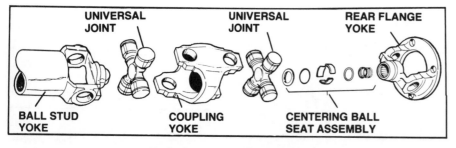

Typical constant velocity joint.

driveshaft and when placed together, both yokes engage a center member, or cross, with four arms spaced 90° apart. A bearing cup is used on each arm of the cross to accommodate movement as the driveshaft rotates.

The second type is the ball and trunnion universal, a T-shaped shaft which is enclosed in the body of the joint. The trunnion ends are each equipped with a ball mounted in needle bearings and move freely in grooves in the outer body of the joint, in effect creating a slip-joint. This type of joint is always enclosed.

A conventional universal joint will cause the driveshaft to speed up or slow down through each revolution and cause a corresponding change in the velocity of the driven shaft. This change in speed causes natural vibrations to occur through the driveline necessitating a third type of universal joint—the constant velocity joint. A rolling ball moves in a curved groove, located between two yoke-and-cross universal joints, connected to each other by a coupling yoke. The result is uniform motion as the driveshaft rotates, avoiding the fluctuations in driveshaft speeds.

Front-Wheel Drive

Front wheel drive cars (Omni/Horizon, GM X-Body, Rabbit, Honda, to name a few) do not have conventional rear axles or driveshafts. Instead, power is transmitted from the engine to a transaxle, or combination of transmission and drive axle, in one unit. See Section 21, "Clutch and Manual Transmission" for more information on the transaxle. Both the transmission and drive axle accomplish the same function as their counterparts in a front-engine/rear-drive axle design. The difference is in the location of components.

In place of a conventional driveshaft, a front-wheel-drive design uses two driveshafts,

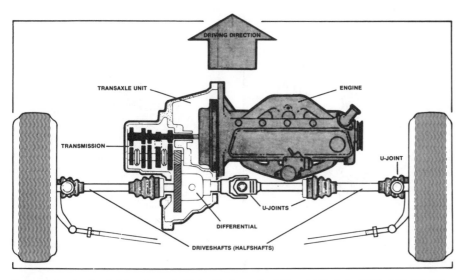

Typical front-wheel-drive layout. Note that most of the parts are similar to conventional rear-wheel drive, except for location.

sometimes called halfshafts, which couple the drive axle portion of the transaxle to the wheels. Universal joints or constant velocity joints are used just as they would in a rear-wheel-drive design.

Rear (Drive) Axle and Differential

The drive axle must transmit power through a 90° angle. The flow of power in conventional front-engine/rear-wheel-drive cars moves from the engine to the drive axle in approximately a straight line. But, at the drive axle, the power must be turned at right angles (from the line of the driveshaft) and directed to the rear wheels.

This is accomplished by a pinion drive gear which turns a circular ring gear. The ring gear is bolted to a differential housing, containing a set of smaller gears which are splined to the inner end of each axle shaft. As the differential gear housing is rotated, the internal differential gears turn the axle shafts, which are also attached to the rear wheels.

Differential Operation

The differential is an arrangement of gears with two functions: to permit the rear wheels to turn at different speeds when cornering and to divide the power flow between both rear wheels.

How this happens is somewhat complicated, but basically, the drive pinion, which is turned by the driveshaft, turns the ring gear (1).

The ring gear, which is bolted to the differential case, turns the case (2).

The pinion shaft, located in a bore in the differential case, is at right angles to the axle shafts and turns with the case (3).

The differential pinion (drive) gears are mounted on the pinion shaft and rotate with the shaft (4).

Differential side gears (driven gears) are meshed with the pinion gears and turn with the differential housing and ring gear as a unit (5).

The side gears are splined to the inner ends of the axle shafts and rotate the shafts as the housing turns (6).

Where both wheels have equal traction, the pinion gears do not rotate on the pinion shaft, since the input force of the pinion gears is divided equally between the two side gears (7).

When it is necessary to turn a corner, the differential gearing becomes effective and allows the axle shafts to rotate at different speeds (8).

As the inner wheel slows down, the side gear splined to the inner wheel axle shaft also slows down. The pinion gears act as balancing levers by maintaining equal tooth loads to both gears, while allowing unequal speeds of rotation at the axle shafts. If the car

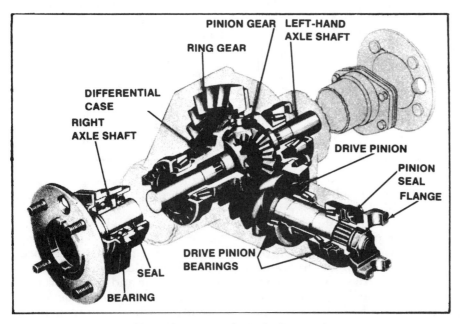

Component parts of a typical rear axle.

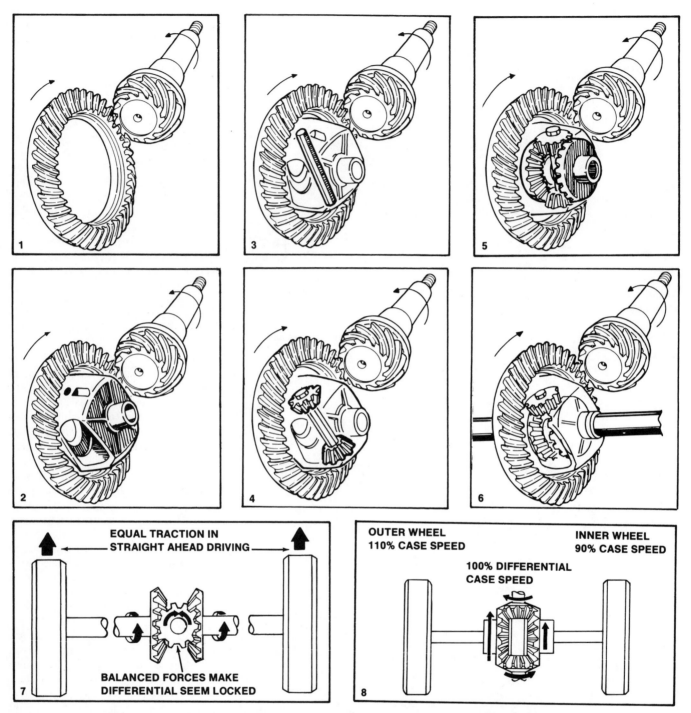

speed remains constant, and the inner wheel slows down to 90 percent of car speed, the outer wheel will speed up to 110 percent.

Limited-Slip Differential Operation

Limited-slip differentials provide the driving force to the

wheel with the best traction before the other wheel begins to spin. This is accomplished through clutch plates or cones. The clutch plates or cones are located between the side gears and the inner walls of the differential case. When they are squeezed together through spring tension and outward force from the side gears, three reactions occur. Re-

sistance on the side gears cause more torque to be exerted on the clutch packs or clutch cones. Rapid one-wheel spin cannot occur, because the side gear is forced to turn at the same speed as the case. Most important, with the side gear and the differential case turning at the same speed, the other wheel is forced to rotate in the same direction and at

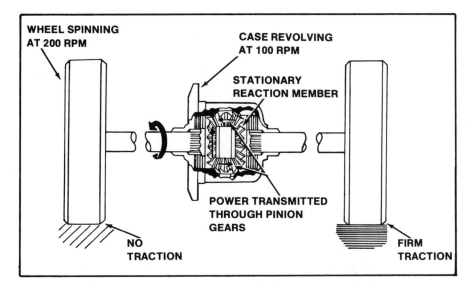

Limited slip differential transmits power through clutches or cones to drive the wheel having the best traction.

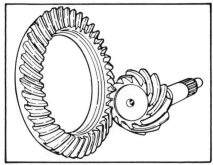

The numerical ratio of the rear axle is the number of teeth on the ring gear divided by the number of teeth on the pinion gear.

the same speed as the differential case. Thus, driving force is applied to the wheel with the better traction.

Identifying a Limited-Slip Rear Axle

Metal tags are normally attached to the axle assembly at the filler plug or to a bolt on the cover. During the life of the car, these tags can become lost and other means must be used to identify the rear axle.

To determine whether a car has a limited-slip or a conventional rear axle by tire movement, raise the rear wheels off the ground. Place the transmission in PARK (automatic) or LOW (manual), and attempt to turn a wheel by hand. If the rear axle is a limited-slip type, it will be very difficult to turn the wheel. If the rear axle is the conventional (open) type, the wheel will turn easily, and the opposite wheel will turn in the opposite direction.

Place the transmission in neutral and again rotate a rear wheel. If the axle is a limited-slip type, the opposite wheel will rotate in the same direction. If the axle is a conventional type, the opposite wheel will rotate in the opposite direction, if it rotates at all.

■

Chilton Tip

It should be noted that whenever the rear of a car, equipped with a limited-slip differential, is jacked up or supported, both rear wheels must be raised off the ground. Movement of either wheel that may be in contact with the ground, can cause the car to move off the jack or supports.

■

Gear Ratio

The drive axle of a car is said to have a certain axle ratio. This number (usually a whole number and a decimal fraction) is actually a comparison of the number of gear teeth on the ring gear and the pinion gear. For example, a 4.11 rear means that theoretically, there are 4.11 teeth on the ring gear for each tooth on the pinion gear or, put another way, the driveshaft must turn 4.11 times to turn the wheels once. Actually, on a 4.11 rear, there might be 37 teeth on the ring gear and 9 teeth on the pinion gear. By dividing the number of

teeth on the pinion gear into the number of teeth on the ring gear, the numerical axle ratio (4.11) is obtained. This also provides a good method of ascertaining exactly which axle ratio one is dealing with.

Another method of determining gear ratio is to jack up and support the car so that both rear wheels are off the ground. Make a chalk mark on the rear wheel and the drive shaft. Put the transmission in neutral. Turn the rear wheel one complete turn and count the number of turns that the driveshaft makes. The number of turns that the driveshaft makes in one complete revolution of the rear wheel is an approximation of the rear axle ratio.

Four Wheel Drive

When the vehicle is driven by both the front and rear wheels, two complete axle assemblies are used and power from the transmission is directed to both drive axles at the same time. A transfer case is attached to, or mounted near, the rear of the transmission and directs the power flow to the front and rear axles through two driveshafts.

Since the angles between the front and rear driveshafts change constantly, slip joints are used on the shafts to accommodate the changes in distance between axles and transfer case.

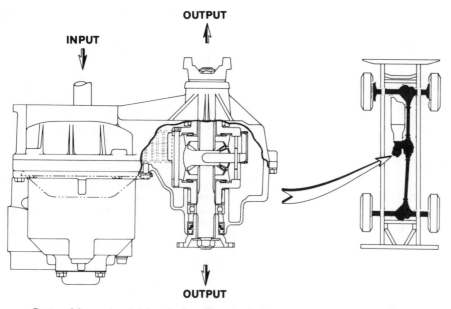

INPUT

Parts of four-wheel-drive design. The shaded area represents power flow.

Shifting devices attached to transfer cases disengage the front drive axle when four-wheel-drive capability is not needed. However, some newer transfer cases are in constant mesh and cannot be totally disengaged. These are known as "full-time" four-wheel drive and are just what the name says, four-wheel drive operating all the time. This is made possible by a differential in the transfer case.

Jeep® vehicles use a full-time system called Quadra-Trac, which is full-time four-wheel drive with a limited slip differential in the transfer case. All you have to do is drive.

Other four-wheel-drive manufacturers use a New Process unit which has a differential which is not limited slip. Instead a lock position on the shifter, in effect, converts the system to the equivalent of a part-time system with

four-wheel drive engaged for rough going. The big advantage of full-time four-wheel drive is that all those expensive four-wheel-drive components are working for you all the time.

AMC's Viscous Coupling Transfer Case

In 1980, American Motors introduced the Eagle, a four-wheel-drive sedan or station wagon. The Eagle utilizes a full-time four-wheel-drive system that requires no action by the driver to activate the system, and take advantage of the improved traction and handling of four-wheel drive.

The heart of the system is a new transfer case which distributes the torque between front and rear axles by means of a viscous or fluid coupling. The coupling provides a slip-limiting action and also absorbs minor driveline vibrations, giving smoother and quieter operation.

The new transfer case is known as Model NP 119, a single-speed unit. The rear driveshaft is driven directly from the rear of the transfer case, while the front is offset to the left, driven via a silent chain. The viscous coupling acts as a limited-slip differential between the drives and there is no mechanical lock-up between the two shafts.

When the front and rear driveshafts turn at the same speed, as they do when the Eagle drives straight down the road, there is no differential action. In a turn or other maneuvers where front and rear wheels must travel slightly different distances, differential action is required because the driveshafts must be able to rotate at slightly different speeds. When this happens, the fluid in the coupling—a liquid silicone—permits normal differential action.

Greater variations in speed between the driveshafts, such as occur when a wheel or pair of

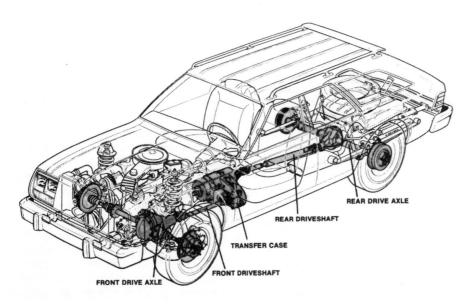

REAR DRIVE AXLE

REAR DRIVESHAFT

TRANSFER CASE

FRONT DRIVESHAFT

FRONT DRIVE AXLE

Essential parts of the automatic four-wheel-drive design used in the AMC Eagle.

wheels encounter reduced traction and tend to spin, bring the viscous coupling's slip-limiting characteristics into action. The action of the viscous coupling is velocity-sensitive, permitting the comparatively slow movements typical of normal differential action but quickly building up resistance and effectively transmitting available torque to the axle with the best traction.

The action of the fluid between the plates in the coupling could be compared to the action of water against a body when wading across a pool. In waist-deep water, a person can walk with comparatively little effort as long as he moves slowly and gently. But when he tries to hurry, the additional effort that is required is proportionate to the increase in speed one attempts to achieve. So it is with the viscous coupling. But, instead of water, there is liquid silicone with a viscosity nearly the consistency of honey.

The Eagle's four-wheel-drive system is more efficient than other automatic four-wheel-drive systems because there is no "open" differential (as opposed to a limited-slip differential) between the driveshafts. In the "open" differential system, the loss of traction at one wheel results in no torque being delivered to the other wheels, since it is the nature of the open differential to deliver motion to the "easy" shaft—the one that is slipping. When using a viscous coupling, the loss of traction at one wheel brings the slip-limiting character of the viscous coupling into action, causing drive torque to be transferred to the axle with the greatest traction.

In addition to the differential function, the viscous coupling also improves braking effectiveness. It acts as a skid deter-

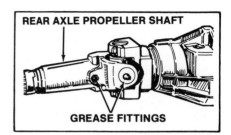

Some driveshaft U-joints are equipped with grease (zerk) fittings. Lubricate these with a grease gun.

rent, tending to equalize driveshaft speeds when the wheels at one end or the other want to lock and slide.

Periodic Maintenance

Maintenance includes inspecting the level of and changing the gear lubricant, and lubricating the universal joints if they are equipped with "zerk" or grease fittings.

Most modern universal joints are of the "extended life" design, meaning that they are sealed and require no periodic lubrication. However, it is wise to inspect the joints for hidden grease plugs or fittings, initially.

Also inspect the driveline for abnormal looseness, whenever the car is serviced.

Rear Axle Lubricants

In general, rear axles use either SAE 80 or 90 weight gear oil for lubrication, meeting API (American Petroleum Institute) GL-4 or GL-5 specifications. This will be stated on the top of the can.

In the case of limited-slip rear axles, it is very important that the proper gear lube be used. The wrong lubricant can damage the clutch packs and cause grabbing or chattering on turns. If this condition exists, try draining the oil and refilling with the proper gear lube before having it serviced.

DRIVESHAFT AND REAR AXLE PERIODIC MAINTENANCE

The driveshaft and rear (drive) axle should give trouble-free service if they are maintained at these intervals.

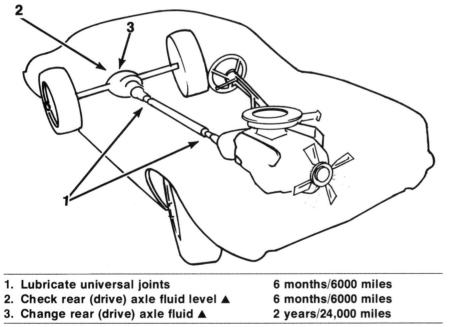

1. Lubricate universal joints	6 months/6000 miles
2. Check rear (drive) axle fluid level ▲	6 months/6000 miles
3. Change rear (drive) axle fluid ▲	2 years/24,000 miles

▲ If the vehicle is used for severe service (trailer pulling, continual stop/start driving, off-road operation) cut the maintenance interval in half.

■

Chilton Tip

Lubricants specified for use in limited-slip axles can be used in conventional (open) axles, but conventional axle lubricants cannot be used in limited-slip axles.

■

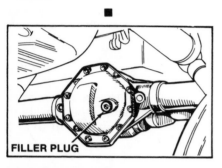

Integral carrier axles sometimes have only a filler plug. In these cases, either remove the rear cover to drain the fluid or use a suction gun through the filler opening.

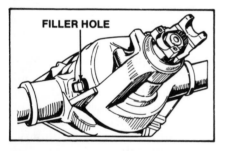

Removable carrier axles usually have only a fill plug. Remove the plug and suck the fluid out with a suction gun.

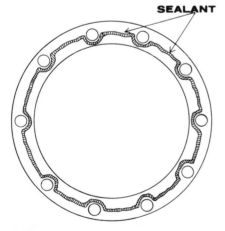

To form your own gasket, apply the sealant in an ⅛" continuous bead as shown. Follow the manufacturers' directions for hardening time.

Changing Rear Axle Lubricant

There are basically two types of rear axle design. Some have a removable (bolted-on) rear cover (integral carrier) and some have no rear cover (removable carrier).

Integral carrier axles usually have a drain and fill plug to use when changing lubricant. If there is no drain plug, the rear cover must be unbolted and removed. If this is the case, be sure to have a replacement gasket or a tube of gel gasket on hand, since the gasket has to be replaced.

An alternative to removing the cover is to purchase an inexpensive suction gun which can be used to suck the fluid out through the filler hole, and also will make installing new fluid easier.

Removable carrier axles are sometimes only equipped with a fill plug. If this is the case, the fluid must be sucked out with a suction gun.

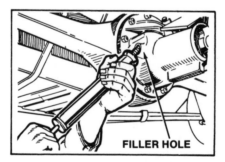

Fluid can be removed or installed with a suction gun.

Basic Drive Axle Problems

Drive axle problems frequently give warnings in the form of abnormal noises. Unfortunately, they are often confused with noise produced by other parts.

First, determine when the noise is most noticeable.

Drive noise: Produced during vehicle acceleration.

Coast noise: Produced while the car coasts with a closed throttle.

Float noise: Occurs while maintaining constant car speed on a level road.

Second, make a thorough check to be sure the noises are coming from the drive axle, and not from some other part of the car.

Road Noise

Brick or rough concrete roads produce noises that seem to come from the drive axle. Road noise is usually identical whether driving or coasting. Driving on a different type of road will tell whether the road is the problem.

Tire Noise

Tire noises are often mistaken for drive axle problems. Snow treads or unevenly worn tires produce vibrations seeming to originate elsewhere. *Temporarily* inflating the tires to 40 psi will significantly alter tire noise, but will have no effect on drive axle noises (which normally cease below about 30 mph).

Engine/Transmission Noise

Determine at what speed the noise is most pronounced, then stop the car in a quiet place. With the transmission in Neutral, run the engine through speeds corresponding to road speeds where the noise was noticed. Noises produced with the car standing still are coming from the engine or transmission.

Front Wheel Bearings

While holding the car speed steady, lightly apply the footbrake; this will often decrease bearing noise, as some of the load is taken from the bearing.

Drive Axle Noises

Eliminating other possible sources can narrow the cause to the drive axle, which normally produces noise from worn gears or bearings. Gear noises tend to peak in a narrow speed range, while bearing noises will usually vary in pitch with engine speeds.

CHECKING LUBRICANT LEVEL

As a rule, the level of the rear axle lubricant should be even with, or within ½" below the level of the filler plug. Remove the filler plug and check the level with a bent metal rod or with your finger.

To check the level in a transaxle (which often shares a common lubricant supply with the drive axle) see Section 21, Clutch and Manual Transmission.

INTEGRAL CARRIER	**REMOVABLE CARRIER**

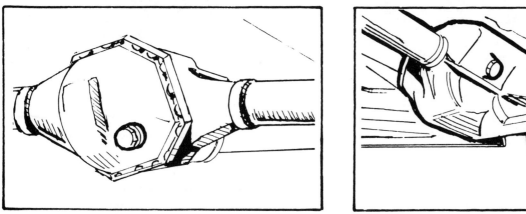

1. Locate the filler plug on the rear of the axle housing. If there are two plugs, the filler plug will be the upper plug.

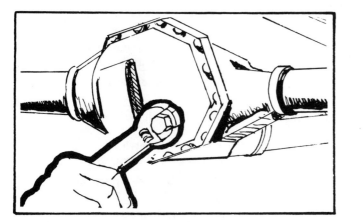 

2. Wipe the plug area clean and remove the plug. If an Allen plug is used, remove it with a ½" drive extension. A lot of fluid seeping past the plug as it's removed indicates the level may be too high.

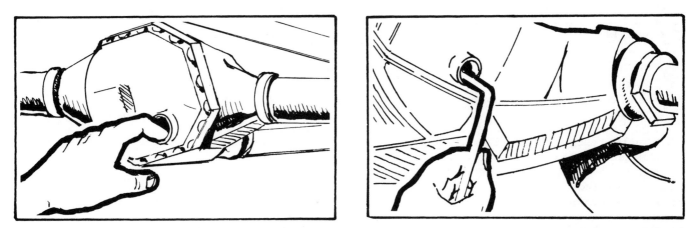

3. Check the level with your finger or a bent piece of wire. It should be within ½" below the level of the filler hole.

INTEGRAL CARRIER

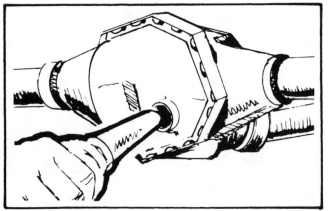

REMOVABLE CARRIER

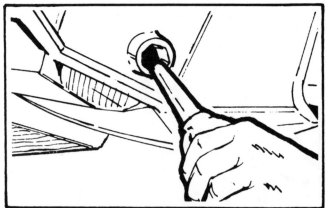

4. If the fluid level is low, fluid can be added with a hand bulb syringe or suction gun. Replace and tighten the filler plug.

TROUBLESHOOTING BASIC DRIVESHAFT PROBLEMS

When abnormal vibrations or noises are detected in the driveshaft area, this chart can be used to help diagnose possible causes. Remember that other components such as wheels, tires, rear axle and suspension can also produce similar conditions.

BASIC DRIVESHAFT PROBLEMS

The Problem	Is Caused By	What to Do
Shudder as car accelerates from stop or low speed	• Loose U-joint • Defective center bearing	• Tighten U-joint or have it replaced • Have center bearing replaced
Loud clunk in driveshaft when shifting gears	• Worn U-joints	• Have U-joints replaced
Roughness or vibration at any speed	• Out-of-balance, bent or dented driveshaft • Worn U-joints • U-joint clamp bolts loose	• Have driveshaft serviced • Have U-joints serviced • Tighten U-joint clamp bolts
Squeaking noise at low speeds	• Lack of U-joint lubrication	• Lubricate U-joint; if problem persists, have U-joint serviced
Knock or clicking noise	• U-joint or driveshaft hitting frame tunnel • Worn constant velocity joint	• Correct overloaded condition • Have constant velocity joint replaced

NOISE DIAGNOSIS

The Noise Is	Most Probably Produced By
1. Identical under Drive or Coast	Road surface, tires or front wheel bearings
2. Different depending on road surface	Road surface or tires
3. Lower as the car speed is lowered	Tires
4. Similar with car standing or moving	Engine or transmission
5. A vibration	Unbalanced tires, rear wheel bearing, unbalanced driveshaft or worn U-joint
6. A knock or click about every 2 tire revolutions	Rear wheel bearing
7. Most pronounced on turns	Damaged differential gears
8. A steady low-pitched whirring or scraping, starting at low speeds	Damaged or worn pinion bearing
9. A chattering vibration on turns	Wrong differential lubricant or worn clutch plates (limited slip rear axle)
10. Noticed only in Drive, Coast or Float conditions	Worn ring gear and/or pinion gear

24
Suspension and Steering

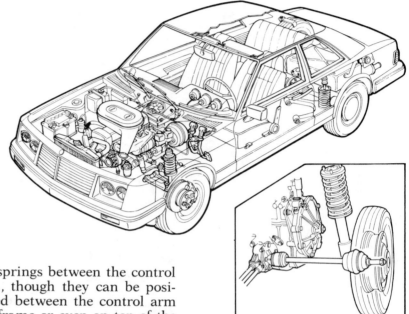

Types of Front Suspensions

The most common front suspensions used on cars today are the independent (unequal length control arms), McPherson strut, torsion bar and transverse torsion bar used exclusively on VW.

Independent Front Suspension

This is also called an unequal length A-arm or control arm type, because the upper and lower control arms attached to the frame are of different lengths. This design is typical of American sedans and is designed this way to reduce tire scuffing.

Ball joints are used to attach the outer ends of the control arms to the spindle. This type of front suspension most often uses coil springs between the control arms, though they can be positioned between the control arm and frame or even on top of the upper control arm. Shock absorbers are used to dampen vibrations.

McPherson Strut

McPherson strut front suspension differs considerably from unequal length A-arm suspension. McPherson strut suspension is found most frequently on subcompact cars, both domestic and imported. With this type of suspension, the shock absorber,

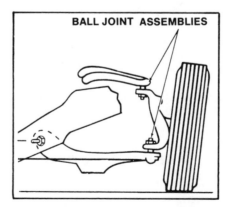

BALL JOINT ASSEMBLIES

Arrows show the upper and lower ball joints.

strut and spindle are a combined unit, which is supported by the coil spring at the upper end and the lower control arm (sometimes called track control arm or transverse link) at the bottom.

There is only one ball joint in this design, and it is attached to the lower part of the spindle. Generally, this ball joint is not a load carrying ball joint, but a follower ball joint, which means it is isolated from vehicle weight.

The shock absorber is built into the strut outer casing and a coil spring sits on a seat welded to the strut casing. The upper mount of the shock absorber bolts to the vehicle body. On some models, the strut cartridge may be replaced, while on others the entire strut must be replaced. Due to the design of this type of suspension, the only front end alignment procedure possible is toe-in adjustment, since caster and camber are fixed.

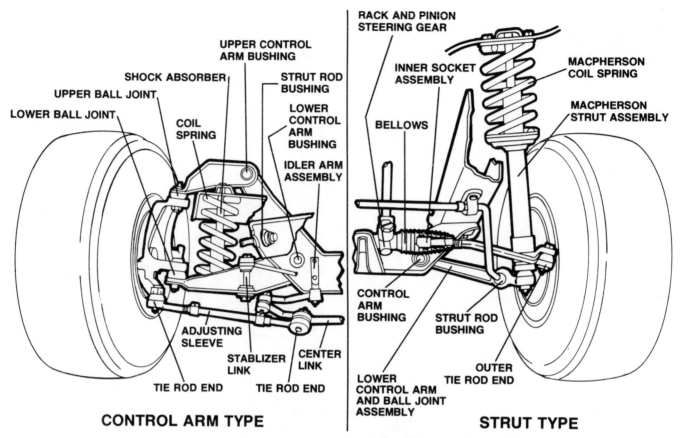

RACK AND PINION
STEERING GEAR

UPPER CONTROL
ARM BUSHING

SHOCK ABSORBER

STRUT ROD
BUSHING

UPPER BALL JOINT

INNER SOCKET
ASSEMBLY

MACPHERSON
COIL SPRING

LOWER BALL JOINT

COIL
SPRING

LOWER
CONTROL
ARM
BUSHING

BELLOWS

MACPHERSON
STRUT ASSEMBLY

IDLER ARM
ASSEMBLY

CONTROL
ARM
BUSHING

STRUT ROD
BUSHING

ADJUSTING
SLEEVE

STABLIZER
LINK

CENTER
LINK

OUTER
TIE ROD END

TIE ROD END

TIE ROD END

LOWER
CONTROL ARM
AND BALL JOINT
ASSEMBLY

CONTROL ARM TYPE

STRUT TYPE

Parts locator for two basic front suspension designs in use on cars today.

Torsion Bar

Torsion bar suspensions are used almost exclusively by Chrysler Corporation. Basically, the torsion bar is a coil spring stretched out straight, and used instead of a coil spring to control wheel action. The torsion bars are attached to the chassis at one end and to the upper or lower control arm at the other end. As the control arm moves up or down in response to road surface, it twists the torsion bar, which resists the twisting force and returns the control arm to the normal position.

The outer ends of the control arms are kept an equal distance apart by spindles sometimes called steering knuckles, which are held in place by ball joints at the top and bottom. Ball joints permit upward and downward motion of the steering knuckle, and the turning motion required for turning corners, while keep-ing the steering knuckles vertical.

Transverse Torsion Bar

The transverse torsion bar suspension is peculiar to VW and uses 8–10 leaves in the upper tubes or round torsion bars to suspend the vehicle weight. The tubes are connected by upper and lower trailing arms and are splined to the leaves or torsion bar. The trailing arms are connected to the spindle by ball joints, which are pressed into the arms and bolted to the spindle. Shock absorbers are used to control vibration and most models use a stabilizer bar for better handling.

Manual Steering

There are two types of manual steering in general use today. They are worm and sector steering, also known as recirculating ball, and rack and pinion steering.

Recirculating Ball Steering

In this type of steering, the end of the steering input shaft, called the wormshaft, is machined with a continuous spiral groove holding ball bearings. These ball bearings move a ball nut assembly up or down the wormshaft when the steering wheel is turned.

Since the wormshaft is coupled directly to the steering column shaft, turning the steering wheel causes the wormshaft to turn in the same direction. This action moves the ball nut assembly along its length. The balls circulate in one direction for a right-hand turn and in the other direction for a left-hand turn. Teeth on the ball nut assembly then engage teeth on the sector shaft (also called the Pitman

PERMANENTLY ADJUSTED TYPE

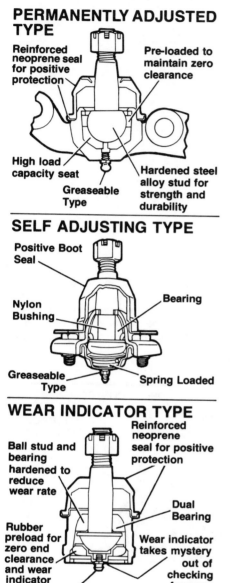

Reinforced neoprene seal for positive protection

Pre-loaded to maintain zero clearance

High load capacity seat

Greaseable Type

Hardened steel alloy stud for strength and durability

SELF ADJUSTING TYPE

Positive Boot Seal

Nylon Bushing

Bearing

Greaseable Type

Spring Loaded

WEAR INDICATOR TYPE

Ball stud and bearing hardened to reduce wear rate

Reinforced neoprene seal for positive protection

Rubber preload for zero end clearance and wear indicator operation

Dual Bearing

Wear indicator takes mystery out of checking for wear

Greaseable Type

Three basic types of ball joint designs.

shaft since it is connected to the Pitman arm) causing the Pitman or sector shaft to move the Pitman arm, thereby converting the rotating force of the steering wheel into the slower, higher torque rotation of the Pitman arm. The Pitman arm in turn transmits the desired directional movement to the front wheels through the steering linkage. Tubes connect the locknut/sleeve unit and allow the balls to constantly recirculate, distributing wear evenly among them.

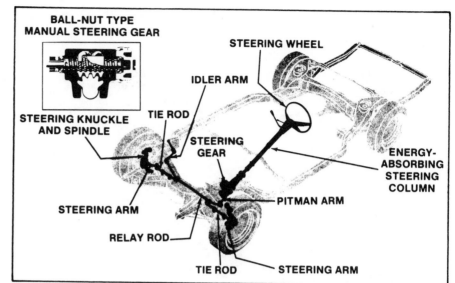

BALL-NUT TYPE MANUAL STEERING GEAR

STEERING WHEEL

IDLER ARM

STEERING KNUCKLE AND SPINDLE

TIE ROD

STEERING GEAR

ENERGY-ABSORBING STEERING COLUMN

STEERING ARM

PITMAN ARM

RELAY ROD

TIE ROD

STEERING ARM

Typical automotive steering system (recirculating ball type shown).

Rack and Pinion Steering

This steering design uses a steering gear connected to the steering column shaft by a flexible coupling. This gear, similar in design to the pinion gear used in a differential, is cut on an angle and meshed on one side with a steel bar or rack which also has teeth cut in it. This rack is contained in the steering gearbox, which is positioned between the tie rods in the steering linkage. When the steering wheel is turned, the pinion gear operates directly on the rack, causing it to move from side to side and transmitting motion to the front wheels. This type of steering gear avoids the use of a Pitman arm and is a more direct and precise

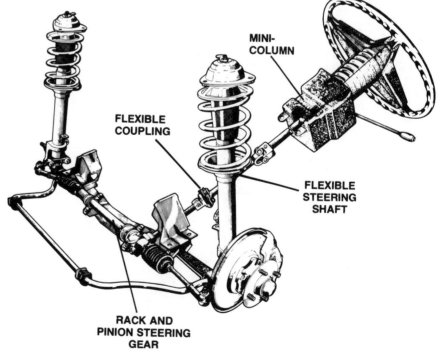

MINI-COLUMN

FLEXIBLE COUPLING

FLEXIBLE STEERING SHAFT

RACK AND PINION STEERING GEAR

Typical rack and pinion steering gear, used on many smaller cars.

FRONT SUSPENSION DESIGNS (CARS)

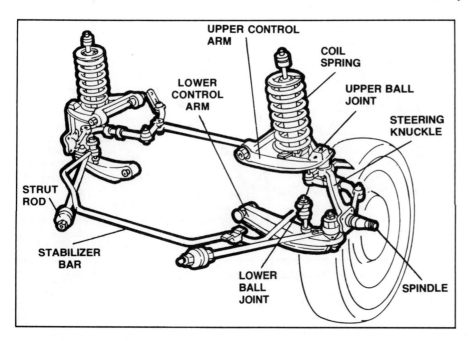

This design is used mainly on Ford vehicles. The coil spring is mounted on top of the control arm with the shock absorber in the center of the coil spring. Only the upper control arm is of A-arm design.

Typical unequal length A-arm suspension used on many American sedans. In this design, the shock absorber and coil spring is positioned between the upper and lower control arms. Note that the control arms (A-arms) are not the same length.

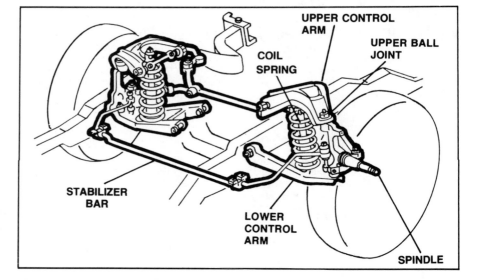

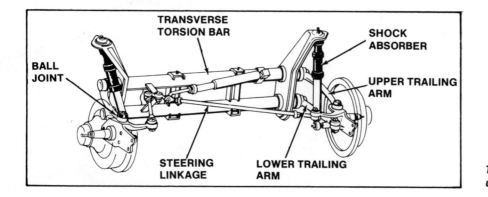

Transverse torsion bar front suspension used primarily by VW.

FRONT SUSPENSION DESIGNS (CARS), continued

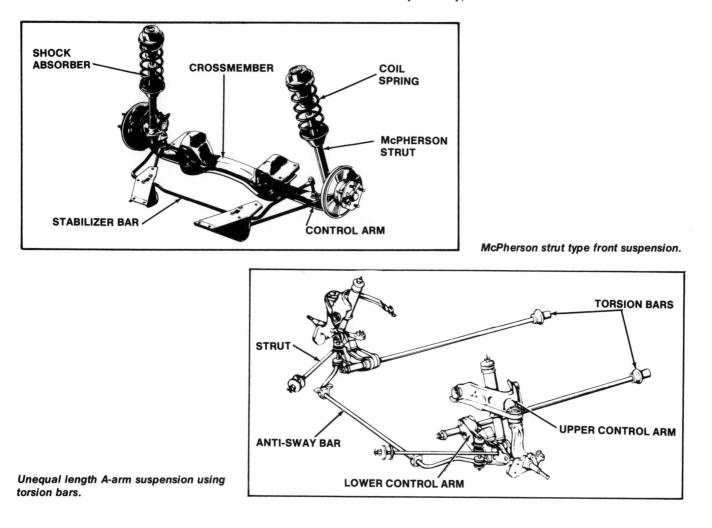

McPherson strut type front suspension.

Unequal length A-arm suspension using torsion bars.

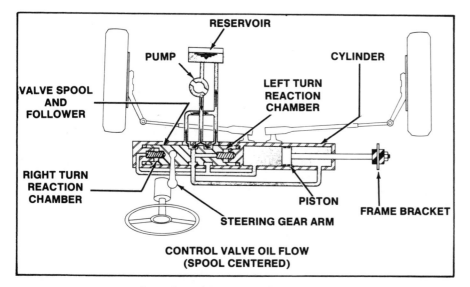

Operation of power steering system.

type of steering, although drivers accustomed to recirculating ball steering occasionally find its directness disconcerting.

Power Steering

Power steering units are mechanical steering gear units incorporating a power assist. A worm shaft, which is rotated by the shaft coming down from the steering wheel via a flexible coupling, causes a rack piston nut to slide up and down inside the housing. This motion is changed into rotating force by the action of an output shaft sector gear. The rack piston nut is forced up and down inside the housing by

FRONT SUSPENSION DESIGNS (TRUCKS)

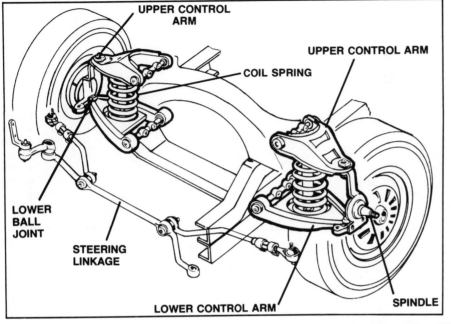

UPPER CONTROL ARM

UPPER CONTROL ARM

COIL SPRING

LOWER BALL JOINT

STEERING LINKAGE

LOWER CONTROL ARM

SPINDLE

This independent front truck suspension is very similar to the unequal length A-arm suspension used by American sedans. It functions in the same manner, but the components are beefier to handle the added stress.

This is a straight I-beam front suspension. It is uncomplicated and meant to handle heavy loads, rather than give a comfortable ride.

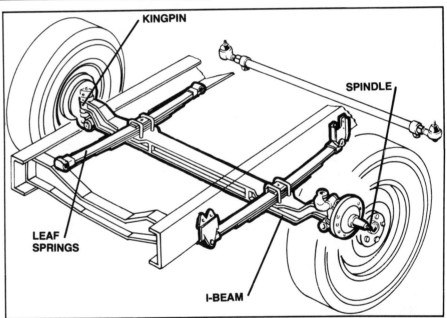

KINGPIN

SPINDLE

LEAF SPRINGS

I-BEAM

the rotation of the worm gear, which forces the nut to move through the action of recirculating balls. The nut fits tightly inside the housing, and is sealed against the sides of the housing by a ring seal. Power assist is provided by forcing hydraulic fluid into the housing on one side or the other of the rack piston nut.

The hydraulic pressure is sup-

plied by a rotary vane pump, driven by the engine via V belts. The pump incorporates a flow control valve that bypasses the right amount of fluid for the proper operating pressure. The pump contains a fluid reservoir, located above the main body of the pump. The same fluid lubricates all parts of the power steering unit.

A rotary valve, spool valve, or

pivot lever located in the steering box senses the rotation of the steering wheel and channels fluid to the upper or lower surface of the rack piston nut.

Steering Geometry

Front wheel alignment (also known as front end geometry) is the position of the front wheels relative to each other and to the

FRONT SUSPENSION DESIGNS (TRUCKS), continued

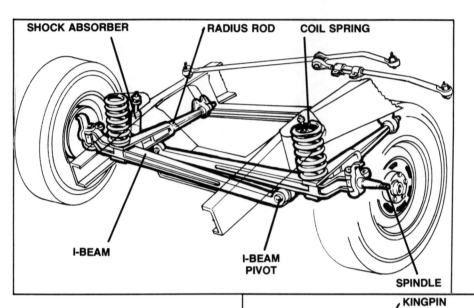

SHOCK ABSORBER   RADIUS ROD   COIL SPRING

I-BEAM

I-BEAM PIVOT

SPINDLE

The twin I-beam front suspension is used almost exclusively by Ford trucks. The coil spring is mounted between the frame and an I-beam that carries each wheel. The I-beam is pivoted at the other end, and a radius rod serves to locate the fore-and-aft position of each I-beam.

KINGPIN

LEAF SPRING

DRIVE AXLE

STEERING LINKAGE

WHEEL HUB

The four-wheel-drive suspension is basically the same as an I-beam suspension, except that a front drive axle takes the place of the I-beam.

vehicle. Correct alignment must be maintained to provide safe, accurate steering, vehicle stability and minimum tire wear. The factors which determine wheel alignment are interdependent. Therefore, when one of the factors is adjusted, the others must be adjusted to compensate.

Front end alignment can only be checked with sophisticated equipment.

Caster Angle

Caster angle is the number of degrees that a line, drawn through the center of the upper and lower ball joints and viewed from the side, can be tilted forward or backward. Positive caster means that the top of the upper ball joint is tilted toward the rear of the car, and negative caster means that it is tilted toward the front. A car with a slightly positive caster setting will have its lower ball joint pivot slightly ahead of the tire's center. This will assist the directional stability of the car by causing a drag at the bottom center of the wheel when it turns, thereby resisting the turn and tending to hold the wheel steady in whatever direction the car is pointed. A car with too much (positive) caster will be hard to steer and shimmy at low speeds. A car with insufficient (negative) caster may tend to be unstable at high speeds and may respond erratically when the brakes are applied.

Camber Angle

Camber angle is the number of degrees that the wheel itself is tilted from a vertical line, when

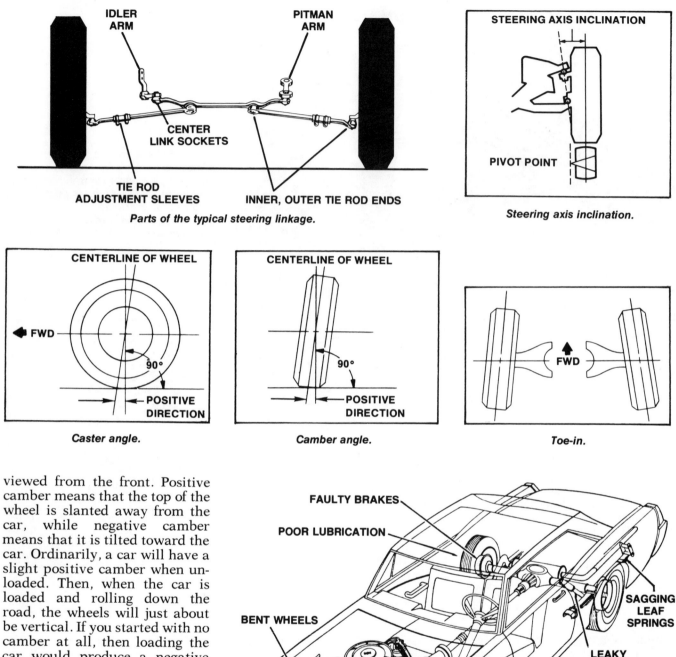

Parts of the typical steering linkage.

Steering axis inclination.

Caster angle.

Camber angle.

Toe-in.

viewed from the front. Positive camber means that the top of the wheel is slanted away from the car, while negative camber means that it is tilted toward the car. Ordinarily, a car will have a slight positive camber when unloaded. Then, when the car is loaded and rolling down the road, the wheels will just about be vertical. If you started with no camber at all, then loading the car would produce a negative camber. Excessive camber (either positive or negative) will produce rapid tire wear, since one side of the tire will be more heavily loaded than the other side.

Steering Axis Inclination

Steering axis inclination is the number of degrees that a line drawn through the upper and lower ball joints and viewed from the front, is tilted to the left or the right. This, in combination

These 9 points should be checked or examined whenever the front suspension or rear suspension is serviced.

with caster, is responsible for the directional stability and self-centering of the steering. As the steering knuckle swings from lock to lock, the spindle generates an arc, causing the car to be raised when it is turned from the straight-ahead position. The reason the car body must rise is straightforward: since the wheel is in contact with the ground, it cannot move down. However, when it is swung away from the straight-ahead position, it must move either up or down (due to the arc generated by the steering knuckle). Not being able to move down, it must move up. Then, the weight of the car acts against this lift, and attempts to return the spindle to the straight-ahead position when the steering wheel is released.

Toe-In

Toe-in is the difference (in inches) between the front and the rear of the front tires. On a car with toe-in, the distance between the front wheels is less at the front than at the rear. Toe-in is normally only a few fractions of an inch, and is necessary to ensure parallel rolling of the front wheels and to prevent excessive tire wear. As the car is driven at increasingly faster speeds, the steering linkage has a tendency to expand slightly, thereby allowing the front wheels to turn out and away from each other. Therefore, initially setting the front wheels so that they are pointing slightly inward (toe-in), allows them to turn straight ahead when the car is underway.

Rear Suspensions

Rear suspensions, in general, can be much simpler than front suspensions since all they have to do is support the rear of the car and provide some sort of suspension control. However, some rear suspensions, especially those found on sports cars, are quite complex.

SUSPENSION AND STEERING SYSTEM MAINTENANCE INTERVALS

Your car's suspension and steering system will work efficiently if it is maintained at these intervals.

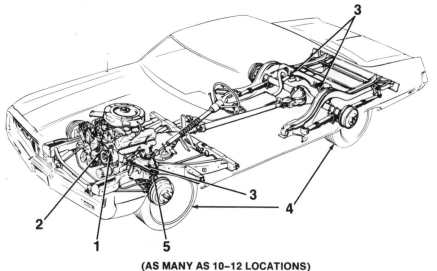

(AS MANY AS 10–12 LOCATIONS)

1. Check/add power steering fluid	Every 3 months or 3000 miles
2. Check/adjust belt tension	Every 3 months or 3000 miles
Replace power steering belt ▲	Every 2 yrs or 24,000 miles
3. Check shock absorbers	Every year or 12,000 miles
4. Check tires for abnormal wear	Every month or 1000 miles
5. Grease front end	Every 3 months or 3000 miles

▲Retighten the belt after 300 miles of use. New belts have a tendency to stretch.

Periodic Maintenance

Adjusting Power Steering Belt Tension

A loose power steering belt is frequently the cause of hard steering. Check the belt at the recommended intervals, and if it needs adjusting, use the following procedure.

1. Locate the adjusting bolt first. It will be the bolt located in the long, narrow adjusting slot. Sometimes there are two adjusting bolts.
2. Locate and loosen the pivot bolt or bolts.
3. Loosen the adjusting bolt or bolts and pry the pump in the correct direction with a pry bar of some sort. Try not to pry too hard on the pump body itself as it can be damaged by vigorous prying.

4. The belt is correctly tensioned when there is approximately ½" of play in the middle of the belt. Once you have the

Quite often, there are a number of bolts on the power steering pump that must be loosened in order to adjust it. The bolts shown here are the pivot bolts and must be loosened.

REAR SUSPENSION DESIGNS

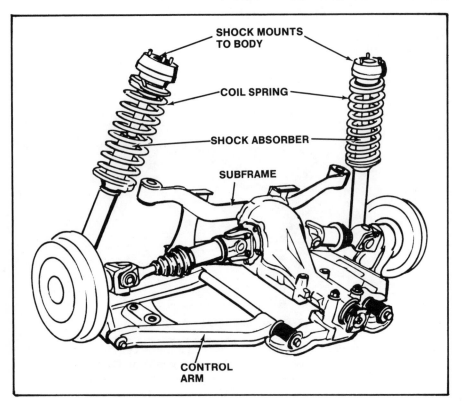

This is a strut suspension with coil spring, shock absorber and strut combined in one unit and attached to the body and wheel spindle. In this type of suspension the lower control arm, strut and rear axle usually mount on some sort of sub-frame which is attached to the car body.

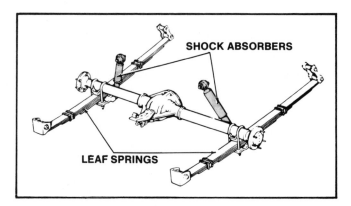

This is a basic, uncomplicated leaf spring rear suspension with shock absorbers to control vibration and up and down movement of the axle.

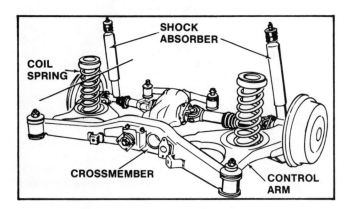

This is an independent rear suspension used on many sports cars. Coil springs are used between the control arm and the vehicle body, and the control arms pivot on a cross-member and are attached at the other end to a spindle. A shock absorber attached to the spindle or control arm absorbs vibrations.

REAR SUSPENSION DESIGNS, continued

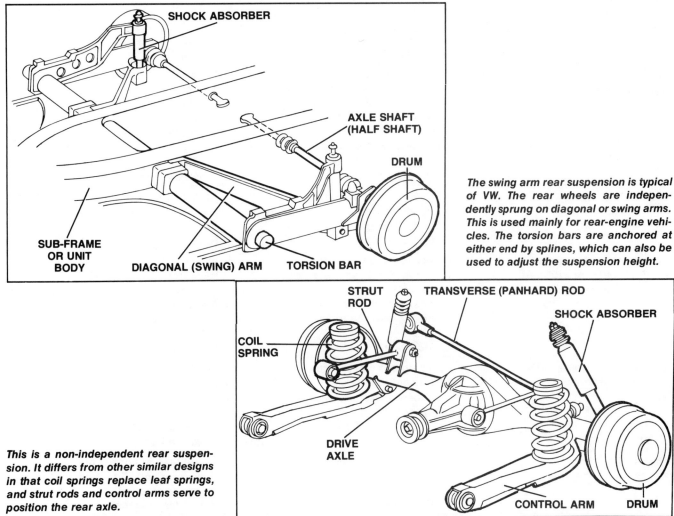

SHOCK ABSORBER

AXLE SHAFT (HALF SHAFT)

DRUM

SUB-FRAME OR UNIT BODY

DIAGONAL (SWING) ARM   TORSION BAR

The swing arm rear suspension is typical of VW. The rear wheels are independently sprung on diagonal or swing arms. This is used mainly for rear-engine vehicles. The torsion bars are anchored at either end by splines, which can also be used to adjust the suspension height.

STRUT ROD   TRANSVERSE (PANHARD) ROD

SHOCK ABSORBER

COIL SPRING

DRIVE AXLE

CONTROL ARM   DRUM

This is a non-independent rear suspension. It differs from other similar designs in that coil springs replace leaf springs, and strut rods and control arms serve to position the rear axle.

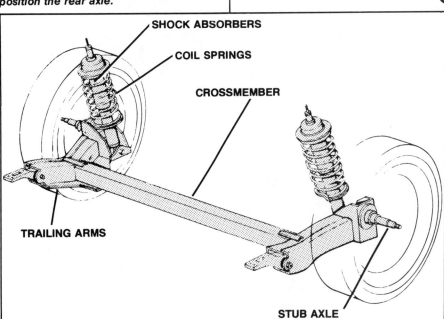

SHOCK ABSORBERS

COIL SPRINGS

CROSSMEMBER

TRAILING ARMS

STUB AXLE

An independent (dead) axle used with front-wheel-drive cars. Trailing arms holding the wheel and shock absorber are attached to a rigid crossmember.

TROUBLESHOOTING BASIC STEERING AND SUSPENSION PROBLEMS

Most problems in the front end and steering are caused by improperly maintained tires which you can correct yourself, or by incorrect wheel alignment, which requires the services of a professional mechanic. Get in the habit of checking tires frequently; this is usually the first place that problems in the front end or steering will show up.

The Condition	Is Caused By	What to Do
Hard Steering (steering wheel is hard to turn)	• Low or uneven tire pressure • Loose power steering pump drive belt • Low or incorrect power steering fluid • Incorrect front end alignment • Defective power steering pump • Bent or poorly lubricated front end parts	• Inflate tires to correct pressure • Adjust belt • Add fluid as necessary • Have front end alignment checked/adjusted • Have pump checked/repaired • Lubricate and/or have defective parts replaced
Loose Steering (too much play in the steering wheel	• Loose wheel bearings • Loose or worn steering linkage • Faulty shocks • Worn ball joints	• Adjust wheel bearings • Have worn parts serviced • Replace shocks • Have ball joints checked/serviced
Car Veers or Wanders (car pulls to one side with hands off the steering wheel)	• Incorrect tire pressure • Improper front end alignment • Loose wheel bearings • Loose or bent front end components • Faulty shocks	• Inflate tires to correct pressure • Have front end alignment checked/adjusted • Adjust wheel bearings • Have worn components checked/serviced • Replace shocks
Wheel oscillation or vibration transmitted through steering wheel	• Improper tire pressures • Tires out of balance • Loose wheel bearings • Improper front end alignment • Worn or bent front end components	• Inflate tires to correct pressure • Have tires balanced • Adjust wheel bearings • Have front end alignment checked/adjusted • Have front end checked/serviced
Uneven tire wear (see Section 26—Tires)	• Incorrect tire pressure • Front end out of alignment • Tires out of balance	• Inflate tires to correct pressure • Have front end alignment checked/adjusted • Have tires balanced

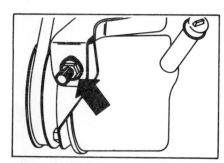

This is the actual adjustment bolt on this pump. By turning the bolt, you can adjust the pump inward or outward. On others you may have to loosen the adjusting and pivot bolts and pry on the pump to move it.

belt correctly tensioned, tighten the bolts. Tighten the pivot bolt first and the pump won't move when you tighten the others.

Checking and Adding Power Steering Fluid

If the system isn't leaking, you shouldn't need to add fluid very often at all. Nonetheless, it's a

Remove the pump dipstick and check the fluid level.

Keep the level between the "Full" and "Add" marks (arrows).

good idea to check the fluid with the engine at operating temperature and the wheels pointed straight ahead. The engine should be off. Fluid must be maintained between the "full"

Bounce the car several times to get it moving up and down. Let go. If the shocks are good, the car shouldn't continue to bounce more than once.

and the "add" marks. Use power steering fluid to top up the reservoir. While you're adding fluid, check the power steering hoses for wear or chafing. Ordinarily, there should be no problem, but it's always a good idea to check.

Spotting Worn Shocks

Worn shocks can cause a considerable number of problems, ranging from excessive tire wear to erratic handling. Fortunately, the test for worn shocks is quite simple. The first step is to crawl underneath the car and check all the shocks for oil streaks. If you spot any shocks streaked with oil, they need replacing. Plain road grime doesn't count.

The next step is to stand at the front or rear of the car and bounce the car up and down a few times. Let go and see how long it takes the car to stop rocking. If the shocks are good, the car shouldn't bounce more than one time after you let go. Repeat the operation for the other end of the car. Remember, if any shocks need replacing, always replace them in pairs (front pair or rear pair).

Grease the Front End

Depending on the age of your car and the intentions of the manufacturer, there may be as many as 10 or 12, or as few as 2 lubrication fittings on the front end. Typical places to look for grease nipples are the ball joints, control arm pivot points, steering linkage and tie-rod ends.

Lubricate any of these fittings with a small, hand-operated grease gun filled with EP chassis lubricant. If you plan on buying a grease gun to do this, buy a flexible extention to go with it. This will allow you to get at those hard-to-reach fittings.

Pump grease into the fitting until you see grease ooze out around the joint, indicating that it's full.

Occasionally, these grease nipples will get clogged with dirt. If so, simply unscrew them with a small wrench and clean them out. When you put them back, cover them with a small piece of tin foil to seal out dirt.

Servicing the Steering System

Power Steering Belt Replacement

Various methods are used to adjust the belt tension on power steering pumps. Most are fairly obvious and a casual study of the pump will reveal the method of

Use a hand grease gun and EP chassis lube to grease the front end.

TREAD WEAR PATTERNS

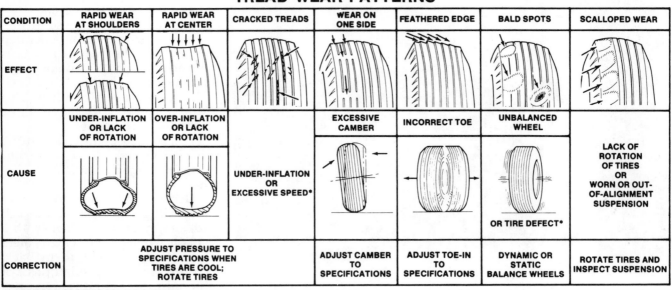

CONDITION	RAPID WEAR AT SHOULDERS	RAPID WEAR AT CENTER	CRACKED TREADS	WEAR ON ONE SIDE	FEATHERED EDGE	BALD SPOTS	SCALLOPED WEAR
EFFECT							
CAUSE	UNDER-INFLATION OR LACK OF ROTATION	OVER-INFLATION OR LACK OF ROTATION	UNDER-INFLATION OR EXCESSIVE SPEED*	EXCESSIVE CAMBER	INCORRECT TOE	UNBALANCED WHEEL OR TIRE DEFECT*	LACK OF ROTATION OF TIRES OR WORN OR OUT-OF-ALIGNMENT SUSPENSION
CORRECTION	ADJUST PRESSURE TO SPECIFICATIONS WHEN TIRES ARE COOL; ROTATE TIRES			ADJUST CAMBER TO SPECIFICATIONS	ADJUST TOE-IN TO SPECIFICATIONS	DYNAMIC OR STATIC BALANCE WHEELS	ROTATE TIRES AND INSPECT SUSPENSION

*HAVE TIRE INSPECTED FOR FURTHER USE.

adjustment. Sometimes a pivot bolt must be loosened to swing the pump inward, sometimes only an adjustment bolt must be loosened. Often the power steering belt is located behind other accessory drive belts, which will have to be removed before the power steering pump belt can be removed.

When adjusting the tension of the belt, do not pry on the power steering pump housing neck; the pump itself is fairly delicate and easily damaged. A wooden hammer handle works well used between the engine block and the body of the pump, or better yet, use your hand to force the pump outward.

Tighten the adjusting bolt first and check the tension on the belt. It should be about ½" at the middle of the longest span. Be sure to recheck the tension after about 200 miles of use—new belts will stretch and need readjusting.

Shock Absorber Replacement

There are various types of shock mountings, but as a general rule, shock replacement is a fairly easy task. The only exception to this is McPherson strut suspension cartridge replacement, which requires a spring compressor and some expertise. If your car is equipped with Mc-Pherson strut suspension, we recommend you leave cartridge re-

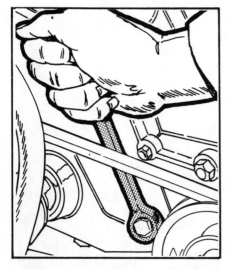

Loosen the pivot bolts. You may have to remove other belts that are in the way to allow removal of the power steering belts.

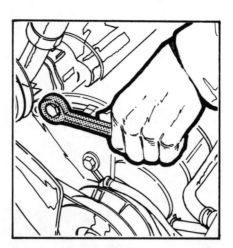

Loosen the adjustment bolt. Grab the belt and pull it upward to move the pump inward toward the engine. Remove the old belt.

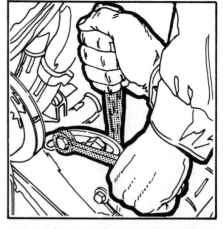

Install the new belt in the pulley grooves and carefully pry the pump outward, unless the pump has a built-in adjustment. Tighten the adjustment and pivot bolts when the tension is correct.

This is a common type of shock mount. The entire shock tower can be removed (arrows) or the shock itself can be removed from the tower.

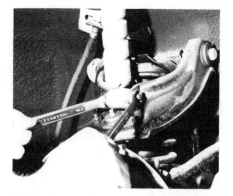

On some shocks you have to hold one nut while turning the other.

Shock mounts like these are generally easy to remove.

On some shocks you have to hold the stem (arrow) while loosening the nut.

Often the upper mount of rear shocks is hard to reach.

placement to a professional. However, if your car is equipped with conventional shock absorbers, it's not too hard a job.

1. Jack up the car and support it with safety stands. Use genuine safety stands, not cinder blocks or pieces of wood.

2. Squirt the shock mounting studs with some penetrating oil before trying to loosen them. If the car is fairly new, there shouldn't be much problem, but on older cars, the mounting nuts are generally rusted in place.

3. Remove the shock absorber mounting nuts. This sounds easy, but sometimes it isn't. A lot of top shock mounts require you to hold the top of the shock with a pair of vise grips while you turn the mounting nut. There are other variations on this, depending on the type of shock mounting.

4. Once you have the mounting nuts removed, remove the old shock and install the new one. Note which way the rubber bushings went so the new ones can be reinstalled correctly.

5. Install the new shock using the new hardware. Tighten the mounting bolts and lower the car.

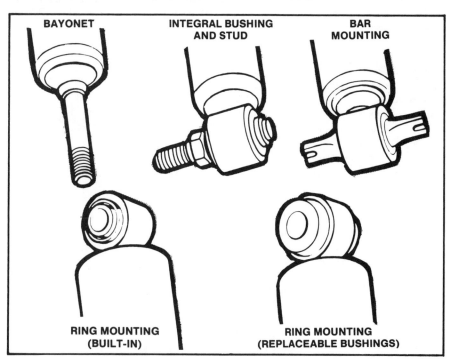

There are five basic types of shock mounts.

25
Wheels

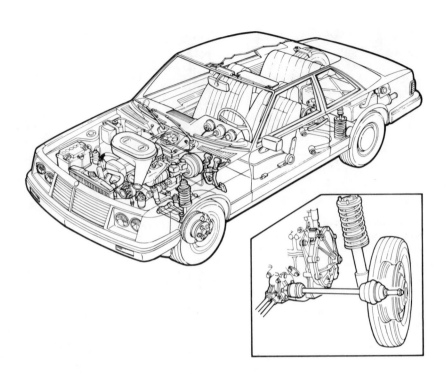

Any discussion of wheels inevitably involves tires. The only reason you would want new wheels is for appearance (custom wheels) or to use larger tires. The failure rate of wheels is small, but custom wheels are extremely popular. The subject of wheels is complex and technical, but there are a few tips for those shopping around for new wheels.

The correct capacity, rim width, type of wheel, offset, bolt pattern and diameter all must be considered when selecting a replacement or custom wheel. Having the right wheel is just as important as having one that's not defective. At highway speeds, the wheels on an average car will rotate close to 600 times a minute, about 10 times every second. The wrong type or size of wheel can destroy tires and bearings very quickly at that rate.

Wheel Construction

A wheel is made up of a rim and center member, known as a disc or spider. The rim supports the tire and the spider (disc) connects the vehicle with the rim.

Wheels are usually of two types—the drop center (DC) and the semi-drop center (SDC). Drop center wheels are used on all cars and light trucks; semi-drop center wheels are usually only used with large multi-ply, heavy-duty tires on over-the-road trucks. The SDC wheel has a removable outer ring that allows easier installation and higher inflation pressure. Above six plies, tires would be extremely rigid in

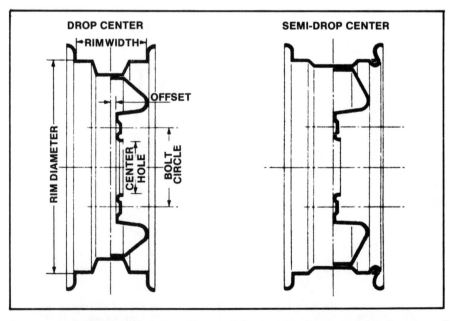

Two types of wheel construction. The semi-drop center has removable flanges and does not need the severe drop in the center of the rim. These wheels are only used on heavy equipment.

the bead and be very difficult to mount on a single-piece wheel without damaging the bead.

Most passenger car wheels fall into two types. The all-steel wheel is the type found on cars as original equipment from the factory. Custom or "mag" wheels are named for their resemblance to magnesium racing wheels. True magnesium wheels are too porous to hold the air pressure of a street tire and never should be used on the street. Custom wheels are either a cast aluminum alloy, a steel rim with cast aluminum alloy spider or a two-piece steel wheel.

Wheel Capacity

Just as tires have a maximum load capacity and inflation pressure, so do wheels. Any wheels you install should have a greater load capacity and inflation pressure capacity than the tires, or you could have problems. Obviously the load-carrying capacity of the vehicle is only as strong as the weakest part. If you have selected your tires to carry an anticipated load of, say, 1500 lbs., then the wheel should be capable of carrying at least that, preferably more.

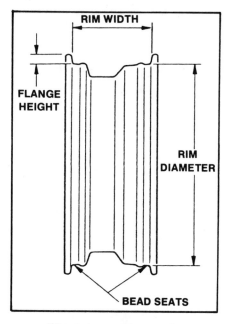
Wheel rim measurements.

Wheel Dimensions

Size

Wheel sizes are determined by three measurements—rim diameter, rim width and flange height. A typical wheel size might be 14 x 7JJ. Rim diameter and rim width are always expressed in inches, so this wheel is 14" in diameter and has a rim width of 7". The letter combination following the rim width indicates the flange height in inches. A J rim has .68" high flanges while a K rim has .77" high flanges. The circumference on which the centers of the wheel bolt holes are located is the bolt circle. It is usually shown as a double number: 5–5½. The first number indicates the number of holes, and the second, the diameter of the bolt circle.

The rim width will be dictated by the tire section width and/or the tread width. The general rule is that the flange-to-flange width of the rim should be a minimum of three-quarters of the tire section width. The maximum flange-to-flange wheel width should be equal to the width of the tire tread. Narrow tires on wide rims tend to make the outer edges of the tire curl in toward the center. The result is less tread on the road, increased tire wear and a harsher ride. At high speeds, centrifugal action can pull the tire beads away from the bead seat on the rim.

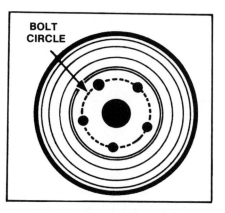
The dotted line indicates the bolt circle.

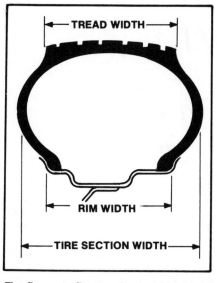
The flange-to-flange wheel width should never be more than the tread width of the tire.

Wide tires on narrow rims create a poor bead seal and force the tread to assume a convex shape causing abnormal tire wear, loss of control with a somewhat smoother ride.

The general rule is that the tire and wheel combination is satisfactory if, when the tire is flat, no part of the underside of the vehicle touches the ground. This will prevent a shower of sparks, should a blowout occur.

Offset

Another important dimension to be considered when looking for wheels is offset. Offset is the distance from the mounting face of the wheel spider to the rim centerline. Offset is positive when the mounting face (lug circle) is outboard of the centerline and negative if the lug circle is inboard of the centerline. All wheels are designed for either positive, negative or zero offset, usually for disc brake clearance or for handling characteristics.

Generally, you should not increase the offset more than ½" or tire width by 1", or you'll create further problems. Increasing offset ½" (or tire width 1") will put the entire extra tire width ½" to the outside, where it may not

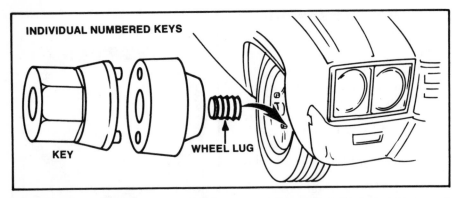

Wheel locks are unlocked with a key. Be sure to keep the lock lubricated to prevent freezing. Other wheel locks use an individually shaped adapter to remove the lock. Supposedly, no two adapters are alike.

WHEEL MAINTENANCE INTERVALS

Wheels require little maintenance, other than occasional cleaning and checking that the wheel weights are still intact.

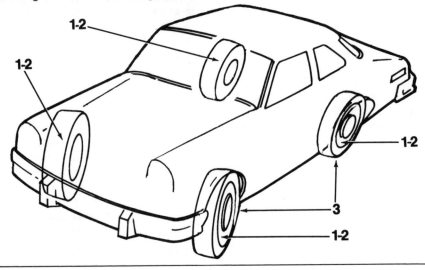

1. Clean the wheels (custom wheels)	As necessary
2. Check wheel weights	Every fuel stop/2 weeks (when you check tire pressure)
3. Rotate wheel/tire See Section 26 "Tires"	Every 6000 miles/6 months

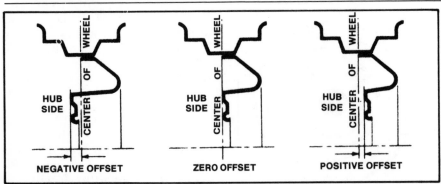

Wheel offset is the distance between the rim centerline and the mounting face of the spider. Offset should never be increased more than ½".

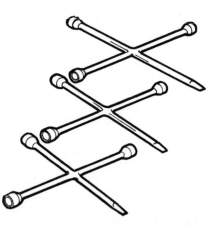

A lug wrench of this type works best. Check the lug nut torque with a torque wrench.

clear the wheelwell. Increasing the offset also has the effect of loading the front wheel bearings past their design limits and can actually "cock" the bearings causing rapid wear or premature failure.

Occasionally, disc brakes cause a mounting problem; some wheels were not designed for use with disc brakes and will not clear the brake caliper or will interfere with the disc. Be sure to check before buying wheels, especially used wheels, that they will fit your vehicle. Be sure that the tires on wider wheels will clear the wheelwells, especially when turned at full lock, and that the tires do not interfere with suspension travel.

Caring for Wheels

Tire Mounting

Most wheels, with the exception of custom wheels, require little care. Tires must be mounted carefully to avoid scratching expensive wheels. Wheels with steel rims and alloy spiders are somewhat easier than all-alloy wheels, but many service facilities charge extra to mount tires on custom wheels, or will refuse to work on them at all.

Custom wheels are balanced in the same way as steel wheels, but adhesive backed weights are used instead of the hammered on type. Adhesive weights must be checked more frequently than the others, and, as with mounting tires, many service stations charge extra to dynamically (spin) balance custom wheels, or will not do it at all.

Tightening Wheels

Torque specifications for lug nuts should be adhered to and applied evenly in a criss-cross pattern. Overtightening lugs can lead to broken studs, and overtightening or tightening in the wrong sequence can lead to warped brake drums or rotors.

■
Chilton Tip
Under no circumstances should an electric or air impact gun be used to tighten the lugs on custom alloy wheels.
■

Keeping Your Wheels & Keeping Them Clean

Oxidation and theft are the main enemies of custom wheels. Oxidation is caused by a chemical reaction between air and water which causes the alloy to pit. Various waxes and cleaners are available to hold the oxidation process to a minimum and keep the wheels looking like new. Theft is a man-made problem, and about the only thing you can do is stay out of the evil parts of town or lock your wheels and hope for the best. There are many wheel locks available, some using a key and others using a special individual adaptor to get the lock off.

TROUBLESHOOTING BASIC WHEEL PROBLEMS

Wheels very seldom give problems. Many times a suspected wheel problem is actually a problem in the tires or the car's front end. Before going to the trouble of having wheels removed or replaced, check section 26 "Tires" and section 24 "Suspension and Steering."

The Problem	Is Caused By	What to Do
The car's front end vibrates at high speed	• The wheels are out of balance • Wheels are out of alignment	• Have wheels balanced—See Section 26 "Tires" • Have wheel alignment checked/adjusted—See Section 26 "Tires"
Car pulls to either side	• Wheels are out of alignment • Unequal tire pressure • Different size tires or wheels	• Have wheel alignment checked/adjusted • Check/adjust tire pressure See Section 26 "Tires" • Change tires or wheels to same size
The car's wheel(s) wobbles	• Loose wheel lug nuts • Wheels out of balance • Damaged wheel • Wheels are out of alignment • Worn or damaged ball joint • Excessive play in the steering linkage (usually due to worn parts) • Defective shock absorber	• Tighten wheel lug nuts • Have tires balanced—See Section 26 "Tires" • Raise car and spin the wheel. If the wheel is bent, it should be replaced • Have wheel alignment checked/adjusted—See Section 26 "Tires" • Check ball joints—See Section 24 "Suspension and Steering" • Have steering linkage checked—See Section 24 "Suspension and Steering" • Check shock absorbers—See Section 24 "Suspension and Steering"
Tires wear unevenly or prematurely	• Incorrect wheel size • Wheels are out of balance • Wheels are out of alignment	• Check if wheel and tire size are compatible • Have wheels balanced—See Section 26 "Tires" • Have wheel alignment checked/adjusted

TORQUE WHEEL LUG NUTS CORRECTLY

Many car manufacturers are putting more emphasis on tightening wheel lug nuts properly. Overtightening the lug nuts can break the wheel studs and damage the wheel. Tightening in the wrong sequence can distort brake drums or brake discs.

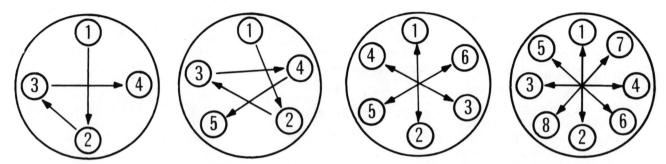

Most common wheel bolt tightening patterns are illustrated. If in doubt, tighten in a criss-cross pattern.

26

Tires

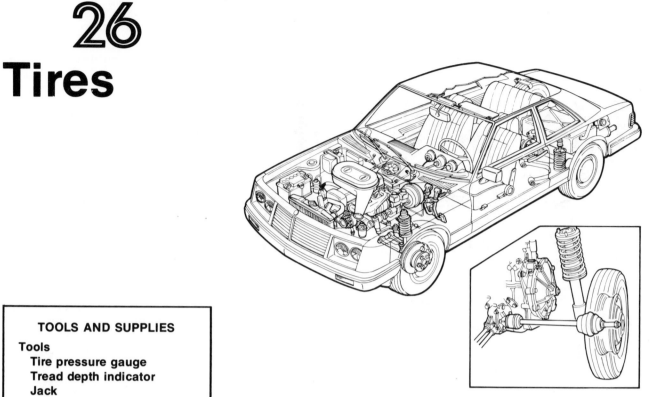

Tires are among the most important, and least understood parts of the car. Everything concerned with driving—starting, moving and stopping—involves the tires. Because of their importance to driving ease and safety, learning the basics of tires will pay off in dollar savings and safe driving.

Types of Tires

Modern tires use a combination of materials to contain pressurized air. The foundation of the tire is the plies (layers of nylon, polyester, fiberglass or steel) just beneath the tread that provides flexibility and strength.

Regardless of size, cost or brand, there are basically only three types of tires—bias, bias belted and radial.

Bias tires, the old stand-by, are constructed with cords running across the tread (from bead-to-bead) at an angle about 35° to the tread centerline; alternate plies reverse direction. Crisscrossing adds strength to the tire sidewalls and tread. When properly inflated, these tires give a relatively soft, comfortable ride.

Bias belted tires are similar, but additional belts of fiberglass or rayon encircle the tire under the tread. The belts stabilize the tread, holding it flatter against the road with less squirm (side movement). Belted tires offer a firmer ride, better traction, improved puncture resistance and longer life than bias ply tires.

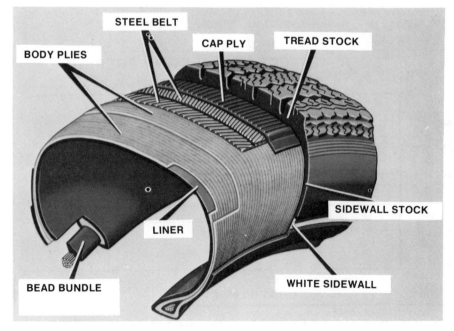

Various parts of a tire are shown in this cutaway of a radial tire.

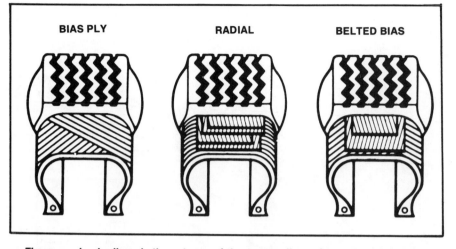

There are basically only three types of tires, regardless of cost, brand or size.

Radial tires are constructed with steel or fabric carcass plies crossing the tread at approximately a 90° angle, and two or more belts circle the tire under the tread. The sidewalls flex while the tread remains rigid, accounting for the characteristic sidewall bulge of a radial. The tread runs flatter on the road with a better grip and the inherently harsher ride is offset by superior handling and mileage.

New Tire Technology

Between now and 1985, when the 27.5 mpg CAFE (Corporate Average Fuel Economy) standards take effect, there are going to be a lot of changes in tires. Tires will be very important in meeting the CAFE standards because they are responsible for 20% of a car's total drag. But whatever is developed, it will have to be a compromise. A tire that handles well sacrifices tread wear; a soft-riding tire sacrifices traction; a tire that reduces rolling resistance and delivers good fuel economy sacrifices braking stability.

Elliptic Tires

A recent variation of the radial tire is the elliptic tire—a polyester cord body within steel belts. It resembles a conventional radial, except that it has a slightly more squatty appearance. The elliptically shaped sidewall forms a curve to the point where the tire meets the wheel rim, allowing up to 50% higher inflation pressures without causing an uncomfortable ride. The higher inflation pressure reduces rolling resistance and can increase fuel economy up to 3 or 4% at highway speeds.

A conventional radial inflated to 35 to 40 pounds per square inch delivers better gas mileage, but also transmits more road shocks from the tread to the wheel because the sidewall is almost vertical. Lower inflation pressures tend to lessen road shocks because the curved sidewall absorbs much of the vibration. The elliptic tire has extremely thick sidewalls that maintain the curved shape even at high inflation pressures.

The problem with elliptic tires is that they require an entirely new wheel to hold the tire on the rim. A special "low flange rim" required for the elliptic tire will not support a conventional radial, nor will a conventional rim support an elliptic tire. Fortunately, even though the elliptic tire has a 65 aspect ratio, a 15-inch elliptic tire has the same outside diameter as a 78 series 14-inch tire, and an elliptic

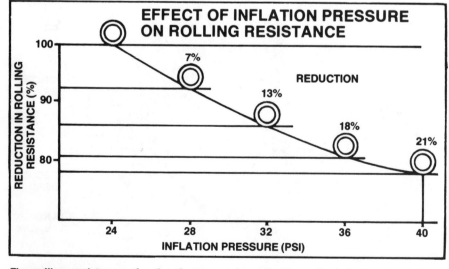

The rolling resistance of a tire decreases dramatically as the inflation pressure increases.

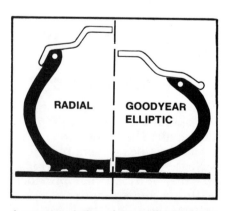

A recent variation of the radial tire is the elliptic tire, using inflation pressures as much as 50% higher than conventional radials.

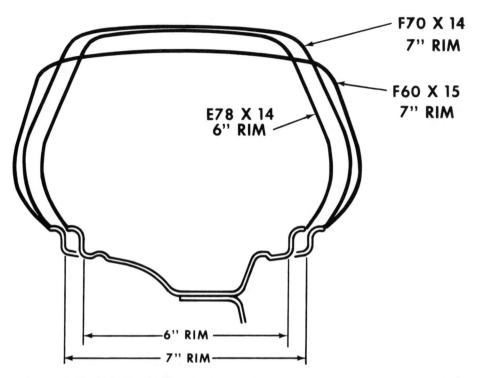

F70 X 14
7" RIM

F60 X 15
7" RIM

E78 X 14
6" RIM

6" RIM

7" RIM

Comparison of 78, 70 and 60 series (aspect ratio) tires mounted on 6 and 7 inch rims. Note that as the aspect ratio between the height and width of the tire increases, there is more tread contact with the road and a larger rim is required.

tire/wheel combination can be marketed as a replacement for existing wheels and tires.

Spare Tires

A conventional wheel and spare tire weigh about 38 pounds, and the jack another 10 pounds, so the auto industry has turned a good deal of attention here toward saving weight by eliminating the conventional spare. There are three alternatives to the spare tire problem.

Space-Saver® Spares

The most prevalent alternative today is the Space-Saver spare used on many new cars. The Space-Saver is a special, emergency-only tire that is stored deflated and folded around the wheel when not in use. It is designed to be mounted on the car and inflated only with a special inflation canister which is supplied with the tire. Once used, the canister is discarded and a new one purchased from

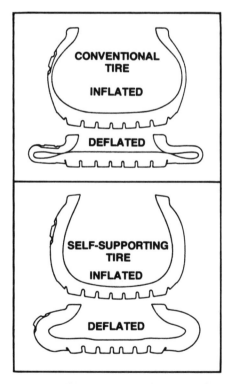

A conventional and a self-supporting tire. Note the extremely thick sidewalls used on a self-supporting tire.

the auto dealership, tire manufacturer or an auto supply store.

Self-Supporting Tires

Self-supporting tires look like conventional radials with super-thick sidewalls. They retain the shape of an under-inflated radial, even with no pressure inside. When deflated they can be driven as far as 50 miles with no handling problems. They can also be re-inflated without damage. The main roadblock to their use is the development of a workable low-pressure warning system to alert the driver that the tire is flat.

Run-Flat Tires

For years, tire engineers have been trying to develop a "run-flat" tire—one that would allow the car to run a given distance, even if the tire loses air pressure due to a puncture. Drawbacks on prototypes developed by major manufacturers have been the need for expensive "tire-within-a-tire" designs, lubricants to cool the tire sidewall due to high temperatures generated when the tire operates at low air pressure, and the need for special wheels to support unconventional tires.

Recently, Japanese tire engineers developed a run-flat tire that uses a simple design, requires a conventional air valve and can be mounted on the wheel with conventional tire changing equipment. It is based on a steel-belted radial tire, but uses rein-

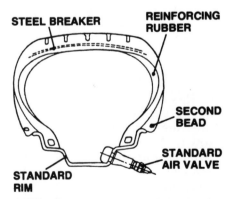

STEEL BREAKER
REINFORCING RUBBER
SECOND BEAD
STANDARD AIR VALVE
STANDARD RIM

Crossectional view of recently developed N-type "run-flat" tire.

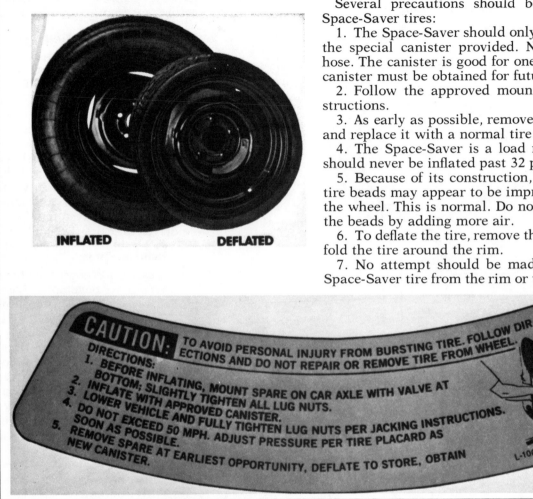

INFLATED   DEFLATED

Several precautions should be followed with Space-Saver tires:

1. The Space-Saver should only be inflated with the special canister provided. Never use an air hose. The canister is good for one use only; a new canister must be obtained for future use.

2. Follow the approved mounting and use instructions.

3. As early as possible, remove the Space-Saver and replace it with a normal tire.

4. The Space-Saver is a load range B tire and should never be inflated past 32 psi.

5. Because of its construction, the Space-Saver tire beads may appear to be improperly seated on the wheel. This is normal. Do not attempt to seat the beads by adding more air.

6. To deflate the tire, remove the valve stem and fold the tire around the rim.

7. No attempt should be made to remove the Space-Saver tire from the rim or to repair the tire.

CAUTION: TO AVOID PERSONAL INJURY FROM BURSTING TIRE. FOLLOW DIRECTIONS AND DO NOT REPAIR OR REMOVE TIRE FROM WHEEL.

DIRECTIONS:
1. BEFORE INFLATING, MOUNT SPARE ON CAR AXLE WITH VALVE AT BOTTOM; SLIGHTLY TIGHTEN ALL LUG NUTS.
2. INFLATE WITH APPROVED CANISTER.
3. LOWER VEHICLE AND FULLY TIGHTEN LUG NUTS PER JACKING INSTRUCTIONS.
4. DO NOT EXCEED 50 MPH. ADJUST PRESSURE PER TIRE PLACARD AS SOON AS POSSIBLE.
5. REMOVE SPARE AT EARLIEST OPPORTUNITY, DEFLATE TO STORE, OBTAIN NEW CANISTER.

L-100A B.F. Goodrich

Space-Saver spares must be handled carefully to preserve their usefulness.

forced sidewalls for support in a run-flat condition. The tire weighs about 25% more than a conventional tire, but about 15 pounds per vehicle can be saved because the spare and the jack are unnecessary. The deflated tire can run about 100 miles at a maximum speed of about 50 mph.

Tire Selection

Bias tires cost the least to buy and give the poorest wear, but are fine for short trips around town. Radials are relatively expensive, but give superior performance and wear. Bias belted tires strike a middle ground between bias and radials in almost all areas.

Retreaded tires can save as much as half over the cost of comparable new tires. Retreads are made by replacing the tread on salvageable, but closely inspected, tire casings. Forget the reputation of older recaps— today's retreaded tires are difficult to distinguish from new tires. They are so reliable that 98% of the world's airlines as well as many heavy equipment and trucking firms use retreads.

When replacing tires, it's best to buy four of the same size and type. Because of different handling and traction characteristics, it is also best not to mix types or sizes of tires on any one car or axle. In particular, radials should not be mixed with other types. Ideally, radials should be used in sets of five but, if absolutely unavoidable, radials can be used in pairs, on the rear axle only—never on the front axle only.

Before buying wider tires, check carefully that there will be sufficient clearance in the wheelwells, especially when turning. Generally, most cars will accept wider tires within the same letter size group, but check to be sure. Also check to be sure that the wheels are wide enough to accommodate wider tires.

For maximum mileage and wear, tires (new or old) should be balanced every time they are mounted on a rim. Balancing involves installing small lead weights on the edge of the wheel,

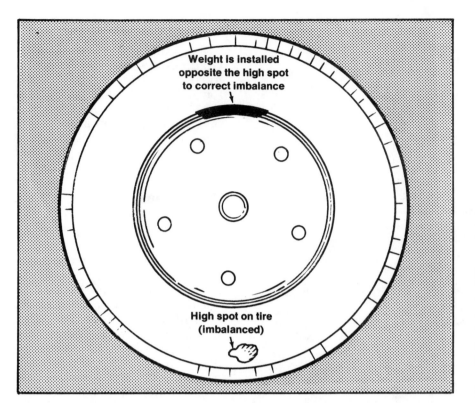

Whenever a tire is installed on the wheel it should be balanced to offset minor tolerances.

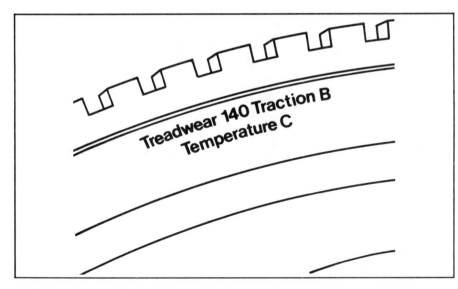

Beginning April 1979, tires are required to be graded for three characteristics.

formance oriented cars and trucks to more modern, lighter cars with considerably better suspensions and handling characteristics. It is only natural that drivers want tires that match the car's capabilities.

The original push for high performance tires started in Europe, where tire manufacturers worked together with auto manufacturers to perfect the handling characteristics of high performance cars and where tires are speed rated for performance.

Many drivers of high performance cars are familiar with the European speed ratings, where the speed rated tire is matched with the speed of the automobile. The most common speed ratings were:

VR—for cars that can speed over 130 mph
HR—for cars that can speed up to 130 mph
SR—for cars speed rated up to 112 mph.

There is no such rigid rating system in the U.S., although there is a minimum standard established by the Department of Transportation (DOT) which includes testing of the tire at 85 mph and a plunger test. A new car sold in the U.S. must also have a tire that meets the capabilities of the car, but the standards are much looser than they are in Europe. U.S. tires that do meet the European standards have the ratings, but it's a moot point in a country where the official speed limit is 55 mph.

Just as U.S. tire manufacturers have begun to adopt the European speed rating system, the Europeans have adopted a new system, using a single letter:

to correct any out-of-balance condition. Spin balancing is done on a machine that rotates the tire at highway speeds and will give the best results (for extra cost). Bubble or static bal- ancing gives adequate results at less cost.

High Performance Tires

Lately, American drivers have been moving from older, less per-

Old Speed Rating	New Speed Rating	Maximum Speed (mph)
SR	P	93
	Q	99
	R	106
	S	113
HR	T	116
	H	130
VR	V	Over 130

EAGLE VR

Racing does improve the breed. This high performance Eagle VR was the first European speed-rated tire with a unidirectional tread pattern, adapted from Goodyear's Formula One racing rain tire tread design. These tires should always maintain the same direction of rotation.

Tire Grading

The Uniform Tire Quality Grading System took effect in April 1979. This system provides for a gradual phasing-in (bias tires first, followed by bias-belted) of a uniform grading system to compare tires in three areas: traction, treadwear and resistance to heat.

Treadwear

The treadwear grade is expressed by a number in multiples of 10—a higher number indicating a comparatively longer tread life. The number 100 is assigned as the standard of 30,000-mile tread life on a test track under controlled conditions, and other numbers represent a percentage up or down from 100. As an example, a grade of 150 represents a tread life 50% greater than 30,000 miles, or 45,000 miles.

Traction

The test for traction involves towing a trailer mounted with the test tires over a concrete and an asphalt course wetted with a controlled amount of water. As the brakes are slammed on, the tire's coefficient of friction is measured. An "A" grade means that its traction exceeds a predetermined standard on both courses. A "B" grade indicates that it exceeds a lower predetermined standard on both courses. If the tire can't make the "B" grade on either concrete or asphalt, it receives a "C" grade.

Temperature Resistance

The test for temperature resistance is to roll the tire against a large steel wheel at increasing speeds until the tire either is destroyed or achieves a grade of "A," indicating that it can survive a sustained run of 115 mph at 95° F. A grade of "B" indicates endurance at 100 mph, and anything less, but still above the federal minimum tire safety standard, receives a grade of "C".

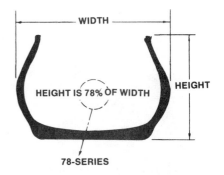

Even though the width of the tire stays the same, the height can vary with different series. When the height is a lower percentage of the width, it gives the tire a lower profile.

EAGLE GT

The Eagle GT also traces its heritage to Goodyear's racing/high-performance program. Race-prepared Chevrolet Camaros complete exclusively in the International Race of Champions (IROC) series on Eagle race tires and autos compete in showroom stock classes on original equipment Eagle street radials. The Eagle GT, and simiular tires, offer upgraded handling and performance compared to standard-size high performance tires

Reading the Tire Sidewall

The tire sidewall contains just about anything you would want to know about a tire, most of it required by federal law. Up to 1978, tires were designated in the alpha-numeric system. To conform to standards, most tire manufacturers now use the metric designation, but will continue to use "old" information as well.

Size—Tire width and diameter are identified on the sidewall as shown in the accompanying illustrations and tire size comparison chart.

Maximum pressure and load—This is the maximum load the tire should carry when inflated at its maximum cold inflation pressure. Consult your owners manual or tire dealer for the recommended inflation pressure for your vehicle. Very seldom will the tires be inflated to their maximum pressure.

Load range—The load range in the alpha-numeric designation is a letter indicating the number of plies at which the tire is rated.

Load Range	Replaces Ply-Rating
A	2
B	4
C	6
D	8
E	10

Tires using the metric labeling system are divided into two load ranges:

SL = Standard Load (35 psi max)

XL = Extra load (41 psi max.)

Type of cord and number of plies—Each of these is dependent on the other and will vary with tire construction.

Dot compliance—Since 1971,

After tires have been mounted on wheels, its important that they be balanced. Dynamic balancing is perferrable to static (bubble) balancing. Note that the paint spot on the tire (which will wash off), if there is one, is adjacent to the valve stem on the wheel. This is intentional.

After the tire and wheel is mounted on the dynamic balancer, the safety hood is put in place and the wheel and tire are spun to simulate road speeds.

A computer in the dynamic balancer computes the amount and position of weights that need to be added to the wheel and tire to balance out any heavy spots.

Performance tires will dress up any vehicle and make it handle considerably better compared to standard type tires.

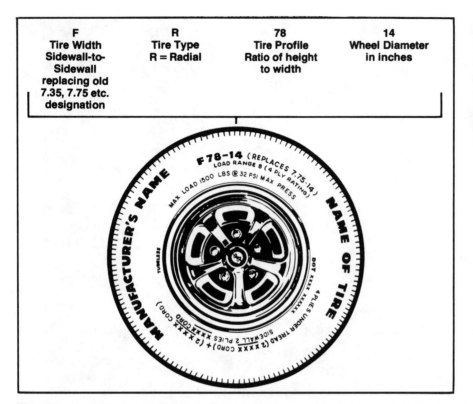

F	R	78	14
Tire Width Sidewall-to-Sidewall replacing old 7.35, 7.75 etc. designation	Tire Type R = Radial	Tire Profile Ratio of height to width	Wheel Diameter in inches

The alpha-numeric tire designation, shown here, is gradually being replaced by the newer metric designation. An older metric designation (175R14, for example) is similar to the alpha-numeric system. 175 is the sidewall-to-sidewall width in millimeters, R is radial construction and 14 is the rim diameter in inches.

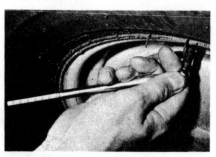

Check tire inflation pressure with a pocket-type gauge.

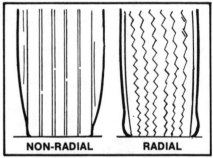

Radial tires have a characteristic sidewall bulge which makes them appear under-inflated when compared with a standard tire.

all tires are required to carry certain standard coded information, prefixed by DOT. This indicates that the tire conforms to U.S. Department of Transportation safety standards. The coded information also identifies the manufacturer, date of manufacture and other significant characteristics on the tire.

Tire Care

Caring for tires is easy and important for safety, but many car owners neglect this important part of vehicle maintenance.

A survey by a major tire manufacturer found that:

· Nine of every 10 cars in-spected had improperly inflated tires.

· One of every five cars inspected had at least one tire with too little tread for safe use.

· One of every 20 tires inspected was in danger of imminent failure.

· Nearly one of every five tires inspected showed unusual tread

The DOT code supplies identifying information about the tire.

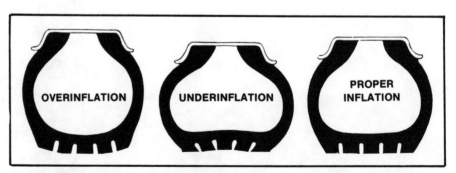

Tire inflation pressure is the major factor in determining how long your tires last and how well they perform.

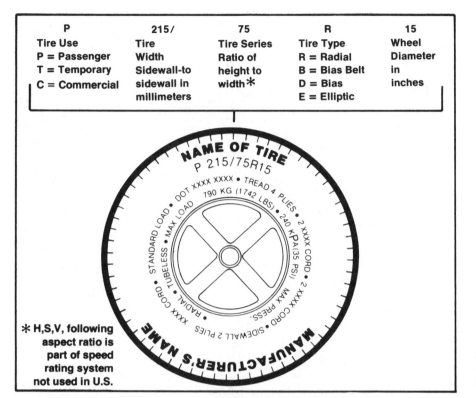

P	215/	75	R	15
Tire Use	Tire	Tire Series	Tire Type	Wheel
P = Passenger	Width	Ratio of	R = Radial	Diameter
T = Temporary	Sidewall-to	height to	B = Bias Belt	in
C = Commercial	sidewall in	width✱	D = Bias	inches
	millimeters		E = Elliptic	

✱ H,S,V, following aspect ratio is part of speed rating system not used in U.S.

The sidewall of a tire using metric designations looks similar to this. Since the new metric labeling does not interchange with the alpha-numeric labeling, refer to the Tire Size Comparison Chart when replacing tires. Even though the new designation is metric, wheel diameter is still given in inches, and load and pressure are given in both metric (kg/kPA) and English (lb/psi).

TIRE MAINTENANCE INTERVALS

For maximum wear and safety from your tires, they should be maintained at the following intervals.

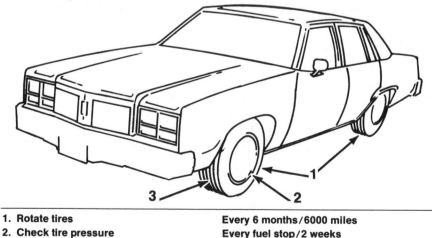

1. Rotate tires	Every 6 months/6000 miles
2. Check tire pressure	Every fuel stop/2 weeks
3. Check tread depth	Every 6 months/6000 miles
Clean tread of stones, glass, debris	As necessary

wear due to alignment, improper inflation or improper balance.

Inflation Pressure

Tire inflation is the most ignored item of auto maintenance. Gasoline mileage can drop as much as .8% for every one pound per square inch (psi) of under inflation.

Two items should be a permanent fixture in every glove compartment; a tire pressure gauge and a tread depth gauge. Check the tire air pressure (including the spare) regularly with a pocket-type gauge on a cool tire. Kicking the tire won't tell you a thing, and the gauge on the service station air hose is notoriously inaccurate.

The tire pressures recommended for your car are usually found on the glove compartment door, on the door post or in the owner's manual. Ideally, inflation pressure should be checked when the tires are cool. When the air becomes heated it expands and the pressure increases. Every 10° F. rise (or drop) in temperature means a difference of one psi, which also explains why the tire appears to lose air on a very cold night. When it is impossible to check the tires "cold," allow at least 15 psi over the recommended "cold" inflation pressure to allow for pressure build-up due to heat. If the "hot" pressure exceeds the "cold" pressure by more than 15 psi, reduce your speed, load or both. Otherwise, internal heat is created in the tire. When the heat approaches the temperature at which the tire was cured, during manufacture, the tread can separate from the body.

■ Chilton Tip

Never counteract excessive pressure build-up by bleeding off air pressure (letting some air out). This will only further raise the tire operating temperature.

■

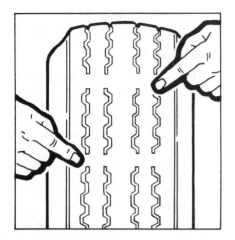

Since 1968, tread wear indicators are built into the tire tread and appear when 1/16" tread remains.

Before starting a long trip with lots of luggage, you can add about two to four psi to the tires to make them run cooler, but never exceed the maximum inflation pressure on the side of the tire.

Tread Depth

Tires are grooved to give many road-gripping edges for traction. These grooves also carry off water that is squeezed out from between the tread and the road, when driving in the rain. At high speeds in the rain, the tires may not be able to carry off all the water and will actually begin to slide on a thin film of water between the tire and the road. This phenomenon is known as hydroplaning, and the car is out of con-

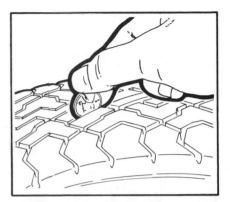

A Lincoln penny can be used to check approximate tread depth. If you can see the top of Lincoln's head in two adjacent grooves, you need new tires.

trol until speed is reduced. Worn tires only make this condition worse and will tend to hydroplane at lower speeds.

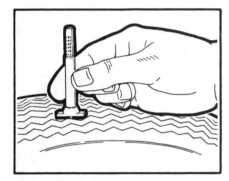

Checking tread depth with an inexpensive tread depth gauge.

While you are checking tread depth, remove any debris from the tread.

TIRE SIZE COMPARISON CHARTS

These charts provide a cross-reference to compare various replacement tire sizes. Most common tire sizes are listed, but replacement tires should always be checked for clearance.

IF VEHICLE TIRE PLACARD SPECIFIES AN ALPHA-NUMERIC TIRE SIZE:
(All sizes are Load Range B or Standard Load unless noted.)

Alpha-Numeric Size (78 & 70 SERIES)	Acceptable Substitute Size. Important—Add 3 PSI Above the Pressure Specified on the Vehicle Tire Placard to Assure Adequate Load Capacity
AR78-13	P165/80R13, P175/75R13, P185/70R13
BR78-13	P175/80R13, P185/75R13, P195/70R13
CR78-13	P185/80R13, P205/70R13
BR78-14	P175/75R14
CR78-14	P185/75R14
DR78-14	P195/75R14, P205/70R14
ER78-14	P195/75R14, P215/70R14
FR78-14	P205/75R14, P225/70R14
GR78-14	P215/75R14, P235/70R14
HR78-14	P225/75R14, P245/70R14
BR78-15	P165/80R15
ER78-15	P195/75R15
FR78-15	P205/75R15
GR78-15	P215/75R15, P225/70R15
HR78-15	P225/75R15, P235/70R15
JR78-15	P225/75R15
LR78-15	P235/75R15, P255/70R15

TIRE SIZE COMPARISON CHART

This chart provides a cross-reference to compare various older tire sizes. It does not take into account the new metric designations.

"60 Series"	"70 Series"	"78 Series"	1965-77	"60 Series"	"70 Series"	"80 Series"
			5.50-12, 5.60-12	165/60-12	165/70-12	155-12
		Y78-12	6.00-12			
		W78-13	5.20-13	165/60-13	145/70-13	135-13
		Y78-13	5.60-13	175/60-13	155/70-13	145-13
			6.15-13	185/60-13	165/70-13	155-13, P155/80-13
A60-13	A70-13	A78-13	6.40-13	195/60-13	175/70-13	165-13
B60-13	B70-13	B78-13	6.70-13	205/60-13	185/70-13	175-13
			6.90-13			
C60-13	C70-13	C78-13	7.00-13	215/60-13	195/70-13	185-13
D60-13	D70-13	D78-13	7.25-13			
E60-13	E70-13	E78-13	7.75-13			195-13
			5.20-14	165/60-14	145/70-14	135-14
			5.60-14	175/60-14	155/70-14	145-14
			5.90-14			
A60-14	A70-14	A78-14	6.15-14	185/60-14	165/70-14	155-14
	B70-14	B78-14	6.45-14	195/60-14	175/70-14	165-14
	C70-14	C78-14	6.95-14	205/60-14	185/70-14	175-14
D60-14	D70-14	D78-14				
E60-14	E70-14	E78-14	7.35-14	215/60-14	195/70-14	185-14
F60-14	F70-14	F78-14, F83-14	7.75-14	225/60-14	200/70-14	195-14
G60-14	G70-14	G77-14, G78-14	8.25-14	235/60-14	205/70-14	205-14
H60-14	H70-14	H78-14	8.55-14	245/60-14	215/70-14	215-14
J60-14	J70-14	J78-14	8.85-14	255/60-14	225/70-14	225-14
L60-14	L70-14		9.15-14	265/60-14	235/70-14	
	A70-15	A78-15	5.60-15	185/60-15	165/70-15	155-15
B60-15	B70-15	B78-15	6.35-15	195/60-15	175/70-15	165-15
C60-15	C70-15	C78-15	6.85-15	205/60-15	185/70-15	175-15
	D70-15	D78-15				
E60-15	E70-15	E78-15	7.35-15	215/60-15	195/70-15	185-15
F60-15	F70-15	F78-15	7.75-15	225/60-15	205/70-15	195-15
G60-15	G70-15	G78-15	8.15-15/8.25-15	235/60-15	215/70-15	205-15
H60-15	H70-15	H78-15	8.45-15/8.55-15	245/60-15	225/70-15	215-15
J60-15	J70-15	J78-15	8.85-15/8.90-15	255/60-15	235/70-15	225-15
	K70-15		9.00-15	265/60-15	245/70-15	230-15
L60-15	L70-15	L78-15, L84-15	9.15-15			235-15
	M70-15	M78-15				255-15
		N78-15				

Note: Every size tire is not listed and many size comparisons are approximate, based on load ratings. Wider tires than those supplied new with the vehicle, should always be checked for clearance.

IF VEHICLE TIRE PLACARD SPECIFIES A P-METRIC TIRE SIZE:
(All sizes are Load Range B or Standard Load, unless noted. Do not exceed maximum pressure marked on tire sidewall.)

P-Metric Size	Acceptable Substitute Size
P155/80R13	P165/75R13, P175/70R13
P165/80R13	P175/75R13, P185/70R13, AR78-13, AR70-13
P175/80R13	P185/75R13, P195/70R13, CR78-13, CR70-13
P185/80R13	
P165/75R13	P165/80R13, P185/70R13, AR78-13, AR70-13
P175/75R13	P175/80R13, P195/70R13, BR78-13, BR70-13
P185/75R13	P185/80R13, P205/70R13, CR78-13, CR70-13
P185/70R13	P175/80R13, P185/75R13, BR78-13, BR70-13
P195/70R13	P185/80R13, CR78-13, CR70-13
P205/70R13	
P165/80R14	P175/75R14, BR78-14
P175/75R14	BR78-14
P185/75R14	P205/70R14, DR78-14, DR70-14
P195/75R14	P215/70R14, ER78-14, ER70-14
P205/75R14	P225/70R14, FR78-14, FR70-14
P205/75R14 (Extra Load)	FR78-14 (Load Range D), FR70-14 (Load Range D)
P215/75R14	P235/70R14, GR78-14, GR70-14
P225/75R14	P245/70R14, HR78-14, HR70-14
P205/70R14	P205/75R14, FR78-14, FR70-14
P215/70R14	P215/75R14, GR78-14, GR70-14
P225/70R14	P225/75R14, HR78-14, HR70-14
P235/70R14	JR78-14
P245/70R14	
P155/80R15	P165/75R15
P165/80R15	CR78-15
P165/75R15	P165/80R15, BR78-15
P195/75R15	FR78-15, FR70-15
P205/75R15	P225/70R15, GR78-15, GR70-15
P215/75R15	P235/70R15, HR78-15, HR70-15
P225/75R15	JR78-15
P235/75R15	P255/70R15
P225/70R15	P225/75R15, HR78-15, HR70-15
P235/70R15	P235/75R15, LR78-15
P255/70R15	

INFLATION PRESSURE CONVERSION CHART   kPa to psi 6.9 kPa = 1 psi

kPa	psi	kPa	psi	kPa	psi
140	20	185	27	235	34
145	21	190	28	240	35
155	22	200	29	275	40
160	23	205	30	310	45
165	24	215	31	345	50
170	25	220	32	380	55
180	26	230	33	415	60

IF VEHICLE TIRE PLACARD SPECIFIES A EUROPEAN METRIC TIRE SIZE:
(All sizes are Load Range B or Standard Load, unless noted.)

European Metric Size	Acceptable Substitute Size. Important—Add 3 PSI Above the Pressure Specified on the Vehicle Tire Placard to Assure Adequate Load Capacity
155R13	P155/80R13, P165/75R13, P175/70R13
165R13	P165/80R13, P175/75R13, P185/70R13
175R13	P175/80R13, P185/75R13, P195/70R13
185R13	P185/80R13, P205/70R13
175/70R13	P165/80R13, P175/75R13, P185/70R13
185/70R13	P175/80R13, P185/75R13, P195/70R13
165R14	P165/80R14, P175/75R14
175R14	P185/75R14
185R14	P195/75R14, P205/70R14
185/70R14	P185/75R14
195/70R14	P195/75R14, P205/70R14
155R15	P155/80R15, P165/75R15
165R15	P165/80R15
175R15	

All tires made since 1968, have eight built-in tread wear indicator bars that show up as ½" wide smooth bands across the tire when ¹/₁₆" of tread remains. The appearance of tread wear indicators means that the tires should be replaced. In fact, many states have laws prohibiting the use of tires with less than ¹/₁₆" tread, and studies have shown that 90% of all tire problems will occur in the last 10% of tire life.

You can check your own tread depth with an inexpensive gauge or by using a Lincoln-head penny. Slip the Lincoln penny into several tread grooves. If you

Mark the tires when you remove them to preserve direction of rotation.

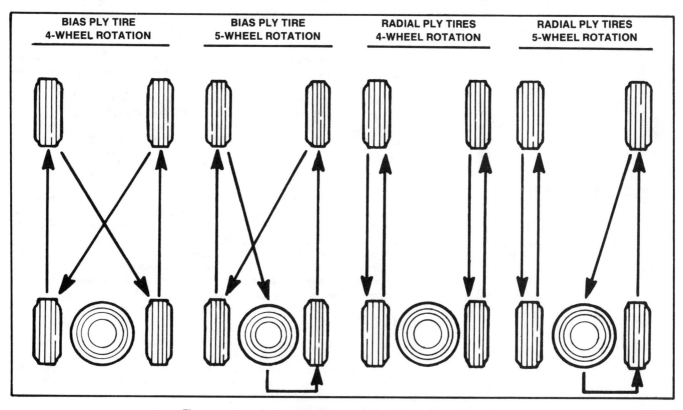

Tire wear can be equalized by rotating tires every 6000 miles.

HOW TO READ TIRE WEAR

The way your tires wear is a good indicator of other parts of your car. Abnormal wear patterns are often caused by the need for simple tire maintenance, or for front end alignment.

Tires should be inspected at every opportunity; once a week isn't too often. Learning to read the early warning signs of trouble can prevent wear that shortens tire life or indicates the need for having other parts of the car serviced. Tires should be inspected 3 ways. First, visually examine all 4 tires; second, feel the tread by hand to detect wear such as feathering and third, check all 4 tires with a pocket type pressure gauge.

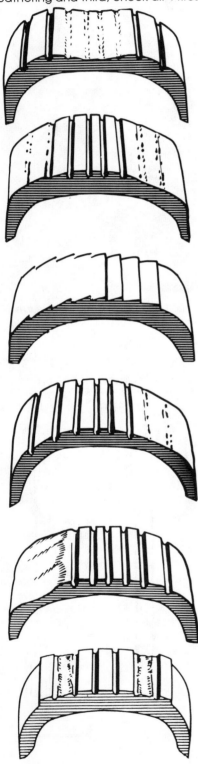

Over Inflation

Excessive wear at the center of the tread indicates that the air pressure in the tire is consistently too high. The tire is riding on the center of the tread and wearing it prematurely. Many times, the "eyeball" method of inflation (pumping the tires up until there is no bulge at the bottom) is at fault; tire inflation pressure should always be checked with a reliable tire gauge. Occasionally, this wear pattern can result from outrageously wide tires on narrow rims. The cure for this is to replace either the tires or the wheels.

Under Inflation

This type of wear usually results from consistent under inflation. When a tire is under inflated, there is too much contact with the road by the outer treads, which wear prematurely. Tire pressure should be checked with a reliable pressure gauge. When this type of wear occurs, and the tire pressure is known to be consistently correct, a bent or worn steering component or the need for wheel alignment could be indicated. Bent steering or idler arms cause incorrect toe-in and abnormal handling characteristics on turns.

Feathering

Feathering is a condition when the edge of each tread rib develops a slightly rounded edge on one side and a sharp edge on the other. By running your hand over the tire, you can usually feel the sharper edges before you'll be able to see them. The most common cause of feathering is incorrect toe-in setting, which can be cured by having it set correctly. Occasionally toe-in will be set correctly and this wear pattern still occurs. This is usually due to deteriorated bushings in the front suspension, causing the wheel alignment to shift as the car moves down the road.

One Side Wear

When an inner or outer rib wears faster than than the rest of the tire, the need for wheel alignment is indicated. There is excessive camber in the front suspension, causing the wheel to lean too much to the inside or outside and putting too much load on one side of the tire. The car may simply need the wheels aligned, but misalignment could be due to sagging springs, worn ball joints, or worn control arm bushings. Because load has a great effect on alignment, be sure the vehicle is loaded the way it's normally driven when you have the wheels aligned; this is particularly important with independent rear suspension cars.

Cupping

Cups or scalloped dips appearing around the edge of the tread on one side or the other, almost always indicate worn (sometimes bent) suspension parts. Adjustment of wheel alignment alone will seldom cure the problem. Any worn component that connects the wheel to the car (ball joint, wheel bearing, shock absorber, springs, bushings, etc.) can cause this condition. Worn components should be replaced with new ones. The worn tire should be balanced and possibly moved to a different location on the car. Occasionally, wheels that are out of balance will wear like this, but wheel imbalance usually shows up as bald spots between the outside edges and center of the tread.

Second-rib Wear

Second-rib wear is normally found only in radial tires, and appears where the steel belts end in relation to the tread. Normally, it can be kept to a minimum by paying careful attention to tire pressure and frequently rotating the tires. Some car and tire manufacturers consider a slight amount of wear at the second rib of a radial tire normal, but that excessive amounts of wear indicate that the tires are too wide for the wheels. Be careful when having oversize tires installed on narrow wheels.

WHEN YOU HAVE A FLAT TIRE

Safety is the first consideration when you have a flat tire. Switch on the hazard warning lights, pull well off the road, set the parking brake and, if possible, chock the wheel diagonally opposite the flat tire. Use the jack and lug wrench provided with the car, according to the instructions on the jack or in the owner's manual.

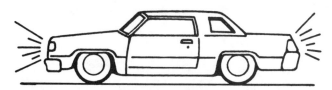

1. When you have a flat tire, pull well off the road onto a level surface and set the parking brake. Switch on the hazard flashers and if possible, chock the wheel diagonally opposite the flat. Automatic transmissions should be in PARK and manual transmissions in Reverse.

2. Remove the wheel cover. To make the job a little easier, loosen all of the lug nuts a few turns, while the wheel is resting on the ground.

3. Operating instructions for the jack supplied with your car can be found in the owner's manual or in the jack stowage area on a decal. Regardless of the type of jack used, make sure the jack is seated firmly and not angled away from the vehicle.

4. Operate the jack slowly and smoothly according to the directions supplied. Raise the vehicle so that the tire just clears the ground (flexible body panels may deform slightly while the car is raised). Remove the lug nuts and wheel and replace it with the spare. Tighten the lug nuts finger-tight.

5. If your car is equipped with a Space-Saver spare, read the directions and cautions supplied with the tire (see Space-Saver Tires) in this section. Place the inflator over the valve stem and push squarely until the tire inflates. It is normal for the tire to move slightly on the rim while it is expanding.

6. Lower the vehicle and fully tighten the wheel lug nuts. Install the wheel cover and stow the jack and flat tire. Have the flat tire repaired as soon as possible and if you have a Space-Saver spare, obtain a new canister or have the old one refilled at a fire extinguisher service facility.

can see the top of Lincoln's head in two adjacent grooves, the tires have less than 1/16" tread left and should be replaced. You can measure snow tires in the same manner by using the "tails" side of the Lincoln penny. If you can see the top of the Lincoln memorial, it's time to replace the snow tires.

Rotate the Tires

Tires will wear differently on the front and rear of a car or truck. Tire wear can be equalized by switching the position of the tires about every 6000 miles. Including the spare in the rotation pattern can give up to 20% more tire life.

Caution

Do not include the new "space-saver" spare tires in the rotation pattern. These are for temporary emergency use only.

There are certain exceptions to tire rotation, however. Studded snow tires should not be rotated, and radials should be kept on the same side of the car (maintain the same direction of rotation). The belts on radial tires get set in a pattern. If the direction of rotation is reversed, it can cause rough ride and vibration.

■

Chilton Tip

When radials or studded snows are taken off the car, mark them, so you can maintain the same direction of rotation.

■

Storing the Tires

Store the tires at proper inflation pressures if they are mounted on wheels. All tires should be kept in a cool, dry place. If they are stored in the garage or basement, do not let them stand on a concrete floor; set them on strips of wood.

TROUBLESHOOTING BASIC TIRE AND WHEEL PROBLEMS

The most common cause of tire problems is improperly inflated tires. The majority of tire problems can be cured by maintaining the proper inflation pressure, rotating the tires regularly and by correct good driving habits.

Problem	Is Caused by	What to Do
The car's front end vibrates at high speeds and the steering wheel shakes	• Wheels out of balance • Front end needs aligning	• Have wheels balanced • Have front end alignment checked
The car pulls to one side while cruising	• Unequal tire pressure (car will usually pull to the low side) • Mismatched tires • Front end needs aligning	• Check/adjust tire pressure • Be sure tires are of the same type and size • Have front end alignment checked
Abnormal, excessive or uneven tire wear See "How to Read Tire Wear"	• Infrequent tire rotation • Improper tire pressure • Sudden stops/starts or high speed on curves	• Rotate tires more frequently to equalize wear • Check/adjust pressure • Correct driving habits
Tire squeals	• Improper tire pressure • Front end needs aligning	• Check/adjust tire pressure • Have front end alignment checked

27
Brakes

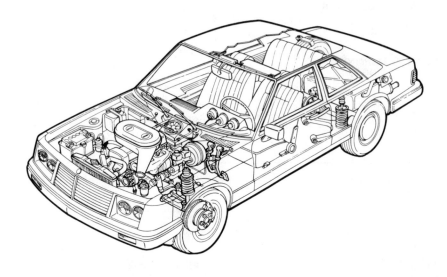

Hydraulic System

When you step on the brake pedal, you expect the vehicle to stop. The brake pedal operates a hydraulic system that is used for two reasons. First, fluid under pressure can be carried to all parts of the car by small hoses or metal lines without taking up a lot of room or causing routing problems. Second, the hydraulic fluid offers a great mechanical advantage—little foot pressure is required on the pedal, but a great deal of pressure is generated at the wheels.

The brake pedal is linked to a piston in the brake master cylinder, which is filled with hydraulic brake fluid. The master cylinder consists of a cylinder containing a small piston and a fluid reservoir.

Most modern master cylinders are actually two separate cylinders. Such a system is called a dual circuit, because the front cylinder is connected to the front brakes and the rear cylinder to the rear brakes.(Some cars are connected diagonally.) The two cylinders are actually separated, allowing for emergency stopping power should one part of the system fail.

The entire hydraulic system from the master cylinder to the wheels is full of hydraulic brake fluid. When the brake pedal is depressed, the pistons in the master cylinder are forced to move, exerting tremendous force on the fluid in the lines. The fluid has nowhere to go, and forces the wheel cylinder pistons (drum brakes) or caliper pistons (disc brakes) to exert pressure on the brake shoes or pads. The resulting friction between the brake shoe and wheel drum or the

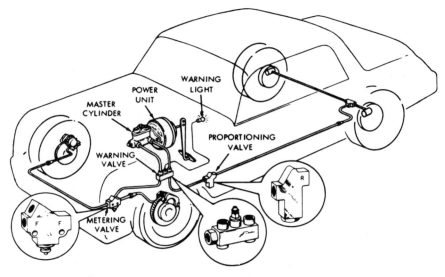

Typical parts of a front disc/rear drum brake system.

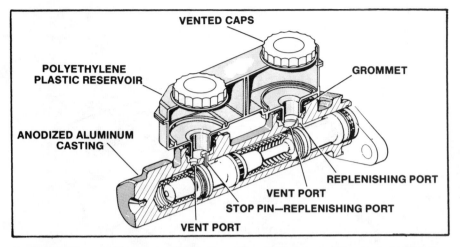

Typical master cylinder. Since 1967, all master cylinders are of the dual circuit type.

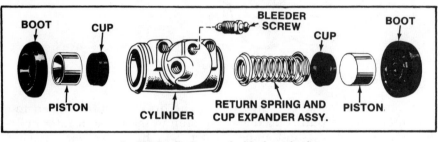

A wheel cylinder used with drum brakes

brake pad and disc slows the car and eventually stops it.

Also attached to the brake pedal is a switch which lights the brake lights as the pedal is depressed. The lights stay on until the brake pedal is released and returns to its normal position.

Each wheel cylinder in a drum brake system contains two pistons, one at either end, which push outward in opposite directions. In disc brake systems, the wheel cylinders are part of the caliper (there can be as many as four or as few as one). Whether disc or drum type, all pistons use some type of rubber seal to prevent leakage around the piston, and a rubber dust boot seals the outer ends of the wheel cylinders against dirt and moisture.

When the brake pedal is released, a spring pushes the master cylinder pistons back to their normal positions. Check valves in the master cylinder piston allow fluid to flow toward the wheel cylinders or calipers as the piston returns. Then as the brake shoe return springs pull the brake shoes back to the released position, excess fluid returns to the master cylinder through compensating ports, which have been uncovered as the pistons move back. Any fluid that has leaked from the system will also be replaced through the compensating ports.

All dual circuit brake systems use a switch to activate a light, warning of brake failure. The switch is located in a valve mounted near the master cylinder. A piston in the valve receives pressure on each end from the front and rear brake circuits. When the pressures are balanced, the piston remains stationary, but when one circuit has a leak, greater pressure during the application of the brakes will force the piston to one side or the other, closing the switch and activating the warning light. The light can also be activated by the ignition switch during engine starting or by the parking brake.

Disc brake systems also have a metering valve to prevent the front disc brakes from engaging before the rear brakes have contacted the drums. This ensures that the front brakes will not normally be used alone to stop the car. A proportioning valve is also used to limit pressure to the rear brakes to prevent rear wheel lock-up during hard braking.

Drum Brakes

Drum brakes use two brake shoes mounted on a stationary backing plate on each wheel. These shoes are positioned inside a circular cast iron drum which rotates with the wheel assembly. The shoes are held in place by springs; this allows them to slide toward the drums (when they are applied) while keeping the linings and drums in alignment.

The shoes are actuated by a wheel cylinder which is usually mounted at the top of the backing plate. When the brakes are applied, hydraulic pressure forces the wheel cylinder's two actuating links outward. Since these links bear directly against the top of the brake shoes, the tops of the shoes are then forced outward against the inner side of the drum. This action forces the bottoms of the two shoes to contact the brake drum by rotating the entire assembly slightly (known as servo action). When pressure within the wheel cylinder is relieved, return springs pull the shoes away from the drum.

Most modern drum brakes are designed to self-adjust during application when the vehicle is moving in reverse. This motion causes both shoes to rotate very slightly with the drum, rocking an adjusting lever. The self-adjusters are only intended to compensate for normal wear. Although the adjustment is "automatic," there is a definite

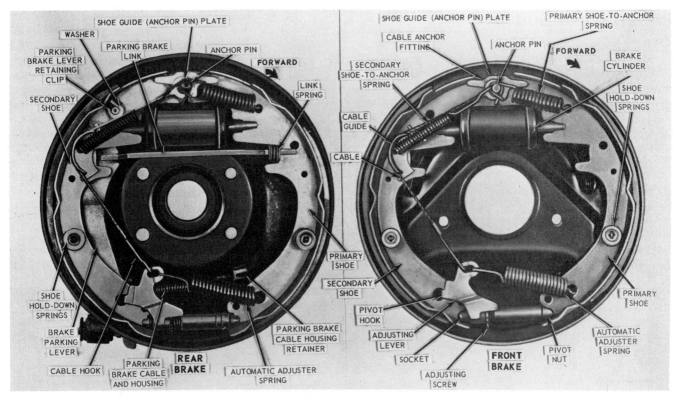

Typical drum brake components.

method to actuate the self-adjuster, which is done during normal driving. Driving the car in reverse and applying the brakes usually activates the automatic adjusters. If the brake pedal was low, you should be able to feel an increase in the height of the brake pedal.

Disc Brakes

Instead of the traditional expanding brakes that press outward against a circular drum, disc brake systems utilize a cast iron disc with brake pads positioned on either side of it. Braking effect is achieved in a manner similar to the way you would squeeze a spinning disc between your fingers. The disc (rotor) is a one-piece casting with cooling fins between the two braking surfaces. This enables air to circulate between the braking surfaces making them less sensitive to heat buildup and more resistant to fade. Dirt and water do not affect braking action since

contaminants are thrown off by the centrifugal action of the rotor or scraped off by the pads. Also, the equal clamping action of the two brake pads tends to ensure uniform, straightline stops. All disc brakes are inherently self-adjusting.

There are three general types of disc brake:

1. A fixed caliper, four-piston type.

2. A floating caliper, single piston type.

3. A sliding caliper, single piston type.

The fixed caliper design uses two pistons mounted on either side of the rotor (in each side of the caliper). The caliper is mounted rigidly and does not move.

The sliding and floating designs are quite similar and often considered as one. The pad on the inside of the rotor is moved into contact with the rotor by hydraulic force. The caliper, which is not held in a fixed position, moves slightly, bringing the out-

side pad into contact with the rotor. There are various methods of attaching floating calipers; some pivot at the bottom or top, and some slide on mounting bolts.

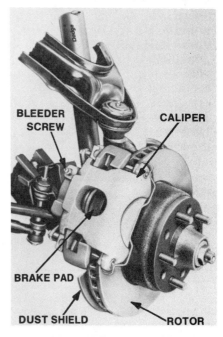

Sliding caliper disc brake.

Power Brake Boosters

Power brakes operate just as standard brake systems, except in the actuation of the master cylinder pistons. A vacuum diaphragm is located behind the master cylinder and assists the driver in applying the brakes, reducing both the effort and travel he must put into moving the brake pedal.

The vacuum diaphragm housing is connected to the intake manifold by a vacuum hose. A check valve at the point where the hose enters the diaphragm housing ensures that during periods of low manifold vacuum brake assist vacuum will not be lost.

Depressing the brake pedal closes the vacuum source and allows atmospheric pressure to enter on one side of the diaphragm. This causes the master cylinder pistons to move and apply the brakes. When the brake pedal is released, vacuum is applied to both sides of the diaphragm, and return springs return the diaphragm and master cylinder pistons to the released position. If the vacuum fails, the brake pedal rod will butt against the end of the master cylinder actuating rod, and direct mechanical application will occur as the pedal is depressed.

The hydraulic and mechanical problems that apply to conventional brake systems also apply to power brakes.

Emergency Brake

The emergency or parking brake is used simply for parking. It has no hydraulic connection and is simply a means of activating the rear wheel brakes with a cable attached to a floor-mounted lever or dash-mounted pedal or lever.

Periodic Maintenance

Caution

Breathing asbestos dust is hazardous to your health. Dust and dirt present on brake assemblies may contain asbestos fibers that are hazardous to your health when made airborne by dry brushing or cleaning with compressed air. Dust and dirt should be cleaned using a vacuum cleaner recommended for use with asbestos fibers, and should be disposed of in a manner that prevents dust exposure. If cleaning by vacuuming is not possible, work on brake assemblies should be done in a well-ventilated area using an approved toxic-dust respirator.

Checking Fluid Level

The most important item in brake system maintenance is periodic checking of the brake fluid level. Check the level *at least* once a month, more often if possible.

Before checking the level, carefully wipe off the master cylinder

BRAKE SYSTEM MAINTENANCE INTERVALS

Your car's brake system will work efficiently if it is maintained at these intervals.

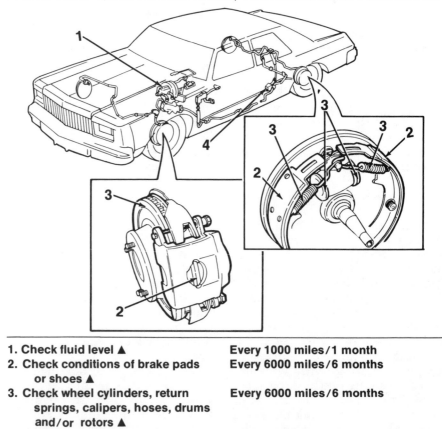

1. Check fluid level ▲	Every 1000 miles/1 month
2. Check conditions of brake pads or shoes ▲	Every 6000 miles/6 months
3. Check wheel cylinders, return springs, calipers, hoses, drums and/or rotors ▲	Every 6000 miles/6 months
4. Adjust parking brake	As necessary

▲ If the vehicle is used for severe service, (trailer pulling, constant stop/start driving, off-road operation, etc.) cut the maintenance interval in half.

Parking Brake Linkage

The parking brake linkage normally operates the rear brakes. Depressing the pedal or pulling up on the lever expands the rear brake shoes against the drum.

TROUBLESHOOTING BASIC BRAKE PROBLEMS

These are examples of basic brake problems and usually mean something is wrong in the brake system. Left alone, any of these problems will likely only get worse, so have the brakes checked as soon as possible.

The Problem	Is Caused By	What to Do
The brake pedal goes to the floor	• Leak somewhere in the system • Brakes out of adjustment	• Check/correct fluid level; have system checked • Check automatic brake adjusters
Spongy brake pedal	• Air in brake system • Brake fluid contaminated	• Have brake system bled • Have system drained, refilled and bled
The brake pedal is hard	• Improperly adjusted brakes • Worn pads or linings • Kinked brake lines • Defective power brake booster • Low engine vacuum (power brakes)	• Have brakes adjusted • Check lining/pad wear • Have defective brake line replaced • Have booster checked • Check engine vacuum (see Section 8, Engine)
The brake pedal "fades" under pressure (repeated hard stops will cause brake fade; brakes will return to normal when they cool down)	• Air in system • Incorrect brake fluid • Leaking master cylinder or wheel cylinders • Leaking hoses/lines	• Have brakes bled • Check fluid • Check master cylinder and wheel cylinders for leaks • Check lines for leaks
The car pulls to one side or brakes grab	• Incorrect tire pressure • Contaminated brake linings or pads • Worn brake linings • Loose or misaligned calipers • Defective proportioning valve • Front end out of alignment	• Check/correct tire pressure • Check linings for grease; if greasy, replace • Have linings replaced • Check caliper mountings • Have proportioning valve checked • Have wheel alignment checked
Brakes chatter or shudder	• Worn linings • Drums out-of-round • Wobbly rotor • Heat checked drums	• Check lining thickness • Have drums and linings ground • Have rotor checked for excessive wobble • Check drums for heat checking; if necessary, replace drums
Brakes produce noise (squealing, scraping, clicking)	• Worn linings • Loose calipers • Caliper anti-rattle springs missing • Scored or glazed drums or rotors	• Check pad and lining wear • Check caliper mountings • Check calipers for missing parts • Check for glazing (light glazing can be removed with sandpaper)
Brakes drag (will not release)	• Incorrect brake adjustment • Parking brake stuck or adjusted too tight • Caliper pistons seized • Defective metering valve or master cylinder • Broken brake return springs	• Have brakes checked • Check cable where it enters the brake backing plate. In winter, water frequently freezes here • Have calipers checked • Have system checked • Check brake return springs, replace if necessary
Brake system warning light stays lit	• One part of dual circuit inoperative, defective warning light switch, differential pressure valve not centered	• Have brake system checked

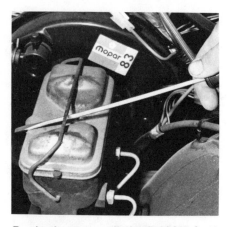

To check master cylinder fluid level, pry the retaining clip off the cap with a screwdriver. Some master cylinder caps are bolted on and still others unscrew.

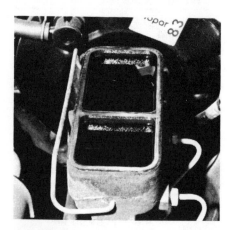

On unmarked master cylinders, the fluid level should be about here.

Most import cars have see-through master cylinders with maximum and minimum level markings. On this type, the reservoir cap usually unscrews.

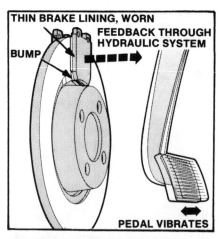

If the master cylinder needs fluid, carefully add fluid from a fresh can. Don't spill any on painted surfaces. The brake fluid is extremely corrosive and will eat through paint.

cover to remove any dirt or water that would fall into the reservoir. Then remove the retaining clip (sometimes a bolt) and cap. The fluid level should be kept about ¼" from the top on cylinders that are not marked. On marked cylinders, simply keep the fluid up to the specified line. If the master cylinder needs fluid, add heavy-duty brake fluid meeting DOT 4 (disc brake and heavy-duty use) or 3 (all others) specifications.

■

Chilton Tip

Be very careful not to spill brake fluid on paint. It is very corrosive and will destroy paint.

■

While a certain amount of fluid loss over a long period of time is normal, if you find you are continually adding fluid, obviously something is wrong with your brake system, and you should have it checked. The color of the brake fluid can also warn of trouble. The fluid should not appear overly dark or have a "burned" appearance. If it does, something is probably wrong, but this doesn't happen very often.

Brake fluid will deteriorate

with age. Buy only as much as you need, and store it in a cool dark place in a tightly capped container.

Inspecting the Brakes

Brakes should be inspected every 6000 miles or 6 months. The rate at which the linings wear will be influenced by many variables, among them where and how you drive, whether or not you pull a trailer, etc.

Some disc brakes have built-in pad wear indicators. When wear reaches the replacement point, a bump in the disc produces a vibration in the pedal when the brakes are applied.

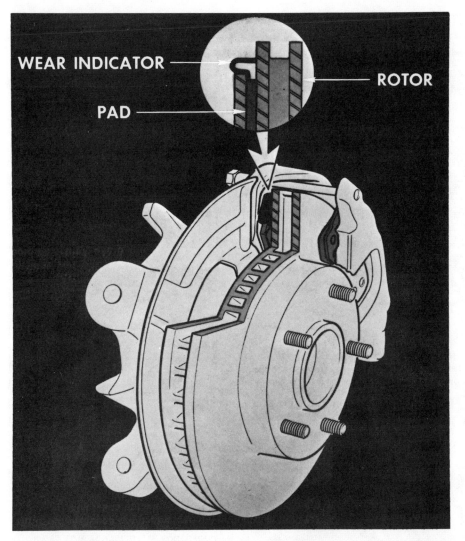

Some disc brakes have a wear indicator that produces a screech when the pad wears to a minimum level. The screeching sound indicates the need for brake pad replacement.

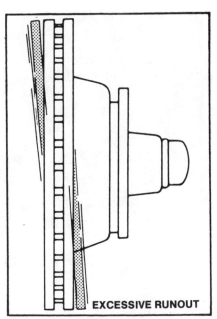

EXCESSIVE RUNOUT

A wobbly rotor can cause chatter and vibration during braking.

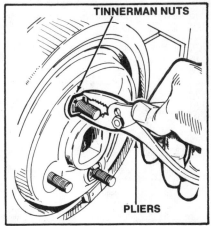

TINNERMAN NUTS

PLIERS

Rear brake drums are often retained by Tinnerman nuts. Remove these or the drum will never come off.

Inspecting Disc Brakes

Inspecting disc brakes is very easy. Normally, all you have to do is remove a wheel and maybe an anti-rattle clip from the caliper. Unfortunately, there are few cars that require that the caliper actually be removed to inspect the pads.

Some pads on later models have a disc brake wear indicator, which will screech or provide a pedal vibration as the brakes are applied to warn the driver that the pad lining is low.

Inspect the brake discs (rotors) for a wobbly movement of the rotor from side to side as it rotates. Check the rotor surface for grooves worn in the surface (very small grooves are OK) and for "bluing" caused by severe overheating. Check around the calipers and brake lines for leaks.

Pads should be replaced when ⅛" or less of pad material remains on the backing plate.

Inspecting Drum Brakes

To inspect drum brakes, it is first necessary to remove the brake drum. For front drums, you'll have to pull the dust cover in the center of the wheel, and remove the cotter pin and spindle nut. The drum will then pull straight off. The wheel bearings will come off with the drum so don't drop them in the dirt. Be sure to adjust the front bearing when replacing the drum (see "Wheel Bearing Adjustment," this section). Use a new cotter pin also.

Rear drums require you to first remove the wheel and then the drum. Once the wheel is removed, the drum should pull straight off, provided the parking brake is not on and the brakes are not too tightly adjusted. Do not pry the drum off. If it's stubborn, apply some penetrating oil

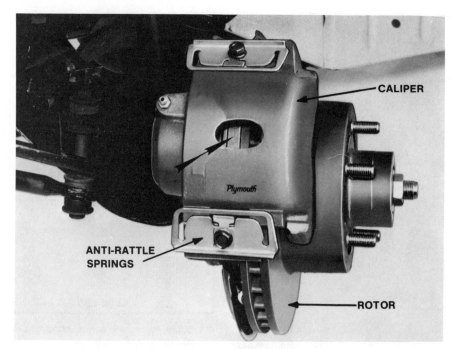

Many disc brakes have easily visible pads (arrow). While the pads must be removed for actual measurement, a quick look will tell whether the pads are worn to the point of replacement. Depending on design, the anti-rattle springs may have to be removed for a clearer view.

This disc (rotor) is ruined. Note the deep grooves in the rotor (right) and brake pad (left). The lining is also worn off the brake pad backing plate, which allowed it to score the rotor. Some light scoring is normal, but deep grooves indicate the need for service.

Chilton Tip

Do not, under any circumstances, depress the brake pedal with the drum removed; you'll explode the wheel cylinders.

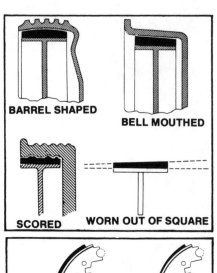

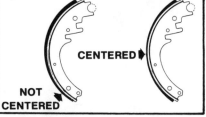

Improperly worn linings are cause for concern only if braking is unstable and noise is objectionable. Compare the lining and drum wear pattern, the drum being more important, since the drum shapes the wear of the shoe.

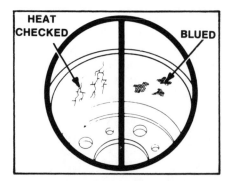

A "blued" or severely heat-checked drum and "blued," charred or heavily glazed linings are the result of overheating. The brakes should be checked immediately.

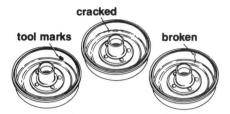

Check brake drums for breaks. Small cracks or tool marks from turning the drums on a brake lathe.

to the lugs and then tap lightly with a hammer around the perimeter of the drum. Don't risk breaking any parts. If the drum is too stubborn, leave the job to a pro.

Once the drum is off, clean the shoes and springs with a stiff brush to remove the accumulated brake dust. Grease on the shoes can be removed with alcohol or fine sandpaper.

After cleaning, examine the brake shoes for glazed, oily, loose, cracked or improperly worn linings. Light glazing is common and can be removed with fine sandpaper. Linings that are worn improperly or below $1/16''$ above rivet heads or brake shoe should be replaced. The NHSTA advises states with inspection programs to fail vehicles with brake linings less than $1/32''$. A good "eyeball" test is to replace the linings when the thickness is the same as or less than the thickness of the metal backing plate of the shoe.

Wheel cylinders are a vital part of the brake system and should be inspected carefully. Gently pull back the rubber boots; if any fluid is visible, it's time to replace or rebuild the wheel cylinders. Boots that are distorted, cracked or otherwise damaged also point to the need for service. Check the flexible

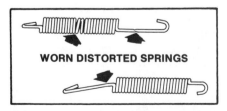

Check for weak or distorted retracting springs.

BRAKE SYSTEM TUNEUP PROCEDURE

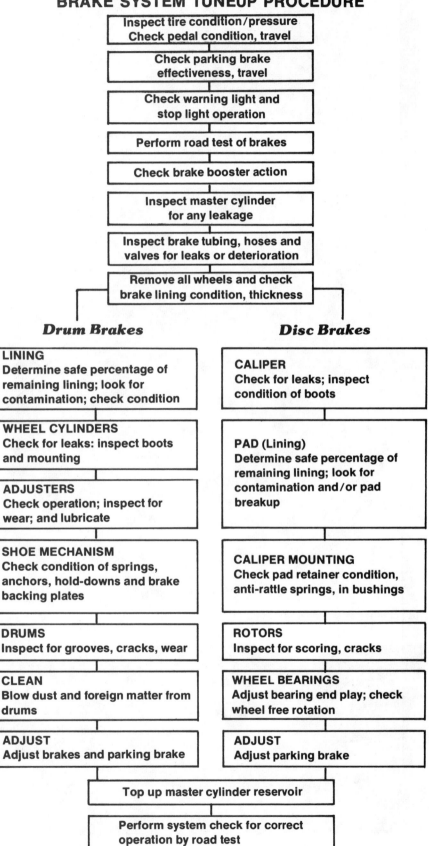

Inspect tire condition/pressure
Check pedal condition, travel

Check parking brake
effectiveness, travel

Check warning light and
stop light operation

Perform road test of brakes

Check brake booster action

Inspect master cylinder
for any leakage

Inspect brake tubing, hoses and
valves for leaks or deterioration

Remove all wheels and check
brake lining condition, thickness

Drum Brakes

LINING
Determine safe percentage of remaining lining; look for contamination; check condition

WHEEL CYLINDERS
Check for leaks: inspect boots and mounting

ADJUSTERS
Check operation; inspect for wear; and lubricate

SHOE MECHANISM
Check condition of springs, anchors, hold-downs and brake backing plates

DRUMS
Inspect for grooves, cracks, wear

CLEAN
Blow dust and foreign matter from drums

ADJUST
Adjust brakes and parking brake

Disc Brakes

CALIPER
Check for leaks; inspect condition of boots

PAD (Lining)
Determine safe percentage of remaining lining; look for contamination and/or pad breakup

CALIPER MOUNTING
Check pad retainer condition, anti-rattle springs, in bushings

ROTORS
Inspect for scoring, cracks

WHEEL BEARINGS
Adjust bearing end play; check wheel free rotation

ADJUST
Adjust parking brake

Top up master cylinder reservoir

Perform system check for correct
operation by road test

Pull back the edge of the wheel cylinder boot and check for fluid leakage. If you see any fluid, the wheel cylinders need rebuilding or replacing.

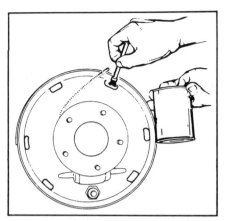

Lubricate the brake shoe pads on the backing plate with a thin coat of brake shoe paste.

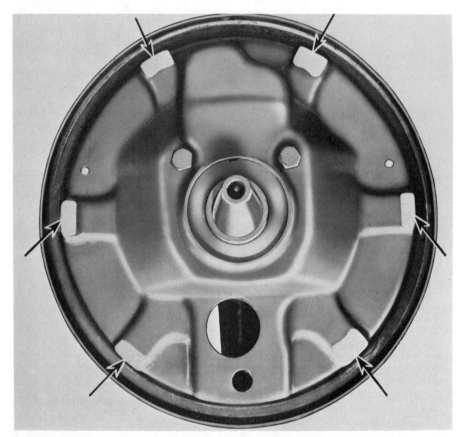

Rust at these areas (arrows) indicates that brake shoes may not be moving properly.

Parking brake adjusters located underneath the car (arrow) are generally difficult to turn unless you spray them with penetrating lubricant first.

brake lines for cracks, chafing or wear.

Check the brake shoe retracting and hold-down springs; they should not be worn or distorted. Be sure that the adjuster mechanism moves freely. The points on the backing plate where the shoes slide should be shiny and free of rust. Rust in these areas suggests that the brake shoes are not moving properly.

Parking Brake Adjustment

Parking brakes generally do not require adjustment if the automatic adjusters are working properly. If adjustment is required, proceed as follows:

1. Put the vehicle on a lift so neither rear wheel is touching the ground.

2. Engage the parking brake about halfway.

3. Loosen the locknut on the equalizer yoke located under the car, and then turn the adjusting nut until drag can be felt on both rear wheels.

4. Release the brake and check for free rotation of the rear wheels.

On systems where a floor-mounted hand-lever is used, the adjustment is usually contained under the rubber boot which covers the base of the lever. Tighten each of the adjusting nuts on these systems until an equal, slight torque is required to turn each rear drum.

WHEEL BEARING ADJUSTMENT

Whenever you remove the front brake drums or rotors, it will be necessary to adjust the front wheel bearings. All manufacturers have specific procedures for front wheel bearing adjustment, and it would be a good idea to use the factory procedure if you intend to perform this job regularly, but the following procedure will work well.

1. After removing the wheel, use a screwdriver to pry the dust cap off.

2. Remove the cotter pin (that holds the spindle nut) using side cutters or needle-nosed pliers. Make sure you have a new cotter pin handy before you do this, since the cotter pin is not reusable.

3. Spin the rotor or brake drum with one hand while tightening the spindle nut with a pair of pliers or a wrench. As soon as wheel drag or friction becomes apparent, back off the nut until you reach the nearest cotter pin hole, and insert a new cotter pin. Do not back the nut up more than a quarter turn under any circumstances. This will only cause a loose wheel bearing.

4. After inserting the cotter pin, bend the ends upward to prevent the cotter pin from working its way out. Tap the dust cover back on the spindle. Reinstall the wheel and tire, grasp it at the top and bottom and shake it. Wheel bearing play should be negligible.

28
Trailer Towing

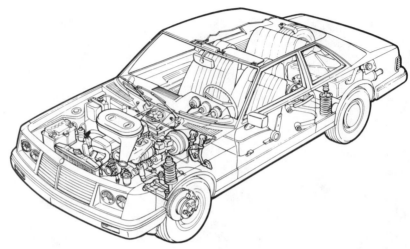

Towing a trailer is not the nervewracking experience many people imagine, but proper equipment is a must. Is your car powerful enough to pull your trailer? Is your car properly equipped for towing?

Trailer Weight

The weight of the trailer is the most important factor. A good weight-to-horse-power ratio is about 35:1–35 pounds of GCW for every horsepower your engine develops. Multiply the engines' rated horsepower by 35 and subtract the weight of the car, passengers and luggage. The result is the approximate ideal max-imum weight you should tow, although a numerically higher axle ratio can help compensate for heavier weight.

Hitch Weight

Figure the hitch weight to select a proper hitch. Hitches fall into three types—those that mount on the frame and rear bumper, and bolt-on or weld-on load distributing types used for larger trailers.

Axle mounted hitches or clamp-on bumper hitches should never be used.

Installation of a bolt-on hitch

Compare the actual hitch weight (plus any load in the trunk) with your hitch's capacity. Set up a 2″ thick piece of lumber as shown; be sure the trailer is level. For heavier weights add 1-2 feet to the 2″ dimension. Always multiply the scale reading by the number of feet between the pipes to get the hitch weight.

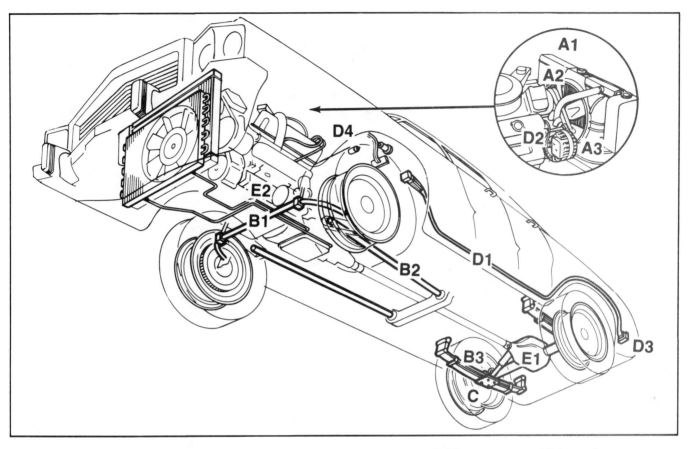

How to equip your car for trailer towing. These items are recommended for most cars and light trucks.

A. Heavy duty Cooling
   1. Large Capacity Radiator
   2. Fan Shroud
   3. Coolant Reserve System
B. Heavy Duty Suspension
   1. Larger Sway Bar
   2. Larger Torsion Bars or Springs
   3. Heavy Duty Rear Springs
C. Wide Wheels

D. Wiring Package
   1. Trailer Harness
   2. Heavy Duty Alternator
   3. Variable load flasher
   4. Heavy Duty Stop Light Switch
E. Other items
   1. Optional rear axle
   2. Automatic transmission oil cooler

is easy. When the hitch is installed, the tongue should be level and parallel to the road, and in the exact center of the car.

If your vehicle has a unitized body, a piece of steel plate ¼" x 9½" wide and as long as necessary should be welded to the car for reinforcement.

If you're installing a load distributing hitch, the car will "squat" front and rear when the trailer is coupled. You will have to get the hitch ball at the height where the car will be when fully loaded. Add the average "squat" to the distance from the ground to the top of the coupler to get the ball height.

To determine the average "squat," multiply the hitch weight by two-thirds. Load this weight into the front seat (use approximate weight of people) and measure how much the car squats from the unloaded height both front and rear. Average the front and rear figures.

Load distributing hitches generally use equalizer bars and chain links to level the tow car after the trailer is hooked up.

With the trailer directly behind the car, measure the car height front and rear. Hook up the trailer and adjust the chain links so that it levels the car and provides approximately the

same car height, front and rear, with maybe ½" difference. These hitches also have sway controls. While testing the rig, you should be able to let go of the wheel and feel no fish-tailing.

Wiring the Vehicle

Wiring the car and trailer is also easy. All you really need is some electrical tape, a wiring harness plug to match the trailer plug, some tap connectors, and, if you own an imported car, an isolation unit.

Fortunately, most trailer harnesses use only four wires (some have five or six) and the color

RECOMMENDED EQUIPMENT CHECKLIST*

Equipment	Class I Trailers Under 2,000 pounds	Class II Trailers 2,000–3,500 pounds	Class III Trailers 3,500–5,000 pounds	Class IV Trailers 5,000 pounds and up
Hitch	Frame or Equalizing	Equalizing	Equalizing	Equalizing with anti-sway
Tongue Load Limit**	Up to 200 pounds	200–350 pounds	15% of max. GTW	15% of max. GTW
Trailer Brakes	Not Required	Required	Required	Required
Safety Chain	3/16" diameter links	1/4" diameter links	5/16" diameter links	—
Fender Mounted Mirrors	Useful, but not necessary	Recommended	Recommended	Recommended
Turn Signal Flasher	Standard	Constant Rate or heavy duty	Constant Rate or heavy duty	Constant Rate or heavy duty
Coolant Recovery System	Recommended	Required	Required	Required
Transmission Oil Cooler	Recommended	Recommended	Recommended	Recommended
Engine Oil Cooler	Recommended	Recommended	Recommended	Recommended
Air Adjustable Shock Absorbers	Recommended	Recommended	Recommended	Recommended
Flex or Clutch Fan	Recommended	Recommended	Recommended	Recommended
Tires	***	***	***	***

NOTE: The information in this chart is a guide. Check the manufacturer's recommendations for your car if in doubt.

  *Local laws may require specific equipment such as trailer brakes or fender-mounted mirrors. Check your local laws. Hitch weight is usually 10–15% of trailer gross weight and should be measured with trailer loaded.

*** Most manufacturers do not recommend towing trailers of over 1,000 pounds with compacts. Some intermediates cannot tow Class III trailers.

*** Check manufacturer's recommendations for your specific car/trailer combination.

—Does not apply

code is more or less standard. Your vehicle probably does not have the same color code, but your car dealer can supply the

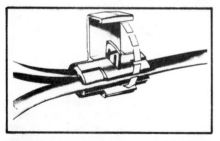

Tap connectors are readily available and make electrical connections quick and easy. Pierce the two wires with the metal blade using pliers.

color of your car's turn signal and running light wires.

Locate the turn signal/stop light wires and the common wire for running lights. The rear wiring harness usually runs through the trunk or under the rear floorpan and is probably encased in a protective wrap. Splice into the proper wires. If you "pigtail" the connections, tape them securely. The last wire to be connected should be the white ground wire. Scrape away the paint or undercoating to get a good ground. On five or six wire harnesses, the other wires are for 12V (direct to battery) and power for electric

brakes. Plug the trailer and vehicle together and test all services. The trailer should be hitched to the vehicle; otherwise, a good ground may not be established.

If you own an imported vehicle, the wiring problem is slightly more complicated. Domestic vehicles use a single bulb for signal and brake lights, while many foreign vehicles use a separate bulb for each.

The most practical way around this is to use a commercially available isolation unit, which takes separate brake and turn signal impulses and combines them into a common output to

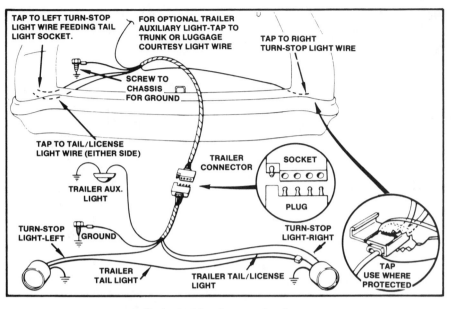

Typical wiring harness hook-up

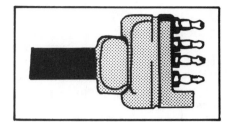

White = ground
Green = tail/clearance
Red = left turn
Brown = right turn
Black = 12-volt power

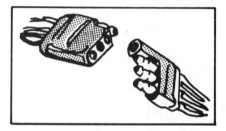

White = ground
Green = tail/clearance
Red = left turn
Brown = right turn

the trailer, allowing use of the standard harness. Otherwise, the wiring is the same as for domestic cars, except that you tap into the isolation unit. Be sure to tape all wires where there is any chance of chafing.

You should also use a variable load or heavy duty flasher to take care of heavier demands.

Trailer Brakes

Electric brakes are the most popular because of their reliability and simplicity of operation, but installation and set-up is usually beyond the scope of the casual do-it-yourselfer.

Cooling

Note: See Section 9, The Coding System, for more information on flex-fans and transmission oil coolers.

Engine

A frequent hazard of towing is engine overheating, due to increased load. To aid cooling, most manufacturers include a heavy-duty cooling system as part of the trailer package. It usually consists of a larger capacity radiator, heavy-duty water pump and coolant recov-

ery system. A/C equipped cars also use a clutch-type fan, which uses a heat sensor, allowing the fan to free-wheel, or push air, depending on engine temperature.

Flex-fans also aid cooling. Flexible fan blades are designed to push more air at slow speeds when more cooling is needed. At higher speeds when less cooling is needed, the blades flatten out, saving fuel and reducing noise with more efficient engine performance.

Flex fans can replace an OEM standard or clutch-type fan for increased cooling at low speeds. The plastic blades are curved and flatten out at high speeds to save power. (Photo Courtesy Hayden, Inc.)

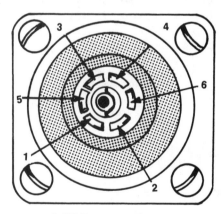

1. White = ground
2. Blue = brakes
3. Green = tail/clearance
4. Black = 12-volt power
5. Red = left turn
6. Brown = right turn

These are the accepted industry color codes, and are the ones most often used. The color may not be the primary color of the wire, however; it may be a trace color (the color of a small stripe on the wire).

Transmission

In recent years, the automatic has become the recommended transmission for trailer towing. The overall reliability and power of the automatic makes pulling easier than having to ride the clutch and lug the rig to get moving. On the negative side, the automatic transmission is far more complicated than a manual, and overheating is responsible for the majority of automatic transmission failures. Under normal service, fluid is designed to last about 50,000 miles at operating temperatures of 195°F. As the temperature of the fluid increases, the life of the fluid decreases rapidly (a 20°F temperature rise will halve the life of the fluid:

At 212°F, fluid life is 25,000 miles

At 235°F, fluid life is 12,500 miles

At 255°F, fluid life is 6,250 miles

At 275°F, fluid life is 3,000 miles.

Installation of an oil cooler will protect against high heat and premature transmission failure. A 20° drop in transmission fluid temperature will approximately double the fluid life; most coolers will reduce temperatures by 30° or more.

To select a cooler:

1. Estimate the combined weight of the vehicle plus the load pulled or carried.

2. Select a cooler of at least equal capacity.

3. Determine the mounting location. Be sure that cooling is adequate and that the cooler will fit.

4. If you are planning a by-pass installation, select a cooler two sizes larger.

Approximate Vehicle Weights

Compact car	3500 lbs
Intermediate car	4000 lbs
Full-size car	5000 lbs
Pick-up, utility or van	5000 lbs
Boat trailer	100 lbs/ft
Camper (pop-up)	200 lbs/ft
Travel trailer	250 lbs/ft
Utility trailer	300 lbs/ft
Motorhome (van chassis)	400 lbs/ft

Handling a Trailer

Towing a trailer with ease and safety requires a certain amount of experience. The handling and braking characteristics of any tow vehicle may be radically changed by the added weight of a trailer. It's a good idea to learn the "feel" of a trailer by practicing turning, stopping and backing in an open area (an empty parking lot is a good place). Make mental notes of space requirements and trailer response and follow these common sense tips to help avoid accidents.

Load with Safety

When loaded, the trailer should be heavier at the front; this will transfer most of the weight to the rear of the tow car. Approximately 60% of the gross trailer weight should be forward of the axle. If the load is centered, or toward the rear, it will cause the trailer to sway, sometimes violently.

Mirrors

Fender-mounted mirrors are essential, especially with larger trailers. Be sure the mirrors are properly adjusted for the driver.

Turning

Be sure to signal all turns well in advance. Remember that the trailer wheels will be closer to the inside of a turn than the car wheels.

The arc of the turn is greater with a trailer; you cannot turn as tightly. Starting a turn near the center of the street will place you on the far right side of the new street when the turn is complete. Starting the turn at the outside

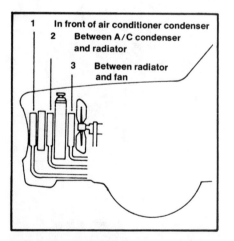

The location of the cooler is important. Position 1 provides 100% of capacity; Position 2, 75%, and Position 3 gives 60%, when installed in series with the original cooler. Alternate mounting locations should be chosen where the maximum, coldest air flow will pass over the cooler. (Photo courtesy Hayden, Inc.)

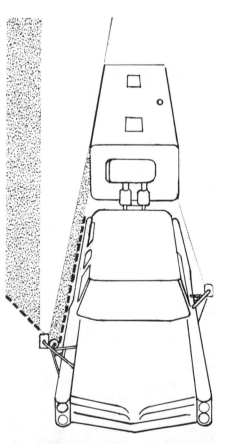

Mirrors should be adjusted so that there is an unobstructed view of the shaded areas. A convex mirror can be used on the passengers side for greater visibility (dotted lines).

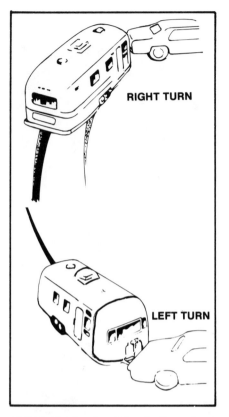

Notice the track of the trailer wheels compared to the car wheels.

portion of the road will complete the turn near the center of the new street. This means that you have to drive slightly "deeper" into the turn, or beyond your normal turning point.

Passing

Never pass on a hill or curve. Leave enough room before start-

Allow extra room for the trailer length when passing.

When being passed by a large truck or bus, slow down a little to counteract sway.

ing to pass; acceleration is considerably slower with the added weight. Remember to allow for extra length when pulling back in after passing.

You may notice when a large truck or bus passes you, that the displaced air pushes the trailer to the right and then affects the front of the trailer. Don't hit the brakes or make any sudden maneuvers; this will only make it worse. Slow down a little and the trailer will straighten itself out.

Following and Stopping

It takes longer to stop with a trailer. Allow at least twice your normal stopping distance and try to anticipate all stops. Avoid panic stops, which cause the trailer to "jacknife" or try to catch up with the car. Taking your foot off the brakes will usually cure this condition. Remember that everything must be done slowly—starting and stopping.

Driving on Hills

On down grades, use lower gears and let engine compression slow the car and trailer. Overuse of the brakes will only result in overheating and loss of effectiveness.

When going up long hills, you can reduce the chance of over-

heating using a lower gear. The engine will turn faster, causing the fan to push more air. Should overheating occur, pull off the road, turn off all accessories except the heater and run the engine at fast idle until the temperature returns to normal. Check for leaks, broken drive belts, cracked hoses, etc., but never open the radiator cap.

Learn the "Maximum Controllable Speed"

Every rig has a maximum speed, above which, it is out of control. Above this speed many external factors can cause sudden, violent and uncontrolled trailer sway. Gusts of wind, passing vehicles, rough road surface, crosswinds and sudden maneuvers can all have disastrous consequences when driving above the rigs maximum controllable speed.

Backing a Trailer

One of the worst experiences for a new trailer owner is backing a trailer. It can be a source of annoyance and frustration until you learn the trick to it.

There is no substitute for experience and one of the best places to practice is an empty parking lot. Practice backing between two trash cans, gradually decreasing the space between them.

Every driver has his own technique, but above all, go slowly. The trick is to turn the car steering wheel in the opposite direction that you want the trailer to go.

An easy way to remember this is to put your right hand on the bottom of the steering wheel. To move the trailer left, turn your hand to the left; to move the trailer right, turn your hand right. Once the trailer is moving in the right direction, turn the wheels back in the opposite direction, so the car will "follow"

HOOKING UP THE TRAILER

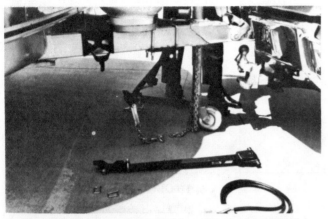

1. *Back the car up until the ball is under the coupler. A second person is usually needed for this. Lower the trailer coupler onto the ball. It is easiest to slide the coupler over the front edge of the ball and down over it.*

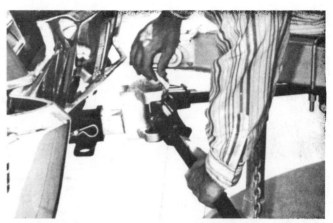

2. *Attach the equalizer bars to the car hitch. This only applies to load distributing hitches used with larger trailers.*

3. *On load distributing hitches, attach the equalizer bars to the struts on the trailer tongue.*

4. *On load distributing hitches, attach the equalizer bar struts to the trailer tongue using a preselected chain link.*

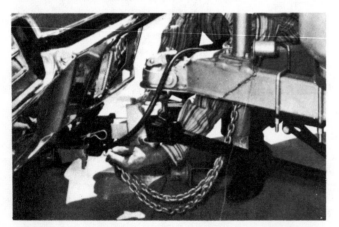

5. *Attach the safety chains. Plug in the wiring harness connector.*

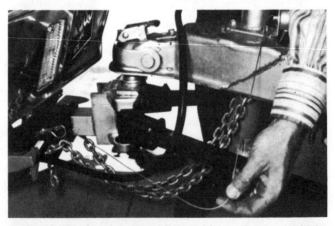

6. *Attach the break-away switch cable to the tow vehicle. Check the turn signals, running and brake lights. (Photos courtesy Airstream Trailers)*

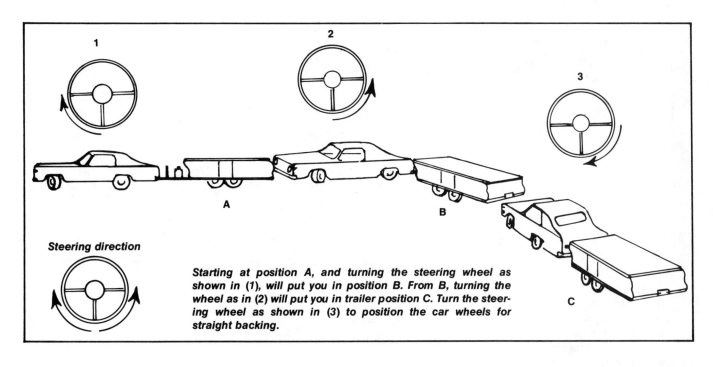

Steering direction

Starting at position A, and turning the steering wheel as shown in (1), will put you in position B. From B, turning the wheel as in (2) will put you in trailer position C. Turn the steering wheel as shown in (3) to position the car wheels for straight backing.

the trailer through the turn. If you find the trailer is not going where you want it, pull forward, straighten the rig and try again.

Be patient. Turn the steering wheel a little at a time to start out. It's easier to begin backing with the vehicle and trailer in a straight line. This minimizes the corrections required, although, with practice, this becomes less important.

29
Body Care and Repair

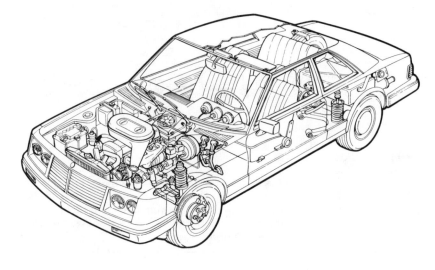

TOOLS AND SUPPLIES

Tools
- Body hammer
- Dent puller
- Sanding block
- Drill and drill bits
- Drill grinder attachment
- Plastic file
  (the half-round kind)

Supplies
- Wax
- Chrome cleaner
- Various grades of sandpaper (#120, 180, 320, 600 both wet and dry)
- Glazing putty
- Auto body plastic
- Spreaders (for plastic)
- Can or cans of primer
- Can of touch-up paint

The list of tools and equipment you will need to perform minor body care ranges from practically nonexistent to fairly complex. Obviously, if you only intend to keep your car washed and polished, all you'll need is some soap and wax. On the other hand, if you intend to repair minor dents, dings, and holes, you may end up with a fairly complete collection of body working tools. So, depending on your level of involvement, you may need none of the articles listed, some of them or all of them.

Keep in mind that most auto body repair kits contain everything you need to do the job right in the kit. If you have a small rust spot or dent you want to fix, check the contents of the kit before you buy any additional tools.

Washing

You may view polishing and waxing your car as a pleasant way to spend a Sunday after-noon, or as a boring chore, but either way, it's got to be done if you want to keep your car looking like new.

There are hundreds—maybe thousands—of products on the market, all designed to protect or aid your car's finish in some manner. There are as many different products as there are ways

Most auto body repair kits contain all of the materials and supplies that you'll need to do a job.

to use them, but they all have one thing in common—the surface must be clean. This means you have to wash the car first. Just becaue it looks clean, doesn't mean it's ready to be waxed. Waxing a dirty car will only grind the dirt into the paint.

The primary ingredient for washing your car is water, preferrably "soft" water. In many areas of the country, the local water supply is "hard" containing many minerals. The little rings or film that is left on your car's surface after it has dried is the result of "hard" water.

Since you usually can't change the local water supply, the next best thing is to dry the surface before it has a chance to dry itself.

Into the water you usually add soap. Don't use detergents or common, coarse soaps. Your car's paint never truly dries out, but is always evaporating residual oils into the air. Harsh detergents will remove these oils, causing the paint to dry faster than normal. Instead, use warm water and a non-detergent soap made especially for waxed surfaces, a liquid soap made for waxed surfaces, or a liquid soap made for washing dishes by hand. Other products that can be used on painted surfaces include baking soda or plain soda water for stubborn dirt.

Wash the car completely, starting at the top, and rinse it completely clean. Abrasive grit should be loaded off under water pressure; scrubbing them off will scratch the finish. The best washing tools are sponges, cleaning mitts or soft towels. Whatever you choose, replace them often as they tend to absorb grease and dirt.

Other ways to get a better wash include:

· Don't wash your car in the sun or when the finish is hot.

· Use water pressure to remove caked-on dirt.

· Remove tree-sap and bird effluence immediately. Such sub- stances will eat through wax, polish and paint.

One of the best implements to dry your car is a turkish towel or an old, soft bath towel. Anything with a deep nap will hold any dirt in suspension and not grind it in to the paint.

Harder cloths will only grind the grit into the paint making more scratches. Always start drying at the top, followed by the hood and trunk and sides. You'll find there's always more dirt near the rocker panels and wheelwells which will wind up on the rest of the car if you dry these areas first.

Cleaners, Waxes and Polishes

Before going any farther you need to know the function of various products.

Cleaners—remove the top layer of dead pigment or paint.

Compounds—rubbing compounds are used to remove stubborn dirt, get rid of minor scratches, smooth away imperfections and partially restore badly weathered paint.

Polishes—polishes contain no abrasives or waxes; they shine the paint by adding oils to the paint.

Waxes—a protective coating for the polish.

Cleaners

Before you apply any wax, you'll have to remove oxidation, road film and other types of pollutants that simply washing will not remove.

The paint on your car never dries completely. There are always residual oils evaporating from the paint into the air. When enough oils are present in the paint, it has a healthy shine (gloss). When too many oils evaporate the paint takes on a whitish cast known as oxidation. The idea of polishing and waxing is to keep enough oil present in the painted surface to prevent oxida- tion; but when it occurs, the only recourse is to remove the top layer of "dead" paint, exposing the healthy paint underneath.

Products to remove oxidation and road film are sold under a variety of generic names— polishes, cleaner, rubbing compound, cleaner/polish, polish/ cleaner, self-polishing wax, pre- wax cleaner, finish restorer and many more. Regardless of name there are two types of cleaners— abrasive cleaners (sometimes called polishing or rubbing compounds) that remove oxidation by grinding away the top layer of "dead" paint, or chemical cleaners that dissolve the "dead" pigment, allowing it to be wiped away.

Abrasive cleaners, by their nature, leave thousands of minute scratches in the finish, which must be polished out later. These should only be used in extreme cases, but are usually the only thing to use on badly oxidized paint finishes. Chemical cleaners are much milder but are not strong enough for severe cases of oxidation or weathered paint.

The most popular cleaners are liquid or paste abrasive polishing and rubbing compounds. Polishing compounds have a finer abrasive grit for medium- duty work. Rubbing compounds are a coarser abrasive and for heavy-duty work. Unless you are familar with how to use compounds, be very careful. Excessive rubbing with any type of compound or cleaner can grind right through the paint to primer or bare metal. Follow the directions on the container—depending on type, the cleaner may or may not be OK for your paint. For example, some cleaners are not formulated for acrylic lacquer finishes.

When a small area needs compounding or heavy polishing, it's best to do the job by hand. Some people prefer a powered buffer for large areas. Avoid cutting through the paint along styling edges on the body. Small, hand operations where the compound is applied and rubbed using cloth folded into a thick ball, allow you to work in straight lines along such edges.

To avoid cutting through on the edges when using a power buffer, try masking tape. Just cover the edge with tape while using power. Then finish the job by hand with the tape removed. Even then work carefully. The paint tends to be a lot thinner along the sharp ridges stamped into the panels.

Compounding by machine or by hand, only work on a small area and apply the compound sparingly. If the materials are spread too thin, or allowed to sit too long, they dry out. Once dry they lose the ability to deliver a smooth, clean finish. Also, dried-out polish tends to cause the buffer to stick in one spot. This in turn can burn or cut through the finish.

Waxes and Polishes

Your car's finish can be protected in a number of ways. A cleaner/wax or polish/cleaner followed by wax or variations of each all provide good results. The two-step approach (polish followed by wax) is probably slightly better but consumes more time and effort. Properly fed with oils, your paint should never need cleaning, but despite the best polishing job, it won't last unless it's protected with

wax. Without wax, polish must be renewed at least once a month to prevent oxidation.

The thing that makes wax so good for protecting surfaces is its hydrophobic character—it rejects water. And the things which cause paint to deteriorate include water, light and air.

The film of wax applied to a surface will not exclude these completely, but it does slow the attack. Detergents tend to remove wax in spite of the fact that it will not readily dissolve in water. To help it get through several washings, a chemical called aminofunctional-silicone is added to the blend of waxes. The wax is blended to get toughness in an extremely thin film.

The layer of wax is perhaps only one molecule thick at some points. While this is difficult to measure, it isn't hard to detect. And the method used even by experts is the water beading test. If water "beads" on the surface, the wax layer is present. If it doesn't bead, it's time to clean and wax again.

Years ago (some still swear by it today), the best wax was made from the Brazilian palm, the Carnuba, favored for its vegetable base and high melting point. However, modern synthetic waxes are harder, which means they protect against moisture better, and chemically inert silicone is used for long-lasting pro-

tection. The only problem with silicone wax is that it penetrates all layers of paint. To repaint or touch up a panel or car protected by silicone wax, you have to completely strip the finish to avoid "fisheyes."

Under normal conditions, silicone waxes will last four to six months, but you have to be careful of wax build-up from too much waxing. Too thick a coat of wax is just as bad as no wax at all; it stops the paint from breathing.

Combination cleaner/waxes have become popular lately because they remove the old layer of wax plus light oxidation, while putting on a fresh coat of wax at the same time. Some cleaner/waxes contain abrasive cleaners which require caution, although many cleaner/waxes use a chemical cleaner.

Applying Wax or Polish

You may view polishing and waxing your car as a pleasant way to spend an afternoon, or as a boring chore, but it has to be done to keep the paint on your car. Caring for the paint doesn't require special tools, but you should follow a few rules.

1. Use a good quality wax.

2. Before applying any wax or polish, be sure the surface is completely clean. Just because the car looks clean, doesn't mean it's ready for polish or wax.

3. If the finish on your car is weathered, dull, or oxidized, it will probably have to be compounded to remove the old or oxidized paint. If the paint is simply dulled from lack of care, one of the non-abrasive cleaners known as polishing compounds will do the trick. If the paint is severely scratched or really dull, you'll probably have to use a rubbing compound to prepare the finish for waxing. If you're not sure which one to use, use the polishing compound, since you can easily ruin the finish by using too strong a rubbing compound.

4. Don't apply wax or polish

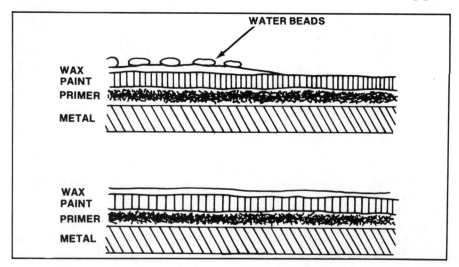

WATER BEADS

WAX
PAINT
PRIMER
METAL

WAX
PAINT
PRIMER
METAL

compound in direct sunlight, even if the directions on the can say you can. Most waxes will not cure properly in bright sunlight and you'll probably end up with a blotchy looking finish.

5. Don't rub the wax off too soon. The result will be a wet, dull finish. Let the wax dry thoroughly before buffing it off.

6. A constant debate among car enthusiasts is how wax should be applied. Some maintain pastes or liquids should be applied in a circular motion, but body shop experts have long thought that this approach results in barely detectable circular abrasions, especially on cars that are waxed frequently. They advise rubbing in straight lines, especially if any kind of cleaner is involved.

7. If an applicator is not supplied with the wax, use a piece of soft cheesecloth or very soft lint-free material. The same applies to buffing the surface.

Special Surfaces

One-Step combination cleaner and wax formulas shouldn't be used on many of the special surfaces which are used on cars. The one-step materials contain abrasives to achieve a clean surface under the wax top coat. The abrasives are so mild that you could clean a car every week for a couple of years without fear of rubbing through the paint. But this same level of abrasiveness might, through repeated use, damage decals used for special trim effects. This includes wide stripes, wood-grain trim and other appliques.

Painted plastics must be cleaned with care. If a cleaner is too aggressive it will cut through the paint and expose the primer. If bright trim such as polished aluminum or chrome is painted, cleaning must be performed with even greater care. If rubbing compound is being used, it will

cut faster than polish. Thus, the possibility of getting into trouble is increased.

If you attempt to protect these more-porous-than-usual surfaces, don't turn to low-luster furniture waxes. They aren't formulated for automotive finishes. They may even cause damage.

Just the opposite gloss problem is found with acrylic finishes. They have their highest gloss as sprayed. Abrasive cleaners will dull the finish. The best way to clean these newer finishes is with a non-abrasive liquid polish. Only dirt and oxidation, not paint, will be removed.

Taking a few minutes to read the instructions on the can of polish or wax will help prevent serious mistakes. The information on the label is there because it is important. Not all preparations will work on all surfaces. And some are intended for power application while others will only work when applied by hand.

Don't get the idea that just pouring on some polish and then hitting it with a buffer will suffice. Power equipment speeds the operation, but it also adds a measure of risk. It's very easy to damage the finish if you use the wrong methods or materials.

Rust, Undercoating and Rustproofing

Rust

About the only technical information the average backyard mechanic needs to know about rust is that it is an electrochemical process that works from *the inside out*. It works on ferrous metals (iron and steel) from the inside out due to exposure of unprotected surfaces to air and moisture. The possibility of rust exists practically nationwide—anywhere humidity, industrial pollution or chemical salts are present, rust can form. In coastal areas, the problem is

high humidity and salt air; in snowy areas, the problem is chemical salt (de-icer) used to keep the roads clear; and in industrial areas, sulpher dioxide is present in the air from industrial pollution and is changed to sulphuric acid when it rains. The rusting process is accelerated by high temperatures, especially in snowy areas, when vehicles are driven over slushy roads and then left overnight in a heated garage.

Automotive styling also can be a contributor to rust formation. Spot welding of panels creates small pockets that trap moisture and form environments for rust formation. Fortunately, auto manufacturers have been working hard to increase the corrosion protection of their products. Galvanized sheet metal enjoys much wider use, along with the increased use of plastic and various rust-retardant coatings. Manufacturers are also changing designs to eliminate areas in the body where rust-forming moisture can collect.

Rustproofing

To prevent rust, you must stop it before it gets started. On new cars, there are two ways to accomplish this.

First, the car should be treated with a commercial rustproofing compound. There are many different brands of franchised rustproofers, but most processes involve spraying a waxy "self-sealing" compound under the chassis, inside rocker panels, inside doors and fender liners and similar places where rust is likely to form. Prices for a quality rustproofing job range from $100-$250, dependng on the area, the brand name and the size of the vehicle.

Ideally, the vehicle should be rustproofed as soon as possible following the purchase. The surfaces of the car or truck have begun to oxidize and deteriorate during shipping. In addition, the car may have sat on a dealer's lot or on a lot at the factory, and once the rust has progressed past the stage of light, powdery surface oxidation, rustproofing is not likely to be worthwhile. Professional rustproofers feel that once rust has formed, rustproofing will simply seal in moisture already present. Most franchised rustproofing operations offer a three to five year warranty against rust-through, but will not support that warranty if the rustproofing is not applied within three months of the date of manufacture.

Second, keep a garden hose handy for your car in winter. Use it a few times on nice days during the winter for underneath areas, and it will pay big dividends when spring arrives. Spraying under the fenders and other areas which even carwashes don't reach will help remove road salt, dirt and other build-ups which help breed rust. Adjust the nozzle to a high-force spray. An old brush will help break up residue, permitting it to be washed away more easily.

It's a somewhat messy job, but it will be worth it in the long run because a car's rust often starts in those hidden areas.

At the same time, wash grime off the door sills and, more importantly, the under portions of the doors and the tailgate if you have a station wagon or truck. Applying a coat of wax to those areas at least once before and once during winter will help fend off rust.

When applying the wax to the under parts of the doors, you will note small drain holes. These holes often are plugged with undercoating or dirt. Make sure they are cleaned out to prevent water build-up inside the doors. A small punch or penknife will do the job.

Water from the high-pressure sprays in carwashes sometimes can get into the housings for parking and taillights, so take a close look, and if they contain

water merely loosen the retaining screws and the water should run out.

Undercoating

Undercoating should not be mistaken for rustproofing. Undercoating is a black, tar-like substance that is applied to the underside of the vehicle.

Contrary to what most people think, the primary purpose of undercoating is not to prevent rust, but to deaden noise that might otherwise be transmitted to the car's interior. Undercoating simply cannot get into the crevices and seams where moisture tends to collect, and in fact may clog up drainage holes and ventilation passages.

Since cars are pretty quiet these days anyway, dealers are only too willing to promote undercoating as a rust preventative. Undercoating will of course, prevent some rust, but only if applied when the car is brand-new. In any case, undercoating doesn't provide the protection that a good rustproofing does. If you do decide to undercoat your car and it's not brand-new, you have a big clean-up job ahead of you. It's a good idea to have the underside of the car professionally steam-cleaned and save yourself a lot of work. Spraying undercoat on dirty or rusty parts is only going to make things worse, since the undercoat will trap any rust-causing agents.

Drain Holes

Rusty rocker panels are a common problem on nearly every car, but they can be prevented by simply drilling some holes in your rocker panels to let the water out, or by keeping the ones that are already there clean and unclogged. Most cars these days have a series of holes in the rocker panels to prevent moisture collection there, but they frequently become clogged. Just use a small screwdriver or penknife to keep them clean. If your car doesn't have drain holes, it's

Drilling drain holes in the rocker panels is a simple job. Drill at least two holes for each panel. One at either end and one in the middle is probably best. If your car already has drain holes in the rocker panels, clean them out periodically with a large nail or an icepick.

a simple matter to drill a couple of holes in each panel.

Repairing Minor Body Damage

Unless your car just rolled off the showroom floor, chances are it has a few minor scratches or dings in it somewhere, or a small rust spot you've been meaning to fix. You just haven't been able to decide whether or not you can really do the job. Well, if the damage is anything like that presented here, the answer is yes. There are a number of auto body repair kits that contain everything you need to repair minor scratches, dents and rust spots.

If you're unsure of your ability, start with a small scratch. Once you've mastered small scratches and dings, you can work your way up to the more complicated repairs. When doing rust repairs, remember that unless *all* the rust is removed, it's going to come back in a year or less. Just sanding the rust down and applying some paint won't work.

RUSTPROOFING YOUR CAR

Professional rustproofing jobs consist of drilling holes in exactly the right places through which the rustproofing is sprayed, by special equipment. Naturally, the location of the holes is different on each model, requiring precise specifications. Also, the equipment is not inexpensive, which somewhat justifies the high price.

The alternative to a professional rustproofing job is a do-it-yourself kit, at a fraction of the cost of a professional aftermarket job. The kits consist of aerosol spray cans of rustproofing, plastic wands to reach inside panels, doors and fenders, and small rubber or plastic plugs to close the access holes that must be drilled.

Inside the Doors

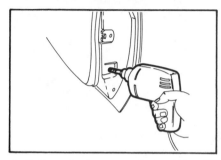

1. If there is no access hole, drill a ½" hole on the lower half of the door. Be sure the windows are rolled up and there is nothing behind the door panel.

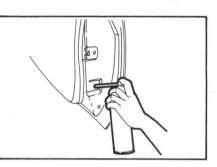

2. Attach a wand to the spray can and insert in the door as far as possible. Coat the entire inside metal door surface.

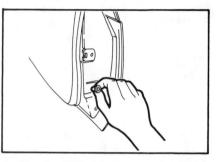

3. Plug the drilled hole with a ½" rubber or plastic plug. Repeat the operation on all doors and tailgates.

Quarterpanel, Rocker Panel and Trunk

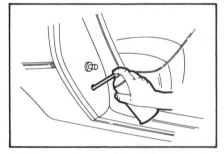

4. The quarterpanel can normally be reached through the trunk or through an access hole drilled in the front part. Follow the directions for inside doors.

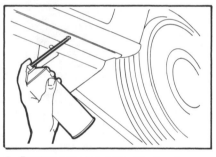

5. Rocker panels are the most rust-prone areas, and access depends on the individual car. There may be drain or access holes; if not, you'll have to drill some and fill them with plugs.

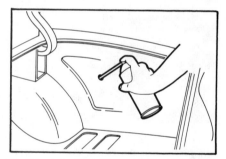

6. Remove the floor mats and completely clean the trunk. Spray between the rear wheel, floor and rear quarterpanels. Spray the bottom of trunk, and the walls.

Underhood, Underbody and Wheel Openings

7. Spray all exposed areas of sheet metal, the front quarterpanel and the wheelwells.

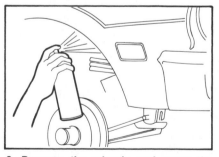

8. Remove the wheels and cover the brake drums or discs. Spray the entire area evenly after thoroughly cleaning away dirt.

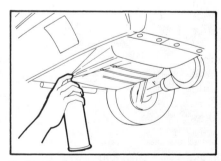

9. Block the wheels and support the car. Clean away all loose dirt and spray the gas tank, floorpan and accessible parts of fenderwells. Do not spray brake drums, driveshaft, exhaust system, shock absorbers or rubber parts.

REPAIRING MINOR SURFACE RUST OR SCRATCHES

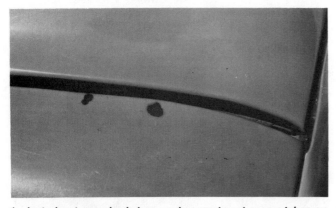

1. Just about everybody has a minor rust spot or scratches on their car. Spots such as these can be easily repaired in an hour or two. You'll need some sandpaper, masking tape, primer and a can of touch-up paint.

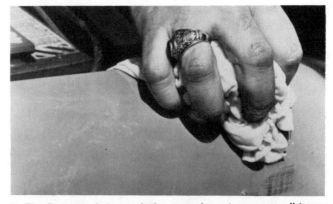

2. The first step is to wash the area down to remove all traces of dirt and road grime. If the car has been frequently waxed, you should wipe it with thinner or some other wax remover so that the paint will stick.

3. Small rust spots and scratches like these will only require light hand sanding. For a job like this, you can start with about grade 320 sandpaper and then use a 400 grit for the final sanding.

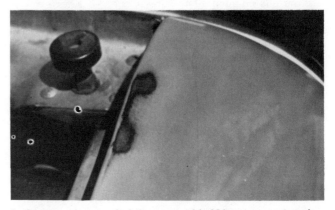

4. Once you've sanded the area with 320 paper, wet a piece of 400 paper and sand it lightly. Wet sanding will feather the edges of the surrounding paint into the area to be painted. For large areas, you could use a sanding block, but it's not really necessary for a small job like this.

5. The area should look like this once you're finished sanding. Wipe off any water and run the palm of your hand over the sanded area with your eyes closed. You shouldn't be able to feel any bumps or ridges anywhere. Make sure you have sanded a couple of inches back in each direction so you'll get good paint adhesion.

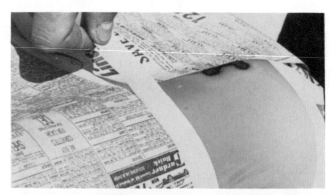

6. Once you have the area sanded to your satisfaction, mask the surrounding area with masking tape and newspaper. Be sure to cover any chrome or trim that might get sprayed. You'll have to mask far enough back from the damaged area to allow for overspray. If you mask right around the sanded spots, you'll end up with a series of lines marking the painted area.

7. You can avoid a lot of excess overspray by cutting a hole in a piece of cardboard that approximately matches the area you are going to paint. Hold the cardboard steady over the area as you spray the primer on. If you haven't painted before, it's a good idea to practice on something before you try painting your car. Don't hold the paint can in one spot. Keep it moving and you'll avoid runs and sags.

8. The primered area should look like this when you have finished. It's better to spray several light coats than one heavy coat. Let the primer dry for several minutes between coats. Make sure you've covered all the bare metal.

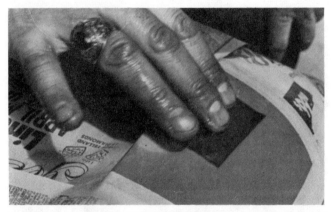

9. After the primer has dried, sand the area with wet 400 paper, Wash it off and let it dry. Your final coat goes on next, so make sure the area is clean and dry.

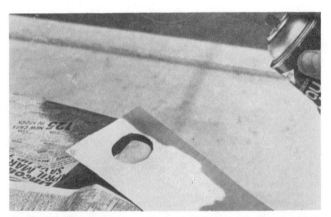

10. Spray the touch-up paint on using the cardboard again. Make the first coat a very light coat (known as a fog coat). Remember to keep the paint can moving smoothly at about 8–12 inches from the surface.

11. Once you've finished painting, let the paint dry for about 15 minutes before you remove the masking tape and newspaper.

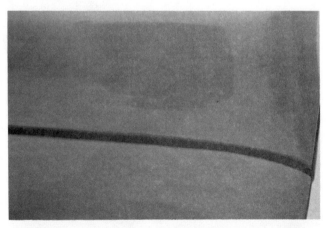

12. Let the paint dry for several days before you rub it out lightly with rubbing compound, and the finished job should be indistinguishable from the rest of the car. Don't rub hard or you'll cut through the paint.

REPAIRING MINOR DENTS AND DEEP SCRATCHES

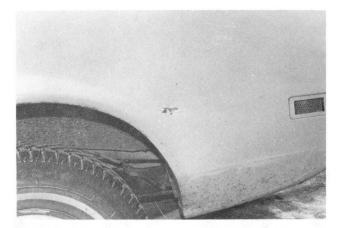

1. This dent (arrow) is typical of a deep scratch or minor dent. If deep enough, the dent or scratch can be pulled out or hammered out from behind. In this case no straightening was necessary.

2. Using an 80-grit grinding disc on an electric drill, grind the paint from the surrounding area down to bare metal. This will provide a rough surface for the body filler to grab.

3. The area should look like this when you're finished grinding.

4. Mix the body filler and cream hardener according to the directions.

5. Spread the body filler evenly over the entire area. Be sure to cover the area completely.

6. Let the body filler dry until surface can just be scratched with your fingernail.

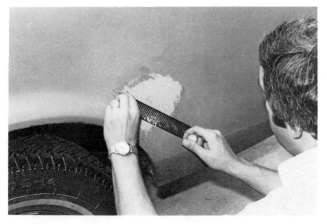

7. *Knock the high spots from the body filler with a body file.*

8. *Check frequently with the palm of your hand for high and low spots. If you wind up with low spots, you may have to apply another layer of filler.*

9. *Block sand the entire area with 320 grit paper.*

10. *When you're finished, the repair should look like this. Note the sand marks extending 2–3 inches out from the repaired area.*

11. *Prime the entire area with automotive primer.*

12. *The finished repair ready for the final paint coat. Note that the primer has covered the sanding marks (see Step 10). A repair of this size should be spotpainted with good results.*

REPAIRING RUST HOLES WITH FIBERGLASS

1. Rust areas such as this are common and are easily fixed.

2. Grind away all traces of rust with a 24-grit grinding disc. Be sure to grind back 3–4 inches from the edge of the hole down to bare metal.

3. Be sure all rust is removed from the edges of the metal. The edges must be ground back to un-rusted metal.

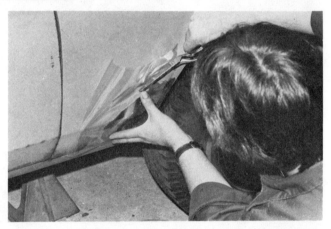

4. If you are going to use release film, cut a piece about 2″ larger than the area you have sanded. Place the film over the repair and mark the sanded area on the film. Avoid any unnecessary wrinkling of the film.

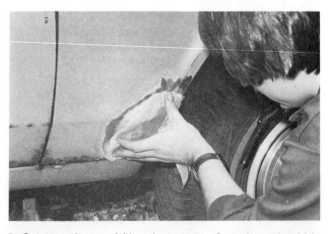

5. Cut two pieces of fiberglass matte. One piece should be about 1″ smaller than the sanded area and the second piece should be 1″ smaller than the first. Use sharp scissors to avoid loose ends.

6. Check the dimensions of the release film and cloth by holding them up to the repair area.

7. Mix enough repair jelly and cream hardener in the mixing tray to saturate the fiberglass material or fill the repair area. Follow the directions on the container.

8. Lay the release sheet on a flat surface and spread an even layer of filler large enough to cover the repair. Lay the smaller piece of fiberglass cloth in the center of the sheet and spread another layer of repair jelly over the fiberglass cloth. Repeat the operation for the larger piece of cloth. If the fiberglass cloth is not used, spread the repair jelly on the release film, concentrated in the middle of the repair.

9. Place the repair material over the repair area, with the release film facing outward.

10. Use a spreader and work from the center outward smoothing the material, following the body contours. Be sure to remove all air bubbles.

11. Wait until the repair has dried tack-free and peel off the release sheet. The ideal working temperature is 65–90° F. Cooler or warmer temperatures or high humidity may require additional curing time.

12. Sand and feather-edge the entire area. The initial sanding can be done with a sanding disc on an electric drill if care is used. Finish the sanding with a block sander.

13. When the area is sanded smooth, mix some topcoat and hardener and apply it directly with a spreader. This will give a smooth finish and prevent the glass matte from showing through the paint.

14. Block sand the topcoat with finishing sandpaper.

15. To finish this repair, grind out the surface rust along the top edge of the rocker panel.

16. Mix some more repair jelly and cream hardener and apply it directly over the surface.

17. When it dries tack-free, block sand the surface smooth.

18. If necessary, mask off adjacent panels and spray the entire repair with primer. You are now ready for a color coat.

30
Anti-Theft Systems

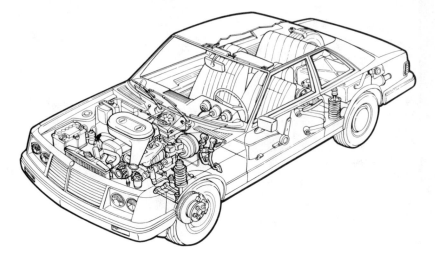

TOOLS AND SUPPLIES

Tools
  Wrenches
  Screwdrivers
  Electric drill
  Wire-cutting pliers
  Test light
    (for finding hot wires)
  Wire splicers
Supplies
  Alarm system (read the instructions carefully)
  Electrical tape
  Wire terminal hardware

Every 32 seconds, a car is stolen somewhere in the United States. Automotive theft is big business—more than a million cars were stolen last year, along with untold numbers of auto stereos, batteries, tires, wheels, and valuables left in car trunks. Even whole engines disappear in what is still referred to as "the midnight auto sale."

If your car is next on the list, it's going to set you back a bundle, regardless of whether the entire vehicle or just some part of it vanishes some dark night. What can you do to protect your car and everything in it from the sticky fingers of your local car thief?

For starters, *never* leave your keys in your car. Don't leave the doors unlocked either, or the windows rolled down even a crack. Contrary to what you may think, most car thieves are amateurs. They're not interested in a car that might be even the slightest bit difficult to steal. There are plenty of cars around that present no problem at all: 80% of all the cars stolen last year were unlocked; 40% had the keys in the ignition. So if you lock the car and keep the windows rolled up tight, most amateurs won't bother you. They'll simply keep looking for another car that's easier to steal.

Simple Steps You Can Take to Protect Your Car

Besides never leaving the keys in the car and rolling the windows up tight, there are a couple of other simple things you can do to protect your car and all its parts. One of the simplest things you can do is replace the standard door locks with the tapered kind. They're almost impossible to pull up with a coat hanger and will deter most ama-

Tapered door locks are extremely easy to install and effective.

teurs. Quite a few cars these days have different locks for the ignition, doors, and trunk, but if your car doesn't, it's a good idea to have them installed. That way, a thief who gets your door key won't have your ignition key. On the subject of keys, if you keep a spare key for your car (and you should), keep it in your wallet, not in the car or under the hood. If a professional thief is interested in stealing your car, he'll know where to find the key, so don't hide it on the car somewhere.

327

A good car thief can disappear with your car in less than a minute, unless you slow him down somehow.

Locking gas caps, hood locks, and wheel locks are cheap insurance. Locking gas caps are easy to install, and the only sure way to keep that expensive gas in your tank where it belongs and to keep other things from finding their way into your tank. They can be forced open, of course, but

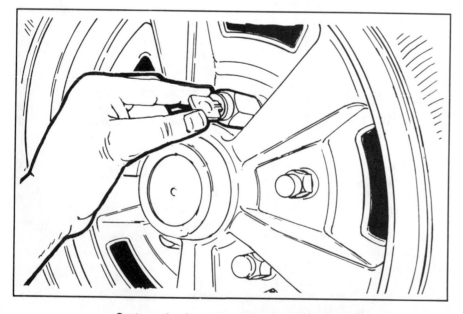

Custom wheels can be secured with wheel locks.

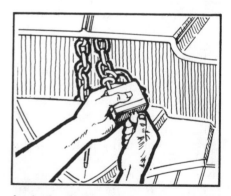

Lock the hood with a case-hardened chain and lock or hood pin.

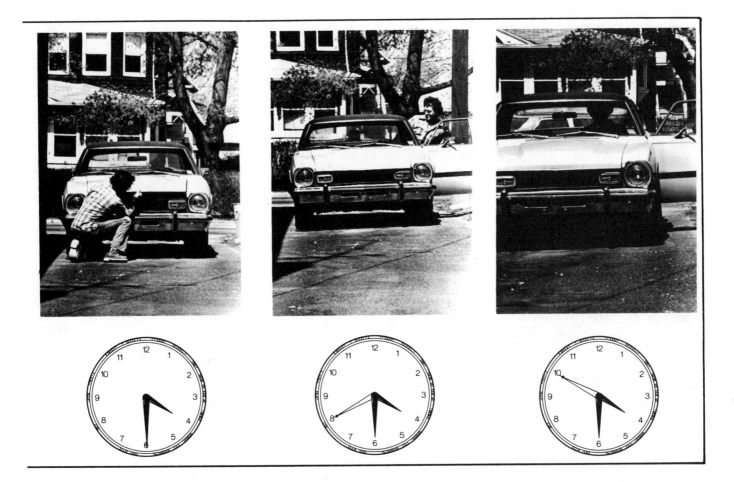

most thieves aren't about to take the time.

If you have custom wheels, either factory-installed or after-market items, wheel locks are the best thing you can do for them. Simply take the old lug nuts off, and screw the new ones on. Cus-tom wheels are high on car thieves "most wanted" list, but generally the sight of wheel locks will deter the average thief.

Hood locks are an excellent way to keep what's under the hood where it's supposed to be. There are two basic types of hood

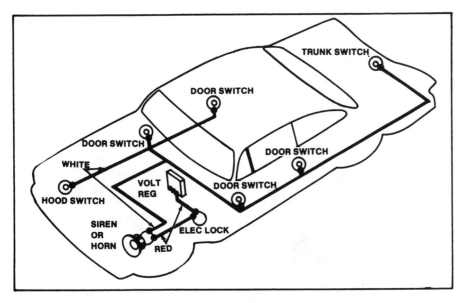

Self-contained alarm system schematic.

Locking gas caps keep gas in and other things out.

locks—one uses a strap or length of heavy chain and limits the distance the hood can be opened until the lock is released. The other type is just like a trunk lock with a key, and requires that you cut a hole in the hood to install the locks (usually one on each side of the hood).

Insurance

Auto theft coverage is usually included with the Comprehensive portion of your policy, as is the theft of components or contents. You may find that the insurer has specifically exempted some items (such as CB radios) unless they are installed in the dash or are factory equipment.

Check your individual policy for fine print, such as:

· Is there a deductible for contents or for the car itself? The higher the deductible (the amount you pay), the lower the premium.

· Does the policy cover CBs, stereos, and tape decks if not installed in the dash or as factory equipment?

· Does the policy cover items stolen along **with** the car, or only **from** the car?

If your car or contents of the car are stolen, be prepared to provide the police with a list of what was stolen, along with any identifying marks.

How Anti-Theft Systems Work

With the widespread and increasing rate of auto theft, automotive anti-theft systems have come into general use. Many auto manufacturers now offer anti-theft or alarm systems as optional equipment. In addition, there are literally dozens of aftermarket suppliers who manufacture these systems.

Most systems can be installed with hand tools in a few hours, but more complicated systems are best left to professionals.

There are two basic types of automotive anti-theft systems—alarm systems and movement inhibitors.

Alarm Systems

There are two basic types of burglar alarm systems for automobiles—those which actuate the car horn, and those which set off an auxiliary siren or bell. Regardless of which type it is, each one can be broken down into its separate components: the trigger, trigger control and the alarm itself.

Trigger Mechanisms

The trigger mechanism is the device used to activate the alarm. In most cases, the trigger consists of a switch or switches,

and a drop relay. A drop relay is a relay that, once activated, will not recycle until reset manually; therefore, the alarm will not stop functioning even if the trigger switch is deactivated.

Motion sensitive switches such as mercury switches, pendulum switches, etc. are excellent means of detecting tampering. The switch may be mounted anywhere in the car, and its sensitivity adjusted to the desired level. The disadvantage of a motion-sensitive switch is the accuracy with which it must be adjusted. The switch must respond to the opening of a door, the hood or trunk, but not to such things as parking on an incline, being bumped by a pedestrian, or traffic passing by. Once the proper sensitivity is determined, it is a good idea to include a timer in the trigger circuit, to shut the alarm off after a certain period of time if it is accidentally triggered.

Pushbutton switches (such as interior light doorjamb switches) mounted on all doors and the hood and trunk may also be used to trigger an alarm. These spring-loaded, normally closed switches may be positioned adjacent to the existing switches on the doorjambs and on the hood and trunk latch plates. A combination system of motion sensitive and pushbutton switches will provide excellent protection. Mercury switches used to activate hood and trunk lights may be used as triggers, in lieu of pushbutton switches, on the hood and trunk.

Trigger Control Switches

The trigger control switch acts as an on-off switch for the alarm system. It must be arranged in such a manner so that the owner may enter the car without triggering the alarm, but a thief must be unable to detect or disarm it.

The simplest type of control switch is a toggle switch mounted outside the car in an inconspicuous place. Inside the

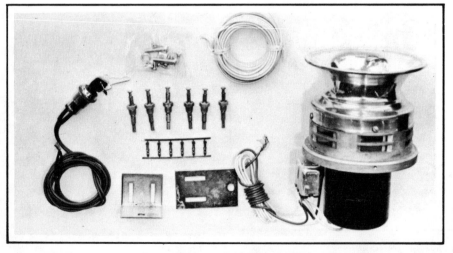

Typical aftermarket alarm system.

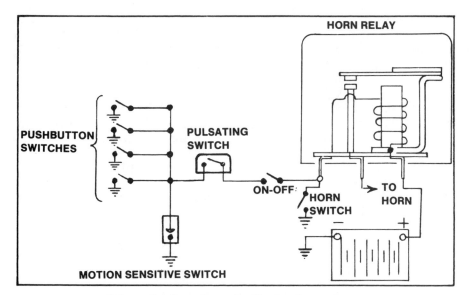

Schematic of an alarm circuit using the car horn.

fender well or under the rocker panel are two typical places that this type of switch is mounted. The only drawbacks to this type of switch are that the switch and wiring must be waterproofed, and that someone may find the switch and deactivate the alarm.

The most popular type of switch is the locking type which may be mounted anywhere on the outside of the car. These switches use cylindrical "pick-proof" locks, and provide excellent protection, in addition to acting as a visual deterrent.

Alarms

An alarm may be devised as an integral part of the electrical system to set off the horn, or the warning system may contain its own alarm. To connect an alarm

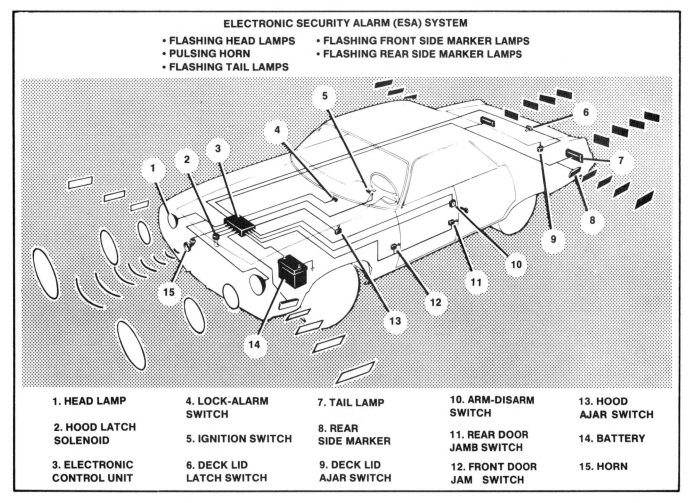

Typical factory alarm system.

1. HEAD LAMP	4. LOCK-ALARM SWITCH	7. TAIL LAMP	10. ARM-DISARM SWITCH	13. HOOD AJAR SWITCH
2. HOOD LATCH SOLENOID	5. IGNITION SWITCH	8. REAR SIDE MARKER	11. REAR DOOR JAMB SWITCH	14. BATTERY
3. ELECTRONIC CONTROL UNIT	6. DECK LID LATCH SWITCH	9. DECK LID AJAR SWITCH	12. FRONT DOOR JAM SWITCH	15. HORN

system utilizing the car horn, proceed as follows: Locate the terminal on the horn relay that will sound the horn when it is bridged to ground. Connect one lead from the on-off switch to this terminal. Connect the other lead from the on-off switch to a pulsating (flasher-type) terminal. Connect the open terminal of the pulsating switch to the trigger mechanism. Now firmly ground the trigger mechanism.

Non-integral, self-contained alarm systems may be connected to the accessory position in the fuse box. The alarm itself (siren, bell, buzzer, etc.) must be loud enough to attract attention at a reasonable distance, and should be positioned somewhere where full advantage can be taken of its capabilities (such as behind the grill). A drop relay and/or a timer should be installed somewhere in the circuit. The drop relay will keep the alarm activated, even after the trigger is deactivated, unless all current is removed from the alarm circuit. The timer is used to deactivate the alarm a certain period of time after the trigger is deactivated, to prevent the alarm running down the battery, and also to prevent disturbing the peace after accidental triggering.

One of the best things you can do after you install one of these alarm systems is to mount the "protected by alarm" sticker that comes with the system. A casual thief seeing this sticker isn't going to stick around to see if it's telling the truth or not.

Movement Inhibitors

The most common systems available inhibit the movement of the brake pedal and/or the steering wheel. Of these, the most prevalent (best known by its trade name—Krooklok®) is a locking, telescoping steel bar, with a hook at each end. In use, one hook is positioned around a steering wheel spoke and the other around the brake pedal arm. The steel shaft is then telescoped down and locked into po-

sition, preventing movement of the brake pedal and limiting movement of the steering wheel. A similar system utilizes a long steel bar which hooks and locks onto the steering wheel, and prevents it from turning beyond a certain point by wedging against interior components.

Both of these devices have the advantage of being easily visible from outside the car, thereby acting as a visual deterrent. Their

main disadvantage is that they are somewhat awkward and must be removed and installed each time that car is moved.

Fuel Shut-Off Valves

One method of limiting the movement of a vehicle is to install a fuel shut-off valve in an inconspicuous place in the fuel line. Once the valve is installed, simply turn it to the off position

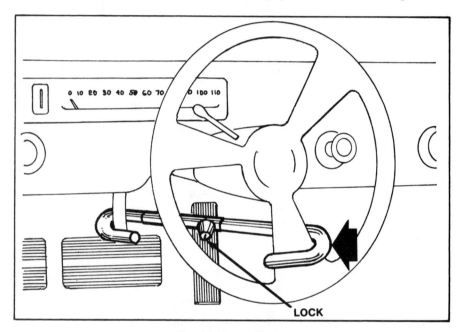

Krooklok® installed.

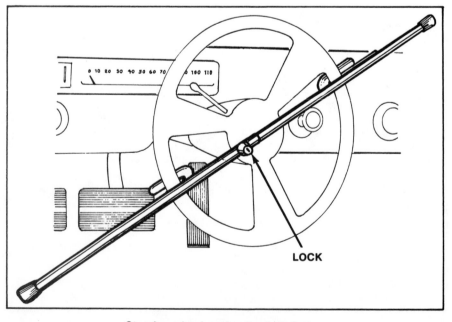

Steering wheel wedge bar installed.

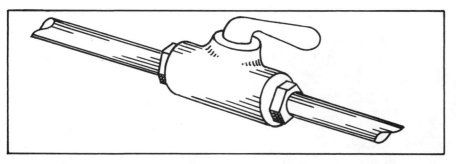

Fuel shut-off valve.

whenever you leave the car. The major disadvantage is that the engine will run until the fuel supply in the float bowl runs out, which means the car can be moved a short distance.

Electrical Cut-Outs

NOTE: *Ignition ground switches are not recommended for cars with electronic ignition.*

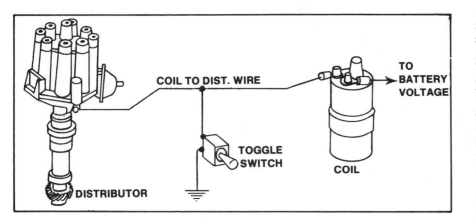

Ignition ground switch.

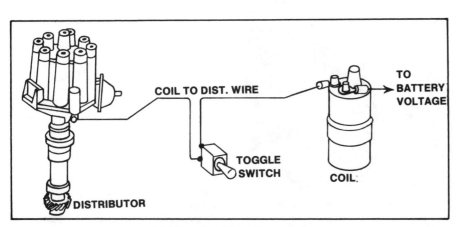

Ignition circuit breaker switch.

One of the simplest and most effective anti-theft devices is an ignition ground switch. A device such as this will prevent the engine from being started when it is activated. A single pole, single throw switch is wired between the distributor primary lead and ground and mounted inconspicuously, preferably in the interior. When the switch is open, the ignition will function normally. When the switch is closed, the engine's ignition system is grounded and the car will not run.

An alternate method utilizes a switch located in the distributor primary wire. If the car is wired like this, the ignition system will only function when the switch is closed, thereby completing the circuit.

The disadvantage of both these systems is the location of the switch. If the switch can be found easily, the system is useless. If the switch is located under the hood, the hood will have to be locked in some manner. Many modern cars have hoods which can only be opened from the car's interior, but a good many of these inside hood latches can be easily broken.

CB Radios, Stereos and Accessories

Thefts of CBs and stereos are reaching epidemic proportions, seemingly increasing in direct relation to the number of sets sold. The situation is so bad that the police in a certain anonymous metropolitan area estimate the average CB lasts 28 days before it is stolen. Some motels are posting signs advising travelers to remove their CB's and stereos and take them inside overnight.

Insurance companies are faring no better than their customers. Most insurers want CBs excluded from the regular automobile coverage offering, in its place, an optional CB policy for a nominal amount, usually about $4.00 per hundred dollars of value. There are some companies, however, that are willing to waive exclusion if the unit is permanently installed (in-dash). But it's up to you to check with your insurance company as to exactly what is covered and what isn't.

Is there anything you can do to prevent your precious CB or stereo from becoming a police statistic? The most important item of the system to protect is the set itself, and the best way to

A combination CB/AM/FM/Tape deck is the ultimate in both sound and protection from theft.

protect it is to remove it and take it with you when you leave the vehicle. This can become monotonous and time consuming, unless you had the foresight to install the set on a slide mount, like those used for tape decks. These allow you to slide the set off the stationary part of the mount and stow it out of sight. In-dash combination AM/FM/CB radios are gaining in popularity, but the radio is sometimes just as vulnerable, depending on the accessibility of the dashboard. Likewise, remote-control CB radios are seen with increasing frequency. The set is comprised of several parts: an electronic box housing the transmitting and receiving components, a control box and a microphone. A variation on the theme sometimes eliminates the control housing, putting all the controls in the microphone housing. In any case, everything is compact and can be disconnected from the electronic box and stowed in a pocket or glove compartment, leaving the electronics concealed beneath the dash.

CB Antennas

Some consideration should be given to your CB antenna which, to a thief, broadcasts the presence of a CB like a beacon. Unfortunately, almost anything you do to make your antenna easily removable is going to compromise the performance or aesthetics of your installation. Several companies market combination AM/FM/CB "ears" which replace your regular entertainment radio antenna, but these frequently have a loading coil in the antenna, which leaves you where you started—with a CB antenna permanently affixed. One antenna specialist company, however, makes a replacement AM/FM antenna that uses a hidden loading coil to electrically

Remove the CB antenna from the car. The thing sticks out in a parking lot like a divining rod.

transform it for CB use. Similarly, other companies market a loading box with built-in matchbox to convert the stock AM/FM antenna to AM/FM/CB.

Base-load antennas can be unscrewed from their mounts and quick-disconnects can be used for whips. There are even adaptors to use a ⅜" x 24 threaded whip on a base-load mount. Even though the distinctive CB mount is always present, most thieves are not going to risk breaking into a car or truck on the off chance that a CB may be lurking under the seat. One of the most recent solutions to this problem is the folding antenna mount which can be folded into the trunk when not in use. The disadvantage is that the side of the trunk is not the ideal place for the antenna either, but, you can't have everything.

Identify Your Equipment

Once the CB or stereo is stolen, it's not lost and gone forever, if you take certain precautions. Many stolen sets are recovered, but the tragedy is that the owner cannot positively identify the set, or the police cannot trace the owner through the serial number because the owner did not send in the warranty card. The "That's my set! I recognize that little nick on the front," line just

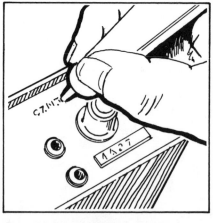

Some police departments will provide an etching tool free of charge to engrave your drivers license or similar easily traceable number on the chassis of your CB or tape deck.

doesn't work unless you report the identifying features beforehand. In a move to ease stolen CB identification, the FCC, since Jan. 1, 1977, has required manufacturers to engrave the serial number or other unique identifying number on the chassis of the set.

Police are encouraging people to engrave an identifying number on the CB, stereo, or other component and will often supply the engraver free of charge. Your social security number is not the best number for this purpose, because the social security office in Washington will not release the name and address of the social security number's owner—not even to the police. Use your driver's license number, your name and address, or some other number that can be easily and officially traced to you and no one else.

There are also national computer registration programs, which for a set one-time fee, provide an identifying number (guaranteed yours and yours alone) and a complete kit for engraving it. The number is registered with the computer service. Police can easily trace the number to you through a toll-free phone number to the computer service. No matter what number you use, be sure you have a copy of it, and be sure you can prove the number is used only by you. It is also a good idea to register it with the local police.

Safety Precautions

Most thieves work fast. Once inside a car, prying at the CB or stereo hung under the dash with a stout screwdriver usually frees it in seconds. A couple of snips with the sidecutters and the thief is on his way. Because speed is of the essence, anything that will slow a thief down may be a deterrent. Alarms and mounting brackets are sometimes useful, but alarms can be disabled in seconds (by a professional) and locking mounting brackets are generally pried loose with a stout crowbar, tearing up your dash in the process. Locking barrels over the mounting nuts offer approximately the same resistance, are dealt with in the same crude manner, and gain the same net result. The simple truth is, if you leave your rig in plain sight regularly, you're inviting trouble.

To sum the whole thing up:

1. Don't park in the evil parts of town and leave your radio in the vehicle.

2. When you do park on the streets or in a lot for short periods of time, try to park under a light.

3. When you are going to be gone for a while, remove the set and stow it out of sight. If you don't remove it, AT LEAST cover it with something.

4. Don't forget to remove the CB antenna (if you've equipped it with a quick-disconnect). If you don't the thing sticks out like a divining rod.

5. Many local law enforcement agencies provide a number etching service. A number (driver's license, call letters) is etched onto your set and logged in police files. It won't keep the set from being stolen, but it may aid recovery.

31
Buying and Owning a Car

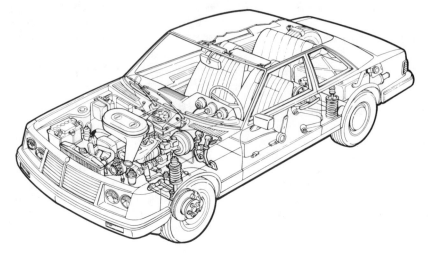

For most people, next to a house, their car represents the single, largest purchase they will make. While you wouldn't think of buying a house that wasn't "just right" for what you need, many people blunder into the showroom and drive a new car home that night because "it was cute," "the color was right," or a hundred other reasons, many supplied by the salesman. Some estimates put the number of buyers who even bother to take a test drive at less than four out of five.

Buying a New Car

Naturally, everyone is influenced to some degree by brand loyalty, advertising, or reputation, but the obvious point is to buy what you really need. Once you have decided that you want or need another car, set down some basic limits—subcompact or intermediate, room for four people, type of engine, etc. Then start shopping around for what fits your needs.

Some factors to consider are:

Weight—If maximum fuel economy is your goal, weight of the car is the single most important factor. Roughly each 500-lb gain in weight over 2,000 lbs will cost you 2 to 5 mpg. On the other hand, the fuel economy penalty for heavier cars is less if most of your driving is at sustained highway speeds.

Body Style—This will largely be determined by your needs and the way you use a car or truck. Generally, the smallest car that fits your needs will be most economical.

Engines—All other factors being equal, smaller engines are considered more economical to operate, but this can be deceiving. One of the biggest mistakes new car buyers make is to underpower their car. This is particularly true with intermediate and larger size cars. In fact, compared to weight, engine size is not a significant factor in fuel economy at highway speeds.

Ease of Service—If you plan to maintain the car yourself, look for easy accessibility of parts frequently replaced (plugs, filters, lube fittings, etc.). Even if you don't want to get your hands dirty, easy accessibility will lower your mechanic's bill.

Options

If you're looking for a "loaded" popular model, you may be lucky enough to find just the car you want already on a dealer's lot. Otherwise, don't count on it.

After you've finally narrowed your choices down to about three models, how do you decide which car is going to give you the most for your money? Start by taking a look at the sticker prices of all three, and paying close attention to exactly what equipment each includes. "Standard equipment" is a flexible term, and there is a lot of difference in its meaning from one domestic car maker to another. What one car maker offers as standard equipment may be considered an accessory by others.

Beyond the essential parts needed to make the car run, the more equipment you get for the same money, the better off you are. The cost of options can add up fast, though. They can drive up the price of your car by the hundreds before you know it.

Performance-related parts are things like radial tires, disc brakes, and overdrive transmis-

WHAT SIZE CAR IS BEST FOR YOU?

Size	Advantages	Disadvantages
Subcompact	Cost least Best gas mileage Easiest to handle Simpler engines Cheapest to run, maintain	Stiff ride Very limited space All options not available
Compact	Costs a little more Good gas mileage Good for commuting Easy to handle Cheap to run, maintain	Somewhat stiff ride Limited space Options somewhat limited
Intermediate	Good room and comfort Fairly easy to handle Good choice of engines, options Fairly cheap to run, maintain	Costs quite a bit more Lower gas mileage Not as good for big families, heavy loads as full size
Full size	Most comfortable Widest choice of engines, options Best long-trip car Best for heavy loads	Costs most to buy, run, maintain Hardest to handle Lowest gas mileage

sion, which no one will know you have, but will make all the difference in the way your car handles and performs. And they can help you achieve the maximum degree of economy.

Radial tires and disc brakes may be either standard or optional equipment. And both are options you really ought to have.

Overdrive transmission is great to have if you do a lot of highway driving. It saves gas and reduces wear and tear on your car. If you plan to use your car for quick jaunts around town, forget it. Look at it as one of those things that's nice to have if the car maker throws it in free. But don't order it unless you really need it.

Comfort/convenience accessories are usually optional on domestic models. This is an area where import cars have a definite edge. It's not unusual to find tinted glass, radio, and rear window defogger as part of the standard equipment on one of these models. You probably shouldn't let the presence or lack of a radio influence your decision very

much, especially since you can always buy one later and have it installed in your car for a lot less, including labor.

Air conditioning is almost never considered standard equipment. Where you live plays an important part in your decision as to whether you need it or not. And remember that the performance and the fuel economy of your car are probably going to suffer, but you will be comfortable.

Style/trim accessories have no real function, and are usually described in glowing terms like "deluxe custom interior," "custom wheel covers," "sport package," etc. If you're really shopping for a bargain, forget about these. There are many kits available for the do-it-yourselfer to customize his car nicely without the expense of the factory doing it for you.

Best Time to Buy

Usually the best time to buy a new car is toward the end of the month. Many dealerships run monthly sales incentive pro-

grams, and many salesmen have quotas to meet each month. Depending on circumstances, the salesman may be willing to take slightly less commission to sell a car somewhere between what you want to pay and what the sales manager will accept.

Time of year also is important to new car sales. New cars are in short supply shortly after the fall introductions, so prices are slightly higher then. The winter months are traditionally slow for new car sales, and sometimes you can find a good deal then.

Trade Ins

If you plan to trade in your old car, don't discuss this until you have arrived at a price for your new car. This avoids a lot of confusion about what the car is costing and how much trade you're allowed.

All car dealers subscribe to one of several used car valuation books that list the average wholesale and retail value for a car depending on condition. If the dealer can't make money on selling you a new car, he may try to get your "cherry" used car at rock-bottom trade in.

A good rule of thumb is to accept a dealer's trade-in offer if it is within $200 of the price your car commands in the local papers. The aggravation and cost of selling your car is worth that much at least. If the dealer can't come closer than $200, sell it yourself.

It is almost impossible to tell how much your car will depreciate or what it will be worth several years after you have owned it. Determining your car's trade-in value are such factors as gasoline availability vs. your car's fuel economy, frequency of repairs, general public acceptance (popularity), and whether it is an import or American made.

In general, import cars have been holding their value slightly better than their American counterparts, and due to the uncertain gasoline situation, small

EPA Mileage Estimates

How realistic are the EPA mileage estimates? There is no question that fuel economy in a particular car will vary widely, depending on the driver. Complicating the estimate is the fact that cars are even more variable than drivers.

There has been considerable criticism of the EPA fuel consumption figures as being too optimistic. The EPA procedure is useful as a simplified representation of the wide variation in conditions that affect customer fuel consumption. In addition to the driving cycle itself, the EPA procedure establishes many standard test conditions for variables such as type of fuel, ambient temperature, and "soak-time" (elapsed time since vehicle was last operated, which affects warm-up conditions). Though the specifications are meant to be representative, each introduces into the measurement of fuel consumption a variable which tends to make it higher or lower than customer usage indicates.

As an example, look at the dynamometer tests. The car is run in a stationary position on large rollers that allow the wheels to spin, simulating road speed. Tire rolling resistance is affected by vehicle weight distribution and tire pressure, among other factors. But only one pair of tires (front or rear) is cradled on the dynamometer rollers. Because of this, front-wheel-drive cars can experience higher losses due to tire rolling resistance than rear-wheel-drive cars. Tire pressure also influences rolling resistance, and the EPA specifies an artificially high tire pressure to increase durability during the tests.

Other factors contributing small biases toward the final EPA economy number include road surface, state of road repair, wind, weather conditions, altitude, engine accessory loads, and customer maintenance. All will affect the actual in-use fuel economy.

Fuel economy labels are meant to be useful in comparing *relative* economy of cars and in *estimating* the actual fuel consumption experienced in use. Obviously, the in-use fuel economy obtained by any given driver/vehicle combination is subject to many variables and cannot be determined exactly.

Diesel Payback

Is the diesel really worth buying? Some manufacturers advertise a "negative premium" to buy a diesel car, which means that a diesel model is less expensive to purchase than the gasoline engine model. Mercedes-Benz, for example, sells the 6-cylinder, gasoline-engine 280E, for $26,243, but you could have virtually the same car, called the 300D with a 5-cylinder diesel engine for $24,584, a saving of $1659.

And that's not the only saving.

According to the 1979 EPA Mileage Guide, the 280E gets 14 mpg at an average annual fuel cost of $750, whereas the 300D gets 23 mpg at a fuel cost of $392 per year. It's not hard to see that in this case, the savings in purchase price and fuel costs alone are considerable. Mercedes-Benz can afford to sell the diesel at a lower price because the diesel has no costly emission control hardware and they have been building diesels since 1937, so initial costs were long ago amortized.

But not every manufacturer offers a diesel model at a negative premium. In fact, most manufacturers *charge* a premium for a diesel engine that ranges from $200 to $850 over the cost of a comparable gasoline engine model. Let's look at two popular models, the VW Rabbit Diesel and the Oldsmobile Cutlass Diesel.

Volkswagen charges a $195 premium to get the diesel model, and Oldsmobile charges about $750 over the base V8 to get the Oldsmobile diesel V8. Using the latest available EPA mileage ratings, does it really make sense to buy a diesel? Let's look at the numbers in the accompanying table.

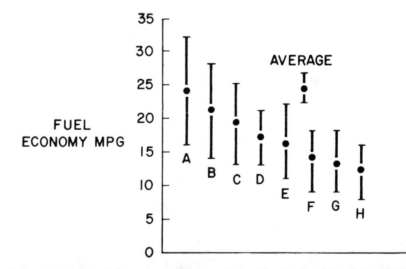

This chart shows the results of tests, published by the Society of Automotive Engineers, that measured the real-world fuel economy of eight different kinds of cars (identified A through H). Drivers of these cars recorded their fuel mileage for three successive tank fillings. The range of fuel economy indicated by the highs and lows is compared to the EPA estimates, shown by the dots.

Counting fuel costs alone, at the current price of fuel it will take less than a year to pay the diesel premium on a Rabbit, and just short of three years to pay the diesel premium on an Olds Cutlass diesel. If you're the average driver who puts 12,000 miles per year on a car and keeps the car between five and six years, you will probably save money on either diesel. Similar comparisons could probably be made with other diesel models.

There are other financial benefits to owning the diesel. In general, the diesel costs less to maintain. Even though some maintenance operations, such as oil changes, must be done more frequently on a diesel, the diesel has no conventional ignition system and does not require costly tune-ups. It is not unreasonable to assume that a diesel will run 45,000 to 50,000 miles without any major attention. In the same number of miles, a comparably sized gasoline engine would have required almost two complete tune-ups (spark plugs, ignition system servicing, and labor).

In general, the depreciation at resale is less on a diesel model than on a comparable gasoline engine model. According to both the *NADA Official Used Car Guide* and the *Kelly Blue Book,* the 1977 Mercedes-Benz 240D and 300D models retain more value than any of the other Mercedes-Benz models of that year.

The situation is the same at other manufacturers. The VW Rabbit Diesel is in such demand that the major publishers of used car trade-in values (*NADA Official Used Car Guide, Kelly Blue Book,* and *National Market Reports, Inc. Red Book*) do not list a value for Rabbit Diesels. At Oldsmobile, in 1978 you could purchase identically equipped new Delta 88 Royale Town Sedans for $6,224 (V6 gas engine) or $7,074 (diesel V8). According to the end-of-1979 edition of the *Red Book,* the diesel model retained 76.6%

of its value compared to 73.3% for the gas engine V6.

As the cost of fuel goes up, the savings of the diesel will be even more substantial, because it will deliver more miles per gallon than a comparable gasoline-powered vehicle.

But the diesel is not for those who make an occasional trip to the grocery store. Its efficiency shows to greater advantage when the miles begin to pile up on the odometer. In short, the more you drive and the more fuel costs, the more you will save with a diesel.

At present, the diesel is the one alternative to allow those who need a 5- or 6-passenger automobile to get reasonable fuel economy in the process.

Making the Deal

Now that you have your choice narrowed down, it's time to shop for the best deal. A dealer has to make between $125 and $300 on each car to stay in business. But that doesn't mean that the sticker price on the window reflects this profit margin—it's probably much more. You can easily figure the approximate cost of the car to the dealer by looking in any of several publications available on newsstands or by using the following chart:

Size	Dealer Discount
Subcompact	13%
Compact	14%
Intermediate	18%
Full-Size	20%
Luxury	22%
Specialty	15%

The suggested retail price is shown on the window and probably looks something like this:

Basic Price	$4,295.00
Includes:	
Front disc brakes	no charge
Color-keyed wheel covers	no charge
Bright side molding	no charge
Outside rear-view mirror	no charge
Air-conditioning	$482.00
2.73:1 rear axle	16.00
Rear window defogger	21.00
Automatic transmission	184.00
H.D. cooling system	27.00
Front stabilizer bar	16.00
Hi-torque V8 engine	120.00
Power steering	84:00
	$5245.00

Depending on the model of car you're considering, figure what it cost the dealer. If this hypothetical car were an intermediate it would cost the dealer about $4292 (sticker price minus about 18% of sticker price). To this you have to add dealer preparation, transportation, taxes, and tags. A good deal on a car is this bottom line plus the dealer profit of $125–300.

Arriving at what you consider a fair price is relatively easy. But that doesn't mean the dealer or salesman has to sell the car at that price. Get the salesman to put his best offer in writing, then go to different dealers and try to bargain for a lower price. Remember, too, that no price a salesman quotes is binding until the sales manager accepts it.

	EPA Mpg Rating	EPA Average Annual Fuel Cost
1980 VW Rabbit (gas)	24	$563
1980 VW Rabbit (diesel)	40	$300
1979 Olds Cutlass (gas V8)	17	$617
1979 Olds Cutlass (diesel V8)	25	$360

Buying Used Cars

With new car prices skyrocketing, many car buyers are turning to used cars. The old saw that you're only buying someone else's trouble is really not true today.

Approximately 13 to 14 million used cars are sold every year in the United States by dealers, private sellers, and renting/leasing agencies, totaling more than $21 billion. Almost 75% of all passenger cars purchased for private use are previously owned.

Obviously, there are a lot of buyers who are convinced that a quality used car is a bargain. The Hertz Corporation annually publishes its compilation of car operating costs, and their figures show a used car can be a bargain. The figures in the accompanying chart are rounded off to the nearest cent per mile.

Age of Car when Purchased (in Years)	Ownership/ Operating Cost	
	Cents per Mile	Percent Saved
New	28	—
1	25	10
2	20	30
3	15	48
4	14	51
5	13	52
6	13	53
7	13	53

People sell or trade cars for all kinds of reasons, and if you're willing to compromise a little on the car of your dreams, you may get a good buy. First decide what kind of car you want and start looking for it, either privately or on new or used car lots.

Cars on used car lots are easier to find, but they frequently cost more than those offered for sale privately in newspapers. The reason is simple—the dealer has to make money over what he paid for the car to stay in business. While private cars may be less expensive, they require considerably more leg work to track down and weed out the clunkers. You are also strictly on your own when buying a used car from a private party. True, you don't have to deal with a used car salesman who's a pro. But there's no law requiring honesty from private citizens selling used cars, either.

Once you've located a promising car, how can you lessen the chances that you're buying someone else's trouble? Start by following these shopping rules:

1. Never shop for used cars at night. The glare of bright lights make it easy to overlook body imperfections.

2. Take along a small pocket magnet. Casually try the magnet in locations all along the fenders. Anywhere the magnet doesn't stick—beware. The fender has been filled with plastic.

3. Ask to see the title. Many states identify cars that were bought out of state with a code, and the codes are usually explained somewhere on the title. Cars on a lot were frequently bought at an auction. Occasionally, a used-car dealer may get an exceptional car at auction, but for the most part, the auction is a dumping ground for cars that other dealers took in trade and were not worth reselling. As a general rule, you should beware of a car that was bought out of state or at an auction.

4. If the car is on a lot, ask for the name and address of the former owner from the title and try to contact the owner. No reputable dealer will refuse the information. If he does, walk away.

5. Write down the year, model, and serial number before you buy any used car. Then dial 1-800-424-9393, the toll-free number of the NHTSA (National Highway Traffic Safety Administration) and ask the clerk if the car has ever been included on any manufacturer's recall list. If so, make sure the needed repairs were made.

Used Car Inspection Checklist

In addition to making sure everything works (wipers, radio, clock, gauges, heater, defroster, lights, turn signals, etc.), carefully evaluate these areas on any used car you are considering buying. The number preceding each paragraph corresponds to the numbers in the accompanying drawing.

1. Mileage—Average mileage is about 12,000 miles per year. The numbers should be straight across the odometer. If a 1975 or later car is near 50,000 miles, the catalytic converter probably needs service.

2. Paint—Check around tailpipe, molding, and windows for

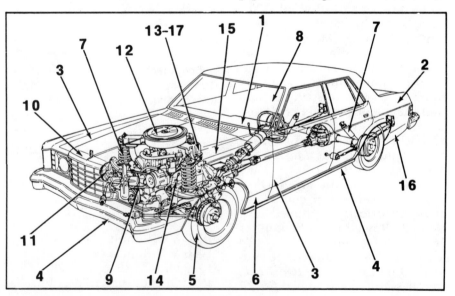

overspray indicating the car has been repainted.

3. Body damage—Check where the body panels meet; severe misalignment indicates crash work. Sight down the contours of the body panels; ripples indicate body work. Check overall condition of moldings, bumpers, and grille.

4. Leaks—Look under the car. There are no normal "leaks," other than water from the A/C condenser.

5. Tires—Check the tire pressure. A common used-car trick is to pump the tire pressure up to make the car easier to roll. Check the tread wear. Uneven wear is a clue that the front end needs alignment.

6. Rust—Check all around the car (fenders, doors, rocker panels, rain gutters, window moldings, wheelwells, under floormats) for signs of rust. Any rust at all will be a problem. There is no inexpensive way to stop the spread of rust. The only sure way is to replace the rusted part.

7. Shocks—Check the shock absorbers by bouncing each corner of the car. Good shocks will not bounce more than twice after you let go.

8. Interior—Check the entire interior. You're looking for an interior condition that doesn't agree with the overall condition of the car. Reasonable wear is expected, but be suspicious of new seatcovers on sagging seats, new pedal pads, and worn armrests. These indicate an attempt to cover up hard use. Pull back the carpets and look for evidence of water leaks or flooding.

Look for evidences of a leak or rust in the trunk. New welds indicate recent crash work. Look for missing door handles, control knobs, and other miscellaneous pieces of hardware. Check for proper operation of all lights and signals. Look for scratches and cracks in all glass.

9. Hoses, belts—Check all belts and hoses for wear or weak spots.

10. Battery terminals—Low electrolyte level, corroded terminals, and/or cracked case indicate a lack of maintenance.

11. Radiator/coolant—Look for corrosion or rust around the radiator, signifying a leak. Rust in the coolant indicates a lack of maintenance.

12. Air filter—A dirty air filter usually means a lack of preventive maintenance.

13. Ignition wires—Check the ignition wires for cracks, burned spots, or wear. Worn wires will have to be replaced.

14. Oil level—If the oil level is low, chances are even that the engine uses oil. Beware of water in the oil (cracked block), excessively thick oil (used to quiet a noisy engine), or thin dirty oil with a distinct gasoline smell (internal problems in the engine).

15. Automatic transmission—Pull the automatic transmission dipstick out when the engine is running. The level should read "Full," and the fluid should be clear and bright red. Dark brown or black fluid, or fluid that has a distinct burnt odor, signals a transmission in need of repair or overhaul.

16. Exhaust—Check the color of the exhaust smoke. Blue smoke indicates worn rings; black smoke can indicate burnt valves or that a tune-up is needed.

17. Spark plugs—Remove one of the spark plugs (the most accessible will do). An engine in good condition will show plugs with a light tan or gray firing tip.

Once you have checked the car out thoroughly and taken careful note of any problems as outlined above, you can come to a fairly reliable initial evaluation of the condition of the car and the care it has received. Below is a guide to help you. If your inspection turns up problems in two of the areas below, or in only one of them but a problem shows up in your road test, proceed with caution. That car is in less than excellent condition.

Illustration numbers 1–8: Problems in more than two areas indicate a lack of maintenance, and you should beware.

Illustration numbers 9–13: Problems in any of these areas indicate a lack of proper care, too, but can usually be corrected with a tune-up or relatively simple parts replacement.

Illustration numbers 14–17: Be very wary of problems in either the engine or automatic transmission. These can mean major expense. Walk away from any car with problems in *both* areas.

Road Test and Mechanic's Opinion

If you are satisfied with the apparent condition of the car, take it out on a road test. The results of the road test should agree with your original evaluation. Check for these things on the road:

Engine performance—Should be peppy whether cold or warm, with plenty of power and good pickup. It should respond smoothly through all the gears.

Brakes—Should provide quick, firm stops with no signs of noise, pulling, or fading pedal.

Steering—Should provide sure control with no binding, harshness, or looseness and no shimmy in the wheel. Noise or vibration from the steering wheel when turning the car means trouble.

Clutch, manual transmission—Should give quick, smooth response with easy shifting. The clutch pedal should have about 1 to 1½" play before it disengages the clutch. Start engine, set parking brake, put in first gear, and slowly release the clutch pedal. Engine should stall when pedal is one-half to three-quarters of the way up.

Automatic transmission—Should shift rapidly and smoothly, with no hesitation and no noise.

Differential—No noise or thumps.

Driveshaft, universal joints—Vibration and shimmy could

mean driveshaft problems. Clicking sound at low speeds means worn U joints.

Suspension—Hit bumps going slow and fast. A car that bounces has weak shocks. Shimmying may be due to driveshaft problems.

Frame—Wet the tires and drive in a straight line on concrete. Tracks should show two straight lines, not four.

It won't take a good mechanic more than an hour to check the car over. If your opinion coincides with that of a trusted mechanic, that's about the best you can expect. The rest is up to you.

Warranties

The time to find about warranties, either a new car or used, is before you actually purchase the car. After you buy, it's too late to realize that what you thought would be fixed, might not be. Find out about the warranty in detail. There is considerable variation from one car maker to another, and the differences are not always obvious.

There are basically two kinds of warranties: expressed and implied. An expressed warranty is that which is stated, either in black and white or as an assurance by the salesperson. An implied warranty is intended, suggested, or understood, though it doesn't have to be specifically stated (and in fact, is not). It is usually these implied warranties that manufacturers are guarding against when they state words to the effect that "there are no warranties, either expressed or implied, other than those stated herein. . . ."

New car warranties generally run for 12 months or 12,000 miles, whichever comes first, from the date of purchase, though a few new car warranties run longer. For an extra fee that varies with manufacturers, you can purchase an extended warranty plan, which amounts to

buying insurance. As an example, Ford's extended warranty covers a new car or truck for 36 months/36,000 miles, provided the plan is purchased within 90 days from date of car purchase. It is only available to the original buyer or lessee. Cost of the plan varies from $150 for small cars to $275 for big cars.

No two used-car warranties are the same. A new car dealer selling a used car, or a used car dealer, will probably offer a 30-day or 1,000-mile warranty. Some dealers will want to split the cost of repairs 50/50 with you, while others will offer a 100% warranty. Be sure that you get the warranty in writing and signed by the seller before you buy the car.

Virtually no car warranty will cover:

· Tires—these are warranted for defects by the tire manufacturer.

· Travel in Mexico—most car warranties are applicable only to the U.S. and Canada.

· Abuse—most warranties carry a statement to the effect that the car must be properly maintained.

· Installation of "non-stock" equipment. This could apply to custom exhaust systems, speed or high performance equipment, or work that requires altering the emission systems.

Emission Control Systems Warranty

The emission control and related system parts are warranted differently than other parts of the car. According to federal law, if:

· Your car is less than 5 years old and has less than 50,000 miles, *and*

· An original engine part fails because of a defect in materials or workmanship, *and*

· The part failure causes your car to exceed federal emissions standards,

then the car manufacturer must

repair or replace the defective part. This protection is afforded by the Emissions Design and Defect Warranty required by the Clean Air Act.

The emissions warranty applies to all motor vehicles manufactured since 1972, including cars, pick-ups, recreational vehicles, trucks, and motorcycles. However, the length of the warranty coverage, as expressed by a time or mileage limitation called "useful life," is different for each type of vehicle. The length of warranty coverage or useful life that applies to your vehicle is stated in the emissions warranty description in your owner's manual or warranty booklet (beginning with 1972 models). For most cars this is 5 years or 50,000 miles, whichever comes first.

Parts that do not have a stated replacement interval in the maintenance instructions are warranted for the useful life of the vehicle. Parts with a stated replacement interval, such as, "replace at 15,000 miles or 12 months," are warranted up to the first replacement point only. Finally, parts that are the subject of some maintenance instruction that requires them to be "checked and replaced if necessary" are warranted for the entire period of warranty coverage.

Under the law, each manufacturer must honor the warranty if the three conditions listed above are met. It does not matter if you brought your car new or used, from a dealer or from anyone else. As long as your vehicle has not exceeded the warranty time or mileage limitations, the warranty applies.

What Parts Are Covered?

Coverage of parts under the emission control systems warranty includes (1) any part whose primary purpose is to control emissions, and (2) any part that has an effect on emissions. Emission-control parts are often given different names by different manufacturers, and one manufacturer may use more parts than another. Parts that affect emissions can include the carburetor, choke, fuel injector, fuel distributor, thermostatically controlled air cleaner, air box, distributor, electronic ignition controls, spark plugs, ignition wires and coil, and any hoses, gaskets, brackets, clamps, and other accessories used with these parts.

If you or your mechanic can show that a part in one of the emissions or related systems is defective and has failed in a way that would be likely to cause your car's emissions to exceed federal standards, that part is probably covered under the emissions warranty. When you believe you have identified a defective part that may be covered, you should make a warranty claim to the manufacturer using the procedures outlined in your owner's manual or warranty booklet.

Lack of Scheduled Maintenance

Performance of scheduled maintenance is your responsibility. You are expected to perform scheduled maintenance yourself or have a qualified mechanic perform it for you. If a part failure is a direct result of your car not being maintained or used according to the manufacturer's recommendations, the manufacturer may not be required to repair or replace the failed part under the emissions warranty.

Proof of maintenance is not required in order to obtain coverage under the emissions warranty. However, when lack of scheduled maintenance could have caused the particular part failure, you may be asked to show that scheduled maintenance was performed.

Use of Leaded Gas

When leaded gas is used in cars requiring unleaded fuel, the emission controls (particularly the catalytic converter) may be affected. In addition, lead deposits will form inside the engine and, under certain circumstances, may contribute to the failure of an engine part. The emissions warranty does not cover any part failures that result from the use of leaded fuel in a car that requires unleaded fuel.

Costs of Owning a Car

The costs of owning a car can be broken down into two categories—variable and fixed. Variable costs include fuel, oil, maintenance, and tires and are directly related to the number and type of miles driven. The cost of repairs is also included in this category.

Fixed costs include insurance, license and registration, taxes, and depreciation. Though these may vary from car to car or place to place, these costs are established by business conditions beyond control of the car owner and have less to do with how or when the car is driven.

Variable Costs

Fuel and Oil—The best way to determine your fuel and oil operating costs is to develop your own figures. As an example, see the accompanying table.

Oil consumption, though not a major expense, also varies, and it should be figured in the same way. Remember to add the cost of every oil change. For example, a typical motorist may have the oil changed every 6,000 miles, less often if his car is a recent model. One or two quarts of oil may be added between changes. Simply add what you spend on oil during the year, divide the total by the number of miles driven, and add this amount to your variable costs. Generally, the cost of oil represents approximately 3% of the cost per mile for gasoline.

While the most accurate figures are obtained by keeping a record each time you buy gas or oil, it may be sufficient to make the test several times during the year.

Maintenance—Expenses for tune-ups, maintenance, and service items depend largely on the age of the car. The newer it is, the smaller these expenses probably will be. However, even a car under warranty requires regular checkups and service. Money "saved" by neglecting needed service and repairs will usually show up in the form of increased depreciation. This can be prevented by following a regular maintenance schedule.

The only way to determine accurately the cost of maintenance is to keep a record of all expenditures. It's a good idea to keep a small notebook in the glove compartment for this purpose.

Tires—If the car is driven with reasonable care and the wheels are kept properly aligned, tire wear will be kept to a minimum. On the other hand, over- or underinflation, high speeds, hard cornering, rapid acceleration, and quick stops all contribute to fast tire wear and increased costs of car operation.

Fixed Costs

Insurance—There is nothing uniform about insurance pre-

Tank filled		odometer reading: 8850
Buy gas	9.7 gallons cost $ 9.89	9008
Buy gas	9.9 gallons cost $10.10	9168
Buy gas	10.7 gallons cost $10.92	9343
TOTAL:	30.3 gallons cost $30.91	

Miles driven: 9343 − 8850 = 493
Miles per gallon: 493 ÷ 30.3 = 16.3
Cost of gas per mile: $19.68 ÷ 493 = 6.27¢

miums. The costs depend on the amount of coverage, where you live, and the purpose for which the car is used. To determine insurance costs, simply add the premiums of all policies you carry that are directly related to car operation, such as property damage and liability, comprehensive and collision.

License, Registration Fees and Taxes—These payments are usually due once a year. No two states use exactly the same schedules. Determine what you spend for license and registration and add the total to your fixed costs. Taxes, such as property or use taxes, should be treated in the same way. Sales or excise taxes which are paid only when the car is bought should be considered a part of the total purchase price and not included in calculating annual operating costs.

Depreciation—Depreciation is the largest single expense in owning a car. It is the difference between what you paid for it and what you would get in a trade-in or resale. Depreciation also is the most difficult cost to determine. Cars depreciate at different rates, depending on their appearance, mileage on the odometer, and the demand for your particular model at the time you want to dispose of it.

Due to economic conditions and fuel availability, the depreciation of specific makes and

Expected Average Retained Value, 1979 Models

	Standard Cars	Compact Cars	Sub-compact Cars
1979	71.9%	83.2%	87.6%
1980	57.2	70.5	76.0
1981	46.0	59.8	64.5
1982	36.0	49.8	53.7
1983	27.5	40.2	43.0
1984	20.5	31.0	33.2
1985	14.2	22.3	24.0
1986	9.0	14.1	15.2
1987	4.0	6.4	7.2
1988	0.0	0.0	0.0

Source: Office of Highway Statistics, U.S. Department of Transportation.

FIGURE YOUR CAR COSTS

Fixed Costs	Yearly Totals
Depreciation (divide by number of years of ownership)	_____
Insurance	_____
Taxes	_____
Licenses and registration	_____
TOTAL FIXED COSTS	_____
Variable Costs	
Gas and oil per mile	_____
Number of miles driven	_____
Cost per year (multiply miles driven by gas and oil per mile)	_____
Maintenance	_____
Tires	_____
Other costs (car wash, repairs, accessories, etc.)	_____
TOTAL VARIABLE COSTS	_____
TOTAL DRIVING COSTS PER YEAR	_____
COST PER MILE (divide yearly total by total miles driven)	_____

TYPICAL DEPRECIATION RATES

Depreciation from list price

Calendar Year	1977 models	1976 models	1975 models	1974 models	1973 models	1972 models
Standard cars (mid-sized and larger)						
1977	25%	15%	13%	10%	7%	6%
1978	15%	13%	10%	7%	6%	6%
1979	13%	10%	7%	6%	6%	6%
1980	10%	7%	6%	6%	6%	6%
1981	7%	6%	6%	6%	6%	6%
Compact cars						
1977	14%	13%	11%	10%	10%	10%
1978	13%	11%	10%	10%	10%	9%
1979	11%	10%	10%	10%	9%	8%
1980	10%	10%	10%	9%	8%	7%
1981	10%	10%	9%	8%	7%	6%
Subcompact cars						
1977	12%	11%	11%	11%	10%	10%
1978	11%	11%	11%	10%	10%	10%
1979	11%	11%	10%	10%	10%	9%
1980	11%	10%	10%	10%	9%	8%
1981	10%	10%	10%	9%	8%	7%

Source: "Cost of Owning and Operating an Automobile, 1976," U.S. Department of Transportation, Federal Highway Administration.

models will vary considerably. One figure the average motorist might use to estimate depreciation is the difference between the current market price of his used car and the price of a comparable new one with the same optional equipment.

Insurance

There are nearly 132,000,000 motorists driving over 90,000,000 insured cars on the nation's highways. Millions of other cars are not insured simply because owners cannot afford it.

Car insurance is a $15 billion business that is essentially a huge book-making operation. Insurance companies collect premiums from the people they insure, betting on the chance that they will not have to pay off for bodily injury or property damage claims. It's a risky business with a small profit margin (less than 5%) and the cost that you pay (your premium) is determined by the degree of risk.

How Your Rate is Determined

The business of insuring cars is based on statistics and probabilities. There are basically seven factors taken into consideration by an insurer.

1. Geographic Environment—Rates are based on the geographic area in which you live. Statistics have shown that most accidents occur within 25 miles of your residence. No matter where an insured person has an accident, if he is at fault or if a claim is paid, it is statistically recorded in the area in which he resides. The territories are rated high or low depending on the experience of the company with drivers living in the territory. If your territory has a high accident record, high medical costs, or high repair costs, your insurance will probably cost more.

2. Who Uses the Car—The age of the persons driving the car will affect the amount of the premium. Drivers under the age of 24 are involved in 25% of all accidents and are therefore higher risks. The statistics also reveal that male drivers are involved in

accidents more than female drivers and that married males under 30 and married females under 25 are less likely to be involved in an accident than their single counterparts.

3. How the Car is Used—You will usually be charged a higher premium if you drive your car more than 10 miles to work, less if it is used for pleasure purposes only. Cars not driven to and from work are usually subject to lower premiums.

4. Driving Record—Statistics prove that the drivers who have had accidents previously or who have been convicted of serious traffic violations are more likely to be involved in an accident than drivers with clean records. Many companies surcharge traffic violations and "at-fault" accidents within the last three years.

5. Type of Car—The make, model, and engine size are prime rate determining factors. Studies by the Insurance Institute for Highway Safety show that:

· Within each size group, 2-door models have more injury claims than 4-door models.

· Sports and specialty cars have the highest injury claims.

· Subcompacts have the highest percentage of collision claims.

· Among cars of the same size, sports and specialty models have larger collision claims than other models, and 2-door models frequently have larger claims than 4-door models.

6. Cost of each claim—Car repair charges, hospital bills, and financial awards vary greatly from area to area. Inflation in the costs of body parts, hospital costs, and repair costs, result in higher premiums.

7. Discounts—Most companies will offer discounts to young drivers who have successfully completed a driver education course, owners of compact cars, and families with more than one car (on the theory that each car is driven less).

Types of Car Insurance

Car insurance protects you against three kinds of risks:

1. In case someone is hurt in a car accident in which you are involved (liability).

2. In case you destroy someone else's property (property damage).

3. In case your car is stolen or damaged (collision or comprehensive).

Liability Insurance

Until 1970, insurance policies protected you in the event someone was hurt in an accident through "bodily injury" liability and "medical payments" insurance. If the accident was judged your fault, the bodily injury portion of your policy covered the medical payments of those you injured. Your medical payments insurance covered the medical bills of yourself and any passengers in your car. If the accident was the other person's fault, you collected from his insurance policy under the same arrangement. This system is known as "fault-based," since it involves a question of who was at fault and often resulted in interminable court cases.

Since 1971, 26 states have adopted what has come to be known as "no-fault" insurance. Basically, this means that anyone involved in an accident submits claims to, and collects from, their own insurance company, regardless of who is at fault. On the surface, this seems a smooth and equitable way of handling things. But there is a hitch. In some states, under certain circumstances, even if you are covered under a no-fault policy, persons who are badly injured in accidents can take you to court and sue for additional amounts. In order to sue, damages must exceed a "threshold" amount, which varies from state to state, but it can be as low as $400.

For maximum protection, even

though you may have no-fault, you need "Bodily Injury Liability."

Property Damage Insurance

As the name implies, this part of the policy covers damages caused to other people's property by your car. It usually covers you if you are driving your own car, someone else's car (with their permission), or if someone else is driving your car with your permission.

Comprehensive and Collision Insurance

Comprehensive insurance covers damage to your car that results from anything other than a collision. Collision insurance pays the bills if your car is damaged in an accident with another car or if you damage your car, backing into a telephone pole for example.

Both Comprehensive and Collision are sold on a deductible basis. This means that for any claim that you submit, you must pay the deductible amount yourself, before the insurance takes over.

Reading the Fine Print

Most auto insurance policies follow a regular form, with each part setting down specific information and conditions.

Declarations Includes information about the person taking out the policy, the amount of the policy, the kind of coverage, cost, the date and time coverage begins and the date the policy expires.

Insuring agreements states what the policy will cover.

Exclusions state what the policy will *not* pay for, sometimes referred to as the "fine print." Some typical exclusions are:

· Intentional damage to your own automobile.

· Damages caused when your automobile is being used as a public or delivery vehicle unless the declarations portion of your policy states that it will be used for this purpose.

· Damages caused while your automobile is being driven by employees of a garage, parking lot or auto sales agency.

Conditions give the policy rules and your duties in case of a loss, such as:

· Report a loss to the company as soon as possible.

· Use reasonable care to prevent further damage to your car.

· Cooperate with the company in settling claims.

· File proper proof of loss.

· Forward all documents concerning suits under your policy to your company.

Endorsements cover changes which must be made in your insurance policy. When this happens, changes are typed on a form called an endorsement, signed by a company official, and attached to your policy.

Typical Coverage

Some of the typical coverages afforded by insurance are described below.

Liability covers damages that are the result of negligence on your part. $10,000/$20,000/$5,000 means that if you have an accident that is your fault, you are covered for $10,000 for any one person you injure, $20,000 for more than one person, and $5,000 for property damage. Bodily injury liability is the $10,000/$20,000 portion of the policy. Property damage liability is the $5,000 portion of the 10/20/5.

You may decide that you need more than just the basic amounts of liability insurance, and higher limits are available. Higher liability coverage will protect you from losing any assets you may have, such as savings accounts or property, should you lose a lawsuit and the person you injured is awarded a sum higher than that covered by no fault.

Personal injury protection or PIP (known as "no-fault") pays for reasonable medical expense and loss of income or earning capacity. PIP is usually available with deductibles, and your premiums will be lower if you choose one of these deductibles.

Physical damage coverage includes those coverages available to a car owner for damages to his car, such as comprehensive, collision, fire, lightning, combined additional coverage, theft, towing, and labor costs.

Collision coverage protects you from losses when your own car is damaged in an accident. Carrying collision insurance is usually voluntary. But you will be required to reject it in writing.

Basic property protection is a less expensive form of collision that pays for full damages to your car if an accident is not your fault.

Broad form collision is full collision coverage. It pays for all damages to your car if an accident is not your fault and for damages above a deductible if the accident *is* your fault.

Comprehensive coverage protects your car from losses other than those caused by collision. Common losses such as fire, theft, windstorm, hail, flood, vandalism and glass breakage, malicious mischief, or riot are covered under comprehensive.

Fire, theft, and combined additional coverage is an alternative to comprehensive coverage and usually covers the same as comprehensive except for glass breakage. It applies to "named perils" which are specifically listed in your insurance policy.

Towing and labor costs pays a stated amount for towing and labor costs in an emergency.

Medical payments insurance pays for medical, surgical, or dental expenses. It will pay up to the limits you have chosen regardless of fault.

Uninsured motorist coverage pays if you are hit by an uninsured motorist and your loss of income and medical bills are more than the $5,000 paid under

RATE COMPARISON WORKSHEET

COMPANY NAMES: _____ _____ _____

Type of Coverage	Amount of Coverage	Annual Rates	Annual Rates	Annual Rates
Liability	$_____	$_____	$_____	$_____
Medical payments	_____	_____	_____	_____
Property damage	_____	_____	_____	_____
Uninsured motorist	_____	_____	_____	_____
Collision	_____ (Deductible)	_____	_____	_____
Comprehensive	_____ (Deductible)	_____	_____	_____
Other	_____	_____	_____	_____
	_____	_____	_____	_____
TOTAL		$_____	$_____	$_____

the personal injury protection portion of your no-fault policy.

Your car insurance shopping should include a close scrutiny of all discounts and rate structures available.

Shaving Insurance Costs

Auto insurance rates take a big bite of the family budget, especially when young drivers are involved. Here are a few suggestions on how to save money on your policy.

First, you might consider buying collision and comprehensive coverage with higher deductibles. Collision coverage can be reduced about 17% when the deductible is changed from $100 to $200. Going from $50 to $100 deductible for comprehensive could work out to a 20% savings. Carefully evaluate the need for collision and the amount of deductible, but don't skimp on bodily injury or property damage liability.

Another possibility is to drop collision insurance entirely on an older car, because regardless of how much coverage you carry, the insurance company will pay only up to the car's "book value." For example, if your car requires $1,000 in repairs but its book value is only $500, the insurance company is required only to pay $500.

Investigate special discounts offered by some companies in some states. They may be available for young drivers who have successfully completed driver education courses. There also are special discounts for those with good driving records, for college students attending a school more than 100 miles from home, for women over 30, and for families with two or more cars.

The lowest premium should not be your only goal. You should consider that you want to get the satisfaction you're entitled to when you make a claim and that your claim will neither increase your premium in the future nor be grounds for cancelling your policy.

If you stay with your present company and have an accident, your company will take your previous record into consideration. If you are getting good service from your present company, making a switch may not be to your advantage in the long run.

32

How to Deal with Motor Vehicle Emergencies

At one time or another, most drivers encounter some sort of emergency involving a malfunction of their vehicle or a situation requiring emergency driving techniques. If these emergency situations are not handled properly, the result can be accident, injury or even death.

In an emergency, panic is the real enemy. Emergency plans, like the ones described here, can help prevent panic and possibly save lives. Following are some of the most common emergency situations and how they can be handled, with accident prevention and pedestrian and motorist safety being the prime concerns.

Stopping on the Highway

Many emergency situations require stopping on the highway. Stopping on a highway for any reason is dangerous, so if you *must* stop, observe the following precautions:

· If the highway has paved shoulders, signal your intention to pull off the highway, pull off at near traffic speed, then slow down. If the shoulder is unpaved,

signal a right turn and slow down to a safe speed before pulling off the paved roadway.

· In dusk, darkness, or bad weather, leave your low-beam headlights on and turn on your interior lights and your four-way flasher.

· If you have to stop in a risky location (e.g., over the crest of a hill or on a curve), get everyone out of the car and well away from traffic.

· Place a flare or other warning device just behind the car and another at least 300 feet farther back. Retrieve them before you drive away.

· If you need help, raise the hood and tie a white cloth to the antenna or left door handle.

NOTE: The hazard (emergency) lights on most cars will not operate when the brakes are applied. Once you are off the road (or if stranded on the road), you should shut off the engine, put the car in "park," apply the parking brake, and take your foot off the brake pedal.

Throttle Sticking

You're driving along a street or highway and for some reason you

must slow down. You reduce the foot pressure on the accelerator but the accelerator pedal does not respond and the car does not slow down. Or, for some reason the accelerator pedal is suddenly depressed to the floor, and the car lurches forward, even though you've taken your foot off the accelerator. What can you do?

If this situation occurs on the open highway and you have a lot of distance between you and other traffic, you can first lightly tap the accelerator pedal a few times to see if it will spring back to its normal position. If this fails, try to pull the pedal up with the toe of your shoe, or have a front seat passenger reach down and do it. Don't reach down yourself because that would divert your attention from the road.

If you must slow down or stop rapidly, turn your ignition to Off and apply the brakes. But be sure you turn the key to Off, not Lock. On most cars you can't turn the steering wheel when the key is in the lock position. If you have power steering and power brakes, turning off the ignition will require increased physical effort to steer and brake the car as the car slows down. Don't pump brakes and some power may be retained. As the car slows down, steer it off the roadway, if possible.

NOTE: By Off is meant any key position that will turn off the engine *but not lock* the steering. Ignition systems on vehicles vary. Make sure you know which position will cut the engine without locking the steering.

After you stop the car, look for the source of trouble. The accelerator pedal may be binding on the floor mat or the rug in your car, and you can easily free the pedal by moving the rug or mat. If the problem is not in the passenger compartment, look in your engine compartment and check the accelerator linkage. Some of the parts may be stuck and binding, and a little oil (from the dipstick used to check your oil) may solve the problem.

If you can't locate and remedy the problem (e.g., it may be caused by a broken or missing accelerator return spring or by a broken motor mount), don't drive the car. Get help so the problem can be corrected.

If you think you've corrected the problem, make certain before driving the car. Apply the emergency (or parking) brake firmly, put the gear selector in Park or Neutral, and start the car. Exercise the accelerator pedal a few times to make sure it returns to its normal position after you remove your foot from the pedal. Then put the car in gear and try revving the engine a few times before releasing the parking brake and proceeding on your way.

Brake Failure

Newer cars have a split braking system designed to reduce the possibility of total brake failure (loss of brakes on all four wheels). They have a warning light on the instrument panel which lights up when your brakes are failing due to such problems as loss of pressure in the braking system. When the brake failure light comes on, slow down, pull off the road, and don't proceed until you have the problem corrected or determine that you can drive safely to the nearest service facility. Because of the split braking system, the chances are that you will have some braking power left when the brake failure light comes on, but you may have to apply more force to the brake pedal and will need a greater distance to stop. If half of the braking system remains, proceed cautiously to the nearest service station or garage.

But, if you have a complete brake failure, what can you do to stop? There are several things you can try, but you must act rapidly.

· First, get off the highway onto the shoulder or other clear area, if possible.

· Try pumping your brakes rapidly to bring up your brake pressure.

· If pumping doesn't work, put the gear selector in a lower range (D1 or extra low in cars with automatic transmissions or shift to a lower gear in cars with manual transmissions) to give some braking power from the engine, and apply the emergency or parking brake with increased force. On vehicles with no manual parking or emergency brake release lever, use a modulated pressure on the pedal, as necessary, to prevent total locking of brakes.

· If none of the above work and you are in danger of crashing into someone or something, or of going down an embankment, there is one more thing you can try—but only as a last resort. Turn the ignition off and move the gear selector to low. This may damage your transmission, but it may help you to stop in a real emergency.

If your brakes fail on a hill or mountain grade and the above remedies do not work, look for something to sideswipe—a snow-bank, a guard rail, dirt mounds on the side of the road, or anything that will slow you down.

Loss of Steering

Loss of steering can occur suddenly and without warning. Something in the steering mechanism or its related components may break, fall off, or jam, leaving the driver with no control of the car's direction.

In such situations there is little you can do except to apply the brakes to come to a stop as quickly as possible. While applying the brakes, some warning to other motorists and pedestrians may be possible by turning on your emergency flashers, using your headlights, blowing your horn, and using hand signals. (See previous note on emergency flashers.)

To those accustomed to power steering or power brakes, a malfunction in the system providing the power may lead the driver to think his brakes or steering have failed. If your car is equipped with these power features, and if you suddenly find that steering is more difficult, or the brakes will not respond when you touch the brake pedal, you can still steer and brake. It takes considerably more effort, but it can be done. Proceed with caution until your vehicle is repaired.

Fires
Under the Hood or Under the Dash

Fires are generally caused by a fault in the electrical system or by leakage in the fuel system, which may cause raw gas to leak onto a hot engine. When such a fire develops, pull off the roadway just as soon as it is safe to do so. Turn off the ignition, and get out of the vehicle in a safe manner.

Every vehicle should have a

fire extinguisher for emergencies. If you don't have an extinguisher, fires in the engine compartment can sometimes be put out by throwing dirt on them. You can also try smothering the fire by using a heavy cloth. Be careful when raising the hood to get at such a fire—use a rag to protect your hand when releasing the hood latch and turn your head aside as the hood is released to prevent facial burns from flashing flames.

Caution:

Consider the severity of the fire and the risk involved before trying to put it out. If the fire is a major one or is a fuel-fed fire, stand clear of the vehicle and wait for the fire department.

If you don't have a fire extinguisher and there is a passenger with you, have him flag down a passing motorist (especially a truck) who may have a fire extinguisher.

If the fire occurs while you're driving in a city or town, ask a passerby to summon the fire department.

Finally, don't attempt to drive the car until the cause of the blaze is determined and the problem corrected, including any damage caused by the fire itself.

Fires in the Rear of the Car

Fires in the rear of the car are potentially the most hazardous since most cars have their gas tanks in the rear. The biggest danger here is explosion of the gas tank.

If you notice smoke or flames coming from the rear of your car, immediately pull off the road to a safe spot. Get all passengers out of the car and remain at a great distance from it. Warn motorists and passersby of the danger, and have someone call the nearest fire department.

Loss of Oil Pressure

A sudden loss of oil pressure, if not promptly corrected, can result in extensive damage to your car's engine as well as a highway breakdown. Most cars have an oil pressure light on the instrument panel. This light comes on as soon as you turn on the ignition. Shortly after the engine starts, this light should go out. If the light doesn't go out when the engine is running, or if it comes on while you're driving, you have trouble. You may not have enough oil in your engine, or your oil pump may be bad and not pumping oil through the engine.

If the oil light comes on and stays lit, the first thing to do after pulling off the road is turn off the ignition and check your oil. If the oil level is at or below the "add" mark on the dipstick, add oil before driving the car any farther. A spare can of oil carried in your trunk is ideal for just such an emergency. If this was the problem, the oil light should go out when you restart the car.

Normally it is not advisable to operate the engine with the oil light on, but if there are no abnormal engine noises and if your check shows you have enough oil, in an emergency you may cautiously drive, with the oil light on, a few miles to the nearest service facility but no farther. Get a good mechanic to check the car, because something else is wrong.

Windshield Wiper Failure

Windshield wipers may fail when you need them most. To lower the odds of your wipers failing, periodically check them. Make sure you have good blades and that they are properly adjusted to conform to the shape of the windshield.

If you have the disappearing-type wipers, periodically check the opening to the front of your windshield. Do this more frequently in the fall and winter. Remove leaves, twigs, snow or ice from the wiper recesses and from around the wiper motor shaft and wiper arms. Such obstructions can place a strain on your wiper motor and result in wiper failure.

If you have a failure on the highway (loose wiper, motor ceases to turn wipers, blade flies off), get off the highway (open the window and stick your head out to see, if necessary) and see if you can correct the problem. Some obstruction may be hampering wiper movement, or it may be possible to push a loose wiper arm on the spindle more firmly.

If you find that you can't fix the wipers yourself, wait until the rain or snowstorm has let up, then proceed with caution to the nearest service facility. If it's impractical to wait, you'll have to get help.

Hood Popup

Failure of hood latch (both primary and secondary) or improper closure of hood and subsequent failure of the secondary latch, can result in the hood popping open while you are driving. When the hood opens in this fashion, it will block your view of the road in front of you.

This problem is not as prevalent as it was prior to 1969. A federal safety standard, which became effective in January 1969, requires that a front opening hood, which in any open position partially or completely obstructs a driver's forward view through the windshield, be provided with a second latch position on the hood latch system or with a second hood latch system. Despite this, hood latch failure can occur and you should know what to do if your hood suddenly pops open while driving.

The first thing to remember is don't panic and don't panic stop. If you apply your brakes suddenly and hard, you may be inviting a rear end collision. Instead, ease the car to the right or left (depending on the lane of traffic you're in and the room you have on either side) and use your limited view from the left window for forward steering reference (you may have to stick your head out the window to look). Also, glance in your rear view mirror to see how much room you have between you and the vehicle behind you. Remove your foot from the accelerator and apply your brakes slowly. Turn on your emergency flashers and give a hand signal to indicate that you are going to stop. After you've signaled drivers to the rear, pull off the road (to the left or the right depending on the type highway and lane you're driving in) and try to remedy your problem.

If for some reason you cannot get the car off the highway (e.g., driving on a bridge, or guard rail to the right), do not leave your car. After traffic has cleared behind you, proceed with caution to the nearest point at which you can exit the highway.

Caution:

A frequent cause of hood popup is the failure to close the hood properly after checking the oil, radiator or battery. Get accustomed to the sound made by your hood when it is closed firmly. Thereafter, if you fail to hear the customary "THUNK" when you or an attendant closes your hood, check the hood before proceeding.

Submersion in Water

Emergencies of this nature are very rare and unpredictable, and speedy and proper reactions by the driver and passengers are critical to survival. If your car goes through a bridge railing, over an embankment into a deep body of water, or is surrounded by flooding waters, the following tips may help you survive:

· Cars with their windows and doors closed will float for a few minutes. Don't try to open a door to get out because the water pressure will hold it shut. Windows can be rolled down easily, so open the window (windows in case of passengers) and use the opening as an escape route.

· If you have power windows, open them immediately before they short out. If they do short out and won't open, your only recourse is to try to break them out with a heavy hard object. The tempered glass used in modern cars is hard to break.

· If you can't open or break a window and must open a door, remember that cars with engines in the front will sink nose first. This will push some air to the rear of the car near the roof, helping to equalize the pressure and making it easier to open a door.

Loss of Lug Nuts on the Wheels

If you notice a wobble in a wheel or hear a rattling noise coming from a wheel, especially at low speeds, the problem may be loose lug nuts or a lug nut that has come off the wheel stud and is rattling inside the hub cap or wheel cover. This problem is often caused by improper tightening of the nuts when a tire is replaced, or by faulty lug bolt threads which will not retain the lug nuts tightly.

Take care of such a problem immediately before you lose a wheel. Pull off the road, display warning devices, remove the hub caps or wheel covers, and check the tightness of all the lug nuts. Tighten all the nuts that may be loose. If all the lug nuts are tight, the sound could be caused by a faulty or burned-out bearing. Drive cautiously to the nearest service facility for repairs.

If you've already lost more than one nut from a wheel, borrow one nut (no more) from another wheel so that you can tighten the wheels adequately. Then, at your first opportunity, replace all the missing lug nuts.

If two or more of the wheel studs are too badly stripped to permit retightening of the nuts, leave the car beside the road and get help. Have all faulty lug nuts or lugs replaced as necessary.

Exhaust System Failures

There's nothing you can do about a blown muffler or broken tailpipe when you're out on the highway except to get the problem taken care of as soon as you can.

Sometimes a hanger holding your muffler or tailpipe in position can break due to rust and corrosion. The muffler or tailpipe may separate and drag along the pavement. You may be able to hear the dragging noise. You'll also hear the loud engine noise caused by a damaged muffler. When this happens, pull off the road and examine your tailpipe and muffler. Often a temporary fix can be made by pushing the muffler/tailpipe in place or raising it and holding it in place with a piece of wire or a coat hanger. **CAUTION:** wait for the exhaust system to cool down. You can be severely burned if you grasp a muffler or tailpipe while it is hot. Until the exhaust system is repaired, drive with a side window at least partially open to prevent carbon monoxide accumulation in the passenger compartment.

Flat Tires and Blowouts

A blowout will be sudden. You'll feel it in the wheel and you may hear it. You may feel a part of the car dip. Control of the car may be difficult. A flat tire will also be felt in the handling of the car and steering may become unnatural, but this is more gradual than a blowout.

If you have a flat tire or a blowout on the highway, get a firm grip on the wheel and apply your brakes gently to slow down. Pull off the road to a safe spot where you have enough room to park and get out of the car without danger to yourself and without causing a traffic hazard for other motorists. *Don't slam on the brakes.* Sudden braking may throw your car into a spin or out of control.

If you can't pull off the road where you are, drive to a spot where you can pull off and change the tire safely. Do this even if you have to drive on a flat or blown-out tire—but drive slowly and put on your emergency flashers.

Don't try to change a tire on uneven or hilly ground. It's better to risk ruining a tire or wheel by driving on a flat tire than to risk having a jack slip when you're changing a tire on uneven ground.

Driving on Flooded Roads or in Heavy Rain

Driving under these conditions can result in several major problems, including engine drownout, brake failure, loss of vehicle control, and hydroplaning, which results in loss of steering control (water builds up between the tires and the road, causing the vehicle to "float" on a layer of water).

Every year people drown trying to drive across flooded roads. Before crossing a flooded road, know the depth of the water or don't cross it. If you drive through a deep puddle—especially if your car is moving fast—water can be thrown up into your engine compartment and cause your car to stall out due to moisture on your spark plug wires, coil, or distributor. A car moving in the other direction can cause the same problem if it's moving too fast and throws a lot of water (or road slush in case of a snowstorm) onto your car. If you encounter deep puddles or high water along the highway, drive through slowly.

If your car stalls out, try to coast to the side of the road and wait for the engine to dry out. If you know the parts of your electrical system, the drying out process can be quickened by taking a dry rag and wiping the plugs, wires, and coil, and by drying the inside of the distributor cap.

If your car stalls in the middle of a puddle and you can't move it, and if you're near a stream that is overflowing onto the highway, be alert to the possibility of a flash flood. For your own safety you may have to leave the car where it is and seek shelter until the water recedes.

After moving through water, your brakes may have lost their stopping power. Apply your brakes lightly while driving to dry out the linings and other components.

Driving on Snow and Ice

Driving safely on snow and ice requires caution, alertness, and skill. Following these tips will help.

Start Gently

· Install snow tires before the first snowfall and add chains when the going is difficult. On loosely packed snow, snow tires increase traction 50% and the tire chains quadruple traction.

· Start with an easy foot on the accelerator and slip the clutch in second gear. Don't spin the wheels. Traction is greatest just before the wheels spin.

· If the wheels start to spin, try rocking the car forward and backward. If you dig yourself a pocket, use sand or traction mats to get out. Keep the front wheels pointed straight ahead when possible.

· Once underway, keep going. When approaching a hill, keep far enough behind the vehicle ahead so you will not have to slow down or stop. A little extra speed at the bottom of the hill will give extra momentum to help carry you over the top. If wheels start to spin, release the accelerator slightly.

· During snow and ice conditions, leave yourself an out when you park. On a downhill slope leave ample space in front of your car so you can pull out without backing. Avoid parking on an upgrade unless there is ample room to back out.

Turn Gradually

· Icy surfaces make steering difficult. Slow down before reaching curves. It may be necessary to creep around curves to avoid side skids.

· When entering a curve, turn the steering wheel gradually and no further than necessary. On icy curves, traction may sometimes be improved by using the shoulder.

· If the rear of the car starts skidding, release the accelerator and steer the front of the car in the direction of the skid. As soon as the car starts to straighten out, straighten the front wheels. Don't oversteer.

· On a winter day when the road surface is clear, watch for icy patches in shaded areas, beneath overpasses, and on bridges. These can easily cause a skid if you are going too fast.

Stop Gently

Experience has shown that stopping on glare ice and hard-packed snow can take up to ten times the braking distance on a dry road. However, a car equipped with studded tires on the rear wheels alone can reduce stopping distance under these conditions by 30% at 32° F. In other words, normal stopping

AVERAGE STOPPING DISTANCES

Two factors are involved with stopping the vehicle: 1) Driver reaction time, and 2) Vehicle braking efficiency. Vehicle weight and velocity are also important considerations in total braking. Here are how the above-named factors enter into overall braking:

Miles Per Hour	20	30	40	50	60	70	80	90
Driver Reaction Time (in feet)[1]	21	31	41	51	62	72	82	92
Braking Distance (in feet)[2]	17	39	70	109	156	213	278	360
Total	38	70	111	160	218	285	360	452

[1] Before a driver's mind and body react to the need for vehicle braking, the vehicle travels this far.

[2] Even excellent brakes require time to "take ahold," and this means the vehicle will travel further when the brakes are first applied than it will when maximum braking is achieved.

Weight/Speed Relationship:

• If weight is doubled—stopping power must be doubled.

• If speed is doubled—stopping power must be increased four times.

• If weight and speed are doubled—stopping power must be increased 8 times.

Coefficient of Friction/Temperature/Fade Relationship:

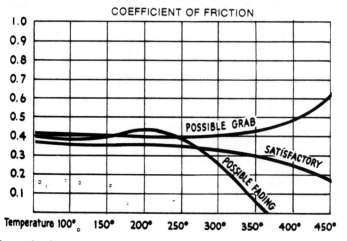

Differently formulated brake lining materials react differently in identical braking/temperature situations, as indicated above. Note that linings with a "cold" coefficient of friction of approximately D.4 behave almost the same up to a temperature of approximately 250°F (121.11°C), thereinafter each lining takes on a different operating characteristic. Only the highest grade linings should be used in every application.

distance of 200 feet on glare ice would be reduced to 140 feet.

• Be especially wary on days when the temperature rises to 32° F. At that temperature, stopping distances on ice are twice as great as at 0° F. Sleet, which is treacherous and slick, also forms at 32° F.

• Follow other cars at greater distances to compensate for longer stopping distances.

• Pump the brakes when stopping. This gives maximum steering control while brakes are off and maximum braking while brakes are on.

• Reduce speed to a minimum when going over the crest of a hill, and starting down. Put the car in second gear or low range and pump the brakes to keep speed down. Avoid use of low gear as this tends to make the rear wheels skid.

• Keep tires properly inflated. To avoid swerving while braking, tire pressures on each axle must be equal.

• Drive defensively. Slow down on slippery roads and at intersections. Increase following distance between you and the car in front of you. Other vehicles may not have the advantage of studded tires and won't stop as quickly as a car that does. Avoid abrupt use of brakes, gas pedal or steering wheel on turns and sharp curves and watch out for wind gusts. Never jam on brakes—pump them to avoid locking wheels which can cause a skid.

If a Skid Starts

• Take foot off gas.

• Keep off the brakes. Braking will only make the skid worse.

• Steer into the skid by turning wheels in the direction in which your rear wheels are sliding.

• When car comes out of the skid, straighten your wheels and pump brakes gently to slow down.

First Aid Supplies for Your Car

Many of the little problems that can disable a car along the roadway can be taken care of by the driver—if he has some simple tool or some little thing like a piece of tape or wire. You don't have to be a good mechanic to fix many of the little things that can go wrong. Your car's fan belt may become loose because the bolt holding the generator/alternator in position became loose—this would be reflected in the warning light on your dash indicating that the alternator/generator is not charging. A wire may become disconnected, a tailpipe hanger may break, and so on. The following is a list of some of the things you can carry in your trunk or glove compartment that you may find useful from time to time:

Necessary Items

Glove Compartment

The name, address, and phone number of someone to call in an emergency

Spare fuses for the electrical system

A good flashlight

An ice scraper for winter driving

A pocket knife

Trunk

Spare tire (with air in it) or temporary spare and inflator

Fire extinguisher

First aid kit

Jack and lug wrench for changing tires

Flares or reflective day/night devices

Very Useful Items

An empty can to carry gasoline (if you run out of gas) and a plastic jug of water (if your engine boils over and you lose your coolant). *NOTE:* **Never carry gasoline in your trunk—this is very dangerous and frequently illegal.**

Pliers—useful for tightening clamps, small nuts that may work loose, and twisting wires

Screwdrivers—several sizes, including a phillips head

Adjustable wrench or small set of open-end wrenches—to tighten nuts and bolts that may have worked loose

Electrical and duct tape—to repair broken or frayed wires and to temporarily stop small leaks in a hose until you can get to a service facility

Wire—to temporarily hold a muffler or tailpipe in place if one of the hangers breaks or falls off.

Rags—to dry up your distributor or wet wires if your motor is drowned out in heavy rain or high water

Battery jumper cables—to get your car started if your battery is weak, especially in the winter. See Section 11—Battery for how to use jumper cables

Piece of sandpaper—useful for cleaning dirty battery terminals when the car won't start

Can of engine oil—nice to have when the oil light comes on and you're far from a service station.

Other Useful Items

Tire pump—to use when one of your tires has developed a slow leak and you'd rather drive to a service station to have it changed than do it yourself; can also be used to dry out a distributor that is wet

Plastic sheet—for use in changing a tire in the rain or if you have to get under the car to check something

For Winter Driving

Tire chains—if you don't have snow tires

A small shovel—to help you get out of ruts and snowbanks

A small bag of sand or traction mats—to throw under the wheels for better traction if you get stuck in ice or snow.

33
55 Ways to Save Fuel

Fuel Economy

There are over 130,000,000 cars and trucks registered in the United States, travelling an average of 10,000 to 12,000 miles per year. In total, private vehicles consume close to 70 billion gallons of gasoline each year, which is about ⅔ of the oil imported by the United States every year.

The federal government's goal is to reduce gasoline consumption 10% by 1985. A variety of methods are either implemented or under serious consideration, all of them affecting your driving and the cars you drive. In addition to "down-sizing," the industry is using and investigating alternative engines, electronic fuel delivery, smaller and lighter cars, and streamlining, to name a few, in an effort to meet the federally mandated Corporate Average Fuel Economy (CAFE) of 27.5 mpg by 1985.

CAFE is not the same as mpg. Miles per gallon refers to the miles that any given vehicle will travel on a single gallon of fuel. The CAFE figure is a measure of average fuel consumption of a

manufacturer's entire fleet. To determine the CAFE number, the manufacturer uses the EPA miles-per-gallon rating for each model in its line. Each manufacturer is assigned an EPA mileage figure based on a weighted (55/45) average of city and highway fuel economy numbers. This number will be somewhat higher than the official EPA rating because the EPA is only publishing city ratings now. Then a fleet, or corporate, average is computed. The mileage of each model contributes to the corporate average

in proportion to the number of units sold of that model.

Consider a hypothetical case. A vehicle getting 20 mpg and a vehicle getting 40 mpg would average 30 mpg, using the mile-per-gallon formula. But the CAFE formula is different. Let's assume that each vehicle is actually driven 100 miles. The 20-mpg-vehicle would use 5 gallons of fuel to travel 100 miles and the 40-mpg-vehicle would use 2.5 gallons of fuel to go the same distance. Add the 5 and 2.5 gallons for a total of 7.5 gallons of fuel

PRESENT AND FUTURE FEDERAL CORPORATE AVERAGE FUEL ECONOMY STANDARDS

Model Year	Average Miles per Gallon	Percent Improvement from 1973
1973 (base year)	13.5	—
Mandated		
1978	18.0	33%
1979	19.0	41%
1980	20.0	48%
1981	22.0	62%
1982	24.0	78%
1983	26.0	92%
1984	27.0	100%
1985	27.5	104%
1990 (projected)	35.0	159%

consumed by the two vehicles to travel a total of 200 miles. Divide the 200 miles by 7.5 gallons and you arrive at a "fleet" average of 26.67 mpg, not 30 mpg, as you would get if you simply averaged the two cars' mpg ratings.

Using the CAFE method, not only are the gas mileage figures of each car taken into account, but also the sales mix of each particular model. It is obvious that it takes more than one high-mileage vehicle to offset the sale of one low-mileage vehicle.

Which brings us to the diesel. The fuel efficiency of the diesel is currently the only way most manufacturers see to meet the increasingly stiffer CAFE requirements set down by the federal government, especially if the individual manufacturer's line is heavily weighted with larger cars. The stakes in the CAFE game are not small, either. The CAFE standard gets much tougher through 1985.

If the manufacturer does not achieve the required CAFE fig-ure, there are provisions that they could be fined $5 per vehicle for every one tenth mile the manufacturer falls short.

Further federal regulation could possibly be avoided if just one gallon of gasoline per week could be saved for every automobile. This would amount to 8% of the government's goal of 10% reduction in fuel consumption.

There are three areas where the motorist can save on fuel—proper maintenance, efficient

TUNE-UP BENEFITS

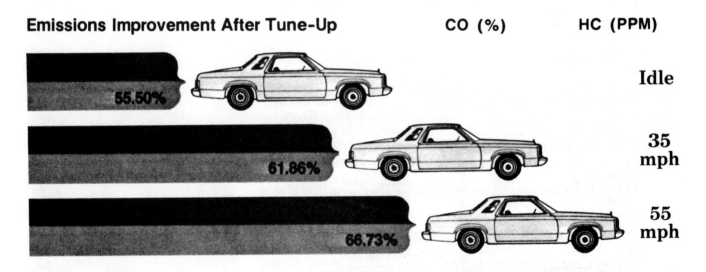

Emissions Improvement After Tune-Up   CO (%)   HC (PPM)

55.50%   Idle

61.86%   35 mph

66.73%   55 mph

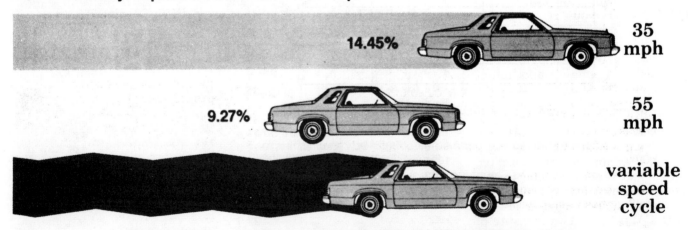

Fuel Economy Improvement After Tune-Up

14.45%   35 mph

9.27%   55 mph

variable speed cycle

Proper maintenance and tune-ups provide better fuel economy and improved emissions.

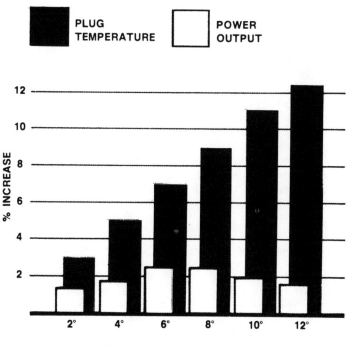

■ PLUG TEMPERATURE   □ POWER OUTPUT

TIMING OVER-ADVANCE (BTDC)

On modern emission controlled engines, it's important that the ignition timing be set to specifications. Advancing the timing past specifications leads to a rapid rise in plug temperature with little appreciable gain in power output.

driving habits, and intelligent purchase of a car.

Care and Maintenance

Proper care and maintenance of your vehicle(s) will save you money and conserve gas. Tune-ups and a regular maintenance program like the one in this book can save up to 20% in fuel.

Tests by the Champion Spark Plug Company showed a tune-up, on cars judged to be in need of one, increased fuel economy by over 11%. The same tests also revealed that of the vehicles checked, ¾ had maintenance deficiencies that adversely affected fuel economy, emissions or performance.

A regular maintenance program should at least include:

1. Replace spark plugs regularly. New plugs alone can increase fuel economy by 3%.

2. Be sure the plugs are the correct type and properly gapped.

3. Be sure the ignition timing is set to specifications.

4. If your vehicle does not have electronic ignition, check the points, rotor, and cap in your distributor as specified.

5. Replace the air filter regularly. A dirty air filter enriches the air/fuel mixture and can increase fuel consumption as much as 10%. Tests show one third of all vehicles have air filters in need of replacement.

6. Replace the fuel filter at least as often as recommended.

7. Be sure the idle speed and carburetor fuel mixture are set to specifications.

8. Check the automatic choke. A sticking or malfunctioning choke wastes gas.

9. Change the oil and filter as recommended. Dirty oil is thick and causes extra friction between the moving parts, cutting efficiency and increasing wear.

10. Replace the PCV valve at regular intervals.

11. Service the cooling system at regular recommended intervals.

12. Be sure the thermostat is operating properly. A thermostat that is stuck open delays engine warm-up, and a cold engine uses twice as much fuel as a warm engine.

13. Be sure the tires are properly inflated. Underinflated tires can cost as much as 1 mpg. Better mileage can be achieved by over inflating the tires (never exceed the maximum inflation pressure on the side of the tire), but the tires will wear faster.

14. Be sure the drive belts (especially the fan belt) are in good condition and properly adjusted.

15. Be sure the battery is fully charged for fast starts.

16. Use the recommended viscosity motor oil to reduce friction.

17. Use the recommended viscosity fluids in the rear axle and transmission.

18. Be sure the wheels are properly balanced.

19. Be sure the front end is correctly aligned. A misaligned front end actually has wheels going in different directions, creating additional drag.

20. Correctly adjust the wheel bearings. Wheel bearings adjusted too tight increase rolling resistance.

21. If possible, install radial tires. Radial tires deliver as much as ½ mpg more than bias belted tires.

22. Install a flex-type fan if you don't have a clutch fan. Flex fans push more air at low speeds when more cooling is needed. At high speeds the blades flatten out for less resistance.

23. Check the radiator cap for a cracked or worn gasket. If the cap doesn't seal properly, the cooling system will not function properly.

24. Check the spark plug wires for bad cracks and burned or broken insulation. Cracked wires decrease fuel efficiency by failing to deliver full voltage to the spark plugs.

Driving Habits

Getting the best gas mileage depends not only on how the vehicle is maintained, but on how it is driven. By planning ahead and driving by intention rather than instinct, gasoline mileage can increase as much as 20%. Here are some fuel-saving driving tips to follow:

25. Avoid extended warm-ups. As soon as your car is driveable, accelerate gently and slowly until the vehicle is fully warmed.

26. Avoid unnecessary idling. One minute of idling uses more gas than it takes to restart the engine. Prolonged idling uses gas at the rate of about ½ gallon per hour.

27. Avoid sudden stops and starts. Hard acceleration uses up to one third more gas. Achieve your desired speed with a steady foot on the accelerator and try coasting to stop.

28. Drive at a steady pace. Plan your route to avoid stop-and-start conditions and heavy traffic. Be aware of the traffic around you and adjust your driving to avoid constant acceleration and deceleration.

29. Many traffic light systems are "timed" for a given speed. Try to pace your speed to make the green lights rather than going faster and stopping for red or yellow lights.

30. Try to anticipate traffic jams and avoid them when possible. Despite stops for traffic signals on other roads, avoiding those expressway traffic jams can lower fuel consumption as much as 50%.

31. Avoid hills. The fuel saved going downhill is less than the fuel used going up.

32. Choose your road surface. The fuel economy penalty for driving on soft or poorly surfaced roads can be 10 to 30%.

33. Avoid excessive braking. The need for braking can often be eliminated by down-shifting or simply taking your foot off the gas.

34. Combine several short trips into a single trip. Short trips (under 5 miles) don't let the engine reach its most efficient operating temperature. By combining numerous short trips, you can save on the total miles driven and take advantage of the vehicle's more efficient warmed-up condition.

35. On long trips, start early in the morning to avoid heavy traffic and to reduce the need for air conditioning in hot weather.

36. If you own more than one car, use the most economical, especially for commuting or stop-and-go driving.

37. Use the transmission properly. If your vehicle has a manual transmission, shift gears as soon as the engine can run smoothly in the next gear. Low gear at 20 mph gives only about two-thirds the mileage as high gear at the same speed. In 2nd gear, it's four-fifths the mileage you'd get in high. With an automatic transmission, lifting your foot slightly off the accelerator will make the transmission shift sooner.

38. When approaching hills, don't wait until the vehicle begins to "lug" before shifting gears. Don't accelerate once you have started up the hill, because speed increase is slight and gas consumption is high. You can minimize the speed loss by gradually increasing speed as you approach a hill.

39. If you can, take advantage of good weather, and avoid bad weather driving. Rain or snow can reduce gas mileage as much as 2 mpg. A strong headwind can mean a 10% loss in fuel economy.

40. Summer temperatures (above 70° F) are better for fuel economy than winter temperatures. There is an approximate 85% difference in economy between 70° F and 20° F.

41. If equipped, use the cruise control. A cruise control can gain 1 to 2 mpg by maintaining a steady, preset speed over any kind of terrain.

42. The best fuel economy is obtained at moderate speeds. More fuel is consumed below 35 mph than at 45 mph, and generally you'll lose 1 mpg for every 5 mpg over 50.

43. Use the A/C at highway speeds. Even though the weight and operation of the air conditioner reduce economy, tests have shown that wind drag at 55 mph with the windows open can consume more fuel that using the air conditioner with the windows shut. The least efficient time to use the air conditioner is at lower speeds.

44. Don't carry unnecessary equipment in the trunk. Weight is the largest single factor in fuel usage, and every extra hundred pounds in cargo costs about 1% in fuel economy.

45. Don't load cargo on a roof rack. This just creates more frontal area, increases air resistance, and lowers your mpg.

46. Turn off the air conditioning and use the vents when the outside temperature is in the comfort range.

47. Learn to drive by instruments. Reading the tachometer (if equipped) can keep the engine in the optimum 1000–3000 rpm operating range. A vacuum gauge indicates the highest engine vacuum (best mileage).

48. Relax while driving. Find a comfortable driving position; fidgeting in the seat leads to constant speed changes and decreases gas mileage.

49. Avoid buying super-wide tread tires. They only create extra rolling resistance. Stick to the manufacturer's recommendations.

50. If you drive a manual transmission car, start in second when going downhill.

51. On a 4-barrel carburetor engine, learn how to move the gas pedal to avoid activating the

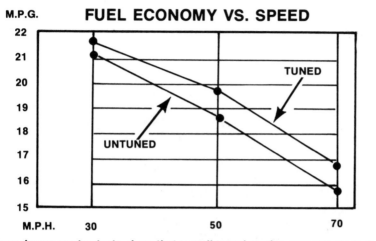

FUEL ECONOMY VS. SPEED

Champions dynamometer tests show that a well-tuned engine can get up to 2 mpg more than an untuned engine. (Courtesy Champion Spark Plug Co.)

secondary circuit, except in an emergency.

52. Avoid using large mud-flaps or oversize rear view mirrors unless necessary. They only create extra drag (air resistance).

53. Don't drive fast until the engine has fully warmed to normal operating temperature.

54. In winter, clean accumulated snow and ice from the trunk, hood, and roof before driving. Carrying heavy, wet snow uses fuel.

55. Keep accurate records. Over a period of time you can check your fuel economy; a sudden drop in miles per gallon may mean it's time for a tune-up or other maintenance.

Buying a Car

Fuel consumption is the biggest contributor to operating cost, and it is a primary consideration when buying a car. Some things to remember about options and fuel economy are:

How you will use the car— Your driving needs may be adequately served by a compact instead of a full-size car.

Engines—Smaller engines generally require less gas than larger V8's, but an underpowered car will use more gas than one with sufficient power. Likewise, on a larger engine, a 4-barrel may provide better fuel distribution than a 2-barrel carburetor.

Transmissions—If used properly, a manual transmission can provide up to 8% better mileage than an automatic, in city driving. At highway speeds the difference is negligible.

Axle ratios—Numerically higher axle ratios give more power, but numerically lower ratios save gas at highway speeds because the engine doesn't have to rotate as many times.

Weight—The lighter the car, the less gas it will use. On an average car, every extra hundred pounds will cost about 1% in fuel economy.

Tires—Radial tires can deliver as much as ½ mpg over bias or bias-belted tires.

Cruise control—If you do a lot of highway driving, a cruise control can gain 1 to 2 mpg.

Fuel Injection—Fuel injection is generally more efficient than a carburetor because it meters fuel more precisely.

Electronic ignition—Electronic ignition provides better combustion and less spark plug fouling because there are no parts to wear out, which translates to better fuel economy.

34
Chilton Tips

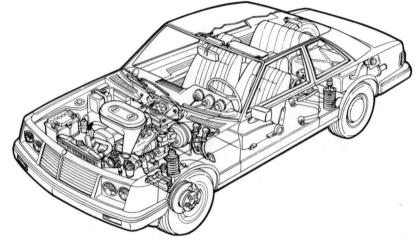

Most vehicle manufacturers issue technical service bulletins on a regular basis. They usually include previously overlooked information that were discovered as a result of field service.

Following are some of the more interesting and basic tips from manufacturers, and some from our own experience.

AMC ignition disruption—Occasional disruption of the ignition may occur on all 1977 AMC cars if the distributor sensor wires for the electronic ignition are not routed as shown.

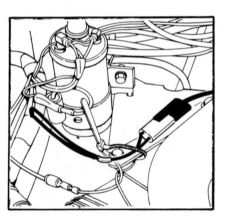

V-8 Engine

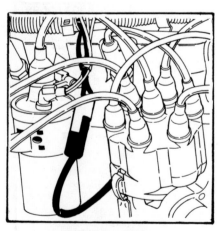

6-Cylinder Engine

Colt/Arrow radiator drain plug—The radiator drain plug on 1600 cc models was designed to be loosened only—not removed. Removing it completely can damage the threads in the radiator.

Mazda oil dipstick—The difference between the L (low) and F (Full) mark on the Mazda rotary engine dipstick is actually 2½ qts., not the usual 1 qt. It is important to keep the level near F, since at L, the engine is only half full.

Hard-to-reach spark plugs—Spark plug installation in hard-to-reach places can be eased

somewhat by slipping a length of vacuum hose over the end of the plug. This will provide something to start the plug.

Maverick/Comet engine cooling—To improve cooling on 1974 Maverick/Comet with V8 and/or air conditioning, Ford recommends repositioning the front license plate from the center to the left side.

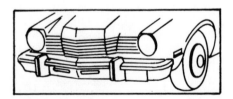

VW/Audi crankcase lubricant—Volkswagen and Audi warn that 10W-50 motor oil is not to be used in any engine.

Dodge radio static—Radio static or intermittent radio operation on 1974 Dodges could be due to a loose or missing rear radio support bracket. The bracket makes a ground for the radio and must be securely attached to the radio and instrument panel.

Storing oil—The plastic top from a small tub of margarine makes a good cover for partly used cans of oil.

Inadequate grounding—Chevrolets have a wire connecting the negative battery terminal to the fender. A poor or loose ground wire can cause dim head-

lights or intermittent operation of other accessories.

Capri battery tray modification—To replace the European-style battery in 1973–74 Capris with an American style, modify the battery tray as shown. You need 2 hold-down brackets (Part No. DORY-10718-A) and 2 marine battery terminals (Part No. WXC-5433).

Pontiac radiator hose interference—The upper radiator hose on a 1974 Ventura 6-cylinder may contact the air pump pulley. If so, cutting ½″ off each end of the hose will shorten it enough.

Wind whistle—If you hear a whistle from your 1973 Ford, filling the deep holes in the front parking lamp lenses with sealer may cure the problem.

Chevelle/Monte Carlo vibration—A vibration or noise from the rear of a 1973 Chevelle or Monte Carlo can be cured by slitting a 5″ piece of ¾″ hose lengthwise and wrapping it around the stabilizer bar as shown. Use a hose clamp to hold it in place.

Radiator hose wear—The up-

per radiator hose on 1975 Imperial, Chrysler, Gran Fury and Monaco can be worn by the air conditioning discharge line rubbing against it. Chrysler provides foam insulation to attach to the air conditioning line. A replacement hose (Part No. 3870146) can also be installed to eliminate the problem.

Intermittent fuel gauge—The fuel gauge on some 1975 Fords may operate erratically due to a faulty sending unit ground connection. Replace the ground wire screw in the trunk as shown with a #10 sheet metal screw and toothed washer. Plug the old hole with sealant.

Loose ignition connectors—If your Ford (conventional ignition) is having problems with erratic

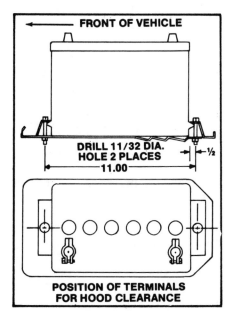

FRONT OF VEHICLE

DRILL 11/32 DIA. HOLE 2 PLACES

11.00

POSITION OF TERMINALS FOR HOOD CLEARANCE

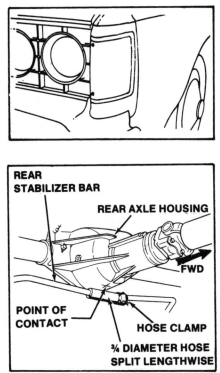

REAR STABILIZER BAR

REAR AXLE HOUSING

FWD

POINT OF CONTACT

HOSE CLAMP

¾ DIAMETER HOSE SPLIT LENGTHWISE

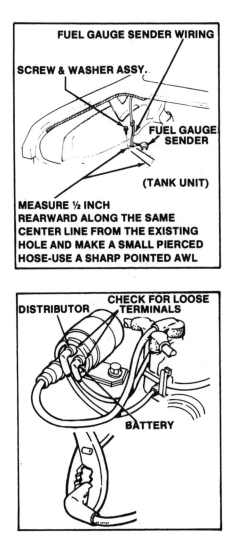

FUEL GAUGE SENDER WIRING

SCREW & WASHER ASSY.

FUEL GAUGE SENDER

(TANK UNIT)

MEASURE ½ INCH REARWARD ALONG THE SAME CENTER LINE FROM THE EXISTING HOLE AND MAKE A SMALL PIERCED HOSE-USE A SHARP POINTED AWL

DISTRIBUTOR

CHECK FOR LOOSE TERMINALS

BATTERY

ignition system operation, check the ignition coil post connectors. If they are spread too far, causing poor contact, carefully squeeze the connectors together (not too far) with pliers and reinstall the connectors.

Chevette wheels—Two-piece Chevette wheel covers are optional and must be carefully removed. The covers appear to be one piece, but they must be removed by prying against the outer edge of the wheel cover, not the trim ring. The cover holds the trim ring, which will fall free when the cover is removed.

Ford fuses—1975 Torino and Elite models with air conditioning originally had a 10-amp fuse to protect the AC compressor, turn signals and back-up lights. If this fuse blows, it should be replaced with a 20-amp fuse as specified on the fuse panel.

Monza spark plug replacement—Chevrolet says that the easiest way to replace the No. 3 spark plug on a 1975 Monza with a V-8 engine is to loosen the engine mount bolts about 4 turns and raise the engine about ½ in. Loosen the plug with a spark plug socket, 3″ extension and flex head ratchet. Remove the ratchet and turn the plug out with the extension and socket. Reverse the procedure to install the plug. Lower the engine and tighten the engine mounts.

Pontiac radiator hose interference—The upper radiator hose on a 1974 6-cylinder Ventura may hit the air pump pulley. If so, cutting ½″ from each end of the hose will give enough clearance.

Ford/Mercury timing marks—On 1975 and later Ford and Mercury air-conditioned models with 351M and 400 V-8 engines, the timing marks are viewed over the edge of the power steering bracket between the water pump and front cover. On all other 351M and 400 V-8 engines, the timing marks can be seen from the right-hand side of the engine.

GM timing marks—The harmonic balancers on 1977 and later 350 V-8s and 231 V-6s have two timing marks. The smaller mark is ¹⁄₁₆″ wide and is located on the harmonic balancer boss. It is the one used for setting timing with a hand-held light. The other mark is ⅛″ wide and only to be used with magnetic timing equipment used by dealers.

GM 6-cylinder crossfiring—On 250 and 292 6-cylinder engines used in Chevrolet and GMC trucks and Chevrolet and Pontiac cars, the coil lead must be routed differently. On 250 engines, route the coil lead **over** the No. 4, 5 and 6 plug wires. On the 292 engine, route the coil lead **under** No. 4, 5 and 6 plug wires. This will prevent crossfiring between plug wires.

Capri erratic engine operation—Erratic engine operation on 1974 Capris may be due to excessive vertical movement of the distributor rotor. The situation can be cured by installing a different rotor with a longer spring (Part No. D4RY-12200-A).

Temporarily plugging vacuum lines—Some manufacturers call for the vacuum line to be disconnected and plugged when timing the engine or adjusting the idle. A golf tee makes a good temporary plug for vacuum lines.

Vega plug fouling—1975 Vegas with a 2-barrel carburetor that start hard in cold weather because of fouled plugs, can be helped by changing the plug gap from .060″ to .035″. For general driving Chevrolet recommends R43TS plugs or the equivalent.

Ford V-6 ignition misfire—Some cases of ignition miss on Bobcat, Pinto and Mustang II V-6 engines have been traced to electrical interference from the battery ground cable. If the guide bracket behind the distributor is bent upward (toward the distributor), ignition misfire could result. The bracket should be bent down toward the bell housing.

Emergency hose repair—Broken radiator hoses and many

other problems can be temporarily fixed with duct tape (sometimes called racer's tape). The silver-colored tape resists heat and moisture and will effect a temporary repair of many materials.

Chrysler Corp. brake drums—Some Chrysler Corp. brake drums are being manufactured with a new process. The finished friction surface may appear slightly grooved but feel smooth to the touch. This type of finish is completely normal and does not affect brake performance or lining life in any way.

Dodge Colt oil pressure light—The oil pressure light may flicker on and off or fail to go out on Dodge Colts. This can be caused by air trapped in the oil pressure sending unit. The air can be bled out using the following procedure. Start the engine, and remove the wire from the oil pressure sending unit, located on the right side of the engine block. Then loosen the screw on the electrical connection of the oil pressure switch momentarily. Retighten the screw after bleeding out the air.

If the oil pressure light fails to go out after bleeding, check the engine oil pressure with a master gage before replacing the oil pressure switch.

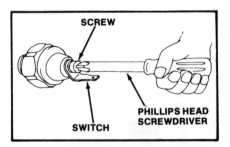

Chevrolet inverted air cleaner lid—Some owners of 1973–75 Chevrolets are inverting the air cleaner lid in the mistaken belief that it will improve fuel economy and performance. In fact, it can result in loss of power, poor driveability in cold weather, excessive noise.

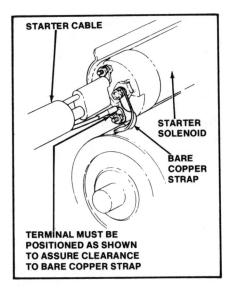

TERMINAL MUST BE POSITIONED AS SHOWN TO ASSURE CLEARANCE TO BARE COPPER STRAP

Lincoln-Mercury starter wiring—If the engine starts but quits when the key is released on some 1974 Lincoln-Mercury cars, the problem may be a mispositioned wiring terminal at the starter motor solenoid. The terminal must be properly positioned on the solenoid "R" terminal to avoid contact with the uninsulated copper strap.

Dodge delayed hot starting—Delayed hot starting on 1972–74 Dodge cars equipped with the charcoal canister can be caused by a dip in the vapor hose from the carburetor to the canister.

Solid fuel may collect in the hose dip.

The vapor canister hoses should be directed between the air conditioning hoses and the heater hoses. The vapor canister hose harness must be free of dips and take a downhill path from the carburetor to the vapor canister.

Chevrolet knock—Some 1974 Chevrolets may have a metallic knocking noise when the outside temperature is below freezing. The noise may come from the fuel pump return hose.

With the engine running, pinch shut the fuel return hose. If the noise stops, you can cure the problem permanently by installing a T, an accumulator and two clamps in the fuel feed line. These pieces carry part numbers 338109, 1523319, and 1470029.

To install these parts, cut the fuel feed hose and use the new hose clamps. Temporarily install them away from the cut ends.

Then preassemble the T and accumulator.

Install them into the hose end completely with the accumulator pointing upwards. Move the clamps into position at the T and tighten securely. Start the engine and check for leaks.

Mustang/Capri starter cable—Some Mustangs and Capris built before January 2, 1979 have an improperly positioned starter cable. If the cable is too tight at the starter end, the cable can be repositioned in the support brackets. Pry open the support brackets and pull the cable through until there is about two inches of slack between the support bracket and the starter. Recrimp both support brackets.

Cadillac Seville battery drain—A constantly drained battery on a Cadillac Seville with a diesel engine can be caused by a loose purple wire leading to the glow-plug controller. If it is loose or disconnected, the glow plugs may stay on and drain the battery.

Grand Prix thumping noise—A thumping noise from the rear of a 1978 Grand Prix may be caused by the parking brake cable hitting the floor pan whenever the car goes over a bump. To eliminate the noise, pull the cable

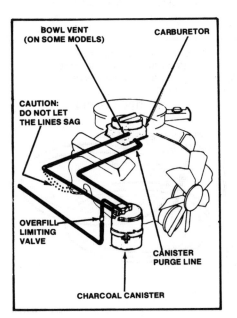

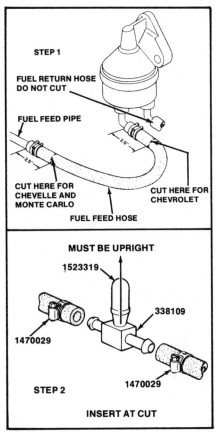

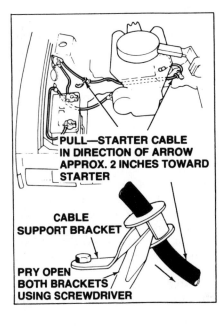

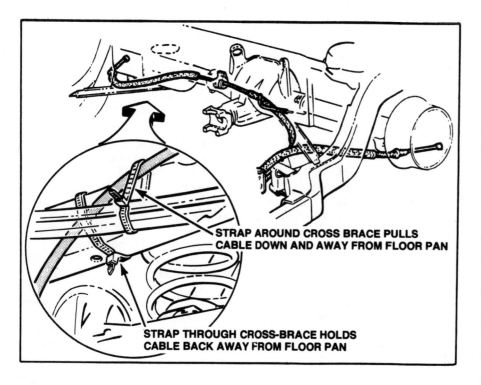

STRAP AROUND CROSS BRACE PULLS CABLE DOWN AND AWAY FROM FLOOR PAN

STRAP THROUGH CROSS-BRACE HOLDS CABLE BACK AWAY FROM FLOOR PAN

away from the floor pan and fasten it to the crossmember.

Omega tire chains—Oldsmobile Omegas equipped with the LS package tires and wheels (FR78 x 15) can use only the type of tire chain designated SAE class "S". Use of any other type chain will cause sheet metal damage.

Volvo power steering fluid—Although DEXRON® automatic transmission fluid is recommended for use in the power steering pump of 240 and 260 models, type F fluid may be used as an alternative. However, type F fluid is not recommended for 140 and 160 power steering pumps.

Omni/Horizon towing—If an Omni or Horizon with automatic transmission is to be towed by the rear, the front wheels must be placed on dollies, or the automatic transaxle will be damaged. The car can be towed a short distance from a hazardous location without the aid of a dolly, but the dolly should be used as soon as possible.

Oldsmobile Toronado discharged battery—A discharged battery on these 1979 vehicles could be caused by the use of the wrong generator warning light bulb. The correct bulb can be identified by the number 168 or a three-candlepower rating. A dim warning light bulb while the engine is running indicates that the wrong bulb is installed.

GM 301 CID V-8 engines—Some GM 301 V-8 engines may develop a knocking noise which disappears a few seconds after starting the engine when cold. This is caused by the use of a filter with no oil drain-back check valve. The original equipment AC PF-46 oil filter has no drain-back valve to prevent oil from draining back into the engine after shutting the engine off. An AC PF-44 filter (which has the necessary valve) or the equivalent should be used (the PF-46 has been discontinued). When the PF-44 or equivalent filter is used, the engine requires only five (instead of six) quarts of oil. The other alternative is to install a check-valve equipped AC PF-24 or equivalent filter, provided that you use the thicker filter gasket from the original PF-46 filter. If you don't use the thicker filter gasket, it won't seal at all.

Chevrolet truck whistle—Some 1975–78 Chevrolet four-wheel drive trucks may exhibit a whistling sound at cruising speeds. This is caused by the position of the slot in the tie-rod sleeve, which causes air turbulence, producing the whistle. Do not attempt to reposition the slot; fill the slot with a non-hardening sealer.

Dodge/Plymouth trucks—1979 one-ton trucks may have an EGR maintenance reminder light that comes on intermittently or con-

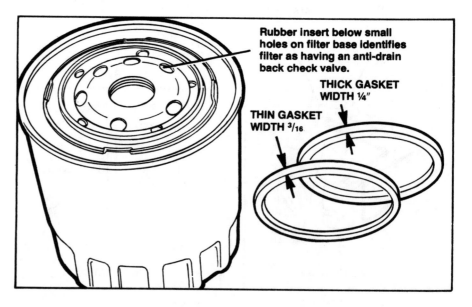

Rubber insert below small holes on filter base identifies filter as having an anti-drain back check valve.

THICK GASKET WIDTH ¼"

THIN GASKET WIDTH 3/16

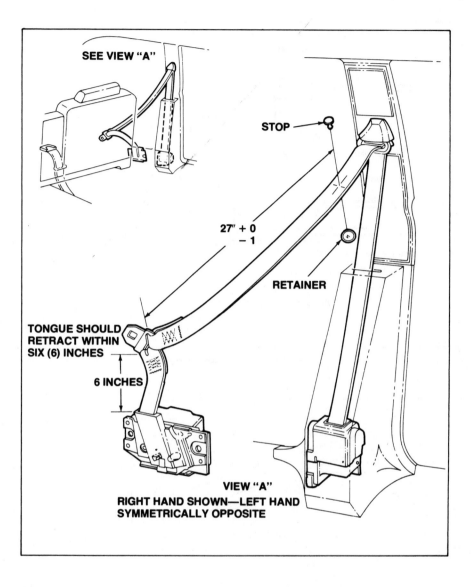

SEE VIEW "A"

STOP

27" + 0 − 1

RETAINER

TONGUE SHOULD RETRACT WITHIN SIX (6) INCHES

6 INCHES

VIEW "A"
RIGHT HAND SHOWN—LEFT HAND SYMMETRICALLY OPPOSITE

tinually before the prescribed mileage is attained. This is due to reversed wires in the connector that allow premature operation of the light if accidental grounding through the switch case occurs. The condition can be corrected by connecting the wires to their proper cavities.

Oldsmobile diesel engine noise—A rumbling noise may be heard in some 88 and 98 models equipped with diesel engines, most noticeable during acceleration. The noise is probably caused by the air cleaner resonator contacting the brace between the fender and dash. Loosen each

end of the the brace and move it inward so that there is at least ¾ in. clearance between the brace and resonator. Tighten the bolts.

Lincoln/Mercury lap-belt retractors—If the lap-belt retractors on the front seatbelt of early 1978–79 Versailles models do not retract the tongue to within six inches of the retractor, the free-wheeling solenoid switch stays "closed" allowing a constant current sufficient to discharge the battery. This usually occurs when the shoulder-harness retractor reacts faster than the lap-belt retractor. A stop and retainer kit (KIT D6FZ-6260286-A)

is available to correct this condition. The stop and retainer should be installed 27 inches from the buckle.

1979 Mustang/Capri radio interference—Interference in these vehicles equipped with monaural AM/FM radios is caused by a missing windshield wiper noise-suppression assembly. Interference is possible when the wipers are operating and the radio is in the FM mode. Interference can be reduced by installing an interference suppressor (Part No. D8BZ-18A832-A). Disconnect the existing 14290 wire from the wiper motor. Connect the sup-

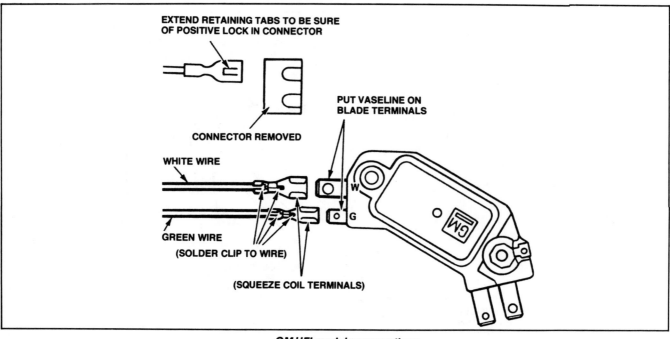

GM HEI module connections

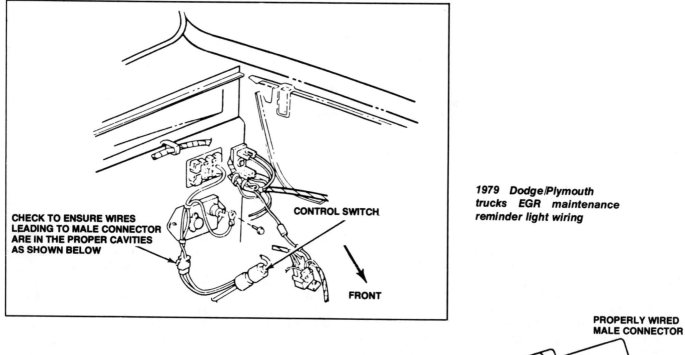

1979 Dodge/Plymouth trucks EGR maintenance reminder light wiring

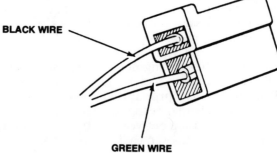

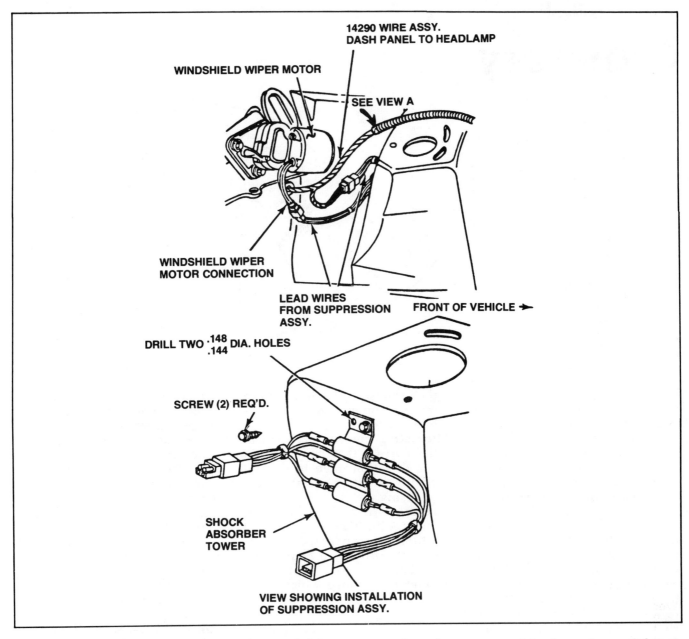

14290 WIRE ASSY.
DASH PANEL TO HEADLAMP

WINDSHIELD WIPER MOTOR

SEE VIEW A

WINDSHIELD WIPER
MOTOR CONNECTION

LEAD WIRES
FROM SUPPRESSION
ASSY.

FRONT OF VEHICLE ➡

DRILL TWO .148 DIA. HOLES
         .144

SCREW (2) REQ'D.

SHOCK
ABSORBER
TOWER

VIEW SHOWING INSTALLATION
OF SUPPRESSION ASSY.

pressor between the wiper motor and the 14290 wire. Install the suppressor on the rear face of the left shock absorber tower with sheet metal screws (the sheet metal screws must be capable of conducting electricity).

GM HEI modules—In some cases, problems with GM High-Energy Ignition (HEI) modules have been traced to faulty connections. Before any component of the HEI system (especially the module) is assumed to be faulty, check the connections as shown.

Remove the module and clean the terminals with emery cloth to remove any oxide deposits.

Remove the connector body from the pick-up coil leads and inspect the connections. If the connections are loose, they should be recrimped. Squeeze the side rails of the terminals with needle-nosed pliers to as-sure a tight fit on the module terminals.

Apply a thin film of petroleum jelly on the module terminals to prevent future oxidation.

Apply a thin film of silicone heat transfer grease (AC D-1290 or the equivalent) to the base of the module.

Reinstall the module and re-connect the leads making sure there is good metal-to-metal contact.

35
Glossary

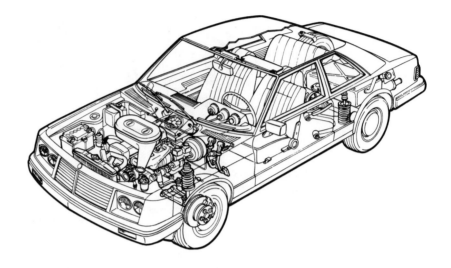

Understanding your mechanic is as important as understanding your car. Just about everyone drives a car, but many drivers have difficulty understanding automotive terminology. Talking the language of cars makes it easier to effectively communicate with professional mechanics. It isn't necessary (or recommended) that you diagnose the problem for him, but it will save **him** time, and **you** money, if you can accurately describe what is happening. It will also help you to know why your car does what it is doing, and what repairs were made.

Accelerator pump—A small pump located in the carburetor that feeds fuel into the air/fuel mixture during acceleration.

Advance—Setting the ignition timing so that spark occurs earlier before the piston reaches top dead center (TDC).

Air bag—Device on the inside of the car designed to inflate on impact of crash, protecting the occupants of the car.

Air pump—An emission control device that supplies fresh air to the exhaust manifold to aid in more completely burning exhaust gases.

Alternating current (AC)—Electric current that flows first in one direction, then in the opposite direction, continually reversing flow.

Alternator—A device which produces AC (alternating current) which is converted to DC (direct current) to charge the car battery.

Ammeter—A gauge which measures current flow (amps). Am-

Automotive alternator.

meters show whether the battery is charging or discharging.

Ampere (amp)—Unit to measure the rate of flow of electrical current.

Amp/hr. rating (battery)—Measurement of the ability of a battery to deliver a stated amount of current for a stated period of time. The higher the amp/hr. rating, the better the battery.

Antifreeze—A substance (ethylene glycol) added to the coolant to prevent freezing in cold weather.

Anti-roll bar—See stabilizer bar.

ATDC—After Top Dead Center. Spark occurs after the piston has reached top dead center and is on the downward stroke.

ATF—Automatic transmission fluid.

Axle capacity—The maximum load-carrying capacity of the axle itself, as specified by the manufacturer. This is usually a higher number than the GAWR.

Axle ratio—This is a number (3.07:1, 4.56:1, for example) expressing the ratio between driveshaft revolutions and wheel revolutions. A low numerical ratio allows the engine to work easier because it doesn't have to turn as fast. A high numerical ratio means that the engine has to turn more rpm's to move the wheels through the same number of turns.

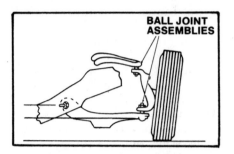

Front suspension ball joints.

Ball joint—A ball and matching socket connecting suspension components (steering knuckle to lower control arms). It permits rotating movement in any direction between the components that are joined.

Bead—The portion of a tire that holds it on the rim.

Belted tire—Tire construction similar to bias-ply tires, but using two or more layers of reinforced belts between body plies and the tread.

Bezel—Piece of metal surrounding radio, headlights, gauges or similar components; sometimes used to hold the glass face of a gauge in the dash.

Bias-ply tire—Tire construction, using body ply reinforcing cords which run at alternating angles to the center line of the tread.

Block—The basic engine casting containing the cylinders.

Book value—The average value of a car, widely used to determine trade-in and resale value.

Bore—Diameter of a cylinder.

Brake caliper—The housing that fits over the brake disc. The caliper holds the brake pads, which are pressed against the discs by the caliper pistons when the brake pedal is depressed.

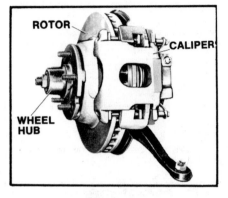

Disc brake.

Brake horsepower—Usable horsepower of an engine measured at the crankshaft.

Brake fade—Loss of braking power, usually caused by excessive heat after repeated brake applications.

Brake pad—The friction pad on a disc brake system.

Brake proportioning valve—A valve on the master cylinder which restricts hydraulic brake pressure to the rear wheels to a specified amount, preventing wheel lock-up.

Brake shoe—The friction lining on a drum brake system.

Breaker points—A set of points inside the distributor, operated by a cam, which make and break the ignition circuit.

BTDC—Before Top Dead Center. Spark occurs on the compression stroke, before the piston reaches top dead center.

Bushing—A plain, replaceable bearing of soft metal or rubber.

California engine—An engine certified by the EPA for use in California only; conforms to more stringent emission regulations than Federal engine.

Camber—One of the factors of wheel alignment. Viewed from the front of the car, it is the inward or outward tilt of the wheel. The top of the tire will lean outward (positive camber) or inward (negative camber).

Camshaft—A shaft that rotates at half the engine speed, used

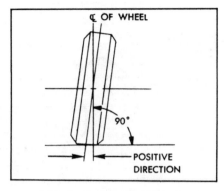

Camber angle (front view).

to operate the intake and exhaust valves. In most engines, the cam bears upon a hydraulic lifter which opens the valve.

Cancer—Rust on a car body.

Carbon monoxide (CO)—One of the by-products of the combustion process. Carbon monoxide is odorless and deadly.

Caster—The forward or rearward tilt of an imaginary line drawn through the upper ball joint and the center of the wheel. Viewed from the sides, positive caster (forward tilt) lends directional stability, while negative caster (rearward tilt) produces instability.

Catalytic converter—A mufflerlike device installed in the exhaust system to help control automotive emissions, specifically NOx (nitrous oxide).

Cetane rating—A measure of the ignition value of diesel fuel. The higher the cetane rating, the better the fuel. Diesel fuel cetane rating is roughly comparable to gasoline octane rating.

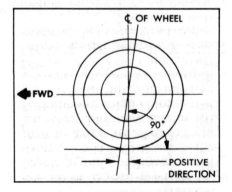

Caster angle (side view).

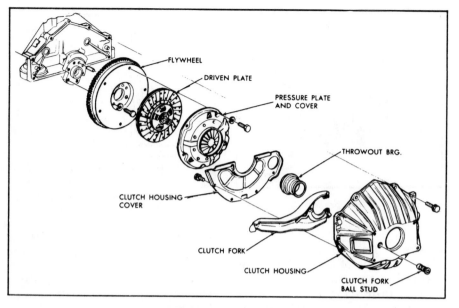

Exploded view of typical clutch.

Choke—The plate near the top of the carburetor that is closed to restrict the amount of air taken into the carburetor, making the fuel mixture richer.

Clutch—Part of the power train used to connect/disconnect power to the rear wheels.

Coil—Part of the ignition system that boosts the relatively low voltage supplied by the car's electrical system to the high voltage required to fire the spark plugs.

Combustion chamber—The part of the engine in the cylinder head where combustion takes place.

Compression check—A test involving removing each spark plug and inserting a gauge. When the engine is cranked, the gauge will record a pressure reading in the individual cylinder. General operating condition can be determined from a compression check.

Compression ratio—The ratio of the volume between the piston and cylinder head when the piston is at the bottom of its stroke (bottom dead center) and when the piston is at the top of its stroke (top dead center).

Condenser—A small device in the ignition system which absorbs the momentary surge of current produced when the breaker points open. It protects the points from burning.

Connecting rod—The connecting link between the crankshaft and piston.

Control arm—The upper or lower A-shaped suspension components which are mounted on the frame and support the ball joints and steering knuckles.

Conventional ignition—Ignition system which uses breaker points.

Coolant—Mixture of water and anti-freeze circulated through the engine to carry off heat produced by the engine.

Crankcase—The part of the engine that houses the crankshaft.

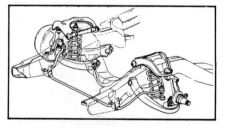

Typical coil spring front suspension.

Crankshaft—Engine component (connected to pistons by connecting rods) which converts the reciprocating (up and down) motion of pistons to rotary motion used to turn the driveshaft.

Curb weight—The weight of a vehicle without passengers or payload, but including all fluids (oil, gas, coolant, etc.) and other equipment specified as standard.

Detergent—An additive in engine oil to improve its operating characteristics.

Detonation—Instantaneous combustion of fuel, resulting in excessive heat and pressure which can damage engine components. Fuel should burn in the cylinders in a controlled manner, rather than exploding immediately.

Dexron®—A brand of automatic transmission fluid.

Dieseling—The engine continues to run after the car is shut off; caused by fuel continuing to be burned in the combustion chamber.

Differential—The part of the rear suspension that turns both axle shafts at the same time, but allows them to turn at different speeds when the car turns a corner.

Diode—A part of the alternator which converts alternating current to direct current.

Direct current (DC)—Electrical current that flows in one direction only.

Displacement—The total volume of air that is displaced by all pistons as the engine turns

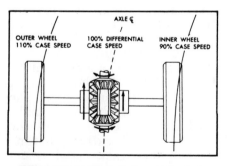

Differential action during cornering.

through one complete revolution.

Distributor—Device containing the breaker points which distributes high voltage to the proper spark plug at the proper time.

DOHC—Double overhead camshaft engine. Two overhead camshafts are used—one operates exhaust valves, and the other operates intake valves.

Drive train—The components that transmit the flow of power from the engine to the wheels. The components include the clutch, transmission, driveshafts (or axle shafts in front wheel drive), U-joints and differential.

Dry charged battery—Battery to which electrolyte is added when the battery is placed in service.

Dwell angle—The number of degrees on the breaker cam that the points are closed.

Electrode—Conductor (positive or negative) of electric current.

Electrolyte—A solution of water and sulphuric acid used to activate the battery. Electrolyte is extremely corrosive.

Electronic ignition—Type of ignition system which uses no breaker points.

Enamel—Type of paint that dries to a smooth, glossy finish.

EP Lubricant—EP (extreme pressure) lubricants are specially formulated for use with gears involving heavy loads (transmissions, differentials, etc.).

Ethyl—A substance added to gasoline to improve its resistance to knock, by slowing down the rate of combustion.

Ethylene glycol—The base substance of antifreeze.

Fast Idle—The speed of the engine when the choke is on. Fast idle speeds engine warmup.

Federal engine—An engine certified by the EPA for use in any of the 49 states (except California).

Filament—The part of a bulb that glows; the filament creates high resistance to current flow and actually glows from the resulting heat.

Final drive—See axle ratio.

Firing order—The numerical sequence in which an engine's cylinders fire.

Flame front—The term used to describe certain aspects of the fuel explosion in the cylinders. The flame front should move in a controlled pattern across the cylinder, rather than simply exploding immediately.

Flat engine—Engine design in which the pistons are horizontally opposed. Porsche and VW are common examples of flat engines.

Flat spot—A point during acceleration when the engine seems to lose power for an instant.

Flooding—A condition created when too much fuel reaches the cylinders; Starting will be difficult or impossible.

Flywheel—A heavy disc of metal attached to the rear of the crankshaft. It smooths the firing impulses of the engine and keeps the crankshaft turning during periods when no firing takes place. The starter also engages the flywheel to start the engine.

Foot-pound—A measurement of torque (turning force).

Freeze plug—A plug in the engine block which will be pushed out if the coolant freezes. Sometimes called expansion plugs, they protect the block from cracking should the coolant freeze.

Frontal area—The total frontal area of a vehicle exposed to air flow.

Front end alignment—A service to set caster, camber and toe-in to the correct specifications. This will ensure that the car steers and handles properly and that the tires wear properly.

Fuel injection—A system replacing the carburetor that sprays fuel into the cylinder through nozzles. The amount of fuel can be more precisely controlled with fuel injection.

Full floating axle—An axle in which the axle housing extends through the wheel giving bearing support on the outside of the housing. The front axle of a four-wheel drive vehicle is usually a full floating axle, as are the rear axles of many larger (¾ ton and over) pick-ups and vans.

Full-time four-wheel drive—A four-wheel drive system that continuously delivers power to all four wheels. A differential between the front and rear driveshafts permits variations in axle speeds to control gear wind-up without damage.

Fuse—A device containing a piece of metal rated to pass a given number of amps. If more current than the rated amperage passes through the fuse, the metal will melt and interrupt the circuit.

Fusible link—A piece of wire in a wiring harness that performs the same job as a fuse. If overloaded, the fusible link will melt and interrupt the circuit.

FWD—Front wheel drive.

GAWR—(Gross axle weight rating) the total maximum weight an axle is designed to carry.

GCW—(Cross combined weight) total combined weight of a tow vehicle and trailer.

Gearbox—Transmission.

Gear ratio—A ratio expressing the number of turns a smaller gear will make to turn a larger gear through one revolution. The ratio is found by dividing the number of teeth on the smaller gear into the number of teeth on the larger gear.

Gel coat—A thin coat of plastic resin covering fiberglass body panels.

Generator—A device which produces direct current (DC) necessary to charge the battery.

GVW—(Gross vehicle weight) total weight of fully equipped and loaded vehicle including passengers, equipment, fuel, oil, etc.

GVWR—(Gross vehicle weight rating) total maximum weight a vehicle is designed to carry including the weight of the vehicle, passengers, equipment, gas, oil, etc.

Header tank—An expansion tank for the radiator coolant. It can be located remotely or built into the radiator.

Heat range—A term used to describe the ability of a spark plug to carry away heat. Plugs with longer nosed insulators take longer to carry heat off effectively.

Heat riser—A flapper in the exhaust manifold that is closed when the engine is cold, causing hot exhaust gases to heat the intake manifold providing better cold engine operation. A thermostatic spring opens the flapper when the engine warms up.

Hemi—A name given an engine using hemispherical combustion chambers.

Horsepower—A measurement of the amount of work; one horsepower is the amount of work necessary to lift 33,000 lbs one foot in one minute. Brake horsepower (bhp) is the horsepower delivered by an engine on a dynamometer. Net horsepower is the power remaining (measured at the flywheel of the engine) that can be used to turn the wheels after power is consumed through friction and running the engine accessories (water pump, alternator, air pump, fan etc.)

Hydrocarbon (HC)—A combination of hydrogen and carbon atoms found in all petroleum-based fuels. Unburned hydrocarbons (those not burned during normal combustion) are about .1% of exhaust emissions.

Hydroplaning—A phenomenon of driving when water builds up under the tire tread, caus-

ing it to lose contact with the road. Slowing down will usually restore normal tire contact with the road.

Idle mixture—The mixture of air and fuel (usually about 14:1) being fed to the cylinders. The idle mixture screw(s) are sometimes adjusted as part of a tune-up.

Idler arm—Component of the steering linkage which is a geometric duplicate of the steering gear arm. It supports the right side of the center steering link.

Lacquer—A quick-drying automotive paint.

Limited slip—A type of differential which transfers driving force to the wheel with the best traction.

Lithium-base grease—Chassis and wheel bearing grease using lithium as a base. Not compatible with sodium-base grease.

Load range—Indicates the number of plies at which a tire is rated. Load range B equals four-ply rating; C equals six-ply rating; and, D equals an eight-ply rating.

Locking hubs—Accessories used on part-time four-wheel drive systems that allow the front wheels to be disengaged from the drive train when four-wheel drive is not being used. When four-wheel drive is desired, the hubs are engaged, locking the wheels to the drive train.

Manifold—A casting connecting a series of outlets to a common opening.

Master cylinder—Reservoir containing hydraulic brake fluid which forces brake fluid to the wheel cylinders or caliper pistons as the brake pedal is depressed.

McPherson strut—A suspension component combining a shock absorber and spring in one unit.

Misfire—Condition occurring when the fuel mixture in a cylinder fails to ignite, causing the engine to run roughly.

Multiweight—Type of oil that provides adequate lubrication at both high and low temperatures.

Nitrous oxide (NOx)—One of the three basic pollutants found in the exhaust emission of an internal combustion engine. The amount of NOx usually varies in an inverse proportion to the amount of HC and CO.

Octane rating—A number, indicating the quality of gasoline based on its ability to resist knock. The higher the number, the better the quality. Higher compression engines require higher octane gas.

OEM—Original Equipment Manufactured. OEM equipment is that furnished standard by the manufacturer.

Offset—The distance between the vertical center of the

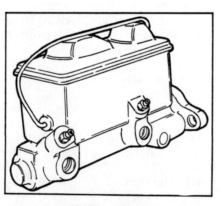

Master cylinder.

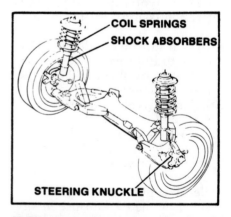

McPherson struts combine shocks and springs in one unit.

wheel and the mounting surface at the lugs. Offset is positive if the center is outside the lug circle; negative offset puts the center line inside the lug circle.

Ohm—Unit used to measure the resistance to flow of electricity.

Oscilloscope—A piece of test equipment that shows electric impulses as a pattern on a screen. Engine performance can be analyzed by interpreting these patterns.

Overdrive—A device attached to or incorporated in a transmission that allows the engine to turn less than one full revolution for every complete revolution of the wheels. The net effect is to reduce engine rpm, thereby using less fuel. A typical overdrive gear ratio would be .87:1, instead of the normal 1:1 in high gear.

Overhead camshaft—Camshaft mounted above the cylinder head. Overhead camshafts usually operate the valves directly rather than through hydraulic valve lifters.

Oversteer—The tendency of a car to steer itself increasingly into a corner, forcing the driver to reduce steering pressure. Opposite of understeer.

Oxides of nitrogen—See nitrous oxide (NOx).

Part-time four-wheel drive—A system that is normally in the two-wheel drive mode and only runs in four-wheel drive when the system is manually engaged because more traction is desired. Two- or four-wheel drive is normally selected by a lever to engage the front axle, but if locking hubs are used, these must also be manually engaged in the Lock position. Otherwise, the front axle will not drive the front wheels.

Payload—The weight the vehicle is capable of carrying in addition to its own weight. Payload includes weight of the driver, passengers and cargo, but not coolant, fuel, lubricant, spare tire, etc.

PCV Valve—A valve usually located in the rocker cover that vents crank-case vapors back into the engine to be reburned.

Percolation—A condition in which the fuel actually "boils," due to excess heat. Percolation prevents proper atomization of the fuel causing rough running.

Pick-up Coil—The coil in which voltage is induced in an electronic ignition.

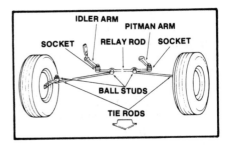

Steering linkage.

Ping—A metallic rattling sound produced by the engine during acceleration. It is usually due to incorrect ignition timing or a poor grade of gasoline.

Pinion—The smaller of two gears. The rear axle pinion drives the ring gear which transmits motion to the axle shafts.

Piston ring—Metal rings (usually three) installed in grooves in the piston. Piston rings seal the small space between the piston and wall of the cylinder.

Pitman arm—A lever which transmits steering force from the steering gear to the steering linkage.

Ply rating—A rating given a tire which indicates strength (but not necessarily actual plies). A two-ply/four-ply rating has only two plies, but the strength of a four ply tire.

Polarity—Indication (positive or negative) of the two poles of a battery.

Power-to-weight ratio—Ratio of horsepower to weight of car.

Powertrain—See Drivetrain.

Ppm—Parts per million; unit used to measure exhaust emissions.

Preignition—Early ignition of fuel in the cylinder, sometimes due to glowing carbon deposits in the combustion chamber. Preignition can be damaging since combustion takes place prematurely.

Pressure plate—A spring-loaded plate (part of the clutch) that transmits power to the driven (friction) plate when the clutch is engaged.

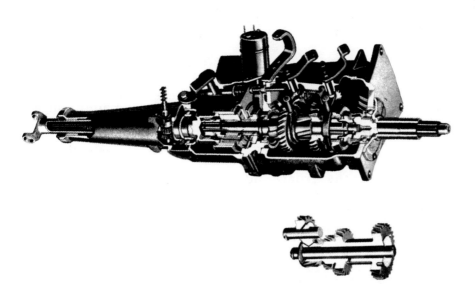

Cutaway view of manual transmission with overdrive unit attached.

Psi—Pounds per square inch; a measurement of pressure.

Pushrod—A steel rod between the hydraulic valve lifter and the valve rocker arm in overhead valve (OHV) engines.

Quarter panel—Body shop term for a fender. Quarter panel is the area from the rear door opening to the tail light area and from rear wheelwell to the base of the trunk and roofline.

Rack and pinion—A type of automotive steering system using a pinion gear attached to the end of the steering shaft. The pinion meshes with a long rack attached to the steering linkage.

Radial tire—Tire design which uses body cords running at right angles to the center line of the tire. Two or more belts are used to give tread strength. Radials can be identified by their characteristic sidewall bulge.

Rear main oil seal—A synthetic or rope-type seal that prevents oil from leaking out of the engine past the rear main crankshaft bearing.

Rectifier—A device (used primarily in alternators) that permits electrical current to flow in one direction only.

Reluctor—An iron wheel that rotates inside the distributor and triggers the release of voltage in an electronic ignition.

Refrigerant 12 (R-12)—The generic name of the refrigerant

used in automotive air-conditioning systems.

Resin—A liquid plastic used in body work.

Resistor spark plug—A spark plug using a resistor to shorten the spark duration. This suppresses radio interference and lengthens plug life.

Retard—Set the ignition timing so that spark occurs later (fewer degrees before TDC).

Rocker arm—A lever which rotates around a shaft pushing down (opening) the valve with an end when the other end is pushed up by the pushrod. Spring pressure will later close the valve.

Rocker panel—The body panel below the doors between the wheel opening.

Rotor (distributor)—Rotating piece attached to the distributor shaft that triggers the release of voltage to the spark plug.

Rpm—Revolutions per minute (usually indicates engine speed).

Run-on—Condition when the engine continues to run, even when the key is turned off. See dieseling.

Sealed beam—A modern automotive headlight. The lens, reflector and filament from a single unit.

Seatbelt interlock—A system whereby the car cannot be started unless the seatbelt is buckled.

Semi-floating axle—In this design, a wheel is attached to the axle shaft, which takes both drive and cornering loads. Almost all solid axle passenger cars and light trucks use this design.

Shimmy—Vibration (sometimes violent) in the front end caused by misaligned front end, out of balance tires or worn suspension components.

Short circuit—An electrical malfunction where current takes the path of least resistance to ground (usually through damaged insulation). Current flow

is excessive from low resistance resulting in a blown fuse.

Skidplate—A metal plate attached to the underside of the body to protect the fuel tank, transfer case or other vulnerable parts from damage.

Sludge—Thick, black deposits in engine formed from dirt, oil, water, etc. It is usually formed in engines when oil changes are neglected.

SOHC—Single overhead camshaft.

Solenoid—An electrically operated, magnetic switching device.

Specific gravity (battery)—The relative weight of liquid (battery electrolyte) as compared to the weight of an equal volume of water.

Spongy pedal—A soft or spongy feeling when the brake pedal is depressed. It is usually due to air in the brake lines.

Sprung weight—The weight of a car supported by the springs.

Stabilizer (sway) bar—A bar linking both sides of the suspension. It resists sway on turns by taking some of added load from one wheel and putting it on the other.

Steering geometry—Combination of various angles of suspension components (caster, camber, toe-in); roughly equivalent to front end alignment.

Straight weight—Term designating motor oil as suitable for use within a narrow range of temperatures. Outside the narrow temperature range its flow characteristics will not adequately lubricate.

Stroke—The distance the piston travels from bottom dead center to top dead center.

Synchromesh—A manual transmission that is equipped with devices (synchronizers) that match the gear speeds so that the transmission can be downshifted without clashing gears.

Synthetic oil—Non-petroleum based oil.

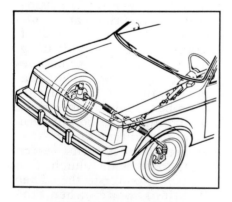

Rack and pinion steering.

Tachometer—Instrument which measures engine speed in rpm.

TDC—Top dead center. The exact top of the piston's stroke.

Thermostat—A temperature-sensitive device in the cooling system that regulates the flow of coolant.

Throwout bearing—As the clutch pedal is depressed, the throwout bearing moves against the spring fingers of the pressure plate, forcing the pressure plate to disengage from the driven disc.

Tie-rod—A rod connecting the steering arms. Tie-rods have threaded ends that are used to adjust toe-in.

Timing chain (belt)—A chain or belt that is driven by the crankshaft and operates the camshaft.

Tire rotation—Moving the tires from one position to another to make the tires wear evenly.

Tire series—A number expressing the ratio between the height and width of a tire. The height of a 78 series tire is 78% of its width.

Toe-in (out)—A term comparing the extreme front and rear of the front tires. Closer together at the front is toe-in; farther apart at the front is toe-out.

Torque—Measurement of turning or twisting force, expressed as foot-pounds or inch-pounds.

Torsion bar suspension—Long rods of spring steel which take the place of springs. One end of the bar is anchored and the

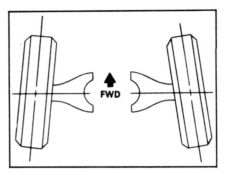

Wheel toe-in (top view).

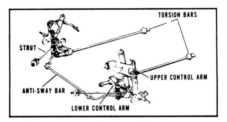

Torsion bar front suspension.

other arm (attached to the suspension) is free to twist. The bars' resistance to twisting causes springing action.

Track—Distance between the centers of the tires where they contact the ground.

Transaxle—A single housing containing the transmission and differential. Transaxles are usually found on front engine/front wheel drive or rear engine/rear wheel drive cars.

Transfer Case—A gearbox driven from the transmission that delivers power to both front and rear driveshafts in a four-wheel drive system. Transfer cases usually have a high and low range set of gears, used depending on how much pulling power is needed.

Tread wear indicator—Bars molded into the tire at right angles to the tread that appear as horizontal bars when 1/16th in. of tread remains.

Tread wear pattern—The pattern of wear on tires which can be "read" to diagnose problems in the front suspension.

Turbocharged—A system to increase engine power by using exhaust gas to drive a com-

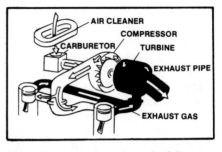

The turbocharged engine principle uses exhaust gas to spin the turbocharger, increasing maximum engine power output.

pressor. As engine speed and load increases, the compressor forces a greater air/fuel mixture into the cylinder. Under light load, or cruising conditions, the turbocharger "idles" and a normal air/fuel mixture reaches the cylinders.

U-joint (universal joint)—A flexible coupling in the drive train that allows the driveshafts or axle shafts to operate at different angles and still transmit rotary power.

Understeer—The tendency of a car to continue straight ahead while negotiating a turn.

Unit Body—Design in which the car body acts as the frame.

Unleaded fuel—Fuel which contains no lead (a common gasoline additive). The presence of lead in fuel will destroy the functioning elements of a catalytic converter, making it useless.

Unsprung weight—The weight of car components not supported by the springs (wheels, tires, brakes, rear axle, control arms, etc.).

Vacuum advance—A method of advancing the ignition timing by applying engine vacuum to a diaphragm mounted on the distributor.

Valve guides—The guide through which the stem of the valve passes. The guide is designed to keep the valve in proper alignment.

Valve lash (clearance)—The operating clearance in the valve train.

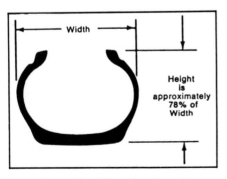

Tire series (78 series shown).

Valve train—The system that operates intake and exhaust valves, consisting of camshaft, valves and springs, lifters, pushrods and rocker arms.

Vapor lock—Boiling of the fuel in the fuel lines due to excess heat. This will interfere with the flow of fuel in the lines and can completely stop the flow. Vapor lock normally only occurs in hot weather.

Varnish—Term applied to the residue formed when gasoline gets old and stale.

Viscosity—The ability of a fluid to flow. The lower the viscosity rating, the easier the fluid will flow. 10 weight motor oil will flow much easier than 40 weight motor oil.

Volt—Unit used to measure the force or pressure of electricity. It is defined as the pressure needed to move one amp through a resistance of one ohm.

Voltage regulator—A device that controls the current output of the alternator or generator.

Wankel engine—An engine which uses no pistons. In place of pistons, triangular-shaped rotors revolve in specially shaped housings.

Wheel alignment—Inclusive term to describe the front end geometry (caster, camber, toe-in/out).

Wheelbase—Distance between the center of front wheels and the center of rear wheels.

Wheel cylinder—A small cylinder in drum brake system that receives pressure from the master cylinder and forces the brake shoes into contact with the brake drum.

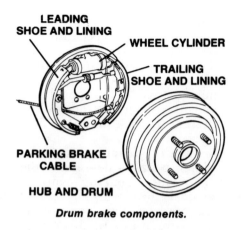

Drum brake components.

Wheel weight—Small weights attached to the wheel to balance the wheel and tire assembly. Out-of-balance tires quickly wear out and also give erratic handling when installed on the front.

TUNE-UP SPECIFICATIONS

CONTENTS

Domestic Cars

AMERICAN MOTORS 379
CHRYSLER CORPORATION
  Rear Wheel Drive 384
  Front Wheel Drive 389
FORD MOTOR COMPANY
  Front Wheel Drive 393
  Rear Wheel Drive 396
GENERAL MOTORS
  Buick Rear Wheel Drive 409
  Cadillac Rear Wheel Drive 419
  Chevrolet Corvette 423
  Chevrolet Rear Wheel Drive 426
  Oldsmobile Rear Wheel Drive 437
  Pontiac Rear Wheel Drive 448
  "A" & "X" Body 458
  "C" Body 462
  "E" & "K" Body 465
  "F" Body 471
  "H" Body 482
  "J" Body 486
  "P" Body 489

  "T" Body 491
  Sprint 495

Import Cars

AUDI 497
BMW 500
CHRYSLER 503
DATSUN/NISSAN 507
HONDA 513
ISUZU 518
MAZDA 521
MERCEDES-BENZ 524
MITSUBISHI 533
PORSCHE 924, 928, 944 535
RENAULT 538
SAAB 542
SUBARU 545
TOYOTA 547
VOLKSWAGEN
  Front Wheel Drive 552
  Rear Wheel Drive 557
VOLVO 560

Note: These specifications are as complete as possible at the time of publication, and are also contained in your owner's manual. Part numbers listed in this book are not recommendations by Chilton for any product by brand name. They are references that can be used with interchange manuals and aftermarket supplier catalogs to locate each brand supplier's discrete part number.

AMERICAN MOTORS
AMX, Concord, Eagle, SX-4, Gremlin, Hornet, Matador, Pacer, Spirit
VEHICLE IDENTIFICATION NUMBER (VIN)

It is important for servicing and ordering parts to be certain of the vehicle and engine identification. The VIN (vehicle identification number) is a 13 or 17 digit number visible through the windshield on the driver's side of the dash and contains the vehicle and engine identification codes. It can be interpreted as follows:

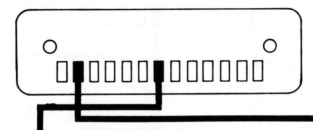

ENGINE CODE						MODEL YEAR CODE	
Code	Cu. In.	Liters	Cyl.	Carb.	Eng. Mfg.	Code	Year
G	121	2.0	4	2	VW	8	1978
B	151	2.5	4	2	Pontiac	9	1979
E	232	3.8	6	1	AMC	0	1980
A	258	4.2	6	1	AMC		
C	258	4.2	6	2	AMC		
H	304	5.0	8	2	AMC		
N	360	5.9	8	2	AMC		

The thirteen digit Vehicle Identification Number can be used to determine engine application and model year. The second digit indicates model year, and the seventh digit indicates engine code.

VEHICLE IDENTIFICATION NUMBER (VIN)

It is important for servicing and ordering parts to be certain of the vehicle and engine identification. The VIN (vehicle identification number) is a 13 or 17 digit number visible through the windshield on the driver's side of the dash and contains the vehicle and engine identification codes. It can be interpreted as follows:

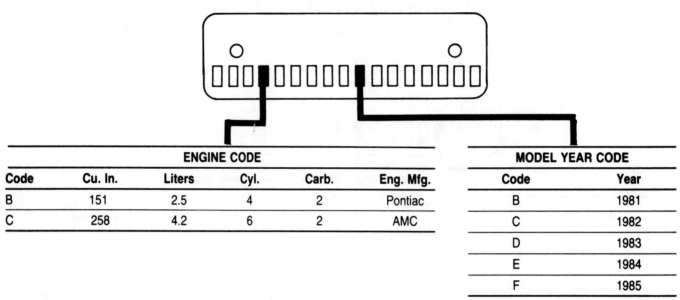

ENGINE CODE						MODEL YEAR CODE	
Code	Cu. In.	Liters	Cyl.	Carb.	Eng. Mfg.	Code	Year
B	151	2.5	4	2	Pontiac	B	1981
C	258	4.2	6	2	AMC	C	1982
						D	1983
						E	1984
						F	1985

The seventeen digit Vehicle Identification Number can be used to determine engine identification and model year. The tenth digit indicates model year, and the fourth digit indicates engine code.

TUNE-UP SPECIFICATIONS

(When analyzing compression test results, look for uniformity among cylinders rather than specific pressures.)

Year	No. Cyl. Displacement (cu. in.)	Eng VIN Code	HP	Eng Mfg	Spark Plugs Orig. Type	Gap (in.)	Distributor Point Dwell (deg)	Point Gap (in.)	Ignition Timing (deg) ▲ Man. Trans. ●	Auto. Trans.	Valves Intake Opens ■ (deg)	Fuel Pump Pressure (psi)	Idle Speed ● (rpm) ▲ Man Trans	Auto Trans*
'78	4-121	G	2 bbl	VW	N-8L	.035	47	.018	12B	12B(8B)	41¾	4–6	900	800
	6-232	E	1 bbl	AMC	N-13L	.035	electronic		8B	10B	12	4–5	600	550
	6-258	A	1 bbl	AMC	N-13L	.035	electronic		(6B)①	(8B)①	12	4–5	600(850)	550(700)
	6-258	C	2 bbl	AMC	N-13L	.035	electronic		6B	8B	14½	4–5	600	600
	8-304	H	2 bbl	AMC	N-12Y	.035	electronic		—	10B(5B)①	14¾	5–6½	—	600(700)
	8-360	N	2 bbl	AMC	N-12Y	.035	electronic		—	10B	14¾	5–6½	—	600(650)
'79	4-121	G	2 bbl	VW	N-8L	.035	47	.018	12B②	12B(8B)	41¾	4–6	900	800
	6-232	E	1 bbl	AMC	N-13L	.035	electronic		8B	10B	12	4–5	600	550
	6-258	A	1 bbl	AMC	N-13L	.035	electronic		—	8B	12	4–5	—	700
	6-258	C	2 bbl	AMC	N-13L	.035	electronic		4B	8B	12	4–5	700	600
	8-304	H	2 bbl	AMC	N-12Y	.035	electronic		5B	8B	14¾	5–6½	800	600
'80	4-151	B	2 bbl	Pontiac	R44TSX	.060	electronic		10B(12B)	12B(10B)	33	6½–8	900	700
	6-258	C	2 bbl	AMC	N14LY④	.035	electronic		6B	10B③	14½	4–5	700	600
'81–'82	4-151	B	2 bbl	Pontiac	R44TSX	.060	electronic		10B⑤	12B③	25	6½–8	900	700
	6-258	C	2 bbl	AMC	RFN-14LY	.033	electronic		⑥	⑦	9	5–6½	700	600
'83	4-151	B	2 bbl	Pontiac	R44TSX	.060	electronic		10B⑤	12B③	25	6½–8	900	700
	6-258	C	2 bbl	AMC	RFN14LY	.033	electronic		⑥	⑦	9	5–6½	700	600
'84–'85	4-150	U	1 bbl	AMC	RFN14LY	.035	electronic		12B	12B	27B	6½–8	750	750
	6-258	C	2bbl	AMC	RFN14LY	.033	electronic		⑥	⑦	9	5–6½	700	600

▲ If underhood emissions decal differs, always use the specifications on the decal.
* With transmission in Drive
● Figure in parentheses indicates California engine
■ All figures before Top Dead Center
B Before Top Dead Center
TDC Top Dead Center (zero degrees)
— Not applicable
① High Altitude—10B

② 16B for models with code EH on upper right corner of emission information label.
③ 8B—Eagle for Calif. and all Pacer
④ N13L—Eagle
⑤ Eagle except for Calif.—11B
⑥ Concord, Spirit—6B
Eagle except Calif.—8B
Eagle Calif.—4B High Alt.—15B
⑦ Concord, Spirit—6B
Eagle Except Calif.—8B
Eagle Calif.—6B High Alt.—15B

FIRING ORDER

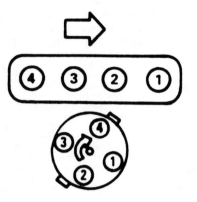

AMC 150-4 cylinder firing order: 4-3-2-1

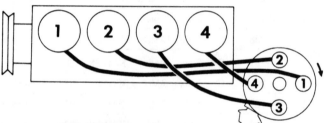

AMC 151 4-cyl.
Engine firing order: 1-3-4-2
Distributor rotation: clockwise

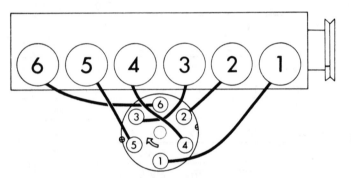

AMC 232, 258 6-cyl. 1978 and later
Engine firing order 1-5-3-6-2-4
Distributor rotation: clockwise

AMC 121 4-cyl.
Engine firing order: 1-3-4-2
Distributor rotation: clockwise

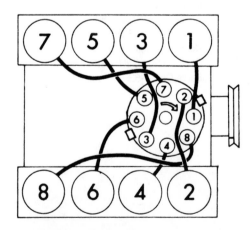

AMC 304, 360, 401 V8
Engine firing order: 1-8-4-3-6-5-7-2
Distributor rotation: clockwise

CAPACITIES

Year	Engine No. Cyl. Displacement (cu. in.)	Model	Engine Crankcase Add 1 Qt. For New Filter	Transmission (Pts. To Refill After Draining) Manual 3-Speed	4-Speed	Automatic	Drive Axle (pts)	Cooling System (qts) With Heater	With A/C
'78	4-121	Gremlin	3.5	—	2.4①	14.2	3	6.5	—
	6-232	Gremlin	4	3.5②	3.5	17	3	11	14
	6-232	Hornet, Concord	4	3.5②	3.5	17	3	11	11.5③
	6-232	Pacer	4	3.5②	3.5	17	3	14	14
	6-258	Gremlin	4	3.5②	3.5	17	3	11	14
	6-258	Hornet, Concord	4	3.5②	3.5	17	3	11	11.5③
	6-258	Pacer	4	3.5②	3.5	17	3	14	14
	6-258	Matador coupe	4	—	—	17	4	13.5	13.5
	6-258	Matador sedan, wagon	4	—	—	17	4	11.5	11.5
	8-304	Hornet, Concord, Pacer	4	—	—	17	4	16④	16④
	8-304	Matador coupe	4	—	—	17	4	18.5	18.5
	8-304	Matador sedan, wagon	4	—	—	17	4	16.5	16.5
	8-360	Matador coupe	4	—	—	19⑤	4	17.5	17.5
	8-360	Matador sedan, wagon	4	—	—	19⑤	4	15.5	15.5
'79	4-121	Spirit, Concord	3.5	2.5	2.8	14.2	3⑥	6.5	6.5
	6-232	Spirit, Concord	4	2.5	2.8	17	3⑥	11	14
	6-258	Spirit, Concord, Pacer, AMX	4	2.5	2.8	17	3⑥	11	14
	8-304	Spirit, Concord, Pacer, AMX	4	2.5	2.8	17	3⑥	18	18
'80	4-151	Spirit, Concord	3.5⑦	—	3.3	17	3	6.5	6.5
	6-258	Spirit, Concord Pacer, AMX	4	—	3.3	17	3	11⑧	11⑧
	6-258	Eagle	4	—	3.3⑨	17⑨	3⑩	11	14
'81–'83	4-151	Spirit, Concord	3.0	—	3.5⑪	14.2	3	6.5	6.5
	4-151	Eagle	3.0	—	3.5⑪	14.2	3⑩	6.5	6.5
'81–'85	6-258	Spirit, Concord	4.0	—	3.5⑪	17.0	3	11	14
	6-258	Eagle	4.0	—	3.5⑪	17.0	3⑩	14	14
'84–'85	4-150	Eagle	4.0	—	7.4	15.8	2.5	10.0	10.0

① 2.8—1978
② 3 pts—1978
③ 14.0—1978
④ 18.0–1978
⑤ 16.4—1978
⑥ 8.875 ring gear—4 pts

⑦ Add ½ qt. for new filter
⑧ 14.5 qts. in Pacer
⑨ Transfer case: 3.0 pts. until March 1980; 4.0 pts. thereafter
⑩ 2.5—front axle

⑪ 82 and later:
T4 Spirit-Concord; 4.0 pts.
T4 Eagle; 3.5 pts.
T5 Spirit-Concord; 4.5 pts.
T5 Eagle; 4.0 pts.
— Not applicable

CHRYSLER CORP. REAR WHEEL DRIVE
Cordoba, Fifth Avenue, Imperial, LeBaron, Newport, New Yorker, Aspen, Charger, Magnum XE, Mirada, Monaco, Royal Monaco, St. Regis, Caravelle, Fury, Gran Fury, Volare, Diplomat SE

VEHICLE IDENTIFICATION NUMBER (VIN)

It is important for servicing and ordering parts to be certain of the vehicle and engine identification. The VIN (vehicle identification number) is a 13 or 17 digit number visible through the windshield on the driver's side of the dash and contains the vehicle and engine identification codes. It can be interpreted as follows:

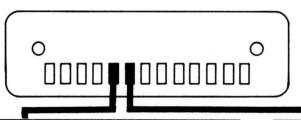

Engine Code						Model Year Code	
Code	Cu. In.	Liters	Cyl.	Carb.(Bbl.)	Eng.Mfg.	Code	Year
C	225	3.7	6	1	Chrys.	8	1978
D	225	3.7	6	2	Chrys.	9	1979
G	318	5.2	8	2	Chrys.	A	1980
H	318	5.2	8	4	Chrys.		
K	360	5.9	8	2	Chrys.		
L	360HP①	5.9	8	4	Chrys.		
J	360	5.9	8	4	Chrys.		
N	400	6.6	8	4	Chrys.		
P	400HP①	6.6	8	4	Chrys.		
T	440	7.2	8	4	Chrys.		
U	440HP①	7.2	8	4	Chrys.		

The thirteen digit Vehicle Identification Number can be used to determine engine application and model year. The 6th digit indicates the model year, and the 5th digit identifies the factory installed engine.

① High Performance

VEHICLE IDENTIFICATION NUMBER (VIN)

It is important for servicing and ordering parts to be certain of the vehicle and engine identification. The VIN (vehicle identification number) is a 13 or 17 digit number visible through the windshield on the driver's side of the dash and contains the vehicle and engine identification codes. It can be interpreted as follows:

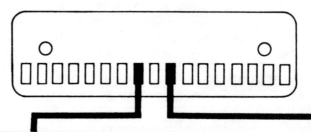

Engine Code						Model Year Code	
Code	Cu. In.	Liters	Cyl.	Carb.(Bbl.)	Eng.Mfg.	Code	Year
E	225	3.7	6	1	Chrys.	B	1981
H	225	3.7	6	1	Chrys.	C	1982
F	225	3.7	6	1 H.D.	Chrys.	D	1983
J	225	3.7	6	1 H.D.	Chrys.	E	1984
G	225	3.7	6	2①	Chrys.	F	1985
K	225	3.7	6	2①	Chrys.		
H	225	3.7	6	2 H.D.①	Chrys.		
L	225	3.7	6	2 H.D.①	Chrys.		
K	318	5.2	8	2	Chrys.		
P	318	5.2	8	2	Chrys.		
L	318	5.2	8	2 H.D.	Chrys.		
J	318	5.2	8	EFI	Chrys.		
N	318	5.2	8	EFI	Chrys.		
R	318	5.2	8	4	Chrys.		
M	318	5.2	8	4	Chrys.		
N	318	5.2	8	4 H.D.	Chrys.		
S	318	5.2	8	4 H.D.	Chrys.		

H.D. = Heavy Duty
EFI = Electronic Fuel Injection
① = Canada Only

The seventeen digit Vehicle Identification Number can be used to determine engine application and model year. The seventeen digit code supercedes the thirteen digit code which ended in 1980. The 10th digit indicates the model year, and the 8th digit identifies the factory installed engine.
EFI Electronic Fuel Injection

TUNE-UP SPECIFICATIONS

(When analyzing compression test results, look for uniformity among cylinders rather than specific pressures.)

Year	Eng. V.I.N. Code	Engine No. Cyl. Displacement (cu.in.)	Carb. (bbl.)	Spark Plugs Orig. Type	Spark Plugs Gap (in.)	Distributor Point Dwell (deg)	Distributor Point Gap (in.)	Ignition Timing (deg)▲ Man Trans●	Ignition Timing (deg)▲ Auto Trans	Valves Intake Opens ■(deg)	Fuel Pump Pressure (psi)	Idle Speed (rpm)▲ Man Trans●	Idle Speed (rpm)▲ Auto Trans
'78	C	6-225	1	RBL-16Y	.035	Electronic		12B(8B)	12B(8B)	16	3½–5	700(750)	700(750)
	D	6-225	2	RBL-16Y	.035	Electronic		12B(10B)	12B(10B)	16	3½–5	700(750)	700(750)
	G	8-318	2	RN-12Y	.035	Electronic		16B	16B	10	5¾–7¼	700(750)	700(750)
	H	8-318①	4	RN-12Y	.035	Electronic		—	10B	10	5¾–7¼	700(750)	700(750)
	K	8-360①	2	RN-12Y	.035	Electronic		—	20B	18	5¾–7¼	—	750
	L,J	8-360HP	4	RN-12Y	.035	Electronic		—	16B(6/8B)	18	5¾–7¼	—	750
	N	8-400①	4	OJ-13Y	.035	Electronic		—	20B	18	5–7	—	750
	T	8-440①	4	OJ-13Y	.035	Electronic		—	12B(8B)	18	5¾–7¼	—	750
	U	8-440①	4	OJ-11Y	.035	Electronic		—	16B(8B)	18	6–7½	—	750
'79	C	6-225	1	RBL-16Y	.035	Electronic		12B(8B)	12B (8B)	16	3½–5	700(750)	700(750)
	D	6-225	2	RBL-16Y	.035	Electronic		12B	12B	16	3½–5	700(750)	700(750)
	G	8-318	2	RN-12Y	.035	Electronic		—	16B	10	5–7	—	750
	H	8-318	4	RN-12Y	.035	Electronic		—	16B	10	5–7	750	750
	K	8-360	2	RN-12Y	.035	Electronic		—	16B	18	5–7	—	750
	L,J	8-360HP	4	RN-12Y	.035	Electronic		—	16B	18	5–7	750	750
'80	C	6-225	1	P-560 PR	.035	Electronic		12B	12B	16	3½–5	725	725(750)
	D	6-225	2	P-560 PR	.035	Electronic			12B	16	3½–5	725	725②
	G	8-318	2	P-65 PR	.035	Electronic		—	12B	10	5–7	—	700
	H	8-318	4	P-65 PR	.035	Electronic		—	10B②(16B)	10	5–7	—	750②(700)
	K	8-360	2	P-65 PR	.035	Electronic		—	16B	18	5–7	—	750
	L	8-360	4	P-65 PR	.035	Electronic		—	16B	18	5–7	—	750
'81	E	6-225	1	P-560 PR4Y	.048	Electronic		—	12B③	6	4.0– 5.5	—	600
	J	8-318	EFI	P-68 ER	.048	Electronic		—	12B	10	15.2–19.4	—	580
	K	8-318	2	P-65 PR4Y	.048④	Electronic		—	16B	10	5.75–7.25	—	600
	M	8-318	4	P-65 PR4Y	.048	Electronic		—	16B	10	5.75–7.25	—	600
'82	E,F,G,H	6-225	1 & 2	560PR	.035	Electronic		—	⑤	6	4.0–5.5	—	750
	J	8-318	EFI	65PR	.048	Electronic		—	⑤	10	5.75–11.5	—	600
	K,L,M,N	8-318	2 & 4	RN-12YC	.035	Electronic		—	⑤	10	5.75–7.25	—	700
'83	H,J,K,L	6-225	1 & 2	RBL-16Y	.035	Electronic		—	⑤	6	4.0–5.5	—	750
	N,P,R,S	8-318	2 & 4	RN-12Y	.035	Electronic		—	⑤	10	5.75–7.25	—	700
'84–'85	P,R,S	8-318	2 & 4	RN-127	.035	Electronic		—	⑤	10	5.75–7.25	—	700

NOTE: The underhood specifications sticker often reflects tune-up specification changes made in production. Sticker figures must be used if they disagree with those in this chart.

Part numbers in this chart are not recommendations by Chilton for any product by brand name.

▲ See text for procedure
■ All figures Before Top Dead Center
● Figure in parentheses indicates California engine
HP High Performance

EFI Electronic Fuel Injection
B Before TDC
① Lean Burn
② Canada

③ California 16B
④ Late Production .035—See underhood sticker
⑤ See underhood sticker

FIRING ORDERS

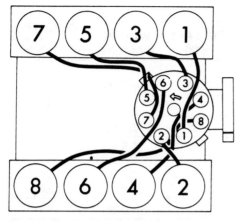

Chrysler Corp.: 400, 440 V8 Engine firing order:1-8-4-3-6-5-7-2 Distributor rotation: counterclockwise

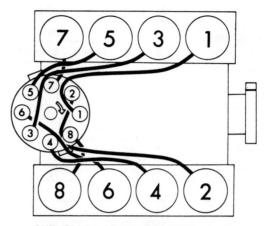

CHRYSLER CORP. 318, 360 V8 Engine firing order: 1-8-4-3-6-5-7-2 Distributor rotation: clockwise

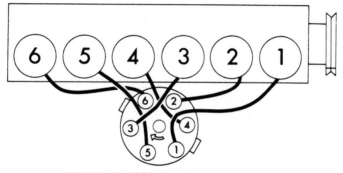

CHRYSLER CORP. 6-cyl. Engine firing order: 1-5-3-6-2-4 Distributor rotation: clockwise

CAPACITIES

Year	Engine No. Cyl. Displacement (Cu. In.)	Engine Crankcase Add 1 Qt For New Filter	Transmission Pts to Refill After Draining			Drive Axle (pts)	Gasoline Tank (gals)	Cooling System (qts)	
			Manual						
			3-Speed	4-Speed	Automatic			With Heater	With A/C
'78	6-225	4	4.75	7.0④	17⑪	2.1⑥	18⑤⑩	12	14
	8-318	4	4.75	7.0④	17⑪	2.1⑥	20⑩	16	17.5
	8-360	4	—	—	17⑪	4.5	20⑩	16	17.5
	8-400	4	—	—	16.5⑪	4.5	25.5⑤	16.5	16.5
	8-400HP	4	—	—	19.0⑪	4.5	20.5	16.5	16.5
	8-440	4	—	—	16.5⑪	4.5	26.5⑬	16.0	16.5
'79	6-225	4	4.75	7.0④	17⑧⑭	③	18⑩⑫	11.5	12.5
	8-318	4	—	—	17⑧⑭	③	19.5	15①	16.5
	8-360	4	—	—	17⑧⑭	③	19.5	15	15
'80–'85	6-225	4	4.75	7.0④	17⑧⑭	③	18⑫	11.5	14.5②
	8-318	4	—	—	17⑧⑭	③	18.0⑮	15.0⑦	16.5⑨
	8-360	4	—	—	17⑧⑭	③	18.0⑮	16.0	16.0

① Calif.—16.5
② 15 qts on Cordoba, Mirada
③ 7¼″ axle—2.1 pts., 8¼″ axle—4.4 pts., 9¼″ axle—4.5 pts.
④ Aspen/Volare
⑤ 20 gal. on wagon
⑥ 4.4 pts for station wagon or High Altitude models.
⑦ 15.5 qts. on Imperial
⑧ A904 trans.; 15.9 pts.—A727 trans.
⑨ 17.5 on Imperial and heavy duty coding systems
⑩ 19.5 gal. on Diplomat, LeBaron; 25.5 gal. on Fury, Monaco, Royal Monaco, Charger, Gran Fury; 26.5 gal on Cordoba, Newport, New Yorker
⑪ 7.3–7.8 pts. if converter isn't drained.
⑫ 19.5 on Aspen/Volare wagon; 21 gal. on 1979 and later Cordoba, Mirada, Gran Fury, St. Regis and Magnum
⑬ 24 gal. on wagons; 25.5 gal. Cordoba
⑭ 16.3 pts. on Aspen/Volare with A904 trans.; 15.9 pts. on A727 trans.
⑮ 21 gal. on '78–'79 Cordoba/Newport and '78–'81 New Yorker, Dodge/Plymouth full size. 19.5 gal. on 1980 Dodge/Plymouth midsize.

CHRYSLER CORP. FRONT WHEEL DRIVE
Omni, Horizon, Aries, Reliant, LeBaron, Dodge 400, Dodge 600, E Class, New Yorker, Daytona, Laser, Charger, Turismo, TC3, 024

VEHICLE IDENTIFICATION NUMBER (VIN)

It is important for servicing and ordering parts to be certain of the vehicle and engine identification. The VIN (vehicle identification number) is a 13 or 17 digit number visible through the windshield on the driver's side of the dash, and contains the vehicle and engine identification codes. It can be interpreted as follows:

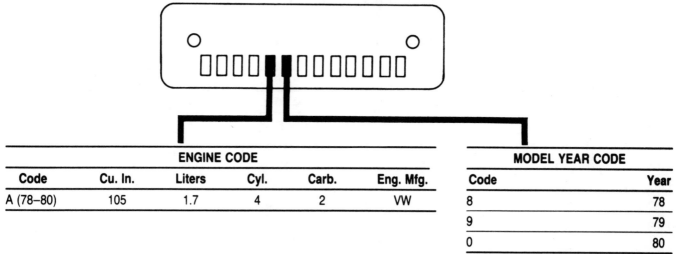

ENGINE CODE						MODEL YEAR CODE	
Code	Cu. In.	Liters	Cyl.	Carb.	Eng. Mfg.	Code	Year
A (78–80)	105	1.7	4	2	VW	8	78
						9	79
						0	80

The thirteen digit Vehicle Identification Number can be used to determine engine application and model year. The sixth digit indicates the model year, and the fifth digit indicates engine displacement.

VEHICLE IDENTIFICATION NUMBER (VIN)

It is important for servicing and ordering parts to be certain of the vehicle and engine identification. The VIN (vehicle identification number) is a 13 or 17 digit number visible through the windshield on the driver's side of the dash, and contains the vehicle and engine identification codes. It can be interpreted as follows:

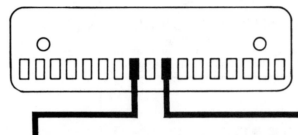

ENGINE CODE

Code	Cu. In.	Liters	Cyl.	Carb.	Eng. Mfg.
A (84–85)	98	1.6	4	2	Peugeot
A (81–82)	105	1.7	4	2	VW
B (83)	105	1.7	4	2	VW
B (81–82)	135	2.2	4	2	Chrysler
C (83–85)	135	2.2	4	2	Chrysler
D (83–85)	135	2.2	4	EFI	Chrysler
E (84–85)	135	2.2	4	Turbo	Chrysler
D (81–82)	156	2.6	4	2	Mitsubishi
G (83–85)	156	2.6	4	2	Mitsubishi

MODEL YEAR CODE

Code	Year
B	81
C	82
D	83
E	84
F	85

The seventeen digit Vehicle Identification Number can be used to determine engine application and model year. The tenth indicates the model year, and the eighth digit identifies engine displacement.

TUNE-UP SPECIFICATIONS

Year	Eng. V.I.N. Code	No. Cyl. Displ. Cu. In.	Eng. Mfg.	h.p.	Spark Plugs Orig. Type	Gap (in.)	Ignition Timing (deg.) ▲ Man. Trans.	Auto Trans.	Intake Valve Opens (deg.)■	Fuel Pump Pressure (psi)	Idle Speed (rpm) ▲ Man. Trans.	Auto Trans.	Valve Lash (in.) ▲ Intake	Exhaust
'84–'85	A	4–98	Peugeot	64	RN12YC	.035	12B	12B	16	4.5–6.0	850	1000	.012C	.014C
'78	A	4–105	VW	75	RN-12Y	.035	15B	15B	23	4.5–6.0	900	900	.008–.012H	.016–.020H
'79	A	4–105	VW	75	RN-12Y	.035	15B	15B	14	4.4–5.8	900	900	.008–.012H	.016–.020H
'80	A	4–105	VW	75	RN-12Y	.035	15B	15B	14	4.4–5.8	900	900	.008–.012H	.016–.020H
'81–'82	A	4–105	VW	63	P65-PR4	.048②	12B④	10B	14	4.5–6.0	900	900	.008–.012H	.016–.020H
'83	A	4–105	VW	63	65PR	.035	20B	12B	14	4.4–5.8	900	900	.008–.012H	.016–.020H
'81–'82	B	4–135	Chrysler	84	P65-PR4	.035	10B	10B	12	4.5–6.0	900	900	Hyd.	Hyd.
'84–'85	C	4–135	Chrysler	All	RN12YC	.035	10B	10B	12	4.5–6.0	900	900	Hyd.	Hyd.
'84–'85	E	4–135	Chrysler	146	RN12YC	.035	12B	12B	12	73–122	900	800	Hyd.	Hyd.
'81–'82	D	4–156	Mitsubishi	92	P65-PR4	.041③	7B	7B	25	4.5–6.0	800①	800①	.006H	.010H
'83–'85	G	4–156	Mitsubishi	92	RN11YC4	.041③	7B	7B	25	4.5–6.0	800①	800①	.006H	.010H

NOTE: The underhood specifications sticker often reflects tune-up specification changes made in production. Sticker figures must be used if they disagree with those in this chart. Part numbers in this chart are not recommendations by Chilton for any product by brand name.

▲See text for procedure   H Hot   ②.035-Canada
■Before top dead center   C Cold   ③.030-Canada
Hyd. Hydraulic   ①750 rpm-Canada   ④1982-20B

FIRING ORDERS

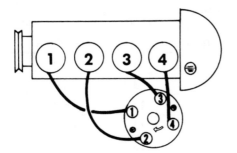

Chrysler Corp. 1.7L 1978 and later
Engine Firing Order: 1-3-4-2
Distributor Rotation: Clockwise

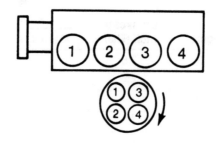

Chrysler Corp. 2.2L
Engine Firing Order: 1-3-4-2
Distributor Rotation: Clockwise

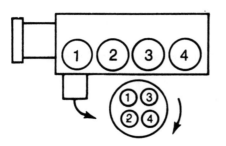

Chrysler Corp. (Mitsubishi) 2.6L
Engine Firing Order: 1-3-4-2
Distributor Rotation: Clockwise

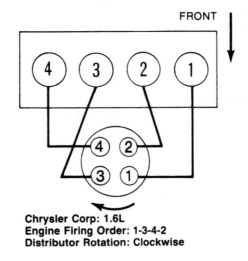

Chrysler Corp: 1.6L
Engine Firing Order: 1-3-4-2
Distributor Rotation: Clockwise

CAPACITIES

Year	Engine	Crankcase Incl. Filter	Pints To Refill After Draining		Final Drive (pts.)	Fuel Tank (gal.)	Cooling System (qts.)	
			Manual	Automatic			With Heater	With A/C
'84–'85	4–98	3.5	③	16②	—	13	7.0	—
'78–'80	4–105	4	2.65	13.0②	2.4	13	6.0①	6.0①
'81–'82	4–105	4	2.60	14.5②	2.4	13	6.0	6.0
'83	4–105	4	③	16.75②	2.4	13	6.0	6.0
'81–'82	4–135	4	2.60	15.0②	2.4	13	7.5	7.5
'83–'85	4–135	4④	③	17.75②	2.4	13	9	9
'81–'82	4–156	5	3.75	15.0②	2.4	13	8.5	8.5
'83–'85	4–156	5	③	17.75②	2.4	13	9	9

NOTE: If the starter motor is located on the radiator side of the engine the car is equipped with an A-412 manual transaxle; Use GL-4 Hypoid Lubricant. If the starter motor is located on the firewall side of the engine the car is equipped with an A-460 manual transaxle; Use only Dexron II lubricant.

① 1978 models with A/C: 6.5 qts., without A/C: 8.0 qts.

② Includes torque converter. Approx. 6 pts without draining converter.

③ 4 speed: 3.75–use Dexron® II lubricant
  5 speed: 4.55–use Dexron® II lubricant

④ '84–'85 2.2 Turbo engines: 5 qts. (Effective 4-24-84 Chrysler Corp. increased the oil capacity from 4 to 5 qts.)

FORD MOTOR CO. FRONT WHEEL DRIVE
Escort, Lynx, EXP, LN7, Tempo, Topaz

VEHICLE IDENTIFICATION NUMBER (VIN)

It is important for servicing and ordering parts to be certain of the vehicle and engine identification. The VIN (vehicle identification number) is a 13 or 17 digit number visible through the windshield on the driver's side of the dash and contains the vehicle and engine identification codes. It can be interpreted as follows:

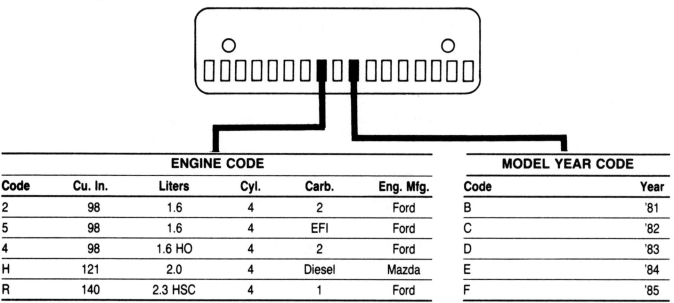

ENGINE CODE						MODEL YEAR CODE	
Code	Cu. In.	Liters	Cyl.	Carb.	Eng. Mfg.	Code	Year
2	98	1.6	4	2	Ford	B	'81
5	98	1.6	4	EFI	Ford	C	'82
4	98	1.6 HO	4	2	Ford	D	'83
H	121	2.0	4	Diesel	Mazda	E	'84
R	140	2.3 HSC	4	1	Ford	F	'85

The seventeen digit Vehicle Identification Number can be used to determine engine application and model year. The tenth digit indicates model year, and the eighth digit identifies engine code.

TUNE-UP SPECIFICATIONS

(When analyzing compression test results, look for uniformity among cylinders rather than specific pressures.)

| Year | Engine | | | Spark Plugs | | Distributor | | Ignition Timing (deg) ▲ | | Valves Intake Opens ■ (deg) | Fuel Pump Pressure (psi) | Idle Speed (rpm) ▲ | |
	Eng V.I.N. Code	No. Cyl. Displacement cu in. (cc)	Eng Mfg	Orig. Type ●	Gap (in.)	Point Dwell (deg)	Point Gap (in.)	Man Trans ●	Auto Trans			Man Trans	Auto Trans
'81	2	4-97.6 (1597)	Ford	AGSP-32	.042–.046	Electronic		10B①	10B①	—	4–6	①	①
'82	2	4-97.6 (1597)	Ford	AWSF-32	.042–.046	Electronic		①	①	—	4–6	①	①
'83–'85	—	4-97.6 (1597)	Ford	AWSF-34②	.042–.046	Electronic		①	①	—	4–6③	①	①
'84–'85	R	4-140 (2300)	Ford	AWSF-62	.044	Electronic		10B	15B	—	5	①	①

NOTE: The underhood specifications sticker often reflects tune-up specification changes made in production. Sticker figures must be used if they disagree with those in this chart. Part numbers in this chart are not recommended by Chilton for any product by brand name.

▲See text for procedure
■All figures Before Top Dead Center
●Figure in parenthesis is for California
B Before Top Dead Center

—Not applicable
①Calibration levels vary from model to model. Always refer to the underhood sticker for your

cars requirements.
②EFI Models: AWSF24
③EFI pressure: 35–45 psi

FIRING ORDERS

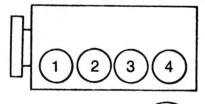

Ford Motor Co. 1600 cc
Engine Firing Order: 1-3-4-2
Distributor rotation: counterclockwise

CAPACITIES

| Year | Engine No. Cyl. Displacement (cc) | Engine Crankcase Capacity Including Filter (qts.) | Transmission Pts To Refill After Draining | | Drive Axle (pts) | Gasoline Tank (gals) | Cooling System (qts) | |
			Manual	Automatic (Total Capacity)			With Heater	With A/C
'81–'85	4-1597	4.0	5.0①	②	③	④	6.7	8.1
'84–'85	4-2000	7.2⑤	①	—	③	⑥	8.1	8.1

① 5 speed: 6.1
② Total dry capacity–converter, cooler and sump drained.
1981–82: 20 pts, 1983–85: 16.6 pts. Partial fluid change (pan sump only), add 8 pts, start engine and check level. Add necessary fluid until correct level is reached.
③ Included in transmission capacity
④ 1981–'82: 10 gal. Standard
11.3 gal. Extended range
1983–'85: 10 gal. FE models
13 gal. Standard
13 gal. EXP/LN7

⑤ Capacity for complete system-pan capacity is 5.3 qts.
⑥ 1984: 14 gal; 1985; 15.2 gal.
⑦ After filter replacement, add 4 qts of oil and run engine. Shut engine off and check oil level. Add ½ qt if necessary.

FORD MOTOR CO. REAR WHEEL DRIVE
Ford, Lincoln, Mercury—All Models

VEHICLE IDENTIFICATION NUMBER (VIN)

It is important for servicing and ordering parts to be certain of the vehicle and engine identification. The VIN (vehicle identification number) is a 13 or 17 digit number visible through the windshield on the driver's side of the dash and contains the vehicle and engine identification codes. It can be interpreted as follows:

Engine Code						Model Year Code	
Code	Cu. In.	Liters	Cyl.	Carb.	Eng. Mfg.	Code	Year
Y	140	2.3	4	2	Ford	8	1978
W('79)	140	2.3	4	Turbo	Ford	9	1979
T('80)	140	2.3	4	Turbo	Ford	0	1980
A('80)	140	2.3	4	2	Ford		
Z	170	2.8	6	2	Ford		
T	200	3.3	6	1	Ford		
B('80)	200	3.3	6	1	Ford		
L	250	4.1	6	1	Ford		
C('80)	250	4.1	6	1	Ford		
D	255	4.2	8	2(W)	Ford		
F	302	5.0	8	2①	Ford		
H②	351W	5.8	8	2③	Ford		
Q	351M	5.8	8	2	Ford		
S	400	6.6	8	2	Ford		
A	460	7.5	V8	4	Ford		
C	460PI	7.5	V8	4	Ford		

The thirteen digit Vehicle Identification Number can be used to determine engine application and model year. The first digit indicates model code, and the fifth digit indicates engine application.

NOTE: Windsor and Modified Cleveland 351 V8 engines were used thru 1979. A quick visual means of identification is the location of the thermostat housing water outlet. Windsor engines have the housing mounted on the front of the intake manifold, while the Modified Cleveland engine has the thermostat housing mounted on the engine block.

① EFI on various models in 1980 ③ VV carburetor on various models in 1980
② G or E in 1980 ④ A in Canada

VEHICLE IDENTIFICATION NUMBER (VIN)

It is important for servicing and ordering parts to be certain of the vehicle and engine identification. The VIN (vehicle identification number) is a 13 or 17 digit number visible through the windshield on the driver's side of the dash and contains the vehicle and engine identification codes. It can be interpreted as follows:

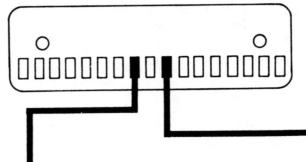

Engine Code						Model Year Code	
Code	Cu. In.	Liters	Cyl.	Carb.	Eng. Mfg.	Code	Year
A	140	2.3	4	2(1)	Ford	B	1981
T	140	2.3	4	Turbo	Ford	C	1982
6	140	2.3	4	Propane	Ford	D	1983
W('83–'85)	140	2.3	4	Turbo	Ford	E	1984
B	200	3.3	6	1	Ford	F	1985
3	232	3.8	V6	①	Ford		
D	255	4.2	V8	2(VV)	Ford		
F	302	5.0	V8	①	Ford		
M	302HO	5.0	V8	①	Ford		
G	351W	5.8	V8	①	Ford		
G	351HO	5.8	V8	①	Ford		

The seventeen digit Vehicle Identification Number can be used to determine engine application and model year. The tenth digit indicates the model year, and the eighth digit identifies the engine code.
① EFI, VV, 2 bbl. or 4 bbl. depending on model

TRANSMISSION CODES

1.	Three speed
2.	Five speed overdrive
4.	Four speed overdrive (SROD)
5.	Five speed
5.	Five speed overdrive (RAP)
6.	Four speed (Borg Warner)
7.	Four speed overdrive (RUG)
7.	Four speed (ET) (Hummer)
C.	C5 automatic
S.	JATCO automatic
T.	AOD (automatic overdrive)
U.	C6 automatic
V.	C3 automatic
W.	C4 automatic
X.	FMX automatic
Y.	Borg Warner automatic
Z.	C6 police automatic

Refer to the vehicle certification plate on the driver's door frame for transmission identification code.

TUNE-UP SPECIFICATIONS—PINTO/BOBCAT/MUSTANG II

(When analyzing compression test results, look for uniformity among cylinders rather than specific pressures.)

Year	Engine No. Cyl. Displacement cu in. (cc)	Spark Plugs		Distributor		Ignition Timing (deg) ▲		Valves Intake Opens ■ (deg)	Fuel Pump Pressure (psi)	Idle Speed (rpm) ▲	
		Orig. Type	Gap ● (in.)	Point Dwell (deg)	Point Gap (in.)	Man Trans ●	Auto Trans			Man Trans	Auto Trans
'78	4-140 (2300)	AWRF-42	.034	Electronic		6B	20B	22	5½–6½	850①	800(750)①
	6-171 (2800)	AWSF-42	.034	Electronic		10B	12B(6B)	20	3½–5¾	700①	650⑤(600)①
	8-302 (4950)	ARF-52 (ARF-52-6)	.050 (.060)	Electronic		6B	4B(12B)	16	5½–6½	900①	700①
'79	4-140 (2300)	AWSF-42	.034	Electronic		6B	20B	22	5½–6½	850①	800(750)①
	6-171 (2800)	AWSF-42	.034	Electronic		NA	9B(6B)	28	3½–5½	NA	650(600)①
'80	4-140 (2300)	AWSF-42	.034	Electronic		6B	20B(12B)	22	5½–6½	850②	750②

NOTE: The underhood specifications sticker often reflects tune-up specification changes made in production. Sticker figures must be used if they disagree with those in this chart. Part numbers in this chart are not recommendations by Chilton for any product by brand name.

▲ See text for procedure
■ All figures Before Top Dead Center
● Figure in parentheses is for California
B Before Top Dead Center

— Not applicable
① See underhood sticker for TSP-OFF or A/C-OFF idle speeds
② TSP-off idle speed—550 rpm

TUNE-UP SPECIFICATIONS—MID SIZE MODELS

(When analyzing compression test results, look for uniformity among cylinders rather than specific pressures.)

Year	Eng. V.I.N. Code	No. Cyl. Displacement (cu. in.)	Eng. mfg.	Spark Plugs Orig. Type	Gap ● (in.)	Distributor Point Dwell* (deg)	Point Gap (in.)	Ignition Timing (deg) ▲ Man Trans ●	Auto Trans	Valves Intake Opens ■ (deg)	Fuel Pump Pressure (psi)	Idle Speed (rpm) ▲ Man Trans ●	Auto Trans
'78	Y	4-140	Ford	AWRF-42	.034	Electronic		6B	20B	22	5½–6½	850	800
	T	6-200	Ford	BRF-82	.050 (.060)	Electronic		10B	10B(6B)	20	5½–6½	800	650
	L	6-250	Ford	BRF-82	.050	Electronic		4B	14B(6B)	18	5½–6½	800	600
	F	8-302	Ford	ARF-52 (ARF-52-6)	.050 (.060)	Electronic		10B	6B(12B)④	16	5½–6½	500	650
	H	8-351W	Ford	ARF-52 (ARF-52-6)	.050 (.060)	Electronic		—	14B	16	4–6	—	650
	Q	8-351M	Ford	ARF-52 (ARF-52-6)	.050 (.060)	Electronic		—	14B(16B)	19½	6½–7½	—	650
	S	8-400	Ford	ARF-52 (ARF-52-6)	.050 (.060)	Electronic		—	13B(16B)	17	6½–7½	—	650
'79	Y	4-140	Ford	AWSF-42	.034	Electronic		6B	20B	22	5½–6½	850	850(750)
	W	4-140T	Ford	AWSF-32	.034	Electronic		2B	—	22	6½–7½	900	—
	Z	6-170	Ford	AWSF-42	.034	Electronic		—	9B(6B)	28	3½–5½	—	650(600)
	T	6-200	Ford	BRF-82	.050 (.060)	Electronic		8B	10B	20	5½–6½	800	650
	L	6-250	Ford	BSF-82	.050	Electronic		4B	10B(6B)	18	5½–6½	800	600
	F	8-302	Ford	ASF-52 (ASF-52-6)	.050 (.060)	Electronic		12B	6B④	16	5½–6½	800	600
	H	8-351W	Ford	ASF-52	.050	Electronic		—	15B	23	6½–8	—	650
	Q	8-351M	Ford	ASF-52	.050	Electronic		—	12B(14B)	17⑤	6–8	—	600
'80	A	4-140	Ford	AWSF-42	.035	Electronic		6B	20B(12B)	22	5½–6½	850	750
	T	4-140T	Ford	AWSF-32	.050	Electronic		6B(2B)	8B(2B)	22	6½–7½	900	800(600)
	B	6-200	Ford	BRF-82	.050	Electronic		10B	12B	20	5½–6½	700⑥	550(600)⑦
	C	6-250	Ford	BSF-82	.050	Electronic		8B	10B	18	5½–6½	700	550
	D	8-255	Ford	ASF-42	.050	Electronic		8B	8B(6B)④	16	4–6	500	550(500)④
	F	8-302	Ford	ASF-52 (ASF-52-6)	.050 (.060)	Electronic		—	8B④	16	5½–6½	—	550④
'81	A	4-140	Ford	AWSF-42	.034	Electronic		6B	6B	22	5½–6½	700	700
	T	4-140T	Ford	AWSF-32	.034	Electronic		6B	8B	22	6½–7½	850	750(65)
	B	6-200	Ford	BSF-92	.050	Electronic		10B	10B	20	5½–6½	700⑥	600(700)⑦
	D	8-255	Ford	ASF-52	.050	Electronic		10B	10B	16	5½–6½	700⑥	550⑦
	F	8-302	Ford	ASF-52	.050	Electronic		8B	8B	16	5½–6½	800	800
'82	A	4-140	Ford	AWSF-42	.034	Electronic		①	①	22	5½–6½	850	750
	B	6-200	Ford	BSF-92	.050	Electronic		①	①	20	6–8	700①	600(700)①
	3	6-232	Ford	AGSP-52	.044	Electronic		①	①	13	6–8	①	①
	F	8-302	Ford	ASF-52	.050	Electronic		—	①④	16	6–8⑧	①④	①④

TUNE-UP SPECIFICATIONS

(When analyzing compression test results, look for uniformity among cylinders rather than specific pressures.)

Year	Engine Eng. V.I.N. Code	Engine No. Cyl. Displacement (cu. in.)	Engine Eng. mfg.	Spark Plugs Orig. Type	Spark Plugs Gap ● (in.)	Distributor Point Dwell* (deg)	Distributor Point Gap (in.)	Ignition Timing (deg) ▲ Man Trans ●	Ignition Timing (deg) ▲ Auto Trans	Valves Intake Opens ■ (deg)	Fuel Pump Pressure (psi)	Idle Speed (rpm) ▲ Man Trans ●	Idle Speed (rpm) ▲ Auto Trans
'83–'85	A	4-140	Ford	AWSF-44	.044	Electronic		①	①	22	5½–6½	850	800
	—	4-140P	Ford	AWSF-34	.034	Electronic		①	①	—	—	—	750
	W	4-140T	Ford	AWSF32C	.034	Electronic		①	①	—	—	①④	①④
	B	6-200	Ford	BSF-92	.050	Electronic		①	①	20	6–8	—	550
	3	6-232	Ford	AWSF-52⑪	.044	Electronic		①	①	13	6–8⑨	—	700(650)①
	F	8-302	Ford	ASF-42①⑫	.044	Electronic		①	①④	16	6–8⑧⑩	700①	550①

NOTE: The underhood specifications sticker often reflects tune-up specification changes. Sticker data must be used if they disagree with those shown in this chart.
NOTE: Part numbers listed in this chart are not recommendations by Chilton for any product by part number or brand name.

▲ See text for procedure
■All figures are in degrees Before Top Dead Center
T Turbocharged
P Propane
①Calibrations vary depending upon model: refer to the underhood specifications sticker

②Electric fuel pump mounted in the gas tank
③California models and Versailles use figures in parentheses
④EEC equipped depending on model—Ignition timing, idle speed and mixture are non-adjustable.
⑤California; 19½

⑥900 rpm w/AC
⑦700 rpm w/AC
⑧EFI models; 39 psi
⑨In tank pump 40–45
⑩6 low pressure pump 39 EFI pressure
⑪CFI models: AWSF-54
⑫'85–ASF52, HO–ASF42

TUNE-UP SPECIFICATIONS—FULL SIZE MODELS

(When analyzing compression test results, look for uniformity among cylinders rather than specific pressures.)

Year	Engine No. Cyl. Displacement (cu. in.)	Eng V.I.N. Code	hp	Eng MFG	Spark Plugs Orig. Type	Gap ● (in.)	Distributor Point Dwell (deg)	Point Gap (in.)	Ignition Timing (deg) ▲ Man Trans ●	Auto Trans	Valves Intake Opens ■ (deg)	Fuel Pump Pressure (psi)	Idle Speed (rpm) ▲ Man Trans*	Auto ● Trans
'78	8-302	F	All	Ford	ARF-52 (ARF-52-6)	.050 (.060)	Electronic		—	14B	16	5½–6½	—	650
	8-351W	H	All	Ford	ARF-52 (ARF-52-6)	.050 (.060)	Electronic		—	4B	23	4–6	—	650
	8-351M	Q	All	Ford	ARF-52 (ARF-52-6)	.050 (.060)	Electronic		—	12B(16B)	19½	6½–7½	—	650
	8-400	S	All	Ford	ARF-52 (ARF-52-6)	.050 (.060)	Electronic		—	13B(16B)	17	6½–7½	—	650
	8-460	A	All	Ford	ARF-52 (ARF-52-6)	.050 (.060)	Electronic		—	10B	8	7½–8½	—	580
	8-460	C	PI	Ford	ARF-52-6	.060	Electronic		—	16B	18	7½–8½	—	580
'79	8-302	F	All	Ford	ASF-52 (ASF-52-6)	.050 (.060)	Electronic		—	6B	16	5½–6½	—	550
	8-351 W	H	2 V	Ford	ASF-52	.050	Electronic		—	15B	23	6½–8	—	550
	8-351 W	H	VV	Ford	ASF-52	.050	Electronic		—	EEC	23	6½–8	—	550
	8-400	S	2 V	Ford	ASF-52 (ASF-52-6)	.050 .060	Electronic		—	14B	17	6.0–8.0	—	575(600)
'80–'82	8-255	D	VV	Ford	ASF-52	.050	Electronic		—	①②	16	6–8	—	500②
	8-302	F	VV	Ford	ASF-52	.050	Electronic		—	①②	17	6½–8	—	550②
	8-302	F	EFI	Ford	ASF-52	.050	Electronic		—	①②	17	39.2	—	550②
	8-351 W	H	VV	Ford	ASF-52	.050	Electronic		—	①②	23	6½–8	—	550②

TUNE-UP SPECIFICATIONS—FULL SIZE MODELS

(When analyzing compression test results, look for uniformity among cylinders rather than specific pressures.)

Year	Engine				Spark Plugs		Distributor		Ignition Timing (deg) ▲		Valves Intake Opens ■ (deg)	Fuel Pump Pressure (psi)	Idle Speed (rpm) ▲	
	No. Cyl. Displacement (cu. in.)	Eng V.I.N. Code	hp	Eng MFG	Orig. Type	Gap ● (in.)	Point Dwell (deg)	Point Gap (in.)	Man Trans ●	Auto Trans			Man Trans*	Auto ● Trans
'83–'85	8-302	F	EFI	Ford	ASF-52	.050	Electronic		—	①②	16	39.2	—	550②
	8-302	F	VV	Ford	ASF-52	.050	Electronic		—	①②	16	6½–8	—	600②
	8-351	G	VV	Ford	ASF-52③	.050	Electronic		—	①②	23	6½–8	—	600②

NOTE: The underhood specifications sticker often reflects tune-up specification changes made in production. Sticker figures must be used if they disagree with those in this chart.

▲ See text for procedure

●Figure in parentheses indicates California engine

■All figures Before Top Dead Center

*In all cases where two idle speed figures are separated by a slash, the first is for idle speed with solenoid energized and the automatic transmission in Drive, while the second is for idle speed with solenoid disconnected and automatic transmission in Neutral.

Part numbers in this chart are not recommendations by Chilton for any product by brand name.

B Before Top Dead Center

M Modified Cleveland

PI Police Interceptor

W Windsor

EEC Electronic Engine Control. Ignition timing, idle speed and mixture are non-adjustable. See text for description.

VV Variable Venturi

— Not applicable

①See Underhood specifications Sticker

②Some models: EEC controls timing and idle speed.

③'85—ASF-42 .044

FIRING ORDERS

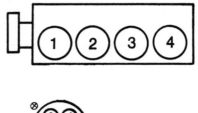

FORD MOTOR CO. 2300 cc 4-cyl.
Engine firing order: 1-3-4-2
Distributor rotation: clockwise

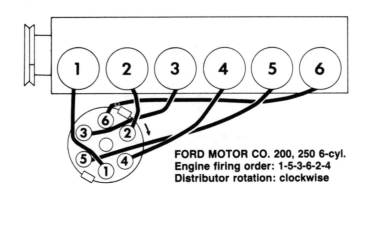

FORD MOTOR CO. 200, 250 6-cyl.
Engine firing order: 1-5-3-6-2-4
Distributor rotation: clockwise

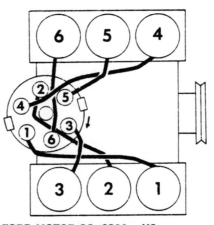

FORD MOTOR CO, 2800cc V6
Engine firing order: 1-4-2-5-3-6
Distributor rotation: Clockwise

FIRING ORDERS

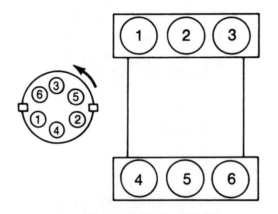

FORD MOTOR CO. 232 V6
Engine firing order: 1-4-2-5-3-6
Distributor rotation: counterclockwise

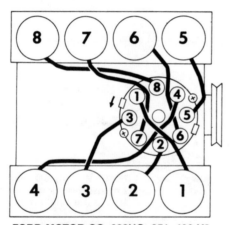

FORD MOTOR CO. 302HO, 351, 400 V8
Engine firing order: 1-3-7-2-6-5-4-8
Distributor rotation: counterclockwise

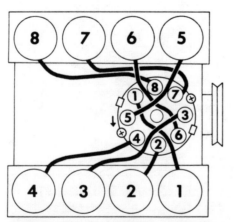

FORD MOTOR CO. 255,302 (exc. HO) 460
V8 Engine firing order: 1-5-4-2-6-3-7-8
Distributor rotation: counterclockwise

CAPACITIES—PINTO/BOBCAT/MUSTANG II

Year	Engine No. Cyl. Displacement (Cu. In.)	Engine Crankcase Add 1 Qt For ■ New Filter	TRANSMISSION Pts To Refill After Draining		Drive Axle (pts)	Gasoline Tank (gals)	Cooling System (qts)	
			4-Speed Manual	Automatic (Total capacity)			With Heater	With A/C
'78	4-140 (2300cc) Pinto, Bobcat	4.0	2.8	①	2.3②	13③	8.6	9.0
	4-140 (2300cc) Mustang II	4.0	3.5	①	3.0	13④	8.8	9.1
	6-171 (2800cc) Pinto, Bobcat	4.5	2.8	①	4.5	13③	8.5	9.2
	6-171 (2800cc) Mustang II	4.5	3.5	①	4.5	13④	8.5	9.0
	8-302 (4950)	4.0	3.5	①	4.5	13④	16.3	16.3
'79–'80	4-140 (2300cc)	4.0	2.8	①	2.5②	13③ ⑤	8.6	9.0
	6-171 (2800cc)	4.5	2.8	①	4.5	13③ ⑤	8.5	9.1

■ ½ quart for 2800
— Not applicable
① C3 trans.—16; C4 trans.—14
② 8.00 in. axle—4.5
③ 14 gals on station wagon
④ 16.5 gals with auxiliary tank in Mustang II
⑤ Optional on some 1979–80 models— 11.7

CAPACITIES—MID SIZE MODELS

Year	Engine No. Cyl. Displacement (Cu. In.)	Engine Crankcase Add 1 Qt For New Filter	Transmission Pts to Refill After Draining			Drive Axle (pts)	Gasoline Tank (gals)	Cooling System (qts)	
			Manual		Automatic (Total Capacity)			With Heater	With A/C
			3-Speed	4/5-Speed					
'78–'80	Versailles								
	8-302	4	—	—	20.5[3]	5.0	19.2	14.6	14.6
	8-351W	4	—	—	20.5	5.0	19.2	15.7	15.7
'78–'80	Granada, Monarch								
	6-200	4	3.5	4.0[4]	—	4.0[5]	19.2[6]	9.9	9.9
	6-250	4	3.5	4.0[4]	17.0[7]	4.0[5]	19.2[6]	10.5	10.7
	8-255	4	3.5	4.0[4]	17.2	4.5	18.0	14.2	14.3
	8-302	4	3.5	4.0[4]	20.0[8]	4.0[5]	19.2[6]	14.6	14.6
	8-351	4	—	—	20.0	4.0[5]	19.2[6]	15.7	16.7
'78–'79	LTD II, Thunderbird, Cougar, Cougar XR-7								
	8-302	4	—	—	[1]	5.0	21.0[9]	14.3[10]	14.6
	8-351W	4	—	—	[1]	5.0	21.0[9]	15.5	16.0
	8-351M	4	—	—	[1]	5.0	21.0[9]	17.1[11]	17.5[11]
	8-400	4	—	—	[1]	5.0	21.0[9]	17.1[11]	17.5[11]
'78–'82	Fairmont, Futura, Zephyr								
	4-140	4	—	2.8[4]	16[12]	[13]	16[14][15][16]	8.6[17]	10.2
	6-200	4	3.5	2.8[4]	19[12]	[13]	16[14][16]	9.0[18][19]	9.0[18][19]
	8-255	4	—	—	16[12]	[13]	16[14][16]	13.4	13.5
	8-302	4	—	—	20.5[12]	[13]	16[14]	13.9	14.0
'79–'82	Mustang, Capri					[13]			
	4-140	4	—	2.8	20[20][12]	[13]	11.5[24]	8.6[17]	10[27]
	4-140T	4.5	—	3.5	20[20][12]	[13]	11.5[24]	8.6[26]	10.2[26]
	6-170	4.5	—	4.5	20[20][12]	[13]	12.5	9.2	9.2
	6-200	4	—	4.5	12[20][23]	[13]	16[25][24]	9[18]	9[18]
	8-255	4	—	4.5	19[23]	[13]	12.5[24]	13.4[28]	13.7[29]
	8-302	4	—	4.5	19	[13]	12.5[24]	13.9	14.2
'80–'81	Cougar XR-7, Thunderbird								
	6-200	4	—	—	16[23]	3.5	17.5	13.0	13.2
	8-255	4	—	—	20[30]	3.5	17.5	13.2	13.3
	8-302	4	—	—	20[30]	3.5	17.5	12.7	12.8
'81	Cougar, Granada								
	4-140	4	—	2.8	16	3.5	14.7	8.6	8.6
	6-200	4	—	—	16	3.5	16.0	8.1	8.1
	8-255	4	—	—	19	3.5	16.0	13.4	13.5

CAPACITIES—MID SIZE MODELS

Year	Engine No. Cyl. Displacement (Cu. In.)	Engine Crankcase Add 1 Qt For New Filter	Transmission Pts to Refill After Draining			Drive Axle (pts)	Gasoline Tank (gals)	Cooling System (qts)	
			Manual		Automatic (Total Capacity)			With Heater	With A/C
			3-Speed	⅘-Speed					
'82	Cougar XR-7, Thunderbird, Lincoln Continental								
	6-200	4	—	—	22	3.25	21	8.4	8.4
	6-232	4	—	—	24	3.25	21③①	8.3	8.6
	8-255	4	—	—	24	3.25	21	14.9	15
	8-302	4	—	—	24	3.25	22.6	13.3	13.4
'82	Cougar, Granada								
	4-140	4	—	—	16	⑬	16.0③②	10.2	10.2
	6-200	4	—	—	22	3.25	16.0③②	8.4	8.4
	6-232	4	—	—	22	3.25	16.0③②	8.3	8.3
'83–'85	LTD/Marquis								
	4-140	4	—	2.8	16	3.25③③	16	8.6	9.4
	4-140P	4	—	—	16	3.25③③	24	8.6	9.4
	6-200	4	—	—	22	3.25③③	16	8.4	8.5
	6-232	4	—	—	22③④	3.25③③	16	10.7	10.8
'83–'85	Mustang/Capri								
	4-140	4③⑥	—	2.8③⑤	16	3.25③③	15.4	8.6	9.4③④
	6-232	4	—	—	22	3.25③③	15.4	8.4	8.4
	8-302	4	—	4.5	—	3.55	15.4	13.1	13.4
'83	Fairmont Futura								
	4-140	4	—	2.8	16	3.25③③	16	10.2	10.2
	6-200	4	—	—	22	3.25③③	16	8.4	8.4
'83–'85	Thunderbird, Cougar Continental								
	4-140 Turbo	4.5③⑥	—	4.75	—	3.25③③	18	8.4	8.7
	6-232	4	—	—	22③④	3.25③③	21	10.4	10.7
	8-302	4	—	—	22③④	3.25③③	20.7③⑦	13.3	13.4

T—Turbocharged
P—Propane
N/A—Specs not available at time of printing
① C4-20 pts; C6-25 pts; FMX-22 pts
② Station wagon; 21.2 gal
③ '79 and later; 20 pts
④ 4 speed overdrive, 4.5 pts
⑤ 8 in.-4.5 pts
  8.7 in.-4.0 pts
  9 in.-5.0 pts
⑥ 1 gal less on certain '76 models; '78-'80; 18 gals
⑦ 16.5 pts with C4
⑧ 17 pts for '76
⑨ '79 optional tank-27.5 gals

⑩ '77-13.5 qts
⑪ '78–'79; 16.5 qts
⑫ '81-13.25 pts with C4; 14.5 pts w/6 cyl; 19 pts w/V8
⑬ 6.75 in. axle-2.5 pts; 7.5 in. axle-3.5 pts
⑭ '80–'81 Station wagon; 14 gals
⑮ '81; 14.7 gals
⑯ '82; 20 gal optional
⑰ '82; 10.2 qts
⑱ '80–'82; 8.1 qts
⑲ '82; 8.4 qts
⑳ C3-16 pts; C4-14 pts
㉑ add ½ qt with filter change
㉒ '79; 14 pts
㉓ '82; C5-22 pts

㉔ '82; 15.4 gal
㉕ '80–'81; 12.5 gal
㉖ '80–'81; 9.2 qts
㉗ '80–'81; 9.0 qts-'82; 10.2 qts
㉘ '82; 14.7 qts
㉙ '82; 15 qts
㉚ AOD transmission; 24 pts
㉛ Continental; 20 gals std; 22.6 optional
㉜ 20 gals optional
㉝ Traction-Lok; 3.55 pts
㉞ AOD transmission; 24 pts
㉟ 5 speed transmission; 4.75 pts
㊱ 4.5 Turbo add .5 with filter
㊲ 22.3 Continental
㊳ 10.5—Turbo models

CAPACITIES—FULL SIZE MODELS

Year	Engine No. Cyl. Displacement (Cu. In.)	Engine Crankcase Add 1 Qt For New Filter	Automatic Transmission (Total capacity)	Drive Axle (pts)	Gasoline Tank (gals) ■	Cooling System With Heater	Cooling System With A/C
'78	8-302	4	①	4④	24.2	15.1	15.1
	8-351W	4	①	4④	24.2	16.2	16.2
	8-351M	4	①	4④	24.2	16.9	16.9⑤
'78	8-400	4	①	4④	24.2	16.9	16.9⑤
	8-460	4	①	5	24.2	18.6	19.0
	8-460PI	6②	①	5	24.2	19.7	19.7
'79	8-302	4	①	⑥	19	13.3	13.8
	8-351W	4	①	⑥	19	14.6	15.2
'80	8-302	4	①	⑥	19	13.3	13.4
	8-351W	4	①	⑥	19	14.4	14.5
'81	8-255	4	24	⑥	20	14.8	15.2
	8-302	4	24	⑥	20	13.0	13.3
	8-351	4	24	⑥	20	13.9	14.0
'82–'85	8-225⑦	4	24	⑥	20	14.8	15.2
	8-302	4	24	⑥	20⑧	13.3	13.4
	8-351	4	24	⑥	20	13.8	13.8

■ Station wagons:
'79–'80—20 gals
through '78—21 gals
M Modified Cleveland
PI Police Interceptor
— Not applicable
① See Automatic Trans. Capacities Chart
② 7.5 w/oil cooler

③ With auxiliary fuel tank; sedan—32.3 gals; wagon—29.0 gals.
④ 5 with locker or 3.0:1 ratio
⑤ Trailer Towing: 17.4
⑥ 7.5 inch axle—3.5
8.5 inch axle—4.0
⑦ Discontinued for 1983
⑧ Lincoln: 18

① AUTOMATIC TRANSMISSION CAPACITIES
(Pts)

Year	Code	Capacities
'78–'80	X	22
'78–'80	W	20.5
'78–'80	U, Z	25
'80–'84	T	24

BUICK REAR WHEEL DRIVE
Electra, Century, Regal, Riviera, Skylark, LeSabre

VEHICLE IDENTIFICATION NUMBER (VIN)

It is important for servicing and ordering parts to be certain of the vehicle and engine identification. The VIN (vehicle identification number) is a 13 or 17 digit number visible through the windshield on the driver's side of the dash and contains the vehicle and engine identification codes. It can be interpreted as follows:

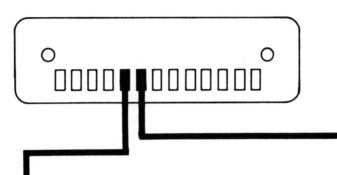

ENGINE CODE						MODEL YEAR CODE	
Code	Cu. In.	Liters	Cyl.	Carb.	Eng. Mfg.	Code	Year
C (78–79)	196	3.2	6	2	Buick	8	78
A	231	3.8	6	2	Buick	9	79
G	231①	3.8	6	2	Buick	A	80
2	231	3.8	6	2	Buick		
3	231①	3.8	6	4	Buick		
4	252	4.1	6	4	Buick		
S	265	4.3	8	2	Pont.		
Y	301	4.9	8	2	Pont.		
W	301	4.9	8	4	Pont.		
U	305	5.0	8	2	Chev.		
H	305	5.0	8	2	Chev.		
G	305	5.0	8	2	Chev.		
L	350	5.7	8	4	Chev.		
R	350	5.7	8	4	Olds.		
X	350	5.7	8	4	Buick		
N	350	5.7	8	Diesel	Olds.		
Z	400	6.5	8	4	Pont.		
K	403	6.6	8	4	Olds.		

The thirteen digit Vehicle Identification Number can be used to determine engine application and model year. The 6th digit indicates the model year, and the 5th digit identifies the factory-installed engine.
① Turbocharged

VEHICLE IDENTIFICATION NUMBER (VIN)

It is important for servicing and ordering parts to be certain of the vehicle and engine identification. The VIN (vehicle identification number) is a 13 or 17 digit number visible through the windshield on the driver's side of the dash and contains the vehicle and engine identification codes. It can be interpreted as follows:

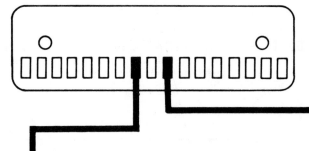

Engine Code

Code	Cu. In.	Liters	Cyl.	Carb.	Eng. Mfg.
A	231	3.8	6	2	Buick
3	231①	3.8	6	4	Buick
8	231①	3.8	6	4	Buick
9	231	3.8	6	M.F.I.	Buick
4	252	4.1	6	4	Buick
V	263	4.3	6	Diesel	Olds.
S	265	4.3	8	2	Pont.
J	267	4.4	8	2	Chev.
W	301	4.9	8	4	Pont.
H	305	5.0	8	4	Chev.
Y	307	5.0	8	4	Olds.
X	350	5.7	8	4	Buick
N	350	5.7	8	Diesel	Olds.

MODEL YEAR CODE

Code	Year
B	81
C	82
D	83
E	84
F	85

The seventeen digit Vehicle Identification Number can be used to determine engine application and model year. The 10th digit indicates the model year, and the 8th digit identifies the factory-installed engine.

① Turbocharged

TUNE-UP SPECIFICATIONS

When analyzing compression test results, look for uniformity among cylinders rather than specific pressures

Year	Engine V.I.N. Code	Engine Type	Engine Manufacturer	Spark Plugs Type①	Gap (in.)	Ignition Timing (deg. B.T.D.C.)② Manual Transmission③	Automatic Transmission③	Intake Valve Opens (°B.T.D.C.)	Fuel Pump Pressure (psi)	Idle Speed (rpm)④ Manual Transmission③	Automatic Transmission③
'78	C	6-196	Buick	R46TSX	.060	15 @ 800	15	18	4½–5½	800/600	600
	A	6-231	Buick	R46TSX	.060	15 @ 800	15	17	4½–5½	800/600	670/600
	G	6-231	Buick	R44TSX	.060	—	15 @ 600	17	4½–5½	—	650
	3	6-231	Buick	R44TSX	.060	—	15 @ 600	17	4½–5½	—	650
	Y	8-301	Pont.	R46TSX	.060	—	12 @ 550	27	7–8.5	—	650/550
	H,U	8–305	Chev.	R45TS	.045	—	4 @ 500 (6 @ 500) [8 @ 600]	28	7½–9	—	600/500 (650/500) [700/600]
	L	8-350	Chev.	R45TS	.045	—	8 @ 500 [8 @ 600]	28	7½–9	—	600/500 [650/600]
	R	8-350	Olds.	R46SZ	.060	—	20 @ 1100	16	5½–6½	—	650/550 [700/600]
	X	8-350	Buick	R46TSX	.060	—	15 @ 600	16	7½–9	—	550
	Z	8-400	Pont.	R45TSX	.060	—	16	29	7–8½	—	650
	K	8-403	Olds.	R46SZ	.060	—	20 @ 1100	16	5½–6½	—	650/550 [700/600]
'79	C	6-196	Buick	R45TSX or R46TSX	.060 .060	15 @ 800	15 @ 600	16	4¼–5¾	800/600	670/550
	A	6-231	Buick	R45TSX or R46TSX	.060 .060	15 @ 800	15 @ 600	16	4¼–5¾	800/600	670/550 (600) [600]
	2	6-231	Buick	R45TSX or R46TSX	.060 .060	—	15 @ 580	16	4¼–5¾	—	670/580
	3	6-231	Buick	R44TSX	.060	—	15	16	4¼–5¾	—	650
	Y	8-301	Pont.	R46TSX	.060	—	12 @ 650	27	7–8½	—	650/500
	W	8-301	Pont.	R45TSX	.060	—	12 @ 650	27	7–8½	—	650/500
	G	8-305	Chev.	R45TS	.045	—	4 @ 600	28	7½–9	—	⑤
	H	8-305	Chev.	R45TS	.045	—	4 @ 500 [8 @ 600]	28	7½–9	—	600/500 [650/600]
	L	8-350	Chev.	R45TS	.045	—	8 @ 600 [8 @ 500]	28	7½–9	—	600/500 [650/600]
	R	8-350	Olds.	R46SZ	.060	—	20 @ 1100	16	6–7½	—	650/550 (600/500) [700/600]
	X	8-350	Buick	R45TSX or R46TSX	.060 .060	—	15	13½	6–7½	—	550
	K	8-403	Olds.	R46SZ	.060	—	20 @ 1100	16	6–7½	—	650/550 (600/500) [700/600]

TUNE-UP SPECIFICATIONS

When analyzing compression test results, look for uniformity among cylinders rather than specific pressures

Year	Engine V.I.N. Code	Engine Type	Engine Manufacturer	Spark Plugs Type①	Spark Plugs Gap (in.)	Ignition Timing (deg. B.T.D.C.)② Manual Transmission③	Ignition Timing (deg. B.T.D.C.)② Automatic Transmission③	Intake Valve Opens (°B.T.D.C.)	Fuel Pump Pressure (psi)	Idle Speed (rpm)④ Manual Transmission③	Idle Speed (rpm)④ Automatic Transmission③
'80	A	6-231	Buick	R45TSX	.060	15 @ 550	15 @ 550	16	5½–6½	800/600	670/550⑥ (620/550)⑦ 550⑧
	3	6-231	Buick	R45TS	.040	—	15 @ 650	16	5½–6½	—	650
	4	6-252	Buick	R45TSX	.060	—	15 @ 550	—	5½–6½	—	680/550⑨ 550⑧
	S	8-265	Pont.	R45TSX	.060	—	10 @ 700	27	7–8½	—	650/550⑨ 550⑧
	W	8-301	Pont.	R45TSX	.060	—	12 @ 500	27	7–8½	—	650/500⑨ 550⑧
	H	8-305	Chev.	R45TS	.035	—	4 @ 550	28	7½–9	—	650/550⑨ 550⑧
	R	8-350	Olds.	R46SX or R47SX	.080 .080	—	18 @ 1100	16	5½–6½	—	650/550
	X	8-350	Buick	R45TSX	.060	—	15 @ 550	13½	6–7½	—	550
'81	A	6-231	Buick	R45TS8	.080	—⑩—		16	5½–6½	—⑩—	
	3	6-231	Buick	R45TS	.040	—⑩—		16	5½–6½	—⑩—	
	4	6-252	Buick	R45TS8	.080	—⑩—		16	5½–6½	—⑩—	
	S	8-265	Pont.	R45TSX	.060	—⑩—		27	5½–6½	—⑩—	
	J	8-267	Chev.	R45TS	.045	—⑩—		28	5½–6½	—⑩—	
	W	8-301	Pont.	R45TSX	.060	—⑩—		27	5½–6½	—⑩—	
	H	8-305	Chev.	R45TS	.045	—⑩—		28	5½–6½	—⑩—	
	Y	8-307	Olds.	R45TS4	.060	—⑩—		20	5½–6½	—⑩—	
	X	8-350	Buick	R45TSX	.060	—⑩—		13½	5½–6½	—⑩—	
'82	A	6-231	Buick	R45TS8	.080	—⑩—		16	5½–6½	—⑩—	
	3	6-231	Buick	R45TSX	.060	—⑩—		16	5½–6½	—⑩—	
	4	6-252	Buick	R45TS8	.080	—⑩—		16	5½–6½	—⑩—	
	J	8-267	Chev.	R45TS	.045	—⑩—		28	5½–6½	—⑩—	
	H	8-305	Chev.	R45TS	.045	—⑩—		28	5½–6½	—⑩—	
	Y	8-307	Olds.	R46SX	.080	—⑩—		20	5½–6½	—⑩—	
'83	A	6-231	Buick	R45TS8	.080	—⑩—		16	5½–6½	—⑩—	
	8	6-231	Buick	R45TSX	.060	—⑩—		16	5½–6½	—⑩—	
	4	6-252	Buick	R45TS8	.080	—⑩—		16	5½–6½	—⑩—	
	Y	8-307	Olds.	R46SX	.080	—⑩—		20	5½–6½	—⑩—	
'84	A	6-231	Buick	R45TSX	.060	—⑩—		16	5½–6½	—⑩—	
	9	6-231	Buick	R44TS	.045	—⑩—		16	26–51	—⑩—	
	4	6-252	Buick	R45TSX	.060	—⑩—		16	5½–6½	—⑩—	
	Y	8-307	Olds	R46SX	.080	—⑩—		20	5½–6½	—⑩—	

TUNE-UP SPECIFICATIONS

When analyzing compression test results, look for uniformity among cylinders rather than specific pressures

| Year | Engine V.I.N. Code | Engine Type | Engine Manufac- turer | Spark Plugs | | Ignition Timing (deg. B.T.D.C.)② | | Intake Valve Opens (°B.T.D.C.) | Fuel Pump Pressure (psi) | Idle Speed (rpm)④ | |
				Type①	Gap (in.)	Manual Transmission③	Automatic Transmission③			Manual Transmission③	Automatic Transmission③
'85	A	6-231	Buick	R45TSX	.060	—⑩—		16	5½–6½	—⑩—	
	9	6-231	Buick	R44TS	.045	—⑩—		16	26–51	—⑩—	
	4	6-252	Buick	R45TSX	.060	—⑩—		16	5½–6½	—⑩—	
	Y	8-307	Olds	R46SX	.080	—⑩—		20	5½–6½	—⑩—	

NOTE: The underhood specifications sticker often reflects tune-up specification changes made in production. Sticker figures must be used if they disagree with those in this chart.

① All models use electronic ignition systems.
B.T.D.C.—Before top dead center (No. 1 cylinder)
C.I.D.—Cubic inch displacement
Min.—Minimum
    Part numbers in this chart are not recommendations by Chilton for any product by brand name.
② On some models, the engine must be held at a specific rpm to accurately check and adjust the ignition timing. See the text for specific procedures.
③ Figure in parenthesis ( ) indicates a special figure for California models; figure in brackets [ ] indicates a special figure for high-altitude models.
④ Most 1979 and later carburetors have idle mixture screws concealed with hardened steel plugs. Normal idle mixture adjustments are not required on these carburetors. Plug removal should be performed only by professional technicians.
⑤ With the solenoid energized, set the solenoid screw to 600 rpm; with the solenoid de-energized, set the carburetor screw to 550 rpm for models with air conditioning, 500 for models without air conditioning.
⑥ With air conditioning, 49 states models only
⑦ With air conditioning, California models only
⑧ All models without air conditioning
⑨ All models with air conditioning
⑩ On vehicles equipped with computerized emissions systems (which have no distributor vacuum advance unit), the idle speed and ignition timing are controlled by the emissions computer. These adjustments should be performed professionally on models so equipped.

DIESEL TUNE-UP SPECIFICATIONS

Year	Engine No. of cyl.- Displacement- Manufacturer	Fuel Pump Pressure (psi)	Compression Pressure (psi)②	Intake Valve Opens (°B.T.D.C.)	Idle Speed (rpm)
'81–'84	8-350-Olds	5.5–6.5	275 minimum	16	①
'82–'84	6-263 Olds	5.8–8.7	275 minimum	16	①

NOTE: The underhood specifications sticker often reflects tune-up specification changes made in production. Sticker figures must be used if they disagree with those in this chart.

B.T.D.C.—Before top dead center (No. 1 cylinder)

① See the underhood specifications sticker.

② The lowest cylinder reading must not be less than 70% of the highest cylinder reading.

FIRING ORDERS

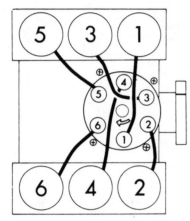

GM (Buick) 231, 252 V6
Engine firing order: 1-6-5-4-3-2
Distributor rotation: clockwise

Buick-manufactured V8 engines
Engine firing order: 1-8-4-3-6-5-7-2
Distributor rotation: clockwise

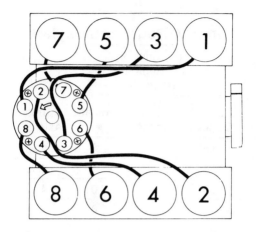

Oldsmobile-manufactured V8 engines
Engine firing order: 1-8-4-3-6-5-7-2
Distributor rotation: counterclockwise

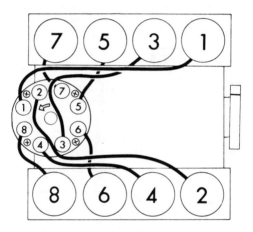

Pontiac-manufactured V8 engines
Engine firing order: 1-8-4-3-6-5-7-2
Distributor rotation: counterclockwise

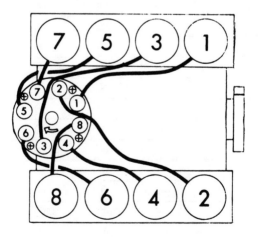

Chevrolet-manufactured V8 engines
Engine firing order: 1-8-4-3-6-5-7-2
Distributor rotation: clockwise

CAPACITIES
Century, Regal and Skylark

Year	Engine No. Cyl. Displacement (cu. in.)	Engine Crankcase Add 1 Qt For New Filter	Transmission Pts to Refill After Draining Manual 3-Speed	4-Speed	Automatic ●	Drive Axle (pts)	Gasoline Tank (gals)	Cooling System (qts) With Heater	With A/C	Heavy Duty
'78	6-196 Buick	4	3.5	—	3.0	4.25	18.1	13.1	13.2	13.1
	6-231 Buick②	4	3.5	3.5	⑤	4.25	18.1	13.1	13.2	13.1
	6-231 Buick⑥	4	3.5	—	3.0	4.25	20.8	13.6	13.7	13.5
	6-231 Buick⑦	4	—	3.5	3.0	3.75	18.5	11.7	12.1	12.6
	8-305 Chev. ②	4	—	—	⑤	4.25	18.1	19.2	18.9	19.6
	8-305 Chev. ④	4	—	—	⑤	4.25	20.8	15.9	16.3	16.9
	8-350 Chev. ②	4	—	—	3.0	4.25	18.1	19.2	18.9	19.6
	8-350 Chev. ④	4	—	—	3.0	4.25	20.8	16.1	16.9	16.9
'79	6-196 Buick	4	3.12	—	③	3.5	18.1	13.5	13.5	13.4
	6-231 Buick④	4	3.12	—	6.0	⑥	21.0	13.7	13.8	—
	6-231 Buick②	4	—	3.5	③	—	18.1	13.4	13.4	—
	8-301 Pont.	4	—	—	③	⑥	18.1	17.6	17.9	17.9
	8-305 Chev. ④	4	—	—	③	⑥	21.0	15.9	16.3	16.9
	8-305 Chev. ④	4	—	—	③	⑥	18.1	17.6	18.1	18.1
	8-350 Chev. ④	4	—	—	③	⑥	18.1	17.6	18.1	18.1
	8-350 Chev. ④	4	—	—	③	⑥	21.0	16.1	16.9	16.9
'80	6-231 Buick②	4	3.5	—	③	⑥	18.1①①	13.4	13.4	—
	8-265 Pont.	4①	—	—	③	⑥	18.0	N.A.	N.A.	—
	8-301 Pont.	4①	—	—	③	⑥	18.0	20.3	21.0	20.8
	8-305 Chev.	4	—	—	③	⑥	18.0	17.6	—	18.1
'81	6-231 Buick	4	3.5	—	③	⑥	18.1⑤	13.4	13.4	—
	6-252 Buick	4	3.5	—	③	⑥	18.1⑤	13.0	13.0	—
	8-265 Pont.	4	—	—	③	⑥	25⑧	N.A.	N.A.	N.A.
	8-350 Diesel	7⑨	—	—	③	⑥	—	N.A.	N.A.	N.A.
'82	6-231 Buick	4	—	—	⑨	⑥	18.1	13	13.1	—
	6-252 Buick	4	—	—	⑨	⑥	18.1	13	13.1	—
	6-263 Diesel	6	—	—	⑨	⑥	18.1⑦	_____	14.8	_____
	8-267 Chev.	4	—	—	⑨	⑥	18.1⑦	_____	21	_____
	8-305 Chev.	4	—	—	⑨	⑥	18.1⑦	_____	19	_____
	8-350 Diesel	6	—	—	⑨	⑥	18.1⑦	_____	17.3	_____
'83–'84	6-231 Buick	4	—	—	⑨	⑥	19	13	13.1	—
	6-252 Buick	4	—	—	⑨	⑥	19	13	13.1	—
	6-263 Diesel	6	—	—	⑨	⑥	19	_____	14.8	_____
	8-350 Diesel	6	—	—	⑨	⑥	19	_____	17.3	_____

CAPACITIES
Century, Regal and Skylark

Year	Engine No. Cyl. Displacement (cu. in.)	Engine Crankcase Add 1 Qt For New Filter	Manual 3-Speed	Manual 4-Speed	Automatic ●	Drive Axle (pts)	Gasoline Tank (gals)	With Heater	With A/C	Heavy Duty
'85	6-231 Buick	4	—	—	⑨	⑥	19	13	13.1	—
	6-252 Buick	4	—	—	⑨	⑥	19	13	13.1	—
	6-263 Diesel	6	—	—	⑨	⑥	19	—	14.8	—
	8-350 Diesel	6	—	—	⑨	⑥	19	—	17.3	—

• Specifications do not include torque convertor
N.A.—Not available
—: Not applicable
① 4 quarts total
② Century and Regal
③ THM 200—6; THM 350—3
④ Skylark
⑤ Wagon—18.2

⑥ 7.5 in. ring gear—3.5; 8.5 in. ring gear—4.25; 8.75 in. ring gear—5.4
⑦ Station wagon—18.2 gal.
⑧ Station wagon—22 gal.
⑨ THM 200 & 200R-4—7 pts.; THM 250C—8 pts.; THM 350C—6.3 pts.

CAPACITIES
Electra, LeSabre, Riviera

Year	Engine No. Cyl. Displacement (cu. in.)	Engine Crankcase Add 1 Qt For New Filter	Manual 3-Speed	Manual 4-Speed	Automatic ●	Drive Axle (pts)	Gasoline Tank (gals)	With Heater	With A/C	Heavy Duty
'78	6-231 Buick	4	—	—	⑦	①	21.0	12.9	12.9	12.9
	8-301 Pont.	5	—	—	⑦	①	21.0④	20.9	20.9	21.6
	8-305 Chev.	4	—	—	⑦	①	21.0④	16.6	16.7	16.7
	8-350 Buick	5	—	—	⑦	①	25.3②⑤	14.1	14.1	14.9
	8-350 Chev.	4	—	—	⑦	①	21.0④	16.6	16.7	18.0
	8-350 Olds.	4	—	—	⑦	①	21.0⑤⑥	14.6	14.5	15.4
	8-403 Olds.	4	—	—	⑦	①	25.3⑤⑥	15.7	16.6	16.6
'79	6-231 Buick④	4	—	—	⑦	①	25.3	12.9	12.9	12.9
	8-301 Pont.④	4	—	—	⑦	①	21.0	20.9	20.9	21.6
	8-305 Chev.④	4	—	—	⑦	①	21.0	20.9	20.9	21.6
	8-350 Buick④	4	—	—	⑦	①	21.0	14.1	14.1	14.9
	8-350 Buick⑧	4	—	—	⑦	①	25.3	14.1	14.1	14.9
	8-350 Olds④	4	—	—	⑦	①	21.0	14.6	14.5	15.4
	8-350 Olds⑧	4	—	—	⑦	①	25.3	14.6	14.5	15.4
	8-403 Olds④	4	—	—	⑦	①	21.0	15.7	16.6	16.6
	8-403 Olds⑧	4	—	—	⑦	①	25.3	15.7	16.6	16.6

CAPACITIES
Electra, LeSabre, Riviera

Year	Engine No. Cyl. Displacement (cu. in.)	Engine Crankcase Add 1 Qt For New Filter	Transmission Pts to Refill After Draining Manual 3-Speed	4-Speed	Automatic ●	Drive Axle (pts)	Gasoline Tank (gals)	Cooling System (qts) With Heater	With A/C	Heavy Duty
'80–'81	6-231 Buick④	4	—	—	⑦	①	25.0④	13.0	13.0	13.0
	6-252 Buick	4	—	—	⑦	①	25.0	13.0	13.0	13.0
	8-301 Pont.④	4	—	—	⑦	①	25.0④	18.9	18.9	18.9
	8-307 Olds.	4	—	—	⑦	①	25.0④	15.6⑩	16.3⑩	16.0⑩
	8-350 Buick④⑧	4	—	—	⑦	①	25.0④	14.3	14.2	14.7
	8-350 Olds.④⑧	4	—	—	⑦	①	25.0④	—	14.5	15.2
	8-350 Diesel	6	—	—	⑦	①	23.0⑨	18.3	18.0	18.0
'82	6-231, 6-252	4	—	—	⑦	①	③	13	13.1	—
	8-307	4	—	—	⑦	①	③	15.4	16.2	16.1
	8-350 Diesel	6	—	—	⑦	①	③	—	17.9	—
'83–'85	6-231, 6-252	4	—	—	⑦	①	25	13	13.1	—
	8-307	4	—	—	⑦	①	25	15.4	16.2	16.1
	8-350 Diesel	6	—	—	⑦	①	25	—	17.9	—

• Specifications do not include torque converter
—: Not applicable

① 7.5 in. ring gear—3.5; 8.5 in. ring gear—4.25; 8.75 in. ring gear—5.4
② Station wagon—18.2 gal.
③ Not available at time of publication
④ LeSabre
⑤ Estate wagon—22 gal.
⑥ Electra—25.3

⑦ THM 200 & 200R-4, 350, 400—Add 6 pts, start engine and allow to warm up, fill as required
⑧ Electra
⑨ Wagon—27 gal.
⑩ Riviera 16.4 (Heater), 16.4 (A.C.), 16.2 (H.D.)

CADILLAC REAR WHEEL DRIVE
Deville, Fleetwood, Seville

VEHICLE IDENTIFICATION NUMBER (VIN)

It is important for servicing and ordering parts to be certain of the vehicle and engine identification. The VIN (vehicle identification number) is a 13 or 17 digit number visible through the windshield on the driver's side of the dash and contains the vehicle and engine identification codes. It can be interpreted as follows:

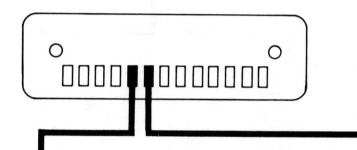

ENGINE CODE					
Code	Cu. In.	Liters	Cyl.	Carb.	Eng. Mfg.
R	350	5.7	8	EFI	Olds.
B	350	5.7	8	EFI	Olds.
N	350	5.7	8	Diesel	Olds.
6	368	6.0	8	4bbl	Cad.
T	425	7.0	8	EFI	Cad.
S	425	7.0	8	4bbl	Cad.

MODEL YEAR CODE	
Code	Year
8	78
9	79
A	80

The thirteen digit Vehicle Identification Number can be used to determine engine application and model year. The 6th digit indicates the model year, and the fifth digit identifies the factory installed engine.

VEHICLE IDENTIFICATION NUMBER (VIN)

It is important for servicing and ordering parts to be certain of the vehicle and engine identification. The VIN (vehicle identification number) is a 13 or 17 digit number visible through the windshield on the driver's side of the dash and contains the vehicle and engine identification codes. It can be interpreted as follows:

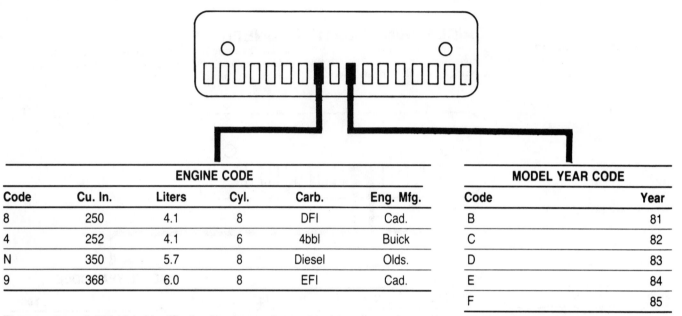

ENGINE CODE						MODEL YEAR CODE	
Code	Cu. In.	Liters	Cyl.	Carb.	Eng. Mfg.	Code	Year
8	250	4.1	8	DFI	Cad.	B	81
4	252	4.1	6	4bbl	Buick	C	82
N	350	5.7	8	Diesel	Olds.	D	83
9	368	6.0	8	EFI	Cad.	E	84
						F	85

The seventeen digit Vehicle Identification Number can be used to determine engine application and model year. The 10th digit indicates the model year, and the 8th digit identifies the factory installed engine.

FIRING ORDERS

NOTE: To avoid confusion, always replace spark plugs and wires one at a time.

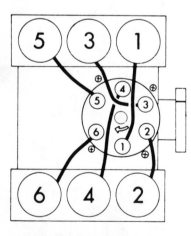

GM (Buick) 252 (4.1 L) V6
Engine firing order: 1-6-5-4-3-2
Distributor rotation: clockwise

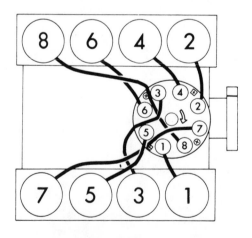

GM (Cadillac) 368,425,
V8 Engine firing order: 1-5-6-3-4-2-7-8
Distributor rotation: clockwise

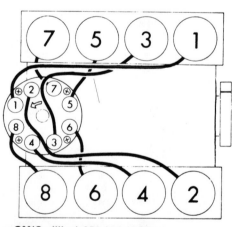

GM(Cadillac) 250 (4.1 L) V8,
GM(Oldsmobile) 350 V8 w/EFI
Engine firing order: 1-8-4-3-6-5-7-2
Distributor rotation: counterclockwise

TUNE-UP SPECIFICATIONS

(When analyzing compression test results, look for uniformity among cylinders rather than specific pressures.)

Year	V.I.N. Code	Displacement (cu in.)	Mfg.	Fuel Delivery	Orig. Type	Gap (in.)	Point Dwell (deg)	Point Gap (in.)	Ignition Timing (deg) ▲ Auto. Trans.	Valves Intake Opens ■ (deg)	Fuel Pump Pressure (psi)	Idle Speed (rpm) ▲ Auto. Trans.
'78	S,T	425	Cad.	⑦	R-45NSX	.060	Electronic		18B @ 1400	21	5¼-6½	650
	B	350	Olds.	EFI	R-47SX	.060	Electronic		10B(8B)	22	5¼-6½	600
	N	350	Olds.	Diesel	—	—	—		5B①	16	8-12③	575
'79	B	350	Olds.	EFI	R-47SX	.060	Electronic		10B	22	5.5-6.5	600
	N	350	Olds.	Diesel	—	—	—		5B①	16	5.5-6.5③	600
	S,T	425	Cad.	⑦	R-45NSX	.060	Electronic		23B②	21	5.5-6.5	650
'80	N	350	Olds.	Diesel	—	—	—		5B①	16	5.5-6.5③	650/575
	6	368	Cad.	4 bbl	R-45NSX	.060	Electronic		18B	11	5.5-6.5	575
	4	252	Buick	4 bbl	R-45TSX	.060	Electronic		15B	16	4¼-5¾	550④
'81	9	368	Cad.	DFI-MD	R-45NSX	.060	Electronic		10B	11	12-14	450⑤
	N	350	Olds.	Diesel	—	—	—		—	16	5½-6½③	⑥
	4	252	Buick	4 bbl	R-45TSX	.060	Electronic		15B	16	4¼-5¾	550④
'82	9	368	Cad.	DFI	R-45NAX	.060	Electronic		⑧	11	12-14	450⑤
	N	350	Olds.	Diesel	—	—	—		⑧	16	5½-6½	⑥
	8	250	Cad.	DFI	R-43NTS6	.060	Electronic		⑧	37	12-14	450
	4	252	Buick	4 bbl	R-45TSX	.060	Electronic		⑧	16	4¼-5¾	550④
'83	8	250	Cad.	DFI	R-43NTS6	.060	Electronic		⑧	37	12-14	⑧
	N	350	Olds.	Diesel	—	—	—		⑧	16	5½-6½	⑧
'84-'85	8	250	Cad.	DFI	R-43NTS6	.060	Electronic		⑧	37	12-14	⑧
	N	350	Olds.	Diesel	—	—	—		⑧	16	5½-6½	⑧

NOTE: The underhood specifications sticker often reflects tune-up specification changes made in production. Sticker figures must be used if they disagree with those in this chart. Part numbers in this chart are not recommendations by Chilton for any product by brand name.

▲ See text for procedure
■ All figures Before Top Dead Center
B Before Top Dead Center
EFI Electronic fuel injection
DFI-MD Digital Fuel Injection-Modulated Displacement
— Not applicable
① Static

② EFI: 18B
③ Injector opening pressure: 1800 psi
④ In drive
⑤ Drive or neutral
⑥ 600 RPM in drive, warm engine; 750 RPM in drive, cold engine
⑦ Eng. Code "S"-4bbl., "T"-E.F.I.
⑧ See underhood decal

CAPACITIES

Year	Engine Displacement (Cu. In.)	Engine Crankcase Add 1 Qt For New Filter	Transmission Automatic Pts To Refill After Draining ●	Drive Axle (pts)	Gasoline Tank (gals)	Cooling System (qts)	
						With Heater	With A/C
'78	350	4	8	4.25	21	18.9	18.9
'78	350 Diesel	6	6	4.25	21	18.9	18.9
'78	425	4	8	4.25	24	19.8	19.8
'79	425	4	9	4.25	①	20.8	20.8
'79	350	4	9	4.25	①	17.2	17.2
'79	350 Diesel	6	7	4.25	①	20.0	20.0
'80-'82	350 Diesel	6	6	4.25	27	23.7	23.7
'80	368	4	8	4.25	25	21.4	21.4
'81-'82	368	4	8	4.25	25	21.4	21.4
'81-'82	252	4	8	4.25	25	18.2	18.2
'82	250	4	8	4.25	25	10.8	10.8
'83-'85	250	4	10	4.25	24	11	11
'83-'85	350 Diesel	6	10	4.25	26	23	23

● Specifications do not include torque converter

① Seville—21; All others—25

CHEVROLET CORVETTE

VEHICLE IDENTIFICATION NUMBER (VIN)

It is important for servicing and ordering parts to be certain of the vehicle and engine identification. The (VIN) (vehicle identification number) is a 13 or 17 digit number visible through the windshield on the driver's side of the dash and contains the vehicle and engine identification codes. It can be interpreted as follows:

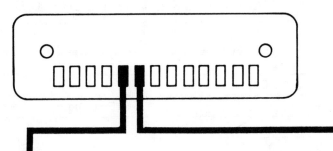

Engine Code						Model Year Code	
Code	Cu. In.	Liters	Cyl.	Carb.	Eng. Mfg.	Code	Year
L①	350	5.7	8	4 bbl.	Chev.	8	78
4②	350	5.7	8	4 bbl.	Chev.	9	79
8①	350	5.7	8	4 bbl.	Chev.	A	80
H	305	5.7	8	4 bbl.	Chev.		
6②	350	5.7	8	4 bbl.	Chev.		

The thirteen digit Vehicle Identification Number can be used to determine engine application and model year. The 6th digit indicates the model year, and the 5th digit identifies the factory installed engine.
① Standard performance L48 engine
② High performance L82 engine

VEHICLE IDENTIFICATION NUMBER (VIN)

It is important for servicing and ordering parts to be certain of the vehicle and engine identification. The VIN (vehicle identification number) is a 13 or 17 digit number visible through the windshield on the driver's side of the dash and contains the vehicle and engine identification codes. It can be interpreted as follows:

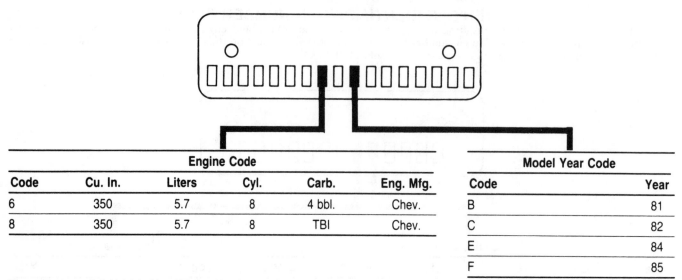

Engine Code

Code	Cu. In.	Liters	Cyl.	Carb.	Eng. Mfg.
6	350	5.7	8	4 bbl.	Chev.
8	350	5.7	8	TBI	Chev.

Model Year Code

Code	Year
B	81
C	82
E	84
F	85

The seventeen digit Vehicle Identification Number can be used to determine engine application and model year. The 10th digit indicates the model year, and the 8th digit identifies the factory installed engine. There is no 1983 Corvette model.
T.B.I.—Throttle body (fuel) injection

TUNE UP SPECIFICATIONS

(When analyzing compression test results, look for uniformity among cylinders rather than specific pressures.)

Year	Engine No. of Cyl.-Displacement (Cu. In.)	V.I.N. Code	Option Code	Horse-power	Spark Plugs Type (A.C.)	Gap (in.)	Ignition Timing (deg) ⑤ ⑥ Man. Trans.	Auto. Trans.	Valves Intake Opens ⑦(deg)	Fuel Pump Pressure (psi)	Idle Speed (rpm) ⑤ Man. Trans.	Auto. Trans.
'78	8-350	L	L48	185	R45TS	.045	6B	6B(8B)	28	7½–9	700	500②
	8-350	4	L82	220	R45TS	.045	12B	12B	52	7½–9	900	700
'79	8-350	8	L48	195	R45TS	.045	6B	③	28	7½–9	④	④
	8-350	4	L82	225	R45TS	.045	12B	12B	25	7½–9	④	④
'80	8-305	H	LG4	180	R45TS	.045	4B	4B	28	7½–9	④	④
	8-350	8	L48	190	R45TS	.045	6B③	6B	28	7½–9	④	④
	8-350	6	L82	230	R45TS	.045	12B	12B	52	7½–9	④	④
'81	8-350	6	L81	190	R45TS	.045	6B	6B	38	7½–9	④	④
'82	8-350	8	L83	200	R45TS	.045	①	④	32	9–13	①	④
'84	8-350	8	L83	205	R45TS	.045	④	④	32	9–13	④	④
'85	8-350	NA	NA	NA	R45TS	.045	④	④	NA	NA	④	④

NOTE: All models use electronic ignition systems. No adjustments are necessary. The underhood specifications sticker often reflects tuneup specification changes made in production. Sticker figures must be used if they disagree with those in this chart. Part numbers in this chart are not recommendations by Chilton for any product by brand name.

B–Before Top Dead Center
① Manual transmission not available
② High Altitude: 600
③ Except Calif. and High Altitude: 6B Calif. and High Altitude: 8B

④ See Underhood Sticker
⑤ See text for procedure
⑥ Figure in parentheses indicates California engine
⑦ All figures Before Top Dead Center

FIRING ORDER

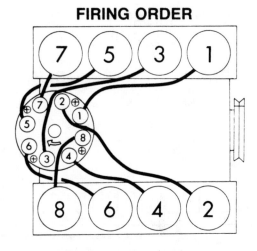

GM (Chevrolet) V8
Engine firing order: 1-8-4-3-6-5-7-2
Distributor rotation: clockwise

CAPACITIES

Year	Engine No. of Cyl.- Displacement (Cu. In.)	Engine Crankcase (Add 1 Qt For New Filter)	Transmission (Pts To Refill After Draining)			Gasoline Tank (gals)	Cooling System (qts)	
			Manual 4-Speed	Automatic ②	Drive Axle (pts)		With Heater	With A/C
'78	8-350	4	3	8	3.75	24	21	21
'79	8-350	4	3①	8	4	24	21	21
'80-'81	8-305, 350	4	3	8	4	24	21	22
'82	8-350	4	—	10	4	24	21	22
'84-'85	8-350	4	3.5③	8	3.75	20	15	15

①Optional close-ratio 4-speed—2.75
②For pan removal and filter change only
—Not applicable
③Four speed overdrive uses Dexron® II
   in the overdrive section

CHEVROLET REAR WHEEL DRIVE
Caprice, Chevelle, Impala, Malibu, Monte Carlo, Nova

VEHICLE IDENTIFICATION NUMBER (VIN)

It is important for servicing and ordering parts to be certain of the vehicle and engine identification. The VIN (vehicle identification number) is a 13 or 17 digit number visible through the windshield on the driver's side of the dash and contains the vehicle and engine identification codes. It can be interpreted as follows:

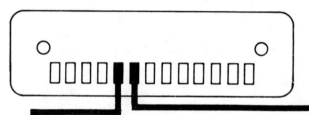

Engine Code						Model Year Code	
Code	Cu. In.	Liters	Cyl.	Carb.	Eng. Mfg.	Code	Year
M	200	3.3	6	2	Chev.	8	1978
D	250	4.1	6	1	Chev.	9	1979
K	229	3.8	6	2	Chev.	A	1980

ENGINE CODE

Code	Cu. In.	Liters	Cyl.	Carb.	Eng. Mfg.
A	231	3.8	6	2	Buick
3	231	3.8	6	Turbo	Buick
J	267	4.4	8	2	Chev.
U	305	5.0	8	2	Chev.
G	305	5.0	8	2	Chev.
H	305	5.0	8	4	Chev.
L	350	5.7	8	4	Chev.
N	350	5.7	8	Diesel	Olds.

The thirteen digit Vehicle Identification Number can be used to determine engine application and model year. The sixth digit indicates the model year, and the fifth digit identifies the factory installed engine.

VEHICLE IDENTIFICATION NUMBER (VIN)

It is important for servicing and ordering parts to be certain of the vehicle and engine identification. The VIN (vehicle identification number) is a 13 or 17 digit number visible through the windshield on the driver's side of the dash and contains the vehicle and engine identification codes. It can be interpreted as follows:

ENGINE CODE

Code	Cu. In.	Liters	Cyl.	Carb.	Eng. Mfg.
K	229	3.8	6	2	Chev.
9	229	3.8	6	2	Chev.
A	231	3.8	6	2	Buick
3	231	3.8	6	Turbo	Buick
V	263	4.3	6	Diesel	Olds.
J	267	4.4	8	2	Chev.
G	305	5.0	8	4	Chev.
H	305	5.0	8	4	Chev.
6	305	5.7	8	4	Chev.
N	350	5.7	8	Diesel	Chev.

MODEL YEAR CODE

Code	Year
B	'81
C	'82
D	'83
E	'84
F	'85

The seventeen digit Vehicle Identification Number can be used to determine engine application and model year. The tenth digit indicates the model year, and the eighth digit identifies the factory installed engine.

TUNE-UP SPECIFICATIONS
Nova

(When analyzing compression test results, look for uniformity among cylinders rather than specific pressures.)

		Engine				Spark Plugs		Distributor		Ignition Timing (deg) ▲ ●		Valves Intake Opens ■ (deg) ●	Fuel Pump Pressure (psi)	Idle Speed (rpm) ▲ *	
Year	Eng. V.I.N. Code	No. Cyl. Displacement (cu. in.)	Eng. Mfg.	hp		Orig. Type	Gap (in.)	Point Dwell (deg)	Point Gap (in.)	Man Trans	Auto Trans			Trans Man ●	Trans Auto
'78	D	6-250	Chev.	All		R-46TS	.035	Electronic		6B	①	16	4–5	800/425	500(600)/ 425(400)
	U	8-305	Chev.	All		R-45TS	.045	Electronic		4B	4B(6B)	28	7.5–9	600	500
	L	8-350	Chev.	All		R-45TS	.045	Electronic		—	8B	28	7.5–9	—	500
'79	D	6-250	Chev.	All		R-46TS	.035	Electronic		8B	10B(6B)	16	4.5–6.0	800	500
	G	8-305	Chev.	All		R-45TS	.045	Electronic		4B	4B	28	7.5–9.0	600	500
	L	8-350	Chev.	All		R-45TS	.045	Electronic		—	8B	28	7.5–9.0	—	500

NOTE: The underhood specifications sticker often reflects tuneup specification changes made in production. Sticker figures must be used if they disagree with those in this chart.
▲See text for procedure
●Figure in parentheses indicates California engine
■All figures before top dead center

*When two idle speed figures are separated by a slash, the lower figure is with the idle speed solenoid disconnected.
①49 states without A/C: 10B
49 states with A/C: 8B
Calif.: 6B

—Not applicable
Part numbers in this chart are not recommendations by Chilton for any product by brand name.

TUNE-UP SPECIFICATIONS
Chevelle, Monte Carlo and Malibu

(When analyzing compression test results, look for uniformity among cylinders rather than specific pressures.)

Year	Eng. V.I.N. Code	Engine No. Cyl. Displacement (cu. in.)	Eng. Mfg.	hp	Spark Plugs Orig. Type	Gap (in.)	Distributor Point Dwell (deg)	Point Gap (in.)	Ignition Timing (deg) ▲ ● Man Trans	Auto Trans	Valves Intake Opens ■ (deg) ●	Fuel Pump Pressure (psi)	Idle Speed (rpm) ▲ * Trans Man ●	Trans Auto
'78	M	6-200	Chev.	95	R-45TS	.045	Electronic		8B	8B	28	7.5–9	700	600
	A	6-231	Buick	105	R-46TSX	.060	Electronic		15B	15B	17	6–7	600	500
	U	8-305	Chev.	145	R-45TS	.045	Electronic		4B	①	28	7.5–9	600	500②
	L	8-350	Chev.	170	R-45TS	.045	Electronic		—	8B	28	7.5–9	—	500
'79	M	6-200	Chev.	All	R-45TS	.045	Electronic		8B	12B	34	4.5–6.0	700	600
	A	6-231	Buick	All	R-46TSX	.060	Electronic		15B	15B	16	4.25–5.75	600	600
	J	8-267	Chev.	All	R-45TS	.045	Electronic		4B	10B	28	7.5–9.0	600	500
	G	8-305	Chev.	All	R-43TS	.045	Electronic		4B	4B	28	7.5–9.0	600	500
	L	8-350	Chev.	All	R-43TS	.045	Electronic		—	8B	28	7.5–9.0	—	500
'80	K	6-229	Chev.	All	R-45TS	.045	Electronic		8B	12B	42	4.5–6.0	700	600
	A	6-231	Buick	All	R-45TSX	.060	Electronic		—	15B	16	4.25–5.75	—	560(600)
	3	6-231	Buick	Turbo	R-45TSX	.060	Electronic		—	15B	16	4.25–5.75	—	550(600)
	J	8-267	Chev.	All	R-45TS	.045	Electronic		—	4B	28	7.5–9.0	—	500
	H	8-305	Chev.	All	R-45TS	.045	Electronic		4B	4B	28	7.5–9.0	700	500(550)
'81	K	6-229	Chev.	All	R-45TS	.045	Electronic		6B	6B	42	4.5–6.0	700	600
	A	6-231	Buick	All	R-45TS	.045	Electronic		—	15B	16	4.25–5.75	—	500
	J	8-267	Chev.	All	R-45TS	.045	Electronic		—	6B	44	7.5–9.0	—	500
	H	8-305	Chev.	All	R-45TS	.045	Electronic		6B	6B	44	7.5–9.0	700	500
'82	K	6-229	Chev.	All	R-45TS	.045	Electronic		6B③	6B③	42	4.5–6.0	700	600
	A	6-231	Buick	All	R-45TS	.045	Electronic		—	15B③	16	4.25–5.75	—	500
	V	6-263	Olds.	Diesel	—	—	—		—	③	16	5.5–6.5	—	③
	J	8-267	Chev.	All	R-45TS	.045	Electronic		—	6B③	44	5.5–7.0	—	500
	H	8-305	Chev.	All	R-45TS	.045	Electronic		—	6B③	44	5.5–7.0	—	500
	N	8-350	Olds.	Diesel	—	—	—		—	③	16	5.5–6.5	—	③
'83	9	6-229	Chev.	All	R-45TS	.045	Electronic		—	6B③	42	4.5–6.0	700③	600③
	A	6-231	Buick	All	R-45TS	.045	Electronic		—	15B③	16	4.25–5.75	—	500③
	V	6-263	Olds.	Diesel	—	—	—		—	③	16	5.5–6.5	—	③
	H	8-305	Chev.	All	R-45TS	.045	Electronic		—	6B③	44	5.5–7.0	—	500③
	N	8-350	Olds.	Diesel	—	—	—		—	③	16	5.5–6.5	—	③

TUNE-UP SPECIFICATIONS
Chevelle, Monte Carlo and Malibu

(When analyzing compression test results, look for uniformity among cylinders rather than specific pressures.)

Year	Eng. V.I.N. Code	Engine No. Cyl. Displacement (cu. in.)	Eng. Mfg.	hp	Spark Plugs Orig. Type	Spark Plugs Gap (in.)	Distributor Point Dwell (deg)	Distributor Point Gap (in.)	Ignition Timing (deg) ▲ ● Man Trans	Ignition Timing (deg) ▲ ● Auto Trans	Valves Intake Opens ■ (deg) ●	Fuel Pump Pressure (psi)	Idle Speed (rpm) ▲ * Trans Man ●	Idle Speed (rpm) ▲ * Trans Auto
'84-85	9	6-229	Chev.	All	R-45TS	.045	Electronic		—	③	42	4.5–6.0	③	③
	A	6-231	Buick	All	R-45TS	.060	Electronic		—	③	16	4.25–5.75	③	③
	H	8-305	Chev.	All	R-45TS	.045	Electronic		—	⑤	44	5.5–7.0	③	③
	G	8-305	Chev.	All	R-45TS	.045	Electronic		③	③	NA	7.5–9.0	③	③
	N	8-350	Olds.	Diesel	—	—	—		—	③	16	5.5–6.5	③	③

NOTE: The underhood specifications sticker often reflects tune-up specification changes made in production. Sticker figures must be used if they disagree with those in this chart.

▲See text for procedure

●Figure in parentheses indicates California engine

■All figures Before Top Dead Center

*When two idle speed figures are separated by a slash, the lower figure is with the idle speed solenoid disconnected

B   Before Top Dead Center
TDC   Top Dead Center
—Not applicable
NA—Not available
Part numbers in this chart are not recommendations by Chilton for any product by brand name.

① 49 states: 4B
  Calif.: 6B
  High Altitude: 8B
② High Altitude: 600
③ Refer to underhood specifications sticker

TUNE-UP SPECIFICATIONS
Chevrolet

(When analyzing compression test results, look for uniformity among cylinders rather than specific pressures.)

Year	Eng. V.I.N. Code	No. Cyl. Displacement	Eng. Mfg.	Hp (cu. in.)	Orig. Type	Gap (in.)	Point Dwell (deg)	Point Gap (in.)	Man Trans	● Auto Trans	Intake Opens ■ (deg) ●	Fuel Pump Pressure (psi)	Man Trans	Auto Trans
'78	D	6-250	Chev.	110	R-46TS	.035	Electronic	—	—	①	16	4–5	—	550(600)
	U	8-305	Chev.	145	R-45TS	.045	Electronic	—	—	4B(6B)	28	7–9	—	500
	L	8-350	Chev.	170	R-45TS	.045	Electronic	—	—	6B(8B)	28	7–9	—	500
'79	D	6-250	Chev.	110	R-46TS	.035	Electronic	—	—	10B(6B)	16	4.5–6.0	②	②
	H	8-305	Chev.	145	R-45TS	.045	Electronic	—	—	4B	28	7.5–9.0	②	②
	L	8-350	Chev.	170	R-45TS	.045	Electronic	—	—	6B(8B)	28	7.5–9.0	②	②
'80	K	6-229	Chev.	All	R-45TS	.045	Electronic	—	—	②	42	4.5–6.0	②	②
	A	6-231	Buick	110	R-45TS	.045	Electronic	—	—	②	16	4.5–6.0	②	②
	J	8-267	Chev.	All	R-45TS	.045	Electronic	—	—	②	28	7.5–9.0	②	②
	H	8-305	Chev.	All	R-43TS	.045	Electronic	—	—	②	28	7.5–9.0	②	②
	N	8-350	Olds.	Diesel	—	—	—	—	—	—	16	5.5–6.5	②	②
'81	K	6-229	Chev.	110	R-45TS	.045	Electronic	—	—	6B	42	4.5–6.0	—	②
	A	6-231	Buick	110	R-45TS	.045	Electronic	—	—	15B	16	4.25–5.75	—	②
	J	8-267	Chev.	115	R-45TS	.045	Electronic	—	—	6B	44	7.5–9.0	—	②
	H	8-305	Chev.	150	R-45TS	.045	Electronic	—	—	6B	44	7.5–9.0	—	②
	N	8-350	Olds.	Diesel	—	—	—	—	—	—	16	5.5–6.5	—	②
'82	K	6-229	Chev.	115	R-45TS	.045	Electronic	—	—	6B②	42	4.5–6.0	—	②
	A	6-231	Buick	110	R-45TS	.045	Electronic	—	—	15B②	16	4.25–5.75	—	②
	J	6-267	Chev.	115	R-45TS	.045	Electronic	—	—	6B②	44	5.5–7.0	—	②
	H	8-305	Chev.	150	R-45TS	.045	Electronic	—	—	6B②	44	5.5–7.0	—	②
	N	8-350 Diesel	Olds.	105	—	—	—	—	—	②	16	5.5–6.5	—	②
'83	9	6-229	Chev.	115	R-45TS	.045	Electronic	—	—	②	42	4.5–6.0	—	②
	A	6-231	Buick	110	R-45TS	.045	Electronic	—	—	②	16	4.25–5.75	—	②
	H	8-305	Chev.	150	R-45TS	.045	Electronic	—	—	②	44	5.5–7.0	—	②
	N	8-350	Olds.	Diesel	—	—	—	—	—	②	16	5.5–6.5	—	②
'84-85	9	6-229	Chev.	All	R-45TS	.045	Electronic	—	—	②	42	4.5–6.0	—	②
	A	6-231	Buick	All	R-45TS8	.060	Electronic	—	—	②	16	4.25–5.75	—	②
	H	8-305	Chev.	All	R-45TS	.045	Electronic	—	—	②	44	5.5–7.0	—	②
	N	8-350	Olds.	Diesel	—	—	—	—	—	②	16	5.5–6.5	—	②

NOTE: The underhood specifications sticker often reflects tune-up specification changes made in production. Sticker figures must be used if they disagree with those in this chart.

▲ See text for procedure
● Figure in parentheses indicates California engine
■ All figures Before Top Dead Center
B Before Top Dead Center
TDC Top Dead Center
— Not applicable

Part numbers in this chart are not recommendations by Chilton for any product by brand name.

① Non-California, non-air conditioning: 10B
  Non-California, with air conditioning: 8B
  California: 6B
② See underhood specifications sticker

FIRING ORDERS

NOTE: To avoid confusion, always replace spark plug wires one at a time.

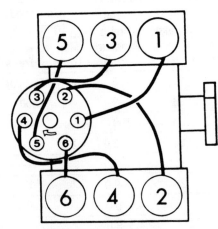

Chevrolet-built V6 engine
Engine firing order: 1-6-5-4-3-2
Distributor rotation: clockwise

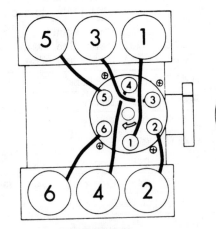

GM (Buick) 231 V6
Engine firing order: 1-6-5-4-3-2
Distributor rotation: clockwise

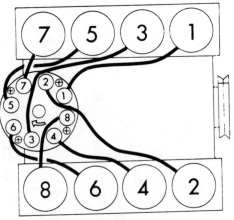

GM (Chevrolet) V8
Engine firing order: 1-8-4-3-6-5-7-2
Distributor rotation: clockwise

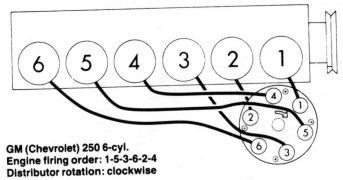

GM (Chevrolet) 250 6-cyl.
Engine firing order: 1-5-3-6-2-4
Distributor rotation: clockwise

CAPACITIES
Chevrolet

Year	Engine No. Cyl. (Cu. In.) Displacement	Engine Crankcase Add 1 Qt For New Filter	Manual 3-Speed	Manual 4-Speed	Automatic ●	Drive Axle (pts) ▲	Gasoline Tank (gals) ■	Cooling System (qts) With Heater	Cooling System (qts) With A/C
'78	6-250	4	—	—	6.0	3.25	21	14.2	14.2
	8-305	4	—	—	6.0	3.25	21	16.6	16.6
	8-350	4	—	—	6.0	3.25	21	16.6	16.6
'79	6-250	4	—	—	7.0	4.0	21	14.2	14.2
	8-305	4	—	—	8.0	4.0①	21	16.6	16.6
	8-350	4	—	—	8.0	4.0①	21	16.6	16.6
'80–'82	6-229	4③	—	—	7.0	4.0	18.5	—	14¼④
	6-231	4③	—	—	7.0	4.0①	18.5	—	11¾④
	8-267	4	—	—	6.0②	4.0①	18.5	—	16¾
	8-305	4	—	—	6.0	4.0①	18.5	—	15½
	8-350⑤	4	—	—	6.0	4.0①	18.5	—	16¼
	8-350 Diesel	7	—	—	6.0	4.0①	18.5	—	16¼
'83	6-229	4	—	—	6.0	⑥	⑦	—	14¼④
	6-231	4	—	—	6.0	⑥	⑦	—	11¾④
	8-305	4	—	—	6.0⑧	⑥	⑦	—	15½
	8-350 Diesel	6	—	—	6.0	⑥	⑦	—	18.3
'84–'85	6-229	4	—	—	6.0	⑥	⑦	—	14¼
	6-231	4	—	—	6.0	⑥	⑦	—	11¾
	8-305	4	—	—	6.0⑧	⑥	⑦	—	15½
	8-350 Diesel	6	—	—	6.0	⑥	⑦	—	18.3

●Specifications do not include torque converter
Add just enough fluid to fill the transmission to the proper level. It takes only one pint to raise the level from "ADD" to "FULL" with a hot transmission. Do not overfill.
■Station wagons: 22 gals
▲'78 and later 8.5 and 8.75: 4.0 pts
—Not applicable
①with 7.5 inch ring gear: 3.25
②7.5 pt. w/200 T.H. Trans.

④Cooling system capacity, Station wagon heavy duty capacity 16¾ qts.
⑤Not available after 1980.
⑥7.5" ring gear: 3.5 pts
 8.75" ring gear: 5.0 pts
⑦Gasoline coupe and sedan—25 gal; diesel—27 gal.
 All station wagons—22 gal.
⑧Automatic Overdrive; 10 pts

CAPACITIES
Chevrolet

Year	Engine No. Cyl. (Cu. In.) Displacement	Engine Crankcase Add 1 Qt For New Filter	Transmission Pts To Refill After Draining			Drive Axle (pts) ▲	Gasoline Tank (gals) ■	Cooling System (qts)	
			Manual		Automatic ●			With Heater	With A/C
			3-Speed	4-Speed					
	8-305	4	—	—	6.0⑧	⑥	⑦	—	15½
	8-350 Diesel	6	—	—	6.0	⑥	⑦	—	18.3

● Specifications do not include torque converter
Add just enough fluid to fill the transmission to the proper level. It takes only one pint to raise the level from "ADD" to "FULL" with a hot transmission. Do not overfill.
■ Station wagons: 22 gals
▲ '78 and later 8.5 and 8.75: 4.0 pts
— Not applicable
① with 7 .5 inch ring gear: 3.25
② 7.5 pt. w/200 T.H. Trans.
③ 4 qt. with filter change

④ Cooling system capacity, Station wagon heavy duty capacity 16¾ qts.
⑤ Not available after 1980.
⑥ 7.5" ring gear: 3.5 pts
8.75" ring gear: 5.0 pts
⑦ Gasoline coupe and sedan—25 gal; diesel—27 gal.
All station wagons—22 gal.
⑧ Automatic Overdrive; 10 pts

CAPACITIES
Chevelle, Monte Carlo, Malibu and Nova

Year	Engine No. Cyl. Displacement (Cu. In.)	Engine Crankcase Add 1 Qt For New Filter ■	Transmission (Pts To Refill After Draining)		Automatic ●	Drive Axle (pts)	Gasoline Tank (gals)	Cooling System (qts)	
			Manual 3-Speed	4-Speed				With Heater	With A/C
'78	6-200 Chev.	4	3	—	6.0	3.5	18.1⑪	16.8	16.8
	6-231 Buick	4	3	3	6.0	3.5	18.1⑪	14.79	14.79
	6-250 Chev.	4	3	—	6.0	⑧	18.1⑪	14.6	14.6
	8-305 Chev.	4	—	3	6.0	⑧	18.1⑪	①	①
	8-350 Chev.	4	—	3	6.0	⑧	18.1⑪	②	②
'79	6-200 Chev.	4	3.0	—	8.0	3.25	18.1⑪	18.8	18.8
	6-231 Buick	4	3.0	—	8.0	3.25	18.1⑪	15.4	15.4
	6-250 Chev.	4	3.0	—	8.0	⑧	18.1⑪	⑨	⑨
	8-267 Chev.	4	—	3.4	8.0	3.25	18.1⑪	20.6	20.6
	8-305 Chev.	4	—	3.4	8.0	⑧	18.1⑪	①	①
	8-350 Chev.	4	3.0	3.4	8.0	⑧	18.1⑪	②	②
'80–'81	6-229 Chev.	4	3.0	3.4	8.0③	3.25	18.1	18.8⑩	18.8⑩
	6-231 Buick	4	3.0	3.4	8.0③	3.25	18.1	15.4⑤	15.4⑤
	8-267 Chev.	4	3.0	3.4	8.0③	3.25	18.1	20.6⑪	20.6⑯
	8-305 Chev.	4	3.0	3.4	8.0③	⑧	18.1	①	①
	8-350 Chev.	4	3.0	3.4	8.0	4.25	18.1	16.4⑫	16.4
'82	6-229 Chev.	4	—	—	6.0	3.5	18.1	15.0	15.0
	6-231 Buick	4	—	—	6.0	3.5	18.1	12.5	12.2
	6-263 Diesel	6④	—	—	6.0	3.5	18.1	15.0	15.0
	8-267 Chev.	4	—	—	6.0	3.5	18.1	18.9	18.0
	8-305 Chev.	4	—	—	6.0	3.5	18.1	16.5	16.5
	8-350 Diesel	7④	—	—	6.0	3.5	18.1	18.0	18.0
'83	6-229 Chev.	4	—	—	6.0	3.5	18.1	15.0	15.0
	6-231 Buick	4	—	—	6.0	3.5	18.1	15.0	15.0
	6-263 Diesel	6④	—	—	6.0	3.5	18.1	15.0	15.0
	8-305 Chev.	4	—	—	6.0	3.5	18.1	15.0	15.0
	8-350 Diesel	7④	—	—	6.0	3.5	18.1	18.0	18.0

CAPACITIES
Chevelle, Monte Carlo, Malibu and Nova

Year	Engine No. Cyl. Displacement (Cu. In.)	Engine Crankcase Add 1 Qt For New Filter ■	Transmission (Pts To Refill After Draining)		Automatic ●	Drive Axle (pts)	Gasoline Tank (gals)	Cooling System (qts)	
			Manual					With Heater	With A/C
			3-Speed	4-Speed					
'84	6-229 Chev.	4	—	—	6.0	3.5	18.1	15.0	15.0
	6-231 Buick	4	—	—	6.0	3.5	18.1	15.0	15.0
	8-305 Chev.⑫	4	—	—	6.0	3.5	18.1	16.6	16.6
	8-305 Chev.	4	—	—	6.0	3.5	18.1	16.3	16.3
	8-350 Diesel	7④	—	—	6.0	3.5	19.8	17.3	17.3

●Specifications do not include torque converter
Add just enough fluid to fill the transmission to the proper level. It takes only one pint to raise the level from "ADD" to "FULL" with a hot transmission. Do not overfill.

■On models with micro oil filters, capacity is the same with or without new filter
① Malibu, Monte Carlo 19.2 (thru 1980), 16.5 (1981)
Nova: 16.0
② Malibu: 19.2
Nova: 16.1
③ 1981–82: 7.0 pts. w/200, 200C, 200-4R; 8.0 pts w/250, 250C; 6.3 pts w/350, 350C

④ Includes mandatory filter change
⑤ 1981: 12.5 w/heater, 12.2 w/A/C
⑥ With 7.5 inch ring gear: 3.5 with 8.5 inch ring gear: 4.25
⑦ Nova: 13.6
⑧ 1981: 15.2 w/heater, 15 w/A/C
⑨ 1981: 18.9 w/heater, 18 w/A/C
⑩ 1981: 16.61 w/heater, 16.63 w/A/C
—Not applicable
⑪ '78–'79—Nova: 21 gal
⑫ Eng. Code G

OLDSMOBILE REAR WHEEL DRIVE
Cutlass, Omega, 88, 98

VEHICLE IDENTIFICATION NUMBER (VIN)

It is important for servicing and ordering parts to be certain of the vehicle and engine identification. The VIN (vehicle identification number) is a 13 or 17 digit number visible through the windshield on the driver's side of the dash and contains the vehicle and engine identification codes. It can be interpreted as follows:

ENGINE CODE

Code	Cu. In.	Liters	Cyl.	Carb.	Eng. Mfg.
C	231	3.8	6	2bbl	Buick
A	231	3.8	6	2bbl	Buick
2	231	3.8	6	2bbl	Buick
F	260	4.3	6	2bbl	Olds.
P	260	4.3	8	Diesel	Olds.
S	265	4.3	8	2bbl	Pont.
Y (79)	301	4.9	8	2bbl	Pont.
U	305	5.0	8	2bbl	Chev.
H	305	5.0	8	4bbl	Chev.
G	305	5.0	8	2bbl	Chev.
Y (80)	307	5.0	8	4bbl	Olds.
R	350	5.7	8	4bbl	Olds.
L	350	5.7	8	4bbl	Chev.
N	350	5.7	8	Diesel	Olds.
X	350	5.7	8	4bbl	Buick
8	350	5.7	8	4bbl	Chev.

MODEL YEAR CODE

Code	Year
8	1978
9	1979
A	1980

The thirteen digit Vehicle Identification Number can be used to determine engine application and model year. The 6th digit indicates the model year, and the 5th digit identifies the factory installed engine.

VEHICLE IDENTIFICATION NUMBER (VIN)

It is important for servicing and ordering parts to be certain of the vehicle and engine identification. The VIN (vehicle identification number) is a 13 or 17 digit number visible through the windshield on the driver's side of the dash and contains the vehicle and engine identification codes. It can be interpreted as follows:

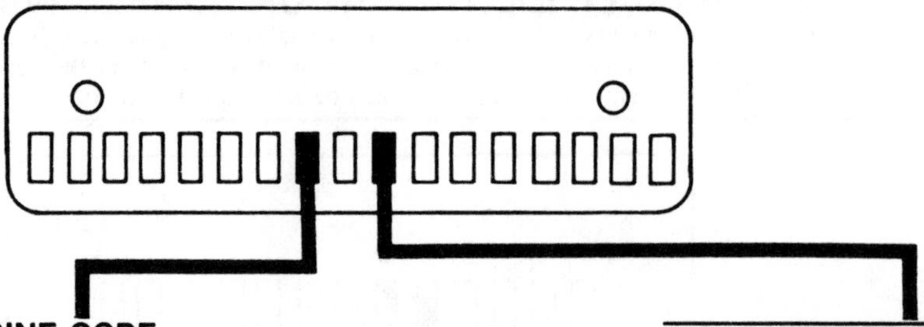

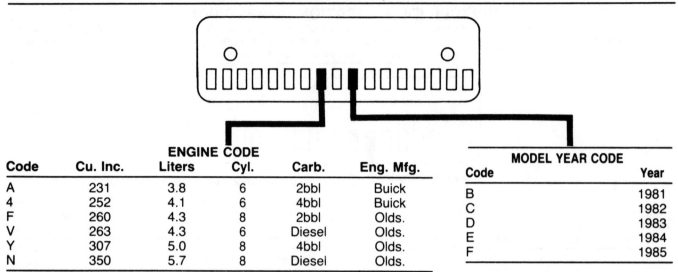

ENGINE CODE

Code	Cu. Inc.	Liters	Cyl.	Carb.	Eng. Mfg.
A	231	3.8	6	2bbl	Buick
4	252	4.1	6	4bbl	Buick
F	260	4.3	8	2bbl	Olds.
V	263	4.3	6	Diesel	Olds.
Y	307	5.0	8	4bbl	Olds.
N	350	5.7	8	Diesel	Olds.

MODEL YEAR CODE

Code	Year
B	1981
C	1982
D	1983
E	1984
F	1985

The seventeen digit Vehicle Identification Number can be used to determine engine application and model year. The 10th digit indicates the model year and the 8th digit identifies the factory installed engine.

TUNE-UP SPECIFICATIONS
Oldsmobile 88, 98

(When analyzing compression test results, look for uniformity among cylinders rather than specific pressures.)

	Engine				Spark Plugs		Distributor		Ignition Timing (deg) ▲		Valves	Fuel	Idle Speed (rpm) ▲	
Year	Eng. V.I.N. Code	No. Cyl. Displacement (cu in.)	Eng. Mfg.	hp	Orig. Type	Gap (in.)	Point Dwell (deg)	Point Gap (in.)	Man Trans	Auto Trans	Intake Opens ■ (deg)	Pump Pressure (psi)	Man Trans ●	Auto Trans
'78	A	6-231	Buick	105	R-46TSX	.060	Electronic		—	15B	17	5.5-6.5	—	600
	F	8-260	Olds.	110	R-46SZ	.060	Electronic		—	20B @ 1100	14	5.5-6.5	—	500
	X	8-350	Buick	170	R-46TSX	.060	Electronic		—	15B	19	5.5-6.5	—	550
	R	8-350	Olds.	170	R-46SZ	.060	Electronic		—	20B @ 1100	16	5.5-6.5	—	650①
	K	8-403	Olds.	185	R-46SZ	.060	Electronic		—	18B② @ 1100	16	5.5-6.5	—	550③
'79	A	6-231	Buick	115	R-46TSX	.060	Electronic		—	12B	16	5.5-6.5	—	550
	F	8-260	Olds.	110	R-46SZ	.060	Electronic		—	18B @ 1100	14	5.5-6.5	—	550
	Y	8-301	Pont.	All	R-46TSX	.060	Electronic		—	12B	16	5.5-6.5	—	650(500)
	R	8-350	Olds.	170	R-46SZ	.060	Electronic		—	20B @ 1100	16	5.5-6.5	—	550
	K	8-403	Olds.	185	R-46SZ	.060	Electronic		—	24B(20B) @ 1100	16	5.5-6.5	—	550

TUNE-UP SPECIFICATIONS
Oldsmobile 88, 98

(When analyzing compression test results, look for uniformity among cylinders rather than specific pressures.)

	Engine				Spark Plugs		Distributor		Ignition Timing (deg) ▲		Valves Intake Opens ■ (deg)	Fuel Pump Pressure (psi)	Idle Speed (rpm) ▲	
Year	Eng. V.I.N. Code	No. Cyl. Displacement (cu in.)	Eng. Mfg.	hp	Orig. Type	Gap (in.)	Point Dwell (deg)	Point Gap (in.)	Man Trans	Auto Trans			Man Trans ●	Auto Trans
'80	A	6-231	Buick	All	R-45TS④	.040⑤	Electronic		—	15B	16	3-4.5	—	670/550⑥
	Y	8-307	Olds.	All	R-46SX	.080	Electronic		—	20B	20	5.5-6.5	—	600/500
	R	8-350	Olds.	All	R-46SX	.080	Electronic		—	18B	16	5.5-6.5	—	600(650)/ 500(550)
'81	A	6-231	Buick	All	R45TSX	.080	Electronic		—	⑦	16	4.25-5.75	—	⑦
	4	6-252	Buick	All	R45TSX	.080	Electronic		—	⑦	16	4.25-5.75	—	⑦
	F	8-260	Olds.	All	R-46SX	.080	Electronic		—	18B	14	5.5-6.5	—	⑦
	Y	8-307	Olds.	All	R-46SX	.080	Electronic		—	15B	20	6-7.5	—	⑦
'82	A	6-231	Buick	All	R-45TS	.040	Electronic		—	⑦	16	4.25-5.75	—	⑦
	4	6-252	Buick	All	R-45TS8	.080	Electronic		—	⑦	16	4.25-5.75	—	⑦
	F	8-260	Olds.	All	R-465X	.080	Electronic		—	⑦	14	5.5-6.5	—	⑦
	Y	8-307	Olds.	All	R-465X	.080	Electronic		—	⑦	—	6-7.5	—	⑦
'83	A	6-231	Buick	All	R-45TS	.040	Electronic		—	⑦	16	4.25-5.75	—	⑦
	4	6-252	Buick	All	R-45TS8	.080	Electronic		—	⑦	16	4.25-5.75	—	⑦
	Y	8-307	Olds.	All	R-46SX	.080	Electronic		—	⑦	—	6-7.5	—	⑦
'84-'85	A	6-231	Buick	All	R45TS	.040	Electronic		—	⑦	16	4.25-5.75	—	⑦
	Y	8-307	Olds.	All	R46SX	.080	Electronic		—	⑦	—	6-7.5	—	⑦

NOTE: The underhood specifications sticker often reflects tuneup specification changes made in production. Sticker figures must be used if they disagree with those in this chart. Part numbers in this chart are not recommendations by Chilton for any product by brand name.

NOTE: Most 1979 and later carburetors have idle mixture screws concealed by staked-in plugs. These are not meant to be removed, except at carburetor overhaul.

① High Altitude: 700
② 88 sta. wgn.: 20B @ 1100
③ High Altitude: 600
④ With C-4 ignition—R45TSX
⑤ With C-4 ignition—.060
⑥ With C-4 ignition—620/550
⑦ See underhood sticker
▲ See text for procedure
■ All figures are in degrees Before Top Dead Center

● Figures in parentheses apply to California engines. Where two idle speed figures appear separated by a slash, the first is idle speed with solenoid energized, the second is idle speed with solenoid disconnected.

B Before Top Dead Center

DIESEL TUNE-UP SPECIFICATIONS

Year	Eng. V.I.N. Code	Engine No. Cyl. Displacement (Cu. in.)	Eng. Mfg.	Fuel Pump Pressure (psi)	Compression (lbs)	Intake Valve Opens (deg)	Idle Speed ● (rpm)
'78	N	8-350	Olds.	5.5-6.5	275 min.	16	650/575
'79	P	8-260	Olds.	5.5-6.5	275 min.	16	650/590
	N	8-350	Olds.	5.5-6.5	275 min.	16	650/675
'80	N	8-350	Olds.	5.5-6.5	275 min.	16	750/600
'81	N	8-350	Olds.	5.5-6.5	275 min.	16	①
'82	V	6-263	Olds.	5-6	②	②	①
	N	8-350	Olds.	5.5-6.5	275 min.	16	①
'83	V	6-263	Olds.	5-6	②	②	①
	N	8-350	Olds.	5.5-6.5	275 min.	16	①
'84–'85	V	6-263	Olds.	5-6	②	—	①
	N	8-350	Olds.	5.5-6.5	275 min.	—	①

NOTE: The underhood specifications sticker often reflects tuneup specification changes made in production. Sticker figures must be used if they disagree with those in this chart.

① See underhood specifications sticker

② Not available

● Where two idle speed figures appear separated by a slash, the first is idle speed with solenoid energized, the second is idle speed with solenoid disconnected.

TUNE-UP SPECIFICATIONS
Cutlass, Omega

(When analyzing compression test results, look for uniformity among cylinders rather than specific pressures.)

Year	Eng. V.I.N. Code	No. Cyl Displacement (cu in.)	Eng. Mfg.	hp	Spark Plugs Orig. Type	Spark Plugs Gap ● (in.)	Distributor Point Dwell (deg)	Distributor Point Gap (in.)	Ignition Timing (deg)▲●* Man Trans	Ignition Timing (deg)▲●* Auto Trans	Valves Intake Opens ■(deg)●	Fuel Pump Pressure (psi)	Idle Speed (rpm)▲ Man Trans ●	Idle Speed (rpm)▲ Auto Trans
'78	A	6-231	Buick	105	R-46TSX	.060	Electronic		15B	15B	17	5-6	①	600
	F	8-260	Olds.	110	R-46SZ	.060	Electronic		18B	20B⑤	14	5-6	800	500④
	U	8-305	Chev.	145	R-45TS	.045	Electronic		4B	②	28	7-9	600	500③
	H	8-305	Chev.	160	R-45TS	.045	Electronic		—	4B	28	7-9	—	500
	L	8-350	Chev.	170	R-45TS	.045	Electronic		—	8B	28	7-9	—	600(500)
'79	A	6-231	Olds.	115	R-46TSX	.060	Electronic		15B	15B	17	4-5	800/600	670/550(600)③
	F	8-260	Olds.	110	R-46SZ	.060	Electronic		18B	20B⑤	14	5.5-6.5	800/650	625/500⑩
	P	8-260	Olds.	Diesel	—	—	—		—	5B⑦	16	8-12⑥	660/575	650/590
	G	8-305	Chev.	145	R-45TS	.045	Electronic		4B	4B⑧	28	7.5-9	700/600	600(650)/500(600)
	H	8-305	Chev.	160	R-44TS	.045	Electronic		4B	4B⑨	28	7.5-9	700	600/500⑪
	8	8-350	Chev.	160	R-45TS	.045	Electronic		—	8B	2B	7.5-9	—	650(600)/600(500)
'80	A	6-231	Buick	110	R-45TS (R-45TSX)	.040 (.060)	Electronic		15B	15B	16	3-4.5	800/600	670/550 (620/550)
	F	8-260	Olds.	All	R-46SX	.080	Electronic		—	20B⑦	—	5.5-6.5	—	625/500
	H	8-305	Chev.	All	R-45TS	.045	Electronic		—	4B	28	7.5-9	—	600(650)/500(550)
	R	8-350	Olds.	All	R-46SX	.080	Electronic		—	18B	16	5.5-6.5	—	600(650)/500(550)
'81	A	6-231	Buick	All	R-45TSX	.080	Electronic		15B	15B	16	4.25-5.75	⑥	⑥
	F	8-260	Olds.	All	R-46SX	.080	Electronic		—	20B⑫	14	5.5-6.5	—	⑥
	Y	8-307	Olds.	All	R-46SX	.080	Electronic		—	15B	14	5.5-6.5	—	⑥
'82	A	6-231	Buick	All	R45TX	.040	Electronic		—	⑥	16	4.25-5.75	—	⑥
	F	8-260	Olds.	All	R46SX	.080	Electronic		—	⑥	—	5.5-6.5	—	⑥
	Y	8-307	Olds.	All	R46SX	.080	Electronic		—	⑥	—	6-7.5	—	⑥
'83	A	6-231	Buick	All	R45TX	.040	Electronic		—	⑥	16	4.25-5.75	—	⑥
	Y	8-307	Olds	All	R46SX	.080	Electronic		—	⑥	—	6-7.5	—	⑥
'84-'85	A	6-231	Buick	All	R45TX	.040	Electronic		—	⑥	16	4.25-5.75	—	⑥
	Y	8-307	Olds.	All	R46SX	.080	Electronic		—	⑥	—	6-7.5	—	⑥

NOTE: The underhood specifications sticker often reflects tune-up specification changes made in production. Sticker figures must be used if they disagree with those in this chart. Part numbers in this chart are not recommendations by Chilton for any product by brand name.

▲ See text for procedure
■ All figures Before Top Dead Center
● Figure in parentheses indicates California engine. Where two idle speed figures appear separated by a slash, the second is with the idle speed solenoid disconnected.
* See sticker for timing rpm.
① MT: 49 states Cutlass except sta. wgn., 49 states Omega, 800 All others—600
② 49 states: 4B
  Calif.: 6B
  High Altitude: 8B

③ High Altitude: 600
④ High Altitude Cutlass, except Sta. Wgn.: 550
⑤ Calif. Cutlass, except Sta. Wgn.: 18B @ 1100
⑥ See underhood sticker
⑦ Cutlass wagon—18B @ 1100
⑧ Calif: 2B
⑨ High Altitude: 8B
⑩ High Altitude: 650/550
⑪ High Altitude: 650/600
⑫ Station wagon—18B @ 1100
B Before Top Dead Center
— Not applicable

FIRING ORDER

NOTE: To avoid confusion, always replace spark plug wires one at a time.

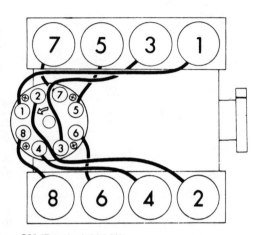

GM (Pontiac) 301 V8
Engine firing order: 1-8-4-3-6-5-7-2
Distributor rotation: counterclockwise

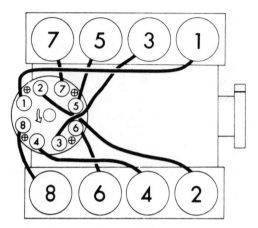

GM (Oldsmobile) 260 V8
Engine firing order: 1-8-4-3-6-5-7-2
Distributor rotation: counterclockwise

FIRING ORDERS

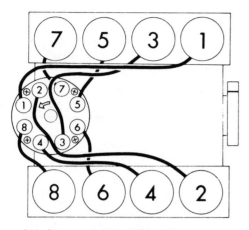

GM (Oldsmobile) 307, 350, 403
Engine firing order: 1–8–4–3–6–5–7–2
Distributor rotation: counterclockwise

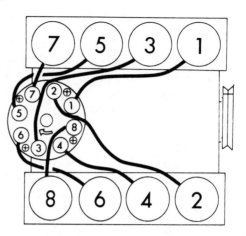

GM (Chevrolet) V8
Engine firing order: 1-8-4-3-6-5-7-2
Distributor rotation: clockwise

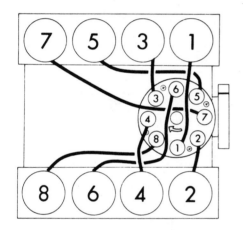

GM (Buick) Omega 350 V8
Engine firing order: 1-8-4-3-6-5-7-2
Distributor rotation: clockwise

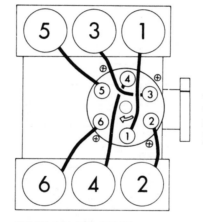

GM (Buick) 231, 252 V6
(3.2 L, 3.8 L, 4.1 L)
Engine firing order: 1–6–5–4–3–2
Distributor rotation: clockwise

V6 harmonic balancers have two
timing marks: one is 1/8 in. wide, and
one is 1/16 in. wide. Use the 1/16 in.
mark for timing with a hand held light.
The 1/8 in. mark is used only with a
magnetic timing pick-up probe.

CAPACITIES
Cutlass, Omega

Year	Engine No. Cyl. Displacement (Cu. In.)	Engine Crankcase Add 1 Qt For New Filter	Transmission (Pts To Refill After Draining)			Drive Axle (pts)	Gasoline Tank (gals)	Cooling System (qts)		
			3 sp	4sp/5sp	Automatic•			With Heater	With A/C	Heavy Duty Cooling
'78	6-231 Buick④	4	3.5	3.5	6	③	20.75	12.75	12.75	12.75
	6-231 Buick⑤	4	3.5	3.5	6	3.5	18.0⑥	12.0	12.0	12.0
	6-231 Buick	4	—	3.5	6	3.5	18.5	11.75	12.25	—
	8-260 Olds.	4	—	3.5	6	3.5	18.0⑥	16.25	16.25	16.75
	8-305 Chev.④	4	—	3.5	6	③	20/75	15.75	16.0	16.75
	8-305 Chev.⑤	4	—	3.5	6	3.5	18.0⑥	15.5	15.5	16.25
'78	8-305 Chev.	4	—	3.5	6	3.5	18.5	16.25	16.25	—
	8-350 Chev.④	4	—	—	6	③	20.75	16.0	16.75	16.75
	8-350 Chev.⑤	4	—	—	6	3.5	18.0⑥	15.5	16.25	16.25
'79	6-231 Buick	4	—	3.0①	6	3.5	18.5	11.75	11.75	12.25
	6-231 Buick	4	3.5	—	6	③	21.0	12.75	12.75	—
	6-231 Buick⑤	4	3.5	3.0	6	3.5	18.2	13.3	13.3	—
	8-260 Olds.⑤	4	—	3.5	6	3.5	18.2	16.25	16.25	16.75
	8-260 Diesel⑤	7②	—	3.5	6	3.5	19.75	19.75	19.75	19.5
	8-305 Chev.	4	—	3.0	6	3.5	18.5	16.2	16.2	—
	8-305 Chev.	4	—	3.0	6	③	21.0	15.8	16	16.75
	8-350 Chev.⑤	4	—	3.0	6	3.5	18.2	15.5	15.5	16.25
	8-350 Chev.④	4	—	—	6	③	21.0	16	16.75	—
	8-350 Olds.⑤	4	—	—	6	3.5	18.2	17.5	17.5	17.5
	8-350 Diesel	7②	—	—	6	3.5	18.2	17.5	17.5	17.5
'80	6-231 Buick	4	—	3	6	3.5	18.5	11.9	12.4	—
	6-231 Buick	4	3	3	6	3.5	18⑥	13	13	—
	8-260 Olds.	4	—	3	6	3.5	18⑥	16	16.5	—
	8-350 Chev.	4	—	3	6	3.5	18	15.25	15.25	16
	8-350 Olds.	4	—	—	6	3.5	18	15	15	—
	8-350 Diesel	7②	—	—	6	3.5	18	17.25	17.25	—
'81	6-231 Buick	4	3	—	6	3.5	18.1	N.A.	N.A.	N.A.
	8-260 Olds.	4	—	—	6	3.5	18.1	15.9	15.6	15.5
	8-307 Olds.	4	—	—	6	3.5	18.1⑥	14.9	15.6	15.5
	8-350 Diesel	7②	—	—	6	3.5	19.8⑥	17.4	17.3	17.3
'82	6-231 Buick	4	3	⑦	6	3.5	18.2	13.3	13.3	—
	6-263 Diesel	6②	—	⑦	6	⑦	19.8	⑦	⑦	—
	8-260 Olds.	4	—	—	6	3.5	18.2	20.0	20.0	—
	8-305 Olds.	4	—	—	6	3.5	18.2	15.5	15.5	—
	8-350 Diesel	7②	—	—	6	3.5	19.8	18	18	—

'83	6-231 Buick	4	—	—	6	3.5	18.2	13.3	13.3	—
	6-263 Diesel	6②	—	—	6	3.5	19.8	12.9	12.9	—
	8-307 Olds	4	—	—	6	3.5	18.2	15.5	15.5	—
	8-350 Diesel	7②	—	—	6	3.5	19.8	18	18	—
'84–'85	6-231 Buick	4	—	—	6	3.5	19.8	13.3	13.3	
	6-263 Diesel	6②	—	—	6	3.5	19.8	12.9	12.9	
	8-307 Olds.	4	—	—	6	3.5	18.2	15.5	15.5	
	8-350 Diesel	7②	—	—	6	3.5	19.8	18	18	

● Check dip stick and gradually fill to correct level. See the General Maintenance section of Unit Repair.
① 3 pts. with 70mm 4-speed, 3½ with 5-speed
② Includes mandatory filter change
③ 7.5 inch ring gear: 3.5
8.5 inch ring gear: 4.25 (Omega only)
④ Omega
⑤ Cutlass
⑥ Stawgn.: 18.25
— Not applicable
⑦ Not available at time of publication

CAPACITIES
Oldsmobile 88, 98

Year	Engine No. Cyl. Displacement (Cu. In.)	Engine Crankcase Add 1 Qt For New Filter*	Transmission (Pts To Refill After Draining) Automatic•	Drive Axle (pts)	Gasoline Tank (gals)	Cooling System (qts)		Heavy Duty Cooling
						With Heater	With A/C	
'78	6-231 Buick	4	6	④	25.25	12.25	12.25	12.25
	8-260 Olds.	4	6	④	22.25③	16.25	16.25	16.75
	8-350 Buick	4	6	④	22.25③	14.5	14.5	15.5
	8-350 Olds.	4	6	④	⑤	14.5	14.5	15.5
	8-350 Diesel	7⑥	6	④	22.0	18.0	18.0	18.0
	8-403 Olds.	4	6	④	⑤	15.75	16.5	16.5
'79	6-231 Buick	4	6	4.25	25.0②	13.3	13.3	—
	8-260 Olds.	4	6	4.25	25.0②	16.25	16.25	17.25
	8-350 Olds.	4	6	4.25	25.0②	14.5	14.5	15.5
	8-350 Diesel	7⑥	6	4.25	27	18.0	18	—
	8-403 Olds.	4	6	4.25	25.0②	15.75	16.4	16.25
'80	6-231 Buick	4	6	④	20.75	13.0	13.0	—
	8-307 Olds.	4	6	④	25①	15.5	15.25	16.25
	8-350 Olds.	4	6	④	25	14.5	14.5	15.5
	8-350 Diesel	7⑥	6	④	27③	18.25	18.0	—
'81	6-231 Buick	4	6	4	N.A.	N.A.	N.A.	N.A.
	6-252 Buick	4	6	4	N.A.	N.A.	N.A.	N.A.
	8-260 Pont.	4	6	4	25③	15.9	15.5	16.6
	8-307 Olds.	4	6	4	25③	14.9	15.6	15.6
	8-350 Diesel	7⑥	6	4	27③	18.0	18.0	18.0
'82	6-231 Buick	4	6	4	25③	13.7	13.7	⑦
	6-252 Buick	4	6	4	25③	13.7	13.7	⑦
	8-260 Olds.	4	6	4	25③	16	16.5	⑦
	8-263 Diesel.	6⑥	6	4	27	⑦	⑦	⑦
	8-307 Olds.	4	6	4	25③	17.5	17.5	⑦
	8-350 Diesel	7⑥	6	4	27③	18.0	18.0	18.0
'83	6-231 Buick	4	6	4	25③	13.7	13.7	⑦
	6-252 Buick	4	6	4	25③	13.7	13.7	⑦
	8-307 Olds.	4	6	4	25③	17.5	17.5	⑦
	8-350 Diesel	7⑥	6	4	27③	18	18	⑦

CAPACITIES
Oldsmobile 88, 98

Year	Engine No. Cyl. Displacement (Cu. In.)	Engine Crankcase Add 1 Qt For New Filter*	Transmission (Pts To Refill After Draining) Automatic•	Drive Axle (pts)	Gasoline Tank (gals)	Cooling System (qts) With Heater	With A/C	Heavy Duty Cooling
'84–'85	6-231 Buick	4	6	4	25③	13.7	13.7	⑦
	8-307 Olds.	4	6	4	25③	17.5	17.5	⑦
	8-350 Diesel	7⑥	6	4	27③	18	18	⑦

• Check dipstick and gradually fill to the correct level. See the General Maintenance section of the Unit Repair.
① Royale, Royal Brougham Coupe and Sedan: 20.75
② 20.75 for Calif. 350 or w/power seats
③ 22 gals on station wagon
④ 7.5 inch ring gear: 3.5
   8.5 and 8.75 inch ring gear: 4.25
⑤ 88 Sedan and Calif. Coupe: 21.0
   All others: 25.25
⑥ Includes mandatory filter change
⑦ Not available at time of publication
— Not applicable

PONTIAC REAR WHEEL DRIVE
Bonneville, Catalina, Parisienne, Grand Prix, LeMans, Phoenix, Grand Am

TUNE-UP SPECIFICATIONS
LeMans, Grand Am, 1982–'85 Bonneville

(When analyzing compression test results, look for uniformity among cylinders rather than specific pressures.)

Year	Eng. V.I.N. Code	No. Cyl. Displacement (cu in.)	Eng. Mfg.	hp	Spark Plugs Orig. Type	Gap (in.)	Point Dwell (deg)	Point Gap (in.)	Ignition Timing (deg) ▲ Man Trans ●	Auto Trans	Valves Opens ■ (deg)	Fuel Pressure (psi)	Idle Speed ● (rpm) ▲ Man Trans	Auto Trans
'78	A	6-231	Buick	105	R-46TSX	.060	Electronic		15B	15B	27	7-8.5	800	670(600)
	Y	8-301	Pont.	135	R-46TSX	.060	Electronic		—	12B	17	4.5-5.5	—	550
	W	8-301	Pont.	150	R-45TSX	.060	Electronic		—	12B	17	4.5-5.5	—	550
	U	8-305	Chev.	145	R-45TS	.045	Electronic		—	④	29	4.5-5	—	⑤
	L	8-350	Chev.	170	R-45TS	.045	Electronic		—	8B	17	4-5	—	650
'79	2,A	6-231	Buick	115	R-46TSX	.060	Electronic		15B	15B	16	4.5-5.5	800	600
	Y	8-301	Pont.	140	R-46TSX③	.060	Electronic		—	12B	16	5.5-6.5	—	650
	W	8-301	Pont.	150	R-45TSX	.060	Electronic		14B	12B	16⑥	5.5-6.5	750	650
	H	8-305	Chev.	160	R-45TS	.045	Electronic		—	4B	28	5.5-6.5	—	500
	L	8-350	Chev.	160	R-45TS	.045	Electronic		—	8B	28	5.5-6.5	—	600
'80	A	6-231	Buick	115	R-45TSX⑦	.060⑦	Electronic		—	15B	16	3-4½	—	620/550①
	K	6-229	Chev.	All	R-45TS	.045	Electronic		—	6B	42	4.5-6.0	②	②
	S	8-265	Pont.	120	R-45TSX	.060	Electronic		—	10B	27	7-8½	—	650/550①
	W	8-301	Pont.	150	R-45TSX	.060	Electronic		—	12B	16	7-8½	—	650/500①
	H	8-305	Chev.	160	R-45TS	.045	Electronic		—	4B	28	7½-9	—	650/550①
'81	A	6-231	Buick	115	R-45TSX	.080	Electronic		15B	15B	16	4.25-5.75	800⑧	500⑧
	K	6-229	Chev.	All	R-45TS	.045	Electronic		—	6B	42	4.5-6.0	②	②
	S	8-265	Pont.	119	R-45TSX	.060	Electronic		—	12B	16	7-8.5	—	450⑧
	W	8-301	Pont.	155	R-45TSX	.060	Electronic		—	12B	16	7-8.5	—	450⑧
'82	A	6-231	Buick	110	R-45TS8	.080	Electronic		—	15B	16	4.25-5.75	—	②
	4	6-252	Buick	125	R-45TS8	.080	Electronic		—	15B	16	4.25-5.75	—	②
	N	8-350	Olds	105	—	—	—		—	②	16	5.5-6.5	—	②
'83–'84	A	6-231	Buick	110	R-45TS8	.080	Electronic		—	15B	16	4.25-5.75	—	②
	H	8-305	Chev.	All	R-45TS	.045	Electronic		—	②	44	5.5-7.0	—	②
	N	8-350	Olds.	105	—	—	—		—	②	16	5.5-6.5	—	②
'85	A	6-231	Buick	All	R-45TS8	.080	Electronic		—	②	16	4.25-5.75	—	②
	H	8-305	Chev.	All	R-45TS	.045	Electronic		—	②	44	5.5-7.0	—	②
	N	8-350	Olds.	All	—	—	—		—	②	16	5.5-6.5	—	②

NOTE: The underhood specifications sticker often reflects tuneup specification changes made in production. Sticker figures must be used if they disagree with those in this chart. Part numbers in this chart are not recommendations by Chilton for any product by brand name.

▲ See text for procedure
● Figure in parentheses indicates California engine
■ All figures are in degrees Before Top Dead Center. Where two figures appear, the first represents timing with manual transmission, the second with automatic transmission.
① Lower figure indicates idle speed with solenoid disconnected

② See underhood sticker
③ High altitude and Calif.: R-45TSX
④ Except California and High Altitude: 4B
　California: 6B
　High Altitude: 8B
⑤ Except California and High Altitude: 600
　California: 650
　High Altitude: 700

⑥ High performance: 27
⑦ Low Altitude w/o C-4, R-45TS, gap .040
⑧ Curb Idle; for base idle see underhood sticker
B Before Top Dead Center
— Not applicable
N.A. Not available

TUNE-UP SPECIFICATIONS
1978-'81 Bonneville, Catalina, Grand Prix, Parisienne

(When analyzing compression test results, look for uniformity among cylinders rather than specific pressures.)

Year	Eng. V.I.N. Code	No. Cyl. Displacement	Eng. Mfg.	hp (cu in.)	Spark Plugs Orig. Type ●	Gap (in.)	Point Dwell (deg)	Point Gap (in.)	Ignition Timing (deg) ▲ Man Trans ●	Ignition Timing (deg) ▲ Auto Trans	Valves Intake Opens ■ (deg)	Fuel Pump Pressure (psi)	Idle Speed ● (rpm) ▲ Man Trans	Idle Speed ● (rpm) ▲ Auto Trans
'78	A	6-231	Buick	105	R-46TSX	.060	Electronic		15B	15B	17	4.5-5.74	800	600
	Y,W	8-301	Pont.	All	R-46TSX④	.060	Electronic		—	12B	27	7-8.5	—	550
	U,H	8-305	Chev.	All	R-45TS	.045	Electronic		—	8B(6B)	28	3-4.5	—	600 (500)
	X	8-350	Buick	170	R-46TSX	.060	Electronic		—	15B	16	4.5-5.5	—	550
	R	8-350	Olds.	170	R-46SZ	.060	Electronic		—	20B @ 1100	17	5.5-6.5	—	550
	Z	8-400	Pont.	180	R-45TSX	.060	Electronic		—	16B	29	7-8.5	—	575
	K	8-403	Pont.	185	R-46SZ	.060	Electronic		—	20B @ 1100	16	6-7.5	—	600 (550)
'79	2,A	6-231	Buick	115	R-46TSX	.060	Electronic		15B	15B	16	4.5-5.5	800	600
	Y	8-301	Pont.	140	R-46TSX	.060	Electronic		—	12B	16	7.0-8.5	—	650
	W	8-301	Pont.	150	R-45TSX	.060	Electronic		14B	12B	16⑤	7.0-8.5	750	500 (650)
	H	8-305	Chev.	160	R-45TS	.045	Electronic		—	4B	28	4.5-5.5	—	①
	X	8-350	Buick	155	R-46TSX	.060	Electronic		—	15B	16	4.5-5.5	—	550
	R	8-350	Olds.	170	R-46SZ	.060	Electronic		—	20B @ 1100	16	5.5-6.5	—	550
	K	8-403	Olds.	185	R-46SZ	.060	Electronic		—	18B(20B) @ 1100	16	5.5-6.5	—	500 (500)
'80	A	6-231	Buick	115	R-45TSX⑥	.060⑥	Electronic		—	15B	16	3-4½	—	620/550
	S	8-265	Pont.	120	R-45TSX	.060	Electronic		—	10B	27	7-8½	—	650/550
	W	8-301	Pont.	150	R-45TSX	.060	Electronic		—	12B	16	7-8½	—	650/500
	H	8-305	Chev.	160	R-45TS	.045	Electronic		—	4B	28	7½-9	—	650/550
	R	8-350	Olds.	160	R-43TS	.045	Electronic		—	6B	28	7½-9	—	650/550
	N	8-350	Olds.	105	—	—	Electronic		—	5B③	16	5½-6½	—	600
'81	A	6-231	Buick	110	R-45TS8	.080	Electronic		—	②	16	4.25-5.75	—	②
	S	8-265	Pont.	120	R-45TSX	.060	Electronic		—	12B	16	7-8.5	—	②
	Y	8-307	Olds.	148	R-46SX	.080	Electronic		—	15B	14	5.5-6.5	—	②
	N	8-350	Olds.	105	—	—	—		—	②	16	5.5-6.5	—	②
'82	A	6-231	Buick	110	R-45TS8	.080	Electronic		—	15B	16	4.25-5.75	—	②
	4	6-252	Buick	125	R-45TS8	.080	Electronic		—	15B	16	4.25-5.75	—	②
	N	8-350	Olds.	105	—	—	Electronic		—	②	16	5.5-6.5	—	②
'83-'84	A	6-231	Buick	110	R-45TS8	.080	Electronic		—	15B	16	4.25-5.75	—	②
	H	8-305	Chev.	NA	R-45TS	.045	Electronic		—	②		5.5-7.0	—	②
	N	8-350	Olds.	105	—	—	—		—	②	16	5.5-6.5	—	②
'85	A	6-231	Buick	All	R-45TS8	.080	Electronic		—	②	16	4.25-5.75	—	②
	H	8-305	Chev.	All	R-45TS	.045	Electronic		—	②	44	5.5-7.0	—	②
	N	8-350	Olds.	All	—	—	—		—	②	16	5.5-6.5	—	②

▲ See text for procedure
● Figure in parentheses indicates California engine. Where two idle speeds appear separated by a slash, the second is with the solenoid disconnected.
■ All figures are in degrees Before Top Dead Center.

Where two figures appear, the first represents timing with manual transmission, the second with automatic transmission.
① Calif.: 500, High Altitude: 600
② See the underhood sticker

③ Static
④ with 4 bbl: R-45TSX
⑤ High performance: 27
⑥ Low Altitude without C-4: R-45TS; gap: .040
B Before Top Dead Center

TUNE-UP SPECIFICATIONS
Phoenix

(When analyzing compression test results, look for uniformity among cylinders rather than specific pressures.)

	Engine				Spark Plugs		Distributor		Ignition Timing (deg) ▲		Valves Intake Opens ■ (deg)	Fuel Pump Pressure (psi)	Idle Speed ● (rpm) ▲	
Year	Eng. V.I.N. Code	No. Cyl. Displace-ment	Eng. Mfg.	hp (cu in.)	Orig. Type	Gap (in.)	Point Dwell (deg)	Point Gap (in.)	Man Trans ●	Auto Trans			Man Trans	Auto Trans
'78	V	4-151	Pont.	87	R-43TSX	.060	Electronic		14B	①	33	4-5.5	—	②
	A	6-231	Buick	105	R-46TSX	.060	Electronic		15B	15B	17	3-4.5	800	600
	H	8-305	Chev.	135	R-45TS	.045	Electronic		4B	6B	29	4.5-5	700	③
	L	8-350	Chev.	170	R-45TS	.045	Electronic		—	8B	17	4-5	—	600
'79	V	4-151	Pont.	85	R-43TSX	.060	Electronic		12B(14B)	12B(14B)	33	5.0-6.5	900 (1000)	650
	2,A	6-231	Buick	115	R-46TSX	.060	Electronic		15B	15B	16	4.0-6.5	800	600
	G	8-305	Chev.	145	R-45TS	.045	Electronic		4B	4B	28	5.5-6.5	600	500
	L	8-350	Chev.	160	R-45TS	.045	Electronic		—	8B	28	5.5-6.5	—	600

NOTE: The underhood specifications sticker often reflects tuneup specification changes made in production. Sticker figures must be used if they disagree with those in this chart. Part numbers in this chart are not recommendations by Chilton for any product by brand name.

▲ See text for procedure
■ All figures Before Top Dead Center
● Figure in Parentheses for California. When two figures are separated by a slash, the lower figure is idle speed with solenoid disconnected.

① Phoenix: 14B
② Air conditioned models: 650
   Without air conditioning: 500

③ Phoenix with air conditioning, except Calif. and high alt.: 600
   Phoenix, high altitude: 700
   All others: 650

VEHICLE IDENTIFICATION NUMBER (VIN)

It is important for servicing and ordering parts to be certain of the vehicle and engine identification. The VIN (vehicle identification number) is a 13 or 17 digit number visible through the windshield on the driver's side of the dash and contains the vehicle and engine identification codes. It can be interpreted as follows:

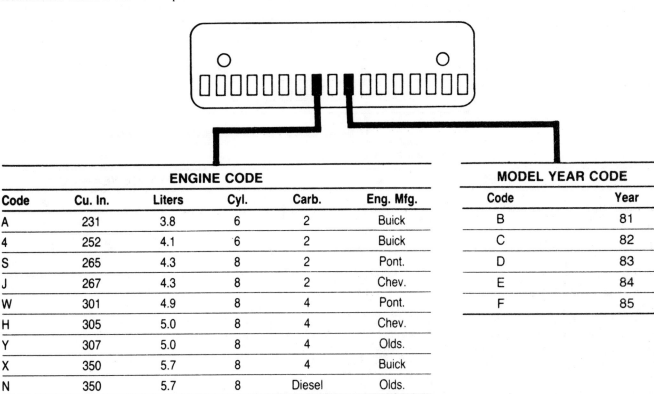

ENGINE CODE						MODEL YEAR CODE	
Code	Cu. In.	Liters	Cyl.	Carb.	Eng. Mfg.	Code	Year
A	231	3.8	6	2	Buick	B	81
4	252	4.1	6	2	Buick	C	82
S	265	4.3	8	2	Pont.	D	83
J	267	4.3	8	2	Chev.	E	84
W	301	4.9	8	4	Pont.	F	85
H	305	5.0	8	4	Chev.		
Y	307	5.0	8	4	Olds.		
X	350	5.7	8	4	Buick		
N	350	5.7	8	Diesel	Olds.		

The seventeen digit Vehicle Identification Number can be used to determine engine application and model year. The 10th digit indicates the model year, and the 8th digit identifies the factory installed engine.

VEHICLE IDENTIFICATION NUMBER (VIN)

It is important for servicing and ordering parts to be certain of the vehicle and engine identification. The VIN (vehicle identification number) is a 13 or 17 digit number visible through the windshield on the driver's side of the dash and contains the vehicle and engine identification codes. It can be interpreted as follows:

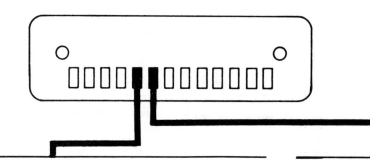

ENGINE CODE							MODEL YEAR CODE	
Code	Cu. In.	Liters	Cyl.	Carb.	Eng. Mfg.		Code	Year
V	151	2.5	4	2	Pont.		8	78
K	229	3.8	6	2	Chev.		9	79
C	231	3.8	6	2	Buick		A	80
A	231	3.8	6	2	Buick			
2	231	3.8	6	2	Buick			
S	265	4.3	8	2	Olds.			
Y	301	4.9	8	2	Pont.			
W	301	4.9	8	4	Pont.			
T	301	4.9	8	4	Pont.			
U	305	5.0	8	2	Chev.			
H	305	5.0	8	4	Chev.			
G	305	5.0	8	2	Chev.			
L	350	5.7	8	4	Chev.			
P	350	5.7	8	4	Pont.			
R	350	5.7	8	4	Olds.			
X	350	5.7	8	4	Buick			
N	350	5.7	8	Diesel	Olds.			
Z	400	6.6	8	4	Pont.			
K	403	6.6	8	4	Olds.			

The thirteen digit Vehicle Identification Number can be used to determine engine application and model year. The 6th digit indicates the model year, and the 5th digit identifies the factory installed engine.

FIRING ORDERS

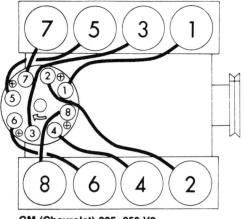

GM (Chevrolet) 305, 350 V8
Engine firing order: 1-8-4-3-6-5-7-2
Distributor rotation: clockwise

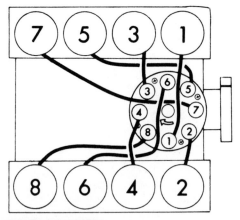

GM (Buick) 350 V8
Engine firing order: 1-8-4-3-6-5-7-2
Distributor rotation: clockwise

FIRING ORDERS

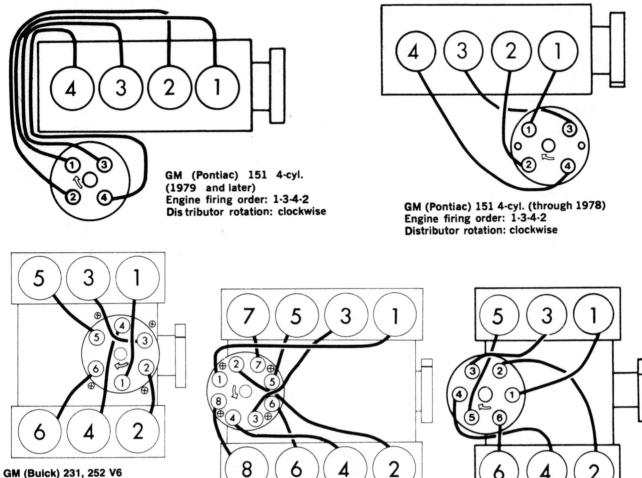

GM (Pontiac) 151 4-cyl.
(1979 and later)
Engine firing order: 1-3-4-2
Distributor rotation: clockwise

GM (Pontiac) 151 4-cyl. (through 1978)
Engine firing order: 1-3-4-2
Distributor rotation: clockwise

GM (Buick) 231, 252 V6
Engine firing order: 1-6-5-4-3-2
Distributor rotation: clockwise

V6 harmonic balancers have two timing marks: one is 1/8 in. wide, and one is 1/16 in. wide. Use the 1/16 in. mark for timing with a hand held light. The 1/8 in. mark is used only with a magnetic timing pick-up probe.

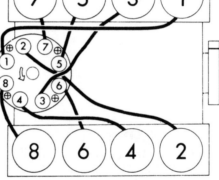

GM (Oldsmobile) 260 V8
Engine firing order: 1-8-4-3-6-5-7-2
Distributor rotation: counterclockwise

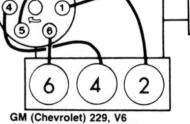

GM (Chevrolet) 229, V6
Engine firing order: 1-6-5-4-3-2
Distributor rotation: clockwise

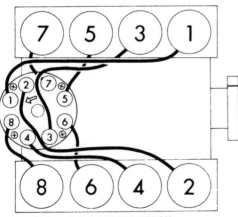

GM (Oldsmobile) 307,350,403 V8
Engine firing order: 1-8-4-3-6-5-7-2
Distributor rotation: counterclockwise

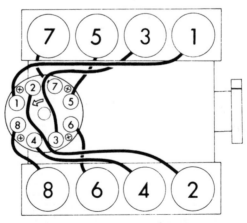

GM (Pontiac) 265, 301, 350, 400, V8
Engine firing order: 1-8-4-3-6-5-7-2
Distributor rotation: counterclockwise

CAPACITIES
Phoenix

Year	Engine No. Cyl. Displacement (Cu. In.)	Engine Crankcase Add 1 Qt For New Filter	Transmission (Pts To Refill After Draining)		Automatic ●	Drive Axle (pts)	Gasoline Tank (gals)	Cooling System (qts)		With Super-Cooling
			Manual ▲					With Heater	With A/C	
			3-Speed	4/5 Speed						
'78	4-151 Pont.	3	—	3.5/3.5	6	3.5	20.8	11.8	11.8	—
	6-231 Buick	4	3.5	3.5/3.5	7.5	3.5	20.8	14.0	14.1	14.1
	8-305 Chev.	4	—	3.5	7.5	4.25	20.8	16.8	17.0	17.2
	8-350 Chev.	4	—	—	7.5	4.25	20.8	17.1	17.1	17.8
'79	4-151 Pont.	3	—	3.0	6	3.5	15.0	13.5	13.5	13.3
	6-231 Buick	4	3.0	—	6	3.5	20.8	14.0	14.1	14.0
	8-305 Chev.	4	—	3.0	6	3.5	20.8	16.8	17.0	17.7
	8-350 Chev.	4	—	—	6	4.25	20.8	17.1	17.8	17.9

▲ 5-speed uses Dexron®
● Specifications do not include torque converter
— Not applicable

CAPACITIES
1978-81 Bonneville, Catalina

Year	Engine No. Cyl. Displacement (cu. in.)	Engine Crankcase Add 1 Qt For New Filter	Transmission Pts to Refill After Draining		Automatic ●	Drive Axle (pts)	Gasoline Tank (gals) ▲	Cooling System		With Super Cooling
			Manual					With Heater	With A/C	
			3-Speed	4-Speed						
'78	6-231 Buick	4	—	—	①	②	21	14.2	14.1	14.1
	8-301 Pont.	5	—	—	①	②	21	20.2	20.1	20.8
	8-350 Buick Sedan Sta. Wgn.	5 5	— —	— —	7.5 7.5	② 5.4	21 22	16.6 18.6	18.5 19.1	19.2 19.1
	8-350 Olds.	4	—	—	7.5	②	21	16.5	16.5	16.4
	8-400 Pont.	5	—	—	7.5	②	21	26.3	20.3	20.3
	8-403 Olds.	4	—	—	7.5	②	21	17.7	23.0	23.0
'79	6-231 Buick	4	—	—	6	3.5	21	13.9	13.9	13.9
	8-301 Pont.	4	—	—	6	3.5③	21	20.2	20.1	20.8
	8-350 Buick	4	—	—	6	3.5③	21	16.6	18.5	16.6
	8-350 Olds.	4	—	—	6	3.5③	21	16.5	16.4	17.1
	8-403 Olds.	4	—	—	6	3.5③	21	17.7	23.0	18.5

CAPACITIES
1978-81 Bonneville, Catalina

Year	Engine No. Cyl. Displacement (cu. in.)	Engine Crankcase Add 1 Qt For New Filter	Transmission Pts to Refill After Draining Manual 3-Speed	4-Speed	Automatic ●	Drive Axle (pts)	Gasoline Tank (gals) ▲	Cooling System With Heater	With A/C	With Super Cooling
'80	6-231 Buick	4	—	—	8	3.4	20.7	12.6	12.6	—
	8-265 Pont.	4	—	—	8	3.4	20.7	20.0	20.0	20.0
	8-301 Pont.	4	—	—	6	3.4	20.7	20.0	20.0	20.0
	8-350 Chev.	4	—	—	6	3.4	20.7	—	15.5	15.5
	8-350 Olds.	7	—	—	6	3.4	20.7	—	17.0	17.0
'81	6-231 Buick	4	—	—	8	3.4	25.0	13.1	13.3	13.3
	8-265 Pont.	4	—	—	8	3.4	25.0	20.0	20.0	20.0
	8-307 Olds.	4	—	—	8	3.4	25.0	14.9	15.6	15.6
	8-350 Diesel	7	—	—	8	3.4	27.0	—	17.0	17.0

① Turbo Hydra-Matic 200: 6.0
Turbo Hydra-Matic 350: 7.5
② with 8.5 in. ring gear: 4.25
with 8.75 in. ring gear: 5.4

③ Sta. Wgn.: 4.25
● Specifications do not include torque converter

— Not applicable
▲ Station wagon fuel tank (gals) '78-'81, 22

CAPACITIES
Grand Prix and Parisienne

Year	Engine No. Cyl. Displacement (cu. in.)	Engine Crankcase Add 1 Qt For New Filter	Transmission Pts to Refill After Draining		Automatic ●	Drive Axle (pts)	Gasoline Tank (gals)	Cooling System (qts)		With Super Cooling
			Manual					With Heater	With A/C	
			3-Speed	4-Speed						
'78	6-231 Buick	4	—	—	7.5	3.5	18.1	14.3	14.2	14.2
	8-301 Pont.	5	—	—	①	3.5	18.1	20.3	20.2	20.9
	8-305 Chev.	4	—	—	①	3.5	18.1	17.7	17.4	18.1
'79	6-231 Buick	4	3.5	—	6	3.4	18.2	14.2	14.0	14.3
	8-301 Pont.	4	3.5	—	6	3.4	18.2	20.3	20.2	20.8
	8-305 Chev.	4	—	—	6	3.4	18.2	17.7	18.3	18.3
'80	6-231 Buick	4	—	—	6	3.4	18.1	12.6	12.6	—
	8-265 Pont.	4	—	—	6	3.4	18.1	19.2	19.2	19.2
	8-301 Pont.	4	—	—	6	3.4	18.1	19.2	19.2	19.2
	8-305 Chev.	4	—	—	6	3.4	18.1	17.2	17.2	17.2
'81	6-231 Buick	4	—	—	8	3.4	18.1	13.1	13.1	—
	8-265 Pont.	4	—	—	8	3.4	18.1	20.3	20.3	20.3
	8-350 Diesel	7	—	—	8	3.4	19.1	—	17.0	—

CAPACITIES
LeMans, Grand Am, 1982-85 Bonneville

Year	Engine No. Cyl. Displacement (Cu. In.)	Engine Crankcase Add 1 Qt For New Filter	Transmission (Pts To Refill After Draining)			Drive Axle (pts)	Gasoline Tank (gals)	Cooling System (qts)		
			Manual		Automatic ●			With Heater	With A/C	With Super-Cooling
			3-Speed	4/5 Speed						
'83–'84	6-231 Buick	4	—	—	6	3.5	17.5	—	12.9	—
	8-305 Chev.	4	—	—	6	3.5	17.5	—	15.3	—
	8-350 Diesel	7①	—	—	6	3.5	19.8	—	17.2	—
'85	6-231 Buick	4	—	—	6	3.5	17.5	—	12.9	—
	8-305 Chev.	4	—	—	6	3.5	17.5	—	15.3	—
	8-350 Diesel	7①	—	—	6	3.5	19.8	—	17.2	—

● Specifications do not include torque converter
① Includes mandatory filter change

② w/THM 350C—6 pt.
③ On micro-filter equipped cars, capacity is the same with or without filter

④ StaWgn: 20.9
⑤ StaWgn: 18.2

GENERAL MOTORS "A" & "X" BODY
Celebrity, Century, Cutlass Ciera, 6000, Citation, Omega, Phoenix, Skylark

VEHICLE IDENTIFICATION NUMBER (VIN)

It is important for servicing and ordering parts to be certain of the vehicle and engine identification. The VIN (vehicle identification number) is a 13 or 17 digit number visible through the windshield on the driver's side of the dash and contains the vehicle and engine identification codes. It can be interpreted as follows:

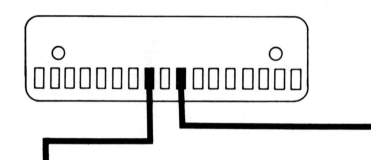

ENGINE CODE

Code	Cu. In.	Liters	Cyl.	Carb.	Eng. Mfg.
5	151	2.5	4	2	Pont.
R	151	2.5	4	TBI	Pont.
X	173	2.8	V6	2	Chev.
Z	173(HO)	2.8	V6	2	Chev.
E	183	3.0	V6	2	Buick
3	231	3.8	V6	MFI	Buick
T	263	4.3	V6	Diesel	Olds

MODEL YEAR CODE

Code	Year
B	1981
C	1982
D	1983
E	1984
F	1985

The seventeen digit Vehicle Identification Number can be used to determine engine application and model year. The 10th digit indicates the model year and the 8th digit identifies the factory installed engine.

T.B.I.: Throttle Body Injection

MFI: Multi-Point Fuel Injection

VEHICLE IDENTIFICATION NUMBER (VIN)

It is important for servicing and ordering parts to be certain of the vehicle and engine identification. The VIN (vehicle identification number) is a 13 or 17 digit number visible through the windshield on the driver's side of the dash and contains the vehicle and engine identification codes. It can be interpreted as follows:

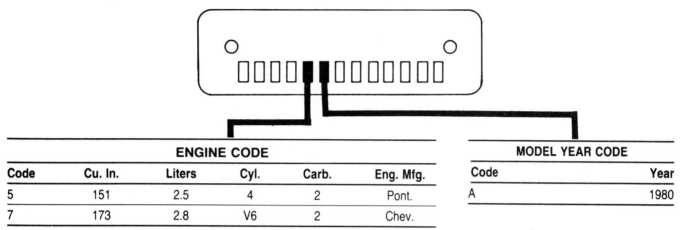

ENGINE CODE						MODEL YEAR CODE	
Code	Cu. In.	Liters	Cyl.	Carb.	Eng. Mfg.	Code	Year
5	151	2.5	4	2	Pont.	A	1980
7	173	2.8	V6	2	Chev.		

The thirteen digit Vehicle Identification Number can be used to determine engine application and model year. The 6th digit indicates the model year, and the 5th digit identifies the factory installed engine.

TUNE-UP SPECIFICATIONS

(When analyzing compression test results, look for uniformity among cylinders rather than specific pressures.)

Year	V.I.N. Code	Eng. No. Cyl. Displ. Cu. In.	Eng. Mfg.	hp	Spark Plugs Orig Type	Spark Plugs Gap (in.)	Ignition Timing (deg) ▲ Man Trans	Ignition Timing (deg) ▲ Auto Trans	Intake Valve Opens (deg)■	Fuel Pump Pressure (psi)	Idle Speed (rpm) ▲ Man Trans	Idle Speed (rpm) ▲ Auto Trans
'80	5	4-151	Pont.	All	R-43TSX	0.060	10B③	10B	33	6.5–8.0	1000	650
	X	6-173	Chev.	All	R-44TS	0.045	2B④	6B⑤	25	6.0–7.5	750⑥	750⑥
'81	5	4-151	Pont.	90	R-44TSX	0.060	4B	4B	33	6.5–8.0	1000	675
	X	6-173	Chev.	110	R-43TS	0.045	6B	10B	25	6.0–7.5	850	850⑦
	Z	6-173 HO	Chev.	135	R-42TS	0.045	10B	10B	31	6.0–7.5	700	700
'82–'85	5,R	4-151	Pont.	90	R-44TSX	0.060	8B	8B	33	6.0–8.0	950①	750②
	X	6-173	Chev.	112	R-43CTS	0.045	10B	10B	25	6.0–7.5	800	600
	Z	6-173 HO	Chev.	135	R-42CTS	0.045	6B	10B	31	6.0–7.5	850⑧	750
	E	6-183	Buick	110	R-44TS8	0.080	—	15B	16	6.0–8.0	—	see text
	3	6-231	Buick	125	R-44TS8	0.080	⑨	⑨	4.0–6.5	⑨	⑨	
	T	6-263	Olds.	85	—	—	—	6A	N.A.	5.8–8.7	—	650

NOTE: The underhood specifications sticker often reflects tune-up specification changes made in production. Sticker figures must be used if they disagree with those in this chart.

▲ See text for procedure
■All figures Before Top Dead Center
B: Before Top Dead Center
A: After Top Dead Center
Part numbers in this chart are not recommendations by Chilton for any product by brand name.

N.A.: Information not available
①Without air conditioning: 850
②Without air conditioning: 680
③Calif.: 12B
④Calif.: 6B
⑤Calif.: 10B

⑥Calif.: 700
⑦With A/C: 900
⑧Calif.: 750
⑨See underhood specifications sticker

FIRING ORDERS

NOTE: To avoid confusion, always replace spark plug wires one at a time.

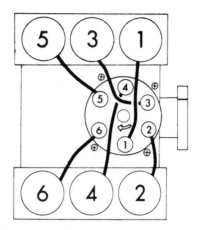

Buick 181, 231 V6 (3.0L, 3.8L) Engine firing order: 1-6-5-4-3-2 Distributor rotation: clockwise.

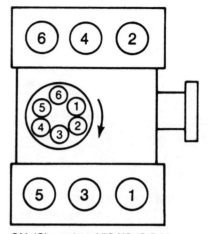

GM (Chevrolet) 173 V6 (2.8 L)
Engine firing order: 1-2-3-4-5-6
Distributor rotation: clockwise

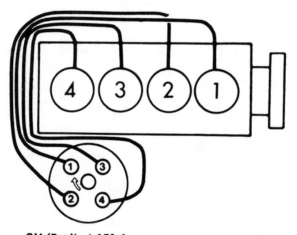

GM (Pontiac) 151-4
Engine firing order: 1-3-4-2
Distributor rotation: clockwise

CAPACITIES
A-Body

Year	V.I.N. Code	Engine Displacement Cu. In.	Eng. Mfg.	Crankcase Quarts		Transaxle Pints		Gas Tank Gal	Cooling System Qts	
				w/filter	wo/filter	4 speed	Auto		w/heater	w/AC
'82–'85	R	4-151	Pont.	3.0	2.8	6.0	10.0	16.0	9.5	9.75
	X	6-173	Chev.	4.0	3.0	6.0	10.0	16.0	11.5	11.75
	E	6-181	Buick	4.0	3.0	—	10.0②	16.0	13.5	14.25
	3	6-231	Buick	4.0①	4.0	—	13.0	16.0	12.25	12.75
	T	6-263	Olds.	6.0	5.5	—	10.0②	16.0	13.25	13.75

①Add as necessary to bring to appropriate level.
②13.0 pts w/440T4 transaxle.

CAPACITIES
X-Body

Year	Engine No. Cyl. Displacement (Cu. In.)	Engine Crankcase Add 1 Qt For New Filter ■	Transmission (Pts To Refill After Draining)			Drive Axle (pts)	Gasoline Tank (gals)	Cooling System (qts)	
			Manual		Automatic ●			With Heater	With A/C
			3-Speed	4-Speed					
'80–'81	4-151 Pont.	3	—	5.9	10.5	①	14	8.3	8.6
	6-173 Chev.	4	—	5.9	10.5	①	14	10.2	10.6
'82	4-151 Pont.	3	—	5.9	10.5	①	14	8.3	8.6
	6-173 Chev.	4	—	5.9	10.5	①	14	10.6	10.8
'83–'85	4-151 Pont.	3	—	5.9	10.5	①	14	8.3	8.6
	6-173 Chev.	4	—	5.9	10.5	①	14	10.6	10.8
	6-173 HO Chev.	4	—	5.9	10.5	①	14	10.6	10.8

① Transaxle refill given with transmission capacity

GM "C" BODY
Buick Electra Limited, Park Avenue, T-Type, Cadillac Fleetwood Brougham, DeVille, Oldsmobile 98 Regency, 98 Regency Brougham

VEHICLE IDENTIFICATION NUMBER (VIN)

It is important for servicing and ordering parts to be certain of the vehicle and engine identification. The VIN (vehicle identification number) is a 17 digit number visable through the windshield on the driver's side of the dash and contains the vehicle and engine identification codes. It can be interpreted as follows:

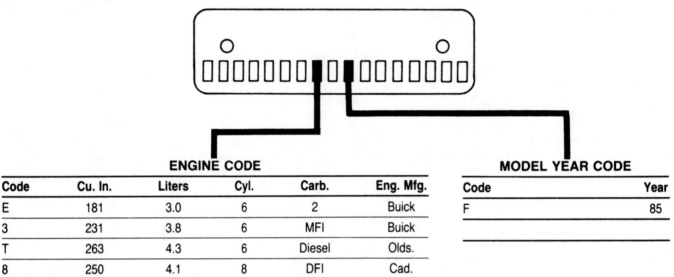

ENGINE CODE

Code	Cu. In.	Liters	Cyl.	Carb.	Eng. Mfg.
E	181	3.0	6	2	Buick
3	231	3.8	6	MFI	Buick
T	263	4.3	6	Diesel	Olds.
8	250	4.1	8	DFI	Cad.

MODEL YEAR CODE

Code	Year
F	85

The seventeen digit Vehicle Identification Number can be used to determine engine application and model year. The 10th digit indicates the model year, and the 8th digit identifies the factory installed engine.

MFI Multi-point Fuel Injection
DFI Digital Fuel Injection

GASOLINE ENGINE TUNE-UP SPECIFICATIONS

(When analyzing compression test results, look for uniformity among cylinders rather than specific pressures.)

	Engine				Spark Plugs		Distributor		Ignition Timing (deg) ▲	Valves Intake Opens ■ (deg)	Fuel Pump Pressure (psi)	Idle Speed (rpm) ▲
Year	Eng. V.I.N. Code	No. Cyl. Displacement (cu. in.)	Eng. Mfg.	Fuel Delivery	Orig. Type	Gap (in.)	Point Dwell (deg)	Point Gap (in.)	Auto. Trans.			Auto. Trans.
'85	E	6-181	Buick	2 bbl	R44TSX	.060	Electronic		① ②	16	3.9-6.5	① ②
'85	3	6-231	Buick	MFI	R44TS8	.080	Electronic		① ②	NA	28-36	① ②
'85	8	8-250	Cad.	DFI	R42CLTS6	.060	Electronic		① ②	37	40	① ②

NOTE: The underhood specifications sticker often reflects tune-up specification changes made in production. Sticker figures must be used if they disagree with those in this chart. Part numbers in this chart are not recommendations by Chilton for any product by brand name.

▲ See text for procedure.

■ All figures Before Top Dead Center

① See Underhood Specifications Sticker

② Only vehicles equipped with computerized emissions systems (which have no distributor vacuum advance unit), the idle speed and ignition timing are controlled by the emissions computer. These adjustments should be performed professionally on models so equipped.

FIRING ORDER

NOTE: To avoid confusion, always replace spark plug wires one at a time.

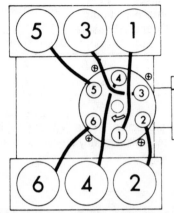

V 6 harmonic balancers have two timing marks: one is ⅛ in. wide. Use the 1/16 in. mark for timing with a hand held light. The ⅛ in. mark is used only with a magnetic timing pick-up probe.

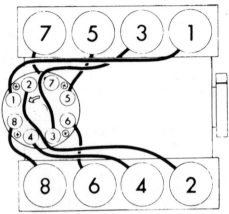

Buick 181, 231 V6 (3.0L, 3.8L) Engine firing order: 1-6-5-4-3-2 Distributor rotation: clockwise.

Cadillac 250 V8 (4.1L) Engine firing order: 1-8-4-3-6-5-7-2 Distributor rotation: counterclockwise

DIESEL ENGINE TUNE-UP SPECIFICATIONS

Year	Engine No. of cyl.- Displacement- Manufacturer	Fuel Pump Pressure (psi)	Compression Pressure (psi)②	Intake Valve Opens (°B.T.D.C.)	Idle Speed (rpm)
'85	6-263-Olds.	5.5–6.5	275 minimum	16	①

① See the Underhood Specifications Sticker

CAPACITIES

Year	Engine No. Cyl. Displacement (Cu. In.)	Engine Crankcase Add 1 Qt For New Filter	Transaxle Automatic Pts To Refill After Draining ●	Gasoline Tank (gals)	Cooling System (qts) With Heater	With A/C
'85	6-181	4.0	13	18	13.3	13.6
'85	6-231	4.0	13	18	13.1	13.2
'85	6-263	5.5	13	18	13.3	13.3
'85	8-250	4	13	NA	NA①	NA①

● Specifications do not include torque converter
NA Not available at time of publication
① The 4.1L V8 uses a coolant solution specifically designed for use in aluminum engines. Be sure that the coolant you choose meets GM spec. #1825M or is labeled for use in aluminum engines.

GENERAL MOTORS "E" & "K" BODY
Riviera, Eldorado, Seville, Toronado

DIESEL TUNE-UP SPECIFICATIONS

Year	Engine No. Cyl Displacement (cu in.)	Fuel Pump Pressure (psi)	Compression (lbs)	Intake Valve Opens (deg)	Idle Speed (rpm) •
'79	8-350	5.5-6.5	275 min.	16	650/675
'80	8-350	5.5-6.5	275 min.	16	750/600
'81-'85	8-350	5.5-7.0	275 min.	16	①

NOTE: The underhood specifications sticker often reflects tune-up specification changes made in production. Sticker figures must be used if they disagree with those in this chart.

① See underhood specifications sticker

• Where two idle speed figures appear separated by a slash, the first is idle speed with solenoid energized, the second is idle speed with solenoid disconnected.

VEHICLE IDENTIFICATION NUMBER (VIN)

It is important for servicing and ordering parts to be certain of the vehicle and engine identification. The VIN (vehicle identification number) is a 13 or 17 digit number visible through the windshield on the driver's side of the dash and contains the vehicle and engine identification codes. It can be interpreted as follows:

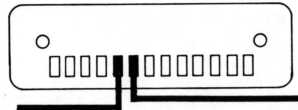

ENGINE CODE					MODEL YEAR CODE	
Code	Cu. In.	Liters	Cyl.	Carb.	Eng. Mfg.	Code	Year

Code	Cu. In.	Liters	Cyl.	Carb.	Eng. Mfg.
3	231	3.8	6	4	Buick
Y	307	5.0	8	4	Olds.
R	350	5.7	8	4	Olds.
B	350	5.7	8	EFI	Olds.
N	350	5.7	8	Diesel	Olds.
9	368	6.0	8	DFI	Cad.
K	403	6.6	8	4	Olds.
S	425	7.0	8	4	Cad.

Code	Year
8	78
9	79
A	80

The thirteen digit Vehicle Identification Number can be used to determine engine application and model year. The 6th digit indicates the model year, and the 5th digit identifies the factory installed engine.

VEHICLE IDENTIFICATION NUMBER (VIN)

It is important for servicing and ordering parts to be certain of the vehicle and engine identification. The VIN (vehicle identification number) is a 13 or 17 digit number visible through the windshield on the driver's side of the dash and contains the vehicle and engine identification codes. It can be interpreted as follows:

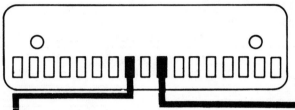

ENGINE CODE

Code	Cu. In.	Liters	Cyl.	Carb.	Eng. Mfg.
8	231	3.8	6	4	Buick
3	231	3.8	6	4	Buick
9	231	3.8	6	FI-Turbo	Buick
8	250	4.1	8	DFI	Cad.
8	250	4.1	8	4	Cad.
4	252	4.1	6	4	Buick
4	252	4.1	6	DFI	Buick
Y	307	5.0	8	4	Olds.
N	350	5.7	8	Diesel	Olds.
9	368	6.0	8	DFI	Cad.

MODEL YEAR CODE

Code	Year
B	81
C	82
D	83
E	84
F	85

The seventeen digit Vehicle Identification Number can be used to determine engine application and model year. The 10th digit indicates the model year, and the 8th digit identifies the factory installed engine.

EFI   Electronic Fuel Injection   DFI   Digital Fuel Injection

GASOLINE ENGINE TUNE-UP SPECIFICATIONS

(When analyzing compression test results, look for uniformity among cylinders rather than specific pressures.)

Year	Eng. Code	Engine No. Cyl. Displacement (cu. in.)	Eng. Mfg.	Spark Plugs Orig Type	Gap (in.)	Distributor	Ignition Timing (deg) Auto Trans ●	Valves Intake Opens (deg) ●	Fuel Pump Pressure (psi)	Idle Speed (rpm) Auto Trans ●
TORONADO										
'78	K	8-403	Olds.	R-46SZ	.060	Electronic	20B(22B)	16B	5.5-6.5	650/550(600)
'79	R	8-350	Olds.	R-46SZ	.060	Electronic	20B	16B	6-7.5	550
'80	Y	8-307	Olds.	R-46SX	.080	Electronic	20B	20	6-7.5	600/500
	R	8-350	Olds.	R-46SX	.080	Electronic	18B(16B)	16	6-7.5	600/500 (650/550)
'81-'82	4	6-252	Buick	R-45TS8	.080	Electronic	15B	16	6-7.5	①
	Y	8-307	Olds.	R-46SX	.080	Electronic	15B	20	6-7.5	①
'83	4	6-252	Buick	R-45TS8	.080	Electronic	15B	16	6-7.5	①
	Y	8-307	Olds.	R-46SX	.080	Electronic	15B	20	6-7.5	①
'84-'85	4	6-252	Buick	R-45TS8	.080	Electronic	①	16	6-7.5	①
	Y	8-307	Olds.	R-46SX	.080	Electronic	①	20	6-7.5	①
RIVIERA										
'79	3	6-231 Turbo	Buick	R-44TSX	.060	Electronic	15B	16	4.25-5.75	650
	R	8-350	Olds.	R-46SZ	.060	Electronic	15B	16	4.25-5.75	550
'80	3	6-231 Turbo	Buick	R-45TS	.040	Electronic	15B	16	5.0	600
	R	8-350	Olds.	R-46SX	.080	Electronic	18B @ 1100	16	5.5-6.5	500
'81-'82	3	6-231 Turbo	Buick	R-45TS	.040	Electronic	15B	16	4.2-5.8	①
	4	6-252	Buick	R-45TS8	.080	Electronic	15B	16	4.2-5.9	①
	Y	8-307	Olds.	R-45TS4	.060	Electronic	15B @ 1100	20	6-7.5	①
'83	8	6-231 Turbo	Buick	R-45TS	.040	Electronic	15B	16	4.2-5.8	①
	4	6-252	Buick	R-45TS8	.080	Electronic	15B	16	6-7.5	①
	Y	8-307	Olds.	R-46SX	.080	Electronic	15B @ 1100	20	6-7.5	①
'84-'85	8⑥	6-231 Turbo	Buick	R-45TS	.040	Electronic	①	16	4.2-5.8	①
	4	6-252	Buick	R-45TS8	.080	Electronic	①	16	6-7.5	①
	Y	8-307	Olds.	R-46SX	.080	Electronic	①	20	6-7.5	①
ELDORADO AND SEVILLE										
'78	S	8-425	Cadillac	R-45NSX	.060	Electronic	18B @ 1400	21	5.25-6.5	650
'79	B	8-350	Olds.	R-47SX	.060	Electronic	10B	22	5.5-6.5	600
'80	9	8-368	Cadillac	R-45NSX	.060	Electronic	18B	11	5.5-6.5	575
'81	4	6-252	Buick	R-45TS8	.060	Electronic	15B	16	4.25-5.75	550③
	9	8-368	Cadillac	R-45NSX	.060	Electronic	10B	16	12-14	470④
'82	8	8-250	Cadillac	R-43NTS6	.060	Electronic	①	37	40	⑤
	4	6-252	Buick	R-45TSV	.060	Electronic	15B @ 550	16	4.25-5.75	550③
'83	8	8-250	Cadillac	R-43NTS6	.060	Electronic	①	37	40	⑤
'84-'85	8	8-250	Cadillac	R-43NTS6⑦	.060	Electronic	①	37	40	⑤

●Where two figures appear separated by a slash, the first is idle speed with solenoid energized, the second is idle speed with solenoid disconnected. Figure in parentheses indicates California engine.

①See Underhood Sticker
②Solenoid energized (higher) idle speed is set with A/C on and compressor clutch wires disconnected.
③In Drive; A/C 680

④Drive or Neutral
⑤Electronic controlled idle, no adjustment
⑥'85: VIN9
⑦R42CLTS6
B Before Top Dead Center

FIRING ORDERS

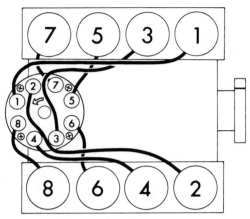

GM 250, 307, 350 V8s, including diesel
Engine firing order: 1-8-4-3-6-5-7-2 Distributor rotation: counterclockwise

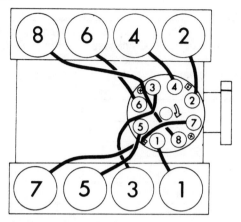

GM 368, 425 V8s
Engine firing order: 1-5-6-3-4-2-7-8 Distributor rotation: clockwise

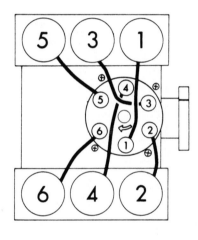

GM (Buick) 231 and 252 V6 (3.8 and 4.1L)
Engine firing order: 1-6-5-4-3-2
Distributor rotation: clockwise
V6 Harmonic balancers have two timing marks: one is ⅛ in. wide, and one is ¹⁄₁₆ in. wide. Use the ¹⁄₁₆ in. mark for timing with a hand held light. The ⅛ in. mark is used only with a magnetic timing pick-up probe.

CAPACITIES
All Models

Year	Engine No. Cyl. Displacement (cu. in.)	Engine Crankcase Add 1 Qt for New Filter	Transmission Pts to Refill After Draining Automatic ●	Drive Axle (pts)	Gasoline Tank (gals)	Cooling System (qts) With Heater	With A/C	With Heavy Duty
'78	8-425	4	8	4.25	24	19.8		—
	8-403	4.75	8	4.25	26	17.5		—
'79	8-350 Cadillac	4	9	4.25	25②	17.2		—
	8-350 Olds.	4	10	3.25	20	15		15.5
	8-350 Olds. ③	4	10	3.25	20.7	14.9		15.6
	8-350 Diesel	7①	9	3.25	③	18.5		—
	6-231	4	10	3.25	20.7	14		14.5
'80	8-368	4	④	3.25	20.7	22.4		—
	8-350	4	④	3.25	20.5	15.2		—
	8-350 Diesel	7①	④	3.25	23	18.5		—
	8-307	4	④	3.25	21	16.5		—
	6-231	4	④	3.25	21	13.6		14.1
'81	8-368	4	④	3.25	20.3	22.4		—
	8-307	4	④	3.25	21	16.25		16.25
	8-350 Diesel	7①	④	3.25	⑤	⑥		—
	6-252	4	④	3.25	21	13.1		—
	6-231	4	④	3.25	21	13.6		14.1
'82	8-350 Diesel	7①	④	3.25	23	⑧		⑧
	8-250	4	④	3.25	20.3	11.8		12.5
	8-307	4	④	3.25	21	⑦		—
	6-252	4	④	3.25	21	13.1		—
	6-231	4	④	3.25	21	13.6		14.1
'83	8-307	4	④	3.25	21	16.2		—
	8-250	4	④	3.25	20.3	11.8		—
	8-350 Diesel	7①	④	3.25	22.8	18.2		—
	8-252	4	④	3.25	21.1	13.1		—
	6-231	4	④	3.25	21.1	13.6		14.1
'84-'85	8-307	4	④	3.25	21.1	16.2		—
	8-250	4	④	3.25	20.3	11.8		12.5
	8-350 Diesel	7①	④	3.25	22.8	18.2		—
	6-252	4	④	3.25	21.1	12.5		—
	6-231	5	④	3.25	21.1	12.9		13.7

●Does not include torque converter
①Includes mandatory filter change
②Seville: 21
③Seville: 21, Eldorado: 19.6, Toronado: 22.8
④Add 6 pts; start engine and allow to warm up. Add fluid necessary to mark on dipstick
⑤Riviera: 27, Eldorado/Seville: 22.8, Toronado: 23
⑥Riviera: 18.2, Eldorado/Seville: 18.4, Toronado: 18
⑦Rivivera: 18.9, Toronado: 16.5
⑧Riviera: 23, Eldorado/Seville: 22.8, Toronado: 23

GENERAL MOTORS "F" BODY
Camaro, Firebird

VEHICLE IDENTIFICATION NUMBER (VIN)

It is important for servicing and ordering parts to be certain of the vehicle and engine identification. The VIN (vehicle identification number) is a 13 or 17 digit number visible through the windshield on the driver's side of the dash and contains the vehicle and engine identification codes. It can be interpreted as follows:

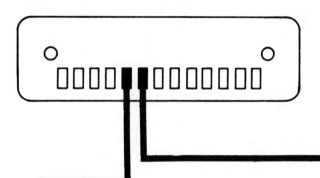

ENGINE CODE					
Code	Cu. In.	Liters	Cyl.	Carb.	Eng. Mfg.
CAMARO					
K	229	3.8	6	2	Chev.
A	231	3.8	V-6	2	Buick
D	250	4.1	6	1	Chev.
J	267	4.4	8	2	Chev.
U	305	5.0	8	2	Chev.
G	305	5.0	8	2	Chev.
H	305	5.0	8	4	Chev.
L	350	5.7	8	4	Chev.
FIREBIRD					
A	231	3.8	V-6	2	Buick
S	265	4.3	8	2	Pont.
Y	301	4.9	8	2	Pont.
W	301	4.9	8	4	Pont.
T	301①	4.9	8	4	Pont.
U	305	5.0	8	2	Chev.
G	305	5.0	8	2	Chev.
H	305	5.0	8	4	Chev.
P	350	5.7	8	4	Pont.
R	350	5.7	8	4	Olds.
L	350	5.7	8	4	Chev.
Z	400	6.5	8	4	Pont.
K	403	6.6	8	4	Olds.

MODEL YEAR CODE	
Code	Year
8	1978
9	1979
A	1980

The thirteen digit Vehicle Identification Number can be used to determine engine application and model year. The 6th digit indicates the model year, and the 5th digit identifies the factory installed engine.

① Turbocharged engine

VEHICLE IDENTIFICATION NUMBER (VIN)

It is important for servicing and ordering parts to be certain of the vehicle and engine identification. The VIN (vehicle identification number) is a 13 or 17 digit number visible through the windshield on the driver's side of the dash and contains the vehicle and engine identification codes. It can be interpreted as follows:

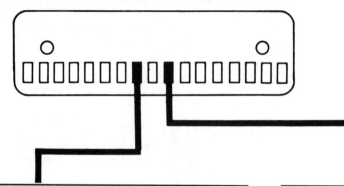

ENGINE CODE

Code	Cu. In.	Liters	Cyl.	Carb.	Eng. Mfg.
CAMARO					
2	151	2.5	4	T.B.I.	Pont.
F	151	2.5	4	2	Pont.
1	173	2.8	V-6	2	Chev.
L	173	2.8	V-6	2	Chev.
K	229	3.8	6	2	Chev.
A	231	3.8	V-6	2	Buick
J	267	4.4	8	2	Chev.
H	305	5.0	8	4	Chev.
7	305	5.0	8	T.B.I.	Chev.
G	305	5.0	8	4	Chev.
S	305	5.0	8	T.B.I.	Chev.
L (81)	350	5.7	8	4	Chev.
FIREBIRD					
2	151	2.5	4	T.B.I.	Pont.
F	151	2.5	4	2	Pont.
1	173	2.8	V-6	2	Chev.
L	173	2.8	V-6	2	Chev.
A	231	3.8	V-6	2	Buick
S (81)	265	4.3	8	2	Pont.
W	301	4.9	8	4	Pont.
T	301 ①	4.9	8	4	Pont.
H	305	5.0	8	4	Chev.
7	305	5.0	8	T.B.I.	Chev.
G	305	5.0	8	4	Chev.
S	305	5.0	8	T.B.I.	Chev.

MODEL YEAR CODE

Code	Year
B	1981
C	1982
D	1983
E	1984
F	1985

The seventeen digit Vehicle Identification Number can be used to determine engine application and model year. The 10th digit indicates the model year, and the 8th digit identifies the factory installed engine.

① Turbocharged engine

T.B.I.—Throttle body (fuel) injection

FIRING ORDERS

NOTE: To avoid confusion, replace spark plugs and wires one at a time.

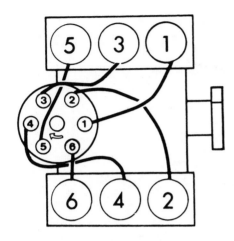

Chevrolet-built 229-V6 engine
Engine firing order: 1-6-5-4-3-2
Distributor rotation: clockwise

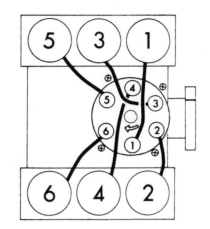

Buick-built 231-V6 engine
Engine firing order: 1-6-5-4-3-2
Distributor rotation: clockwise

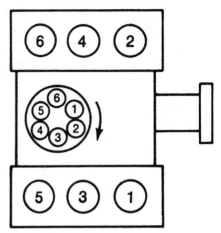

Chevrolet-built 173-V6 engine
Engine firing order: 1-2-3-4-5-6
Distributor rotation: clockwise

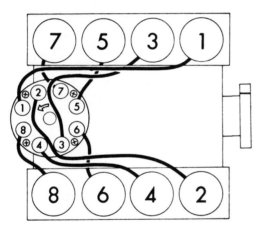

Pontiac-built V8 engines
Engine firing order: 1-8-4-3-6-5-7-2
Distributor rotation: counterclockwise

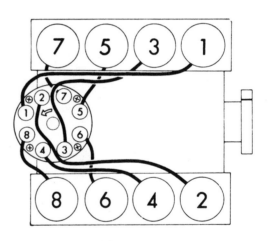

Oldsmobile-built V8 engines
Engine firing order: 1-8-4-3-6-5-7-2
Distributor rotation: counterclockwise

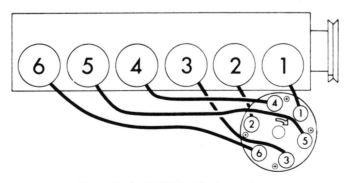

Chevrolet-built 250-6 cylinder engine
Engine firing order: 1-5-3-6-2-4
Distributor rotation: clockwise

FIRING ORDER

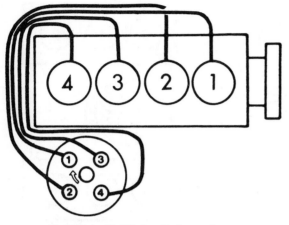

Pontiac-built 151-4 cylinder engine
Engine firing order: 1-3-4-2
Distributor rotation: clockwise

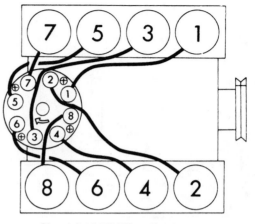

Chevrolet-built V8 engines
Engine firing order: 1-8-4-3-6-5-7-2
Distributor rotation: clockwise

TUNE-UP SPECIFICATIONS
Camaro

Year	Engine V.I.N. Code	Engine No. of Cyl. Displacement (Cu. In.)	Engine Manufacturer	Spark Plugs Type	Gap (in.)	Ignition Timing (deg)① ② Man Trans	Auto Trans	Intake Valve Opens (deg)③	Fuel Pump Pressure (psi)	Idle Speed (rpm)① ② Man Trans	Auto Trans
'78	D	6-250	Chev.	R-46TS	0.035	6B	10B⑥(6B)	16	4½–6	800	550(600)
	U	8-305	Chev.	R-45TS	0.045	4B	4B(6B)	28	7½–9	600	500
	L	8-350	Chev.	R-45TS	0.045	6B	6B(8B)	28	7½–9	700	500⑤
'79	D	6-250	Chev.	R-46TS	0.035	12B	8B(6B)	16	4½–6	800	675(600)
	G	8-305	Chev.	R-45TS	0.045	4B	4B	28	7½–9	600	500(600)
	L	8-350	Chev.	R-45TS	0.045	6B	6B(8B)	28	7½–9	700	500⑤
'80	K	6-229	Chev.	R-T5TS⑥	0.045	8B	12B	42	4½–6	700	600
	A	6-231	Buick	R-45TSX	0.060	—	15B	16	4¼–5¾	—	600
	J	8-267	Chev.	R-45TS	0.045	—	4B	28	7½–9	—	500
	H	8-305	Chev.	R-45TS	0.045	4B	4B	28	7½–9	700	500(550)
	L	8-350	Chev.	R-45TS	0.045	6B	6B	28	7½–9	700	500
'81	K	6-229	Chev.	R-45TS	0.045	6B	6B	42	4½–6	700⑦	600⑦
	A	6-231	Buick	R-45TS8	0.080	—	15B	16	4¼–5¾	—	500⑦
	J	8-267	Chev.	R-45TS	0.045	—	6B	44	7½–9	—	500⑦
	H	8-305	Chev.	R-45TS	0.045	6B	6B	44	7½–9	700	500
	L	8-350	Chev.	R-45TS	0.045	—	6B	38	7½–9	—	500⑦
'82	2	4-151	Pont.	R-44TSX	0.060	⑧	⑧	NA	9–13	⑧	⑧
	F	4-151	Pont.	R-44TSX	0.060	⑧	⑧	NA	5½–6½	⑧	⑧
	1	6-173	Chev.	R-43TS	0.045	⑧	⑧	NA	5½–6½	⑧	⑧
	H	8-305	Chev.	R-45TS	0.045	⑧	⑧	NA	5½–6½	⑧	⑧
	7	8-305	Chev.	R-45TS⑨	0.045	⑧	⑧	NA	9–13	⑧	⑧
'83	2	4-151	Pont.	R-44TSX	0.060	⑧	⑧	NA	9–13	⑧	⑧
	F	4-151	Pont.	R-44TSX	0.060	⑧	⑧	NA	5½–6½	⑧	⑧
	1	6-173	Chev.	R-43CTS	0.045	⑧	⑧	NA	5½–6½	⑧	⑧
	H	8-305	Chev.	R-45TS	0.045	⑧	⑧	NA	5½–6½	⑧	⑧
	7	8-305	Chev.	R-45TS	0.045	⑧	⑧	NA	9–13	⑧	⑧
	S	8-305	Chev.	R-45TS	0.045	⑧	⑧	NA	9–13	⑧	⑧

TUNE-UP SPECIFICATIONS
Camaro

Year	Engine V.I.N. Code	Engine No. of Cyl. Displacement (Cu. In.)	Engine Manufacturer	Spark Plugs		Ignition Timing (deg)① ②		Intake Valve Opens (deg)③	Fuel Pump Pressure (psi)	Idle Speed (rpm)① ②	
				Type	Gap (in.)	Man Trans	Auto Trans			Man Trans	Auto Trans
'84-'85	2	4-151	Pont.	R-44TSX	0.060	⑧	⑧	NA	9–13	⑧	⑧
	F	4-151	Pont.	R-44TSX	0.060	⑧	⑧	NA	5½–6½	⑧	⑧
	1	6-173	Chev.	R-43CTS	0.045	⑧	⑧	NA	5½–6½	⑧	⑧
	L	6-173	Chev.	R42CTS	0.045	⑧	⑧	NA	6–7½	⑧	⑧
	H	8-305	Chev.	R-45TS	0.045	⑧	⑧	NA	5½–6½	⑧	⑧
	G	8-305	Chev.	R-45TS	0.045	⑧	⑧	NA	9–13	⑧	⑧
	S	8-305	Chev.	R-45TS	0.045	⑧	⑧	NA	9–13	⑧	⑧

NOTE: The underhood specifications sticker often reflects tune-up specification changes made during the production run. Sticker figures must always be used if they disagree with those in this chart. Part numbers in this chart are not recommendations by Chilton for any product by brand name.

All models use electronic ignition systems.
B Before Top Dead Center
TDC Top Dead Center
—Not applicable
NA—Not available
① See text for procedure
② Figure in parenthesis indicates California engine
③ All figures Before Top Dead Center (B.T.D.C.)
④ 8B with air conditioning
⑤ High altitude engine—600
⑥ With automatic trans.—R-45TS
⑦ Equipped with Idle Speed Control (I.S.C.)

⑧ These functions are controlled by the emissions computer. In rare instances when adjustment is necessary, refer to the underhood emissions sticker for specifications.
⑨ R-44TS if a colder plug is needed
⑩ With air conditioning—750; without air conditioning—800

TUNE-UP SPECIFICATIONS
Firebird

Year	Engine V.I.N. Code	Engine No. of Cyl.- Displacement (Cu. In.)	Engine Manufac- turer	Spark Plugs Type	Gap (in.)	Ignition Timing (deg)③④ Man Trans	Auto Trans	Intake Valve Opens (deg)⑤	Fuel Pump Pressure (psi)	Idle Speed (rpm)③④ Man Trans	Auto Trans
'78	A	6-231	Buick	R-46TSX	0.060	15B	15B	16	4.5–5.7	800	600
	U	8-305	Chev.	R-45TS	0.045	4B	4B(6B)	29	7–8.5	700	600(650)
	L	8-350	Chev.	R-45TS	0.045	6B	8B	17	4.5–5.7	700	500
	Z	8-400	Pont.	R-45TSX	0.060	—	16B	29	7–8.5	—	650
	Z	8-400⑬	Pont.	R-45TSX	0.060	18B	18B	16	7–8.5	775	700
	K	8-403	Olds.	R-46SZ	0.060	—	20B	16	5.5–6.5	—	700(650)
'79	A	6-231	Buick	R-46TSX	0.060	15B	15B	16	4.5–5.5	800	600
	Y	8-301	Pont.	R-46TSX	0.060	—	12B	16	5.5–6.5	—	650
	W	8-301	Pont.	R-45TSX	0.060	14B	12B	16⑥	5.5–6.5	750	650
	G	8-305	Chev.	R-45TS	0.045	—	4B	28	5.5–6.5	—	500
	L	8-350	Chev.	R-45TS	0.045	—	8B	28	5.5–6.5	—	600
	Z	8-400	Pont.	R-45TSX	0.060	18B	—	16	7–8.5	775	—
	K	8-403	Olds.	R-46SZ	0.060	—	18B(20B)	16	5.5–6.5	—	550(500)
'80	A	6-231	Buick	R-45TSX⑦	0.060⑦	15B	15B	16	3–4.5	800/600①	620/550①
	S	8-265	Pont.	R-45TSX	0.060	—	10B	27	7.5–9	—	650/550①
	W	8-301	Pont.	R-45TSX	0.060	—	12B	16	7.5–9	—	650/500①
	W	8-301⑧	Pont.	R-45TSX	0.060	—	12B	17	7.5–9	700	550
	T	8-301⑨	Pont.	R-45TSX	0.060	—	8B	16	7.5–9	—	650/600①
	H	8-305	Chev.	R-45TS	0.045	—	4B	28	7.5–9	—	650/550①

TUNE-UP SPECIFICATIONS
Firebird

Year	Engine V.I.N. Code	Engine No. of Cyl.- Displacement (Cu. In.)	Engine Manufac- turer	Spark Plugs Type	Gap (in.)	Ignition Timing (deg)③④ Man Trans	Auto Trans	Intake Valve Opens (deg)⑤	Fuel Pump Pressure (psi)	Idle Speed (rpm)③④ Man Trans	Auto Trans
'81	A	6-231	Buick	R-45TS8	0.080	15B	15B	16	4.25–5.75	800	500
	S	8-265	Pont.	R-45TSX	0.060	—	12B	16	7.5–9	—	450 ± 24
	W	8-301	Pont.	R-45TSX	0.060	—	12B	16	7.5–9	—	450 ± 32
	T	8-301⑨	Pont.	R-45TSX	0.060	—	6B	16	7.5–9	—	450 ± 32
	H	8-305	Chev.	R-45TS	0.045	6B	6B	44	7.5–9	800	800
'82	2	4-151	Pont.	R-44TSX	0.060	⑩	⑩	NA	9–13	⑩	⑩
	F	4-151	Pont.	R-44TS	0.060	⑩	⑩	NA	5½–6½	⑨	⑨
	1	6-173	Chev.	R-43TS	0.045	⑩	⑩	NA	5.5–6.5	⑩	⑩
	H	8-305	Chev.	R-45TS	0.045	⑩	⑩	NA	5.5–6.5	⑩	⑩
	7	8-305	Chev.	R-45TS⑯	0.045	⑩	⑩	NA	9–13	⑩	⑩
'83	2	4-151	Pont.	R-44TSX	0.060	⑩	⑩	NA	9–13	⑩	⑩
	F	4-151	Pont.	R-44TS	0.060	⑩	⑩	NA	5½–6½	⑩	⑩
	1	6-173	Chev.	R-43CTS	0.045	⑩	⑩	NA	5.5–6.5	⑩	⑩
	L	6-173HO	Chev.	R-42CTS	0.045	⑩	⑩	NA	6–7½	⑩	⑩
	H	8-305	Chev.	R-45TS	0.045	⑩	⑩	NA	5.5–6.5	⑩	⑩
	7	8-305	Chev.	R-45TS⑯	0.045	⑩	⑩	NA	9–13	⑩	⑩
	S	8-305	Chev.	R-45TS	0.045	⑩	⑩	NA	9–13	⑩	⑩
'84–'85	2	4-151	Pont.	R-44TSX	0.060	⑩	⑩	NA	9–13	⑩	⑩
	F	4-151	Pont.	R-44TSX	0.060	⑩	⑩	NA	5½–6½	⑩	⑩
	1	6-173	Chev.	R-43CTS	0.045	⑩	⑩	NA	5½–6½	⑩	⑩
	L	6-173	Chev.	R-42CTS	0.045	⑩	⑩	NA	6–7½	⑩	⑩
	H	8-305	Chev.	R-45TS	0.045	⑩	⑩	NA	5½–6½	⑩	⑩

TUNE-UP SPECIFICATIONS
Firebird

Year	Engine V.I.N. Code	Engine No. of Cyl.- Displacement (Cu. In.)	Engine Manufac- turer	Spark Plugs Type	Gap (in.)	Ignition Timing (deg)③④ Man Trans	Auto Trans	Intake Valve Opens (deg)⑤	Fuel Pump Pressure (psi)	Idle Speed (rpm)③④ Man Trans	Auto Trans
'84-'85	G	8-305	Chev.	R-45TS	0.045	⑩	⑩	NA	9–13	⑩	⑩
	S	8-305	Chev.	R-45TS	0.045	⑩	⑩	NA	9–13	⑩	⑩

NOTE: The underhood specifications sticker often reflects tune-up specification changes made during the production run. Sticker figures must always be used if they disagree with those in this chart. Part numbers in this chart are not recommendations by Chilton for any product by brand name.

All models use electronic ignition systems.
B Before Top Dead Center
TDC Top Dead Center
——Not applicable
NA—Not available
①Lower figure indicates idle speed with solenoid disconnected
②High altitude and California R-45TSX
③See text for procedure
④Figure in parentheses indicates California engine
⑤All figures are in degrees Before Top Dead Center. Where two figures appear, the first represents timing with manual transmission, the second with automatic transmission
Auto—29
Trans Am—16
⑥High performance—27
⑦All M/T and low altitude A/T—R-45TS, gap 0.040
⑧With performance package
⑨Turbocharged engine
⑩These functions are controlled by the emissions computer. In rare instances when adjustment is necessary, refer to the underhood emissions sticker for specifications.
⑪R-44TS if a colder plug is needed
⑫Trans Am only

CAPACITIES
Camaro

Year	Engine No. Cyl. Displacement (cu. in.)	Engine Crankcase Add 1 qt for New Filter	Transmission Pts to Refill After Draining			Drive Axle (pts)	Gasoline Tank (gals)	Cooling System (qts)	
			Manual					With Heater	With A/C
			3-Speed	4-Speed	Automatic①				
'78	6-250	4	3	—	6	4.25③	21	15.0	16.0
	8-305	4	—	3	6	4.25③	21	17.5	18.5
	8-350	4	—	3	6	4.25③	21	17.5	18.5
'79	6-250	4	3	—	7	4.25③	21	15.0	16.0
	8-305	4	—	3.4	7	4.25③	21	17.5	18.5
	8-350	4	—	3.4	7	4.25③	21	17.5	18.5
'80–'81	6-229	4②	3	—	7④	4.25⑤	21	14.5	15.5
	6-231	4②	—	—	7④	4.25⑤	21	12.0	13.0
	8-267	4	—	—	7④	4.25⑤	21	15.0	16.0
	8-305	4	—	3.4	7④	4.25⑤	21	15.0	16.0
	8-350	4	—	—	7④	4.25⑤	21	16.0	17.0
'82	4-151	3②	—	4.3	8.5	3.5	16	12.8	13.0
	6-173	4②	—	4.3	8.5	3.5	16	12.8	12.8
	8-305⑥	4	—	4.3	8.5	3.5	16	17.2	17.2
	8-305⑦	4	—	4.3	8.5	3.5	16	15.9	15.9
'83	4-151	3②	—	4.3⑧	8.5⑨	3.5	16	12.8	13.0
	6-173	4②	—	4.3⑧	8.5⑨	3.5	16	12.8	12.8
	8-305⑥	4	—	4.3⑧	8.5⑨	3.5	16	17.2	17.2
	8-305⑦	4	—	4.3⑧	8.5⑨	3.5	16	15.9	15.9
'84–'85	4-151	3②	—	3.5⑧	8.5⑨	3.5	16	8.8	9.1
	6-173	4②	—	3.5⑧	8.5⑨	3.5	16	12.5	12.5
	8-305⑥	4	—	3.5⑧	8.5⑨	3.5	16	15.0	15.0
	8-305⑦	4	—	3.5⑧	8.5⑨	3.5	16	15.0	15.0

—Not applicable

① Drain and refill only—does not include torque convertor

② Capacity same with or without filter change

③ With 7½″ ring gear—3.5 pints

④ With 350c—6 pints

⑤ With 7½″ ring gear—3.5 pints; with 8¾″ ring gear—5.4 pints

⑥ With 4 bbl. carburetor

⑦ With throttle body fuel injection

⑧ 5-speed—5.3 pints

⑨ Overdrive transmission—9.9 pints: Add 4 pints, run engine and check dipstick-fill as necessary

CAPACITIES
Firebird

Year	Engine No. Cyl.-Displacement (Cu. In.)	Engine Crankcase (Add 1 Qt For New Filter)	Transmission (Pts To Refill After Draining)			Drive Axle (pts)	Gasoline Tank (gals)	Cooling System (qts)	
			Manual		Automatic (Pts.)①			With Heater	With Air Cond.
			3 Spd.	4 Spd.					
'78	6-231 Buick	4	3.5	—	7.5	4.25	20.8	14.0	14.0
	8-305 Chev.	4	—	3.5	7.5	4.25	20.8	17.2	17.2
	8-350 Chev.	4	—	3.5	7.5	4.25	20.8	17.2	17.2
	8-400 Pont.	5	—	2.44	7.5	4.25	20.8	19.7	③
	8-403 Olds.	5	—		7.5	4.25	20.8	17.4	18.0
'79	6-231 Buick	4	3.5	—	6	4.25	20.8	14.0	14.0
	8-301 Pont.	4	—	3.5	6	4.25	20.8	20.5	20.5
	8-305 Chev.	4	—	—	6	4.25	20.8	17.2	17.2
	8-350 Chev.	4	—	—	7.5	4.25	20.8	17.2	17.8
	8-400 Pont.	5	—	3.5	7.5	4.25	20.8	19.7	20.3
	8-403 Olds.	4	—	—	7.5	4.25	20.8	17.4	18.0
'80	6-231 Buick	4	3.5	3.5	6	4.25	20.8	13.2	13.2
	8-265 Pont.	4②	—	—	6	4.25	20.8	20.4	20.4
	8-301 Pont.	4②	3.5	3.5	6	4.25	20.8	20.4	20.4
	8-301 Pont. Turbo	4②	3.5	3.5	8	4.25	20.8	—	21.4
	8-305 Chev.	4	—	—	6	4.25	20.8	—	16.4
'81	6-231 Buick	4	3.5	—	6	4.25	21.0	20.9	—
	8-265 Pont.	4	—	—	6	4.25	21.0	20.9	—
	8-301 Pont.	4	—	—	6	4.25	21.0	20.9	—
	8-301 Pont. Turbo	4	—	—	6	4.25	21.0	20.9	—
	8-305 Chev.	4	—	—	6	4.25	21.0	20.9	—
'82	4-151 Pont.	3②	—	4.3	8.5	3.5	16.0	12.8	13.0
	6-173 Chev.	4②	—	4.3	8.5	3.5	16.0	12.8	12.8
	8-305 Chev.⑦	4	—	4.3	8.5	3.5	16.0	17.2	17.2
	8-305 Chev.⑧	4	—	4.3	8.5	3.5	16.0	15.9	15.9
'83	4-151 Pont.	3②	—	4.3⑤	8.5⑥	3.5	16.0	12.8	13.0
	6-173 Chev.	4②	—	4.3⑤	8.5⑥	3.5	16.0	12.8	12.8
	8-305 Chev.⑦	4	—	4.3⑤	8.5⑥	3.5	16.0	17.2	17.2
	8-305 Chev.⑧	4	—	4.3⑤	8.5⑥	3.5	16.0	15.9	15.9
'84–'85	4-151 Pont.	3②	—	3.5⑤	8.5⑥	3.5	16.0	8.8	9.1
	6-173 Chev.	4②	—	3.5⑤	8.5⑥	3.5	16.0	12.5	12.5
	8-305 Chev.⑦	4	—	3.5⑤	8.5⑥	3.5	16.0	15.0	15.0
	8-305 Chev.⑧	4	—	3.5⑤	8.5⑥	3.5	16.0	15.0	15.0

—Not applicable
① Drain and refill only—does not include torque convertor.
② Capacity same with or without filter change.
③ With manual trans. 20.3; with automatic trans.—22.1
④ With manual trans.—22.0; with automatic trans.—21.4
⑤ 5-speed—5.3 pints
⑥ Overdrive transmission—9.9 pints. Add 4 pints, run engine and check dipstick-fill as necessary
⑦ With 4 bbl. carburetor
⑧ With throttle body injection

GM "H" BODY
Astre, Monza, Starfire, '78-'80 Skyhawk, '78-'80 Sunbird

VEHICLE IDENTIFICATION NUMBER (VIN)

It is important for servicing and ordering parts to be certain of the vehicle and engine identification. The VIN (vehicle identification number) is a 13 or 17 digit number visible through the windshield on the driver's side of the dash and contains the vehicle and engine identification codes. It can be interpreted as follows:

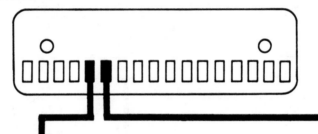

Engine Code						Model Year Code	
Code	Cu. in.	Liters	Cyl.	Carb.	Eng. Mfg.	Code	Year
V	151	2.5	4	2	Pont.	8	1978
C	196	3.2	V-6	2	Buick	9	1979
A	231	3.8	V-6	2	Buick	A	1980
G	305	5.0	V-8	2	Chev.		

The thirteen digit Vehicle Identification Number can be used to determine engine application and model year. The 6th digit indicates the model year, and the 5th digit identifies the factory installed engine.

TUNE-UP SPECIFICATIONS

Year	Model	Eng. V.I.N. Code	Engine No. Cyl. Displacement (cu. in.)	Eng. Mfg.	(hp)	Spark Plugs Orig. Type	Spark Plugs Gap (in.)	Distributor (deg)	Distributor (in.)	Ignition Timing (deg) Man	Ignition Timing (deg) Auto	Intake Valve Opens (deg)	Fuel Pump Pressure (psi)	Idle Speed (rpm) ▲ Man	Idle Speed (rpm) ▲ Auto
'78	Monza	V	4-151	Pont.	85	R43TSX	0.060	Electronic		14B	14B⑥	33	4–5½	1000/500	③
	Starfire	V	4-151	Pont.	90	R43TSX	0.060	Electronic		14B	14B	33	4–5	②	③
	Sunbird	V	4-151	Pont.	87	R43TSX	0.060	Electronic		14B	12B④	33	4–5½	②	⑤
	Monza	C	6-196	Buick	90	R46TSX	0.060	Electronic		15B	15B	17	5–6	800	600
	All	A	6-231	Buick	105	R46TSX	0.060	Electronic		15B	15B	17	3–4½	800⑦	600
	Monza	G	8-305	Chev.	145	R45TS	0.045	Electronic		4B	6B⑧	28	4–5	600	500⑨
'79	Starfire	V	4-151	Pont.	85	R44TSX	0.060	Electronic		14B	14B①	33	4–5½	1000	650
	Sunbird	V	4-151	Pont.	85	R44TSX	0.060	Electronic		12B④	12B④	33	5–6½	1000	650
	Monza	V	4-151	Pont.	85	R43TSX	0.060	Electronic		12B④	12B④	33	4–5.5	1000	650
	Monza	C	6-196	Buick	90	R46TSX	0.060	Electronic		15B	15B	16	4.5–7.5	800	670/550
	All	A	6-231	Buick	115	R46TSX	0.060	Electronic		15B	15B	16	4–6.5	800	600
	Monza	G	8-305	Chev.	130	R45TS	0.045	Electronic		4B	4B	28	7.5–9	700/600	600/500⑧

TUNE-UP SPECIFICATIONS

Year	Model	Eng. V.I.N. Code	Engine No. Cyl. Displacement (cu. in.)	Eng. Mfg.	(hp)	Spark Plugs Orig. Type	Gap (in.)	Distributor (deg) (in.)	Ignition Timing (deg) Man	Auto	Intake Valve Opens (deg)	Fuel Pump Pressure (psi)	Idle Speed (rpm) ▲ Man	Auto
'80	All	V	4-151	Pont.	85	R43TSX⑭	0.060	Electronic	12B	12B	33	4.5–5	1000/550 ⑨ ⑩	650/550 ⑪ ⑫
	All	A	6-231	Buick	115	R46TSX	0.060	Electronic	15B	15B	16	4.5–7.5	800/600	650/550 ⑬

▲ Lines separated by a slash show solenoid on/off

NOTE: The underhood specifications sticker often reflects tune-up specification changes made in production. Sticker figures must be used if they disagree with those in this chart.

NOTE: Where two figures are separated by a slash, the first figure is for idle speed with the solenoid connected, while the second is for the idle speed with the solenoid disconnected.

① Without a/c—1000/500, With a/c—1200/1000
② Calif.—14B
③ With a/c—650, Without a/c—500
④ Calif. without EGR valve—12B
⑤ 600—Skyhawk, Starfire exc. Calif.
⑥ 8B—Calf.
⑦ 600—High Altitude
⑧ Calif.—650/600
⑨ 49 States with a/c—1250/1000
⑩ Calif. without a/c—1000/500, Calif. with a/c—1200/1000
⑪ 49 State with a/c—850/650
⑫ Calif. without a/c—650/550, Calif. with a/c—850/650
⑬ Calif. with a/c—670/620
⑭ Calif. Monza—R44TSX, Sunbird, Starfire—R44TSX

FIRING ORDERS

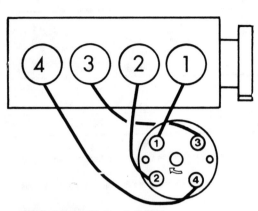

GM Pontiac 151 4 cyl. (1978)
Engine firing order: 1-3-4-2
Distributor rotation: clockwise

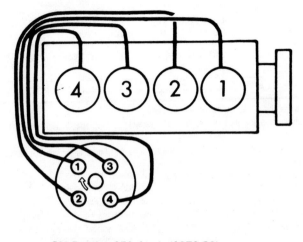

GM Pontiac 151 4-cyl. (1979-80)
Engine firing order: 1-3-4-2
Distributor rotation: clockwise

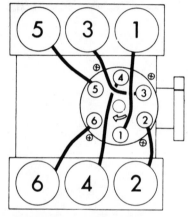

GM (Buick) 196, 231 V6
Engine firing order: 1-6-5-4-3-2
Distributor rotation: clockwise

V6 harmonic balancers have two timing marks: one is 1/8 in. wide, and one is 1/16 in. wide. Use the 1/16 in. mark for timing with a hand held light. The 1/8 in. mark is used only with a magnetic timing pick-up probe.

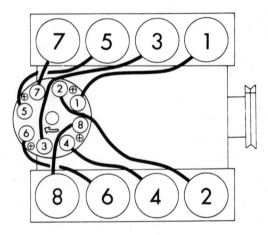

GM (Chevrolet) 305 V8
Engine firing order: 1-8-4-3-6-5-7-2
Distributor rotation: Clockwise

CAPACITIES

Year	Model	Engine Displacement Cu In. (cc)	Engine Crankcase (qts)		Transmission (pts) ▲			Drive Axle (pts)	Gasoline Tank (gals)	Cooling System (qts)	
			With Filter	Without Filter	Manual		Automatic ●			W/ AC	W/O AC
					3-spd	4-5 spd					
'78-'79	Monza	4-151	4	3	—	3①	6	2.8	18.5②	10.8	10.8
	Sunbird	4-151	4	3	—	3.5	6	3.5	18.5③	④	⑤
	Starfire	4-151	4	3	—	3.5	6	3.5	18.5	11.5	11.0
	Monza	6-196	5	4	—	3①	6	2.8	18.5②	11.6	11.6
	Monza	6-231	5	4	—	3①	6	2.8	18.5②	11.6	11.6
	Sunbird	6-231	5	4	—	3.5	7.5	3.5	18.5③	12.8	12.7
	Starfire	6-231	5	4	—	3.5	6	3.5	18.5	12.25	11.75
	Skyhawk	6-231	5	4	—	3.5①	6	3.75	18.5	1.21	11.8
	All	8-305	5	4	—	3①	8	2.8	18.5	18.0	18.0
'80	Monza	4-151	4	3	3.4	—	7.5	3.5	18.5	11.5	11.6
		6-231	5	4	3.4	—	7.0	3.5	18.5	11.9	11.9
	Sunbird	4-151	4	3	3.0	3.5	8.0	3.5	18.5⑥	11.5	11.0
		6-231	5	4	3.4	—	7.0	3.5	18.5⑥	11.9	11.9
	Starfire	4-151	4	3	3.0	—	6.0	3.5	18.5	11.5	11.0
		6-231	5	4	3.0	—	6.0	3.5	18.5	12.4	11.9
	Skyhawk	6-231	5	4	3.0	—	6.0	3.5	18.5	12.2	12.3

● Specifications do not include torque converter
▲ Pints to refill after draining

① 5-speed uses Dexron® II Auto. Trans. Fluid
② Sta. wag. and Monza "S" hatchback—15.0
③ Sta. wag: early production—15.9, late production—15.0
④ Man. trans.—10.9, Auto. trans.—11.6
⑤ Man. trans—10.9, Auto. trans.—11.4
⑥ Sta. wag.—15.0

GM "J" BODY
Cavalier, Cimarron, Firenza, 2000 Sunbird, '82-'85 Skyhawk

VEHICLE IDENTIFICATION NUMBER (VIN)

It is important for servicing and ordering parts to be certain of the vehicle and engine identification. The VIN (vehicle identification number) is a 13 or 17 digit number visible through the windshield on the driver's side of the dash and contains the vehicle and engine identification codes. It can be interpreted as follows:

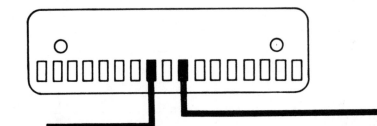

ENGINE CODE						MODEL YEAR CODE	
Code	Cu. In.	Liters	Cyl.	Carb.	Eng. Mfg.	Code	Year
G	110 (OHV)	1.8	4	2 bbl	Chev.	C	1982
O	110 (OHC)	1.8	4	TBI	Pontiac	D	1983
J	110 (OHC)	1.8	4	MFI (Turbo)	Pontiac	E	1984
B	122	2.0	4	①	Chev.	F	1985
P	122	2.0	4	TBI	Chev.		

The seventeen digit Vehicle Identification Number can be used to determine engine application and model year. The 10th digit indicates the model year, and the 8th digit identifies the factory installed engine.

OHV–Overhead valve engine
OHC–Overhead cam engine
TBI–Throttle Body Injection
MFI–Multi-Port Fuel Injection
①–1982: 2 bbl.
    1983: TBI
NOTE: Some 1983–85 Canadian models with the 2.0 Liter engine use a 2 bbl. carburetor

TUNE-UP SPECIFICATIONS

(When analyzing compression test results, look for uniformity among cylinders rather than specific pressures.)

Year	Eng. V.I.N. Code	Engine No. Cyl. Displacement (cu. in.)	Eng. Mfg.	hp	Spark Plugs		Ignition Timing (deg)▲●		Valves Intake Opens (deg)■	Fuel Pump Pressure (psi)	Idle Speed (rpm)▲●	
					Orig Type	Gap (in.)	Man Trans	Auto Trans			Man Trans	Auto Trans
1982–'85	G	4-110	Chev.	88	R-42TS	0.045①	12B	12B	30	4.5–6.0	②	②
	0	4-110	Pont.	84	R-42XLS6④	0.060	8B	8B	N.A.	9–13	②	②
	B	4-122	Chev.	90	R-42CTS	0.035	—	12B	30	4.5–6.0③	②	②
	P	4-122	Chev	86	R-42CTS	0.035	②	②	N.A.	12	②	②
	J	4-110	Pont.	150	R-42CXLS	0.035	②	②	N.A.	12	②	②

NOTE: The underhood specifications sticker often reflects tune-up specification changes made in production. Sticker figures must be used if they disagree with those in this chart.

▲See text for procedure

●Figure in parenthesis indicates California and High Altitude engine

■All figures Before Top Dead Center

B Before Top Dead Center

Part numbers in this chart are not recommendations by Chilton for any product by brand name.

①Certain models may use 0.035 in. Gap—see underhood specifications sticker to be sure

②See underhood specifications sticker

③1983–84 w/T.B.I—12 psi

④1984–85—R44XLS

N.A.: Not Available

FIRING ORDERS

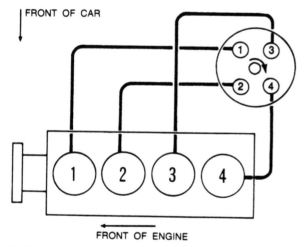

GM (Chevrolet) 110 and 122 overhead valve (OHV)
Engine firing order: 1-3-4-2
Distributor rotation: clockwise

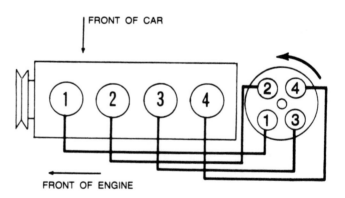

GM (Pontiac) 110 overhead camshaft (OHC)
Engine firing order: 1-3-4-2
Distributor rotation: counterclockwise

CAPACITIES

| Year | Eng. V.I.N. Code | Engine Displacement (Cu. In.) | Eng. Mfg. | Crankcase Quarts (Liters) | | Transaxle Pints (L) | | | Gas Tank Gal (L) | Cooling System Qts (L) | |
				w/filter	wo/filter	4 speed	5 speed	Auto		w/heater	w/AC
1982–'85	G	110	Chev.	4.0 (3.8)	4.0 (3.8)	5.9 (2.8)	—	10.5 (5.0)	14 (53)	8.0 (7.57)	8.0 (7.57)
	0, J	110	Pont.	①	①	—	2.5 (5.3)	10.5 (5.0)	14 (53)	7.8 (7.4)	7.9 (7.5)
	B, P	122	Chev.	4.0 (3.8)	4.0 (3.8)	5.9 (2.8)	—	10.5 (5.0)	14 (53)	8.3 (7.7)	8.3 (7.7)

① Add 3 qts, check oil level at dipstick and add as necessary.

GENERAL MOTORS "P" BODY
Fiero

VEHICLE IDENTIFICATION NUMBER (VIN)

It is important for servicing and ordering parts to be certain of the vehicle and engine identification. The VIN (vehicle identification number) is a 17 digit number visible through the windshield on the driver's side of the dash and contains the vehicle and engine identification codes. It can be interpreted as follows:

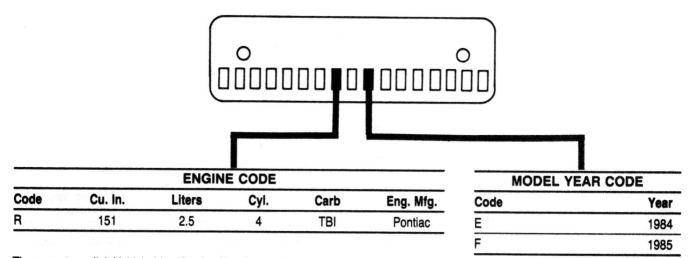

ENGINE CODE

Code	Cu. In.	Liters	Cyl.	Carb	Eng. Mfg.
R	151	2.5	4	TBI	Pontiac

MODEL YEAR CODE

Code	Year
E	1984
F	1985

The seventeen digit Vehicle Identification Number can be used to determine engine application and model year. The 10th digit indicates the model year, and the 8th digit identifies the factory installed engine.
TBI (Throttle body injection)

TUNE-UP SPECIFICATIONS

(When analyzing compression test results, look for uniformity among cylinders rather than specific pressures.)

Year	V.I.N. Code	Eng. No. Cyl. Displ. Cu. In.	Eng. Mfg.	hp	Spark Plugs Orig Type	Spark Plugs Gap (in.)	Ignition Timing (deg)▲ Man Trans	Ignition Timing (deg)▲ Auto Trans	Intake Valve Opens (deg)■	Fuel Pump Pressure (psi)	Idle Speed (rpm)▲ Man Trans	Idle Speed (rpm)▲ Auto Trans
'84–'85	R	151	Pont	90	R44TSX	.060	①	①	33	6-8	①	①

NOTE: The underhood specifications sticker often reflects tune-up specification changes made in production. Sticker figures must be used if they disagree with those in this chart.
①See underhood sticker

FIRING ORDER

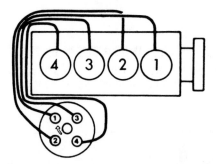

GM (Pontiac) 151-4 engine firing order: 1-3-4-2 Distributor rotation: clockwise

CAPACITIES

Year	V.I.N. Code	Engine Displacement Cu. In.	Eng. Mfg.	Crankcase Quarts	Transaxle Pints		Gas Tank Gal	Cooling System Qts
					Manual	Auto		
'84–'85	R	151	Pont.	3①	6.0	8.0	10.5	②

① With or without filter change
② Manual Trans. 13.8 qts.
  Auto Trans. 14.2 qts.

GENERAL MOTORS "T" BODY
Chevette, 1000

TUNE-UP SPECIFICATIONS

(When analyzing compression test results, look for uniformity among cylinders rather than specific pressures.)

Year	Eng. V.I.N. Code	Engine No. Cyl. Displacement (liters)	Mfg.	SPARK PLUGS Orig. Type	SPARK PLUGS Gap (in.)	DISTRIBUTOR Point Dwell (deg)	DISTRIBUTOR Point Gap (in.)	IGNITION TIMING (deg) ▲ Man Trans	IGNITION TIMING (deg) ▲ Auto Trans	Valves Intake Opens ■ (deg)	Fuel Pump Pressure (psi)	IDLE SPEED (rpm) ▲ Man Trans ◆	IDLE SPEED (rpm) ▲ Auto Trans.
'78	E	4-1.6 base	Chev.	R-43TS	.035	Electronic		8B	8B	28	5-6.5	800	800
	0	4-1.6 HO	Chev.	R-43TS	.035	Electronic		8B	8B	31	5-6.5	800	800
'79	E	4-1.6 base	Chev.	R-42TS	.035	Electronic		12B	18B①	28	5-6.5	800	750
	0	4-1.6 HO	Chev.	R-42TS	.035	Electronic		12B	18B②	31	5-6.5	800	750
'80	9	4-1.6 base	Chev.	R42TS	.035	Electronic		12B	18B	28	5-6.5	800	750③
	0	4-1.6 HO	Chev.	R42TS	.035	Electronic		12B	18B	31	5-6.5	800	750
'81	9	4-1.6	Chev.	R42TS	.035	Electronic		18B	18B	28	2.5-6.5	800	700
'82-'85		4-1.6	See Underhood Specification Sticker										

NOTE: The underhood specifications sticker often reflects tune-up specification changes made in production. Sticker figures must be used if they disagree with those in this chart. Product numbers in this chart are not recommendations by Chilton for any product by brand name.

▲ See text for procedure
● Figure in parentheses indicates California engine
■ All figures Before Top Dead Center
◆ Refer to the Spark Plug Replacement Chart
B Before Top Dead Center
HO High Output
① Calif.—16B
② Calif.—12B
③ Calif.—800

VEHICLE IDENTIFICATION NUMBER (VIN)

It is important for servicing and ordering parts to be certain of the vehicle and engine identification. The VIN (vehicle identification number) is a 13 or 17 digit number visible through the windshield on the driver's side of the dash and contains the vehicle and engine identification codes. It can be interpreted as follows:

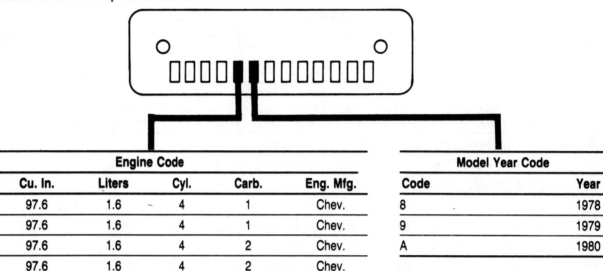

Engine Code						Model Year Code	
Code	Cu. In.	Liters	Cyl.	Carb.	Eng. Mfg.	Code	Year
E	97.6	1.6	4	1	Chev.	8	1978
J	97.6	1.6	4	1	Chev.	9	1979
E('79)	97.6	1.6	4	2	Chev.	A	1980
0	97.6	1.6	4	2	Chev.		
9	97.6	1.6	4	2	Chev.		

The thirteen digit Vehicle Identification Number can be used to determine engine application and model year. The 6th digit indicates the model year, and the 5th digit identifies the factory installed engine.

VEHICLE IDENTIFICATION NUMBER (VIN)

It is important for servicing and ordering parts to be certain of the vehicle and engine identification. The VIN (vehicle identification number) is a 13 or 17 digit number visible through the windshield on the driver's side of the dash and contains the vehicle and engine identification codes. It can be interpreted as follows:

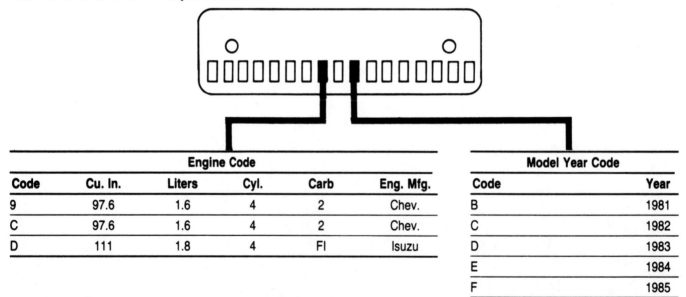

Engine Code						Model Year Code	
Code	Cu. In.	Liters	Cyl.	Carb	Eng. Mfg.	Code	Year
9	97.6	1.6	4	2	Chev.	B	1981
C	97.6	1.6	4	2	Chev.	C	1982
D	111	1.8	4	FI	Isuzu	D	1983
						E	1984
						F	1985

The seventeen digit Vehicle Identification Number can be used to determine engine application and model year. The 10th digit indicates the model year, and the 8th digit identifies the factory installed engine.

DIESEL TUNE-UP SPECIFICATIONS

Year	Engine No. Cyl. Displacement (liters)	Static Injection Timing	Fuel Injection Order	Compression (lbs)	Injection Nozzle Opening Pressure (psi)	Intake Valve Opens (deg)	IDLE SPEED ▲ (rpm)	
							Man.	Auto.
'81-'82	L-4 (1.8)	18°B	1-3-4-2	441①	1707	32	625	725
'83-'85	L-4 (1.8)	11°B	1-3-4-2	441①	1707	32	620	720

NOTE: The underhood specifications sticker often reflects changes made in production. Sticker figures must be used if they disagree with those in the above chart.
▲ See underhood sticker for fast idle speed.
① At 200 rpm

FIRING ORDER

NOTE: To avoid confusion, replace spark plugs and wires one at a time.

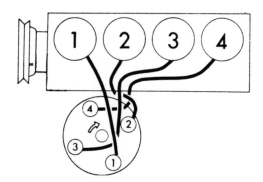

Chevrolet 98 cu. in. (1.6 liter) 4 cyl.
Engine firing order: 1-3-4-2
Distributor rotation: clockwise

CAPACITIES

Year	Engine No. Cyl. Displacement (liters)	Engine Crankcase	TRANSMISSION PTS TO REFILL AFTER DRAINING		Automatic ●	Drive Axle (pts)	Gasoline Tank (gals)	COOLING SYSTEM (qts)	
			Manual						
			4-Speed	5-Speed				With Heater	With A/C
'78	4-1.6	4	3	—	10	2	12.5	8.5	9.0
'79	4-1.6	4	3	—	10	1.75	12.5	8.5	9.0
'80-'85	4-1.6	4	3	4	6	1¾	12.5	9	9¼
'81-'85	4-1.8 Diesel	6①	3	3¼	6	1¾	12.5	8.5	9.0

● Specifications do not include torque converter
① With filter change

CHEVROLET SPRINT

VEHICLE IDENTIFICATION NUMBER (VIN)

It is important for servicing and ordering parts to be certain of the vehicle and engine identification. The VIN (vehicle identification number) is a 17 digit number visible through the windshield on the driver's side of the dash and contains the vehicle and engine identification codes. It can be interpreted as follows:

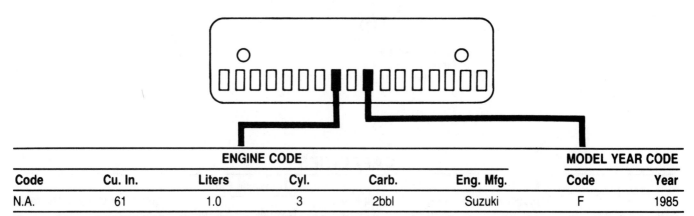

| | ENGINE CODE | | | | | MODEL YEAR CODE | |
Code	Cu. In.	Liters	Cyl.	Carb.	Eng. Mfg.	Code	Year
N.A.	61	1.0	3	2bbl	Suzuki	F	1985

The seventeen digit Vehicle Identification Number can be used to determine engine application and model year. The 10th digit indicates the model year, and the 8th digit identifies the factory installed engine.
N.A.—Not Available

TUNE-UP SPECIFICATIONS

(When analyzing compression test results, look for uniformity among cylinders rather than specific pressures.)

Year	Eng. V.I.N. Code	Engine No. Cyl. Displacement (cu. in.)	Eng. Mfg.	hp	Spark Plugs Orig Type	Spark Plugs Gap (in.)	Ignition Timing (deg)▲● Man Trans	Ignition Timing (deg)▲● Auto Trans	Valves Intake Opens (deg)■	Fuel Pump Pressure (psi)	Idle Speed (rpm) ▲● Man Trans	Idle Speed (rpm) ▲● Auto Trans
'85	N.A.	3-61	Suzuki	48	①	③	③	③	N.A.	3.5②	③	③

①NGK:BPRGES-11 or Nippondenso WIGEXR-U11
②@ 5,000 rpm
③Refer to underhood specifications sticker

FIRING ORDERS

NOTE: To avoid confusion, replace spark plugs and wires one at a time.

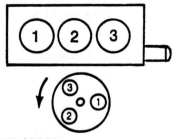

FIRING ORDER
Firing Order: 1-3-2
Distributor rotation: counterclockwise

CAPACITIES

Year	V.I.N. Code	Engine Displacement Cu. In.	Eng. Mfg.	Crankcase Quarts	Transaxle Pints		Gas Tank Gal	Cooling System Qts
					Manual	Auto		
'85		3-61	Suzuki	3.7	4.8	—	.8.3	4.5

AUDI
Fox, 4000, Coupe, 4000S Quattro, 5000, Quattro
SERIAL NUMBER IDENTIFICATION

Vehicle

5000

The chassis number is on the plate on top of the instrument panel, clearly visible through the driver's side of the windshield. It is also stamped into the upper right corner of the firewall. The vehicle identification plate is mounted on the right wheel housing.

4000

The vehicle identification number (VIN) is located on the left (driver's side) windshield pillar and in the engine compartment on the ledge.

FOX

The chassis number is on a plate on the left windshield pillar, clearly visible through the driver's side of the windshield. It is also stamped into the top center of the firewall. The vehicle identification plate is on the right wheel housing.

Engine

5000

The engine number is stamped on the left side of the engine block (clutch housing).

In addition to the engine number, an engine code number is also stamped on the starter end of the cylinder block, just below the cylinder head. This number indicates the exact cylinder bore of the particular engine.

4000

The engine number is located on the left side of the cylinder block, below the cylinder head and next to the distributor.

FOX

The engine number is stamped on the left side of the engine block, just above the fuel pump.

In addition to the engine number, an engine code number is also stamped into the left front side of the cylinder block, just above the water pump. This number indicates the exact cylinder bore of the particular engine.

GASOLINE ENGINE TUNE-UP SPECIFICATIONS

Year and Model	Engine Displacement Cu. In. (cc)	Spark Plugs		Distributor		Ignition Timing (deg)	Intake Valve Opens (deg)	Pressure Fuel Pump (psi)	Idle Speed (rpm)	Valve Clear (in.)	
		Type	Gap (in.)	Point Dwell (deg)	Point Gap (in)					In	Ex
'78–'79 Fox	97 (1,588)	N8Y	.028	44–50	.016	3A @ Idle	4B	4.8–5.4	850–1000	.008–.012	.016–.020
'80 4000	97 (1,588)	N8Y ①	.028	44–50②	.016②	3A @ Idle	4B	64–74	850–1000③	.008–.012	.016–.020
'81–'83 4000	105 (1,715)	N8Y ①⑨	.028	ELECTRONIC		3A @ Idle⑩	6B	64–74	850–1000③	.008–.012	.016–.020
'84–'85 4000	109 (1,780)	N8GY N281BY	.028	ELECTRONIC		6B@ Idle⑭	N.A.	64–74	850–1000	Hyd.	Hyd.
'80–'85 4000 5 cyl	130.8 (2,144)	N8Y ①	.028 ⑤	ELECTRONIC		3A @ Idle⑦⑩	6B⑯	64–74	850–1000④	.008–⑮ .012	.016–⑮ .020
'78–'85 5000	130.8 (2,144)	N8Y ①	.035 ⑥	ELECTRONIC⑧		3A @ Idle⑦⑩	6B	64–74	850–1000④	.008–⑮ .012	.016–⑮ .020
'80–'85 5000 Turbo	130.8 (2,144)	N8Y ⑪	.028	ELECTRONIC		21B @ 3,000⑬	N.A.	72–82	880–1000⑫	.008–⑮ .012	.016–⑮ .020
'82–'85 Quattro	130.8 (2,144)	N6GY	.028	ELECTRONIC		⑬	N.A.	75–85	790–910	.008–.012	.016–.020

NOTE: The underhood specifications sticker often reflects tune-up specification changes made in production. Sticker figures must be used if they disagree with those in this chart.

N.A. Not available at time of publication
IN Intake
EX Exhaust
A After top dead center
B Before top dead center
① Calif: N8GY
② Calif: Electronic ignition system; not adjustable
③ Calif: 920–960

④ 1980–81 Calif: 880–1000
    1982–85 All: 775–925
⑤ 1980: .035
⑥ 1981–84: .028
⑦ 1982: 49 States and Calif. w/MT—6B
⑧ 1978–80 models have adjustable air gap; set to .01 in.
⑨ Canada: N10Y
⑩ 1983–85: 6B (USA only)—'83 MT only; '84

Canada 5000S, GT Coupe—34
⑪ 1983–85: N8GY
⑫ 1983–85: 790–910
⑬ Distributor housing aligned with mark on Quattro and '84–'85 5000 Turbo
⑭ Supply hose to idle by-pass pinched shut
⑮ Models after Jan '84 have hydraulic lash adjusters—no adjustment is necessary.
⑯ '84–'85: 1.5° BTDC

DIESEL ENGINE TUNE-UP SPECIFICATIONS

Model/ Year	Engine Displacement Cu. In. (cc)	Warm Valve Clear (in)		Intake Valve Opens (deg)	Injection Pump Setting (deg)	Injection Nozzle Pressure (psi)		Idle Speed (rpm)	Com- pression Pressure (psi)
		In	Ex			New	Used		
'79–'81 5000 Diesel	121 (1,986)	.008– .012	.016– .020	N.A.	Align Marks	1849	1706	700–800	398–483
'82–'83 5000 Turbodiesel	121 (1,986)	.008– .012	.016– .020	N.A.	Align Marks	2306	2139	700–800	493
'82–'83 4000 Diesel	97 (1,588)	.008– .012	.016– .020	N.A.	Align Marks	1885	1740	770–870	398–483
'83–'85 4000 Turbodiesel	97 (1,588)	.008– .012	.016– .020	N.A.	Align Marks	2306	2139	900–1000	493

N.A. Not available at time of publication

FIRING ORDER

NOTE: To avoid confusion, always replace spark plug wires one at a time.

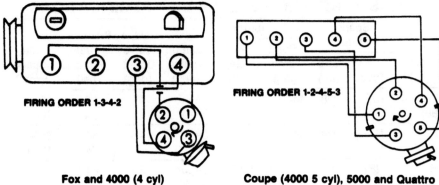

FIRING ORDER 1-3-4-2

Fox and 4000 (4 cyl)

FIRING ORDER 1-2-4-5-3

Coupe (4000 5 cyl), 5000 and Quattro

CAPACITIES

Year/ Model	Engine Displacement cu.in.(cc)	Crankcase (qts)		Transmission (pts)			Gasoline Tank (gals)	Cooling System (qts)
		With Filter	Without Filter	Manual		Automatic		
				4-spd	5-spd			
'78–'79 Fox	97 (1,588)	3.7	3.2	3.4	—	6.4	12.0	6.3
'80–'83 4000	105 (1,715)	3.7③	3.2④	3.4	3.4	6.4	15.9	7.4
'84–'85 4000	109 (1,780)	4.7	4.2	3.4	3.4	6.4	15.9	9.8
'80–'85 Coupe 4000 5cyl	130.8 (2,144)	4.8⑤	4.3⑥	—	5.5⑦	6.4	15.9	8.6
'82–'85 4000 Diesel/ Turbodiesel	97 (1,588)	3.7	3.2	—	3.4	6.4	15.9	6.6
'78–'85 5000	130.8 (2,144)	4.8⑧	4.3⑨	3.4	5.2①	6.4	19.8②	8.6
'79–'83 5000 Diesel/ Turbodiesel	121 (1,986)	4.8	4.3	—	5.2①	6.4	19.8	9.9
'80–'85 5000 Turbo	130.8 (2,144)	4.8⑧	4.3⑨	—	—	6.4	19.8	9.9
'82–'85 Quattro	130.8 (2,144)	4.5	4.0	—	7.6	—	23.8	9.8

① 1980–85: 5.5 ④ 1983–85: 3.0 ⑦ 1983–85: 3.4
② 1978: 15.9 ⑤ 1983–85: 4.0 ⑧ 1983–85: 5.0
③ 1983–85: 3.5 ⑥ 1983–85: 3.5 ⑨ 1983–85: 4.5

BMW
318i, 320i, 325e, 528e, 528i, 530i, 533i, 630CSi, 633CSi, 733i

SERIAL NUMBER IDENTIFICATION

Manufacturer's Plate

The manufacturer's plate is located in the engine compartment on the right side inner fender panel or support, or on the right side of the firewall.

Vehicle Identification Number

The VIN is located on a plate on the upper left of the instrument panel, visible through the windshield.

Chassis Number

The chassis number can be found in the engine compartment on the right inner fender support or facing forward on the right side of the heater bulkhead. A label is also attached to the upper steering column cover inside the vehicle.

Under hood serial number location— typical

Engine Number

The engine number is located on the left rear side of the engine, above the starter motor.

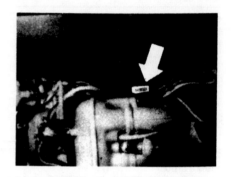

Engine serial number location

FIRING ORDERS

NOTE: To avoid confusion, always replace spark plug wires one at a time.

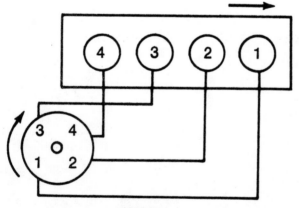

1978–79
4 cylinder firing order: 1-3-4-2

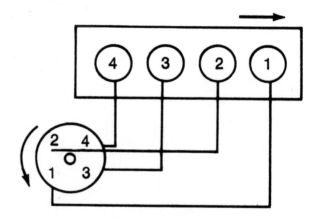

1980–'85
4 cylinder firing order: 1-3-4-2

FIRING ORDER

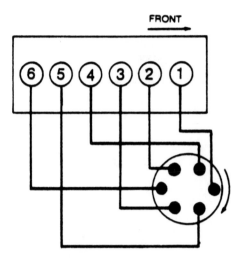

528i, 530i, 630CSi and 1978–81 633CSi and 733i firing order: 1–5–3–6–2–4

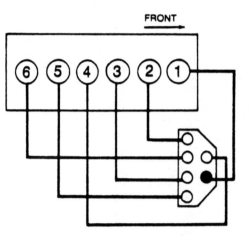

528e, 533i and 1982 and later 633CSi and 733i firing order: 1–5–3–6–2–4

TUNE-UP SPECIFICATIONS

Year	Model	Spark Plugs Type	Gap (in.)	Distributor Dwell (deg.)	Point Gap (in.)	Ignition Timing (deg.)① MT	AT	Intake Valve Opens (deg.)•	Fuel Pump Pressure (psi)	Idle Speed (rpm) MT	AT	Cold Valve Clearance (in.)
'78–'79	320i	Bosch W125T30②	.024③	62	.014	25B@ 2200 (2400)	25B@ 2200 (2400)	4B	64–74	950	950	.007
'80–'83	320i	Bosch WR9DS	.024	Electronic④		25B@ 2200	25B@ 2200	4B	64–74	850	900	.007
'78	530i	Bosch W145T30	.024	38	.014	22B@ 1700 (2700)	22B@ 1700 (2700)	14B	35	950	950	.011
'79–'81	528i	Bosch WR9DS⑤	.024	Electronic④		22B@ 2100	22B@ 2100	7B	35	900	900	.011
'82–'85	325e, 528e	Bosch WR9LS	.024	Electronic		⑥	⑥	NA	43	⑥	⑥	.010
'78–'79	633CSi, 733i	Bosch W145T30	.024	Electronic		22B@ 2400 (2750)	22B@ 2400 (2750)	14B	37	950	950	.011
'80–'81	633CSi, 733i	Bosch WR9DS	.024	Electronic④		22B@ 1650	22B@ 1650	14B	35	900	900	.011
'82–'85	533i, 633CSi, 733i	Bosch WR9LS	.024	Electronic		⑥	⑥	14B	35	⑥	⑥	.011
'84–'85	318i	Bosch WR9DS	.024	Electronic		⑥	⑥	NA	43	⑥	⑥	.008

•.02 in. clearance cam base circle and rocker
NA Not available at time of publication
① Figures in parenthesis are for California
② 1978–79: W145T30

③ 1979: .027
④ Air gap 0.012–0.028 in.
   Dwell 42° ± 10°@ 15 rpm
   52° ± 5° @ 4500 rpm

⑤ 1979: W125T30
⑥ Motronic injection system; controlled by computer

CAPACITIES

Year	Model	Engine Crankcase (qts)		Transmission, Refill After Draining (pts)		Drive Axle (pts)	Gasoline Tank (gals)	Cooling System (qts)
		With Filter Change	Without Filter Change	Manual	Automatic			
'78–'79	320i	4.5	4.25	2.2	4.2	2.0	15.9	7.4
'80–'83	320i	4.5①	4.25②	2.2	4.2	1.9	15.3	7.4
'78	530i	6.0	5.25	2.3	4.2	3.4	16.4	12.7
'78–'85	733i	6.0	5.25	2.4	4.0	3.8	22.5	12.7
'78–'85	633CSi	6.0	5.25	2.4	4.2	3.2	16.5	12.7
'79–'81	528i	6.0	5.25	2.3	4.2	3.4	16.4	12.7
'82–'85	528e	4.5	4.2	3.4	4.2	3.6	16.6	12.7
'83–'85	533i	6.0	5.3	2.65	6.3	3.6	16.6	12.7
'84–'85	318i	4.5	4.2	2.4	6.3	1.9	14.5	7.4
'84–'85	325e	4.5	4.2	2.4	6.3	3.4	14.5	7.4

① With chrome plated guide tube for dipstick:
  4.25
② With chrome plated guide tube for dipstick:
  4.0
③ '83–'85 models—6.3
④ '83–'85 models—3.6

CRYSLER CORP.
Arrow, Colt, Champ, Challenger, Conquest, Sapporo, Vista

SERIAL NUMBER IDENTIFICATION

J B 3 B E 4 4 3 9 C U 4 0 0 0 0 1

1st Digit	2nd Digit	3rd Digit	4th Digit	5th Digit	6th Digit	7th Digit	8th Digit	9th Digit	10th Digit	11th Digit	12th Digit	13th to 17th Digits
Manufacturing country	Sales channel	Vehicle type	Other	Vehicle line	Trim code	Body type	Engine displacement	*Check digit	Model year	Assembly plant	Transmission code	Sequence number
J – Japan	B – Dodge P – Plymouth	3 – Passenger car	B – Manual seat belt	E – Colt/ Champ	2 – Low 3 – Medium 4 – High, High (RS, LS)	4 – 2 door hatchback	2 1.4 litre (86.0 CID) 3 1.6 litre (97.5 CID)	1 2 · · 4 X	C – 1982	U – MIZUSHIMA Plant	1 4 speed M/T Federal 2 · 4 speed M/T California 3 · 4 speed M/T Canada 4 – 4 x 2 speed M/T Federal 5 – 4 x 2 speed M/T California 6 – 4 x 2 speed M/T Canada 7 – 3 speed A/T Federal 8 – 3 speed A/T California 9 · 3 speed A/T Canada	00001 to 99999

NOTE: *"Check Digit" means a single number or letter X used to verify the accuracy of transcription of vehicle identification number.
M/T is an abbreviation for manual transaxle.
A/T is an abbreviation for automatic transaxle.
RS is an abbreviation for "Rally Sports".
LS is an abbreviation for "Luxury Sports".

Typical 1981 and later 17 digit vehicle identification number

Vehicle Number

The vehicle identification plate is mounted on the instrument panel, adjacent to the lower corner of the windshield on the driver's side, and is visible through the windshield. The thirteen digit vehicle number is composed of a seven digit identification code, and a six digit sequential number.

Starting for 1981 and later, a standardized 17 digit Vehicle Identification Number (VIN) was used. The number continues to be visible from the outside of the lower driver's side windshield area.

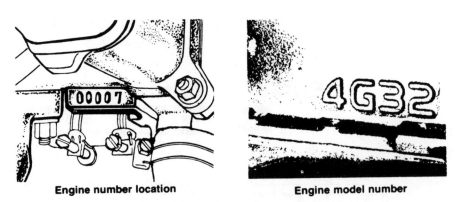

Engine number location

Engine model number

Engine Number

The engine model number in embossed on the lower left side of the block.

The engine model number is stamped near the serial number of the upper right front side of the engine block. The serial number is stamped on a pad at the upper right front of the engine adjacent to the exhaust manifold.

Serial number location

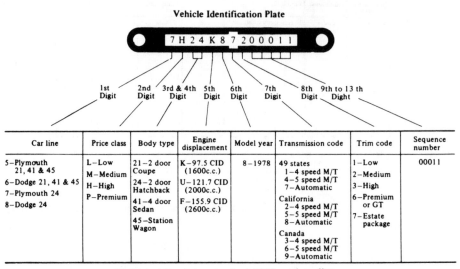

Vehicle Identification Plate

7 H 2 4 K 8 7 2 0 0 0 1 1

| | | 1st Digit | 2nd Digit | 3rd & 4th Digit | 5th Digit | 6th Digit | 7th Digit | 8th Digit | 9th to 13 th Dight |

Car line	Price class	Body type	Engine displacement	Model year	Transmission code	Trim code	Sequence number
5–Plymouth 21, 41 & 45 6–Dodge 21, 41 & 45 7–Plymouth 24 8–Dodge 24	L–Low M–Medium H–High P–Premium	21–2 door Coupe 24–2 door Hatchback 41–4 door Sedan 45–Station Wagon	K–97.5 CID (1600c.c.) U–121.7 CID (2000c.c.) F–155.9 CID (2600c.c.)	8–1978	49 states 1–4 speed M/T 4–5 speed M/T 7–Automatic California 2–4 speed M/T 5–5 speed M/T 8–Automatic Canada 3–4 speed M/T 6–5 speed M/T 9–Automatic	1–Low 2–Medium 3–High 6–Premium or GT 7–Estate package	00011

Vehicle I.D. plate—typical 1980 and earlier

TUNE-UP SPECIFICATIONS

(When analyzing compression test results, look for uniformity among cylinders, rather than specific pressures.)

Year	Engine Displace. cu. in. (cc)	Spark Plugs Type	Spark Plugs Gap (in.)	Distributor Point Dwell (deg)	Distributor Point Gap (in.)	Ignition Timing (deg) MT	Ignition Timing (deg) AT	Intake Valve Opens (deg) BTDC	Fuel Pump Pressure (psi)	Idle Speed (rpm)	Valve Clear (in)● In.	Valve Clear (in)● Ex.
'78	97.5 (1600)	BPR6ES	0.028–0.031	49–55	0.018–0.022	5B ②	5B ②	24 M 19 A	3.7–5.1	①	0.006	0.010
	121.7 (2000)	BPR6ES	0.028–0.031	49–55	0.018–0.022	5B ②	5B ②	24	4.6–6.0	③	0.006	C.010
	155.9 (2600)	BPR6ES	0.039–0.043	52 ± 3	0.018–0.021	7B	7B	25	4.6–6.0	④	0.006⑤	0.010
'79–'82	86.0 (1400)	BPR6ES-11⑫	0.039–⑫0.043	52 ± 3	0.018–0.021 ⑧	5B	—	18	3.7–5.1	700⑨	0.006⑤	0.010
	97.5 (1600)	BPR6ES-11⑫	0.039–⑫0.043	52 ± 3	0.018–0.021 ⑧	5B ⑥	5B ⑥	20	3.7–5.1	650 M 700 A	0.006⑤	0.010
	121.7 (2000)	BPR6ES⑫	0.039–⑫0.043	Electronic		5B	5B	25	4.6–6.0	650 M 700 A	0.006⑤	0.010
	155.9 (2600)	BRP6ES⑫	0.039–⑫0.043	Electronic		7B ⑦	7B ⑦	25	4.6–6.0	④ ⑩	0.006⑤	0.010

TUNE-UP SPECIFICATIONS

(When analyzing compression test results, look for uniformity among cylinders, rather than specific pressures.)

Year	Engine Displace. cu. in. (cc)	Spark Plugs		Distributor		Ignition Timing (deg)		Intake Valve Opens (deg) BTDC	Fuel Pump Pressure (psi)	Idle Speed (rpm)	Valve Clear (in)●	
		Type	Gap (in.)	Point Dwell (deg)	Point Gap (in.)	MT	AT				In.	Ex.
'83–'85	86.0 (1400)	BUR6EA-11⑫	0.039–⑫ 0.043	Electronic		⑪	⑪	18	2.7–3.7	⑪	0.006⑤	0.010
	97.5 (1600)	BUR6EA-11⑫	0.039–⑫ 0.043	Electronic		⑪	⑪	20	2.4–3.4	⑪	0.006⑤	0.010
	121.7 (2000)	BUR6EA-11	0.039– 0.043	Electronic		5B	5B	19	NA	⑭	0.006	0.010
	155.9 (2600)	BPR5ES-11⑫	0.039–⑫ 0.043	Electronic		7B ⑪	7B ⑪	25	4.6–6.0	⑪	0.006⑤	0.010
	155.9⑬ (2600)	BUR6EA-11	0.039– 0.043	Electronic		10B	—	NA	35.6	850	0.006	0.010

NOTE: The underhood specifications sticker often reflects tune-up specifications changes made in production. Sticker figures must be used if they disagree with those in this chart.

B Before top dead center
NA—Not available at time of publication
● All clearances set hot
① Fed: 800–900
  Alt: 900–1000
  Calif.: 900–1000 man.
  800–900 auto.
② Altitude (TDC)
  Calif.: 5A
③ Fed.: 900–1000 man.
  800–900 auto.
  Calif.: 900–1000

④ Fed.: 850 ± 50 rpm—both MT and AT
  Calif. & High Alt.: 700 ± 50 rpm—MT
  Calif.: 750 ± 50 rpm—AT
⑤ Jet valve clearance: 0.006 inch
⑥ High altitude only: 10B
⑦ Actual timing with dual diaphragm advance,
  Calif.: 3 ATDC
  High Alt.—2 BTDC
⑧ 1980 California cars and all 1981 cars:
  electronic reluctor gap not adjustable
⑨ Fed.: 4 speed man. trans. (not available in
  California) 650 rpm

⑩ 1982–83: Man. trans., 50 states 750 rpm
  Auto. trans., 50 states 800 rpm
⑪ See underhood specification sticker
⑫ Canada: 1400—BPR6ES; .028–.031
  1600—BPR6ES; .028–.031
  2000—BPR6ES; .028–.031
  2600—BPR5ES; .028–.031
⑬ 1984 and later Conquest
⑭ Man. Trans.: with AC—750
  without AC—700
  Auto. Trans.: with AC—850
  without AC—750

FIRING ORDERS

NOTE: To avoid confusion, always replace spark plug wires one at a time.

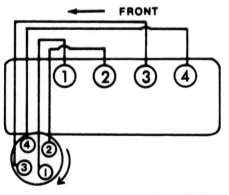

1400cc, 1600cc and 1984 and later 2000cc engines

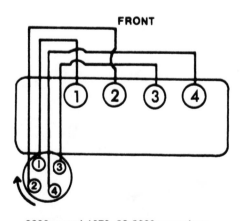

2600cc and 1978–83 2000cc engines

CAPACITIES
Rear Wheel Drive Cars

Year	Model	Engine Displacement (cc)	Engine Crankcase (qts)		Transmission (qts)			Drive Axle (pts)	Gasoline Tank (gals)	Cooling System (qts)	
			With Filter	Without Filter	Manual		Automatic			W/AC	W/O AC
					4-spd	5-spd					
'78	All	1600	4.2	3.7	1.8	2.1	6.8	1.2	15.8	7.7	7.7
		2000	4.5	4.0	—	2.4	6.8	1.2	15.8	9.5	9.5
		2600	4.5	4.0	—	2.4	6.8	1.2	15.8	9.7	9.7
'79–'85	All	1600	4.2	3.7	—	2.1	7.2	1.2	①	7.7	7.7
		2000	4.5	4.0	—	2.4	7.2	1.2	①	9.5	9.5
		2600	4.5	4.0	—	2.4	7.2	1.4②④	①③	9.5	9.5

①Colt Coupe, Sedan and Arrow: 13.2
  Challenger and Sapporo: 15.8
  Sta. Wgn.: 14.0 (1979) 13.2 (1980)
②'81–'84: 2.7
③'81–'84: 15.8; Conquest: 19.8
④Conquest: on complete refills include 4-oz
  of Mopar Hypoid Gear Additive, No.
  4318060

CAPACITIES
Front Wheel Drive Cars

Year	Model	Engine Displacement (cc)	Engine Crankcase (qts)		Transaxle (qts)			Gasoline Tank (gals)	Cooling System (qts)	
			With Filter	W/O Filter	Manual		Automatic		W/AC	W/O AC
					4-spd	Twin Stick				
'79	All	1400	3.7	3.17	2.2	2.2	—	10.6	—	5.2
		1600	4.2	3.67	2.2	2.2	—	10.6	6.9	6.9
'80	All	1400	3.7	3.17	2.3	2.3	—	10.6	—	4.7
		1600	4.2	3.67	2.3	2.3	6.0	10.6	4.7	4.7
'81–'85	All	1400	3.7	3.17	2.4	2.4	—	10.6①	—	4.7
	All	1600	4.2	3.67	2.4	2.4	6.0	10.6①	4.7	4.7
	Vista	2000	4.2	—	2.4	2.4	6.1	13.2	7.4	7.4

①RS, LS: 13.2

DATSUN/NISSAN
200SX, B210, 210, 280Z, 280ZX, 300ZX, 310, 510, 810, F10, Maxima, Pulsar, Sentra, Stanza

SERIAL NUMBER IDENTIFICATION

Engine Number

The engine number is stamped on the right side top edge of the cylinder block, except on the 1984 and later 200SX, and the 1984 and later 300ZX V6. On the V6, the number is stamped on the right rear edge of the right cylinder bank, facing up. On the 1984 and later 200SX (CA20E and CA18ET engines), the number is stamped on the left rear edge of the block, next to the bellhousing. The engine serial number is preceded by the engine model code.

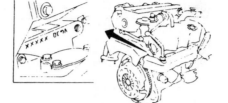

Engine identification number location— 1984 and later V6

Chassis Number

The chassis number is on the firewall under the hood. Late model vehicles also have the chassis number on a plate attached to the top of the instrument panel on the driver's side. The chassis serial number is preceded by the model designation. Late models also have an Emission Control information label on the firewall under the hood.

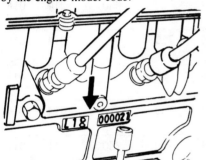

Engine serial and code number, all except V6, CD17 and CA20/CA18ET

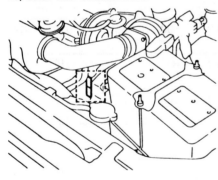

CD17 1.7L diesel engine serial number location

ENGINE I.D. TABLE

Number of Cylinders	Displacement cu. in. (cc)	Type	Engine Model Code
4	119.1 (1952)	OHC	L20B
4	85.24 (1397)	OHV	A14
6	146 (2393)	OHC	L24,L24E
6	168 (2753)	OHC	L28,L28E,L28ET
6	170 (2793)	OHC	LD28①
4	75.48 (1237)	OHV	A12A
4	90.80 (1488)	OHV	A15
4	90.8 (1488)	OHC	E15
4	90.8 (1488)	OHC	E15T,E15ET
4	97.6 (1597)	OHC	E16
4	103.7 (1680)	OHC	CD17①
4	119.1 (1952)	OHC	Z20S,Z20E
4	133.4 (2181)	OHC	Z22E
4	120.4 (1974)	OHC	CA20,CA20E,CA20S
4	110.3 (1809)	OHC	CA18ET
V6	180.6 (2960)	OHC	VG30E,VG30ET

① Diesel

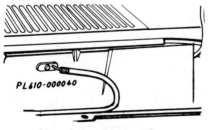

PL610-000040

Chassis number location

VEHICLE IDENTIFICATION PLATE

The vehicle identification plate is attached to the hood ledge or the firewall. This plate is mounted on the left hood ledge panel at

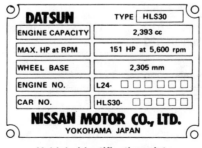

Vehicle identification plate

the back of the strut housing on the 280Z (on the front of the left strut housing on the 300ZX) and on the right side of the firewall, behind the battery, on the 280ZX. The

VIN location

identification plate gives the vehicle model, engine displacement in cc., SAE horsepower rating, wheelbase, engine number and chassis number.

GASOLINE ENGINE TUNE-UP SPECIFICATIONS

(When analyzing compression test results, look for uniformity among cylinders, rather than specific pressures)

Year	Model	Spark Plugs Type	Spark Plugs Gap (in.)	Distributor Dwell (deg)	Distributor Air Gap (in.)	Ignition Timing (deg) MT	Ignition Timing (deg) AT	Fuel Pump Pressure (psi)	Idle Speed (rpm) MT	Idle Speed (rpm) AT▲	Valve Clearance (in.)● In	Valve Clearance (in.)● Ex
'78	F10	BP5ES	.039–.043	Electronic	.008–.016	10B	—	3.8	700	—	.014	.014
'78	B210 Exc. FU	BP5ES	.039–.043	Electronic	.008–.016	10B	8B①	3.9	700	650	.014	.014
'78–'79	B210, 210 FU	BP5EQ	.043–.051	Electronic	.012–.020	5B	—	3.9	700	—	.014	.014
'79–'80	210 Exc. FU	BP5ES	.039–.043	Electronic	.012–.020	10B②③	8B②	3.9	700	650	.014	.014
'81–'82	210	BP5ES-11 BPR5ES-11	.039–.043	Electronic	.012–.020	5B④	5B	3.8	700	650	.014	.014
'79	310	BP5ES⑤	.039–.043	Electronic	.012–.020	10B②	—	3.8	700	—	.014	.014
'80	310	BP5ES⑤	.039–.043	Electronic	.012–.020	8B	—	3.8	750	—	.014	.014
'81	310	BP5ES-11⑤	.039–.043	Electronic	.012–.020	5B	—	3.8	750	—	.014	.014
'82	310	BP5ES-11⑤	.039–.043	Electronic	.012–.020	2A⑦	2A⑦	3.8	750	750⑧	.011	.011
'78–'79	510	BP6ES	.039–.043⑨	Electronic	.012–.020	12B⑩	12B	3.8	600	600	.010	.012
'80	510	BPR6ES⑪	.031–.035	Electronic	.012–.020	12B⑫	12B⑫	3.8	600	600	.010⑬	.012
'81	510	BP6ES⑭	.031–.035	Electronic	.012–.020	6B	6B	3.8	600	600	.012	.012
'78–'79	200SX	BP6ES	.039–.043⑮	Electronic	.012–.020	9B⑯	12B	3.8	600	600	.010	.012
'80	200SX	BP6ES	.031–.035	Electronic	.012–.020	8B⑰	8B⑰	37	700	700	.012	.012
'81	200SX	BP6ES⑭	.031–.035	Electronic	.012–.020	6B⑱	6B⑱	37	750	700	.012	.012
'82–'83	200SX	BPR6ES⑲	.031–.035	Electronic	.012–.020	8B	8B	37	750	700	.012	.012
'78–'85	810 Maxima	BP6ES㉑	.039–.043	Electronic	.012–.020	10B⑳	10B⑳	36	700	650	.010	.012
'78	280Z	BP6ES-11㉓	.039–.043㉔	Electronic	.012–.020	10B	10B	36	800	700	.010	.012
'79	280ZX	B6ES-11㉓	.039–.043	Electronic	.012–.020	10B	10B	36	800㉕	700	.010	.012
'80–'83	280ZX	BP6ES-11⑭	.039–.043	Electronic	.012–.020	10B㉖	10B㉖	36	700	700	.010	.012
'81–'83	280ZX Turbo	BPR6ES-11	.039–.043	Electronic	.012–.020	20B㉟	20B㉟	36	650	650	.010	.012
'82	Sentra	BPR5ES-11	.039–.043	Electronic	.012–.020	4A	6A	3.8	750	650	.011	.011

GASOLINE ENGINE TUNE-UP SPECIFICATIONS

(When analyzing compression test results, look for uniformity among cylinders, rather than specific pressures)

Year	Model	Spark Plugs Type	Spark Plugs Gap (in.)	Distributor Dwell (deg)	Distributor Air Gap (in.)	Ignition Timing (deg) MT	Ignition Timing (deg) AT	Fuel Pump Pressure (psi)	Idle Speed (rpm) MT	Idle Speed (rpm) AT▲	Valve Clearance (in.)● In	Valve Clearance (in.)● Ex
'83	Sentra (E15)	BPR5ES-11	.039–.043	Electronic	.012–.020	2A	2A	3.8	700	700	.011	.011
'83–'85	Sentra, Pulsar (E16)	BPR5ES-11㉘	.039–.043	Electronic	.012–.020	5A㉙	5A㉙	3.8	750㉚	650	.011	.011
'82–'84	Stanza	㉗	.039–.043	Electronic	.012–.020	0	0	3.8	650㉛	650㉛	.012	.012
'84–'85	200SX	BCPR6ES-11㉜	.039–.043	Electronic	.012–.020	0B	0B	37	750	700㉝	.012	.012
'84–'85	200SX Turbo	BCPR6ES-11㉜	.039–.043	Electronic	.012–.020	15B	15B	37	750	700㉝	.012	.012
'84–'85	300ZX	BCPR6ES-11	.039–.043	Electronic	NA	20B	20B	37	700	650	㉞	㉞
'84–'85	300ZX Turbo	BCPR6E-11	.039–.043	Electronic	NA	20B	20B	37	700	650	㉞	㉞

NOTE: Emission control requires a very precise approach to tune-up. Timing and idle speed are peculiar to the engine and its application, rather than to the engine alone. Data for the particular application is on a sticker in the engine compartment on all late models. If the sticker disagrees with this chart, use the sticker figure. The results of any adjustments or modifications should be checked with a CO meter.

●Set hot
▲In Drive
MT: Manual trans.
AT: Automatic trans.
NA: Not available
FU: Hatchback with 5 spd. sold in 49 states but not in Calif.
A: After Top Dead Center
B: Before Top Dead Center
①Calif: 10B
②Calif: 5B
③1980 A14 engine: 8B
④A12A with MT and Canada: 10B
⑤Canada: BPR5ES-11; gap: .031–.035 in.
⑥1980
⑦Canada: 4A
⑧Canada: 650
⑨Canada: .031–.035 in.
⑩1979 49 states cars; 11B
⑪Z20S engine: BP6ES
⑫Z20S engine: 49 states, 8B; Calif/., 6B
⑬Z20S engine: .012 in.
⑭Canada and 1981 280ZX: BPR6ES-11
⑮Canada: .031–.035 in.
⑯Calif. and Canada: 12B
⑰Calif.: 6B
⑱Canada: 8B
⑲Intake side; exhaust side: BPR5ES

⑳1978 Calif. and 1982–85 all: 8B
㉑1978–79; B6ES; 1984 and later BPR6ES-11
㉒1980–81: BP6ES-11
㉓1982–83: BPR6ES-11
㉔Canada: BR6ES
㉕Canada: .028–.031
㉖1981–83 U.S.: 8B
㉗Intake side plugs: BPR6ES-11. 1984 and later: BCPR6ES-11 Exhaust side plugs: BPR5ES-11. 1984 and later: BCPR5ES-11
㉘Canada: BPR5ES; gap: .031–.035
㉙1983 models. 1984 and later:
  5A @ 750 rpm MT, Calif., Canada
  5A @ 650 rpm AT, Calif., Canada
  15B @ 800 rpm MT, 49 states
  8B @ 650 rpm AT, 49 states
㉚1984 and later 49 states w/MT: 800 rpm
㉛1982–83 all models, and 1984 and later Canadian specs. 1984 and later U.S. models (CA20E): 750 MT, 700 AT
㉜Intake side; Exhaust side BCPR5ES-11
㉝630 rpm high altitudes
㉞Hydraulic valve lifters—no adjustment necessary
㉟1983: 24B

DIESEL ENGINE TUNE-UP SPECIFICATIONS

Year Model	Engine Displacement cu. in. (cc)	Warm Valve Clearance (in.)		Intake Valve Opens (deg)	Injection Pump Setting (deg)	Injection Nozzle Pressure (psi)		Idle Speed (rpm)	Compression Pressure (psi)
		In	Ex			New	Used		
'81–'85	170 (2,793)	0.010	0.012	NA	align marks	1,920–2,033	1,778–1,920	650	455
'83–'85	102 (1681)	0.010	0.018	NA	See Text	1,920–2,033	1,778–1,920	750	455

NA: Not Available

FIRING ORDERS

NOTE: To avoid confusion when replacing spark plug wires, always remove them one at a time.

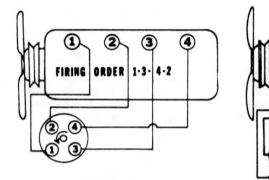

L20B engine

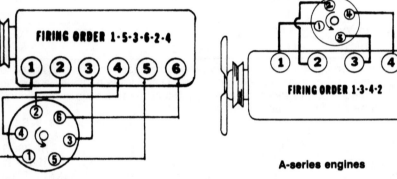

L24, L28 engines

A-series engines

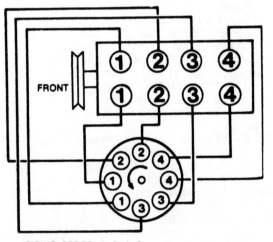

FIRING ORDER: 1–3–4–2
DISTRIBUTOR ROTATION: COUNTERCLOCKWISE

Z20, Z22, Z22E engine—1980 (Calif.), 1981 and later (all)

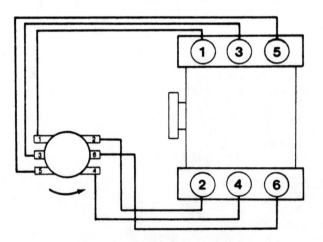

V6 engine firing order: 1-3-5-4-6-2

FIRING ORDERS

NOTE: To avoid confusion when replacing spark plug wires, always remove them one at a time.

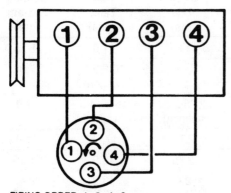

FIRING ORDER: 1–3–4–2
DISTRIBUTOR ROTATION: COUNTERCLOCKWISE

Z20 engine—1980 (49 states)

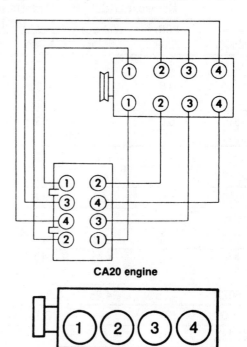

CA20 engine

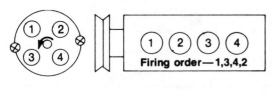

Firing order—1,3,4,2

E15, E16 engine

Firing order 1-3-4-2—CD 17

CAPACITIES

Year	Model	Engine Crankcase (Qts)		Transmission (pts)		Automatic (Total Capacity)	Drive Axle (pts)	Gas Tank (gals)	Cooling System (qts)
		With Filter	Without Filter	4-Spd	5-Spd				
'78	B210	3.8	3.4	2.75	3.6	11.8	1.8	11.5	6.25③
	F10	3.6	3.2	4.90	4.9	—	—	10.6/9.1 (wagon)	7.00
'78	810	6.0	5.5	3.60	—	11.8	2.75/2.2 (wagon)	15.9/14.5 (wagon)	11.0
'78	280Z	5.0	4.25	3.63	4.25	11.8	2.75	17.25	11.0
'78–'79	200SX	4.5	4.0	—	3.6	11.8	2.75	15.9	7.90
'78–'79	510	4.5	4.0	3.6	3.6	11.8	2.4	13.2	9.40
'79–'82	210	①	—	②	2.5	11.8	1.8	13.25	6.25③
'79–'81	310	3.4	2.8	4.9	4.9	—	—	13.25	6.25
'79–'80	810	5.9	5.25	3.7	4.25	11.8	2.0	15.9/14.5 (wagon)	11.00
'79–'83	280ZX	4.75⑤	4.25⑤	3.63	4.25	11.8	2.75	21.12	11.12
'80–'81	510	④	—	3.15	3.6	11.8	2.4	13.25	9.25
'80–'83	200SX	4.4	4.1	—	4.25	11.8	2.4	14/15.9 (hatchback)	10
'82	310	4.12	3.6	4.9	5.74	12.75	—	13.25	6.50
'81	810	5.25	4.75	—	4.25	11.8	2.1	16.4/15.9 (wagon)	11.6
'82–'85	810, Maxima	5.0⑥	4.5⑥	—	4.25	11.8	2.1	16.4/15.9 (wagon)	11.6⑦
'82–'85	Sentra	4.1	3.6	4.8	5.75	13.1	—	13.25	5.0
'83–'85	Pulsar	4.1	3.6	—	5.75	13.1	—	13.25	5.75
'82–'85	Stanza	4.1	3.75	—	5.75	12.75	—	14.3	7.8
'84–'85	300ZX	4.25	3.5	—	4.0	14.5	2.75	19	11.1⑧
'84–'85	200SX	4.0	3.75	—	4.25	14.5	⑨	14	9.1

① A12A, A14 engines: 3.46 qts.
   A15 engine: 3.25 qts.
② A12A engine: 2.5 pts.
   A14 engine: 2.75 pts.
③ Automatic transmission: 6 qts.
④ L20B engine: 4.5 qts.
   Z20S engine: 4.65 qts.
⑤ Turbo: 5.5 with, 5.0 without
⑥ Figures are for gasoline engine. For diesel engine: w/filter—6.5 qts., w/o filter—6.0 qts.
⑦ Figure is for gasoline engine. For diesel engine: 11.0 qts.
⑧ Non-turbo model; turbo 11.5
⑨ Solid rear axle: 2.1 pt
   IRS: 2.75 pt.

HONDA
Accord, Civic, CVCC, Prelude

SERIAL NUMBER IDENTIFICATION

Vehicle Identification (Chassis) Number

Honda vehicle identification numbers are mounted on the top edge of the instrument panel and are visible from the outside. In addition, there is a Vehicle/Engine Identification plate under the hood on the cowl.

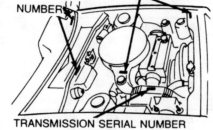

Honda identification numbers

Transmission Serial Number

The transmission serial number is stamped on the top of the transmission/clutch case.

Engine Serial Number

The engine serial number is stamped into the clutch casing. The first three digits indicate engine model identification. The remaining numbers refer to production sequence. This same number is also stamped onto the Vehicle/Engine Identification plate mounted on the hood bracket.

TUNE-UP SPECIFICATIONS

(When analyzing compression test results, look for uniformity among cylinders, rather than specific pressures.)

Year	Model	Engine Displacement (cc)	Original Equipment Spark Plugs Type	Gap (in.)	Distributor Point Dwell (deg)	Point Gap (in.)	Basic Ignition Timing (deg) MT	AT	Intake Valve Fully Opens (deg)	Fuel Pump Pressure (psi)	Idle Speed (rpm) MT	AT	Valve Clearance (in.) Intake (cold)	Auxiliary (cold)	Exhaust (cold)
'78–'79	Civic	1237	BP6ES or W20EP	0.028–0.032	49–55	0.018–0.022	2B ④	2B ④	10A	2.56	650–750 ①	650–750 ②	0.004–0.006	—	0.004–0.006
'78–79	Civic CVCC	1487	B6EB or W20ES-L	0.028–0.032	49–55	0.018–0.022	6B ⑥	6B ⑥	10A	1.85–2.56	650–750 ①	600–700 ②	0.005–0.007	0.005–0.007	0.007–0.009
'78	Accord	1600	B6EB or W20ES-L	0.028–0.032	49–55	0.018–0.022	6B ⑤ ⑥	6B ⑤ ⑥	10A	2.13–2.84	750–850 ①	650–750 ②	0.005–0.007	0.005–0.007	0.007–0.009
'79	Accord Prelude	1751	B7EB	0.028–0.032	Electronic		6B ⑤ ⑧	4B ⑨ ⑦	10A	2.13–2.84	650–750 ①	650–750 ②	0.005–0.007	0.005–0.007	0.010–0.012
'80	Civic	1487	B7EB-11	0.042	Electronic		15B⑤ ⑩	TDC ⑪	—	2.5	700–800 ①	700–800 ②	0.005–0.007	0.005–0.007	0.007–0.009
	Civic	1335	B6EB-11	0.042	Electronic		2B⑤ ⑰	—	10A	2.5	700–800 ①	—	0.005–0.007	0.005–0.007	0.007–0.009
	Accord	1751	B7EB	0.030	Electronic		TDC ⑯	TDC ⑰	—	2.5	750–850 ①	750–850 ②	0.005–0.007	0.005–0.007	0.010–0.012
	Prelude	1751	B7EB	0.030	Electronic		TDC ⑰	TDC ⑰	—	2.5	750–850 ①	750–850 ②	0.005–0.007	0.005–0.007	0.010–0.012
'81	Civic	1487	B6EB-11	0.042	Electronic		10B⑫ ⑤	2A	10A	2.5	700–800 ①	700–800 ②	0.005–0.007	0.005–0.007	0.007–0.009
	Civic	1335	B6EB-11	0.042	Electronic		2B ⑤	—	10A	2.5	700–800 ①	—	0.005–0.007	0.005–0.007	0.007–0.009
	Accord	1751	B6EB-L11	0.042	Electronic		TDC ⑰	TDC ⑰	10A	2.5	750–850 ①	750–850 ②	0.005–0.007	0.005–0.007	0.010–0.012
	Prelude	1751	B6EB-L11	0.042	Electronic		TDC ⑰	TDC ⑰	10A	2.5	750–850 ①	750–850 ②	0.005–0.007	0.005–0.007	0.010–0.012
'82	Civic	1487	BR6EB-11	0.042	Electronic		18B ⑤	18B ⑤	10A	2.5	650–750 ①	650–750 ②	0.005–0.007	0.005–0.007	0.007–0.009
	Civic	1335	BR6EB-11	0.042	Electronic		20B ⑤	—	10A	2.5	650–750 ①	—	0.005–0.007	0.005–0.007	0.007–0.009
	Accord	1751	BR6EB-L11	0.042	Electronic		16B⑬	16B	10A	2.5	750–850 ①	750–850 ②	0.005–0.007	0.005–0.007	0.010–0.012
	Prelude	1751	BR6EB-L11	0.042	Electronic		12B⑭	16B	10A	2.5	700–800 ①	700–800 ②	0.005–0.007	0.005–0.007	0.010–0.012

TUNE-UP SPECIFICATIONS

(When analyzing compression test results, look for uniformity among cylinders, rather than specific pressures.)

Year	Model	Engine Displace- ment (cc)	Original Equipment Spark Plugs Type	Gap (in.)	Distributor Point Dwell (deg)	Point Gap (in.)	Basic Ignition Timing (deg) MT	AT	Intake Valve Fully Opens (deg)	Fuel Pump Pres- sure (psi)	Idle Speed (rpm) MT	AT	Valve Clearance (in.) In- take (cold)	Aux- iliary (cold)	Ex- haust (cold)
'83	Civic	1487	BR6EB-11	0.042	Electronic		18B⑤	18B⑤	10A	2.5	650–750 ①	650–750 ②	0.005–0.007	0.005–0.007	0.007–0.009
	Civic	1335	BR6EB-11	0.042	Electronic		18B⑮ ⑤	—	10A	2.5	600–750 ①	—	0.005–0.007	0.005–0.007	0.007–0.009
	Accord	1751	BR6EB-L11	0.042	Electronic		16B⑬	16B ⑤	10A	2.5	700–800 ①	650–750 ②	0.005–0.007	0.005–0.007	0.010–0.012
	Prelude	1829	BUR6EB-11	0.042	Electronic		10B⑬ ⑤	12B ⑤	N.A.	2.5	750–850 ①	700–800 ②	0.005–0.007	0.005–0.007	0.010–0.012
'84–'85	Civic	1488	BUR6EB-11	0.042	Electronic		⑤	⑤	N.A.	3.0	650–750	650–750	0.007–0.009	0.007–0.009	0.009–0.011
	Civic	1342	BUR6EB-11	0.042	Electronic		⑤	⑤	N.A.	3.0	650–750	—	0.007–0.009	0.007–0.009	0.009–0.011
	Accord	1829	BUR6EB-11	0.042	Electronic		22B ⑯	18B	N.A.	2.5	700–800	650–750	0.005–0.007	0.005–0.007	0.010–0.012
	Prelude	1829	BPR6EY-11	0.042	Electronic		20B	12B	N.A.	2.5	750–850	750–850	0.005–0.007	0.005–0.007	0.010–0.012

NOTE: The underhood specifications sticker often reflects tune-up specification changes made in production. Sticker figures must be used if they disagree with those in this chart.
TDC—Top Dead Center
B—Before top dead center
A—After top dead center
—Not applicable
N.A. Not available
① In neutral, with headlights on
② In drive range, with headlights on
④ Aim timing light at red notch on crankshaft pulley with distributor vacuum hose(s) connected at specified idle speed

⑤ Aim timing light at red mark (yellow mark, '78–'79 Accord M/T) on flywheel or torque converter drive plate distributor vacuum hose connected at specified idle speed
⑥ California (KL) and High Altitude (KH) models: 2B
⑦ Aim light at blue mark (49 states models)
⑧ California (KL) and High Altitude (KH) models: TDC (white mark)
⑨ California (KL) and High Altitude (KH) models: 2A (black mark)

⑩ 49 States Wagon 10B
⑪ California and High Altitude TDC
⑫ Wagon/Sedan—4B, Calif-2A
⑬ Calif.—12B
⑭ Calif.—16B
⑮ 4 speed 20B
⑯ California models: 4A, Aim timing light at red mark
⑰ Aim timing light at white mark
⑱ California models: 18B

FIRING ORDERS

NOTE: To avoid confusion, always replace spark plug wires one at a time.

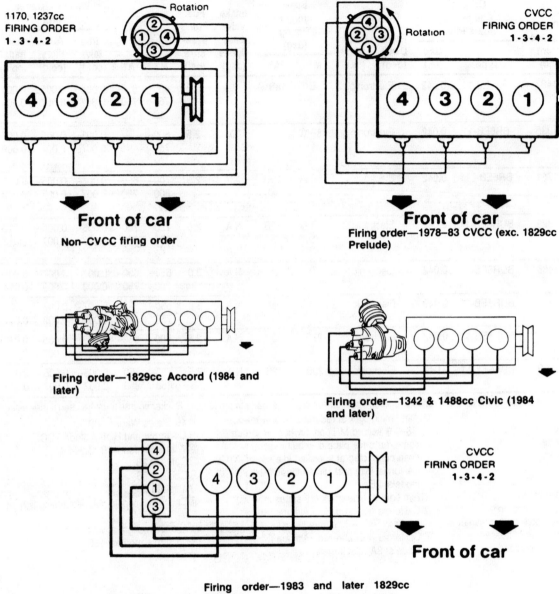

1170, 1237cc
FIRING ORDER
1 - 3 - 4 - 2

Rotation

Front of car

Non–CVCC firing order

CVCC
FIRING ORDER
1 - 3 - 4 - 2

Rotation

Front of car

Firing order—1978–83 CVCC (exc. 1829cc Prelude)

Firing order—1829cc Accord (1984 and later)

Firing order—1342 & 1488cc Civic (1984 and later)

CVCC
FIRING ORDER
1 - 3 - 4 - 2

Front of car

Firing order—1983 and later 1829cc Prelude

CAPACITIES

Year	Model	Engine Displacement (cc)	Engine Crankcase (qts)②	Transmission (pts) Manual 4-sp	Transmission (pts) Manual 5-sp	Transmission (pts) Auto.③	Gasoline Tank (gals)	Cooling System (qts)
'78	Civic	1237	3.8	5.2	—	5.2	10.6	4.2
	Civic CVCC	1487	3.8	5.2	5.2	5.2	10.6①	4.2
	Accord	1600	3.8	5.2	5.2	5.2	13.2	4.2
'79	Civic	1237	3.8	5.2	—	5.2	10.6	4.8
	Civic	1487	3.8	5.2	5.6	5.2	10.6①	4.8
'79	Accord	1751	3.8	5.2	5.2	5.2	13.2	6.4
	Prelude	1751	3.8	5.2	5.2	5.2	13.2	6.0
'80–'81	Civic	1335, 1487	3.8	5.2	5.2	5.2	10.8④	4.8⑤
	Accord & Prelude	1751	3.8	5.0	5.0	5.2	13.2	6.4
'82	Civic	1335, 1487	3.7	5.2	5.2	5.2	10.8④	4.8⑤
	Accord	1751	3.7	5.0	5.0	5.2	15.8	6.0
	Prelude	1751	3.7	5.0	5.0	5.2	13.2	6.0
'83	Civic	1335, 1487	3.7	5.2	5.2	5.2	10.4④	4.8⑤
	Accord	1751	3.7	5.0	5.0	6.0	15.8	6.0
	Prelude	1829	3.7	—	5.0	5.8	15.9	6.3
'84–'85	Civic	1342, 1488	3.7	5.0	5.0	6.0	11.9⑥	4.8⑦
	Accord	1829	3.7	—	5.0	6.0	15.8	6.4
	Prelude	1829	3.7	—	5.0	5.8	15.9	6.3⑧

① Sta. Wgn.: 11.0
② Includes filter
③ Does not include torque converter.
④ 4 Door Sedan: 12.1
⑤ 1335cc: 4.0
⑥ 4 Door Sedan: 12.1, CRX: 10.8
⑦ 1342cc: 3.6
⑧ Auto. trans.: 7.1 qts.

ISUZU
I-Mark, Impulse

SERIAL NUMBER IDENTIFICATION

Vehicle

The vehicle identification number is embossed on a plate attached to the top left of the instrument panel. The number is visible through the windshield from outside the car.

Engine

The engine serial number is stamped on the top right front corner of the engine block on gasoline engines. On diesel models, the engine serial number is stamped on the left rear corner of the engine block.

Transmission

Both manual transmissions have their serial numbers on the side of the main case. The automatic location is similar.

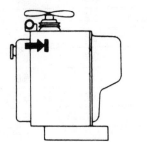

Engine serial number location—gasoline

Engine serial number location—diesel

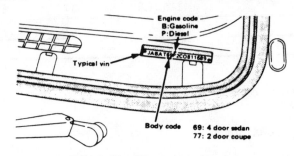

Vehicle identification plate location

GASOLINE ENGINE TUNE-UP SPECIFICATIONS

(When analyzing compression test results, look for uniformity among cylinders, rather than specific pressures)

Year	Engine Displacement (cu. in.)	Spark Plugs Type	Gap (in.)	Distributor Point Dwell (deg)	Point Gap (in.)	Ignition Timing (deg) MT	AT	Intake Valve Opens (deg)	Fuel Pump Pressure (psi)	Idle Speed (rpm)	Valve Clear (in.) (cold) In	Ex
'81–'85	110.8	NGK-BPR6ESII	0.040	Electronic		6B	6B	21	3.6	900	0.006	0.010
'83–'85	118.9	NGK-BPR6ESII	0.040	Electronic		12B	12B	28	2.0–2.5	900	0.006	0.010

NOTE: The underhood specifications sticker often reflects tune-up specification changes made in production. Sticker figures must be used if they disagree with this chart.
B Before top dead center

DIESEL ENGINE TUNE-UP SPECIFICATIONS

Year	Injector Opening Pressure (psi)	Low Idle (rpm)	Valve Clearance		Intake Valve Opens (deg.)	Injection Timing (deg.)	Firing Order
			Intake	Exhaust			
'81–'85	2133③	625①	0.010	0.014	32B	18B②	1-3-4-2

① A/T: 725 rpm
② 12B on 1982 and later
③ 1770–1984 and later

Firing Orders

NOTE: To avoid confusion, always remove spark plug wires one at a time.

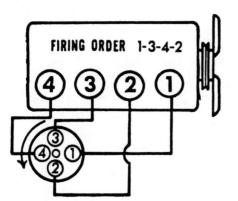

Firing order—gasoline engine

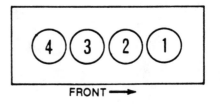

FRONT →

Firing order—diesel engine, 1-3-4-2

CAPACITIES

Year	Model	Engine Displacement (cu.in.)	Engine Crankcase (qts)		Transmission (pts)			Drive Axle (pts)	Gasoline Tank (gals)	Cooling System (qts)	
			With Filter	Without Filter	Manual		Automatic			W/ AC	W/O AC
					4-spd	5-spd					
'81–'85	Gas	110.8	3.8	3.4	2.7	3.2	14①	2.5	13.7	6.4	6.4
	Diesel	111	5.5	5.0	2.7	3.2	14①	2.5	13.7	7.4	7.4
'83–'85	Gas	118.9	3.8	3.4	—	3.2	13.4	2.1	15.1	6.6	6.6

① 26.8 pts with torque converter

MAZDA
Cosmo, GLC, RX-3, RX-4, RX-7, 626

SERIAL NUMBER IDENTIFICATION

Vehicle

The serial number is on a plate located on the driver's side windshield pillar and is visible through the glass.

A vehicle identification number (VIN) plate, bearing the serial number and other data, is attached to the cowl.

Engine

The engine number is located on a plate which is attached to the engine housing, just behind the distributor or on a machined pad at the right front side of the engine block.

The engine number consists of an identification number followed by a six-digit production number.

TUNE-UP SPECIFICATIONS—PISTON ENGINE

(When analyzing compression test results, look for uniformity among cylinders, rather than specific pressures)

Year	Engine Displacement (cu. In.)	Spark Plugs Type	Gap (In.)	Distributor Point Dwell (deg)	Distributor Point Gap (In.)	Ignition Timing (deg) MT	Ignition Timing (deg) AT	Intake Valve Opens (deg)	Fuel Pump Pressure (psi)	Idle Speed (rpm)	Valve Clearance (In.) In	Valve Clearance (In.) Ex
'78	77.6	BP6ES	.031	49–55	.020	7B④	11B	13	2.84–3.84	700–750⑤	.010	.012
'79	86.4	BP5ES, BPR5ES	.031	49–55	.020	7B⑥	7B⑦	15	2.8–3.8	700–750 ⑨⑩	.010	.012
	120.2	BP5ES, BPR5ES	.031	Electronic		8B	8B	10	2.8–3.6	650–700	.012	.012
'80	86.4	BP5ES, BPR5ES	.031	Electronic		5B	5B	15	2.8–3.8	700–750⑨	.010	.012
'80–'82	120.2	BP5ES, BPR5ES	⑬	Electronic		5B⑧	5B⑧	10	2.8–3.6	750–700	.012	.012
'81–'85	90.9	BPR5ES, BPR6ES	⑫	Electronic		8B⑭	8B⑭	15	2.8–3.8 ⑯	850⑪	.010	.012
'83–'85	121.9	BPR5ES, BPR6ES	.031	Electronic		6B	6B	17	2.8–3.5 ⑰	750⑮	.012	.012

NOTE: The underhood specifications sticker often reflects tune-up specification changes made in production. Sticker figures must be used if they disagree with those in this chart.

N.A. Information not available

② California: 8B
③ Automatic: 650–700 in Drive
④ California: 11B
⑤ Automatic: 600–650 in Drive
⑥ California: 5B
Canada: 8A
⑦ California: 5B
Canada: 8B
⑧ Canada: 8B
⑨ Federal:
Automatic: 600–650
⑩ Canada:
Manual: 800–850
Automatic: 700–750
⑪ Automatic 750 in Drive
⑫ BPR5ES—.031, BPR6ES—.031
⑬ '80—.031, '81–'82 BP5ES, BPR5ES—.031, BP6ES, BPR6ES—.031
⑭ '83–'85—6° BTDC
⑮ Automatic: 700 in Drive
⑯ '84–'85—4.27–5.97
⑰ '84–'85—2.8–4.27

TUNE-UP SPECIFICATIONS—ROTARY ENGINE

(When analyzing compression test results, look for uniformity among cylinders, rather than specific pressures)

Year	Engine Displacement (cu. in.)	Spark Plugs		Distributors		Ignition Timing (deg)			Idle Speed (rpm)	
		Type	Gap (in.)	Point Dwell (deg)	Point Gap (in.)	Leading Normal	Leading Retarded	Trailing Normal	MT	AT
'78	70②	RN278B	0.039–0.043	58 ± 3	.018	0	—	20A	725–775	725–775①
'78	80	RN278B	0.039–0.043	58 ± 3	.018	5A	—	25A	725–775	725–775①
'79	70	RN280B	0.039–0.043	58 ± 3	.018	0	—	20A	725–775	725–775①
'80	70	RN280B	0.039–0.043	Electronic		0	—	20A	725–775	725–775①
'81–'85	70④	③	0.053–0.057 ⑤	Electronic		0⑥	—	20A	750⑦	750①

NOTE: The underhood specifications sticker often reflects tune-up specification changes made in production. Sticker figures must be used if they disagree with those in this chart.

TDC—Top dead center
A—After top dead center
B—Before top dead center
MT—Manual transmission
AT—Automatic transmission
deg—degrees
① Transmission in Drive
② Used in RX-3SP only
③ NGK-BR7EQ14, BR8EQ14, BR9EQ14

NIPPONDENSO-W22EDR14, W25EDR14, W27EDR14
④ 13B
  eng: 80
⑤ 13B
  eng: .055
⑥ 13B
  eng: Leading-5A
⑦ 13B
  eng: 800

FIRING ORDERS

NOTE: To avoid confusion, always replace spark plug wires one at a time.

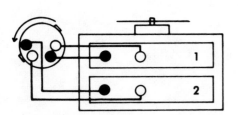

Rotary engine

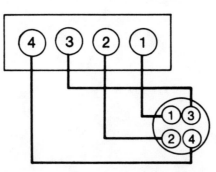

All except 1490 cc engine with front wheel drive

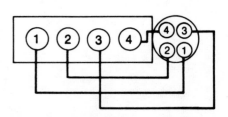

1490 cc engine—GLC front wheel drive

CAPACITIES

Year	Model	Engine Displacement cu. in. (cc)	Engine Crankcase (qts)		Transmission (pts)			Drive Axle (pts)	Gasoline Tank (gals)	Cooling System (qts)
			With Filter	Without Filter	Manual		Automatic			
					4-spd	5-spd				
'78	RX-4, RX-3SP	80 (1308)	6.8	5.3	3.6	4.6	13.2	2.8	16.9②	10.0
	Cosmo	80 (1308)	6.8	5.3	—	3.6	13.2	2.6	17.2	10.0
	GLC	77.6 (1272)	—	3.2	2.8	3.6	12.0	1.6	10.0	6.8
'79–'80	GLC	86.4 (1415)	—	3.2	2.8	3.6	12.0	2.2	10.6③	5.8
'81–'85	GLC	90.9 (1490)	3.9	—	6.8	6.8	12.0	—	11.1	5.8
'79–'82	626	120.2 (1970)	—	4.1④	3.0	3.6	13.2	2.6	14.5	7.9
'83–'85	626	121.9 (2000)	4.8	—	—	7.0	12.0	—	15.8⑦	7.4
'79	RX-7	70 (1146)	5.5	4.4	3.6	3.6	13.2	2.6	14.5	7.6
'80–'85	RX-7	70 (1146)⑥	5.5⑨	4.4⑧	3.6	3.6⑩	13.2⑪	2.6	14.5⑤⑫	10.0

① Station wagon: 10.4
② Station wagon: 17.4
③ Station wagon: 11.9
④ '82—3.8
⑤ '81–'83—16.4

⑥ 13B
 engine: 80 (1308)
⑦ '84–'85: 15.6
⑧ 13B: 4.9 w/o filter, 6.1 full capacity
⑨ 12A: 4.9 full capacity

⑩ 12A: 4.2
 13B: 4.2
⑪ 15.8 total capacity
⑫ '84–'85: 16.4

MERCEDES-BENZ
190, 230, 240, 300, 380, 450, 500, 6.9—All Series

SERIAL NUMBER IDENTIFICATION

Transmission Identification

Mercedes-Benz cars for the U.S. market have been equipped with either a 4 or 5-speed manual transmission or with a fully automatic 3 or 4-speed unit. The automatic transmissions are equipped with a torque converter.

Serial numbers on the manual transmission are located on a pad on the side cover of the transmission (left side).

Automatic transmission serial numbers are located on a metal plate which is attached to the driver's side of the transmission.

Transmission identification number

1. Catalyst and certification tag (left door pillar)
2. Identification tag (left window post)
3. Chassis no.
4. Body no. and paintwork no.
5. Engine no. on rear engine block
6. Emission control information

Location of important information on the 450SL, 450SLC and 380SL

1. Certification tag (left door pillar)
2. Identification tag (left window post)
3. Chassis no.
4. Body no. and paintwork no.
5. Engine no.
6. Emission control tag
7. Emission control tag catalyst information

Location of important information on the 300SD

1. Certification tag (left door pillar)
2. Identification tag (left window post)
3. Chassis no.
4. Body no. and paintwork no.
5. Engine no. on engine block, rear
6. Emission control information

Location of important information on all models not shown

1 Certification Tag (left door pillar)
2 Identification Tag (left window post)
3 Chassis No.
4 Engine No.
5 Body No. and Paintwork No.
6 Emission Control Tag
7 Information Tag
  California version
  Vacuum line routing for emission control system
8 Emission Control Tag
  Catalyst Information

Location of important information on the 380SE, 500SEC and 500SEL

1 Certification Tag (left door pillar)
2 Identification Tag (left window post)
3 Chassis No.
4 Engine No.
5 Body No. and Paintwork No.
6 Information Tag
  California version
  Vacuum line routing for emission control system
7 Emission Control Tag
8 Emission Control Tag
  Catalyst Information

Location of important information on the 300TD

1 Certification Tag (left door pillar)
2 Identification Tag (left window post)
3 Chassis No.
4 Engine No.
5 Body No. and Paintwork No.
6 Information Tag
  California version
  Vacuum line routing for emission control system
7 Emission Control Tag
  Emission Control Tag
  Catalyst Information

Location of important information on the 190D and 190E

Example: Engine Family 80.22.45.30

| | 80 | 22 | 4 | 5 | 30 |

Model Year ──────────────────────────────

Emission System Version ──────────────
- 20 = Federal and California
- 21 = Federal
- 22 = California

Combustion Version ──────────────
- 1 = Carburetor
- 2 = Injection, Gasoline
- 3 = Diesel
- 4 = Diesel, Turbo

Number of Cylinders ──────────────

Piston Displacement ──────────────
3000 cm³ / 183.0 in³

The key to 1980 Vehicle Identification is an 8 digit number

Example: Engine Family B MB 3.8 V 6 F B 4

| | B | MB | 3.8 | V | 6 | F | B | 4 |

Model year ──────────────
A = 1980, B = 1981 etc.

Manufacturer's code ──────────────
MB = Mercedes Benz

Piston displacement ──────────────
here 3800 cc

Vehicles class ──────────────
D = passenger car with diesel engine
V = passenger car with gasoline engine

Type of fuel feed ──────────────
6 = mechanical injection
9 = mechanical injection with turbocharger

Type of catalyst ──────────────
F = 3-way catalyst in combination with lambda control
J = no catalyst (diesel)

For free use of manufacturer ──────────────

Check digit ──────────────

The key to 1981 and later engine identification is a 10 digit number.

ENGINE/VEHICLE IDENTIFICATION

Model	Chassis Type	Engine Model	No. of Cyls.	Engine Type	Engine Description (Fuel, Fuel Delivery, Valve Gear, Displacement)	Years
190D	201.122	OM601	4	601.921	Diesel (2197 cc)	1984–85
190E	102.961	M102	4	102.961	Gas, Fuel Inj. SOHC (2299 cc)	1984–85
230	123.023	M115	4	115.954	Gas, Carb., OHC (2307 cc)	1978
240D	123.123	OM616	4	616.912	Diesel (2404 cc)	1978–83
280E	123.033	M110	6	110.984	Gas, Fuel Inj., DOHC (2746 cc)	1978–81
280CE	123.053	M110	6	110.984	Gas, Fuel Inj., DOHC (2746 cc)	1978–81
280SE	116.024	M110	6	110.985	Gas, Fuel Inj., DOHC (2746 cc)	1978–80
300D	123.130	OM617	5	617.912	Diesel (2998 cc) ①	1978–81
	123.133	OM617	5	617.952	Diesel, Turbocharged (2998 cc)	1982–85
300CD	123.150	OM617	5	617.912	Diesel (2998 cc) ①	1978–81
	123.153	OM617	5	617.952	Diesel, Turbocharged (2998 cc)	1982–85
300SD	116.120	OM617	5	617.950	Diesel, Turbocharged (2998 cc)	1978–80
	126.120	OM617	5	617.951	Diesel, Turbocharged (2998 cc)	1981–85
300TD	123.190	OM617	5	617.912	Diesel (2998 cc)	1979–80
	123.193	OM617	5	617.952	Diesel, Turbocharged (2998 cc)	1981–85
380SE	126.032	M116	8	116.963	Gas, Fuel Inj., OHC (3839 cc)	1984–85
380SEC	126.043	M116	8	116.963	Gas, Fuel Inj., OHC (3839 cc)	1982–83
380SEL	126.033	M116	8	116.961	Gas, Fuel Inj., OHC (3839 cc)	1981–83
380SL	107.045	M116	8	116.960	Gas, Fuel Inj., OHC (3839 cc)	1981–85
380SLC	107.025	M116	8	116.960	Gas, Fuel Inj., OHC (3839 cc)	1981–82
450SEL	116.033	M117	8	117.986	Gas, Fuel Inj., OHC (4520 cc)	1978–80
450SL	107.044	M117	8	117.985	Gas, Fuel Inj., OHC (4520 cc)	1978–80
450SLC	107.024	M117	8	117.985	Gas, Fuel Inj., OHC (4520 cc)	1978–80
500SEC	126.044	M117	8	117.963	Gas, Fuel Inj., OHC (4973 cc)	1984–85
500SEL	126.037	M117	8	117.963	Gas, Fuel Inj., OHC (4973 cc)	1984–85
6.9	116.036	M100	8	100.985	Gas, Fuel inj., OHC (6836 cc)	1978–79

NOTE: 1978–85 models are covered in this section. The years given are not necessarily production years.
Engine designations are as follows: C = 1982, D = 1983, E = 1984, F = 1985
    DMB 2.4D6-J501-2.4 liter Diesel
    DMB 3.0D9-J508-3.0 liter Turbodiesel
    DMB 3.8V6-FSE8-3.8 liter V8 (380SEL/SEC)
    DMB 3.8V6-FSL6-3.8 liter V8 (380 SEL)
   ① 1978: 3005 cc

TRANSMISSION APPLICATIONS

Model	Automatic Transmission	Manual Transmission
190D	W4A020	GL68/20A-5
190E	W4A020	GL68/20B-5
230	W4B 025	—
240D (thru '80)	W4B 025	G-76/18C(4-spd.)
240D ('81 and later)	W4B 025	GL68/20A (4-spd.)
280E, 280CE	W4B 025	—
280SE	W4B 025	—
300D, 300CD, 300TD	W4B 025	—
300D Turbo. 300CD Turbo	W4A 040	—
300TD Turbo 1981–85	W4A 040	—
300SD 1978–80	W4B 025	—
300SD 1981–85	W4A 040	—
380SL, 380SLC, 380SEL, 380SEC, 380SE	W4A 040	—
450SEL, 450SL, 450SLC	W3A 040	—
500SEC, 500SEL	W4A040	—
6.9	W3B 050	—

GASOLINE ENGINE TUNE-UP SPECIFICATIONS
(When analyzing compression test results, look for uniformity among cylinders, rather than specific pressures)

Year	Model	Spark Plugs Type	Gap (in.)	Distributor Point Dwell (deg)	Ignition Timing (deg)	Intake Valve Opens (deg)	Fuel Pump Pressure (psi) Idle●	▲ Idle Speed (rpm)	Valve Clearance* (in.) In (cold)	Ex (cold)
'78–'79	230	N10Y	0.032	Elec.	10B w/vacuum	14B	2–3	850	0.004	0.008
	280E, 280CE, 280SE	N10Y	0.032	Elec.	TDC w/vacuum	7B	75–84 ①	800	0.004	0.010
	450SEL	N10Y	0.032	Elec.	TDC w/vacuum	②	75–84 ①	750	Hyd.	Hyd.
	450SL, 450SLC	N10Y	0.032	Elec.	TDC w/vacuum	②	75–84 ①	750	Hyd.	Hyd.
	6.9	N10Y	0.032	Elec.	TDC w/vacuum	③	75–84 ①	600	Hyd.	Hyd.
'80	280E, 280CE, 280SE	N10Y	0.032	Elec.	10B	7B	④	700–800	0.004	0.010
	450SEL	N10Y	0.032	Elec.	5B	⑤	④	600–700	Hyd.	Hyd.
	450SL, 450SLC	N10Y	0.032	Elec.	5B	⑤	④	600–700	Hyd.	Hyd.

GASOLINE ENGINE TUNE-UP SPECIFICATIONS
(When analyzing compression test results, look for uniformity among cylinders, rather than specific pressures)

Year	Model	Spark Plugs Type	Gap (in.)	Distributor Point Dwell (deg)	Ignition Timing (deg)	Intake Valve Opens (deg)	Fuel Pump Pressure (psi) Idle●	▲ Idle Speed (rpm)	Valve Clearance* (in.) In (cold)	Ex (cold)
'81	280E, 280CE	N10Y	0.032	Elec.	10B	7B	④	700–800	0.004	0.010
	380SEL	N10Y	0.032	Elec.	5B	24A	④	500	Hyd.	Hyd.
	380SL, 380SLC	N10Y	0.032	Elec.	5B	24A	④	500	Hyd.	Hyd.
'82	380SL	N10Y	0.032	Elec.	5B	24A	④	500–600	Hyd.	Hyd.
	380SEL	N10Y	0.032	Elec.	5B	24A	④	500–600	Hyd.	Hyd.
	380SEC	N10Y	0.032	Elec.	5B	24A	④	500–600	Hyd.	Hyd
'83–'84	190E	S12YC	0.032	Elec.	5B	⑥	77–80	700–600	Hyd.	Hyd.
	380SL	N10Y	0.032	Elec.	TDC w/o vacuum	24A	④	500–600	Hyd.	Hyd.
	380SE, 380SEC, 380SEL	N10Y	0.032	Elec.	TDC w/o vacuum	24A	④	500–600	Hyd.	Hyd.
	500SEC, 500SEL	N10Y	0.032	Elec.	TDC w/o vacuum	⑤	④	600–700	Hyd.	Hyd.
'85	All	See Underhood Specification Sticker								

CAUTION: If the specifications listed above differ from those on the tune-up decal in the engine compartment, use those listed on the tune-up decal.

NOTES: 1. On transistor ignitions, only a transistorized dwell meter can be used. Transistor ignitions are recognizable by the "Blue" ignition coil, 2 series resistors and the transistor switchgear.

2. To counteract wear of the fiber contact block, adjust the dwell to the lower end of the range.

A After Top Dead Center
B Before Top Dead Center
w/vacuum—vacuum advance connected
w/o vacuum—vacuum advance disconnected
* Below 0°F; increase valve clearance by 0.002 in.
—Not Available
▲ In Drive
● Timing for test measurements @ 2mm valve lift

① Injection pump pressure
② Right side camshaft—4.5° ATDC
　 Left side camshaft—6.5° ATDC
③ Right side camshaft—12° ATDC
　 Left side camshaft—10° ATDC

④ Approximately 1 quart in 30 seconds
⑤ Left side—22° ATDC
　 Right side—20° ATDC
⑥ New timing chain: 17A
　 Used timing chain (12,000 miles): 18A

DIESEL ENGINE TUNE-UP SPECIFICATIONS

Model	Valve Clearance (cold)① Intake (in.)	Exhaust (in.)	Intake Valve Opens (deg)	Injection Pump Setting (deg)	Injection Nozzle Pressure (psi) New	Used	Idle Speed (rpm) ②	Cranking Compression Pressure (psi)
190D	Hyd.	Hyd.	⑤	15A	1564–1706	1422–1706	700–800	284–327
240D	0.004	0.016	13.5B	24B	1564–1706	1422–1706	750–800	284–327

DIESEL ENGINE TUNE-UP SPECIFICATIONS

Model	Valve Clearance (cold)①		Intake Valve Opens (deg)	Injection Pump Setting (deg)	Injection Nozzle Pressure (psi)		Idle Speed (rpm) ②	Cranking Compression Pressure (psi)
	Intake (in.)	Exhaust (in.)			New	Used		
300D, 300CD, 300TD (5-cylinder, non-turbo)	0.004	0.012	13.5B	24B④	1635–1750 ③	1422	700–800	284–327
300SD, 300TD (5-cylinder, turbo) '78–'81	0.004	0.014	13.5B	24B④	1958–2074	1740	650–850	284–327
300D, 300CD, 300SD, 300TD (5-cylinder, turbo) '82–'85	0.004	0.014	13.5B	24B④⑥	1958–2074	1740	650–850⑦	284–327

B Before Top Dead Center
① In cold weather (below 5°F.), increase valve clearance 0.002 in.
② Manual transmission in Neutral; Automatic in Drive.

③ Difference in opening pressure on injection nozzles should not exceed 71 psi.
④ The injection pump is in start of delivery position when the mark on the pump camshaft is aligned with the mark on the injection pump flange.

⑤ New timing chain: 11A
   Used timing chain (12,000 miles): 12A
⑥ 1984–85: 15A
⑦ 1984–85: 700–800

FIRING ORDERS

NOTE: The position of No. 1 tower on the distributor cap may vary. To avoid confusion when replacing wires, always replace wires one at a time. The notch cut into the rim of the distributor body always indicates No. 1 cylinder.

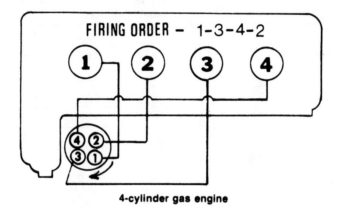

FIRING ORDER - 1-3-4-2

4-cylinder gas engine

FIRING ORDER -1-5-3-6-2-4

6-cylinder gas engine

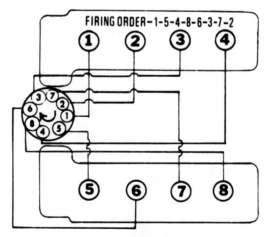

FIRING ORDER -1-5-4-8-6-3-7-2

V8 gasoline engines

CAPACITIES

Year	Model	Cooling System (qts)	Engine Crankcase (qts) ▲		Transmission (pts)		Drive Axle (pts)	Steering Gear (pts)		Level Control (qts)
			With Filter	Without Filter	Manual (4-spd)	Automatic		Power	Manual	
'84	190D	9.0	4.8	4.8	3.2	11.6	1.5	1.0	—	—
'84	190E	9.0	6.3	5.8	3.2	11.6	1.5	1.0	—	—
'78	230	10.5	5.8	5.3	—	11.5	②	3.0	⅝	—
'78–'83	240D	10.5	6.3	5.3	3.4	11.5	②	3.0	⅝	—
'78–'81	280E, 280CE	11.5	6.3	5.8	—	12.3	2.1	3.0	—	—
'78–'80	280SE	11.5	6.3	5.8	—	12.3	2.1	3.0	—	—
'78–'81	300D, 300CD	11.7	6.8	5.3	—	11.5	2.1	3.0	—	—
'82–'85	300D, 300CD	13.2	8.0	6.3	—	13.2	2.2	3.0	—	—
'78–'80	300SD, 300TD	12.7④	6.8	5.3	—	11.5	2.1	3.0	—	6.2③
'81–'85	300SD, 300TD	13.2	8.0	6.3	—	13.2	2.2	3.0	—	3.7
'81	380SL, SLC 380SEL	13.7	8.5	8.0	—	13.0	2.7	⑤	—	—
'82–'85	380SL, 380SE	13.2	8.5	8.0	—	16.2	2.7	3.0	—	—
'82–'83	380SEL 380SEC	13.2	8.5	8.0	—	13.0	2.7	2.5	—	—
'78–'80	450SEL, 450SL, 450SLC	16.0	8.5	8.0	—	16.5	①	3.0	—	6.2③
'84–'85	500SEC 500SEL	13.7	8.5	8.0	—	16.2	2.8	2.6	—	—
'78–'79	6.9	16.0	11.5	10.5	—	16.5	2.7	3.0	—	6.2③

▲Add approximately ½ quart if equipped with
additional oil cooler
—Not Applicable
①450SL, 450SLC—2.7 pts
 450SEL—3.0 pts
②See text:1st version—2.4 pts
 2nd version—2.1 pts
③Approximately 1 qt between dipstick
 maximum and minimum marks
④300SD—13.0 qts
⑤380SEL—2.5
 380SL, SLC—3.0

MITSUBISHI
Cordia, Starion, Tredia

SERIAL NUMBER IDENTIFICATION

Vehicle Number

The vehicle identification number (VIN) is mounted on the instrument panel, adjacent to the lower corner of the windshield on the driver's side and is visible through the windshield.

A standard 17 digit VIN code is used, the tenth digit identifies model year (D, 1983; E, 1984; etc.) and the eighth digit identifies the installed engine (4; 1.8 liter: 7; 2.6 liter).

A vehicle information code plate is riveted onto the front of the right side wheelhouse or onto the firewall (depending on model). The plate shows model code, engine model, transaxle model and body color code.

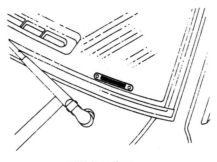

VIN location

A chassis number plate is located on the top center of the firewall in the engine compartment.

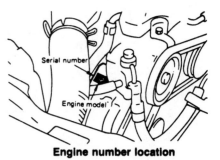

Engine number location

Engine Number

The engine number is stamped at the right front side of the engine on the top edge of the block. The 1.8 engine is model G62B and the 2.6 engine is G54B.

TUNE-UP SPECIFICATIONS

(When analyzing compression test results, look for uniformity among cylinders, rather than specific pressures.)

Year	Engine Displace. (cc)	Spark Plugs Type	Spark Plugs Gap (in.)	Distributor	Ignition Timing (deg) MT	Ignition Timing (deg) AT	Intake Valve Opens (deg) BTDC	Fuel Pump Pressure (psi)	Idle Speed (rpm)	Valve② Clear (in.) In.	Valve② Clear (in.) Ex.
'83	1800	BUR6EA-11	0.039–0.043	Electronic	5B	5B	19	2.4–3.4	650MT 750AT	0.006	0.010
	2600	BUR6EA-11	0.039–0.043	Electronic	10B	—	25	35–47	850	0.006	0.010
'84–'85	1800	BPR7ES-11	0.039–0.043	Electronic	5B	5B	57	35–47	750	0.006	0.010
	2000	BPR6ES-11	0.039–0.043	Electronic	5B	5B	19	2.4–3.4	700MT① 750MT	0.006	0.010
	2600	BUR6EA-11	0.039–0.043	Electronic	10B	10B	25	35–47	750MT 850AT	0.006	0.010

MT Manual Trans.
AT Automatic Trans.

① with A/C: 750MT 850AT

②Jet Valve: 0.010

FIRING ORDERS

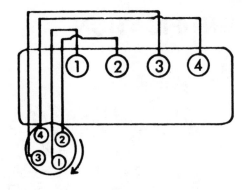

1800 and 2000cc engines

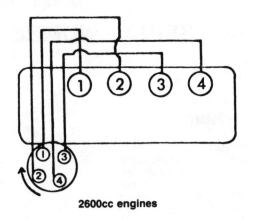

2600cc engines

CAPACITIES
Rear Wheel Drive Cars

Year	Model	Engine Displacement (cc)	Engine Crankcase (qts) With Filter	Engine Crankcase (qts) Without Filter	Transmission (qts) Manual	Transmission (qts) Automatic	Drive Axle (pts)	Gasoline Tank (gals)	Cooling System (qts) W/AC	Cooling System (qts) W/O AC
'83–'85	Starion	2600	4.5	4	2.4	7.4	2.7	19.8	9.7	9.7

CAPACITIES
Front Wheel Drive Cars

Year	Model	Engine Displacement (cc)	Engine Crankcase (qts) With Filter	Engine Crankcase (qts) W/O Filter	Transaxle (qts) Manual 4-spd	Transaxle (qts) Manual 5-spd	Transaxle (qts) Automatic	Gasoline Tank (gals)	Cooling System (qts) W/AC	Cooling System (qts) W/O AC
'83–'85	Cordia Tredia	1800, 2000	4.5	4	2.2	2.2	6.1	13.2	7.4	7.4

PORSCHE
924, 928, 944

SERIAL NUMBER IDENTIFICATION

Vehicle

The chassis serial number is located on the left windshield post and can be viewed from the outside. The vehicle identification plate is in the engine compartment near the battery.

Engine

The engine serial number is stamped on the left of the crankcase near the clutch housing.

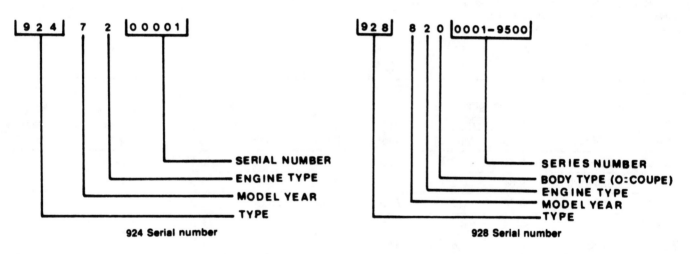

WPO AAO 94 O E N 45 0001–9999

USA/Canada

Serial number
Code for body and engine
Vehicle type together with 7th and 8th digits
Manufacturing site
Model year (E = 1984)
Test code or fill-in letter
Vehicle type together with 12th digit
Fill-in letters or code for USA and Canada cars
World manufacturing code

944 serial number

924 7 2 00001

SERIAL NUMBER
ENGINE TYPE
MODEL YEAR
TYPE

924 Serial number

928 8 2 0 0001–9500

SERIES NUMBER
BODY TYPE (O: COUPE)
ENGINE TYPE
MODEL YEAR
TYPE

928 Serial number

TUNE-UP SPECIFICATIONS

Year	Model	Engine Displacement cc	(cu. in.)	Spark Plugs Type	Gap (in.)	Ignition Timing ① (rpm)	Intake Valve Opens (deg)	Idle Speed (rpm)	Valve Clearance (cold) (in.) Intake	Exhaust
'78–'81	924	1984	(121)	W200-T30	.028–.032	10°A @ 925	5°BTDC	850–1000	0.004	0.016
'79–'81	924 Turbo.	1984	(121)	WR7DS	.024	20°B @ 2000	—	900–1000	0.004	0.016
'82	924	1984	(121)	WR6DS	.028	0° ± 1° @ 750–800③	—	850–1000	0.006	0.016
'82	924 Turbo	1984	(121)	WR6DS	.028④	6°–10°B @ 900⑤	—	900–1000	0.006	0.016
'78–'79	928	4474	(273)	W145-T30	.028–.032	31°B @ 3000	8°ATDC②	800	Hyd.	Hyd.
'80–'81	928	4474	(273)	WR8DS	.028	23°B @ 3000	12°ATDC	700–800	Hyd.	Hyd.
'82	928	4474	(273)	WR8DS	.028–.032	23°B @ 3000	—	700–800	Hyd.	Hyd.
'83–'85	928S	4664	(284)	WR8DS	.028–.032	20°B @ 3000	11°ATDC	700–800⑥	Hyd.	Hyd.
'83–'85	944	2479	(151)	WR8DS	.028–.032	3°–7°B @ 900⑤	1°ATDC	850–950	Hyd.	Hyd.

NA—Not Available at time of publication
A—After Top Dead Center
B—Before Top Dead Center
① With vacuum hose disconnected, if so equipped.
② .0393 in., zero valve clearance
③ With connector above idle stabilizer in front of the left wheel arch disconnected.
④ If Champion N7GY is used, gap should be .024 in.
⑤ Checking specification only; timing is self-adjusting.
⑥ Not adjustable—electronically controlled

CAPACITIES

Year	Model	Engine Displacement cc	(cu. in.)	Engine Crankcase (qts) With Filter	Without Filter	Transaxle (qts.) Manual	Auto.	Gasoline Tank (gal.)	Cooling System (qts.)
'78–'82	924	1984	(121)	5.30	4.75	2.75①	3.17②	16.4④	8.5
'79–'82	924 Turbo.	1984	(121)	5.30	4.75	2.6	5.5	18.6④	8.5
'78–'79	928	4474	(273)	7.90	6.40	4.0③	5.8	22.7	16
'80–'82	928	4474	(273)	8.50	8.00	4.0⑤	5.8	23	17
'83–'85	928S	4664	(284)	8.50	8.00	4.0	6.0	23	17
'83–'85	944	2479	(151)	5.80	—	2.75	3.0⑦	17.4	8.5

NA—Not available.
① SAE 80 or 80W gear oil
② At oil change ATF Dexron®, differential 1.06 qt. SAE 90 gear oil
③ Mid-1978 model year—change manual gear oil usage to Dexron® ATF
④ 1982 and later—17.4
⑤ Use SAE 75w-90 oil, meeting API/GL5 specifications.
⑥ Use SAE 80 oil, meeting API/GL4 specifications.
⑦ Dry refill capacity—6.9 qts. Use Dexron® transmission fluid.

FIRING ORDER

NOTE: To avoid confusion, always replace spark plug wires one at a time.

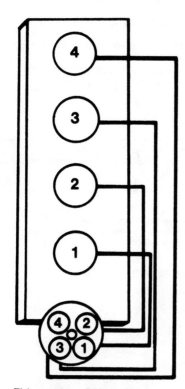

Firing order—944 engine
Distributor rotation—clockwise

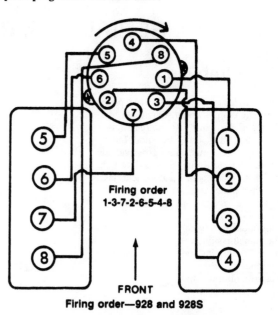

Firing order
1-3-7-2-6-5-4-8

FRONT
Firing order—928 and 928S

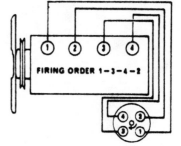

FIRING ORDER 1—3—4—2

Firing order—924 engines

RENAULT
Alliance, Encore, Fuego, LeCar, 18i

SERIAL NUMBER IDENTIFICATION

Vehicle

Renault vehicles are identified by two plates in the engine compartment. One plate, diamond shaped through 1979 and rectangular beginning in 1980, shows the model number, serial number, maximum gross vehicle weight (GVW), maximum gross axle weight rating, date of manufacture and vehicle class.

The other plate, oval in shape, as indicated by the accompanying illustration, shows:

- the model number
- the transmission type
- basic equipment code
- optional equipment code
- manufacturer's number.

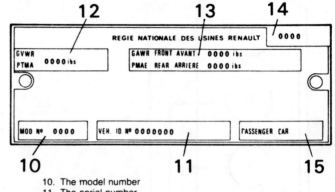

10. The model number
11. The serial number
12. The maximum allowable load for the vehicle
13. The maximum allowable load for the front and rear axles
14. The date of manufacture (month-year)
15. The vehicle class

Rectangular identification plate

Engine

The engine identification plate is attached to the engine block on the left side at the rear, just below the head. On earlier models, all plates were uniformly rectangular on all engines. On later models, however, the size and shape of the plate was determined by available space. Through 1979 the plate showed the engine type, index and manufacturing sequence number. Beginning in 1980, the plate shows, as illustrated:

    A. The engine type

    B. The French Ministry of Mines homologation number

    C. Engine equipment

    D. Manufacturer's identification number

    E. Engine index number

    F. The manufacturing sequence number.

Transaxle

The transaxle identification tag is located under a bolt on the transaxle at the end opposite the engine. The plate shows the type and the manufacturing sequence number.

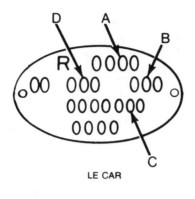

A. Vehicle type
B. Equipment number
C. Manufacturing number
D. Version number

Oval identification plate

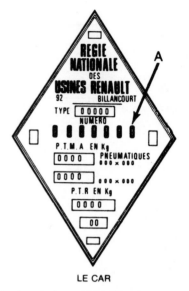

Diamond shaped identification plates

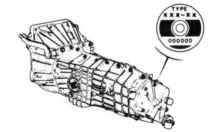

Transaxle identification plate

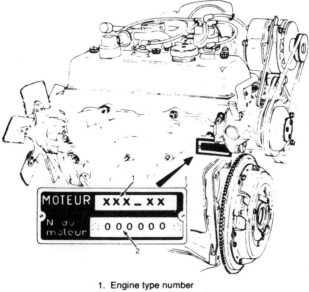

1. Engine type number
2. Engine fabrication number

Engine identification plate

TUNE-UP SPECIFICATIONS

Model	Year	Engine Displacement cu in. (cc)	Spark Plug Type	Gap (in.)	Distributor Point Dwell (deg)	Point Gap (in.)	Ignition Timing (deg) MT	AT	Intake Valve Opens (deg)	Fuel Pump Pressure (psi)	Idle Speed (rpm) MT	AT	Valve Clearance (in.) In	Ex
LeCar, Alliance, Encore	'78–'79	78.6 (1289)	①	②	57	.016–.020	0	—	22B	2.5–3.5	775③	—	.006	.008
	'80–'81	85.2 (1397)	WD9DS	.022–.026	Electronic		3B⑤	—	12B	2.5–3.5	700④	—	.006	.008
	'82–'85	85.2 (1397)	RN-12Y	.032	Electronic		8B	8B	12B	28–36	700	700	.006	.008
18i, Fuego, Sport Wagon	'81–'84	100.5 (1647)	WR7DS	.024–.028	Electronic		10B	10B	22B	28–36	800	650	.008	.010
Fuego	'84–'85	132.0 (2165)					see underhood sticker							

NOTE: The underhood sticker often reflects tune-up specification changes made in production. Sticker figures must be used if they disagree with those in this chart.
B: Before Top Dead Center
① 1978 exc. Calif.: L-874
  1979 exc. Calif.: L-92Y
② 1978 exc. Calif.: .026–.029
  All others: .022–.026
③ W/air pump: 850
④ W/air pump: 750
⑤ Canada: 0

FIRING ORDERS

NOTE: To avoid confusion, always replace spark plug wires one at a time.

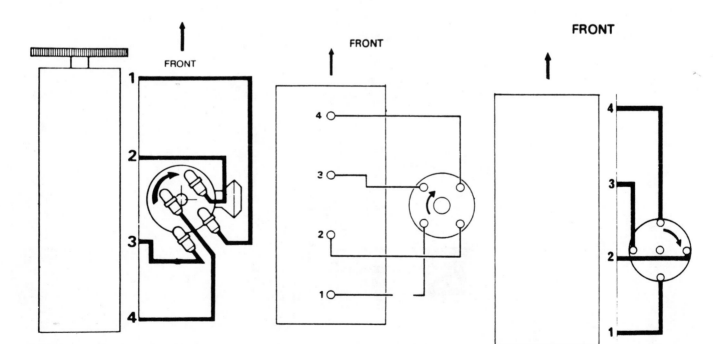

LeCar, Alliance and Encore spark plug wiring diagram

Spark plug wiring diagram for 18i and Fuego engines

Spark plug wiring diagram for R–18 carbureted engines

CAPACITIES

Model	Year	Crankcase Incl. Filter (qts.)	Transmission Pints to Refill After Draining		Fuel Tank (gal.)	Cooling System (qts.)	
			Manual	Automatic●		With Heater	With A/C
LeCar	All	3.5	4.0	—	10.0	6.5	6.5
18,18i, Sport Wagon	'81–'83	4.5	4.5	10.5	①	6.5	6.75
Fuego	'82–'83	4.5	4.5	10.5	15.0	6.4	6.75
Alliance	'82–'83	3.5	7.0	9.0	12.5	4.4	4.8
Alliance, Encore	'84–'85	4.0	②	7.5	12.5	4.4	4.8
Sport Wagon, Fuego	'84–'85	NA	NA	NA	15.0	NA	NA
Fuego Turbo	'84–'85	4.5	4.5	10.5	15.0	6.4	6.75

NA Not Available
● Includes converter
① Sedan: 14
  Sta. Wgn.: 15

② 4sp: 6.4
  5sp: 6.8

SAAB
99, 900
SERIAL NUMBER IDENTIFICATION

Vehicle

The vehicle serial number is located in two places on all SAAB models: the serial number is stamped on a plate at the lower left hand corner of the windshield, and the serial number is punched in the car body under the left side of the rear seat cushion.

Beginning with the 1981 and later models, the vehicle serial number is located on the right side of the rear cross beam in the luggage compartment.

CHASSIS NUMBER
Up To and Including 1980
(11 Digits)

Example—

90 79 2 000001
(1) (2) (3) (4)

(1) Model:
90 = 900
99 = 99
(2) Year:
78 = 1978
79 = 1979
80 = 1980
(3) Assembly Plant:
1 = Trollhättan
2 = Trollhättan
3 = Nystäd (Finland)
(4) Serial number:
000001

CHASSIS NUMBER
Beginning With 1981
and Later (17 Digits)

Example—
YS3 A G 3 1 S X B 1 000001
(1) (2) (3) (4) (5) (6) (7) (8) (9) (10)

(1) Manufacturer:
YS3 = Sweden
YK1 = Finland
(2) Production line:
A = 900

(3) Series:
G = 900
S = 900S
E = 900S
T = Turbo 900
(4) Body Type:
3 = Two side doors and one tailgate
4 = Four side doors
5 = Four side doors and one tailgate
(5) Engine:
1 = B20C
2 = B20T
3 = B20I
4 = B20S
(6) Safety equipment:
A = Air bags
P = Passive safety belts
S = Active safety belts
(7) Check digit:
0–9 or X
(8) Model Year:
B = 1981
C = 1982
D = 1983
E = 1984
F = 1985
(9) Assembly Plant:
1 = Trollhättan—Line one
2 = Trollhättan—Line two
3 = Arlov
4 = Nystäd (Finland)
(10) Serial Number:
000001

ENGINE NUMBER
Up To and Including 1980

Example—
BT 20 P01 000001
(1) (2) (3) (4)

(1) BT = Gasoline engine, twin carburetor
BI = Gasoline engine, mechanical injection

BSI = Gasoline engine, Turbo and mechanical injection
(2) Cylinder volume in deciliter (dl). (deciliter equals 1/10 of liter)
(3) Variant designation, such as engine/transmission combination and geographic location
(4) Serial number in six digits

ENGINE NUMBER
From 1981 and Later

Example—
B 20 S M UC 01 B 000001
(1) (2) (3) (4) (5) (6) (7) (8)

(1) B = Gasoline engine
(2) Cylinder volume in deciliter (dl) (deciliter equal 1/10 of liter)
(3) Model:
C = Single carburetor
T = Twin carburetor
I = Fuel injection
S = Turbo
(4) Transmission type:
M = Manual
A = Automatic
(5) Exhaust emission control level:
UC = USA
SW = Sweden
EU = Europe
(6) Equipment variants, such as engine/transmission combinations and geographic locations
(7) Year designations:
B = 1981
C = 1982
D = 1983
E = 1984
F = 1985
(8) Serial number in six digits

Engine

On the 1985 cc engine the number is stamped on a plate which is secured to the upper portion of the engine directly forward of the fuel injection unit.

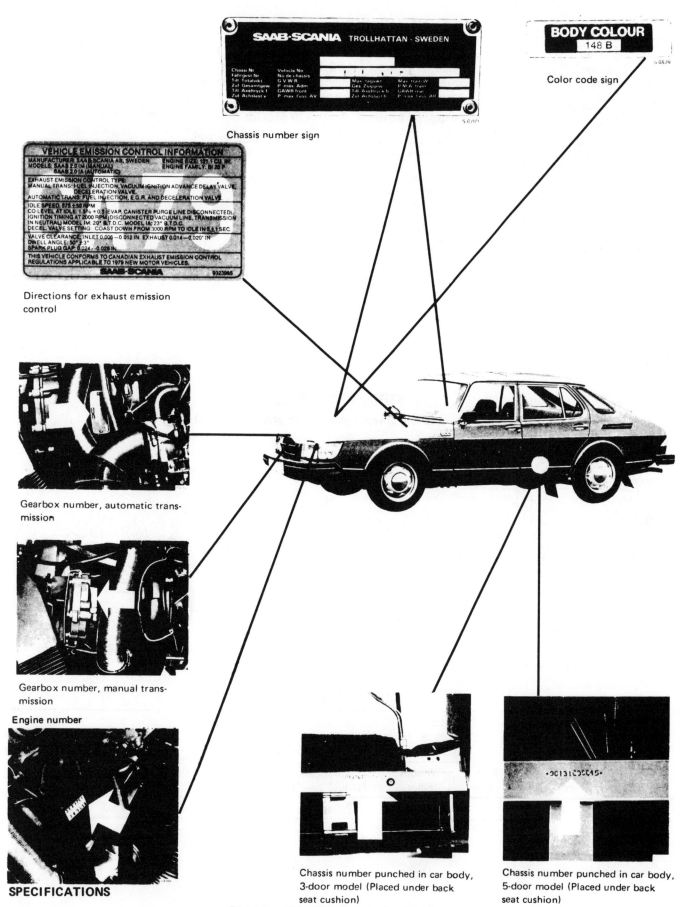

SAAB-SCANIA TROLLHATTAN - SWEDEN

Chassis number sign

BODY COLOUR
148 B

Color code sign

VEHICLE EMISSION CONTROL INFORMATION
MANUFACTURER: SAAB-SCANIA AB, SWEDEN   ENGINE SIZE: 121.1 CU. IN.
MODELS: SAAB 2.0 IM (MANUAL)   ENGINE FAMILY: B 20 P
        SAAB 2.0 IA (AUTOMATIC)
EXHAUST EMISSION CONTROL TYPE:
MANUAL TRANS: FUEL INJECTION, VACUUM IGNITION ADVANCE DELAY VALVE,
              DECELERATION VALVE.
AUTOMATIC TRANS: FUEL INJECTION, E.G.R. AND DECELERATION VALVE.
IDLE SPEED: 875 ± 50 RPM
CO LEVEL AT IDLE: 1.5% + 0.5 (EVAP. CANISTER PURGE LINE DISCONNECTED).
IGNITION TIMING AT 2000 RPM (DISCONNECTED VACUUM LINE, TRANSMISSION
IN NEUTRAL) MODEL IM: 20° B.T.D.C. MODEL IA: 23° B.T.D.C.
DECEL. VALVE SETTING: COAST DOWN FROM 3000 RPM TO IDLE IN 5 ±1 SEC.
VALVE CLEARANCE: INLET 0.008 — 0.012 IN. EXHAUST 0.014 — 0.020 IN.
DWELL ANGLE: 50° ± 3°
SPARK PLUG GAP: 0.024 — 0.028 IN.
THIS VEHICLE CONFORMS TO CANADIAN EXHAUST EMISSION CONTROL
REGULATIONS APPLICABLE TO 1979 NEW MOTOR VEHICLES.
SAAB-SCANIA   9323985

Directions for exhaust emission
control

Gearbox number, automatic transmission

Gearbox number, manual transmission

Engine number

SPECIFICATIONS

Chassis number punched in car body,
3-door model (Placed under back
seat cushion)

Chassis number punched in car body,
5-door model (Placed under back
seat cushion)

Component Identification number locations

TUNE-UP SPECIFICATIONS

Year	Engine Displacement (cc)	Spark Plugs		Distributor		Basic Ignition Timing (deg)	Intake Valve Opens (deg)	Fuel Pump Pressure (psi)	Idle Speed (rpm)	Valve Clearance (in.)	
		Type	Gap	Point Dwell (deg)	Reluctor Gap (in.)⑧					Intake	Exhaust
'78–'85	1985	③	0.024–0.028	Electronic ⑦	0.010 ⑧	②⑥	10 BTDC⑤	①	875	0.008–0.010	0.016–④ 0.018

NOTE: If these specifications differ from those on the engine compartment stickers, use the sticker specifications.

① Fuel injected engines (all models): Fuel line pressure before the control pressure regulator is 66.9–69.7 (setting valve), and 48.5–54.0 psi (warm engine) after the control pressure regulator (located in fuel distributor).

② '78–'85—20° @ 2000 rpm
'78–'85 Canada, manual transmission—20° BTDC @ 2000 rpm
'78–'85 Canada, automatic transmission—23° BTDC @ 2000 rpm

③ Turbo—NGK-BP7ES, Champion N7Y or N7YC; non-Turbo NGK BP6ES, Bosch W70 or Champion N9Y, N9YC

④ Turbo—.018–.020

⑤ Turbo—12° BTDC

⑥ With vacuum hose disconnected

⑦ Canadian models with points ignition, 47–53°

⑧ Point gap (Canadian models) 0.016 in. (0.4mm)

FIRING ORDERS

NOTE: To avoid confusion, always replace spark plug wires one at a time.

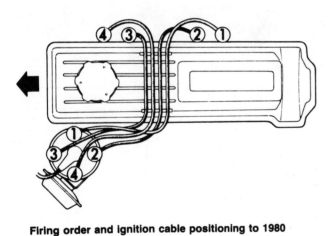

Firing order and ignition cable positioning to 1980

Firing order and ignition cable positioning—1981 and later

CAPACITIES

Year	Engine Displacement (cc)	Engine Crankcase (qts.)		Transmission (pts.)		Drive Axle (pts.)	Fuel Tank (gals.)	Cooling System (qts.) w/o AC
		With Filter	Without Filter	Manual	Automatic			
'78–'85	1985	3.7	3.2	5.2①	17	1.3	14.5③	8.5②

① 6.4—5 speed trans. & 4 speed w/o dipstick

② '79–'80—10.5, '81–'83—10.8 qts

③ '80–'85—16.6 U.S. gals.

SUBARU
1400, 1600, 1800—All Models

SERIAL NUMBER IDENTIFICATION

The Vehicle Identification Number is stamped on a tab located on the top of the dashboard on the driver's side, visible through the windshield. The vehicle identification plate is on the bulkhead in the engine compartment. The engine number is stamped on the crankcase, behind the distributor.

TUNE-UP SPECIFICATIONS

(When analyzing compression test results, look for uniformity among cylinders, rather than specific pressures)

Year	Engine Displacement (cu. in.)	Spark Plugs ⑤ Type	Gap (in.)	Distributor Point Dwell (deg)	Point Gap (in.)	Ignition Timing (deg)	Intake Valve Opens (deg)	Fuel Pump Pressure (psi)	Idle Speed (rpm)	Valve Clearance (in.) In	Ex
'78–'79	(1600)	BP6ES	.032	49–55②	0.018②	8B @ 850	24B	2.6	850①	0.010	0.014
'80	(1600)	BP6ES	.032	Electronic		8B @ 850	24B	2.6	850①	0.009	0.013
	(1800)	BP6ES	.032	Electronic		8B @ 850	24B	2.6	850①	0.009	0.013
'81–'82	(1600)	BPES-11	.040	Electronic		8B @ 700	20B	1.3–2.0	700	0.010	0.014
	(1800)	BPES-11	.040	Electronic		8B @ 700③	20B	1.3–2.0	700④	0.010	0.014
'83	(1600)	BPR6ES-11	.040	Electronic		8B @ 700	20B	1.3–2.0	700④	0.010	0.014
	(1800)	BPR6ES-11	.040	Electronic		8B @ 700③	20B	1.3–2.0	700④	0.010⑥	0.014⑥
	(1800 Turbo)	BPR6ES-11	.040	Electronic		15B @ 800	16B	43.4	800	0	0
'84–'85	(1600)	BPR6ES-11	.040	Electronic		8B @ 650⑦	20B	1.3–2.0	650⑦	.010	.014
	(1800)	BPR6ES-11	.040	Electronic		8B @ 700④	20B	1.3–2.0	700④	.010⑥	.014⑥
	(1800 Turbo)	BPR6ES-11	.040	Electronic		15 @ 800	16B	43.4	800	0	0

NOTE: The underhood specifications sticker often reflects tune-up specification changes made in production. Sticker figures must be used if they disagree with those in this chart.

B—Before top dead center
M—Manual transmission
A—Automatic transmission
① California 900

② California—Electronic ignition
③ Auto trans and 4WD; 8B @ 800
④ 800 rpm w/Auto trans.

⑤ OEM spark plugs or NGK.
⑥ with automatic—O (hydraulic lifters)
⑦ with 5–speed—700

FIRING ORDER

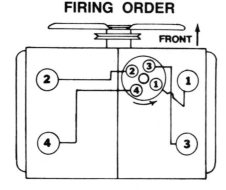

Firing order is 1-3-2-4

CAPACITIES

| Year | Model | Engine Displacement (CC) | Engine Crankcase (Qts) | | Transmission (Pts) | | | | Gasoline Tank (Gals) | Cooling System (Qts) |
			With Filter	Without Filter	4-spd	5-spd	Auto	4WD		
'78–'79	1600 series	1600	3.8	3.5	5.2	5.8	12.5	6.34	13.2	6.3
'80–'82	1600 series	1600	3.8	3.5	5.8	5.8	12.5③	6.34①	13.2②	5.6
'80–'82	1800 series	1800	3.8	3.5	5.8	5.8	12.5③	6.34①	13.2②	5.8
'83–'85	1600 Series	1600	4.2	—	5.8	5.8	10.8–12.6⑤	⑥	15.9⑦	5.6
'83–'85	1800 Series	1800	4.2	—	5.8	5.8	10.8–12.6⑤	⑥	15.9⑦	5.8

①4WD rear differential; 1.7 pts
②4WD vehicles; 11.9 gal
③Automatic transmission differential: 2.5 pts
④Station wagon w/4WD: 14.5 gal.,
  2 dr. hatchback (2WD): 13.2 gal.,
  2 dr: hatchback (4WD): 11.9 gal.

⑤4WD Automatic: 12.6–13.6
  Automatic differential: 2.6
  4WD Rear differential: 1.6
⑥4WD Manual 4 and 5 spd.: 6.4
  4WD Rear differential: 1.6

⑦4WD: 14.5
  Regular Hatchback: 13.2
  4WD Hatchback: 11.9

TOYOTA
Camry, Celica, Corolla, Corona, Cressida, Starlet,
Supra, Tercel, Van

SERIAL NUMBER IDENTIFICATION

Vehicle

All models have the vehicle identification number (VIN) stamped on a plate which is attached to the left side of the instrument panel. This plate is visible through the windshield.

The serial number consists of a series identification number followed by a six-digit production number.

Engine

Bascially, 1978–85 Toyota vehicles have used eight types of engines: The "A" series (1A-C, 3A, 3A-C, 4A-C); "K" series (3K-C, 4K-C, 4K-E); "M" series (4M, 4M-E, 5M-E, 5M-GE); "R" series (20R, 22R, 22R-E); "S" series (2S-E), "T" series (2T-C, 3T-C); "C" series diesel (1C-L, 1C-TL) and the "Y" series (3Y-EC). Engines within each series are similar, as the cylinder block designs are the same. Variances within each series may be due to ignition types (point or electronic), displacements (bore × stroke), cylinder head design (single or double-overhead camshafts) and fuel system type (carburetor or fuel injection). Refer to the accompanying engine I.D. chart.

When ordering engine parts, it may be necessary to obtain the engine serial number. Serial numbers of the engines may be found on the following locations:

"A" series engines—stamped vertically on the left side rear of the engine block.

"K" series engine—stamped on the right side of the engine, below the spark plugs.

"M" series engines—stamped horizontally on the passenger side of the engine block, behind the alternator.

"R" series engine—stamped horizontally on the driver's side of the engine block, behind the alternator.

"T" series engines—stamped horizontally on the driver's side of the engine block, just above the alternator.

"S" and "C" engines—stamped horizontally on the front side of the block.

"Y" series engines—stamped horizontally on the right side of the block.

CHASSIS IDENTIFICATION

Model	Year	Chassis Designation
Corolla 1200	'78–'79	KE
Corolla 1600	'78–'79	TE
Corolla 1800	'80–'82	TE
Corolla (Gasoline Engine)	'83–'85	AE
Corolla (Diesel Engine)	'84–'85	CE
Corona	'78–'82	RT
Celica (exc. Supra)	'78–'85	RA
Celica Supra	'79–'85	MA
Cressida	'78–'84	MX
Starlet	'81–'85	KP
Tercel	'80–'85	AL
Camry (Gasoline Engine)	'83–'85	SV
Camry (Diesel Engine)	'84–'85	CV
Van	'84–85	YR

ENGINE IDENTIFICATION

Model	Year	Engine Displacement Cu. in.(cc)	Engine Series Identification	No. of Cylinders	Engine Type
Camry	'83–'85	121.7 (1995)	2S-E	4	SOHC
	'84–'85	112.2 (1839)	1C-TL	4	SOHC
Celica	'78–'80	133.6 (2189)	20R	4	SOHC
	'81–'85	144.4 (2367)	22R, 22R-E	4	SOHC
Supra	'79½–'80	156.4 (2563)	4M-E	6	SOHC
	'81	168.4 (2759)	5M-E	6	SOHC
	'82–'85	168.4 (2759)	5M-GE	6	DOHC
Corolla	'78–'79	71.2 (1116)	3K-C	4	OHV
	'78–'79	96.9 (1588)	2T-C	4	OHV
	'80–'82	108.0 (1800)	3T-C	4	OHV
	'83–'85	97 (1587)	4A-C	4	SOHC
	'84–'85	112.2 (1839)	1C-L	4	SOHC
Tercel	'80–'85	88.6 (1452)	1A-C, 3A, 3A-C	4	SOHC
Corona	'78–'80	133.6 (2189)	20R	4	SOHC
	'81–'82	144.4 (2367)	22R	4	SOHC
Cressida	'78–'79	156.4 (2563)	4M	6	SOHC
	'80	156.4 (2563)	4M-E	6	SOHC
	'81–'82	168.4 (2759)	5M-E	6	SOHC
	'83–'85	168.4 (2759)	5M-GE	6	DOHC
Starlet	'81–'82	78.7 (1290)	4K-C	4	OHV
	'83–'85	79 (1290)	4K-E	4	OHV
Van	'84–'85	122 (1998)	3Y-EC	4	OHV

DOHC—Double-overhead camshaft   SOHC—Single-overhead camshaft
OHV—Pushrod-actuated Overhead valves

GASOLINE ENGINE TUNE-UP SPECIFICATIONS

Year	Engine Type	Spark Plugs Type (NGK)	Spark Plugs Gap (in.)	Distributor Point Dwell (deg)	Distributor Point Gap (in.)	Ignition Timing (deg)[5] MT	Ignition Timing (deg)[5] AT	Compression Press.	Fuel Pump Press.	Idle Speed (rpm) MT	Idle Speed (rpm) AT	Valve Clearance (in.) (hot) Intake	Valve Clearance (in.) (hot) Exhaust
'78–'79	3K-C	BPR5EA-L	0.031	Electronic		8B	8B	156	3.0–4.5	750	750	0.008	0.012
	2T-C	BP5EA-L	0.031	Electronic[4]		10B[10]	10B[10]	171	3.0–4.5	850	850	0.008	0.013
	4M	BPR5EA-L	0.031	Electronic[4]		10B[10]	10B[10]	156	4.2–5.4	750	750	0.011	0.014
	20R	BP5EA-L[11]	0.031	Electronic[4]		8B	8B	156	2.2–4.2	800	850	0.008	0.012
'80–'81	1A-C	BP6EK-A	0.039	Electronic[4]		5B	—	177	—	650	800	0.008	0.012
	3A	BPR5EA-L	0.031	52	0.018	5B	5B	177	—	650	800[13]	0.008	0.012
	3A-C	BPR5EA-11[14]	0.043	Electronic[4]		5B	5B[5]	177	—	550[13][15]	800[13]	0.008	0.012
	3T-C	BPR5EA	0.043	Electronic[4]		10B[23]	10B[23]	163	—	850[6]	850[6]	0.008	0.013
	4K-C	BPR5EA-11[19]	0.043[19]	Electronic[4]		8B	—	156	2.8–4.2	650[13][20]	—	0.008	0.012
	4M-E	BPR5EA-L	0.031	Electronic[4]		12B	12B	156	33–38	800	800	0.011	0.014

TUNE-UP SPECIFICATIONS

Year	Engine Type	Spark Plugs Type (NGK)	Gap (in.)	Distributor Point Dwell (deg)	Point Gap (in.)	Ignition Timing (deg)⑤ MT	AT	Compression Press.	Fuel Pump Press.	Idle Speed (rpm) MT	AT	Valve Clearance (in.) (hot) Intake	Exhaust
'80–'81	5M-E	BPR5EA-L	0.031	Electronic④		8B	8B	156	33–38	800	800	0.011	0.014
	20R, 22R	BPR5EA-L	0.031	Electronic④		8B	8B	156㉔	2.2–4.3	800⑫	850	0.008	0.012
'82	3A	BPR5EA-L	0.031	52	0.018	5B	5B	177	—	650	800⑬	0.008	0.012
	3A-C	BPR5EA-11⑭	0.043	Electronic④		5B⑤	5B⑤	177	—	550⑬⑮	800⑬	0.008	0.012
	3T-C	BPR5EA-11⑯	0.043⑯	Electronic④		7B⑤⑰	7B⑤⑰	163	—	⑱	⑱	0.008	0.013
	4K-C	BPR5EA-11⑲	0.043⑲	Electronic④		8B	—	156	2.8–4.2	650⑬⑳	—	0.008	0.012
	5M-E	BPR5EA-L	0.031	Electronic④		—	8B	156	33–38	—	800	0.011	0.014
	5M-GE	BPR5EY	0.031	Electronic④		8B⑬	8B⑬	164	35–38	650	650	㉑	㉑
	22R	BPR5EA-L	0.031	Electronic④		8B⑬	8B⑬	171	—	700㉒	750㉒	0.008	0.012
'83	3A	BPR5EA-L	0.031	Electronic④		5B	5B	178	—	㉕	㉕	.008	.012
	3A-C	BPR5EA-11⑭	0.043	Electronic④		5B	5B	178	—	㉖	㉖	.008	.012
	4A-C	BPR5EA-L11㉗	0.043	Electronic④		5B	5B	163	2.5–3.5	㉘	㉘	.008	.012
	4K-E	㉙	0.043	Electronic④		5B	—	185	36–38	700	—	㉑	㉑
	5M-GE	BPR5EP-11	0.043	Electronic④		10B	10B	164	35–38	650	650	㉑	㉑
	22R-E	BPR5EY	0.031	Electronic④		5B	5B	171	35–38	750	750	.008	.012
	22R	BPR5EY	0.031	Electronic④		8B	8B	171	2.5–3.8	700	700	.008	.012
	2S-E	BPR5EA-L11	0.043	Electronic④		5B	5B	156	28–36	㉚	㉚	㉑	㉑
'84	2S-E	BPR5EA-L11	0.043	Electronic④		5B	5B	156	28–36	700	700	Hyd.	Hyd.
	3A-C	BPR5EA-11	0.043	Electronic④		5B	5B	177	2.6–3.5	㉖	㉖	.008	.012
	3Y-EC	BPR5EP-11	0.043	Electronic④		8B	8B	171	33–38	950	950	Hyd.	Hyd.
	4A-C	BPR5EZ-L11③	0.043	Electronic④		5B	5B	163	2.5–3.5	700	700	.008	.012
	4K-E	BPR5EP-11⑦	0.043	Electronic④		5B	—	185	36–38	700	—	Hyd.	Hyd.
	5M-GE	BPR5EP-11	0.043	Electronic④		10B	10B	156	35–38	650	650	㉑	㉑
	22R-E	BPR5EY	0.031	Electronic④		5B	5B	171	35–38	950	950	.008	.012
'85	All	Refer to Underhood Specifications Sticker											

NOTE: If the information given in this chart disagrees with the information on the emission control specification decal, use the specifications on the decal.

MT Manual transmission
AT Automatic transmission
TDC Top dead center
B Before top dead center
Hyd. Hydraulic valve lash adjusters
① Except California
② California only
③ Calif.: BPR5EA-L11
④ Air gap 0.008–0.016 inch
⑤ With vacuum advance disconnected
⑥ M/T without power steering—700 rpm
A/T without power steering—750 rpm
⑦ 5 sp.: BRE529Y-11
⑧ Electric pump (California)—2.4 to 3.8 psi
⑨ California model Celica GT equipped with transistorized ignition
⑩ California—8B
⑪ Celica—BPR5EA-L
⑫ Four-speed manual—700 rpm
⑬ With cooling fan OFF; trans. in Neutral

⑭ California models use BPR5EA-L11
⑮ For 4-speed transmission. 5-speed—650 rpm
⑯ Canada models use BPR5ES, gapped at 0.031 in.
⑰ Canada models—10°BTDC
⑱ Without power steering:
U.S., M.T.—650 rpm
U.S., A.T.—750 rpm
Canada, M.T.—700 rpm
Canada, A.T.—750 rpm
With power steering: 850 rpm
⑲ California models use BPR5EA-L, gapped at 0.031
⑳ California models—700 rpm w/cooling fan OFF, trans. in Neutral
㉑ Self-adusting lash adjusters are used—no adjustment necessary
㉒ Canadian models—850 rpm

㉓ '81 USA models: 7B
㉔ 22R: 171
㉕ W/PS: MT—800
AT—900
W/OPS: MT—650
AT—800
㉖ W/PS: MT—800
AT—900
W/OPS: 4 spd—550
5 spd—650
AT—700
㉗ Canada: BPR5EA-L; gap—0.031
㉘ W/PS: MT—650
AT—800
W/OPS: MT—800
AT—900
㉙ 4 Spd: BPR5EP-11
5 Spd: BRE529-Y11
㉚ Refer to underhood specifications sticker

FIRING ORDERS

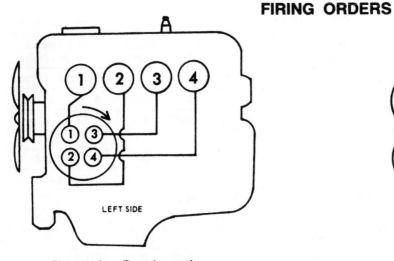

Firing order—R–series engines

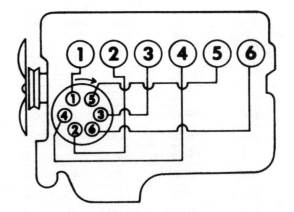

Firing order—5M-GE engines

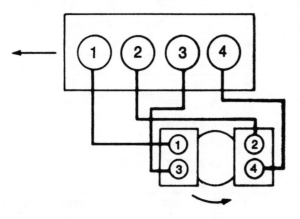

Firing order—A-series engines (1983 shown; others similar)

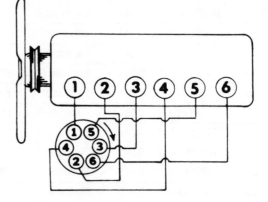

Firing order—4M, 4M–E and 5M–E engines

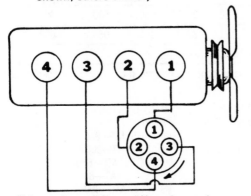

Firing order—all T– and K-series engines

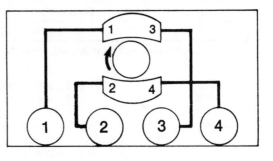

Firing order—2-SE engine

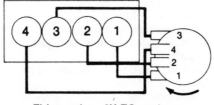

Firing order—3Y-EC engine

CAPACITIES

Model	Year	Crankcase (qt)		Transmission (qt)		Drive Axle (pt)	Fuel Tank (gal)	Cooling System w/Heater (qt)
		W/Filter	W/O Filter	Manual	Automatic			
Corolla								
1200	'78–'79	3.7	2.9	①	—	2.2	12.0	5.1
1600	'78–'79	4.6	3.7	1.6	2.5	2.4	13.2	8.8
1800	'80–'82	4.0	3.5	1.8	2.5	2.2	13.2	8.8
1600	'83–'85	3.5㉒	3.2	1.8	2.5	2.2㉓	13.2⑨	⑭㉑
Tercel	'80–'85	3.5	3.2	3.4⑮	2.3	2.0⑯	11.9⑳	5.4
Corona								
2200	'78–'80	4.8	4.1	2.9②	2.3③	⑤	14.5④	7.4⑥
2400	'81–'82	4.8	4.1	2.9②	2.3③	⑤	16.1	8.5
Celica								
2200	'78–'80	4.9	4.0	2.9②	2.3③	⑤	13.0⑦	8.9
2400	'81–'85	4.9	4.0	2.5	2.5	⑤	16.1	8.9
Cressida								
2600	'78–'80	4.9⑩	4.3⑩	—	2.5⑪	3.0	17.2⑫	11.6
2800	'81–'85	5.4	4.9	2.5	2.5	⑬	17.2⑫	8.8⑲
Supra								
2600	'79½–'80	4.9	4.3	2.8	2.5	3.2	16.1	9.5
2800	'81	4.9	4.3	2.7	2.5	3.2	16.1	9.5
2800	'82–'85	5.4	4.9	2.7	2.5	2.6	16.1	8.5
Starlet	'81–'85	3.7	3.2	2.6	—	2.2	10.6	5.5
Camry	'83–'85	4.2⑱	3.7⑱	2.7	2.5	⑰	13.8	7.4⑧
Van	'84–'85	3.7	3.2	2.3	2.3	2.6	15.9	7.5

① 4 sp: 1.8
   5 sp: 2.6
② 5 speed: 2.8
③ '78–'80: 2.5
④ 1978–79: 15.5; '80: 16.1
⑤ Unitized type: 2.6
   Banjo type: 2.8
⑥ '79–'80: 8.5
⑦ '78–'79: 15.5; '80: 16.1
⑧ Diesel: 8.0

⑨ Sta. Wag.: 12.4
⑩ 1978: 5.7, 4.7
⑪ 1978: 2.3
⑫ Sta. wag.: 16.2
⑬ With 7.5 in. ring gear—1.3; With 8.0 in. ring gear—1.9
⑭ M/T: 5.7
   A/T: 6.6
⑮ W/Transaxle 4 × 4: 4.1
⑯ 4 × 4: 2.2

⑰ M/T: 2.7
   A/T: 2.1
⑱ Diesel: 4.5 w/filter
   4.0 wo/filter
⑲ 1984–85: 9.5
⑳ 1984–85: 13.2
㉑ Diesel: 7.9
㉒ Diesel: 4.5 U.S. & Canada
   4.9 Calif.
㉓ Diesel: 2.1

VOLKSWAGEN FRONT WHEEL DRIVE
Rabbit, Jetta, Dasher, Quantum, Scirocco
SERIAL NUMBER IDENTIFICATION

Vehicle Identification Plate

On the Rabbit, Jetta, Scirocco and Quantum, the vehicle identification plate is on top of the body crossmember above the grille. The same plate on the Dasher is riveted to the inner right fender. The date of manufacture and the chassis number are stamped on the plate.

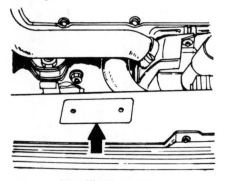

Identification plate

Chassis/VIN Number

The chassis number plate is located on the driver's side windshield pillar on the Scirocco and Dasher, and on the left front corner of the dashboard on the Rabbit, Jetta and Quantum (visible through the wind-

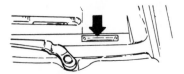

Rabbit, Jetta, Quantum chassis number

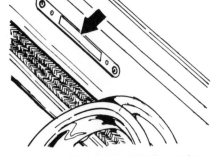

Dasher and Scirocco chassis number

shield). The Dasher and Quantum chassis numbers are also stamped on the firewall over the windshield washer reservoir. The Rabbit, Jetta and Scirocco chassis number is also found on top of the right front suspension strut pillar. It also appears on the vehicle identification plate.

1981 and later models use a seventeen digit code. On seventeen digit codes, the fifth position indicates engine and the tenth, the year. The year code will be a letter. "B"—1981; "C"—1982; etc.

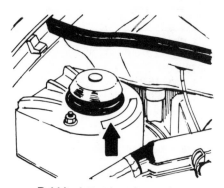

Rabbit, Jetta chassis number

Engine Number

The engine number is stamped on a flat boss on the left side (front on the Rabbit, Jetta,

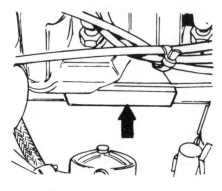

Engine number location

Scirocco and Quantum) of the engine block, just below the cylinder head between the fuel pump and distributor.

Vehicle Identification Label

This label is located in the luggage compartment beside the spare wheel on the Rabbit, Jetta and Scirocco, under the floor covering on the Quantum, and on the left side of the cross panel behind the rear bench seat on the Rabbit Convertible. The label is marked with the Vehicle Identification Number, Vehicle Code, Engine and Transmission Code, Paint and Interior code (needed for matching paint colors) and Option codes.

DIESEL TUNE-UP SPECIFICATIONS

Model	Valve Clearance (cold)①		Intake Valve Opens (deg)	Injection Pump Setting (deg)	Injection Nozzle Pressure (psi)		Idle Speed (rpm)	Cranking Compression Pressure (psi)
	Intake (in.)	Exhaust (in.)			New	Used		
Diesel (All models)	0.008–0.012	0.016–0.020	N.A.	Align marks	1885③	1706③	800–850② ④	406 minimum

N.A. Not Available

①Warm clearance given—Cold clearance:
Intake 0.006–0.010
Exhaust 0.014–0.018

②Volkswagen has lowered the idle speed on early models to this specification. Valve clearance need not be adjusted unless it varies more than 0.002 in. from specification.

③Turbo diesel: New–2306; Used–2139

④Turbo diesel: 900–1000

GASOLINE ENGINE TUNE-UP SPECIFICATIONS

Year Model	Spark Plugs Type	Gap (in.)	Point Dwell (deg)	Point Gap (in.)	Ignition Timing (deg)	Intake Valve Opens (deg)	Compression Pressure (psi)	Idle Speed (rpm)	Valve Clearance (in.) In⑤	Ex⑤
'78–'79 Dasher	W215 T30 N7Y	0.024–0.028	44–50	0.016	3 ATDC @ Idle	4 BTDC	142–184	850–1000	0.008–0.012	0.016–0.020
'78 Rabbit, Scirocco	W175 T30 N8Y	0.024–0.028	44–50	0.016	②	4 BTDC	142–184	850–1000	0.008–0.012	0.016–0.020
'79 Rabbit	W175 T30 N8Y	0.024–0.032	44–50	0.016	3 ATDC @ Idle	4 BTDC	142–184	850–1000	0.008–0.012	0.016–0.020
'79 Scirocco	W175 T30 N8Y	0.024–0.032	44–50	0.016	3 ATDC @ Idle	4 BTDC	142–184	850–1000	0.008–0.012	0.016–0.020
'80–'81 Dasher (49 states)	W175 T30 N8Y	0.024–0.032	44–50⑥	0.016⑥	3 ATDC @ Idle	4 BTDC	142–184	850–1000④	0.008–0.012	0.016–0.020
'80–'81 Dasher (California)	WR7DS N8GY	0.024–0.028	Electronic		3 ATDC @ Idle	4 BTDC	142–184	880–1000	0.008–0.012	0.016–0.020
'80–'85 Rabbit, Jetta, Scirocco, Quantum (49 states)⑧	W175 T30 N8Y	0.024–0.032	44–50⑥	0.016⑥	3 ATDC @ Idle③ ⑫	4 BTDC	142–184⑦	850–1000④	0.008–0.012	0.016–0.020
'80–'85 Rabbit, Jetta, Scirocco, Quantum (California)⑧	WR7DS N8GY	0.024–0.028	Electronic		3 ATDC @ Idle ⑫	4 BTDC	142–184⑦	880–1000	0.008–0.012	0.016–0.020
'83–'85 GTI, GLI, Scirocco⑨, Conv.⑨	WR7DS N8YGY	0.024–0.028	Electronic		6 BTDC @ Idle	—	131–174	880–1000	0.008–0.012	0.016–0.020
'83–'85 Quantum⑩	W7D N8Y⑬	0.024–0.028	Electronic		6 BTDC @ Idle⑪	6 BTDC	142–184	850–1000	0.008–0.012	0.016–0.020

NOTE: The underhood specifications sticker often reflects tune-up specification changes made in production. Sticker figures must be used if they disagree with those in this chart.

① 47°–53° California

② 3 ATDC @ Idle with CIS fuel injection: 7½ BTDC @ Idle with 34 PICT-5 Carburetor

③ Non-California Rabbit w/1 barrel carburetor; timing 7½ BTDC @ Idle

④ W/o Idle stabilizer

⑤ Valve clearance need not be adjusted unless it varies more than 0.002 in. from specifications.

⑥ 1981 and later have electronic ignition

⑦ '82 and later compression pressure 131–174 psi.

⑧ Except 1.8 and 5 cylinder engines

⑨ 1.8 liter engine

⑩ 5 cylinder

⑪ 1983: M/T: 6° BTDC; A/T: 3° ATDC

⑫ 1984 and later: M/T: 6° BTDC; A/T: 3° ATDC

⑬ California: WR7DS: N8GY

FIRING ORDERS

NOTE: To avoid confusion, always replace spark plug wires one at a time.

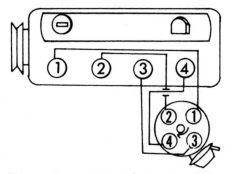

Firing order: 4 cylinder engines; 1–3–4–2

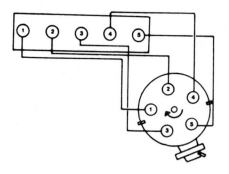

Firing order: 5 cylinder engine: 1–2–4–5– 3

CAPACITIES

Year	Model	Engine Crankcase (qts)		ansmission (pts)		Drive Axle (pts)	Gasoline Tank (gals)	Cooling stem (pts)
		With Filter	Without Filter	Manual	Automatic			
'78–'80	Dasher	3.2	2.6	3.4	12.4②	1.6	12.1	12.6
'78–'80	Rabbit (Diesel)	3.7	3.2	2.6	—	1.6	10.9	12.6
'78–'80	Rabbit	3.7	3.2	2.6②	12.8①	1.6	10.6	9.8
'78	Scirocco	3.7	3.2	3.2②	12.8①	1.6	10.6	9.8
'79–'80	Scirocco	3.7	3.2	3.2②	12.8①	1.6	10.6	9.8
	Dasher (Diesel)	3.7	3.2	3.2②	—	1.6	11.9	9.8
'80	Jetta	3.7	3.2	3.2②	12.8①	1.6	10.5	10.2
'81	Scirocco, Rabbit, Jetta	4.5	4.0	3.2②	12.8①	1.6	10.0③	9.8
'81	Dasher, Rabbit Jetta (Diesel)	3.7	3.2	3.2②	—	1.6	10.0③	14.3④
'82–'85	Rabbit, Jetta, Scirocco, Quantum	4.7	4.2	3.2②	12.8①	1.6	⑤	14.3⑥
	Rabbit, Jetta Quantum (Diesel)	3.7	3.2	3.2②	12.8①	1.6	⑤	14.3

—Not applicable
① Dry refill; normal refill is 6.4 pts
② 5-speed—4.2
③ Dasher: 12.0
④ Dasher: 12.2
⑤ 10.0 Rabbit; 10.6 Jetta, Convertible, Scirocco; 15.8 Quantum
⑥ Except 1.8 and 5 cylinder engine; 1.8 engine: 13.8; 5 cylinder: 14.3.

VOLKSWAGEN REAR WHEEL DRIVE
Beetle, Bus, Camper, Kombi, Vanagon

SERIAL NUMBER IDENTIFICATION

Vehicle (Chassis) Number

The first two numbers are the first two digits of the car's model number and the third digit stands for the car's model year. For example a 0 as the third digit means that the car was produced during the 1980 model year, a 1 would signify 1981, and so forth.

The chassis number is on the frame tunnel under the back seat in the Type 1. In the Type 2, the chassis number is on the right engine cover plate in the engine compartment and behind the front passenger's seat. All models also have an identification plate bearing the chassis number on the top of the instrument panel at the driver's side. This plate is easily visible through the windshield and aids in rapid identification.

Another identification plate bearing the vehicle's serial number and paint, body, and assembly codes, is found in the luggage compartment of the Type 1.

Chassis number location on dashboard

Chassis number location under rear seat

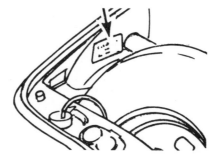

Identification plate in luggage compartment

Engine Number

On the Type 1 which has the upright engine cooling fan housing, the engine number is on the crankcase flange for the generator support. The number can readily be seen by looking through the center of the fan belt.

On Type 2 models with both the suitcase air-cooled engine and the Waterboxer (1984

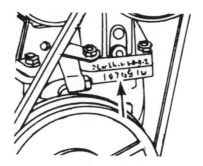

Engine number location on upright fan engine

Engine number location on the suitcase-type air-cooled engine, and on the Waterboxer

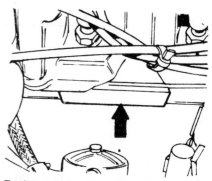

Engine number location—Type 2 with diesel

and later) engine, the number is stamped on the crankcase near the ignition coil and below the crankcase breather. The engine can be identified by the letter or pair of letters preceding the serial number. Engine specifications are listed according to the letters and model year.

Transmission Identification

Transmission identification marks are stamped into the bell housing or on the final drive housing.

DIESEL ENGINE TUNE-UP SPECIFICATIONS

Model	Valve Clearance ①		Intake Valve Opens (deg)	Injection Pump Setting (deg)	Injection Nozzle Pressure (psi)		Idle Speed (rpm)	Cranking Compression Pressure (psi)
	Intake (in.)	Exhaust (in.)			New	Used		
Diesel	.008–.012	.016–.020	NA	Align marks	1885–2001	1740–1885	770–870	406–493

NA Not available at time of publication
① Valve clearance need not be adjusted unless it varies more than .002 in. from specification

ENGINE IDENTIFICATION CHART

Engine Code Letter	Vehicle Type	First Production Year	Last Production Year	Engine Type	Common Designation
AJ	1	1975	1979	Air cooled flat four, fan driven by generator	1600
GD	2	1976	1978	Air cooled flat four, fan driven by crankshaft	2000
GE	2	1979	1980	Air cooled flat four, fan driven by crankshaft	2000
CV	2	1980	1983	Air cooled flat four, fan driven by crankshaft	2000
CS	2	1982	—	Water cooled inline diesel	1600
DH	2	1984	—	Water cooled flat four	Waterboxer

GASOLINE ENGINE TUNE-UP SPECIFICATIONS

Year	Code	Type	Common Designation	Spark Plugs Type①	Gap (in.)	Distributor Point Dwell (deg)	Point Gap (in.)	Ignition Timing (deg) MT	Ignition Timing (deg) AT	Fuel Pump Pressure (psi) @ 4000 rpm	Compression Pressure (psi)	Idle Speed (rpm) MT	Idle Speed (rpm) AT	Valve Clearance (in. cold) In	Valve Clearance (in. cold) Ex
'78	AJ	1	1600	Bosch W145M1 Champ. L288	.028	44–50	.016	5A	5A	28	85–135	800–950	800–950	.006	.006
	GE	2	2000	Bosch W145M2 Champ. N288	.028	44–50	.016	7½B	7½B	28	85–135	800–950	900–1000	Hyd.	Hyd.⑨
'79	AJ	1	1600	Bosch W145M1 Champ. L288	.028	44–50	.016	5A	5A	28	85–135	800–950	800–950	.006	.006
'79–'83	GE, CV	2	2000	Bosch W145M2 Champ. N288	.028	44–50⑤	.016⑤	7½B②	7½B②	28	85–135	800–950③	850–1000④	Hyd.	Hyd.⑨
'84–'85	DH	2	Waterboxer (1900)	Bosch W7CO Champ. N288 Beru 14L-7C	.028	⑥	⑥	5A	5A	⑧	116–189	800–900⑦	800–900⑦	Hyd.	Hyd.⑨

A After Top Dead Center
B Before Top Dead Center
MT Manual trans.
AT Automatic trans.
① Recommended by manufacturer
② 5ATDC, Calif.—idle stabilizer must be bypassed (plugs connected together)
③ Calif.: 850–950

④ Calif.: 850–950
⑤ 1980–83 Vanagon (Calif.)—electronic ignition; point gap and dwell preset and non-adjustable
⑥ 1984 and later: electronic ignition; point gap and dwell preset and non-adjustable

⑦ With vacuum hoses connected
⑧ 29 psi @ idle speed @ approx. 2.0 bar with vacuum hose connected
⑨ Valves must still be adjusted when cylinder heads have been removed; see "Valve Lash" in text.

FIRING ORDERS

NOTE: To avoid confusion, always replace spark plug wires one at a time. The Type 2 Diesel engine's cylinders are numbered 1-2-3-4, starting from the crankshaft pulley and working back. Firing order is 1-3-4-2. Water boxer cylinder numbering and firing order is the same as the air-cooled engine shown below.

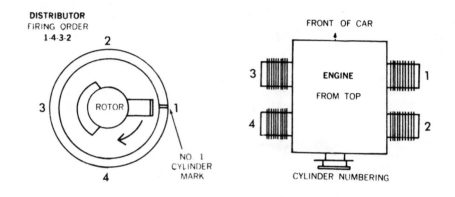

CAPACITIES

Year	Type	Engine Displacement (cc)	Engine Crankcase (qts.)		Transaxle (pts.)			Gasoline Tank (gal.)
			With Filter	Without Filter	Manual	Automatic		
						Conv.	Final Drive	
'78–'79	1	1600	—	2.5	6.3	7.6	6.3①	10.6③
'78–'85	2	1600, 1800, 2000	3.7④	3.2⑤	7.4	②	①	15.9
'84–'85	2	1915	4.7	3.7	⑥	②	①	15.9

Conv. = torque converter
① 5.3 when changed
② 6.4 refill; 12.8 when changed
③ Convertible (11.1)
④ Diesel: 4.2
⑤ Diesel: 3.7
⑥ Type 091: 3.7 qt.
Type 091/1: 3.2 qt. w/gasoline engine; 4.2 qt. with diesel
Type 094: 4.0 qt.

VOLVO

242, 244, 245, 262, 264, 265
DL, GT, GL, GLE, GLT, Coupe

SERIAL NUMBER IDENTIFICATION

Vehicle Type Designation And Chassis Number

Important identification labels appear at several locations on every Volvo, depending on year and model. On 1978–79 models, the type designation (242, 262, etc.) and the chassis number appear on a metal plate riveted to the engine side of the firewall. They also appear on the VIN plate, located at the foot of the left door post, and are stamped into the sheet metal of the right front door pillar.

For 1980–85, the model designations are DL-GL-GT-GLT and Turbo (formerly 242-244-245), GLE (formerly 264-265, to 1982), Coupe (formerly 262C), Diesel, and 760 GLE (1983 and later). The VIN plate on these cars is located on the top left surface of the dash, and is also stamped on the right hand door pillar. Emission control information is on a label located on the left hand shock tower under the hood. There is also a model plate on the right hand shock tower that includes the VIN number, engine type, emission equipment, vehicle weights and color codes.

Model designation and engine availability are related in the following way: from 1978 until 1979, all four cylinder Volvos are in the 240 series—242, 244 and 245. Six cylinder cars are 260 series—262, 264, 265. Starting in 1980, the 240 series became the DL, GL and GLT series. The 260 series evolved into the GLE cars, through 1982. The 760 series took over the GLE designation when launched in 1983.

Engine, Transmission, And Final Drive Identification

The engine type designation, part number, and serial number are given on the left side of the block (4). The last figures of the part number are stamped on a tab and are followed by the serial number stamped on the block.

The transmission type designation, serial number, and part number appear on a metal plate (5) riveted to the underside of the transmission. The final drive reduction ratio, part number, and serial number are found on a metal plate (6) riveted to the left-hand side of the differential.

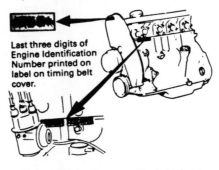

Last three digits of Engine Identification Number printed on label on timing belt cover.

B21 series engine number locations

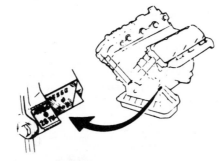

B27F and B28F engine number locations

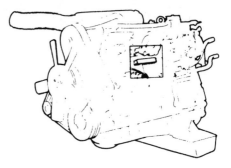

D24 and D24T engine number location

Component Identification

A component data plate is used to specify the manufacturer of major serviceable components such as the brakes, fuel pump, clutch, alternator, and steering gear. The plate is located on the right front door pillar on some models. Each component manufacturer is assigned a code.

CHASSIS NUMBER CHART

Year	Model	Starting Chassis No.
'78	242	122895
	244	274965
	245	163835
	262	2660
	264	46515
	265	10920
'79	242	142125
	244	364650
	245	211325
	262	4330
	264	62105
	265	15735

CHASSIS NUMBER CHART

Year	Model	Starting Chassis No.
'80	DL, GT (2 dr.)	165570
	DL, GL (4 dr.)	482505
	Coupe	6450
	GLE	83055
	4 cyl. wgn.	264755
	6 cyl. wgn.	21755
'81	DL, GL, GLT (2 dr.)	189180
	DL, GL (4 dr.)	592110
	Coupe	8375
	GLE	107610
	4 cyl. wgn.	317940
	6 cyl. wgn.	28320

CHASSIS NUMBER CHART

Year	Model	Starting Chassis No.
'82	DL, GL, GLT (2 dr.)	306780
	DL, GL (4 dr.)	686100
	GLE	125110
	4 cyl. wgn.	368310
'83	760 GLE	3800
	DL, GL (2 dr.)	223940
	DL, GL (4 dr.)	812610
	4 cyl. wagon	434460
'84	760 GLE	33720
	DL, Turbo (2 dr.)	237370
	DL, GL (4 dr.)	939340
	4 cyl. wagon	506270

GASOLINE ENGINE TUNE-UP SPECIFICATIONS

(When analyzing compression test results, look for uniformity among cylinders, rather than specific pressures)

Year	Engine Model and Displacement cu. in.	Spark Plugs Type	Gap (in.)	Distributor Point Dwell (deg)	Point Gap (in.)	Ignition Timing (deg) MT	AT	Intake Valve Opens (deg)	Fuel Pump Pressure (psi)	Idle Speed (rpm) MT	AT	Valve Clearance (cold) (in.) In	Ex
'78	B 21 F 130	Bosch WA175T30	0.030	Electronic		12B ①	12B ①	—	64–75	900	900	0.014–0.016	0.014–0.016
'78–'79	B 27 F 162	Bosch WA200T30	0.030	Electronic		10B ①	10B ①	—	64–75	900	900	0.004–0.006	0.010–0.012
'79	B 21 F 130	Bosch W6DC	0.030	Electronic		10B ①③	10B ①③	—	64–75	900	900	0.014–0.016	0.014–0.016
'80–'83	B 21 F⑤ 130	Bosch WR7DS	0.030	Electronic		8B ⑥⑨④	8B ⑥⑨④	—	64–75	900	900	0.014–0.016	0.014–0.016
'81–'85	B 21 FT⑫ 130	Bosch WR7DS	0.030	Electronic		12B ⑦④	12B ⑦④	—	64–75	900	900	0.014–0.016	0.014–0.016
'81–'85	B 21 A 130	Bosch W7DC	0.030	62	0.016–0.018	12B ⑥⑧④	12B ⑥⑧④	—	64–75	900	900	0.014–0.016	0.014–0.016
'83–'85	B 23 E 140	Bosch W6DC	0.030	Electronic		10B ⑥④	10B ⑥④	—	64–75	900	900	0.014–0.016	0.014–0.016
'83–'85	B 23 F⑩ 140	Bosch WR7DS	0.030	Electronic		12B ⑥④	12B ⑥④	—	64–75	750	750	0.014–0.016	0.014–0.016
'80–'82	B 28 F 174	Bosch WR6DS	0.030	Electronic		10B ⑦④	10B ⑦④	—	64–75	900	900	0.008–0.010	0.012–0.014
'83	B 28 F 174	Bosch WR6DS	0.026	Electronic		10B ④⑪	10B ④⑪	—	64–75	900	900	0.008–0.010	0.012–0.016
'84–'85	B 28 F 174	Bosch WR6DS	0.024	Electronic		10B ④⑪	10B ④⑪	—	64–75	750	750	0.004–0.006	0.010–0.012

NOTE: Some models are equipped with the Constant Idle Speed system (CIS) and cannot be adjusted
① @ 700 rpm
② 9B—left side; 7B—right side
③ Calif: 8B
④ Vacuum advance disconnected, A/C turned off
⑤ Includes Calif. and L-Jetronic models
⑥ @ 750 rpm
⑦ @ 900 rpm
⑧ 7° '82 and later
⑨ 12° '82 and later
⑩ LH-Jetronic injection with Constant Idle Speed and Knock Sensor
⑪ @ 800 rpm
⑫ Turbo
⑬ LH-Jetronic injection (electronic)

DIESEL ENGINE TUNE-UP SPECIFICATIONS

Year	Model	Valve Clearance①		Injection Pump Setting⑧ (in.)	Injector Nozzle Opening Pressure (psi)	Idle Speed (rpm)	Compression Pressure (psi)
		Intake (in.)	Exhaust (in.)				
'80–'85	D24	0.006–0.010	0.014–0.018	0.0265–② 0.0295	1700–1845③	720–④ 880	340 (min.)– 455 (max.)⑤
'83–'85	D24T⑥	0.006–0.010	0.014–0.018	0.0315⑨	2062–2318⑦	750	313 (min.)– 455 (max.)⑤

NOTE: When setting injection timing, distributor plunger stroke must be at Top Dead Center

① Cold
② See text. Acceptable range when checking 0.0287–0.0315 in.
③ Acceptable range. When servicing set to 1775–1920 psi
④ Maximum safe speed: 5100–5200 rpm (high idle)
⑤ Maximum difference between cylinders 115 lbs. psi
⑥ Turbo-Diesel
⑦ Acceptable range. When servicing set to 2205–2318 psi.
⑧ Plunger stroke
⑨ See text. Acceptable range when checking 0.0307–0.0334 in.

FIRING ORDERS

NOTE: To avoid confusion, always replace spark plug wires one at a time.

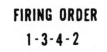

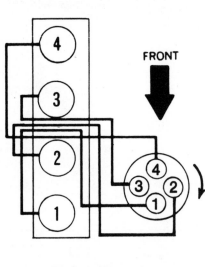

B21F and B23 series

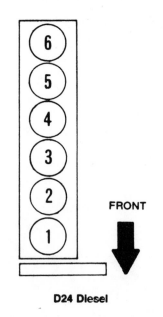

D24 Diesel

FIRING ORDER

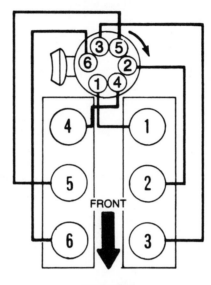

FIRING ORDER
1·6·3·5·2·4

FRONT

B27F, B28

CAPACITIES

Year	Model	Engine Displacement cu. in. (cc)	Engine Crankcase (qt)		Transmission (pts)		Drive Axle (pt)	Gasoline Tank (gal)	Cooling System (qt)
			With Filter	Without Filter	Manual 4-Spd	Automatic			
'78	242, 244, 245	130 (2127)	4.0	3.5	3.8	14.0	3.4	15.8	10.0
	262, 264, 265	162 (2660)	6.8	6.3	4.8	14.0	3.4	15.8	11.5
'79	242, 244, 245	130 (2127)	4.0	3.5	3.8	14.0②	3.4	15.8	10.0
	262, 264, 265	162 (2660)	6.8	6.3	4.8	14.0②	3.4	15.8	11.5
'80–'83	DL, GL, GT④	130 2127)	4.0⑤	3.5⑤	4.8	14.6③	3.4	15.8	10.0
'80–'82	GLE, Coupe	174 (2849)	6.8	6.3	4.8	14.6③	3.4	15.8	11.5
'80–'85	DL, GL Diesel	145 (2383)	7.4	6.6	4.8	14.6③	3.4	15.8	10.0
'83–'85	DL, GL	140 (2320)	3.5	4.0	4.8	14.6③	3.4	15.8	10.0
'82–'85	GLT Wagon, DL Turbo	130 (2127)	4.0⑤	3.5⑤	4.8	14.6③	3.4	15.8	10.0
'83–'85	760 GLE	174 (2849)	6.8	6.3	4.8	14.6③	3.4	15.8⑥	10.5
'83–'85	760 GLE Turbo Diesel	145 (2383)	7.0	6.2	4.8	14.6③	3.4	15.8⑥	11.5⑦

① With extra capacity fluid pan: 14.6
② Fluid capacity for AW70 and AW71 (1982 and later 4-speed) automatics is 15.6 pts.
③ Includes station wagons
④ Cars w/turbo: if oil cooler drained, add 0.7 qt.
⑤ With increased capacity tank 21.6 gal.
⑥ With automatic trans. 10.5 qt.

Index

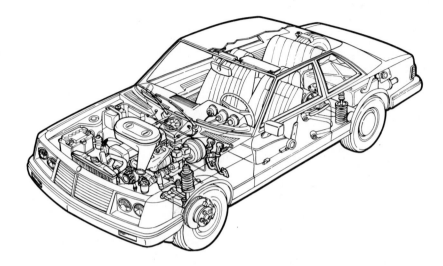

Accelerator, stuck, 348–349
Accessory current draw (chart), 115
Additives, gasoline, 55
Additives, motor oil, 57–58
Air bags, 44–46, *47*
Air conditioning, 106–108
   maintenance for, 63, 109
Air filter, *176, 177*
   inverting lid for, 362
Air injection systems, 172–174
Air pump, 172–174, 177
Alarm systems, for theft, 327–333
Alcohol-impaired driving, deterrents to, 46–47
Allen wrenches, 7–8
Alternator, *See also* Charging system; Starting system, 128–131
   maintenance for, 63, 182
   warning light for, 131
Alternator belt, 132
AMC Eagle, four-wheel drive in, 252
Ammeter gauge, 131, 203
Antennas, CB, 215
   protecting from theft, 333
Antennas, radio, 209
Antifreeze, 91, *See also Coolant*
Anti-theft systems, 327
Autofuse, 159
Automatic Overdrive Transmission, 236–237
Automatic transmission. *See* Transmission, automatic
Automatic transmission fluid, 241–243
   checking for leaks of, 243
Axles, *See* Drive axles, front; Drive axles, rear

Ball joints, 259
Battery, 113
   charging/discharging processes, 115
   jump starting, 122–123
   maintenance for, 63, 117
   tools for cleaning, 10–11

Battery cables, replacing of, 121
Belts. *See specific type*
Blowout, of tire, 351. *See also* Tire, changing flat
Body
   maintenance for, 65
   repairing of, 320–26
   undercoating and rustproofing, 317–18
   washing and waxing of, 314–317
Bolts, 33–36
   SAE, 33
   torque specifications for (chart), 37
   Whitworth, 36
Brake, parking, 298
Brake fluid, 60
   checking level of, 298–300
Brakes, disc, 297
   failure of, 302
   inspecting of, 301
   maintenance for, 65, 298
   tune-up for, 303
   wheels designed for, 274
Brakes, drum, 302–303
   Chrysler finish for, 362
   failure of, 302
   inspecting of, 301–304
   maintenance for, 65, 298
   tune-up procedure for, 303
Brakes, power, 298
Breaker points. *See* Points, ignition
Bumpers, energy-absorbing, 44
Buzzers, for safety systems, 41

Camber angle, 263–264
Capri, erratic engine operation on, 362
Carbon canister, 180
   vapor lock and, 183
Carburetor, 169–170. *See also* Idle mixture; Idle speed
   choke for, 183
   cleaning of, 182
   solenoid for, 181
   tune-up adjustments for, 72

Car dealers, new, 337
   parts from, 24
Caster angle, 263
Catalogs, for parts and supplies, 29
Catalytic converters, 171
CB radios, 214–218
   antennas for, 216
   theft of, 334
Cetane number, for diesel fuel, 56
Chargers, for batteries, 123
Charging system, 128
   maintenance procedures for, 132
Chassis, 65
   lubricants for, 67
Choke, 183
Circuit breakers, 158
Citizens band radio, *See* CB radios
Cleaning
   exterior, 314–326
   interior, 194–200
Clutch, 225–228
   cross-section of, 228
   maintenance for, 65, 231
   pedal free-play for, 232
Coil, ignition, 136, 137
Compression, engine, 83–85
Compression gauge, 13, 83
Compressor belt, inspecting and adjusting, 109
Condenser, air conditioning, 108
Condenser, ignition, 137, 148, 151–152
   replacing of, 148, 151–152
Control arms, 257, 260, 262, 266–267
Coolant, 91. *See also* Antifreeze
   temperature gauge for, 203
Cooling system, air, 103
Cooling system, transmission, 91, 310
Cooling system, water 90–105
   capacities of (chart), 102
   maintenance of, 62, 93–102
Corporate average fuel economy standards, 355–359
Corrosion. *See* Rust

566 • *Index*

Costs, of car ownership, 343–347
Cotter pins, 36
Counterfeit Parts, 27
Crankshaft, operation of, 74
Crossfiring. *See* Misfiring
Cylinders, operation of, 74

Dash gauges, 201–206
Dealer profit margins, 339
Delco-Remy batteries, 119
Density, of gasoline, 55
Dents, repairing of, 322–325
Depreciation, 344–345
  of diesel cars, 338
Detergents
  in gasoline, 55
  in motor oil, 57
Detonation, 53–55, 77, 141
Diesel engine, 78–80, 338
  economy of, 338
  fuel filter for, 169
  oil recommendations for (chart), 85
Diesel fuel, 55
Differential, 249
  for four-wheel drive, 251
  limited-slip, 250
  lubricant in, 249
Dispersants, in motor oils, 56
Distributor, 135–139, 360
  electronic ignition and, 136
  inspecting of, 140
  servicing of, 73
  silicone lubricants for, 141
  timing and, 139
Door panels, cleaning and repairing, 197
Drive axles, front, 251
Drive axles, rear, 249
  lubricants for, 57, 249
  maintenance for, 63, 245
Driveshafts, 247
  maintenance for, 63, 247
Dwell angle, 71, 153
Dwell-tachometer, 13, 71, 153
Drug-impaired driving, deterrents for, 46

EGR emissions systems, 174, 359
Electrolyte, in battery, 118
Electronic ignition, 129
  dwell and, 71
  GM High-Energy Ignition, 363
Emergency checklist (chart), 49, 348
Emergency stopping, on highway, 348
Emissions, affected by maintenance, 174
Emissions systems, 169
  air injection, 172
  exhaust gas recirculation (EGR), 174
  positive crankcase ventilation (PCV), 172
Engine, 74–89
  diesel, 78
  maintenance for, 82
  two-stroke, 81
  Wankel, 78
EPA mileage estimates, 355
Exhaust system, failure of, 357

Fan belt, 81–82, 97–100. *See also* V-belts
Fasteners, 33–38
  metric and SAE sizes of, 33–38
FCC, CB radios and, 214
Feeler gauges, 12

Finish. *See also* Body
  caring for, 314
First-aid supplies, 353
Flashers, 156–166
Flex fans, for increased engine cooling, 309
Flooding, of engine, 182
Flywheel, 225
Four-stroke cycle, 74
Four-wheel drive, 251
Front-wheel drive, 249
Fuel filter, 168–170, 175
Fuel pump, 161, 173, 180
  vapor lock and, 183
Fuel shut-off valve, 355
Fuel system, 161–183
  maintenance for, 61, 161–183
Fuel tank, 161
Fuses, 156–166
Fusible links, 156–166

Gas caps, locking, 357
Gasoline, 51
Gas tank, 161
Gauges, dash, 201–206
  fuel, intermittent, 360
Gear ratios
  in differential, 249
  in manual transmission, 229
Gears
  in automatic transmission, 239
  in manual transmission, 229
Generator, 126
GM High-Energy Ignition, 154
Government
  CB radios and, 214
  fuel economy standards of, 355
  safety regulations by, 37, 42
Grease. *See* Lubricants
Grease gun, 12

Hammers, 6
Headlights, 156–166
  replacing of, 156–166
Hitch, for towing, 306
Hotchkiss drive, 247
Hydrometer, 118

Ice driving on, 352
Idle mixture, adjustment of, 72
Idle speed, adjustment of, 72, 178
Ignition system, 135
  disruption, on AMCs, 360
  electronic, 129
  maintenance for, 135
  tune-up of, 68
Insurance, 345
  determining rate for, 395
  for theft, 327
Interior, maintenance of, 194

Jacks, 16–17
Jackstands, 16–17
Jobbers, as parts source, 25–26
Jump starting, 122
Junkyard, as parts source, 26–27

Knock, engine, 53–55, 77, 141. *See also* Detonation

Lead, in gasoline, 52
Leaks, safety check for, 49, 51

Lighting system. *See also* Headlights; Lights
  rewiring of, 156–166
  safety check of, 49
Lights, 156–166
  for safety systems, 39–41
Locks, 327
Lock-up clutch, for Chrysler torque converter, 234
Lockwashers, 36
Lubricants, 18, 51
  for front end, 268
  for manual transmission, 229
  for rear axle, 249
  for ignition system, 132–33, 135, 141
  for wiper motor and linkage, 188
Lubrication gun, 12
Lugs. *See* Wheel lugs

Manganese, in gasoline, 53
Master cylinder, brake, 295
MacPherson strut suspension, 257, 261, 270
Mileage, 31, 58, 355
  checking of, 361
  EPA estimates of, 355
Mirrors, 49
  rear-view, 198
  for trailers, 306
Misfiring, 143, 360
Motor oil guide (chart), 59

National Highway Traffic and Safety Administration, 39
Noises, 48, 254
Nuts, 35–36

Octane rating, 52
Odors, safety check for, 50
Ohmmeter, 14, 145
Oil, engine, 56, 86
  changing, 86
  checking, 85
Oil, gear, 249
Oil filter, 86
  with drain-back check valve, 360
  wrenches for, 11
Oil pressure, 201–206
  warning light for, 38, 362
Overhead camshaft, four-cylinder, 74, 87

Parts, 23–32
Parts, Counterfeit, 27
PCV emission system, 172
PCV valve, 172
  checking and replacing, 173
Performance, engine, 62, 82
Pinging, 53–55, 77, 141
Pistons, operation of, 75
Planetary gears, in automatic transmission, 239
Plates, in battery, 114
Pliers, 5
Points, ignition, 71, 135
  adjusting and replacing of, 148, 151, 152, 153
  inspecting, 71
Positraction axle, lubricant for, 61
Power steering. *See* Steering, power
Power steering belt, 265, 269, 270

Power steering fluid, 61, 268
  for valves,
Pressure plate, 225

Quadra-Trac, 251

Rack and pinion steering, 259
Radar, police, 218
Radar detectors, 221, 222, 223–24
Radiator, 90, 91. *See also* Cooling system, water
Radiator cap, inspecting of, 94, 96
Radiator hose, 93
Radios, 207
  noise suppression for, 213, 217
  protecting from theft, 327, 333
Ratchets, 8
Refrigerant, for air conditioning, 108, 109
Regulations
  CB radios and, 214–15
  safety and, 39–43
Regulator. *See* Voltage regulator
Release bearing, 228
Rotary engine. *See* Wankel engine
Rubbing compound, 315
Rust, repairing of, 320–326
Rust inhibitors, in motor oils, 57
Rustproofing, 317

Safety
  car systems for, 39
  checks for, 47–51
  federal regulations and, 39
  when servicing car, 21–22
Scratches, repairing of, 320–326
Screwdrivers, 6
Screws, 33
Sealants, 18
Seatbelts, 40–43
Seats, 194
Self-service gasoline, 179
Separators, in battery, 113
Service stations, 179
Shock absorbers, 269, 270, 271
Soldering, 15–17
Solenoid, starter, 127
Solenoid, throttle, 181
Spark plugs, 69, 70, 146, 147–49
  fouling in Vegas, 362
  hard to reach, 360, 362
Spark plug wires, 70, 144, 145
  routing on GM 6-cylinders, 362
Speakers, 208
Spout, oil filter, 11
Starter, 126. *See also* Charging system; Starting system maintenance for, 132
Starter relay, 127
Starting system, 126

Steering, manual, 258
  emergency loss of, 349
  rack and pinion, 259
  recirculating ball, 258
Steering, power, 261
  emergency loss of, 349
  maintenance for, 61, 265
Stopping distances, average, 353
Suction gun, for fluids, 10, 11, 12
Supercharging, 77
Supplies, 23
Suspension, front, 257
  independent, 257
  maintenance for, 62
  McPherson strut, 257–264
  torsion bar, 258
  wheel alignment and, 262–65
Suspension, rear, 62, 265–67
Synchromesh transmissions, 229–30

Tachometer, 204. *See also* Dwell-tachometer
Tailpipe, safety check of, 49
Tape player, 207
Temperature gauge, 203
Temperature warning light, 40
Thermostat, checking and replacing, 96
Theft. *See* Anti-theft systems
Throttle, sticking, 348
Timing, ignition, 72, 139
  adjusting, 154
Timing light, 13
Tire inflation pressure, rolling resistance and (chart), 290
Tires, 277–94
  belted, 277, 278
  bias, 277, 278
  changing flat, 293
  elliptic, 278
  inflation pressure of, 287, 290
  maintenance for, 186
  radial, 278
  size comparison charts for, 288, 289, 290
Toe-in, 265
Tools, 1–22. *See also individual tools*
Torque specifications, for bolts (chart), 37
Torque tube drive, 247
Torque wrench, 10
Torsion bar suspension, 258
Towing
  of cars with automatic transmissions, 238
  of Omni/Horizon, 364
  of trailer, 306–13
Trailer, towing of, 306–13
Transaxles, 231, 232
Transfer cases, for four-wheel drive, 251–253

Transmission, automatic, 234
  cooling system for, 91
  cross-section of, 235
  fluid for, 61
  maintenance for, 239
  starter safety switch on, 127
Transmission, manual, 225
  lubricant for, 60
  maintenance for, 232
  starter safety switch on, 127
Tread wear patterns, 292
Tune-up, 11, 68
  benefitting emissions and mileage (chart), 355–59
Turbocharging, 77
Turns signal, 160–162
Two-stroke engines, 81

U-joints. *See* Universal joints
Undercoating, 317
Universal joints, 247. *See also* Drive-shafts
Used cars, buying of, 336, 340

Vacuum gauge, 11, 69, 88
Valves, adjusting of, 73
Vapor lock, 183
V-belts, 92
Vibration diagnosis (chart), 48
Voltage regulator, 129–130
Voltmeter, 14

Wankel engine, 78
Warning lights and buzzers, 201
  for alternator, 130, 131
  for seatbelts, 41
Waxes, 315
Wheel alignment, 262–65
Wheel bearings, 254
Wheel cylinder, brake, 296, 303–304
Wheel lugs,
  torque sequences for, 276
Wheels, 272
  disc brakes and, 297
  locks for, 274, 328
  maintenance for, 274
  safety check of, 47
  torquing lugs for, 276
Whitworth bolts, 36
Windshield, 60, 177, 179
Windshield washers, 186
Windshield wipers, 65, 184–186
  failure of, 350
Wind whistle, on Fords, 361
Wrenches, 7–10
  allen and star, 7–8
  oil filter, 11
  SAE and metric sizes of, 4
  torque, 10